AUDITING

Philosophy & Technique
Second Edition

JOHN W. COOK, Ph.D., C.P.A.
Georgia State University

GARY M. WINKLE, D.B.A., C.P.A.
Georgia State University

Houghton Mifflin Company Boston
Dallas Geneva, Illinois Hopewell, New Jersey
Palo Alto London

Quotations and textual adaptations from publications copyright © 1963-1979 by the American Institute of Certified Public Accountants, Inc.

Material from the Uniform CPA Examinations and Unofficial Answers, copyright © 1972-1979 by the American Institute of Certified Public Accountants, Inc., is reprinted or adapted with permission.

Material from the Certificate in Management Accounting Examinations, copyright © 1972-1978 by the National Association of Accountants, is reprinted or adapted with permission.

Copyright © 1980 by Houghton Mifflin Company. All rights reserved. No part of this work may be reproduced or transmitted in any form or by any means, electronic or mechanical, including photocopying and recording, or by any information storage or retrieval system, without permission in writing from the publisher.

Printed in the U.S.A.

Library of Congress Catalog Card Number: 79-88718

ISBN: 0-395-28660-3

CONTENTS

PREFACE

This second edition of *Auditing: Philosophy & Technique* endeavors to reflect the many changes in the auditing profession that have taken place since the first edition of the text was published in 1976. Also, there is expanded text coverage in several significant areas. At the same time the balance between concepts and procedures and the conciseness of the first edition is maintained. The overall organization of the text is unchanged. It is divided into three parts: The Auditor's Environment, Techniques for Audit Decisions, and Audit Objectives and Procedures. This organization is designed to acquaint students first with the broad environmental aspects of auditing, and then with more detailed audit considerations. Several appendixes provide supplementary reference material. The material on systems evaluation that appeared in Chapter 11 of the first edition has been integrated into Chapter 7, Internal Controls—Design and Review. A new chapter on special reporting situations (Chapter 6) has been added.

The principal changes and expansions in the second edition include the following:

- Increased illustration of working papers and flowcharts
- Expanded coverage of internal accounting control
- Extensive illustration of audit reports
- A second chapter (Chapter 6) on auditor's reports covering compilation and review services, special reports, reports on internal control, reporting to the SEC, and reviews of interim financial information
- A completely revised treatment of statistical sampling with increased emphasis on attribute sampling (estimation and discovery), mean-per-unit estimation, ratio and difference estimation, and beta risk evaluation
- Illustrative audit programs
- Increased emphasis on integration of audit procedures applicable to elements of operating cycles

- References to Statements on Auditing Standards incorporated throughout the text
- A new section covering considerations involved in completing the audit
- Added coverage on SEC practice and responsibility
- Recent changes in the auditor's professional, ethical, and legal environment
- End-of-chapter reading lists
- Increase in the number and variety of decision problems

The auditing profession is currently undergoing profound changes and is facing challenging opportunities. In this edition of the text, we endeavor to give the student a resource that will establish a thorough understanding of the field and a foundation upon which to build a career in this dynamic profession.

Acknowledgments

We are grateful to the American Institute of Certified Public Accountants for permission to reproduce or quote from a variety of AICPA publications, to the Institute of Management Accounting of the National Association of Accountants for permission to use problem materials from past CMA examinations, to the Institute of Internal Auditors, and the Washington Society of CPAs for permission to use materials.

Our gratitude is extended to the following people, who made a genuine contribution to the preparation of the second edition. Robert Arnold, Youngstown State University, Christopher Dungan, University of Louisville, Daniel O'Mara, Quinnipiac College, and Gerald Smith, Central State University evaluated the first edition and made specific suggestions for the second edition. A special note of appreciation for the comments and suggestions offered in the preparation of this revision is due to Robert Hamilton, University of Minnesota; Thomas McLeod, University of Alabama-Birmingham; Allan Vail, Fairleigh Dickinson University-Teaneck Campus; Gerald McCarley, Deloitte, Haskins and Sells; E. Harold Stokes, Peat, Marwick, Mitchell and Co.; and Wayne Daniel, Georgia State University.

Our sincere thanks also goes to Becky Hooten and Marge Authier, our splendid typists, for their contributions. Finally, the continued support and understanding of our families, Beverly, Alan, Philip, and Laura Cook, and Gail, Karen, and Amy Winkle have sustained us through the long hours.

J. W. C.
G. M. W.

I

The Auditor's Environment

The topics presented in Part I are designed to provide readers with an understanding of the environment in which an auditor works. This environment determines the constraints that shape, broadly, the auditor's task. An early grasp of the auditor's environment is essential to an understanding of auditing, and Chapters 1 through 6 are devoted to this extensive subject.

1

Introduction to the Accounting Profession

Accounting functions

Accounting is the process of providing needed information regarding primarily the financial activities of economic entities so that users of this information may make decisions about the entities. The wide scope of accounting can be recognized when one considers the diversity of economic entities. These range from the simple undertakings of an individual, such as selling a single product, through variously sized corporations engaged in multiproduct lines, and include governmental agencies and programs.

These entities usually use the language of accounting to convey the results of their endeavors to interested parties. Historically, users have been interested primarily in the financial activities of the entities, and accounting has concentrated on conveying financial data. However, as users become more concerned with nonfinancial data, such as the extent of natural resources conserved or the degree of success of certain social endeavors, accounting gains the opportunity to expand into areas other than financial reporting. The information conveyed by accountants likely will continue to expand to meet the ever-increasing needs of users. However, the emphasis in this text is on accounting reports designed to provide financial information useful to present and potential investors, creditors, and other users in making rational decisions.

Users of accounting information fall into two broad categories: those internal to the business enterprise and those external. Managers and employees of a business are obviously internal users; creditors and prospective investors are clearly external users. In some instances owners are engaged directly in managing the operations of a company and are considered internal users. In other cases, the investors are absentee owners, who have no close contact with the operations of the company and obtain their knowledge of the company's financial activities from reports issued to external users. A person working within the company as a member of management may not have first-hand knowledge of the fairness of the accounting information furnished, and an external user certainly cannot directly obtain any assurance of the fairness of the information. Internal users and external users alike need assurance that the accounting information furnished is reliable, accurate, fairly presented, and free from bias. Therefore, both internal and external users require that the information be reviewed by a competent person other than the one who prepares the information. Such a review is called *auditing,* and the reviewer is called an *auditor.*

Auditing—internal and external

Auditing may be defined as the systematic examination and appraisal of transactions, procedures, operations, and resulting financial statements for the purpose of determining the degree of adherence to prescribed criteria and expressing an opinion thereon. If the audit is performed by an employee of the entity whose procedures and statements are being reviewed, that person is called an *internal auditor.* Within an organization internal auditors should be independent of those whose work is reviewed. They occupy a staff position and should report to someone high in the administrative ranks of the organization. Internal auditors fulfill an important function within business corporations, governmental units, or other forms of organization. By reviewing the internal information system, an internal auditor determines whether or not the system is effectively designed to communicate management's directives, to collect necessary data, and to report results of operating activities to management. This review results in an evaluation of the system design, observations about the functioning of the system, and recommendations for its improvement. An internal auditor also investigates activities such as quality control, market penetration, personnel policies, and many other matters only remotely related to financial accounting. The internal auditor must be constantly alert to detect and report matters anywhere within the organization that need to be brought to management's attention. The work of internal auditors is discussed again in Chapters 7 and 11.

Although internal auditors are independent of those within the organization whose work they review, they are still employees of the company. External users of the accounting information would derive little, if any, satisfaction from an internal auditor's assurance about the fairness of accounting reports. Consequently, many external users—including absentee owners, prospective investors, creditors, and governmental regulatory agencies—demand that accounting information be reviewed by an independent auditor. Such a role usually is filled by an external auditor called a *public accountant.* Not an employee of the company whose accounting statements are presented, a public accountant is an independent contractor whose services can be engaged by a business organization much as an individual might engage a doctor, dentist, lawyer, or other professional. Public accountants fulfilling the role of independent auditors realize that many groups external to the reporting entity rely upon their assurance that the accounting information meets established criteria. This assurance is conveyed by the *auditors' report* in which the auditors express their opinion about the fair presentation of the financial statements of the company. Their opinion is not biased toward the needs or desires of any particular group of users. A mental attitude of integrity and objectivity, or *freedom from bias,* is perhaps the paramount trait required of public accountants engaged as independent auditors. The value of their opinion depends directly upon their professional reputation for independence and objectivity. Without such a reputation, the function of independent auditors is of no value.

Auditing is also performed by various governmental agencies, for example, the General Accounting Office, the Army Audit Agency, and the Internal Revenue Service. An investigation by these agencies may be similar to an internal audit, wherein the examination concentrates upon the agency's own operations; or the examination may be centered on the operations of an outside entity that has a business relationship with the governmental agency, and so it may have many aspects of an external independent audit. Audits by governmental agencies vary considerably in scope and purpose. They range from specific single-purpose audits (for instance, determination of compliance with the law on a single point) to very general comprehensive audits that evaluate, say, the performance of management, the accomplishment of a program's goals, or the efficiency in resource management.

Many general concepts of auditing apply to external, internal, and governmental audits. Auditing as practiced by public accountants receives major emphasis in this book.

The public accounting profession

The practice of public accounting developed over the years to meet the needs of various users of financial statements and other accounting reports. As confidence in the work and opinions of public accountants grew, public accounting evolved into a profession. One characteristic of a profession is that it requires specialized training and study generally recognized by colleges and universities. Auditing is one topic usually included within the course of study to prepare for the public accounting profession. Professions are characterized also by the performance of intellectual services, as contrasted with manual or artistic labor. In addition, professions recognize a duty of public service and adopt a code of ethics generally accepted as binding upon their members. Public accounting customarily is considered to possess all these characteristics.

CERTIFIED PUBLIC ACCOUNTANTS

Although the practice of public accountancy in the United States is regulated by each individual state, by the District of Columbia, and by the three territories, all laws and regulations are similar. Most jurisdictions allow a public accountant to practice only after meeting high standards of educational achievement, passing an examination, and obtaining necessary experience. A person meeting these requirements may be licensed to practice as a certified public accountant (CPA). A person who becomes a CPA in one state usually can become a CPA in another state with relative ease. Typically, a certified public accountant must graduate from college with a major in accounting, must pass the Uniform CPA Examination, must supply evidence affirming acceptable personal character, and frequently must have been employed in public accounting or other qualifying accounting positions. In some states the work experience requirement is shortened or eliminated for those with advanced degrees in accounting.

CPA EXAMINATION

While the responsibility for administering the CPA examination rests with the accountancy board of each state, all states use the Uniform CPA Examination, which is prepared and graded under the auspices of the Board of Examiners of the American Institute of Certified Public Accountants (AICPA), the national organization of CPAs. This uniform examination consists of four parts: accounting theory, business law, auditing, and accounting practice. The examination is given in May and November of each year and extends for two and one-half days. Nine hours of examination are devoted to accounting practice, and three and one-half hours are given to each of the other sections. Since the same examination and grading system are used in every state, there is assurance that each person entitled to be called a CPA has met the minimum requirements necessary to pass the examination.

PROFESSIONAL ORGANIZATIONS

Because each state issues CPA certificates, CPAs are necessarily subject to the laws and regulations of the state or states in which they are licensed. In addition, many CPAs are subject to the regulations of the American

Institute of Certified Public Accountants either by their individual membership in this national organization or by their firm's affiliation with it. This organization is instrumental in establishing auditing standards, auditing procedures, and rules of professional conduct; it also maintains appropriate boards and committees to review the activities of members. Failure to adhere to appropriate standards may result in expulsion from membership, public disclosure of improper conduct, and the possibility of fines.

The influence of the AICPA reaches a much broader audience than its own membership. Frequently, state regulations are modeled after AICPA pronouncements. Many court decisions use the statements from the AICPA as criteria to evaluate public accountants and their work. Most CPAs consider the pronouncements of the AICPA to represent the proper guidelines to follow. Although legally CPAs may be governed by differing state regulations, there is much uniformity in the standards of auditing and other areas of professional practice because of the strong influence of the AICPA.

The American Institute of Certified Public Accountants does not have local chapters in the states; it is solely a national organization. However, there is a local society of CPAs in each of the states and territories and in the District of Columbia. These state organizations usually have chapters in major cities, and at this local level the CPAs have their greatest contact and the opportunity to exchange ideas and experiences. The state organizations work closely with the AICPA, and many programs designed by the national organization are carried out through the state societies and their chapters. Most state societies have regulations patterned after AICPA pronouncements, thereby casting the AICPA's influence far beyond its immediate membership.

As the field of auditing has expanded in recent years, many new techniques have developed. Consequently, a major function of the AICPA and state societies is in the area of continuing professional education. Short courses, audio-cassettes, and programmed learning materials have been prepared and presented on many subjects. The public accounting professional organizations have devoted much time and resources in their efforts to keep the knowledge and skills of members current in a rapidly changing environment.

The Institute of Internal Auditors (IIA), also a national organization, has chapters in many locations throughout the United States. The IIA encourages the exchange of ideas among internal auditors, the adherence to professional standards, and the expansion of their services into many phases of business beyond the financial realm. The bimonthly publication of the IIA is *The Internal Auditor.* Additionally, several books on internal auditing have been published under IIA sponsorship. A program of certification is administered by the IIA that enables internal auditors who qualify to become Certified Internal Auditors (CIA).

The nature of auditing

As stated previously, external users of accounting information depend upon public accountants, in the role of auditor, to assure that the accounting data furnished are reliable. These data usually appear in the form of balance sheets, statements of income, statements of changes in owners' equity, statements of changes in financial position, and related notes. At times an auditor may be asked to give assurance on other statements as well. The auditor's assurance usually takes the form of an opinion associated with the client's annual financial statements.

THE AUDITOR'S REPORT

The standard form that the auditor's opinion takes is a two-paragraph report; the first paragraph describes the scope of the examination, and the second expresses the opinion. The traditional wording of the report is reflected in Figure 1-1. Auditors use this form, or one with slight variations, when stating that the presentations of the financial statements are fair according to generally accepted accounting principles. At times auditors must modify the standard form because of restrictions on the scope of the examination or the nature of the findings. The auditor's report and its various modifications are examined in Chapters 5 and 6.

AUDITING STANDARDS AND PROCEDURES

Generally accepted auditing standards guide auditors in conducting their examinations and in preparing their reports. If a proper audit is to be conducted, the auditors cannot deviate from these standards. Using generally accepted auditing standards as guides, auditors must obtain knowledge of a client's operations sufficient to serve as a basis for expressing their opinion on the financial statements. Such knowledge is obtained by examining the design of the accounting system, observing how the system works, inspecting documents, examining assets, reviewing procedures followed by the client's personnel, recomputing certain data, asking questions, and performing numerous other steps. These methods of gathering evidence are known collectively as *auditing procedures.* These procedures are not standardized; rather they are designed for each examination and are influenced by conditions existing at the time. Auditing procedures may be considered applications of generally accepted auditing standards. For many years the AICPA's Auditing Standards Board (and its predecessor committees, the Auditing Standards Executive Committee and the Committee on Auditing Procedure) has issued statements describing various auditing procedures and discussing conditions under which auditors should use them. These statements are today known as *Statements on Auditing Standards,* frequently called SASs. These statements are compiled, by

Figure 1-1 Illustrative Auditor's Report

Board of Directors and Shareholders
DeKalb Manufacturing Company
Atlanta, Georgia

We have examined the balance sheets of DeKalb Manufacturing Company as of December 31, 1982 and 1981, and the related statements of earnings, shareholders' equity and changes in financial position for the years then ended. Our examinations were made in accordance with generally accepted auditing standards and, accordingly, included such tests of the accounting records and such other auditing procedures as we considered necessary in the circumstances.

In our opinion, the financial statements referred to above present fairly the financial position of DeKalb Manufacturing Company as of December 31, 1982 and 1981, and the results of its operations and the changes in its financial position for the years then ended, in conformity with generally accepted accounting principles applied on a consistent basis.

Cook and Winkle
Certified Public Accountants

Atlanta, Georgia
March 3, 1983

subject matter, in Volume 1 of *AICPA Professional Standards* and are assigned section numbers. References to these pronouncements in this text bear the SAS number as well as the section number used in Volume 1 of *AICPA Professional Standards.* By studying this text and by referring to selected sections of the *Statements on Auditing Standards,* students should acquire a general knowledge of the usual procedures of an audit.

GENERALLY ACCEPTED ACCOUNTING PRINCIPLES

The auditor's opinion is that the financial statements are fairly presented in accordance with generally accepted accounting principles. Obviously, to be able to express such an opinion, an auditor must be thoroughly familiar with accounting standards and principles. Knowledge of these standards and principles is a prerequisite for a person to function as an auditor in reviewing the financial activities of a client and in expressing an opinion on the resulting statements.

Accounting principles have evolved throughout the history of the accounting profession. Their development has been affected by authors of accounting texts, court decisions, general practice, pronouncements of regulatory bodies, and statements by various professional organizations. Important among these organizations are the American Accounting Association, the National Association of Accountants, and the Financial Executives Institute. The American Institute of Certified Public Accountants probably exerted the most influence of all through its Committee on Accounting Procedure and the Accounting Principles Board. With the formation in 1973 of the Financial Accounting Standards Board (FASB), the authoritative accounting rule-making group was no longer composed exclusively of CPAs and ceased to be a division of the AICPA. Quite a number of the accounting principles expressed in the *Accounting Research Bulletins* by the Committee on Accounting Procedure and in the *Opinions* of the Accounting Principles Board have been superseded or modified by later pronouncements. Many, however, remain unchanged and represent generally accepted accounting principles along with *Statements of Financial Accounting Standards* issued by the FASB.

In expressing an opinion that financial statements conform with generally accepted accounting principles, an auditor indicates that the principles used by the client's management are appropriate in the circumstances and have been selected from those considered generally accepted. If a client uses an accounting principle that conflicts with one espoused by these official pronouncements, the AICPA's Code of Professional Ethics requires that the auditor demonstrate that, due to unusual circumstances, the financial statements would have been misleading had the official pronouncement been followed.

EARLY AUDITING

Audits of some type have been conducted as long as there has been commerce. The earliest audits were meticulous, detailed reviews of records designed to determine whether each transaction was recorded in the proper account and in the correct amount. The primary purpose of these early audits was to detect defalcations and to determine whether persons in fiduciary positions were acting and reporting responsibly. The earliest audits were meant to assure the owner of a business that hired clerks had maintained the accounts correctly and that all assets were on hand and were in the proper amounts. Somewhat later, when attempting to borrow money, an owner could use the balance sheet to indicate to a banker that the business had sufficient assets to secure a loan. Bankers frequently required that an independent auditor certify the correctness of such balance sheets.

After the Industrial Revolution, the scope and complexity of business expanded greatly. As companies increased in size, they employed larger numbers of people, and their accounting systems became more highly developed. With an expanded accounting system and more people involved, it was possible to divide duties within a company. No one person had the responsibility for handling a complete transaction, the functions of asset custody and record keeping were separated, and other effective internal controls were developed to protect assets and to prevent and detect defalcations. Internal auditors also became a major part of internal control systems. With the increased volume of business activity and the complexity of accounting systems, detailed audits became prohibitively expensive. Additionally, it was realized that the goal of error detection could be accomplished more effectively through an adequate system of internal control. The auditor's role shifted from searching for defalcations and certifying the correctness of a balance sheet to reviewing the system and testing evidence so that an opinion could be expressed on the fair presentation of all financial statements.

The increased widespread ownership of corporations encouraged the development of modern auditing. The stock exchanges in the early part of this century established minimum reporting standards for companies whose stocks were listed. Federal securities legislation in 1933 and 1934 created the Securities and Exchange Commission (SEC), expanded these reporting requirements, and required that financial statements be attested to by independent auditors.

MODERN AUDITING

The present-day audit consists primarily of: (1) a review of the internal accounting control system to determine whether it is designed so that accurate records are maintained, assets are protected, and reliable reports are rendered; (2) tests of the transactions to determine whether the accounting control system functions as designed; and (3) tests of evidence to substantiate the information appearing on the financial statements and in the accompanying notes. The primary purpose of modern auditing is to enable the auditor to express an opinion as to the conformity of financial statements with generally accepted accounting principles.

Errors and Irregularities In this text, the term *error* is used to indicate unintentional mistakes, such as clerical mistakes, misapplication of accounting principles, and misinterpretation or oversight of facts. The term *irregularities* refers to intentional distortions of the financial statements resulting from deliberate misrepresentations by management or misappropriation of assets. SAS No. 16 (AU 327) elaborates upon these definitions and also details the procedures the auditor should follow when circumstances indicate the possible existence of material errors or irregularities. The opinion expressed by the auditor that the statements are presented in conformity with generally accepted accounting principles implies the auditor's belief that they are not materially misstated as a result of errors or irregularities, and users of these statements rely in part, at least, on the auditor's report to give them assurance that the statements are not so misstated. Although the primary purpose of an audit today is not the discovery of errors and irregularities, usual auditing procedures include a search for indications of their existence. When the auditor discovers information indicating that material errors or irregularities may exist, the matter should first be brought to the attention of management at least one level above those involved. If the auditor believes that appropriate corrective action has not been taken, the board of directors or its audit committee should be informed. If it appears that errors or irregularities may materially affect the financial statements, the auditor should modify the standard report or withdraw from the engagement. In either case, the auditor should clearly explain to the client in writing the reasons for such action.

The auditor may determine that material errors or irregularities discovered during the audit do not directly affect the fairness of the financial statements. The matters should still be brought to the attention of appropriate management officials who are at least one level above those involved, and the auditor should consider whether the presence of these errors and irregularities reflect adversely on the company's internal control system.

Illegal Acts by Clients The usual audit examination is not primarily designed for the detection of illegal acts. The assessment of the legality of many acts is beyond the professional competence of most auditors; however, they should be able to recognize that certain acts might be illegal. As part of each examination the auditor should make inquiries about the client's compliance with laws and regulations and about the procedures employed to prevent illegal acts. Normal auditing procedures may bring to the auditor's attention facts that indicate that illegal acts may have occurred. The auditor should expand the investigation of these facts, make inquiries of management, and perhaps consult with the client's lawyer and other specialists.

If it is determined that an illegal act has occurred, SAS No. 17 (AU 328.13) requires that the auditor report the circumstances to personnel within the client's organization who have sufficient authority to take appropriate action. Frequently the board of directors or its audit committee is the appropriate group to inform. Those in authority should be able to initiate remedial action, to have the financial statements adjusted, and to make necessary disclosures. If the financial statements are adjusted and accompanied by disclosure, the auditor's opinion will not be directly affected by the discovery of these acts; however, the implications of illegal acts may affect the auditor's willingness to rely upon the internal accounting controls and representations of management. If the financial statements do not reflect proper accounting and disclosure of the illegal acts, the auditor should modify the standard report or withdraw from the engagement. Generally the auditor is under no obligation to notify anyone other than client personnel of an illegal act. Management has the responsibility of informing other appropriate parties.

Selective Sampling A fundamental approach to modern auditing is *sampling,* in contrast with the earlier approach of detailed examination of transactions and account balances. Items selected for review by the auditor are examined to determine if they meet criteria that are established standards in the field. The tests frequently involve samples of data selected by statistical techniques in order that the auditor may know, with a predetermined degree of confidence, that the samples are representative of the entire group of data under examination. Whether or not statistical sampling procedures are used, the auditor cannot be completely certain that the financial statements present fairly the company's financial position and the results of operations. There always exists the possibility that evidence contained in data not selected for examination might change the auditor's opinion as to the fairness of the financial presentation. The sampling should be extensive enough so that the evidence tested will enable the auditor to express an opinion with professional confidence.

Other public accounting services

Usually the practice of public accounting is divided into the major divisions of auditing, income tax advisory services, management advisory services, and small business services. Auditing was the first service rendered, and it continues to dominate.

INCOME TAX ADVISORY SERVICES

Public accountants have rendered income tax advisory services in the United States since the first passage of income tax legislation. However, the greatest growth in this area has been since the 1940s, when income taxes became a complex and significant business consideration. Because of the correlation between taxable income and the net income figure on financial statements, auditors were in a logical position to extend their services to include advice to their clients on matters related to income taxes. In addition to the actual preparation of income tax returns, many public accountants render a valuable service to both individuals and corporations by advising them in the areas of minimization of their tax liability and compliance with the tax law. In contrast to the audit function, in which public accountants must be certain that financial statements are not biased, the area of income tax services allows accountants to take a position of advocacy and to support the position that, under the tax law, is most favorable to their clients.

MANAGEMENT ADVISORY SERVICES

Auditors have always been alert to detect weaknesses in clients' accounting systems and have been aware of clients' problems in operating their businesses. An auditor was usually willing to enter into engagements to redesign a system or to provide a client with general business advice, but these were traditionally beyond the scope of the normal audit engagement. The nature of such additional engagements began to expand greatly during the 1950s, and many firms of public accountants established separate divisions to render these specialized services. Some CPAs believe management advisory services should be limited to management accounting and control or management information systems. Others, who take a broader view of acceptable professional services, believe that the field should be limited only by an accountant's expertise. Certainly an auditor should not extend services into areas clearly within the domain of other professions. No complete listing of services is possible; however, some to be included are advice on electronic data processing equipment and system design, development and installation of cost accounting systems, advice on budget preparation and analysis of variances, advice on working capital requirements, advice on long-term financing and alternative forms of capitalization, design of forms and reports, advice on pension and profit-sharing plans, advice on pricing, and advice on governmental regulations on such matters as fair trade practices and wage and price controls.

Although there seems to be no general agreement as to the specific services included in management advisory services, all seem to agree that public accountants cannot become so deeply involved in clients' activities that the external users of accounting reports cease to look upon the accountants as independent. Accountants must restrict themselves to advisory services and not become part of the decision-making management team. Services that are primarily commercial in nature and are inconsistent with the professional standing of CPAs should not be among the management advisory services offered. Psychological testing, public opinion polls, and merger and acquisition assistance for a finder's fee are examples of advisory services currently viewed as outside the scope of public accounting. The AICPA is reviewing this matter and perhaps will identify other services deemed to be in conflict with the audit function.

Auditors are required by the Securities and Exchange Commission (SEC), which regulates the listing and sale of securities on the nation's stock exchanges, to present annual statements for each client revealing the nature of all services rendered.[1] The auditor also must indicate the percentage relationship that the fees for nonaudit services bear to the total audit fee stated. The percentage must be computed both separately for each nonaudit service and in the aggregate. This disclosure is required regardless of whether the board of directors or its audit committee approved each nonaudit service. The availability of this information is designed to enable investors and other users of financial statements to understand and evaluate more clearly the relationship between the auditor and the client company. Disclosure information should also indicate whether appropriate consideration was given to the potential effect of these services on the auditor's independence.

SMALL BUSINESS SERVICES

Another aspect of public accounting practice is rendering advisory services to small businesses. Some accountants have specialized in this area, and these services are rendered by a separate department in some large public accounting firms. Many businesses need the services of a controller or financial officer but are not large enough to warrant employing such a person full time. As financial advisors, public accountants can render a valuable service to such businesses. By reviewing financial statements and internal management reports with the personnel of the small business enterprise on a monthly or quarterly basis, accountants can make suggestions about needed actions in many areas—product mix, control over purchasing activities, custody of inventory items, need for temporary financing, and many other business activities. At times financial statements may be compiled from the company's records; in other cases the auditor may perform a review of the statements although an audit is not performed. These services and the related reports are discussed further in Chapter 6. In addition to preparing or reviewing periodic statements and reports, public accountants in the small business services area are usually available at all times for consultation with clients on any management or financial matter concerning them.

Organization of public accounting firms

The practice of public accounting is conducted by firms of accountants that vary greatly in size. Of course, the smallest firm is the single accountant

[1] *Accounting Series Release 250,* Securities and Exchange Commission, Washington, D.C., 1978.

practitioner who has no professional staff. At the other end of the size spectrum are large international public accounting firms with several hundred accountants as partners and thousands of others working at the professional staff level. Many firms have offices in all major cities of the United States and in numerous foreign countries. By employing staff members with many different specialties, these firms are usually able to offer their clients a full range of accounting services. Because of the widespread operations of many commercial enterprises today, only national or international accounting firms are in a position to render the auditing, tax, and management advisory services that such clients request. Ranging between the extremes of the single practitioner and the international firm are local, regional, and smaller national firms.

Accountants who practice as individuals must limit the scope of their services, because no one person can be proficient enough to handle all aspects of auditing, income taxes, and management advisory services. Also, there must be a limit to the size of the business that can be serviced, for a single individual cannot devote sufficient time to serve a large company with widespread operations properly. On the other hand, many businesses need individualized professional accounting services that can be rendered effectively by a single practitioner or a relatively small firm.

In order to serve larger clients, to expand the nature of the services rendered, and to share the overhead costs of operating an office, many public accountants who initially have practiced as single practitioners form partnerships with one or more other accountants. The availability of another professional with whom ideas may be shared and discussed, the opportunity for one to specialize and enhance one's expertise, and the advantages of reviewing one another's work are among the reasons why public accountants decide to form partnerships.

In recent years some local CPA firms have joined together in associations for mutual assistance. The local firms do not lose their identity, yet they receive some of the benefits of being part of a larger organization, such as the availability of other members to assist in audits of clients located in distant geographical areas. Also, by pooling resources, member firms may offer to their personnel educational and training opportunities not usually practicable for a small firm acting alone. Members may also share the services of industry specialists or develop procedures for consultation on technical accounting, auditing, and tax matters.

The laws of most states and the AICPA's Code of Professional Ethics allow public accountants to practice as individuals, to form partnerships, or to form professional associations or corporations. Historically, public accountants, because of the personal nature of their professional services, were prohibited from incorporating their firms. Although today some firms have chosen to incorporate, the nature of their services has not been affected, and their operating structure has been practically unchanged.

Staff organization

In public accounting firms, staff positions and related duties may not be defined as clearly as in industrial operations. During the course of a year, an individual works on the audits of a number of different clients, and the duties assigned may vary in nature as well as in requisite skills. When employed by a small public accounting firm, or when assigned to the audit of a small company, one person may have to perform duties at several levels and at times even perform the complete audit. Consequently, the descriptions of the staff positions that follow are general and may be found to apply more specifically to larger public accounting firms.

THE ASSISTANT ACCOUNTANT

During the first year or two in public accounting, an assistant accountant must follow carefully the instructions of a supervisor who closely reviews the work and makes constructive criticism. Some duties assigned to an assistant accountant include analysis of various accounts, inspection of supporting documents, counts of cash and inventory items, verification of pricing, extensions and additions, and confirmation of accounts receivable. These duties soon are replaced by more responsible assignments. Successful performance of these assignments, as well as possession of necessary personal characteristics, are requisites for advancement. Successful accountants should have inquisitive minds and should want to investigate what lies behind information routinely furnished. They should be willing to pay attention to details, yet be able to maintain a perspective regarding the overall operation of the accounting system. Being alert to situations that appear to be unusual is a desirable trait. They should recognize the limitations of their knowledge and experience and, accordingly, should report errors and irregularities to the supervisor, who will determine what further steps to take. Courtesy and tact are beneficial qualities for auditors, for they must be able to get along with clients' personnel and also with fellow professionals. The ability to communicate effectively is a necessary characteristic of a person who is going to succeed in public accounting. Both orally and in writing, one should be able to give clear instructions and to report findings accurately. The ability of an auditor to communicate is quite important, for the public accounting profession can only be of value to society if its practitioners can furnish users with relevant information in an understandable form.

THE SENIOR ASSISTANT ACCOUNTANT

After acquiring sufficient experience to conduct small audits and important sections of major audits with little or no immediate supervision, an auditor may be advanced to the position of senior assistant and on some audits may be assigned assistant auditors to supervise. Usually the senior assistant has passed some or all parts of the CPA examination and is demonstrating the necessary technical and leadership abilities to advance within the firm. Frequently the rank of senior assistant is not designated; rather, assistant accountants are known either as those with "light" experience or those with "heavy" experience.

THE SENIOR ACCOUNTANT

Customarily, when a professional has received a CPA certificate, has had several years' experience, and has demonstrated the ability to supervise fellow workers, promotion to the position of senior accountant takes place. The senior usually is placed in direct charge of sizable audits, on which several assistants may be assigned, and has the responsibility of assigning duties to the staff, reviewing their work, and preparing or modifying the audit program as necessary. Day-to-day contact with the client includes consultation on routine matters. For major changes in the audit program or for major conferences with a client, the manager or supervisor on the engagement would be consulted. The senior accountant has the ability and training to coordinate all aspects of the audit examination, to determine when sufficient evidence has been gathered, and to write the draft of the audit report.

THE MANAGER OR SUPERVISOR

Auditors who demonstrate the requisite characteristics of leadership and analytical ability and have had a number of years of public accounting experience are normally advanced to the position of manager or supervisor. Having often developed a specialization, they may be assigned the responsibility of managing several engagements at one time in the audit department, tax department, or management services department. The manager is usually the professional who meets with officials of the client to plan the general nature of the audit. Also, the manager may deliver and discuss the final report with the officials. The manager reviews the supporting working papers and the final report to determine not only whether the audit has been satisfactorily performed but also whether the most current standards of reporting are employed. Also, a manager may be given the responsibility of office management or staff training. In a small firm most functions of a manager are often performed by a partner. Managers are expected to stay current in the general developments in accounting, although their in-depth knowledge may be limited to an area of specialization.

PARTNERS

The CPAs who bear the full responsibility of the public accounting practice of the firm are the partners. They spend much time in developing client and public relations, for it is through contacts with partners that most new clients are obtained. In the large public accounting firms, some partners have little if any contact with the day-to-day aspects of auditing. They review the final copies of audit reports with managers and determine whether each audit is in accordance with firm policies and whether the report meets all professional standards. Before signing the auditor's report expressing a professional opinion on the fairness of the financial statements, the partner reviews working papers, discusses the procedures and findings, and makes inquiries necessary for assurance that all aspects of the audit were conducted in a satisfactory manner, that the report is properly written, and that the financial statements do, in fact, present fairly the financial condition of the client company.

To be successful partners, accountants must have superior leadership ability and outstanding management capabilities. They must have general knowledge in all areas of their firm's practice. They cannot be expected to have in-depth knowledge in all specialties, yet they must have sufficient knowledge to review the work of specialists, since the partners are responsible for all aspects of their firm's work.

STAFF TRAINING

The practice in many public accounting firms is to assign all new professional employees to the audit staff. Although the career goal of the employees may be to specialize in taxation or management services, these firms prefer to begin all new employees' training in the auditing area because much information used by both the income tax department and the management services department is gathered during the regular audit. When involved in the examination of a company, auditors have an excellent opportunity to obtain an overall view of the operations. They can gain insight into all aspects of business activities from the very lowest operational level to the top administrative function.

Many public accounting firms enter employees in a formal training program shortly after they join the firm. These programs may deal almost exclusively with firm policies, or they may deal with the detailed aspects of auditing procedures. As employees advance within the firm, they may attend other training programs on more advanced subjects or on currently developing topics. Some firms prefer that employees receive their training on the job, as actual experience is an essential part of every auditor's training and development.

The profession's response to criticism

During the latter part of the 1970s the accounting profession, particularly its auditing activities, met with considerable criticism and with numerous suggestions for changes. The primary sources of criticism and recommendations were:

1. The Commission on Auditors' Responsibilities (an independent commission appointed by the AICPA chaired by Manuel F. Cohen; referred to frequently as the Cohen commission)
2. The Subcommittee on Reports, Accounting and Management of the Committee on Governmental Affairs of the United States Senate and its staff (referred to frequently as the Metcalf committtee)
3. The Subcommittee on Oversight and Investigations of the Committee on Interstate and Foreign Commerce of the United States House of Representatives (referred to frequently as the Moss committee)
4. The Securities and Exchange Commission (a governmental body that has the legal authority to establish accounting principles and auditing procedures for financial statements filed by publicly held companies under its jurisdiction)

The views of various critics were that the auditing profession failed to keep pace with changes in the business environment. They asserted that users of financial statements had needs that were not met by the statements and the accounting principles employed. They noted that because the auditing profession was slow to act, the courts in some instances had established the responsibilities of auditors and the standards for their conduct. Auditors were accused of hiding behind technical jargon, of not clearly communicating their opinions, and of being hesitant to accept responsibility for detection of fraud, illegal payments, and other acts of misconduct.

Some critics viewed the profession as a group dominated by large public accounting firms with control exercised through the AICPA. They contended that the profession restricted competition and as a result did not provide services to clients at the most economical price. Entry into the profession and movement by employees from firm to firm were also restricted, according to these viewers.

Other observers contended that only government regulation of the profession could bring about needed reforms, give assurance of independence of the auditors, and establish uniform accounting principles. Although some continue to favor governmental regulation, the prevailing attitude appears to be that the control of the profession should remain in the private sector with active oversight from the SEC.

Numerous changes have been implemented in response to the criticism. The AICPA has added public members to its governing body; meetings of many of its committees are now open to the public; and it gives greater public disclosure of disciplinary action taken against members. Statements on Auditing Standards have been issued concerning the communication of weaknesses discovered in internal controls, the detection of illegal payments, and other matters. The rules of professional conduct have been amended to permit advertising and other activities that may increase competition. Many of the changes have affected subjects that are discussed in this text, and these changes are incorporated in later chapters when appropriate. Other selected changes are highlighted in the following sections.

REGULATION OF CPA FIRMS

In order to strengthen its self-regulatory requirements and sanctions, the American Institute of Certified Public Accountants created a new division comprised of firms. Prior to creating this division, the AICPA had no mechanism for regulating firms since membership was composed exclusively of individual CPAs. The new division has two sections, one for SEC practice and the other for private companies practice. Both sections are governed by an executive committee, have a public oversight board, require peer reviews of members, and may impose sanctions on member firms.

The SEC practice section has among its goals improvement of the quality of practice of firms before the Securities and Exchange Commission. The section has established a system to monitor and evaluate the activities of its members, strengthening the profession's self-regulation. All of the large public accounting firms in the United States have joined the SEC practice section, as have many smaller firms. Membership in the section is voluntary, and firms need not have SEC clients in order to join. Some of the major requirements imposed upon firms joining the SEC practice section are (1) mandatory continuing professional education of forty hours a year for all partners and professional staff members, (2) mandatory peer review of the firm's quality controls at least every three years, (3) generally a limitation of five years as the period during which a partner may be in charge of any SEC engagement, (4) maintenance of prescribed minimum amounts of liability insurance, (5) required reports to the board of directors or its audit committee describing disagreements with management that would have resulted in a qualification of the auditor's opinion had there not been a resolution, and (6) annual filing of information for public inspection regarding the size, location, fees, number of clients, and so on, of each member firm.

The organization and requirements of the private companies practice section parallels that of the SEC practice section, including provisions for quality controls, continuing education, peer reviews, and a public oversight board. The private companies practice section concentrates on the needs of the type of clients served by these firms and on ways to improve the services provided. Additionally, the section is designed to provide a means whereby the smaller firms may make known their views on professional matters, and to develop ways to establish technical standards that meet the circumstances of smaller and/or privately owned businesses.

Quality Controls At least once every three years each member firm is required to have a peer review to determine whether the firm maintains and applies proper quality controls. Each firm has the responsibility to establish policies and procedures appropriate to its size and the nature of its practice in order to assure that it conforms with professional standards in providing professional services. These policies and procedures must be communicated, usually in writing, to the firm's employees. SAS No. 4 (AU 160.04) describes the policies and procedures that should be established by a firm and gives examples to serve as guidelines. The policies and procedures should be designed to give assurance that

1. independence is maintained in fact and in appearance
2. audits are carried out by individuals having the training and proficiency needed in the circumstances
3. those performing audits seek advice when needed from others having the appropriate expertise
4. the appropriate quality of work is maintained through supervision and review at all organizational levels
5. personnel are hired who have integrity, competence, and motivation to perform competently
6. continuing education and training activities afford employees the knowledge needed to fulfill assigned responsibilities
7. personnel are promoted only when capable of fulfilling increased responsibility
8. clients are selected and continued in a manner to minimize the likelihood of association with those lacking integrity or reliability
9. inspections are made to determine that all other quality control procedures are applied effectively

Peer reviews, conducted either by an AICPA peer review committee or by another CPA firm, include an examination of working papers and other documents to determine that the necessary quality controls have been established and are operative and that other provisions for membership in the AICPA division have been met. The peer review committee may make recommendations for sanctions and other disciplinary action to the executive committee. Sanctions that may possibly be imposed on a firm include monetary fines, suspension or expulsion from membership, censure or reprimand, additional or special peer reviews, additional continuing professional education requirements, and corrective measures dictated by the circumstances. Individuals and firms that are not members of the

AICPA division of firms may participate in a similar voluntary quality review program.

Public Oversight Board A major aspect of the AICPA's response to criticism was the creation of a public oversight board to monitor the operations of each practice section and to report any information deemed appropriate concerning the actions of the peer review or executive committees. Its report may be made to the executive committee of the section, the SEC, congressional committees, or the public. Some observers believe the public oversight board should be given a stronger position by granting it sole authority to impose sanctions, by having it approve the scope and standards of peer reviews, and by its participation in the selection of members of the peer review committee. The public oversight board is composed of five individuals from outside the accounting profession, such as bankers, attorneys, educators, economists, and business executives. The board is supported by a staff to assist members in carrying out their duties.

AUDIT COMMITTEES

The Commission on Auditors' Responsibilities, the SEC, the executive committee of the AICPA, and others have urged that each company to be audited establish an audit committee within its board of directors. An audit committee composed entirely of outside directors, or at minimum a majority of outside directors, is an excellent means of establishing and maintaining communication between the board of directors and the company's independent auditors. The committee should discuss with the auditors the intended scope of the examination and be assured that management has not restricted the auditors' proposed scope. The committee may also examine and approve the estimated fees for the audit. The auditors may choose to discuss with the committee major developments in accounting, such as the effect of any new FASB or SEC pronouncements on the financial statements, or the effect of any proposed changes in accounting policies. Any questionable or possibly illegal activities discovered during the audit should be brought to the audit committee's attention. The auditors should discuss with the committee their suggestions for improving the system of internal accounting control and any recommended changes in accounting procedures. The independence of the auditors is emphasized by their having the opportunity to discuss their findings and recommendations with an audit committee rather than having to communicate primarily with members of management. By attending shareholders' meetings to respond to questions relating to the audit, the auditors can further exemplify their independence from management. The New York Stock Exchange now requires that all companies whose stocks are listed have an audit committee composed of outside directors. Many other companies follow a similar practice.

FUTURE CHANGES

Many of the recommendations for changes in the auditing profession to meet the needs and expectations of users have been implemented; others are in the process of implementation; still others will be accomplished in the future. The Commission on Auditors' Responsibilities recommended several pervasive changes which may take considerable time to achieve and potentially will have profound effects. Among these is a revision of the auditor's report to include paragraphs describing the auditor's work and findings in nontechnical terminology. The suggested report also includes an evaluation of the company's internal controls. Further discussion of the recommendations regarding the auditor's report appears in Chapter 6.

Change is a characteristic of any true profession. Auditing, as a dynamic profession, is subject to continual change. Students of auditing should be prepared to read the current literature and professional pronouncements to expand their knowledge both while studying the discipline and later as active members of the profession.

Supplementary readings

"The AICPA Division of CPA Firms." *Journal of Accountancy* (November 1977), 113-117.

"The Accounting Establishment." *Management Accounting* (April 1977), 51-54.

American Institute of Certified Public Accountants. *Report of Progress: The Institute Acts on Recommendations for Improvements in the Profession.* New York: American Institute of Certified Public Accountants, 1978.

Auerbach, Norman. "ABCs of Audit Committees." *Financial Executive* (October 1976), 22-33.

Boyle, Joseph T., and Thomas L. Holton. "Peer Reviews in the Auditing Profession—Who Audits the Auditor?" *CPA Journal* (January 1975), 15-18.

Breniser, Wayne. "Peer Reviews—A Call for Action." *CPA Journal* (October 1976), 15-19.

Burns, David C., and William J. Haga. "Much Ado About Professionalism: A Second Look at Accounting." *Accounting Review* (July 1977), 705-715.

Burton, John C. "The Profession's Institutional Structure in the 1980's." *Journal of Accountancy* (April 1978), 63-69.

Chetkovich, Michael N. "Current Developments in the Accounting Profession." *CPA Journal* (January 1977), 5-8.

"Improving the Accountability of Publicly Owned Corporations and Their Auditors—Report of the Subcommittee on Reports, Accounting and Management of the Committee on Governmental Affairs United States Senate." *Journal of Accountancy* (January, 1978), 88-96.

Johnson, Johnny R. "Quality Control in a Local Firm." *Journal of Accountancy* (February, 1979), 38-46.

Kapnick, Harvey. "The Changing Role of Public Accounting." *Accounting Forum* (May 1978), 31-39.

Kreiser, Larry. "Maintaining and Improving the Audit Competence of CPAs: CPA and Selected User Reaction." *Accounting Review* (April 1977), 427-437.

McCullers, L. D., and R. P. Van Daniker. "Professionalism in Accounting." *CPA Journal* (August 1974), 39-42.

Mautz, Robert K., and Hussein A. Sharaf. *The Philosophy of Auditing.* Sarasota, Fla.: American Accounting Association, 1961.

Orback, Kenneth N., and Robert H. Strawser. "Public Disclosure Requirements of CPA Firms?" *CPA Journal* (February 1979), 15-21.

Solomon, Kenneth I., and Hymon Muller. "Illegal Payments: Where the Auditor Stands." *Journal of Accountancy* (January 1977), 51-57.

Subcommittee on Reports, Accounting and Management of the Senate Committee on Government Operation. *The Accounting Establishment.* Washington, D.C.: U.S. Government Printing Office, 1977.

Whitehand, Frank. "Management Fraud: What to Look for and What to Do About It." *The Practical Accountant* (October-November 1978), 59-65.

Review questions

1-1. Who are the users of accounting information?

1-2. Why do the users of accounting information require that this information be reviewed by a person independent of the preparer?

1-3. Define *auditing.*

1-4. Describe the work and the objectives of an internal auditor.

1-5. "If a company has an effective internal auditor, there is no need to duplicate his or her work, and services of an external auditor are not needed." Comment on the preceding statement.

1-6. Who has primary responsibility for the accumulation of accounting data and its presentation on financial statements?

1-7. A prospective purchaser and a prospective seller both may rely upon the same set of financial statements attested to by a CPA. Since they are on opposing sides of the transaction, how can they, with confidence, rely upon the same financial statements?

1-8. What are the characteristics that professions are usually considered to possess?

1-9. What are the requirements that a person must usually meet in order to become a CPA?

1-10. Describe the influence that the AICPA has upon its members and also upon nonmembers.

1-11. How does one know which accounting principles are generally accepted? In what way do accounting principles become generally accepted?

1-12. Contrast the purposes of early auditing with those of modern auditing and explain the influence of internal control on each.

1-13. What are the three major phases of a modern-day audit?

1-14. The owner of a small business said, "I'm quite relieved to know that my bookkeeper made no errors last year, for my auditor just delivered the financial statements and gave the usual warranty that everything is correct." Comment on the owner's view of an audit.

1-15. Describe the services that a public accounting firm renders in addition to auditing.

1-16. What are the reasons that a CPA might decide to form a partnership with other CPAs for the practice of public accounting?

1-17. Why were CPA firms traditionally formed as partnerships? Why is this business form no longer required?

1-18. For what reasons would a person entering public accounting with the desire to specialize in management advisory services be urged to work first as an auditor?

1-19. Describe the services that public accountants may render clients in the areas of management advisory services and small business services.

1-20. What is the importance of a public accountant's avoiding the *decision-making role* and stressing the *advisory role* in rendering management advisory services?

1-21. Describe the personal characteristics of a beginning public accountant that would likely contribute to his or her advancement.

1-22. Describe the major duties in the practice of public accounting of:
   a. an assistant accountant
   b. a senior assistant accountant
   c. a senior accountant
   d. a manager or supervisor
   e. a partner

1-23. Why has the public accounting profession established procedures for review of the quality of a firm's operations and practices?

1-24. Describe some steps taken by public accounting firms to help assure the maintenance of proper quality of their services.

Decision problems

1-25. James Wilson, a research professor at Northern Tech, recently organized a consulting firm. He was advised to immediately consult a lawyer and an accountant, which he did.

The CPA, whom he contacted, helped Wilson set up a simple accounting system, which his wife is maintaining. His wife has called the CPA several times and always seems to get an immediate answer to her questions. The CPA has suggested that he be engaged to audit the annual financial statements.

Wilson and his wife have discussed the necessity of having the statements audited. They have decided it is probably a good idea to be assured that she has made no errors in maintaining the records. Also, some other professors have indicated a desire to invest in the consulting firm, and Wilson says he wants the CPA to be able to certify to any new investors that the company accounting records reflect exactly what has gone on.

Mrs. Wilson has indicated that she likely will cease working sometime during the next year, and she has pointed out that it will be good to have the assurance of the CPA that whoever takes her place makes no errors or tries to steal anything.

Discuss the function of a CPA in meeting the desires of the Wilsons.

1-26. Bill Marcotte, a CPA, worked for the public accounting firm of Mullins and Keck for seven years before accepting the job of internal auditor with the Oliver Manufacturing Company. For three years, Marcotte had been the supervisor of the audit of Oliver Manufacturing Company and had become quite familiar with the operations and accounting system as the external independent auditor.

Although Marcotte is not employed in public accounting, he continues to renew his CPA license, attends meetings of the local chapter of the state society of CPAs, is still a member of the AICPA, and attempts to abide by the code of ethics. He says that the scope of his examination is somewhat broader than it was as an external auditor and that his reports are a great deal more detailed. He indicates that he has quite a sense of independence within the Oliver Manufacturing Company organization.

The president of Oliver Manufacturing Company, Philip Oliver, has asked Marcotte to examine the set of financial statements prepared at the end of the past quarter and to express his opinion on them as a CPA. Mr. Oliver intends to show these statements to the bank when he is renewing the company loan there within the next few weeks. Mr. Oliver indicated that he still intends for Mullins and Keck, the CPAs, to perform the regular year-end audit, but he expects the quarterly audits to be performed by Marcotte. With Marcotte doing the quarterly audits and helping the auditors from Mullins and Keck at year end, Mr. Oliver has said he expected the audit fee to be reduced by almost as much as Marcotte's salary.

a. Can Bill Marcotte continue to be a CPA and express his independent opinion on the statements of Oliver Manufacturing Company? Discuss.

b. If the banker is fully aware of Marcotte's background and experience and knows of the independence he has within the Oliver Company, is he justified in relying on the financial statements audited by Bill Marcotte? Discuss.

c. Does it make any difference that the financial statements audited by Marcotte are to be presented to the bank where a loan already exists rather than to prospective owners and creditors? Discuss.

d. Explain what you think Bill Marcotte means by the scope of his internal auditing examination being broader than it was as an external auditor and his report being more detailed.

1-27. "The main reason I entered the public accounting profession was to be an auditor on my own. Independence is the ultimate requisite for being an auditor, and the best way for me to be independent is to work alone without any influences from partners or employees.

"I attend many continuing education courses, I read all the pronouncements from the AICPA, and I have my MBA degree. I know I am knowledgeable of the current developments, and I don't want to be associated with anyone who doesn't keep current. If I take in a partner, I can't force him to keep up.

"A client has the right to expect personal service when engaging a CPA, and as a single practitioner I can render that personal service; I can meet my client's needs for a professional advisor."

Reply to the statement quoted above.

1-28. Perry Key and Co., CPAs, have been rendering services as auditors and consultants to Bruce Co., a small textile company. Ellen Howard, a supervisor with Perry Key and Co., has spent a major portion of the past year redesigning the accounting system and some of the quality control system of Bruce Co. Upon her recommendation, the company purchased a minicomputer, and she was given authority to acquire as many "canned" programs and to design as many others as necessary to get full use from the computer. Presently Howard is supervising company personnel and training some new employees so that the system will function as effectively as possible. Probably by year end, she will have finished most of her duties at Bruce Co.

a. Was Perry Key and Co., as a firm of CPAs, justified in having its employee, Ellen Howard, perform the services described above? Discuss.

b. May Perry Key and Co. continue to serve Bruce Co. as independent CPAs? Discuss.

c. Since Ellen Howard is so familiar with the system at Bruce Co., would you think she is the most logical person to supervise their forthcoming audit? Comment.

1-29. Corporations are establishing audit committees more frequently today than in the past. Commonly accepted guidelines have not been formalized, but their duties and responsibilities are emerging through evolutionary processes.

a. Identify the basic responsibilities a corporation's audit committee are most likely to assume.

b. Identify and discuss the probable benefits that can result from corporations establishing audit committees.

CMA adapted

2

Auditing Standards

The overall guidelines for auditing work are known as *generally accepted auditing standards.* These standards establish the framework within which an auditor decides the necessary action to take in preparing for the examination of financial statements, in performing the examination, and in writing the report. These standards serve to measure the quality of the audit objectives and the acts performed to reach these objectives. The auditing standards described by the AICPA Auditing Standards Board are usually recognized as being accepted by the auditing profession. They are expressed in ten statements divided into three groups: general standards, standards of field work, and standards of reporting. Presented below in their entirety, each standard is discussed individually in subsequent sections of this chapter.

General Standards

1. The examination is to be performed by a person or persons having adequate technical training and proficiency as an auditor.
2. In all matters relating to the assignment, an independence in mental attitude is to be maintained by the auditor or auditors.
3. Due professional care is to be exercised in the performance of the examination and the preparation of the report.

Standards of Field Work

1. The work is to be adequately planned and assistants, if any, are to be properly supervised.
2. There is to be a proper study and evaluation of the existing internal control as a basis for reliance thereon and for the determination of the

resultant extent of the tests to which auditing procedures are to be restricted.

3. Sufficient competent evidential matter is to be obtained through inspection, observation, inquiries, and confirmations to afford a reasonable basis for an opinion regarding the financial statements under examination.

Standards of Reporting

1. The report shall state whether the financial statements are presented in accordance with generally accepted accounting principles.
2. The report shall state whether such principles have been consistently observed in the current period in relation to the preceding period.
3. Informative disclosures in the financial statements are to be regarded as reasonably adequate unless otherwise stated in the report.
4. The report shall either contain an expression of opinion regarding the financial statements, taken as a whole, or an assertion to the effect that an opinion cannot be expressed. When an overall opinion cannot be expressed, the reasons therefor should be stated. In all cases where an auditor's name is associated with financial statements, the report should contain a clear-cut indication of the character of the auditor's examination, if any, and the degree of responsibility he is taking.[1]

Standards v. procedures

Whereas auditing standards are the guidelines for controlling the quality of the examination and the report, auditing procedures describe the actual tasks performed to accomplish the audit. The auditing standards are clearly set forth and no deviation from them is permitted if a satisfactory audit is to be performed. In contrast, generally accepted auditing procedures are described in general terms that must be modified to apply to a specific audit engagement. The auditing procedures to be performed in the audit of a particular company are selected for that specific engagement by the auditors in accordance with their professional judgment. The auditors, as trained professionals, base their judgment upon years of education, training, and experience, and their judgment is the ultimate criterion for all action connected with an audit. Auditors have many guides for their judgment, and generally accepted auditing standards are among the most important.

Although the auditing procedures applicable to a specific engagement depend ultimately on the auditor's judgment, there are guides in the professional literature to aid the auditor in selecting procedures appropriate in a variety of situations. *Statements on Auditing Standards* constitute a major source of such information.

[1] American Institute of Certified Public Accountants, *Statements on Auditing Standards*, No. 1, American Institute of Certified Public Accountants, New York, 1973, p. 5.

General standards

All persons engaged in performing an audit examination must be professionals. They not only must have thorough backgrounds in auditing procedures but also must want to perform a service to clients and to all who rely upon the work performed. The general standards in the first section of generally accepted auditing standards relate primarily to the character, attitudes, and training of auditors. These general standards are also known as personal standards.

Training and proficiency

Because many users of audited financial statements are unacquainted with the auditor whose opinion accompanies the statements, it is essential that they be assured they can rely upon the opinion solely on the basis of the auditor's independence. Even the officers, managers, and employees of a client company, who observe an audit examination being performed, are unable to judge the quality of the work. All users rely upon the professional person to have the necessary education and experience to perform in a professional manner. The technical training and proficiency is required by the first general standard, which states:

> The examination is to be performed by a person or persons having adequate technical training and proficiency as an auditor.

Frequently, attainment of the CPA certificate is considered evidence that an auditor has acquired the requisite technical training and proficiency. Regardless of whether an auditor holds a CPA certificate or not, the public likely will expect the auditor to meet the requirements for a certificate.

TECHNICAL TRAINING

An auditor's advanced formal education should not be exclusively in accounting subjects, nor even be limited to subjects of business administration. Rather, college work should include enough general education to enable an auditor to function as a contributing member of society. Successful auditors need the ability to get along with clients and coworkers, both superiors and subordinates; and, to the extent that general education enables one to function with other people, it is perhaps even more valuable than the technical education. Communication skills need to be singled out as being of utmost importance to auditors. Although much accounting information is expressed in figures, in themselves they are almost meaningless if not conveyed to users in clearly understandable written or spoken language.

Successful auditors realize that technical training received a few years in the past probably is inadequate to satisfy the first general auditing standard. Auditors face the continuous task of updating their technical training, and many opportunities are afforded them to advance their technical training. As mentioned in Chapter 1, professional organizations, on both national and state levels, offer numerous continuing education programs.

Auditors always should keep in mind their ultimate goal: to develop proficiency to the extent that they will be able to consider objectively the various presentations of management and be able to express an opinion on these presentations based upon independent judgment as qualified professional experts.

PROFESSIONAL EXPERIENCE

Just as other professions may require of their members periods of internship, residency, or apprenticeship, the accounting profession expects an auditor to have on-the-job training. Many states require a person to have such experience before becoming a CPA; other states may issue the CPA certificate to a person without experience on the condition that the auditor will obtain such experience before being licensed to practice.

The CPA who employs persons as trainees has a professional duty to provide a wide variety of experiences as well as proper supervision and review of their work. The employing CPA usually is eager to offer the trainees broadly based experience as well as the opportunity to advance, because as the trainees develop judgment of proper auditing procedures, they become more valuable employees. Although many trainees leave their supervising employers to enter practice on their own, to join other public accounting firms, or to pursue other fields of endeavor, supervising employers should train aspiring auditors as though they were certain the auditors would stay with the firm. The professional attitude of experienced auditors leads them to share their knowledge and experience and to help trainees become fully qualified auditors.

Independence in mental attitude

For any profession to exist, it must fulfill some need in society. For auditors, this need is that the public, investors, credit grantors, and other users of financial statements be assured that they can rely upon the representations of management concerning the financial condition of the reporting company. An auditor contributes to the users' assurance by expressing an unqualified opinion on statements only after determining through an examination that the presentations are fair in accordance with generally accepted accounting principles. For users to have confidence in an auditor's unbiased objectivity in expressing such an opinion, they must have confidence in the auditor's ability to view the statements with an attitude of mental independence. Hence, the second general standard of auditing states:

> In all matters relating to the assignment, an independence in mental attitude is to be maintained by the auditor or auditors.

Independence has always been regarded as a fundamental concept of the auditing profession. Defined as the ability to act with integrity and objectivity, independence in mental attitude is an indispensable characteristic of auditors. They must be impartial toward all matters that come under their scrutiny and must recognize their obligation for fairness to each of the various user groups. By being intellectually honest, auditors can assure themselves that their opinions are unbiased. Independence, as required by this general auditing standard, is a mental process and is difficult, if not impossible, for observers to evaluate completely.

The users of financial statements must be convinced of the independence of auditors; the very existence of the profession depends on such confidence. If the users were to suspect a lack of independence, opinions that auditors render would be meaningless to them; consequently there would be no need for the auditors' services. In order for users to have confidence that independence of mental attitude exists, auditors should endeavor to avoid relationships and circumstances that might cause observers to doubt their independence. They must give the appearance of independence in addition to maintaining the mental attitude of independence. Many factors that affect the appearance of independence are the subject of the AICPA Rules of Conduct, discussed in Chapter 3.

Due professional care

No profession can espouse a set of standards that would be sufficiently detailed to describe fully all actions required by its members or all acts prohibited. Hence, some general statements must be made to convey the idea that a high level of quality is expected in all aspects of the profession's endeavors. Such a statement is the third general standard of auditing:

> Due professional care is to be exercised in the performance of the examination and the preparation of the report.

The public has a right to expect an auditor to possess the skill commonly possessed by other professional auditors. Auditors are expected to exercise this skill with reasonable care and diligence. If they do not possess the skill or do not exercise it, they have acted in a manner that is unethical and perhaps illegal. Exercise of due care calls for the auditors to fulfill the requirements of all the other standards. They must properly plan the audit, examine sufficient evidence, carefully prepare working papers, evaluate the financial statements, and meticulously prepare the report containing their opinion. The concept of due care is discussed further in Chapter 4 on legal responsibility.

Standards of field work

Auditors must examine sufficient evidence drawn from clients' financial records and underlying data to be convinced that they are justified in expressing an opinion on the financial statements. Auditors prepare a written record of the evidence examined; collectively these records are called *working papers.* These documents serve as the connecting link between the auditors' report and the client's statements and records. The working papers should be perfectly clear regarding the procedures employed by the auditors, the evidence examined, and the conclusions reached. The recorded information should be complete in itself so that reviewers of the working papers, either at the time of preparation or in the future, do not have to guess or depend on anyone's memory about what was done. The working papers should include the trial balance, descriptions of the internal control system, copies of the minutes of board of directors' meetings, analyses of various accounts, bank reconciliations, memoranda as to findings, and any other types of schedules reflecting information deemed pertinent to the audit.

Perhaps if a client were quite small and an auditor were practicing alone, the auditor could remember what evidence was reviewed and perceive the point at which the fairness of the statements became evident. Even under such a situation, the auditor would be unwise not to prepare comprehensive working papers, for at some time in the future the auditor may have to present evidence about how the opinion was derived. Additionally, a single practitioner should prepare a thorough set of working papers to help focus on the overall plan of proceeding, to keep up with progress on the audit, and to provide evidence for future reference.

When an auditor practices with associates, which is the usual situation, working papers serve the important additional function of allowing a review of the work of assistants. In a large public accounting firm, the partners, who sign the audit report and are fully responsible for the opinion expressed therein, rely almost exclusively upon evidence of an adequate audit as reflected in audit working papers. Chapter 8 presents a thorough description of working papers and a discussion of the evidence they contain.

Planning and supervision

Auditing procedures are not standardized, and those used are selected because they have particular significance for the specific engagement. The planning of auditing procedures and the supervision of the auditors performing these tasks are the subject of the first standard of field work, which states:

The work is to be adequately planned and assistants, if any, are to be properly supervised.

ADEQUATE PLANNING

When an audit is adequately planned, an overall strategy for the examination is developed. The auditor's thorough familiarity with the industry in which the client operates is basic to the examination. The auditor should understand how the industry is affected by economic conditions, tax laws, and other governmental regulations. Knowledge of competitive conditions and financial trends in the industry may be pertinent. As pointed out in SAS No. 22 (AU 311), adequate planning includes the auditor's acquiring an understanding of the nature of the client's business, its organization, the location of its facilities, the products sold or services rendered, its financial structure, related party transactions, methods of compensation, and many other matters. The auditor must learn which accounting principles are followed by the client and should anticipate the extent of reliance on internal controls, the level of materiality, conditions that may require extension of audit tests, and particularly, the nature of reports expected by the client. The level of knowledge acquired by the auditor is frequently less than that possessed by management, but it should be sufficient to enable the auditor to plan and conduct the examination in accordance with generally accepted auditing standards.

To acquire the requisite level of knowledge, the auditor makes use of any prior experience with the client company or industry. Much useful information may be contained in working papers of prior audits. Publications, such as textbooks, industry trade journals, AICPA *Industry Audit Guides,* and financial statements of other companies in the same industry, may be good sources of information. Special consideration should be given to recent pronouncements of the FASB and SEC as they may affect the client's financial reports. Discussions on matters that potentially could influence the examination should be held with personnel in the auditor's own firm who have rendered tax, management advisory, or other services to the client. Discussions with management personnel of the client's organization likely will prove to be an important source of information. Additionally, a review of interim financial statements of the current year may alert the auditor to matters affecting the audit plans. Assistance expected from client personnel, including the internal auditor, and any anticipated use of consultants will also influence the planning.

All planning should be well documented and should include an *audit program*. This is a description of the auditing procedures to be followed in the conduct of the audit to accomplish the objectives of the examination. The prescribed steps should reflect the knowledge acquired during the planning stage by the auditor in charge and the assistants. Although the audit program is developed as expertly as possible during the preliminary planning stage, the procedures may need to be modified as additional information is acquired during the course of the audit.

The client's information system and internal accounting controls have a major impact on the design of the audit program. Documentation in the working papers should indicate how the audit program has been affected by the condition of the client's internal accounting control system. Standardized audit programs exist that describe a multitude of steps to be followed for all possible accounts and activities. Such programs often describe more steps than would normally be applied to a specific client. Several examples of standardized audit programs appear in Part III of this text. An auditor should avoid the inclination to follow a procedure just because it is listed in a generalized program. If such programs serve as guides only, they should assure that the auditor has not overlooked any important audit procedures. Either by modifying a generalized program or by writing an original program, an auditor should tailor-make an audit program to meet the needs of each client.

Early appointment of an auditor contributes to the adequate planning of an audit. With an early appointment, an auditor can review a client's internal accounting control system early in the year (particularly if the client is new) and make recommendations that will strengthen the system. Implementation of the recommendations should reduce the amount of auditing to be done because of the auditor's increased reliance upon internal control. Also, an auditor is able to schedule work and staff assignments more effectively if it can be ascertained in advance what audit engagements are forthcoming. An auditor then will be able to match more closely the needs of a client's audit with the staff's expertise.

Planning requires that an auditor perform audit steps on a timely basis. Certain audit procedures are more conveniently carried out when coordinated with activities of the client. An illustration of timeliness in planning involves the observation of the count of physical inventory, an audit procedure that is generally performed. The auditor not only should be present at the count but also should review the client's plans for taking inventory prior to the actual count. Another auditing procedure generally used is the confirmation of accounts receivable by corresponding with the client's customers. Although, given sufficient internal control, this procedure can be performed at any time during or after the year under examination, planning may allow the confirmation to be performed in conjunction with a regular mailing of accounts receivable statements to customers, thereby increasing the efficiency of the procedure. Another example of timeliness in planning audit procedures is scheduling use of a client's computer at times to cause the least inconvenience to the client's regular computer operations. Sometimes the element of surprise is an important aspect of planning—for example, surprise visits can determine what specific EDP programs are in use.

SUPERVISION OF ASSISTANTS

Supervision of assistants is necessary so that those working at all levels of the audit examination understand the overall objectives of the audit and the procedures necessary to accomplish those objectives. Much of the information obtained during the planning stage concerning the industry, the client company, possible accounting and auditing problems, and the timing of procedures should be conveyed to the assistants. The partner with final responsibility will naturally want to be assured that an adequate examination was performed. Since much of the detailed work is performed by assistants, they should bring to their supervisor's attention significant accounting and auditing problems discovered during the examination. If an audit examination is large enough to demand the services of several auditors, a chain of command is established with one auditor in charge. This supervising auditor, like the partners, will want to know that the persons reporting have performed a proper examination. The auditor in charge of an examination, as well as the partner responsible for the job, uses the working papers created during the examination to review the work performed by others. The working papers may vary somewhat in form according to the skill and experience of the auditor; a more experienced auditor probably could assure the superior of the adequacy of the work with less detailed working papers than could an auditor with little experience. In no case should there be a lack of working paper evidence as to the audit steps actually performed.

An assistant auditor will doubtless encounter many puzzling matters and will need to seek the advice of the supervising auditor. Such matters, including their final disposition, should be recorded in the working papers. Evidence is thereby created to reflect that the assistant was supervised properly. A word of special caution is in order on this matter: An auditor should be certain that, for each question reflected in the working papers, an adequate solution is fully presented and documented. Otherwise questions without corresponding answers could be strong evidence that proper supervision of assistants and due professional care were lacking. If there is a difference of opinion among the professional staff members on an audit engagement, SAS No. 22 (AU 311.12) requires that there should be procedures to "enable an assistant to document his disagreement with the conclusions reached if, after appropriate consultation, he believes it necessary to disassociate himself from the resolution of the matter. In this situation, the basis for the final resolution should also be documented."

Working papers usually are designed so that the person preparing them must initial and date them. In reviewing the work, supervising managers and partners also initial the papers to indicate the work has been reviewed. The audit program may be designed in a form whereby an auditor who performs a particular step must initial a space when the task is completed. This procedure also assists the supervisor in assigning work to assistants, supervising their work, and being aware of progress made on the audit.

Internal control evaluation

Because auditing is a sampling process, auditors select areas to be examined and evidence to be inspected that they believe will have the highest degree of relevance to their ultimate purpose of expressing an opinion on the financial statements. They must work within the restrictions of both limited time and reasonable costs and, therefore, cannot inspect all evidence available. To have the highest degree of assurance that their opinions are correct, auditors want to examine more evidence where the possibility of error is great and, if necessary, may be satisfied with less evidence where the possibility of error is small. In other words, the greater the degree of risk, the stronger the evidence required by auditors for their satisfaction.

An effective internal accounting control system greatly increases the possibilities that resulting financial statements will be accurate. Since auditing procedures are affected by the degree of risk involved, it should be evident that a strong internal control system reduces the risk of errors in the financial reports and thereby reduces the extent of the auditing procedures required.

The second standard of field work states:

> There is to be a proper study and evaluation of the existing internal control as a basis for reliance thereon and for the determination of the resultant extent of the tests to which auditing procedures are to be restricted.

This standard spells out the two purposes for which internal control must be reviewed and evaluated. The first is to establish reliance on the system itself. Auditors cannot reconstruct the records for all transactions that have taken place during the period under examination. They must be able to rely on the dependability of the accounting system with its internal controls for proper recording of transactions and the production of financial statements reflecting those events. If the internal control system does not have a certain minimum level of adequacy, no amount of auditing can compensate for its weakness.

The second purpose for the review and evaluation of internal control is to determine the extent of the auditing tests that the auditor will have to make in order to be satisfied about the fairness of the financial statements. As indicated earlier in this chapter, the plan for an audit is necessarily affected by the strengths and weaknesses of a client's internal control system. Chapter 7 presents a thorough discussion of internal control as an overriding factor in all audits.

Evidence

That point in an audit where sufficient evidence has been examined to enable an auditor to express an opinion is determined by the auditor's professional judgment. Even if all available evidence has been examined, the auditor cannot be absolutely certain that the financial statements are exactly correct or are the only fair presentation possible. There may always be some information withheld, either intentionally or unintentionally. Also, there may be several alternative procedures to record and present financial transactions, each considered to result in a fair presentation under generally accepted accounting principles.

How much evidence should be examined according to the auditor's judgment? The third standard of field work specifies that it is enough to afford a *reasonable* basis for the auditor's opinion. This standard states:

> Sufficient competent evidential matter is to be obtained through inspection, observation, inquiries, and confirmations to afford a reasonable basis for an opinion regarding the financial statements under examination.

Regardless of the amount of evidence examined or its quality, an auditor can never be convinced beyond all doubt that the financial statements are entirely fair. The evidence is usually persuasive rather than completely convincing. Although an auditor cannot remove all doubt regarding the fairness of every item, if there is substantial doubt regarding any material item, the auditor should examine additional evidence to remove such doubt. If this doubt cannot be removed, then either a qualified opinion should be issued or an opinion should be disclaimed on the financial statements. The various types of opinions that an auditor may render are discussed in Chapters 5 and 6.

An auditor should approach an audit with the attitude that the client has prepared financial statements which present fairly the financial position of the company. Although this positive approach is taken, an auditor should not limit evidence to what supports this assumption. An attitude of professional skepticism should be maintained, recognizing that the evidence examined may indicate that the statements contain careless errors or intentional misrepresentation, perhaps to cover up defalcations.

An auditor examines not only the underlying accounting records but also corroborating evidential matter, such as minutes of meetings, contracts, invoices, and correspondence from knowledgeable outsiders. The auditor frequently obtains evidence by asking questions of the company's officers and employees, observing them at work, and examining documents created internally as well as externally. To be competent, the evidence must be valid in its nature and relevant to the matter under consideration. Chapter 8 presents a more detailed discussion of types of evidence and methods of examining it, and Chapter 9 shows how statistical sampling techniques may be used effectively to select evidence to produce the desired degree of confidence. These later chapters give additional guidelines about how much evidence is enough, in an auditor's judgment, to afford a reasonable basis for an opinion.

Standards of reporting

For many users of financial statements, an auditor's report is the only evidence that a professional examination has been made. Consequently, it is extremely important that the report be prepared in a professional manner. Four standards that serve as overall guidelines for preparing the report are described below.

Statement presentation

Presentation in accordance with generally accepted accounting principles is the requirement of the first standard of reporting, which states:

> The report shall state whether the financial statements are presented in accordance with generally accepted accounting principles.

Since the auditor is expressing an opinion that the financial statements present fairly the financial position, changes in financial position, and results of operations of a client company, the auditor must establish a criterion for measuring fairness. The presently accepted measure is *generally accepted accounting principles.* This widely used term covers those conventions, rules, and procedures that define accounting practices accepted at a particular time. As expressed in SAS No. 5 (AU 411.02), this term includes the broad guidelines of general application as well as the detailed practices, procedures, and methods of application. Variations in each of these are quite common, and, as a consequence, a set of financial statements can easily be presented in a variety of ways and still be considered a fair presentation according to generally accepted accounting principles. Such principles, it should be noted, do not depend upon wide acceptance in practice prior to becoming generally accepted principles. It is authoritative support that is the primary requirement for a principle to be generally accepted, and such authoritative support may exist for a principle used only infrequently. As pointed out in Chapter 1, pronouncements by the Financial Accounting Standards Board (FASB) constitute a major source of generally accepted accounting principles and should be followed except in unusual circumstances. In absence of a statement from the FASB, the auditor should seek other authoritative support for the accounting principle used in the financial statements under review. This support may be found in pronouncements of other professional associations, the Securities and Exchange Commission and other regulatory bodies, AICPA *Industry Audit Guides,* court decisions, legislation, textbooks, and industry practices, as well as other sources. Auditors should be alert for changes in accounting practices that are considered generally accepted. Some changes may result from decisions by authoritative bodies; others may evolve from common usage in business.

Although unusual, there may be situations in which the application of selected accounting principles from among generally accepted alternatives may result in misleading financial statements. The auditor has the responsibility to insist upon the use of those principles that will result in a fair presentation of the statements taken as a whole. If the substance of transactions should be different from their form, the accounting principles that present the substance of the transactions should be selected.

Consistency

Consistent application of accounting principles from period to period is necessary for users to know that all significant changes in the financial statements over time result from business activities and not from changed accounting procedures. A statement on consistency normally concludes the opinion paragraph of the auditor's report and thereby satisfies the second reporting standard:

> The report shall state whether such principles have been consistently observed in the current period in relation to the preceding period.

Of course, clients may be justified in changing accounting principles at times. In fact, they may be required to change if the previously used principle is no longer generally accepted. Auditors point out this change and its effects or refer to a note to the financial statements that describes the inconsistency. Auditors must state specifically whether they concur with the change in principle.

At times a client company may use an accounting principle for the first time as a result of changed conditions. For example, convertible preferred capital stock may have been issued, and it has an effect on the computation of earnings per share data. If the client discloses such changes on the financial statements or in related notes, no comment is required by the auditor.

In some situations the effect of a change in an accounting principle may be inseparable from the effect of a change in an estimate. The effect is properly presented on the financial statements as a change in estimate, but the auditor must recognize this change in the consistency statement of the opinion because a different accounting principle is used. Also, a change from an accounting principle that is not generally accepted to one that is generally accepted is accounted for as a correction of an error. This change is presented on the financial statements as a prior period adjustment, not as a change in an accounting principle; however, the auditor must comment on this change in the opinion as to consistency because the accounting principle in use differs from the one previously used.

Changed conditions may result in a revision of an accounting estimate. Much data presented on financial statements result from estimates, and revisions in these estimates are to be expected as additional facts are learned or clearer insight is obtained. If the financial statements and notes reflect these changes in estimates, the auditor should make no comment, because there has been no change in the consistent application of accounting principles. Should the auditor believe that the client's description of the change in estimates is inadequate, the auditor should make a comment as required under the third reporting standard on adequate disclosures discussed below.

Adequate disclosures

Financial statements are considered to present to users, primarily creditors and owners, information relevant to economic decisions that they are making. For the information to bear upon their decisions, it must be as complete as possible, relevant to their decisions, and presented in a manner that is understandable. Neither accountants within a client's organization nor independent auditors have specific knowledge about who the users may be or what type of decisions they may be making. Therefore, the financial statements are designed to give information of a rather general nature, with the hope that it will be meaningful to as many users as possible. If the auditor, after considering the purpose of the statements, believes that they do not present the necessary disclosures, the auditor must state so in the report and modify the opinion. Such an approach is required by the third standard of reporting, which states:

Informative disclosures in the financial statements are to be regarded as reasonably adequate unless otherwise stated in the report.

The concept of informative disclosures embraces not only what information is presented but also how it is presented. The arrangement of information on the financial statements, the classification and captions used, and the terminology chosen are all part of disclosure. Footnotes become an extremely important form of disclosure. This information, like the main portion of the financial statements, is a presentation of management. If the auditor assists the client in writing the footnotes, care should be taken to couch them in terms that management would use and not in terms that show they were prepared by an auditor. In making narrative disclosures, an auditor should remember that excessive information does not necessarily provide full disclosure; important facts may hide among trivia.

Should the financial statements and the related notes not present material information necessary for adequate disclosure, the auditor will be unable to express an unqualified opinion as to the fairness of the statements. As required by SAS No. 1 (AU 430.04), the auditor, in addition to modifying the opinion on the statements, generally should present the omitted information, if practicable. The auditor is not expected to present a statement of changes in financial position or segment information when the client has declined to present that information.

Much information discovered by an auditor in the course of the examination does not have to be reflected on the financial statements or in the accompanying notes. Information received by the auditor may be confidential in nature and should not be revealed unless necessary for full disclosure. Should there be a conflict between the concept of full disclosure and the confidential relationship, the resolution must be in favor of full disclosure. If the client does not agree to present the necessary information, the auditor may present it in the audit report and express the appropriate reservations in the opinion. Since the auditor delivers the report to the client, the ultimate decision to make the disclosure public, in theory at least, rests with the client.

Auditor's opinion

Each time an auditor's name is associated with financial statements, the auditor has the responsibility to inform users of the nature of this association with the statements. Generally, an auditor expresses an *unqualified opinion* about the fairness of presentations of the statements but, at times, may express an *adverse opinion.* An adverse opinion is in effect an unqualified negative opinion stating that the financial statements do not present fairly the financial position and results of operations. An auditor may also express a *qualified opinion,* as when an accounting principle is improperly applied, or in cases of insufficient knowledge may issue a *disclaimer of opinion.* Users of the auditor's report are never left in doubt regarding the nature of the examination or the responsibility the auditor is assuming. Such requirements are set forth in the fourth standard of reporting as follows:

> The report shall either contain an expression of opinion regarding the financial statements, taken as a whole, or an assertion to the effect that an opinion cannot be expressed. When an overall opinion cannot be expressed, the reasons therefor should be stated. In all cases where an auditor's name is associated with financial statements, the report should contain a clear-cut indication of the character of the auditor's examination, if any, and the degree of responsibility he is taking.

Chapters 5 and 6 present a thorough discussion of the types of opinions that may be expressed and the circumstances under which they are appropriate.

The discussion in this chapter of generally accepted auditing standards, the guidelines upon which all auditing is based, has introduced several topics that are treated in greater detail in later chapters. As this additional and more thorough treatment is presented, one should keep in mind that, in all cases, generally accepted auditing standards are the controlling criteria.

Supplementary readings

Blum, James D., and David J. Reiner. "Capsule Summary of Auditing Standards." *CPA Journal* (September 1976), 41-46.

Droppo, Donald R., and Donald F. Arnold. "Compliance with Professional Disclosure Standards." *Journal of Accountancy* (January 1979), 80-88.

"Report of the Special Committee of the AICPA to Study the Structure of the Auditing Standards Executive Committee." *Journal of Accountancy* (October 1978), 131-138.

Warren, Carl S. "Uniformity of Auditing Standards." *Journal of Accounting Research* (Spring 1975), 162-176.

Review questions

2-1. What is the purpose of generally accepted auditing standards? Compare this purpose with the purpose of auditing procedures.
2-2. Why may auditing standards be clearly delineated, whereas auditing procedures vary from audit to audit?
2-3. What criteria are used to determine the auditing procedures to be followed on a particular audit engagement?
2-4. Describe the necessary technical training that an auditor should have in order to meet the requirements of the first general auditing standard.
2-5. In what manner does a beginning auditor acquire the experience necessary to meet the requirements of the first general auditing standard?
2-6. Comment on the statement, "The existence of the auditing profession is dependent upon its members maintaining an attitude of mental independence on all matters relating to an audit assignment."
2-7. Why is it necessary for both a single practitioner and a large public accounting firm to prepare a thorough set of working papers on all engagements regardless of size?
2-8. What are the primary benefits of using standardized audit programs, and what is an inherent danger in using such programs?
2-9. In what ways does the early appointment of an auditor contribute to adequate planning of an audit?
2-10. Name several audit procedures that are carried out in a timely manner when coordinated with activities of a client.
2-11. Describe how working papers serve to implement the auditing standard that requires proper supervision of assistants.
2-12. Why is it necessary that an adequate solution be reflected for each question recorded in the working papers?
2-13. How does the possibility of error in a client's data affect an auditor's selection of areas to be examined and evidence to be inspected?
2-14. Discuss two reasons why an auditor is required by auditing standards to review and evaluate a client's system of internal control.
2-15. Why is it impossible for an auditor to be completely convinced that the financial statements are exactly correct, even when the auditor has examined all the evidence considered necessary? Should the auditor try to remove this doubt?
2-16. How do auditors know they have examined sufficient evidence to justify an opinion on clients' financial statements?
2-17. "If an auditor has substantial doubt regarding a material item, he or she should examine additional evidence. If, after examining the additional evidence, one is unable to remove the doubt, one should in all cases withdraw from the engagement and explain in writing the reasons to the client." Comment on the preceding statement.
2-18. In expressing an unqualified opinion on financial statements, an auditor uses the term *presents fairly.* What criterion is used to measure fairness?
2-19. What is the primary requirement for an accounting principle or practice to be considered generally accepted?

2-20. When a client justifiably changes from one accounting principle to another, what must an auditor do to modify the report?

2-21. Under the third standard of reporting, what action is required by an auditor if the financial statements of a client do not present disclosures considered to be necessary by the auditor?

2-22. Discuss the possible conflict between the concept of full disclosure and the concept of confidential relations. How is this conflict generally resolved?

Decision problems

2-23. Leigh Whitney finished high school at the top of her class and was a straight-A student at Central State College where she was enrolled in the business department for nearly three years. While attending college, she worked in the general accounting office of Dexter Manufacturing Company. She advanced so rapidly at work that she dropped out of college and devoted her time to work and a home-study course in accounting. In addition to completing the study course in accounting, she has assisted the public accountants for three years in the conduct of the audit of Dexter Manufacturing Company. One of the managers of the auditing firm told Whitney, in confidence, that he would rather have her as an assistant than any two of the junior accountants assigned to the audit.

Leigh Whitney has come to you to discuss establishing a firm to practice public accounting. What would you tell her, particularly concerning the first general standard of auditing?

2-24. James O'Brien has been given his first assignment to be in charge of an audit engagement. To assist him on this major job are two relatively inexperienced staff assistants. Shortly after arriving at the client's office, O'Brien calls the assistants to his desk and informs them that it is extremely important for him to make a perfect audit, and the best way to do this is to follow exactly the working papers from last year. "Make no deviations from last year, and we'll be praised for this job," were his closing comments.

Dominic Traverso was assigned the responsibility for the initial examination of B & D Brick Company. The company had been in existence for three years but had not been audited previously. While driving out to the offices of B & D Brick Company, Mr. Traverso informed his two assistants, who were relatively inexperienced, "Forget your book learning about internal control. On a first-time audit like this, I have designed an audit program that is so thorough that no defalcations can get by us. We'll check so many things a single error can't exist without our finding it."

Are the comments of these two auditors justified? Why?

2-25. Robert Hutchins, a CPA, on May 18, 1981, was retained to perform an audit of Harper Import Company, whose year ends December 31. A disagreement arose on June 12, 1981, when Mr. Hutchins arrived with two assistants at the offices of Harper Imports to begin the audit work for the year. Mr. Harper, owner of Harper Imports, insists that he made it clear his company closes its books on December 31, and the CPAs should know not to appear until after the books are closed.

a. What reasons can the CPA give for wanting to begin the audit examination so far in advance of the company's year end?

b. How could the disagreement between Hutchins and Harper have been avoided?

2-26. You have been engaged to perform an audit of Silva's Landscaping Service, an unincorporated business run by Ken Silva. Mr. Silva tells you not to be concerned about the inventory in his greenhouse. He says there is no way a person in your position could tell anything from inspecting the plants. He has offered to give you a letter stating the amount at which the plants should appear on the balance sheet.

Will the letter from Mr. Silva serve as sufficient evidence to satisfy the requirements of the third auditing standard of field work? Discuss.

2-27. Big Star Company changed during 1981 from the pay-as-you-go basis to the accrual basis of accounting for its pension plan. The comparative income statements accompanying your opinion as a CPA cover the two most recent years.

What effect will this change have on your statement as to consistency for the year ended in:

a. 1981?

b. 1982?

2-28. You have accepted the engagement of examining the financial statements of the Salem Company, a small manufacturing firm that has been your client for several years. Because you were busy writing the report for another engagement, you sent a junior accountant to begin the audit with the suggestion that he start with the accounts receivable. Using the prior year's working papers as a guide, the junior prepared a trial balance of the accounts, aged them, prepared and mailed positive confirmation requests, examined underlying support for charges and credits, and performed such other work as he deemed necessary to assure the validity and collectibility of the receivables. At the conclusion of his work, you reviewed the working papers that he prepared and found that he had carefully followed the prior year's work papers.

The opinion rendered by a CPA states ". . . Our examination was made in accordance with generally accepted auditing standards. . . ."

List the three generally accepted standards of field work. Relate them to the above illustration by indicating how they were fulfilled or, if appropriate, how they were not fulfilled.

AICPA adapted

2-29. During your audit of the Classic Co., you note a liability account called *Notes Payable—Miscellaneous,* which has a material balance. Upon further investigation, you find out that the president has all details of the account. As soon as you mention this account to the president, he immediately writes the following on a sheet of paper and gives it to you:

T. Carmichael	$ 20,000
V. Joiner	50,000
L. McRaney	50,000
J. Yost	30,000
	$150,000

He also signs the paper, noting that it is correct to the best of his knowledge. Is this considered evidential matter? Is it adequate?

2-30. *a.* The first generally accepted auditing standard of field work requires, in part, that "the work is to be adequately planned." An effective tool that aids the auditor in adequately planning the work is an audit program.

What is an audit program, and what purposes does it serve?

b. Auditors frequently refer to the terms "Standards" and "Procedures." Standards deal with measures of the quality of the auditor's performance. Standards specifically refer to the ten generally accepted auditing standards. Procedures relate to those acts that are performed by the auditor while trying to gather evidence. Procedures specifically refer to the methods or techniques used by the auditor in the conduct of the examination.

List at least eight different types of procedures that an auditor would use during an examination of financial statements. For example, a type of procedure that an auditor would frequently use is the observation of activities and conditions. *Do not discuss specific accounts.*

AICPA adapted

2-31. The Biggers Co. uses a computer to maintain a current work-in-process total for all of the various jobs worked on at any particular time. The computer program performs all calculations and prints all details of items in work-in-process along with the totals. Your assistant has taken the final print-out for December 31, 1981, the company's year end, and is recomputing the detail and footing the appropriate columns. The controller of Biggers Co. discovers your assistant doing this work and immediately calls you into her office. The controller informs you that she is not going to pay you to re-add figures that a $3,000-a-month computer just prepared. She instructs you to stop checking the computer print-out and take it at face value.

a. If you halt the testing, do you have sufficient competent evidential matter to support work-in-process?

b. If you follow the "request" of the controller, have you maintained an independence in mental attitude?

2-32. Roberta McCray, CPA, is conducting the audit of the Dell Research Company, a new client. Dell Research has been in business for seven years and has had an audit each year by a CPA. McCray has discovered her client has been using consistently over the years an accounting principle with which she is completely unfamiliar. The director of research at Dell insists that this principle has substantial support within the industry.

a. What procedures should the CPA follow in deciding whether this accounting principle is generally accepted?

b. What responsibility does the CPA have if she determines the accounting principle is not generally accepted?

c. What responsibility does the CPA have if she determines the principle is used by only a very small number of companies in the United States, all engaged in technical research?

2-33. Your audit revealed that the bank account for Mama's Family Restaurant was overdrawn by a material amount as of the balance sheet date. This amount was reclassified on the current year's balance sheet. The account had a positive balance at the end of the preceding year and is properly reflected on the comparative balance sheet. Will this change and inconsistency be noted in your audit opinion?

2-34. Dorer, the owner of a small company, asked Toth, CPA, to conduct an audit of the company's records. Dorer told Toth that an audit is to be completed in time to submit audited financial statements to a bank as part of a loan application. Toth immediately accepted the engagement and agreed to provide an auditor's report within three weeks. Dorer agreed to pay Toth a fixed fee plus a bonus if the loan was granted.

Toth hired two accounting students to conduct the audit and spent several hours telling them exactly what to do. Toth told the students not to spend time reviewing the controls but instead to concentrate on proving the mathematical accuracy of the ledger accounts, and summarizing the data in the accounting records that support Dorer's financial statements. The students followed Toth's instructions and after two weeks gave Toth the financial statements which did not include footnotes. Toth reviewed the statements and prepared an unqualified auditor's report. The report, however, did not refer to generally accepted accounting principles nor to the year-to-year application of such principles.

Briefly describe each of the generally accepted auditing standards and indicate how the action(s) of Toth resulted in a failure to comply with *each* standard.

AICPA adapted

3

Professional Ethics

General ethics are guides by which an individual determines proper personal conduct. Usually this takes into account the requirements imposed by society, moral duties, and the effects of one's actions. Professional ethics are merely a special case of general ethics, in which, as a professional person, one is given specific guides of conduct in matters reflecting responsibility to society, to clients, to other members of the profession, and to oneself.

Modern-day auditors are responsible to many users of financial statements who have no firsthand knowledge of the activities of the business enterprise and its management. With the growth of the corporate form of business, there has developed a separation between management and owners. Owners no longer are acquainted intimately with their businesses, and they must rely upon financial reports to learn about their companies' operations. Creditors, potential investors, and other groups also must rely upon these financial statements. The opinion of an independent auditor enhances the reliability of these statements.

Code of professional ethics

By relying upon the opinion of auditors on financial statements, users of the statements express their faith in the individual auditor as well as in the auditing profession. Members of the profession in turn must conduct their affairs in a manner that will justify this confidence. As has been done in other professions, auditors have established a Code of Professional

Ethics to guide members of the profession toward proper conduct. The code proclaims both to clients and to the public that auditors are willing to accept professional status and conduct their affairs accordingly. Certain aspects of the code promote harmonious relations among auditors.

Action by an individual auditor, whether typical of other auditors or not, may be the only experience to come to the attention of some clients, some members of the public, or even entire communities. These people may judge the entire profession by the activities of a single auditor. Consequently, it is imperative that the professional group have a body of rules to suggest conduct for individual members and, when necessary, to provide a mechanism to enforce proper conduct and reprimand those who do not act in the best interest of the profession.

Through the efforts of the American Institute of Certified Public Accountants and other professional groups of accountants at the national and state levels, an effective code of ethics and a mechanism for enforcement have evolved to meet specific needs and to reflect a growing sense of professional responsibility. Although the arrangement of the rules and the extent of coverage may differ somewhat, the codes of conduct of many state societies of CPAs and the regulations of the boards of accountancy in the various states contain the basic principles expressed by the AICPA Code of Professional Ethics. Consequently, most CPAs are subject to similar rules of professional conduct regardless of the state in which they practice or the professional associations to which they belong. The AICPA Code of Professional Ethics is the basis of the material presented in this chapter since it is representative of the rules of ethics of other professional bodies and jurisdictions.

Although the rules of ethical conduct are promulgated by organizations whose members are all CPAs and are expressed in terms applying to CPAs, the concepts are generally applicable to all who practice public accounting. The AICPA's rules of conduct apply to all services rendered by CPAs in the practice of public accounting including tax and management advisory services unless the wording of a rule indicates limited application. Only the rules on integrity and objectivity (Rule 102) and on discreditable acts (Rule 501) apply to CPAs not in public practice. Accountants who are subject to the AICPA's code of ethics may be held responsible for the compliance with the rules of all persons who practice public accounting with them, whether they are fellow partners, shareholders, or employees. Accountants may not ethically permit another party to engage in activities on their behalf if such activities would violate the rules of ethics when performed directly by the accountants.

The AICPA Code of Professional Ethics derives its authority from the AICPA bylaws that establish the mechanism for enforcement. Accountants who are members of the AICPA may be admonished, or they may be suspended or expelled from membership if, after a hearing by a trial board, they are found guilty of violating the rules of conduct. Misconduct of a type that would cause disciplinary action by the AICPA's trial board probably would result in a similar action by the local CPA society or even in revocation of the license to practice by the state board of accountancy. Since any disciplinary action invoked against accountants damages their professional reputation, accountants are known to take extreme care to conduct their professional activities in a manner that adheres to the ideals of the code of ethics.

Presently the AICPA Code of Professional Ethics is divided into three main sections: (1) Concepts of Professional Ethics, (2) Rules of Conduct, and (3) Interpretations of Rules of Conduct. The section on Concepts of Professional Ethics is a philosophical essay discussing the concepts upon which the Rules of Conduct are based. It calls for conduct beyond that of the Rules of Conduct, which is the section of enforceable ethical standards and the only section approved by AICPA membership. The other two sections are approved only by the Professional Ethics Executive Committee of the AICPA and serve mainly as explanations and clarifications. The Interpretations of the Rules of Conduct consists of guidelines as to the scope and application of the rules.

Five ethical principles are presented in the section, Concepts of Professional Ethics. The principles are

Independence, integrity and objectivity. A certified public accountant should maintain his integrity and objectivity and, when engaged in the practice of public accounting, be independent of those he serves.

General and technical standards. A certified public accountant should observe the profession's technical standards and strive continually to improve his competence and the quality of his services.

Responsibilities to clients. A certified public accountant should be fair and candid with his clients and serve them to the best of his ability, with professional concern for their best interests, consistent with his responsibilities to the public.

Responsibilities to colleagues. A certified public accountant should conduct himself in a manner which will promote cooperation and good relations among members of the profession.

Other responsibilities and practices. A certified public accountant should conduct himself in a manner which will enhance the stature of the profession and its ability to serve the public.

These principles serve to organize the following sections of this chapter. The Rules of Conduct relating to each principle are quoted immediately preceding the discussion of the particular principle.[1] The complete essay,

[1] The five ethical principles and the rules on the following pages are quoted from the Code of Professional Ethics, copyright © 1978 by the American Institute of Certified Public Accountants.

Concepts of Professional Ethics, the Rules of Conduct, and the Interpretations of Rules of Conduct appear in Appendix A.

Independence, integrity, and objectivity

Rule 101—Independence

A member or a firm of which he is a partner or shareholder shall not express an opinion on financial statements of an enterprise unless he and his firm are independent with respect to such enterprise. Independence will be considered to be impaired if, for example:

A. During the period of his professional engagement, or at the time of expressing his opinion, he or his firm
   1. (*a*) Had or was committed to acquire any direct or material indirect financial interest in the enterprise; or
      (*b*) Was a trustee of any trust or executor or administrator of any estate if such trust or estate had or was committed to acquire any direct or material indirect financial interest in the enterprise; or
   2. Had any joint closely held business investment with the enterprise or any officer, director, or principal stockholder thereof which was material in relation to his or his firm's net worth; or
   3. Had any loan to or from the enterprise or any officer, director, or principal stockholder thereof. This latter proscription does not apply to the following loans from a financial institution when made under normal lending procedures, terms, and requirements:
      (*a*) Loans obtained by a member or his firm which are not material in relation to the net worth of such borrower.
      (*b*) Home mortgages.
      (*c*) Other secured loans, except loans guaranteed by a member's firm which are otherwise unsecured.

B. During the period covered by the financial statements, during the period of the professional engagement, or at the time of expressing an opinion, he or his firm
   1. Was connected with the enterprise as a promoter, underwriter, or voting trustee, a director or officer or in any capacity equivalent to that of a member of management or of an employee; or
   2. Was a trustee for any pension or profit-sharing trust of the enterprise.

The above examples are not intended to be all-inclusive.

Rule 102—Integrity and Objectivity

A member shall not knowingly misrepresent facts and when engaged in the practice of public accounting, including the rendering of tax and management advisory services, shall not subordinate his judgment to others. In tax practice, a member may resolve doubt in favor of his client as long as there is reasonable support for his position.

As previously discussed, independence is a fundamental characteristic of auditors. Only through maintaining reputations for independence are auditors able to serve properly those who rely upon them. Independence has traditionally been defined as the ability to act with integrity and objectivity. Integrity is an element of character represented by soundness of moral principle, uprightness, and honesty. Objectivity, as applied to auditors, means the ability to maintain an impartial attitude and to handle all matters that come under their review in an unbiased manner. As independent professionals, auditors will not subordinate their judgment to the opinions of clients. Users of audited financial statements have a right to assume an independent state of mind on the part of auditors who express their opinions on the statements. The independent state of mind, also called independence in fact, is required by auditing standards.

Since an auditor's true state of mind cannot be determined by a user of audited financial statements, the user most likely will base any conclusion upon outward signs indicative of the auditor's independence. If the user knows of a close association between the auditor and management, between the auditor and owners, or between the auditor and a particular group of users, the user likely will doubt the independence of the auditor. It therefore behooves auditors to avoid all relationships that might cause users to question their independence.

The conclusion reached by a knowledgeable observer in evaluating an auditor's relationship is the ultimate test of whether such a relationship would cause the auditor's appearance of independence to be impaired. An auditor must take the observer's point of view; then, considering all the facts, normal strength of character, and normal behavior under the circumstances, the auditor must decide whether the relationship threatens his or her integrity and objectivity. Any relationship that fails to give the appearance of independence to a knowledgeable observer should be avoided. Although the appearance of independence does not guarantee independence in fact—which is integrity and objectivity produced by an independence of mental attitude—such appearance is essential to maintain public confidence.

In each of the Rules of Conduct in the Code of Professional Ethics, the examples given should not be considered exhaustive. The code should be viewed as establishing the tenor within which an auditor should work. The rules do not describe all the acts that are prohibited nor all the acts that are required. An accountant should strive to obey the spirit of the code, not just the exact wording of its rules.

INDEPENDENCE

Examples of situations in which an auditor's appearance of independence would be questioned are given in Rule 101. The two main sections of this rule are distinguished by the time period to which they apply. Section A

Table 3-1 Time Chart of Audit Examination

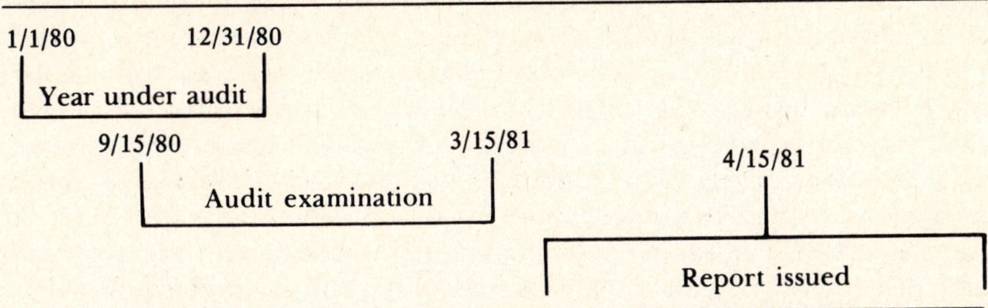

relates to the period of the auditor's professional engagement and the time when the audit report is issued.

In Table 3-1 the time period covered by Section A of Rule 101 begins September 15, 1980, when the auditors begin their examination, and continues through April 15, 1981, when the auditors' report containing their opinion is issued. During this time period, the auditors would not be considered independent if they had financial interests in the client company, or had joint investments in other businesses with an officer or stockholder of the client company, or had loans to or from the client company or any of its officers or major shareholders.

Significantly, the period under audit preceding the initial examination is excluded from coverage by this section of Rule 101. Consequently, auditors may be stockholders in a company at the time they are approached to serve as auditors for that company. If they are engaged to perform the audit, they may dispose of their investments prior to beginning any significant aspect of the examination. A reasonable observer would not question the auditor's independence if all financial ties were relinquished prior to being in a position to influence the financial reports of the company.

Application of this rule on independence extends to all partners or shareholders in a CPA firm and to all professional employees who participate in the audit or are employed in an office where a significant portion of the audit engagement is performed. For example, an audit may be conducted entirely in the San Francisco office of a public accounting firm; but regardless of the office in which they are located, all partners who own stock in the client company would have to dispose of such investments. Professional employees in the San Francisco office must dispose of their investments in the client company, but professional employees in the firm's other offices may retain their investments. Many firms have a more restrictive policy and prohibit all professional employees throughout the firm from having any financial interest in any client company.

Investments by any members of the auditor's immediate household are considered a direct financial interest and are therefore prohibited. Investments by close kin normally are considered indirect interests and thus are prohibited only when they are material.

Auditors are not expected to avoid all relations with client personnel other than those maintained during the audit examination. It is only natural that auditors and client personnel will associate in their normal social, religious, and civic activities. No reasonable observer would doubt the auditor's integrity and objectivity because of such contacts. However, should an auditor enter into a joint investment with any officer, director, or stockholder of the client company, an observer would have reason to question the auditor's independence. Such a relationship is prohibited by Rule 101 A(2). For example, if an auditor owns a one-fifth interest in a real estate venture with four other venturers, the auditor would not be viewed as independent to perform an audit on the textile manufacturing company in which one of the other venturers is a major shareholder.

An auditor or firm could be viewed as lacking independence if there were loans between the auditor and the client (including officers, directors, or stockholders). Such a relationship certainly could lead an observer to suspect an auditor of influencing records or reports for personal benefit. Such loans cause the auditor's independence to be impaired according to Rule 101 A(3), with the exception of loans from a financial institution made under normal lending procedures.

The second major section of Rule 101, Section B, pertains to *the period covered by the financial statements* in addition to the period of the examination and the time of expressing the opinion on the financial statements, which were covered by Section A. Whereas the financial interest, joint investment, and loan restrictions in Table 3-1 relate to the time from September 15, 1980, to April 15, 1981, the prohibitions in Section B apply to the period from January 1, 1980, through April 15, 1981. Auditors would not be viewed as independent if during this period they were associated with their client companies in any capacity of management or as an employee. As auditors, they would be reviewing work with which they were connected and perhaps even supervised. It might be difficult, or even impossible, for them to view objectively the data with which they were so related. Certainly the appearance of independence would be lacking, even if it did exist in fact. Resigning from the company at time of being appointed auditors would not enable them to change their former relationship. Consequently, Rule 101 B(1) states that independence is impaired when such a relationship existed at any time subsequent to the beginning of the audit period.

At times auditors are invited to serve as directors or trustees of not-for-profit organizations in order to lend the prestige of their names to the organizations. These organizations usually have large boards of directors or trustees, and the auditors can limit their participation. The auditors may serve the organization as independent auditors while serving on the board provided the position is purely honorary, all externally circulated documents listing their names state the position is honorary, they do not vote or participate in management functions, and the only participation is use of their names.

Relationships that could cause a practicing auditor's appearance of independence to be questioned have been discussed above. Unanswered so far is the question of what is the proper view of independence of a *retired partner* of an auditing firm engaging in one of these relationships. The Interpretations of Rules of Conduct explain that retired members could serve in any of these capacities or could have such financial interests without affecting the independence of their former firm. They should not hold themselves out as being associated with their former partnership, their retirement benefits should not be materially affected by the fees that the auditing firm receives from the client with whom they are associated, and they should no longer be active in the auditing firm.

Generally auditors are not considered to be independent when there is litigation between the client firm and the auditors, or there is expressed intention to begin litigation. Adverse positions are assumed in cases of litigation, and observers would certainly be justified in questioning both management's willingness to disclose all necessary facts and the auditors' objectivity in examining the client's representations. It is possible, however, for the litigation to be unrelated to the audit work or to involve an immaterial matter, and the auditors' independence, under these circumstances, usually would not be impaired.

MANAGEMENT ADVISORY AND TAX SERVICES

The appearance of independence is not required in the areas of management advisory services or tax practice. However, regardless of the type of service being rendered, accountants should not misrepresent facts nor subordinate their judgment to others. In all cases accountants should express their conclusions honestly and objectively.

Accountants in public practice should be particularly aware that they are rendering management *advisory* services. They are making recommendations to management, not reaching final decisions themselves. Public accountants are not part of the management team where the final responsibility for the decision must be placed. Nevertheless, some observers believe that the accountants' advice cannot be separated from the decision-making process. These people hold the opinion that public accountants often become so closely involved with management in rendering management advisory services that they can no longer view the financial operations objectively. Some public accounting firms have established separate divisions to perform management advisory services and to conduct audits. These divisions are created to take advantage of personnel specialization and to emphasize the ability of the personnel performing the audit to maintain an independent view of the client's operations and financial statements. Also some public accounting firms have restricted the scope of their management advisory services in order to emphasize their independence. Assistance to a client in locating executive personnel is an example of a service that has been eliminated. Currently, the prevailing opinion holds that management services as rendered by most public accountants do not impair their independence in rendering auditing services.

In expressing an opinion on financial statements, an auditor's judgment pertains only to the fairness of the presentation of the results of operating decisions. The auditor is not expressing an opinion on the underlying wisdom of the decision employed by the client to produce the results. Although the auditor, or some other member of the firm, may have affected the client's decision-making process, it is unlikely that the auditor's objectivity would be impaired when judging the fairness of the financial presentation. Although the client may have made a poor decision based upon the auditor's advice, the risks of damaging one's professional reputation are too great for an auditor to compromise integrity and express an unqualified opinion on the financial statements prepared in a manner to cover up the poor decision.

Tax services are another area of specialization wherein public accountants are not expected to maintain an appearance of independence. As long as there is a reasonable basis for their position, accountants, like lawyers, are expected to advocate the position most favorable to their client. Accountants arrive at their position through technical competence and professional integrity. Presenting a client's tax return in the most favorable light is merely the exercise of professional judgment; it does not impair independence.

Although independence is not expected of public accountants in areas of management advisory services and tax practice, in general, the Rules of Conduct apply to all aspects of a public accounting practice, unless the wording of the rule indicates otherwise.

REPRESENTING CONFLICTING INTERESTS

One accountant or one firm may serve as independent auditor for two or more clients whose interests are in conflict. A particular firm may have developed a specialization in one field, such as savings and loan associations or retail grocery chains, and because of extensive knowledge in that field, the firm may be much in demand to serve clients in that industry. With their reputation for independence, integrity, and maintaining confidential relationships, accountants are allowed to represent two or more clients who have conflicting interests. However, they should disclose the relationship to each party involved.

BOOKKEEPING SERVICES

Public accountants may provide bookkeeping services, either manually or by electronic data processing, for clients who are not sufficiently large to employ an adequate internal accounting staff. Even though public accountants perform accounting services, the responsibility for the financial statements remains with the clients. Accountants should make sure that their clients have sufficient understanding of the underlying activities, the valuations used, the accounting policies employed, and the disclosures made so that the clients can accept responsibility for the statements. Public accountants should not function as employees or as managers; neither should they consummate transactions or have custody of clients' assets. The source documents should be prepared by client personnel, and accountants' activities should consist mainly of posting to the general ledger, making monthly closing entries, and preparing monthly financial statements. Accountants should consult clients before making any changes in basic data. If public accountants adhere to these precautions, the AICPA position is that a reasonable observer would consider them independent in performing as auditors even though they also perform the bookkeeping function. That an auditor has been involved in the preparation of the records clearly does not eliminate the duty to perform adequate audit tests.

The Securities and Exchange Commission holds that auditors cannot fulfill the role of outside critic if they are also involved in the bookkeeping function. The SEC takes this position in *Accounting Series Release No. 126:* "The Commission is of the opinion that an accountant cannot objectively audit books and records which he has maintained for a client." Many auditors and public accounting firms comply with the SEC ruling in all their engagements. Such compliance enhances the appearance of the auditor's independence.

The bookkeeping or write-up service performed by some public accountants for small clients is undoubtedly a valuable one. Not only does it serve the client, but also it often provides a source of essential income to an accountant who is just beginning to establish a public accounting practice.

Independence underlies several rules that deal primarily with other aspects of professional conduct. The aspect of independence is noted when these rules are discussed in subsequent sections of this chapter.

General and technical standards

Rule 201—General Standards

A member shall comply with the following general standards as interpreted by bodies designated by Council and must justify any departures therefrom.

A. *Professional competence.* A member shall undertake only those engagements which he or his firm can reasonably expect to complete with professional competence.

B. *Due professional care.* A member shall exercise due professional care in the performance of an engagement.
C. *Planning and supervision.* A member shall adequately plan and supervise an engagement.
D. *Sufficient relevant data.* A member shall obtain sufficient relevant data to afford a reasonable basis for conclusions or recommendations in relation to an engagement.
E. *Forecasts.* A member shall not permit his name to be used in conjunction with any forecast of future transactions in a manner which may lead to the belief that the member vouches for the achievability of the forecast.

Rule 202—Auditing Standards

A member shall not permit his name to be associated with financial statements in such a manner as to imply that he is acting as an independent public accountant unless he has complied with the applicable generally accepted auditing standards promulgated by the Institute. Statements on auditing standards issued by the Institute's auditing standards executive committee are, for purposes of this rule, considered to be interpretations of the generally accepted auditing standards, and departures from such statements must be justified by those who do not follow them.

Rule 203—Accounting Principles

A member shall not express an opinion that financial statements are presented in conformity with generally accepted accounting principles if such statements contain any departure from an accounting principle promulgated by the body designated by Council to establish such principles which has a material effect on the statements taken as a whole, unless the member can demonstrate that due to unusual circumstances the financial statements would otherwise have been misleading. In such cases his report must describe the departure, the approximate effects thereof, if practicable, and the reasons why compliance with the principle would result in a misleading statement.

Rule 204—Other Technical Standards

A member shall comply with other technical standards promulgated by bodies designated by Council to establish such standards, and departures therefrom must be justified by those who do not follow them.

GENERAL STANDARDS

Public accountants have a responsibility when rendering professional services to be competent, to exercise due care, and to observe the technical standards established by their professional bodies. They must have sufficient knowledge and skill to plan and supervise adequately all engagements. The accountant in charge of an engagement need not be qualified to perform all aspects of the work personally but must be able to define the tasks, supervise those performing the tasks, evaluate their performance, and reach an overall conclusion.

Those who present themselves as accountants in public practice claim to have the degree of skill commonly possessed by public accountants. They are expected to complete an engagement according to professional standards. Although they must competently plan the engagement, supervise the work, and gather sufficient data, and should exercise reasonable care and diligence in all phases of the engagement, they are nevertheless not expected to be infallible or free from errors of judgment. Public accounting includes auditing, management advisory services, tax practice, and other related services including some that are highly specialized. Rules 201 and 204 require that accountants adhere to the professional standards when rendering any of these services.

Accountants in public practice not only must be knowledgeable about the appropriate professional standards and technical subject matter applicable to an engagement but they must also comprehend the peculiarities of their clients' businesses. They should have such thorough knowledge about their clients' particular industry and especially about their client companies that they can confidently know they have acquired sufficient data as a basis for the conclusions or recommendations reached on the particular engagement.

When requested to render professional services for a client engaged in a business with which they are unfamiliar, accountants should accept the job only if they have confidence that the necessary knowledge and skills can be acquired. They may acquire the necessary skills perhaps by studying published material on the industry or by consulting colleagues who are familiar with the industry. These are normal aspects of accountants' preparation for conducting an engagement and do not indicate lack of competence. Should some phase of the engagement require specialized knowledge that they cannot acquire, the accountants may engage a specialist on that aspect, or they may refuse the engagement, possibly suggesting another firm for the client to consider.

Continuing education is essential if an accountant is to meet the requirements of competence. Keeping abreast of newly issued *Statements of the Financial Accounting Standards Board, Statements on Auditing Standards, Industry Audit Guides,* positions of the Professional Ethics Division, and other official pronouncements is a minimum requirement. Many accountants have found professional development courses an effective way of maintaining competence in numerous areas. Individual state societies of CPAs present a large number of professional development courses covering a wide range of topics; some are of general interest, such as report writing or managing an accounting practice, and others are specialized, such as filing SEC reports. Technical sessions held at professional society meetings at the local, state, and national levels offer an opportunity for members to acquire knowledge of specialized topics. Additionally, formal training programs are a part of the advancement process in many public accounting firms.

So important is the matter of continuing education that a number of states have legislation requiring CPAs to present evidence of an established number of hours (120 hours during each three-year period, for example) of continuing education endeavors for license renewal. Whether required by law or not, professional persons should accept the responsibility to be competent in all aspects of their work.

FORECASTS

Security analysts and other users of financial statements frequently request financial forecasts and budgets. Nearly all companies have such information available for use by the management team in its planning function, and external users of financial information are pressuring for this information to be available to them. When forecasted data are furnished, it is only natural that the users would like this information to be attested to by an independent reviewer such as a CPA. Many observers believe that an auditor should in no way be associated with forecasted data. Their reasons are that some users of the financial statements might expect a greater degree of responsibility for the accuracy of the forecasts than the auditor is actually assuming. Also, users might lower their esteem for an auditor who is associated with statements that cannot be audited in the usual manner.

Other observers believe that an auditor can fulfill a valuable function in the realm of forecasting by attesting to the soundness of techniques used and the accuracy of the computations. When performing such a service, an auditor should very carefully disclaim an opinion of the achievability of the forecasts, as required by Rule 201 of the Rules of Conduct. Any time an auditor's name is associated with forecasted statements, the auditor must disclose the source of the data, disclose the assumptions made in preparing and analyzing the statements, describe clearly the character of the work performed, and generally disclose that he or she does not vouch for the achievability of the forecasts.

The auditor may assist the client in preparing various types of pro forma financial statements. Cash projections to support a loan application, consolidated financial statements of projected mergers, and statements assuming a new issue of capital stock or additional bank financing are a few examples of pro forma statements with which auditors may assist clients. Since auditors have no control over the uses clients may make of such statements, in order that all users are aware of their position, auditors should make a clear disclosure in writing that they are not assuming responsibility for the achievability of projected information.

AUDITING STANDARDS

The guidelines that measure the quality of audit procedures followed in the conduct of an examination are known as *auditing standards.* They also consider the objectives to be obtained through use of the procedures. Standards are contrasted with procedures, which relate to the acts to be performed. Auditors are required by Rule 202 of the Rules of Conduct to adhere to the generally accepted auditing standards adopted by the AICPA. These standards were discussed in Chapter 2.

Statements on Auditing Standards are the pronouncements issued by the AICPA Auditing Standards Board and are recognized as interpretations of generally accepted auditing standards. An auditor who departs from these statements should be prepared to justify the departure. The AICPA has not issued statements governing all aspects of an audit. Consequently, many auditing procedures performed in an examination are *not* dictated by the *Statements on Auditing Standards.* An auditor, therefore, must have broad knowledge about what acceptable auditing procedures are and must keep informed of developing methods and techniques.

Because an individual auditor's reputation depends to a large extent on the reputation of the CPA profession as a whole, auditors should be concerned that colleagues also observe appropriate auditing standards and procedures. Most accountants welcome the opportunity to learn how they may improve procedures and better fulfill their function. If necessary, a CPA should call any substandard reporting to the attention of the AICPA Practice Review Committee or to the corresponding state society committee. The function of these committees is purely educational so that auditors who are issuing substandard reports through ignorance or carelessness may become aware of their failings, learn what acceptable standards and procedures are, and correct their shortcomings.

ACCOUNTING PRINCIPLES

The Financial Accounting Standards Board is the body designated by the governing body of the AICPA to establish accounting principles that generally must be followed by a client in preparation of financial statements. Rule 203 requires the auditor to be able to demonstrate that any departure from a principle stated by the FASB is necessary to prevent the financial statements from being misleading. Additionally, the auditor must describe the departure, explain why use of the FASB principle would produce a misleading statement, and give the effect of using the different principle. It is quite unusual for the application of an FASB principle to produce a misleading statement; consequently, only rarely are departures from pronounced principles allowed. The accounting principles that Rule 203 requires accountants to follow are not limited to the *Statements of Financial Accounting Standards* issued by the FASB but include previously issued APB Opinions and Accounting Research Bulletins that are not superseded by subsequent FASB pronouncements. *Interpretations* issued by the FASB should be considered by accountants in determining the applicability of previously issued Bulletins, Opinions, or Statements.

OTHER TECHNICAL STANDARDS

When any committee or similar body is designated by council of the AICPA to establish technical standards, auditors generally follow such standards. In 1979 the AICPA council designated the Accounting and Review Services Committee to promulgate standards in the area of compilation and review services. Consequently under Rule 204, auditors who do not follow the standards advocated by this committee must justify such departures.

Responsibilities to clients

Rule 301—Confidential Client Information

A member shall not disclose any confidential information obtained in the course of a professional engagement except with the consent of the client.

This rule shall not be construed (*a*) to relieve a member of his obligation under rules 202 and 203, (*b*) to affect in any way his compliance with a validly issued subpoena or summons enforceable by order of a court, (*c*) to prohibit review of a member's professional practices as a part of voluntary quality review under Institute authorization, or (*d*) to preclude a member from responding to any inquiry made by the ethics division or trial board of the Institute, by a duly constituted investigative or disciplinary body of a state CPA society, or under state statutes.

Members of the ethics division and trial board of the Institute and professional practice reviewers under Institute authorization shall not disclose any confidential client information which comes to their attention from members in disciplinary proceedings or otherwise in carrying out their official responsibilities. However, this prohibition shall not restrict the exchange of information with an aforementioned duly constituted investigative or disciplinary body.

Rule 302—Contingent Fees

Professional services shall not be offered or rendered under an arrangement whereby no fee will be charged unless a specified finding or result is attained, or where the fee is otherwise contingent upon the findings or results of such services. However, a member's fees may vary depending, for example, on the complexity of the service rendered.

Fees are not regarded as being contingent if fixed by courts or other public authorities or, in tax matters, if determined based on the results of judicial proceedings or the findings of governmental agencies.

Clients place their trust in the auditors whom they engage. Usually clients cannot evaluate auditors' technical skills or the competence of their services. Clients have faith in the auditors' competence, honesty, objectivity, and integrity; consequently, they take auditors into their confidence. Auditors in turn should not violate this confidence and should exercise the same care in dealing with clients' affairs as they would exercise in dealing with their own.

Auditors should have their clients' best interests in mind when giving advice and performing professional activities. If several alternatives are available under existing accounting principles or under current laws or regulations, auditors normally should recommend the alternative most favorable to a client. However, auditors must not let this concern for clients surpass responsibility to the public. If certain disclosures are necessary for fair presentation of the financial statements, auditors will insist on making such disclosures. Auditors should not subordinate their judgment or conceal or modify an honest belief in any professional service merely to meet the desires of a client. Should a conflict arise on an important question of principle, a CPA should resign from an engagement rather than submit to an unacceptable position demanded by a client. Many examples can be cited where an auditor lost a client because of a refusal to compromise a position, only to gain other clients because of a reputation for uncompromising integrity and objectivity; and at times the original client later has engaged the same auditor to gain assurance that financial statements were not biased.

CONFIDENTIAL CLIENT INFORMATION

In gathering sufficient evidence to express a professional opinion, auditors naturally acquire knowledge of clients' most private financial and business dealings. They learn of forthcoming mergers, new products, changes in dividend rates, personnel changes, and other confidential information. Should an auditor reveal such confidential information, a client might be damaged severely. Disclosure of confidential information also could be detrimental to an auditor's professional career, as well as damaging to the whole profession.

Although Rule 301 relates specifically to the confidential information obtained from a client, the injunction applies equally to all confidential information obtained in performing professional duties. Auditors respect the confidential nature of information from both prospective clients and former clients.

Auditors should realize that much information about a client's affairs is not known by all of the client's employees, and they must make certain that all such matters are kept confidential. They must not let unauthorized persons have access to working papers that record such information. Payroll information is a prime example of confidential data that could be disturbing if revealed to the employees.

Communications between an auditor and a client are not privileged under common law as are those of lawyers, physicians, and clergymen. In some states statutory provisions have been enacted to provide that public accountants will not be required by the courts to divulge evidence obtained in their confidential capacity. The federal courts have held that state statutes do not apply to federal administrative proceedings. Consequently, state laws on privileged communications do not apply in federal courts or to proceedings that involve a client's federal income tax returns.

There is lack of agreement within the profession on the desirability of statutory provisions creating privileged communications between auditors and their clients. While it is agreed that auditors should not voluntarily divulge confidential information, many believe it would not be in the public interest to impede the courts with laws which prevent auditors from testifying as witnesses. Also, some believe statutes allowing privileged communications would impair auditors' independence. If auditors were prevented from revealing confidential information, they would at times be unable to explain the necessity of qualifications to their opinions on financial statements.

Where there is conflict between the concept of full disclosure and the concept of confidential information, full disclosure dominates without question. In addition, Rule 301 indicates that confidential relations should not prevent auditors from revealing appropriate data when subpoenaed by a court, when submitting information to a quality review board of the AICPA or state society, or when responding to inquiries by investigative or disciplinary bodies of the AICPA or state society.

If sued for negligence, an auditor's reputation and practice are at stake. The auditor surely has a right to self-defense and may disclose whatever information is necessary to that end. Although an auditor tries to avoid the situation, at times a client must be sued for a fee. In such a case the auditor may reveal information needed to substantiate the claim.

Neither the Treasury Department nor the AICPA requires an accountant to breach the confidential relationship when a client refuses to file amended tax returns to correct an understatement of a prior year's taxable income. The confidential relationship would be violated should the accountant notify the tax authorities. A letter to the client pointing out all the relevant facts should urge the client to file an amended return. If the client refuses, the accountant may withdraw from the engagement and specify why in a letter of resignation. An accountant would be prudent to consult an attorney in such a case.

ACCOUNTANTS' FEES

Many accountants base their fees upon per diem or hourly rates for the various classes of staff employees who worked on the job; the fees will also reflect the particular nature of the work. Although engagements may have fees established in advance, some accountants view such fixed-fee arrangements as undesirable because it is difficult to know how much time the professional service will take. At times the auditor may find the internal controls and records in such excellent condition that the time required for the audit is not as great as anticipated. On the other hand, should the auditor find conditions such that more hours than anticipated are necessary to gather sufficient evidence for rendering an opinion, it is only human nature that the auditor would be tempted to take some shortcuts. Probably the client would suffer because of the poor quality of the audit, as would the auditor, who receives inadequate compensation for the time spent on the examination.

When a fixed-fee is not established beforehand, a client has the right to know the general range of an auditor's fee on the forthcoming engagement. An estimate may be given in the form of a probable minimum and maximum, with an understanding that discovery of factors unknown at the time of the estimate could require more work and consequently result in a higher fee.

A former rule of the Code of Professional Ethics prohibiting competitive bidding has been dropped because it was considered to be in violation of the price-fixing prohibitions of federal antitrust laws. The concept of avoidance of competitive bidding remains part of the professional attitude and conduct of many accountants, although the prohibition is no longer stated explicitly.

An auditor is prohibited by Rule 302 from arranging for a fee contingent upon the outcome of an examination. If the auditor's fee were to be a percentage of the net income reflected on the financial statements, for example, there is a possibility that objectivity would be impaired, and the auditor would appear to lack independence. The rule applies not only to fees for opinion audits but also to reports prepared for internal use by management. A client could well question the objectivity of an accountant who recommended a cost system, for instance, if the accountant's fee were set as a percentage of cost reductions. The reductions could all be short-term in nature to increase the fee but in the long term could be detrimental to the company's well-being.

Exceptions to the contingent fee rule are made if the fees are fixed by courts or by other public authorities or in tax work where they may be based upon the findings of a governmental agency or are the results of judicial proceedings. The explanation for this exception is that accountants are not in a position to influence their fees, since the outcome is determined by other authorities.

Accountants' fees need not be based exclusively on per diem or hourly rates. In determining the amount to bill their clients, accountants should consider the time spent by various staff members, their training and skill, the difficulty and unusual nature of the engagement, whether the engagement is of a continuing or casual nature, the value of the services to the client, and the customary charges by colleagues for similar services. Accountants may choose to perform certain jobs below cost or at times for no fee (for example, when auditing a charitable organization). As professional persons, accountants should be concerned with fulfilling their responsibility to clients and to the public above any immediate financial reward.

Responsibilities to colleagues

Cooperation and good relations among accountants are essential for the advancement of the profession. As discussed in connection with the section on competence and technical standards, the reputation of the entire accounting profession is formed frequently by an observer's knowledge of a single accountant. Conversely, other observers know of the cumulative reputation of the accounting profession and judge an individual by this standard. Accountants should conduct their affairs in a manner that will enhance the reputation of the profession, and they should encourage colleagues to do the same.

PROFESSIONAL COOPERATION

Not only does the reputation of the profession depend upon the conduct of individual members, but the improvement of services and the advancement of the profession also depend upon mutual confidence among members. A free interchange of information is essential and is a main source of information about evolving practices and techniques. Generally, members do not keep their ideas and discoveries secret but discuss them at professional meetings, write about them in professional journals, and even make them available for professional development courses.

Cooperation is indispensable in maintaining the standards of the profession. Criteria for admission to the profession are established by individual state laws, and accountants working together through their local state societies have influenced legislation in order to establish the present high standards for admission and other laws that regulate the practice of public accounting.

When kept within reasonable limits, a worthwhile function may be served by professional rivalry. The competitive spirit to achieve and excel can motivate accountants to work assiduously, to strive for more challenging engagements, to obtain clients who will make the practice more profitable, and to increase their concern for clients' welfare while continuing to protect public interests. Accountants should strive to give service that rivals or exceeds that of competitors, and they should charge fees within the range generally charged in their communities. The spirit of rivalry should be constrained by common sense, politeness, and mutual respect.

ENCROACHMENT

A former rule of professional conduct prohibited accountants from seeking to provide professional services to individuals and to businesses that were served by other accountants. The accountants, of course, were not restrained from rendering their services to all who requested them.

The United States Justice Department brought pressure on the AICPA to repeal the rules prohibiting encroachment and direct solicitation of clients, and legal counsel advised that a successful defense by the institute was unlikely. Under such conditions, the membership of the AICPA voted in 1979 to repeal the prohibitions against encroachment on another's practice and against direct solicitation of clients.

Many accountants expect little change to take place in professional activities as a result of these rule changes. In the past most accountants have been able to spread their reputations in a professional manner through social and civic activities, through publications, and by making statements on public policy. These indirect ways of seeking clients may now give way to more direct means of accountants' presenting their credentials to businesses that are not their clients. Some accountants fear that these changes may lead to extreme price cutting, a lowering of quality of services rendered, and competition that could undermine their independence from their clients. Over the years, public accountants have conducted their businesses with professional dignity. Although the rules have recently changed, this professional attitude will likely continue to prevail.

When an auditor is requested by a prospective client to render professional services, certain communication is required to take place with the client's previous auditor. According to SAS No. 7 (AU 315), if the requesting client is currently served by another auditor, the new auditor is required to consult with the former auditor before accepting the engagement. The former auditor may be able to provide information that will influence the new auditor's decision on whether or not to accept the engagement. Questions should be asked about such matters as disagreements with the client's management over accounting principles or auditing procedures to be employed. The successor auditor should try to learn of matters that bear upon the integrity of management and also to learn of the reasons for the change of auditors. Communication with the former auditor not only alerts the new auditor that there was a matter in dispute, but also serves to convey information that may enable the successor auditor to perform a more efficient examination and to serve the new client more effectively.

The matter of the confidential relationship should be considered in determining how much information a former auditor can furnish to a successor. Usually the client requests the former auditor to furnish the successor auditor all the information requested; therefore, with the client's permission, the former auditor may discuss the situation thoroughly and may even permit the new auditor after accepting the engagement to review working papers of previous audits. If the client does not grant permission for the former auditor to discuss confidential matters, the new auditor may be alerted to an undesirable situation in such general terms that no confidential information is disclosed. Often a more satisfactory procedure is for auditors to make a practice of sending clients written memoranda setting forth the details of all disputed matters. Particularly when an auditor resigns from an engagement, the circumstances should be spelled out in a letter of resignation. The former auditor can always suggest that the new one review the letter of resignation or other written memoranda filed with the client.

Other responsibilities and practices

Rule 501—Acts Discreditable

A member shall not commit an act discreditable to the profession.

Rule 502—Advertising and Other Forms of Solicitation

A member shall not seek to obtain clients by advertising or other forms of solicitation in a manner that is false, misleading, or deceptive.

Rule 503—Commissions

A member shall not pay a commission to obtain a client, nor shall he accept a commission for a referral to a client of products or services of others. This rule shall not prohibit payments for the purchase of an accounting practice or retirement payments to individuals formerly engaged in the practice of public accounting or payments to their heirs or estates.

Rule 504—Incompatible Occupations

A member who is engaged in the practice of public accounting shall not concurrently engage in any business or occupation which would create a conflict of interest in rendering professional services.

Rule 505—Form of Practice and Name

A member may practice public accounting, whether as an owner or employee, only in the form of a proprietorship, a partnership, or a professional corporation whose characteristics conform to resolutions of Council.

A member shall not practice under a firm name which includes any fictitious name, indicates specialization, or is misleading as to the type of organization (proprietorship, partnership, or corporation). However, names of one or more past partners or shareholders may be included in the firm name of a successor partnership or corporation. Also, a partner surviving the death or withdrawal of all other partners may continue to practice under the partnership name for up to two years after becoming a sole practitioner.

A firm may not designate itself as "Members of the American Institute of Certified Public Accountants" unless all of its partners or shareholders are members of the Institute.

The final section of the Code of Professional Ethics is concerned with rules that have not logically fallen under another section and are designed primarily to increase public respect and confidence. These rules range from the very general to the very specific. Philosophically, no rule is needed other than Rule 501, which requires that an accountant not commit an act discreditable to the profession. In effect, all other provisions of the Code of Professional Ethics are interpretations of this general rule. The other rules help accountants to know what acts have been interpreted as discreditable to the profession. Under this general rule, anything an accountant does of an illegal or immoral nature that is considered to discredit the profession should result in disciplinary action. In the section of the code on the Concepts of Professional Ethics a statement is made that accountants "should support efforts to achieve equality of opportunity for all, regardless of race, religious background or sex, and should contribute to this goal by their own service relationships and employment practices." An interpretation of Rule 501 by the AICPA Ethics Division states specifically that discrimination based on race, color, religion, sex, age, or national origin in hiring, promotion, or salary practices is considered to be an act discreditable to the profession.

ADVERTISING AND SOLICITATION

In the past recognized professions generally have not engaged in advertising, contending that this would lower their dignity and credibility. The argument was often presented that a professional's reputation was best spread by satisfied clients. The accounting profession adopted its first rule limiting advertising in 1922; over the years the rule has been modified numerous times and for a while prohibited all advertising. A change in the attitude of the accounting profession is reflected by the adoption in 1978 of the current Rule 502 which reduces the restrictions on advertising. This change was engendered in part by the widespread movement of the 1970s to protect the rights of the consumer and provide the public with full information. Actions by the Federal Trade Commission and the United States Justice Department affecting almost all professional groups fostered the movement for increased competition and removal of prohibitions against advertising. The courts, during this period, held that the professions were not exempt from antitrust laws, and restrictions against advertising could be held in violation of these laws. Rather than await decisions to be made through the judicial system, the AICPA modified its rules on advertising to reflect the changing attitudes.

Advertising may be viewed as a method by which the public can obtain information about accounting services and those who offer these services. To grant the public access to this information but at the same time maintain some control over abuses, the present rule prohibits advertising and other forms of solicitation that are false, misleading, or deceptive. The advertisements that first appeared after adoption of this rule were of an institutional nature, informing the readers of services rendered by major accounting firms or stating a particular firm's position on professional matters.

An interpretation of Rule 502 by the Ethics Division of the AICPA indicates approval of advertisements that merely describe the accounting firm, giving its name, address, telephone number, office hours, services offered, fees by hourly rate or fixed fees for specified services, and partners' professional attainments, such as degrees earned, schools attended, certificates awarded, and memberships in professional associations. Advertisements that inform the reader of the accounting firm's policy on a matter related to public accounting practice are also deemed appropriate. On the other hand, certain information in advertisements has been judged inappropriate, or as being false, misleading, or deceptive. Examples are statements that create false expectations of favorable results, or that imply the ability of the accountant to influence any official regulatory agency or similar body. Advertisements or other forms of solicitation should not contain testimonials or endorsements of the accountant's work and should not contain statements of self-praise unless the facts can be verified. Comparisons with other accountants must also be based upon verifiable facts.

Many accountants are cautious of advertising and other forms of solicitation. They believe that contacts established through normal civic, social, political, and public-service activities lead to client-auditor relations in a more professional manner. The best recommendation comes from satisfied clients who spread the accountant's reputation to potential clients.

Accountants are encouraged to participate in programs on accounting topics of public interest. Conducting seminars, delivering speeches, and writing articles are activities that may increase the public's understanding of accounting functions. The profession as a whole benefits from this increased awareness, and the individual accountant's reputation in the community is enhanced.

SPECIALTY DESIGNATIONS

Public accountants may not use specialty designations in any publicity, including business cards, stationery, and directory listings. They may state that they are certified public accountants, describe the services offered by their firms, and may indicate that their practice is limited to certain services. The prohibition against designating a specialization exists because there is no established method of recognizing competence in the various specializations, such as taxation, SEC registrations, or auditing of financial institutions. At times there have been movements to recognize specialization within the profession, including the suggestion that additional examinations and certifications should be established, but so far such procedures have not been adopted.

COMMISSIONS

If a client were to learn that the public accounting firm that performed its audit had paid a commission or fee to the person who recommended the firm, the client might wonder whether the recommendation was based on abilities of the firm's auditors or on fees paid for such recommendation. To preclude such a question, Rule 503 prohibits the payment of commissions to obtain clients. Also prohibited by this rule is the acceptance of commissions by the auditors for products or services recommended. To illustrate, an auditor may recommend a service bureau for processing some of a client's records. If the auditor accepted a fee from the service bureau for the recommendation, one could doubt the objectivity of the recommendation. Unquestionably, an auditor is expected to make payments and receive payments only when professional services have been received or rendered.

SIMULTANEOUS OCCUPATIONS

Auditors may engage in another occupation while practicing public accounting. Rule 504 specifies that the other occupation may not be one that creates a conflict of interest in rendering professional services. There are two major guidelines about types of occupations considered compatible. First, the additional occupation should not lower the auditor's status as a professional person or be contrary to the dignity of the profession. Second, the additional occupation should not be of a nature that would impair the auditor's objectivity in rendering professional services to clients.

Although there are some views to the contrary, generally the practice of law is considered compatible with the practice of public accounting. If an auditor who is not an attorney employs a lawyer as a staff employee, the firm cannot provide legal services. Similarly, should a law firm employ a CPA, the firm cannot render opinions on financial statements. However, the accountant employed by a firm of lawyers may perform tax work for the firm's clients, since taxation is an area where both accountants and lawyers practice. It is left to the professional judgment of each practitioner not to extend practice into areas where one lacks competence. When such a point is reached, the professional owes it to the client to suggest that services of a practitioner of the other profession be engaged.

In recent years many CPAs have formed commercial businesses with non-CPAs to render a variety of consulting services, particularly in the area of computer systems. When the services are of a type normally rendered by public accounting firms, the CPA is required to see that the business follows the rules of conduct of the AICPA's code of ethics if the CPA is actively engaged in the business or has a substantial financial interest. If the interest is not material compared to the net worth of either the CPA or the business enterprise, and the CPA is merely an investor, the business does not have to abide by the AICPA's Code of Professional Ethics.

FORM OF ORGANIZATION

As mentioned in Chapter 1, auditors traditionally have organized their firms either as proprietorships or as partnerships and have been prohibited by state laws and the Code of Professional Ethics from organizing as corporations. There was assumed danger that the corporation would destroy the close personal relationship between auditors and clients or that the corporation would be controlled by nonprofessionals whose primary interest might be profit rather than service and who therefore might engage in nonprofessional activities like advertising. Primarily to permit accountants to have certain tax advantages available only through the corporate form, laws of many states and the Rules of Conduct presently allow the practice of public accounting in the form of professional corporations or professional associations. These regulations were generally drawn in such a manner so as not to detract from the professional responsibility of public accountants to their clients or to the public. The resolution by the AICPA's governing body that describes the characteristics of an approved professional corporation is given below.

RESOLVED, that members may be officers, directors, stockholders, representatives or agents of a corporation offering services of a type performed by public accountants only when the professional corporation or association has the following characteristics:

1. *Name.* The name under which the professional corporation or association renders professional services shall contain only the names of one or more of the present or former shareholders or of partners who were associated with a predecessor accounting firm. Impersonal or fictitious names, as well as names which indicate a specialty, are prohibited.
2. *Purpose.* The professional corporation or association shall not provide services that are incompatible with the practice of public accounting.
3. *Ownership.* All shareholders of the corporation or association shall be persons duly qualified to practice as a certified public accountant in a

state or territory of the United States or the District of Columbia. Shareholders shall at all times own their shares in their own right, and shall be the beneficial owners of the equity capital ascribed to them.

4. *Transfer of Shares.* Provision shall be made requiring any shareholder who ceases to be eligible to be a shareholder to dispose of all of his shares within a reasonable period to a person qualified to be a shareholder or to the corporation or association.
5. *Directors and Officers.* The principal executive officer shall be a shareholder and a director, and to the extent possible, all other directors and officers shall be certified public accountants. Lay directors and officers shall not exercise any authority whatsoever over professional matters.
6. *Conduct.* The right to practice as a corporation or association shall not change the obligation of its shareholders, directors, officers and other employees to comply with the standards of professional conduct established by the American Institute of Certified Public Accountants.
7. *Liability.* The stockholders of professional corporations or associations shall be jointly and severally liable for the acts of a corporation or association, or its employees—except where professional liability insurance is carried, or capitalization is maintained, in amounts deemed sufficient to offer adequate protection to the public. Liability shall not be limited by the formation of subsidiary or affiliated corporations or associations each with its own limited and unrelated liability.

In a report approved by Council at the fall 1969 meeting, the Board of Directors recommended that professional liability insurance or capitalization in the amount of $50,000 per shareholder/officer and professional employee to a maximum of $2,000,000 would offer adequate protection to the public. Members contemplating the formation of a corporation under this rule should ascertain that no further modifications in the characteristics have been made.

Professional ethics of internal auditors

The internal auditing profession recognizes the importance of ethical conduct by its members, and the standards of professional behavior are expressed in the Certified Internal Auditor Code of Ethics adopted by the Institute of Internal Auditors (see Appendix B). Many concepts of professional ethics for internal auditors are the same as those for public accountants, such as the exercise of honesty and objectivity in performing duties, obtaining sufficient evidence to warrant the expression of professional opinions, avoidance of conflicting activities, and the appropriate use of confidential information. A distinctive provision of the internal auditor's code is the requirement of loyalty to employers in all matters of company business. Managers of the employing company or organization rely upon the internal auditor for assistance in fulfilling their responsibilities, and as a consequence internal auditors have a duty to conduct themselves in a manner to advance the interest of their employers.

Supplementary readings

Burton, John C., ed. *Corporate Financial Reporting: Ethical and Other Problems.* New York: American Institute of Certified Public Accountants, 1972.

Hartley, Ronald V., and Timothy L. Ross. "MAS and Audit Independence: An Image Problem." *Journal of Accountancy* (November 1972), 42-51.

Lavin, David. "Perceptions of the Independence of the Auditor." *Accounting Review* (January 1976), 41-50.

Loeb, Stephen E., and Burt A. Leete. "The Dual Practitioner: CPA, Lawyer, or Both?" *Journal of Accountancy* (August 1973), 57-63.

Loeb, Stephen E., and Gordon S. May. "Confidentiality, Privilege and Public Responsibility Under the Attest Function." *Journal of Accountancy* (September 1976), 52-54.

Olson, Wallace. "How Should a Profession Be Disciplined?" *Journal of Accountancy* (May 1978), 59-66.

Ostlund, A. Clayton. "Advertising—In the Public Interest?" *Journal of Accountancy* (January 1978), 59-63.

Weygandt, Jerry J. "The CPA and His Duty to Silence." *Accounting Review* (January 1970), 69-75.

Wood, Thomas D., and Donald A. Ball. "New Rule 502 and Effective Advertising by CPAs." *Journal of Accountancy* (June 1978), 65-70.

Review questions

3-1. Why should a professional group, such as public accountants, have a code of professional ethics?

3-2. Describe the content and purpose of each of the three sections of the AICPA Code of Professional Ethics.

3-3. Define the term *independence* as it is applied to an auditor.

3-4. What criteria can an auditor use to determine whether a relationship will impair the appearance of independence?

3-5. Contrast the appearance of independence and independence in fact.

3-6. If a CPA is a major stockholder in a business enterprise, may the CPA accept appointment as independent auditor of that business? Would your answer be different if the investment was immaterial both as to the CPA's personal fortune and as to the net worth of the business enterprise?

3-7. What restrictions on employees' investments in stocks and bonds are likely to be imposed by public accounting firms?

3-8. What relatives are considered close kin and remote kin for purposes of interpreting the AICPA's Rules of Conduct? Why is this distinction important?

3-9. As a partner in a CPA firm that has the local savings and loan association as a client, may you ethically obtain a home mortgage from this savings and loan association? Explain.

3-10. Regarding the auditor's independence, what distinction is made between the auditor being an investor in the client company and being an officer during that portion of the year under audit prior to the auditor's appointment? Why is such a distinction made?

3-11. If you are the independent auditor for Lowry Corporation, can you also be trustee of the Lowry Corporation's profit-sharing plan? Explain.

3-12. Describe the applicability of a public accountant's independence in tax practice and in rendering management advisory services. How is this position justified?

3-13. How can auditors consider themselves independent when they have performed bookkeeping services for client companies? What bookkeeping services may auditors perform if a client reports to the SEC?

3-14. "Whenever an auditor is requested to perform an audit in an industry that is unfamiliar, the auditor must refuse such an engagement to avoid violation of the code of ethics on the matter of competence." Comment on the preceding statement.

3-15. Barbara Jamison, a senior accounting student at Mid-State University, was heard to say, "I'll be glad to graduate and get to work for a public accounting firm, for I'm tired of having to study." Comment on Jamison's statement.

3-16. What are some ways an auditor is expected to continue professional education while practicing public accounting?

3-17. "In order to become a partner in a CPA firm, a person must have greater knowledge and expertise in all aspects of the business than any of the employees; otherwise, the partner could not appropriately review the work of the others and assume responsibility for the opinions expressed by the firm." Evaluate the previous statement for its accuracy.

3-18. What benefits should ensue to individual CPAs and to the accounting profession when substandard reporting is submitted to the AICPA's Practice Review Committee?

3-19. If asked to audit a company in an industry about which the accountant is unfamiliar, does this lack of knowledge indicate that the accountant lacks competence to perform the audit? Explain.

3-20. By what methods may an accountant acquire knowledge about an unfamiliar industry before accepting the appointment? How much knowledge must be acquired before accepting the appointment?

3-21. Linda Cardillo has been a practicing CPA for 25 years, and she told a client recently, "You probably can use that method of accounting although I know it disagrees with a statement from the FASB. I'll ask around and see if there aren't enough of us CPAs who disagree with the FASB that we won't have to go along with them on that particular statement." Comment on this statement.

3-22. What action does an auditor have to take when discovering that a client's financial statements differ from an accounting principle promulgated by the FASB?

3-23. "Any time an auditor's name is associated with forecasted financial statements, users of the statements will automatically assume the auditor is vouching for the outcome of the statements." Present ideas supporting and refuting this statement.

3-24. Auditors face a constant conflict in protecting confidential information from clients while at the same time making sure there is adequate disclosure on financial statements of all relevant facts. How is this conflict resolved?

3-25. "As a citizen of the United States, a CPA has an obligation to inform the Internal Revenue Service of any underpayment of taxes he or she becomes aware of in performing audits or other professional accounting services." Comment on this statement.

3-26. Describe the factors an accountant may consider in establishing the fee for an audit.

3-27. May a public accounting firm advertise for audits in the public utility industry by stating its success in influencing favorable settlements of rate cases based upon the audited financial statements filed by clients? Discuss.

3-28. Del Chambers, a CPA, states on his letterhead stationery that he is an expert in auditing insurance companies since sixty percent of his clients are engaged in the insurance business. Has Chambers violated the AICPA's code of ethics? Explain.

3-29. Cindy Apt, a CPA, states in her advertisements that she is limiting her practice to companies in the retail business. Has Apt violated the AICPA's code of ethics? Explain.

3-30. If a group of CPAs decide to incorporate their public accounting firm, may they sell shares of the corporation's stock to family members? Explain.

3-31. List some reasons why a newly appointed auditor should consult with the former auditor.

3-32. What are some occupations that may be practiced jointly with public accounting? What are some that may not be? Explain why.

Decision problems

3-33. Financial interests in a client company is one of the factors that affects an auditor's appearance of independence. The following cases involve such financial interests.

a. Robert Mehalik, a CPA, owned 400 shares of capital stock in Mason Company for many years. When approached in March 1981, about serving as auditor of Mason Company for the year ended December 31, 1981, Mehalik refused, saying, "As a stockholder of your company during the year to be examined, I would violate the Code of Professional Ethics if I accepted the appointment." Comment on Mehalik's response to Mason Company.

b. An assistant accountant employed by a CPA firm owned 200 shares of a company that recently became a client to be served by the local office. The accountant was required to dispose of his investment, although he was not assigned to the audit of the client company. Explain why such action was required by the firm. Was the action required by the code of ethics?

c. If you are a partner in a large CPA firm and are located in the Dallas office, can you have a small investment in a client company audited by your firm entirely from the Boston office? Explain.

3-34. An auditor not only must appear to be independent, but also must be independent in fact.

a. Explain the concept of an auditor's independence as it applies to third-party reliance upon financial statements.

b. 1. What determines whether or not an auditor is independent in fact?

2. What determines whether or not an auditor appears to be independent?

c. Explain how an auditor may be independent in fact but not appear to be independent.

d. Would a CPA be considered independent for an examination of the financial statements of:

1. a church for which the CPA is serving as treasurer without compensation?

2. a women's club for which the CPA's wife is serving as treasurer-bookkeeper if he is not to receive a fee for the examination? Explain.

AICPA adapted

3-35. Assume that you examined the financial statements of the Nelson Company in accordance with generally accepted auditing standards and were satisfied with your findings.

a. Would the fact that the company had a loan (of substantial amount to the Nelson Company) payable to a loan company of which your brother was principal stockholder have any effect on your auditor's opinion? Discuss.

b. Your daughter, aged 16, owns 100 shares of the 50,000 shares of the Nelson Company common stock outstanding at the balance sheet date. Would this fact have any effect on your auditor's opinion? Discuss.

AICPA adapted

3-36. You have served as auditor for Magic Markets, Inc., a chain of grocery stores in your state, for a number of years. You recently have been approached by Regional Grocery Corp. to be their auditor. Not only does Regional operate in the same cities where Magic Markets are located, but also Regional has an announced policy of buying out smaller chains. Evidence seems to indicate that the managers of the acquired chains do not stay with Regional very long after acquisition.

a. Ethically, may you serve as independent auditor for both Magic Markets, Inc. and Regional Grocery Corp.?

b. Should either client be informed that you are serving as auditor of the other?

c. What action must you take regarding the previous auditor for Regional Grocery Corp.? Why?

3-37. An auditor's report was appended to the financial statements of Bronowski, Inc. The statements consisted of a balance sheet as of November 30, 1981, and statements of income, changes in financial position, and retained earnings for the year then ending. The first two paragraphs of the report contained the wording of the standard unqualified short-form report, and a third paragraph read as follows:

The wives of two partners of our firm owned a material investment in the outstanding common stock of Bronowski, Inc. during the fiscal year ending November 30, 1981. The aforementioned individuals disposed of their holdings of Bronowski, Inc., on December 3, 1981, in a transaction that did not result in a profit or a loss. This information is included in our report in order to comply with certain disclosure requirements of the Code of Professional Ethics of the American Institute of Certified Public Accountants.

Bell & Davis
Certified Public Accountants

a. Was the CPA firm of Bell & Davis independent with respect to the fiscal 1981 examination of Bronowski's financial statements? Explain.

b. Assume that no members of Bell & Davis or any members of their families held any financial interests in Bronowski during 1981. For each of the following cases, indicate if independence would be lacking on behalf of Bell & Davis, assuming that Bronowski is a profit-seeking enterprise. In each case, explain why independence would or would not be lacking.

1. Two directors of Bronowski became partners in the CPA firm of Bell & Davis on July 1, 1981, resigning their directorships on that date.
2. During 1981 the former controller of Bronowski, now a Bell & Davis partner, was frequently called on for assistance by Bronowski. He made decisions for Bronowski's management regarding fixed-asset acquisitions and the company's product marketing mix. In addition, he conducted a computer feasibility study for Bronowski.

AICPA adapted

3-38. Earl Moss and Mitch Capelli were partners in the firm Moss and Capelli, CPAs. Moss had a financial interest in Baketown, Inc., a local bakery; therefore, he was not independent and refused to serve as auditor when requested. However, he recommended his partner, Capelli, to serve as auditor for Baketown, Inc. Capelli, as an individual CPA, performed the audit for Baketown, Inc. for the year ended September 30, 1983, and issued an unqualified opinion as to the fairness of the financial statements for the year then ended.

a. Did either Moss or Capelli violate the rule of professional conduct concerning independence? Explain.
b. Was any other rule of professional conduct violated? Discuss.
c. If any rules of professional conduct were violated, what disciplinary action would you deem appropriate?

3-39. Mae Gleb, a CPA, has performed bookkeeping services for Globe Employment Agency for several years. Two months before the end of the current fiscal year, the State Street Bank notified Globe that it would be necessary for audited financial statements to accompany the application for any future extensions of the loan which is due to the bank sixty days after Globe's year end. Globe asks Gleb to prepare such audited statements.

May Gleb serve as independent auditor since she has performed bookkeeping services during the year?

3-40. Gilbert and Bradley formed a corporation called Financial Services, Inc., each man taking 50 percent of the authorized common stock. Gilbert is a CPA and a member of the American Institute of CPAs. Bradley is a CPCU (Chartered Property Casualty Underwriter). The corporation performs auditing and tax services under Gilbert's direction and insurance services under Bradley's supervision. The opening of the corporation's office was announced by a three-inch, two-column "card" in the local newspaper.

Identify and discuss the ethical implications of those acts by Gilbert that were in violation of the AICPA Code of Professional Ethics.

AICPA adapted

3-41. In the process of performing your audit of Cascade Lumber Company, you discovered that the company has been giving football tickets to all home games of State College to the key enforcement officers of the State Environmental Agency. Although you do not have complete evidence, there are indications that Cascade's method of burning waste sawdust does not meet state requirements. When you asked questions regarding the environmental laws, the enforcement agency, and the football tickets, you were told that only advertising expense was involved and the financial statements reflected every cent expended. The financial vice president reminded you that your code of ethics required you to keep information learned on the audit confidential.

Discuss what action you should take in this situation, using knowledge of the AICPA's code of ethics to guide you in reaching your decision.

3-42. Alex Jones, a retired partner of your CPA firm, has just been appointed to the board of directors of Palmer Corporation, your firm's client. Jones is also a member of your firm's income tax committee, which meets monthly to discuss income tax problems of the partnership's clients. The partnership pays Jones $200 for each committee meeting he attends and a monthly retirement benefit of $2,000.

Discuss the effect of Jones's appointment to the board of directors of Palmer Corporation on your partnership's independence in expressing an opinion on the Palmer Corporation's financial statements.

AICPA adapted

3-43. The attribute of independence has been traditionally associated with the CPA's function of auditing and expressing opinions on financial statements.

a. What is meant by independence as applied to the CPA's function of auditing and expressing opinions on financial statements? Discuss.

b. CPAs have imposed upon themselves certain rules of professional conduct that induce their members to remain independent and to strengthen public confidence in their independence. Which of the rules of professional conduct are concerned with the CPA's independence? Discuss.

c. The Wallydrag Company is indebted to Anthony Papageorge, a CPA, for unpaid fees and has offered to issue Papageorge unsecured interest-bearing notes. Would Papageorge's acceptance of these notes have any bearing upon his independence in his relations with the Wallydrag Company? Discuss.

d. The Rocky Hill Corporation was formed on October 1, 1981, and its fiscal year will end on September 30, 1982. You audited the corporation's opening balance sheet and rendered an unqualified opinion on it. A month after rendering your report you are offered the position of secretary of the corporation because of the need for a complete set of officers and for convenience in signing various documents. You will have no financial interest in the corporation through stock ownership or otherwise, will receive no salary, will not keep the books, and will not have any influence on its financial matters other than occasional advice on income tax matters and similar advice normally given a client by a CPA.

1. Assume that you accept the offer but plan to resign the position prior to conducting your annual audit with the intention of again assuming the office after rendering an opinion on the statements. Can you render an independent opinion on the financial statements? Discuss.
2. Assume that you accept the offer on a temporary basis until the corporation has gotten under way and can employ a secretary. In any event you would permanently resign the position before conducting your annual audit. Can you render an independent opinion on the financial statements? Discuss.

AICPA adapted

3-44. Nathan Kitrell, a local CPA, was approached by a representative of Randall Adjustment Associates, a firm of public fire adjustors. The adjustment company negotiates settlements of fire losses with insurance companies and needs financial statements on one of its clients for three years. The adjustor asked Kitrell to prepare the statements without audit for a fee based upon the adjustor's fee from the insured. The fee, which the adjustor receives from the insured, is based upon the amount of the settlement from the insurance company.

Discuss the ethical considerations involved in Kitrell's decision to accept or reject such a fee arrangement.

3-45. Sigma Corporation, a locally owned jewelry store, wishes to engage Dab Halvorson, CPA, to examine its annual financial statements. Sigma has been generally pleased with the services provided by its prior CPA, Mar Flanagan, but thought the audit work performed was too detailed and interfered excessively with Sigma's normal office routines. Halvorson asked Sigma to inform Flanagan of the decision to change auditors, but Sigma did not want to do so.

To abide by the Rules of Conduct of the AICPA's code of ethics, Halvorson should follow certain procedures. Describe and discuss these procedures.

AICPA adapted

3-46. Hunter Fesperman, CPA, is a partner in the public accounting firm of Fesperman, Luker and Company. He is conducting a seminar on the effects of the recent changes in the minimum wage law and reporting requirements. Announcements have been mailed to all clients, bankers, and members of the local chamber of commerce inviting them to attend the seminar. His expertise in the field of labor law is widely recognized and can be documented. The announcement elaborates upon this fact. At the conclusion of the seminar, he plans to announce the name, telephone number, and location of his firm, and to invite those who need assistance in meeting the reporting requirements of the new law to contact him. He is aware that clients of other CPAs are likely to be present.

Discuss the actions described above as to whether or not they are in accordance with provisions of the AICPA's code of ethics.

3-47. Lakeview Development Corporation was formed on January 2, 1981, to develop a vacation-recreation area upon land purchased the same day by the corporation for $200,000. The corporation also purchased for $80,000 an adjacent tract of land, which the corporation plans to subdivide into fifty building lots. When the area is developed, the lots are expected to sell for $20,000 each.

The corporation borrowed a substantial portion of its funds from a bank and gave a mortgage on the land. A mortgage covenant requires that the corporation furnish quarterly financial statements.

The quarterly financial statements prepared at March 31 and June 30 by the corporation's bookkeeper were unacceptable to the bank officials. The corporation's president now offers you the engagement of preparing unaudited quarterly financial statements. Because of limited funds your fee would be paid in Lakeview Development Corporation common stock rather than in cash. The stock would be repurchased by the corporation when funds become available. You would not receive enough stock to be a major stockholder.

a. Discuss the ethical implications of your accepting the engagement.

b. Assume that you accepted the engagement and prepared the September 30 statements. After accepting your unaudited September 30 financial statements, the bank notified the corporation that the December 31 financial statements must be accompanied by a CPA's opinion. You were asked to conduct the audit and told that your fee would be paid in cash. Discuss the ethical implications of your accepting the engagement.

AICPA adapted

3-48. You were engaged to examine Barnes Corporation's financial statements for the year just ended. The CPA firm previously engaged declined to make the examination because a son of one of the CPA firm's partners received a material amount of Barnes Corporation common stock in exchange for engineering services rendered to the corporation. The partner in the CPA firm advises his son in business affairs but does not own an interest in his son's engineering firm and had not participated in this examination in past years. Another of the CPA firm's twenty-five partners would have been in charge of this engagement.

This new client wants to receive three different reports from you. In the past the stockholders have considered and discussed the corporation's annual report containing the financial statements and the auditor's opinion at their annual meeting. Because of the shortage of time before the stockholders' meeting, corporation executives are willing to accept (*a*) your report containing unaudited statements to be used for the meetings and (*b*) your final report after your examination is complete. Thereafter, the client would like to receive (*c*) a report containing a forecast of the corporation's 1981–1983 operations.

a. Should the CPA firm previously engaged by Barnes Corporation have declined the examination of the financial statements for the year just ended? Discuss the ethical issues involved.

b. Discuss the issues in the client's request that you render unaudited financial statements prior to rendering your final report.

c. What are the issues for a CPA in rendering a report containing a forecast of a client's future operations? Discuss.

AICPA adapted

3-49. Anita Dekle has been hired by the CPA firm of Noble and Elkins based primarily on the fact that she is an expert in operations research. None of the partners or employees of Noble and Elkins have any knowledge or training in the field of operations research. A number of their clients have had to engage other consulting firms in the past because the CPAs were unable to render services in this area.

a. Would the CPA firm be violating any rules of ethics by sharing fees with Dekle if she is not planning to become a CPA?

b. Is the CPA firm attempting to render services that are in violation of ethical standards?

c. Discuss the possible problems involved with the CPA partners' responsibility for work about which they have no expertise.

3-50. During 1980 your client, Neusel Corporation, requested that you conduct a feasibility study to advise management of the best way the corporation can utilize electronic data processing equipment and which computer, if any, best meets the corporation's requirements. You are technically competent in this area and accept the engagement. Upon completion of your study the corporation accepts your suggestions and installs the computer and related equipment that you recommended.

a. Discuss the effect the acceptance of this management services engagement would have upon your independence in expressing an opinion on the financial statements of the Neusel Corporation.

b. Instead of accepting the engagement, assume that you recommended Ike Mackey, of the CPA firm of Brown and Mackey, who is qualified in specialized services. Upon completion of the engagement your client requests that Mackey's partner, John Brown, perform services in other areas. Should Brown accept the engagement? Discuss.

c. A local printer of data processing forms customarily offers a commission for recommending him as supplier. The client is aware of the commission offer and suggests that Mackey accept it. Would it be proper for Mackey to accept the commission with the client's approval? Discuss.

AICPA adapted

3-51. MacDonald and Nash, both CPAs, each owned 50 percent of the shares in a public accounting firm which was incorporated under the name of Kirchoff and Nash, Certified Public Accountants, the founders of the firm. MacDonald bought out the interest of Kirchoff, also a CPA, when he retired eight years ago. Nash is now ready to retire, and he proposes selling his interest to Louise Marino, who practices as an individual CPA in town. A problem has arisen as to what name the firm can use if Marino purchases Nash's interest. At that time neither Kirchoff nor Nash will be stockholders. Neither MacDonald nor Marino care to use their names in the firm name. MacDonald indicated that for tax reasons he would like to give one half of his shares in the firm to his children and suggests that Marino may want to give some of her shares to her children when she enters the firm.

a. What names are appropriate for the CPA firm to use?

b. Would any provisions of the AICPA's code of ethics be violated if these gifts were made? Discuss.

c. Although Nash has retired from the firm, may he continue to own shares in the corporation?

3-52. Jolynn Taylor has recently passed the CPA examination and has decided to open her own practice of public accounting. She has discussed the matter thoroughly with Maxwell Rosen who plans to join her as a partner within the next three years. Her projections indicate she will employ a part-time secretary immediately and add a staff assistant in about eighteen months. Ms. Taylor desires to list her firm as "Taylor and Company, Certified Public Accountant." After Mr. Rosen joins her in practice, the only change in name necessary will be to add an "s" to make it "Taylor and Company, Certified Public Accountants."

a. Since Ms. Taylor plans to have an employee from the beginning of her practice, is she violating any ethical rules with her choice of firm name? Discuss.

b. Would it be any different from an ethical viewpoint should she omit the *and* from her firm name? Discuss.

3-53. Certified public accountants have imposed upon themselves a rigorous Code of Professional Ethics.

a. Discuss the underlying reasons for the accounting profession's adopting a Code of Professional Ethics.

b. A rule of professional ethics adopted by CPAs is that a CPA may be an officer, director, stockholder, representative, or agent of a corporation engaged in the practice of public accounting. List the restrictions placed upon a CPA firm organized as a corporation.

AICPA adapted

3-54. Andrew Jefferson, CPA, has prepared Mr. Burr's federal income tax return for several years. This year Jefferson has discovered that in the prior year's return he made an error which resulted in a lower tax liability for Burr. The tax return is now under IRS administrative review. What are Jefferson's professional responsibilities in this connection?

AICPA adapted

4

Legal Responsibility

A public accountant, in rendering auditing and other professional services, has both ethical and legal responsibilities. The ethical responsibilities are outlined by the Code of Professional Ethics and related essays and interpretations of the AICPA, the rules of other professional groups, and regulations of the accounting boards in each of the states. Legal responsibilities of the public accountant are defined by common law and statutes. The specific responsibility and related legal liability of the accountant in a particular case may be known only after a jury or a judge reaches a decision and appeals are exhausted. As the philosophy of the courts changes, so changes an accountant's legal responsibility. The large number of legal cases involving public accountants during the past decade or so has resulted in an expanded scope of legal responsibility that is still evolving.

An accountant's liability may arise from either of two sources: (1) *common law* or (2) *statutory law*. Under common law, which is comprised of previous legal decisions, an accountant may incur liability to clients and/or to third parties who are not parties to the auditor-client contract. In addition, both state and federal statutes establish rules that must be followed by accountants, who may be liable for either civil or criminal actions. Criminal action must be initiated by the federal or state government or a governmental agency; imprisonment and/or fines are potential penalties. Civil action may be brought against an accountant under common law as well as under civil sections of statutes by third parties seeking monetary awards as compensation for losses incurred as a result of the accountant's actions.

The presentation in this chapter of the accountant's legal responsibility considers (1) the two sources of liability—common law and statutory law, and (2) the parties to whom the accountant may be liable—clients and third parties. Discussed first is liability to the client under common law; second, liability to third parties under common law; and third, civil and criminal liability under statutory law. Pertinent legal cases are discussed as they relate to the various types of liability.

Liability to the client

An accountant may be liable to clients either for breach of contract or on a tort action for negligence. Failure to carry out a contract for services, such as preparing the client's federal and state income tax returns, is clearly a *breach of contract* and may give rise to liability to the client. *Tort liability* is based upon the failure to carry out a duty created by social policy, or social policy and contract. For example, failure to exercise due professional care in discharging a contract subjects the auditor to a tort action for liability for ordinary negligence based upon failure to perform a duty created by social policy and/or a contract. (Although there are legal distinctions between a breach of contract and a tort, these distinctions are unimportant in this discussion.)

The contract between auditor and client usually is in the form of an engagement letter detailing the type of work expected of the accountant. The importance of an engagement letter is illustrated by the *1136 Tenants' Corporation* case in which the client's successful suit against the audit firm was influenced by the lack of an engagement letter. The accountant had understood that bookkeeping services only were to be performed, but the client stated that an audit had been expected. A properly designed engagement letter would have clarified this matter. In addition to emphasizing the importance of an engagement letter, this case also suggests that accountants not ignore suspicious material coming to their attention, even on a routine bookkeeping engagement. The facts of this case are presented later in the section on representative cases, and engagement letters are discussed more thoroughly later in the chapter.

ORDINARY NEGLIGENCE

An accountant is liable to a client for negligence by failure to exercise due professional care in discharging the duties necessary in the circumstances. For the laity, due care is the exercise of a standard of behavior like that expected of any reasonable person. For professionals who undertake work calling for specialized skills, however, the standard of behavior is that which characterizes others in their profession. As a professional, an auditor is expected to employ the skill, knowledge, and judgment that other professional auditors in a particular locality would employ under similar circumstances. Although not expected to display extraordinary or unusual skill, an auditor should exercise a higher level of care than would an ordinary, nonprofessional, prudent person.

A frequently quoted passage from *Cooley on Torts* describes the responsibility to be exercised in achieving due professional care by those who claim to be professionals.

> In all those employments where peculiar skill is requisite, if one offers his services, he is understood as holding himself out to the public as possessing the degree of skill commonly possessed by others in the same employment, and if his pretensions are unfounded, he commits a species of fraud upon every man who employs him in reliance on his public profession. But no man, whether skilled or unskilled, undertakes that the task he assumes shall be performed successfully, and without fault or error; he undertakes for good faith and integrity, but not for infallibility, and he is liable to his employer for negligence, bad faith, or dishonesty, but not for losses consequent upon mere errors of judgment.[1]

Even if an auditor exercises normal professional care and skill in conducting an audit and in rendering a report, there is no guarantee that false information may not exist in the financial statements. Under such circumstances the auditor usually is not liable for damages that result from the failure to detect false information. Merely making an error in judgment is not considered to subject an auditor to liability. For an auditor to be subject to liability for negligence, (1) there must be a duty with respect to a standard of conduct, (2) the auditor must fail to act in accordance with that duty, (3) there must be causal relationship between the negligence and the injury, and (4) the other party must incur actual loss or damage.

Auditing standards and procedures as well as AICPA rules of professional conduct are generally considered to describe the due care that an auditor should exercise in conducting an audit. These pronouncements indicate that an audit cannot be relied upon to disclose defalcations or deliberate misrepresentations on the financial statements. However, if an auditor's failure to comply with generally accepted auditing standards and the other pronouncements causes the defalcation to go undetected, the auditor clearly has responsibility. In legal suits of negligence against an auditor, a client has the burden to prove that the auditor failed to exercise necessary care.

Whether or not an auditor followed appropriate auditing procedures is not easy to determine, because the procedures that apply to a specific audit depend upon the circumstances. Additionally, procedures are constantly

[1] Thomas M. Cooley, *Cooley on Torts,* 4th ed., rev. by D. Avery Haggard. (Chicago: Callaghan, 1932), III, 335.

being modified to reflect changes in the environment and expectations of clients, outsiders, and auditors. Should an auditor be sued for failure to discover defalcations, a jury may have to decide whether or not the auditor conducted the examination in accordance with standard auditing procedures. If it can be shown that standard auditing procedures would have led to detection of the defalcations, the jury may well determine that the auditor was negligent in not using such procedures and, therefore, is liable to the client. An auditor may also incur liability in cases where the examination is intentionally less than a complete audit and the client does not understand the nature of the auditor's work.

An auditor's best defense, in case of being sued for negligence, is evidence contained in the working papers that the audit was conducted with due professional care. The working papers should indicate that the audit was properly planned, after giving consideration to the client's internal accounting control system, and that the work was properly supervised and reviewed. Additionally, the auditor's report should disclose all relevant information not included in the financial statements and should clearly state the opinion of the auditor.

At times a client may contribute to the negligence of an accountant. If a client withholds information from the accountant or in some way restricts the scope of the professional work the accountant is engaged to perform, there is contributory negligence on the part of the client. If such contributory negligence on the part of a client causes an accountant to fail in performance, then the accountant has a valid defense. But if the accountant ignored the contributory negligence of the client, or if the client's negligence did not influence the accountant's negligent actions, contributory negligence is not a valid defense.

FRAUD

Ordinarily, fraud involves making a statement known to be untrue or without reasonable basis for believing it to be true, as well as the omission of a material fact that is necessary to convey the truth. For fraud to exist, there must be intent that another person act upon the omission or misstatement of the material fact, and the other person must take such action and be injured by doing so. An auditor is generally liable to a client for fraud.

GROSS NEGLIGENCE

There may be negligence to such a great extent that it amounts to fraud—called gross negligence or constructive fraud. An auditor would be guilty of gross negligence, for example, if in the conduct of the audit there was no genuine belief in its adequacy, or not even slight care was exercised, or there was reckless disregard for the truth. For example, gross negligence exists if an auditor fails to perform audit steps required under the circumstances, such as seeing that the subsidiary accounts receivable ledger balance agrees with both the control account and the amount reflected on the financial statements, or determining that the investments are in companies which actually exist and have current worth. An auditor is liable to a client for gross negligence as well as ordinary negligence and fraud.

Liability to third parties at common law

The auditing profession depends upon the fact that creditors, investors, and parties other than clients can rely upon representations of management in financial statements because an auditor has expressed an opinion on those statements. An auditor has a responsibility to these third parties even though they are not parties to the contract with the client. The doctrine of privity of contract, historically, allowed only a party to the contract to bring suit for negligence, thus making an auditor liable only to the client for ordinary negligence. An auditor was liable to third parties for fraud upon proof that the auditor intentionally deceived them for the purpose of inducing them to act upon the deception and that they relied upon the deception and were damaged. Liability could arise if an auditor were guilty of fraud in conducting the examination or in preparing the audit report. An auditor who cooperates with a client in the preparation of misleading financial statements to give false impressions to outside users of the statements has obviously committed fraud.

Court cases over the years have expanded the auditor's liability to third parties beyond that for fraud. In the case of *Ultramares Corp.* v. *Touche,* 255 N.Y. 170, 174 N.E. 441 (1931), the defendant auditors had issued an unqualified opinion on the financial statements of the client company. The plaintiff, a factor, had been furnished a copy of the financial statements and auditor's report and had relied upon the audited financial statements in making loans to the company. Shortly afterward it became known that the financial statements were in error and that the company was actually bankrupt. The factor sued the auditor for negligence, later adding fraud to the complaint. The judge's holding was that an auditor should not be held liable for simple negligence to anyone who happened to rely upon the auditor's opinion. The judge stated that if accountants were to be liable for such simple negligence, "a thoughtless slip or blunder, the failure to detect a theft or forgery beneath the cover of deceptive entries, may expose accountants to a liability in an indeterminate amount for an indeterminate time to an indeterminate class." Although in this specific case the liability for negligence was not extended to the third party, the judge's comments indicate that under other circumstances auditors could be liable for negligence, not only to the party with whom the contract was made, but also to those for whom the audit was explicitly prepared. If the contract clearly has as its "end and aim" a specified person or a limited group to whom the financial statements are to be delivered, the liability for negligence may extend to such designated third party beneficiaries. Also, the judge held that auditors could be guilty of negligence so gross that their liability would extend to third parties, the same as for fraud. For years accountants rested comfortably with this decision, which was generally interpreted to mean that under usual conditions their liability for ordinary negligence extended only to the client.

A position similar to the conclusion of the *Ultramares* case is taken by the American Law Institute in its *Restatement (Second) of Torts,* § 552 (Tentative Draft No. 12, 1966), which constitutes the thinking of leading legal scholars as to what the law should be. The view is that auditors should be responsible only to persons for whose benefit they are intending to provide the information or to persons for whom they know the client will provide the information. Also, loss must be suffered by persons who rely on the information in a transaction, or in a substantially similar transaction which the auditor intended for the information to influence or which the auditor knew the recipients so intended. Accordingly, there would be no liability to a creditor for loss if the auditor knew only that the report would have the usual exposure in a wide variety of transactions. For example, if the auditor were informed that the report would be used by a specific supplier for purposes of extending credit, the auditor would be liable to that supplier, or a comparable supplier, for negligence should the supplier suffer loss. On the other hand, should the supplier, based upon the auditor's report, purchase controlling interest in the company's common stock and subsequently suffer a loss, the auditor would not be liable to the supplier for negligence because the auditor's report was not used for the intended purpose.

The attitude of the court in upholding the concept of privity of contract began to change in the 1950s and 1960s. Previously, a purchaser of a manufactured product, such as a lawnmower, was prevented from collecting damages caused by the manufacturer's breach of warranty because the contractual relationship was between the purchaser and the dealer, not the manufacturer. The law has swung in a different direction, however, and presently the purchaser of a manufactured product generally has little difficulty in pursuing a case against the manufacturer. This change reflects the attitude of the courts in placing the responsibility for the damage on the party who is in a position to correct the wrong or to prevent the loss. Protection of the consumer is quite evident in this attitude.

The courts are tending also to "socialize" the risk of error and harm by placing the responsibility on those who have the ability to spread the costs of the errors over a larger totality. Accountants apparently are included in this new attitude of the courts. If a user of audited financial statements suffers harm because of the negligence of an auditor, there is a tendency to hold the auditor liable for damages because the auditor has the ability to socialize the cost through insurance and increased fees to all clients.

Serious questioning of the doctrine of liability for negligence only to parties of the contract was first indicated through a dissent by Lord Justice Denning in a British case, *Candler* v. *Crane, Christmas & Co.,* High Court of Justice, King's Bench Division 2K.B. 164 (1951). In this case the auditor was found to be extremely careless in the conduct of the audit, but the court determined there was no liability because the auditor owed no duty of care to a user who the auditor knew would be relying upon the financial statements. Lord Denning said that in his opinion "accountants owe a duty of care not only to their own clients, but also to all those whom they know will rely on their accounts in the transactions for which these accounts are prepared." Lord Denning's views became the law in England in *Hedley, Byrne & Co., Ltd.* v. *Heller & Partners, Ltd.,* (1964) A.C. 465 (House of Lords, 1963).

Following similar reasoning, the court ruled in the Rhode Island case of *Rusch Factors, Inc.* v. *Levin,* 284 F. Supp. 85 (1968), that the accountant should be liable for negligence "for careless financial misrepresentations relied upon by actually foreseen and limited classes of persons." In this case the accountant had certified financial statements of Rusch Factors that showed it to be solvent when it was not. The statements were used to support a loan, and after Rusch Factors went into bankruptcy, the lender sued the accountant as a result of his negligence upon fraudulent or negligent misrepresentations in the certified financial statements.

The judge questioned why an innocent party who suffered damages in relying on an accountant's negligent work should have to carry the burden of the loss. The risk of loss could be distributed and spread by imposing it on the accounting profession, which has the capability of passing the cost of insuring against such risks to its clients, who in turn pass the cost to consumers.

Similarly, the Iowa case of *Ryan* v. *Kanne,* 170 N.W. 2d 395 (Iowa, 1969), held that the accountant was responsible for negligence to a third party who relied upon his report and was specifically identified to the accountant at the time of his engagement.

The auditor's liability for negligence to third parties may exist even though an auditor expresses a disclaimer of opinion on the related financial statements. In *Rhode Island Hospital Trust National Bank* v. *Swartz,* 455 F. 2d 847 (4th Cir., 1972), the auditor indicated his disclaimer was based upon the fact that practically all the work on certain warehouse improvements had been performed by employees of the company and that complete detailed cost records were not maintained, thus preventing the exact determination of the actual cost of the improvements. In fact, there were no cost records, and the warehouse improvements were fictitious.

The court held that the auditor was negligent in failing to give a full explanation of the reasons for his disclaimer of opinion and the effect this information would have on the financial statements. The auditors were held liable in negligence for careless financial misrepresentations relied upon by actually foreseen and limited classes of persons. Such decisions seem to be dominant, but some cases can be found in which liability for auditors is more restricted.

Statutory acts and accountants' liability

The ultimate user of audited financial statements has shifted over the years from the individual owner of the company, to the banker or other credit grantors, and finally to the general investing public. To protect this expanding group of users, many of whom suffered great losses in the stock market crash of 1929, the New York Stock Exchange adopted a rule in 1932 that required all companies whose stock was listed by the Exchange to furnish their shareholders certified financial statements on at least an annual basis.

Shortly after this action of the New York Stock Exchange came federal legislation to provide investor protection in the Securities Act of 1933 and the Securities Exchange Act of 1934. These acts seek to protect public investors by requiring each company issuing securities to disclose extensive information about the company, including financial statements attested to by public accountants. Congress, in establishing these acts, considered having the financial statement attested to by federal auditors, but finally specified public accountants who already were rendering expert opinions to an expanding body of users.

Both the acts of 1933 and of 1934 empower the Securities Exchange Commission (SEC), which enforces these acts, to determine the rules and regulations necessary to carry out their provisions. Included specifically are the powers to define accounting terms, prescribe the methods to be followed in preparation of the accounts, specify the items to appear on financial statements, and establish the format for presentation of the information. Although the SEC has the power to establish and enforce accounting and auditing rules, it has generally let the accounting and auditing professions develop the standards in both areas. The SEC works in close liaison, however, with the professional bodies charged with establishing these standards and its views are influential.

STRUCTURE OF THE SEC

The SEC was established by Congress through a provision of the Securities Exchange Act of 1934 to help regulate the securities market in the United

States. (The Securities Act of 1933 was enforced by the Interstate Commerce Commission prior to passage of the 1934 act.) The SEC is directed by five commissioners appointed by the president and approved by the Senate. Their terms are for five years each, and one member is designated by the president as chairman. The commission administers and enforces both the securities acts of 1933 and 1934 as well as several other investment-related acts. A professional staff of accountants, engineers, attorneys, and securities analysts assists the commission in carrying out its duties.

The headquarters of the SEC are in Washington, D.C., and regional and branch offices are located in major cities throughout the United States. As shown on the organization chart, Figure 4-1, there are five divisions of the SEC, with the Division of Corporation Finance being of most importance, perhaps, to accountants and their corporate clients. This division is responsible for establishing and enforcing standards of financial reporting and disclosure by all companies under the SEC jurisdiction. The Division of Corporation Finance reviews all registration statements, prospectuses, proxy statements, and sales literature, as well as quarterly and annual reports filed with the SEC. Additionally, this division provides an advisory service to help clarify the requirements and applications of the securities laws for the issuers of securities, their accountants, attorneys, and underwriters.

On matters of accounting and auditing, the SEC is advised by the Office of the Chief Accountant. The chief accountant directs the development of administrative policies concerning accounting matters and the preparation of accounting rules and regulations. The chief accountant is primarily responsible for implementing the SEC's statutory power to develop accounting and auditing standards that will provide the disclosure sought by the SEC. Consequently, it is the person serving as chief accountant who has the greatest exposure to the accounting community and has major contact with the professional bodies concerned with development of accounting principles. Another responsibility of the chief accountant is to consider matters relating to the independence of public accountants who attest to financial statements filed with the SEC.

These accountants should pay particular attention to pronouncements of the SEC in the form of *Regulation S-X* and *Accounting Series Releases. Regulation S-X,* a codification of rules and regulations, is continually revised, and is the major source of information about the form and content of financial statements included in registration statements and other reports filed with the SEC. *Accounting Series Releases* are pronouncements issued primarily for two purposes: (1) to clarify and explain accounting procedures and practices needing special treatment, and (2) to give notice of disciplinary sanctions imposed by the SEC. These releases are issued at irregular intervals as needed; the frequency of issue has increased considerably in recent years as the SEC has become more active.

Figure 4-1 Organization Chart of the Securities and Exchange Commission

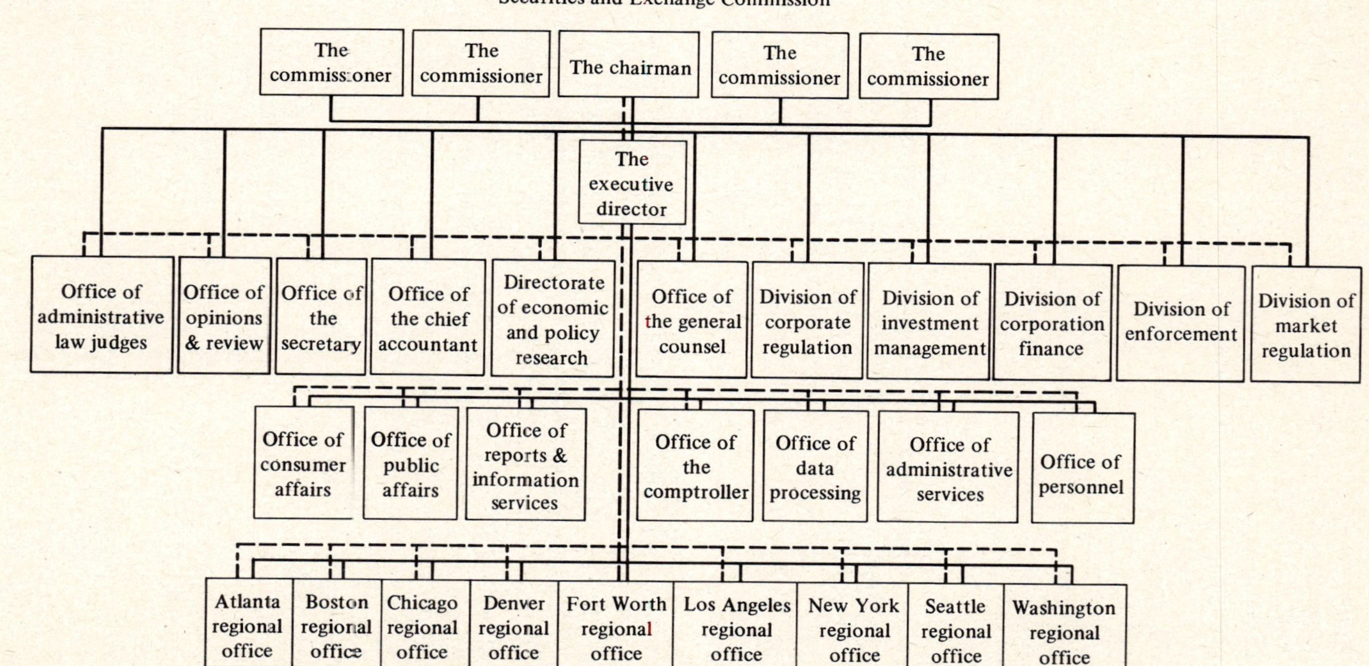
Securities and Exchange Commission
The commissioner
The commissioner
The chairman
The commissioner
The commissioner
The executive director
Office of administrative law judges
Office of opinions & review
Office of the secretary
Office of the chief accountant
Directorate of economic and policy research
Office of the general counsel
Division of corporate regulation
Division of investment management
Division of corporation finance
Division of enforcement
Division of market regulation
Office of consumer affairs
Office of public affairs
Office of reports & information services
Office of the comptroller
Office of data processing
Office of administrative services
Office of personnel
Atlanta regional office
Boston regional office
Chicago regional office
Denver regional office
Fort Worth regional office
Los Angeles regional office
New York regional office
Seattle regional office
Washington regional office
Lines of policy and judicial authority
Lines of budget and management authority

THE SECURITIES ACT OF 1933

Frequently called the "truth in securities" law, the purpose of the Securities Act of 1933 is to regulate the initial offering and original sale of new securities. It does not govern subsequent trading of the securities after their initial distribution. The act requires that investors be provided with adequate information upon which to make their decisions in choosing among alternative investments. Also, the act contains provisions prohibiting misrepresentations and fraudulent practices in the sale of securities. No provision is made for any governmental agency to rule on the financial strength of the company offering the securities or on the potential speculative nature of the securities themselves. The government leaves those determinations to be made by investors; the act merely provides that investors be fully informed of the pertinent facts and that an atmosphere absent of fraud prevails.

With limited exceptions, the Securities Act of 1933 requires each company making a public offering of its securities to file with the SEC a *registration statement* containing audited financial statements, comparative summaries of earnings, and other financial information. The registration statement is a public document, and copies may be obtained by interested parties from the SEC. Much of the information in the registration statement is included in a *prospectus.* A prospectus is a brochure furnished to each person to whom the newly registered securities are offered for sale. It contains information about the company, its history, the nature of the business, and financial statements. This information is filed as a major portion of the registration statement.

The registration statement and prospectus contain financial statements and additional financial data that must be attested to by an independent public accountant. Since the registration may take place several weeks or months after the date of the latest audited financial statements, unaudited interim financial statements are frequently included to update the audited statements. The registration of a company's securities is a major event, and much work goes into preparation of the required information. The independent accountant usually is heavily involved in all phases of the registration process. The accountant normally performs additional inquiries in order to be reasonably assured that conditions since the audit date continue to merit the accountant's name being associated with the statements. This limited review is called an *S-1 review,* named for *Form S-1,* a general form used commonly in filing registrations by commercial and industrial entities. After filing the statements, twenty or more days elapse before the effective date of the registration. The accountant's attestation as of the audit date continues to apply to the financial statements through this effective date. The accountant's association with these and other reports to the SEC is discussed further in Chapter 6.

Comfort Letters The underwriters of a securities issue have the obligation under the Securities Act of 1933 to obtain reasonable assurance as to the accuracy of the registration statement, including any unaudited financial data and other matters relative to the financial statements. The underwriters usually seek a report called a *comfort letter* from the accountants saying that they are not aware of any false or misleading information contained in the registration statement. By stating that no indication was found that the statements are false or misleading at the effective date, the accountant is giving *negative assurance.* The accountant cannot make a positive attestation concerning the statements, for an adequate examination has not been performed. Negative assurance is merely a statement that although no audit was conducted and the review was limited, the accountant has no knowledge of facts contrary to what is reflected on the statements. SAS No. 1 (AU 630) discusses the nature of the accountant's limited review and the content of the comfort letter. Comfort letters are not required by the securities acts or by the SEC. They are, however, a common requirement of underwriting agreements. This topic is discussed further in Chapter 6.

Liability of Independent Accountants Section 11 of the Securities Act of 1933 provides for civil liability of the issuer, underwriter, accountant, engineer, appraiser, or other expert who prepared or certified any portion of the registration statement, should any materially false or inadequate representations be contained therein. Liability appears to be based upon failure to communicate needed information either by making false statements or by omitting material information. Failure to exercise due professional care as measured by professional standards does not seem to be the criterion for determining liability. When independent accountants consent in writing that their opinions may be included in registration statements, they are accepting potential liability to a wider class of users than exists under common law. However, since the 1933 act applies only to registration statements filed when a company is making new offerings of its securities, the situations to which these extended liability provisions apply are somewhat limited.

After a registration statement becomes effective, an investor, although not the public accountant's client or a party to the contract, may sue the accountant, claiming that the financial statements contain an untrue statement of a material fact or omit a material fact necessary to keep the statements from being misleading. An investor must prove that a loss was suffered, but not that the loss resulted from reliance on the financial statements; nor does an investor have to prove that the accountant was negligent or fraudulent in certifying the statements. Under common law, the investor, as plaintiff, would have the burden of proving that the loss was caused by the negligence or fraud of the accountant; but under the

1933 act the accountant has the burden of proving that the loss resulted from other causes. Of course, the claim that the financial statements do not contain false information or omission of material facts is probably the strongest defense. Accountants may use *due diligence* as a defense by proving that they made a reasonable investigation and had reasonable grounds to believe and did believe that the statements were true at the time they became effective. The reasonableness of the investigation is described as that which a prudent individual would use in the management of one's own property. Accountants may offer other defenses, for example, that the investor had prior knowledge of the misstatement, or that excessive time has passed since issuance of the financial statements.

An important case involving the matter of due diligence was the *BarChris* case. (This case is discussed more thoroughly in the section on representative legal cases later in the chapter.) It involved an S-1 review, designed to reveal any information arising between the audit and registration dates that would indicate the audited financial statements were in error. The courts held that an inadequate review was conducted and the accountants did not exercise due diligence.

All parties to a registration statement must show that they exercised due diligence in preparing and reviewing not only their part of the statement but also the entire document. A lesser standard is required of officers, directors, and underwriters if they have relied upon the authority of an expert, such as an accountant. In the *BarChris* case, some newly appointed directors were held to the higher standard of responsibility because they had asked questions only of officers and other directors and had not relied upon opinions of experts. Consequently, accountants are being requested to attest to greater portions of the data filed with the SEC. Accountants who are willing to attest to matters other than the financial statements must realize the expanded area of their responsibility and liability, and also should be careful not to be associated with matters outside their areas of competence.

THE SECURITIES EXCHANGE ACT OF 1934

Regulations for the trading of securities in secondary markets through brokers and exchanges is the focus of the Securities Exchange Act of 1934. As originally enacted, the 1934 act extended to all companies that had securities registered on national stock exchanges. However, through a 1964 amendment, the regulations now apply to companies whose securities are traded on over-the-counter markets if the firms have assets in excess of $1 million and five hundred or more stockholders. The 1934 act requires a registration of outstanding securities similar to, but less extensive than, the one required by the 1933 act. Financial statements for the last fiscal year are included in the registration statement, and updated information is required in the form of annual and quarterly reports, and some special reports in specified situations. The 1934 act also requires the registration of national securities exchanges and brokers dealing in over-the-counter markets.

Liability of Independent Accountants In contrast to the extended period of responsibility for the attestation to financial statements under the 1933 act, the accountant's attestation under the 1934 act is presumed to apply to the statements when the accountant's report is included in the client's filing with the SEC. However, if the accountant has knowledge of relevant material events occurring between the audit report date and the filing date, the accountant should insist upon disclosure of such events. Also in contrast to the 1933 act, provisions of the 1934 act require that investors prove that their reliance upon the financial statements was the cause of losses they incurred. Section 18 of the 1934 act specifically provides that accountants have a valid defense if they can prove they acted in good faith and had no knowledge that the statements were false or misleading. Consequently, it appears that an accountant's liability to third-party investors exists only if there is gross negligence or fraud, the same as at common law.

Section 10(b) of the 1934 act authorized the SEC to prescribe appropriate rules and regulations necessary to protect investors.

> It shall be unlawful for any person, directly or indirectly, by the use of any means, or instrumentality of interstate commerce or of the mails, or of any facility of any national securities exchange. . . .
> (b) To use or employ, in connection with the purchase or sale of any security registered on a national securities exchange or any security not so registered, any manipulative or deceptive device or contrivance in contravention of such rules and regulations as the Commission may prescribe as necessary or appropriate in the public interest or for the protection of investors [15 U.S.C. 78j (b) (1970)].

In order to provide a regulation that would establish a means for apprehending a corporate executive who was committing fraud in the purchase of securities, the SEC in 1942 adopted Rule 10b-5 under the authority of Section 10(b) of the 1934 act.

> It shall be unlawful for any person, directly or indirectly by the use of any means of instrumentality or interstate commerce, or of the mails or of any facility of any national securities exchange,
> (a) To employ any device, scheme, or artifice to defraud,
> (b) To make any untrue statement of a material fact or to omit to state a material fact necessary in order to make the statements made, in the light of the circumstances under which they were made, not misleading, or

(c) To engage in any act, practice, or course of business which operates or would operate as a fraud or deceit upon any person, in connection with the purchase or sale of any security [17 CFR 240.10b-5].

Clauses (a) and (c) clearly enable the courts to impose liability on directors, officers, and professional advisers for fraudulent acts of intentionally deceiving a corporation's existing and potential stockholders and creditors. Clause (b) does not state specifically that the untrue statement or omission of fact had to be made with the intention to defraud. For many years there was confusion and dispute as to whether accountants were liable only for acts with intent to deceive, manipulate, or defraud or were liable also for acts of mere negligence. During this time, particularly during the 1960s and early 1970s, the SEC and various courts, basing their actions on clause (b) of Rule 10b-5, imposed on accountants liability for acts of negligence to a potential group of investors to whom they were not exposed under other provisions of the act. The courts appeared to hold all parties who had any special knowledge of the issuing company liable to all injured third persons in any case where they failed to disclose relevant information known to them.

The uncertainty of interpretation of Rule 10b-5 encouraged litigation that previously would not have been considered. Institutional investors, sensing their responsibility as investing fiduciaries, increased litigation, seeking to recover damages when they thought they were victims of misleading representations. Investors who suffered losses in purchases and sales of securities tended to sue all persons associated with the investee's financial statements, including the independent auditors, in hopes of recovery through an award by a jury or court, or through an out-of-court settlement with the defendants. To avoid the costs and unfavorable publicity associated with extended legal suits, accountants as defendants were frequently eager to reach out-of-court settlements.

In 1976 the U.S. Supreme Court in *Ernst & Ernst* v. *Hochfelder* ruled that action by private third parties for civil damages under Section 10(b) of the 1934 act and related Rule 10b-5 would not be permitted in absence of an allegation that the defendant had intended to deceive, manipulate, or defraud. In cases where the defendant is alleged to have committed ordinary negligence, civil liability to private third parties is no longer allowed. The Supreme Court concluded that the term "any manipulative or deceptive device or contrivance" used in Section 10(b) indicated that intentional misconduct was the meaning of the law. With the absence of *scienter,* which is characterized as an intent to deceive, mislead, or convey a false impression, no civil action can be brought under Section 10(b) of the 1934 act. A regulation cannot expand upon its related statutory provisions; consequently, Rule 10b-5 cannot be used by private plaintiffs to impose liability for negligence against professional advisers such as accountants.

Many accountants expect fewer liability suits as a result of the Supreme Court decision. However, many state statutes have similar provisions to SEC Rule 10b-5, and cases may be brought against accountants under these laws since the decision in the *Hochfelder* case does not directly affect state laws. Additionally, since scienter is a state of mind, lawsuits may continue to be instigated so that the courts may decide whether an accountant's actions are considered willful misconduct or merely negligence. Facts of the *Hochfelder* case are presented in the section on representative legal cases.

Criminal liability

Accountants may incur criminal penalties under either state or federal statutes for fraudulent acts and practices related to the sale of securities. The obtaining of money by false pretenses is a criminal offense according to laws in most states, and accountants could incur liability under these laws if they received money or property, or aided or abetted, or conspired with one receiving such. Although some states have enacted securities legislation establishing criminal responsibilities for those involved in securities frauds, an accountant is more likely to encounter the criminal provisions of federal statutes. Both the 1933 and 1934 securities acts provide for criminal penalties for making false statements or for omitting a true statement either in registration statements or in the statements filed annually. The mailing of false financial statements may subject the auditor to criminal liability under the federal mail fraud statute. Accountants also could be criminally liable under the federal false statements statute, which prohibits false statements in any matter within the jurisdiction of any federal department or agency. Conspiring to commit any offense against the United States also produces criminal liability under the federal conspiracy statute.

The Continental Vending case and the National Student Marketing case, both discussed in the following section on representative legal cases, illustrate action taken against independent accountants under the criminal liability sections of the 1934 act. Although the accountants in neither case benefited directly from the misstatements contained in the financial statements, they were fined and given prison sentences because they failed to disclose essential information known to them. These cases also illustrate clearly that compliance with generally accepted auditing standards and presentation of financial statements in accordance with generally accepted accounting principles do not constitute a complete defense in criminal cases. The accountant must be certain that the financial statements as a whole are not misleading to the average lay investor. The financial statements must provide adequate disclosure of all pertinent information to such a user.

Representative legal cases

Set forth in this section is a description of several legal cases referred to earlier in the chapter. They are arranged according to the topics under which they were previously discussed.

Liability to the client—the *1136 Tenants' Corporation* case
Civil liability under the Securities Act of 1933—the *BarChris* case
Civil liability under the Securities Exchange Act of 1934—the *Hochfelder* case
Criminal liability—the Continental Vending Machine Corp. case and the National Student Marketing case

THE 1136 TENANTS' CORPORATION CASE

Dealing primarily with accountants' responsibility for unaudited financial statements, the case of *1136 Tenants' Corporation* v. *Max Rothenberg & Co.* (319 N.Y.S. 2d 1007, 36 A.D. 2d 804, Supreme Court, Appellate Division, First Department, April 8, 1971) has caused many practitioners to consider the form of their engagement letters and their disclaimers of opinion. A valuable service is rendered to clients when the accountant does *write-up work,* which generally consists of recording and/or summarizing transactions of the client and preparing the financial statements without verifying the transactions. Without such service, many companies would have no financial statements. However, there is quite a distinction between the services an accountant renders in performing write-up work and in conducting an audit. All parties concerned with write-up work and the resulting unaudited financial statements need to have a clear understanding of this great distinction.

The 1136 Tenants' Corporation, an incorporated apartment cooperative, was managed by Riker & Co., Inc., a firm of managing agents, which collected maintenance charges, deposited them in its own account, made disbursements from the account, and maintained its own books. Monthly statements showing receipts and disbursements were prepared for the tenants' association. The accountants, a local firm, were engaged by the cooperative's managing agent, Riker, through an oral agreement in 1963 to render services (the exact nature being in dispute) that resulted in financial statements of the cooperative and in tax information for the tenant-owners.

In the letter of transmittal accompanying the financial statements, the accountants stated in part:

> Pursuant to our engagement, we have reviewed and summarized the statements of your managing agent and other data submitted to us by Riker & Co., Inc. pertaining to 1136 Tenants' Corporation. . . .

> The following statements were prepared from the books and records of the Corporation. No independent verifications were undertaken thereon. . . .

Additionally, the financial statements were marked "Subject to comments in letter of transmittal." These facts support the accountants' claim that they were engaged to perform write-up services for which they received the annual fee of $600. However, in an attached schedule of accrued expenses, the accountants used the term *audit expense.* After the accountants had submitted such statements for 1963 and the first half of 1964, it was charged that the managing agent had reported certain obligations of the cooperative to be paid, when in fact they were not.

Claiming that the accountants had been engaged "to perform all necessary accounting and auditing services for it," the cooperative sued the accountants for damages totaling $174,000 for the alleged failure to detect the defalcations under two alternate theories: (1) the breach of contract to perform an audit and (2) negligence in failing to exercise due care in performing the audit and in meeting generally accepted auditing standards. The working papers of the accountants indicated that they had inspected certain invoices paid by the managing agent. They claimed such examination was necessary to determine proper classification of certain expenditures and other very limited purposes. On the other hand, the cooperative claimed that inspection of the invoices was evidence that an audit had been undertaken. A working paper headed "Missing Invoices 1/1/63-12/31/63 . . ." indicated that the accountants had not pursued the usual audit procedures to determine the cause for their being unavailable for inspection.

The trial court in New York, sitting without a jury, found the accountants were engaged to perform an audit and were negligent in not doing so. The total judgment with interest and costs exceeded $237,000. The aspects of the court's findings which have especially disturbed the accounting profession were the statements that:

> . . . regardless of whether [the accountants] received the invoices for purposes of audit or otherwise [they] had a duty to detect defalcations and on the basis of the evidence adduced could have and should have, noted these defalcations.

> . . . the need for a certain amount of auditing procedures is required even in a "write-up."

> . . . whether the scope of the [accountants'] retainer agreement . . . was to perform a "write-up" or an "audit," certain definitive auditing procedures were necessitated and mandated under this oral retainer. . . .

This case was appealed to the Appellate Division of the Supreme Court of New York, where the trial court's conclusions were affirmed but not its views concerning accountants' duties on write-up engagements. The highest court in New York, the Court of Appeals, affirmed the Appellate Division's decision without expressing any further opinion. Consequently, the trial court's views on the duty of accountants to perform audit procedures and detect defalcations on unaudited engagements appears not to have established a precedent.

However, this case probably substantiates the growing philosophy of the courts that auditors should reveal in their reports, whether an expression of opinion or a disclaimer of opinion, all known facts which they believe to be of material benefit to those relying on the report. As professionals, auditors cannot contract away all their responsibility. Although the contract does not call for an audit examination or the detection of fraud, auditors should be responsible for disclosing circumstances that cause them to believe fraud exists.

THE BARCHRIS CASE

For the first time since the enactment of the Securities Act of 1933, the *BarChris* case caused many auditors to realize that they were actually liable to a broad class of investors for faulty financial statements if they failed to establish their due care. Of course they knew the law existed, but most of the cases involving auditors over the years had involved creditors, banks, suppliers, and other limited groups who could fairly well be foreseen as the "end and aim" of the examination and report. In this case (*Escott* v. *BarChris Construction Corporation,* 283 F. Supp. 643 [1968]), action was taken by purchasers of BarChris's 5½ percent convertible subordinated 15-year debentures, under Section 11 of the Securities Act of 1933, against the officers and directors, the underwriters, and the independent auditor, a large national firm. The financial statements of BarChris, a builder and operator of bowling alleys, had overstated the earnings and the working capital for the year 1960. These misstatements were caused by recording a loan as a sale, recording a sale-leaseback as a sale, overstatement of the percentage of completion on some contracts, inclusion of a receivable from a consolidated subsidiary in accounts receivable, understatement of both recorded and contingent liabilities, and other misstatements.

At the time of this case, the accounting profession had not established the exact accounting procedures for sale-leaseback transactions. Although the court stated that auditors should not be held to standards higher than those recognized in their profession, in this case the standards were not established, and the court took action to indicate proper standards. Such a philosophy on the part of the court may encourage the accounting profession to take the necessary action to establish its own standards and procedures and prevent outside authorities from creating standards that may not be acceptable.

As mentioned earlier in this chapter, auditors are responsible for their opinions on the financial statements as of the effective date of the registration, and they make an S-1 review near the effective date to determine that the financial statements still present fairly the financial position and results of operations at the end of the audited period. In the *BarChris* case, the auditor's program of procedures for the S-1 review was considered adequate, but the court judged the auditors had not been diligent in implementing the audit steps, had not spent sufficient time in examination of supporting evidence, and were too easily satisfied by management's explanations. The court indicated that liability under the 1933 act is not based upon negligence in terms of generally accepted auditing standards established by the profession but is based upon failure to communicate information to an ordinary investor by virtue of making untrue statements or omitting material facts.

THE HOCHFELDER CASE

The case that most auditors hope marks a change in the expanding scope of their legal liability is the *Hochfelder* case (*Ernst & Ernst* v. *Hochfelder,* 425 U.S. 185). In this case, Ernst & Ernst, a national CPA firm, was engaged as auditor for First Securities Company of Chicago, a brokerage firm, from 1946 through 1967. In 1968, the president, who owned 92 percent of the capital stock, stated in a suicide note that the company was bankrupt as a result of his fraudulent activities involving escrow accounts with some clients. From 1942 through 1966, these clients had invested in high-yielding escrow accounts by sending to the president their checks payable to him personally or by sending them to a designated bank for his account. All such payments were addressed to the president's attention. The president established a mail rule within the company that required employees to leave unopened all mail addressed to him or to the company to his attention. During his absences such mail accumulated unopened.

There were, in fact, no escrow accounts. Immediately upon receipt of the clients' funds, the president converted them to his personal use. Neither the financial records of the company nor its filings with the SEC reflected these spurious escrow accounts.

The investors in these escrow accounts filed a suit seeking damages from the auditors under section 10(b) of the 1934 Securities Act. The suit claimed that the auditors were negligent by failure to conduct their audit in accordance with generally accepted auditing standards. Although these investors did not rely on the financial statements examined by the auditors, the suit contended that had the auditors discovered the president's mail rule as an irregular procedure preventing a proper audit, there would have been an investigation of the president's activities and his fraudulent scheme would have been uncovered or prevented. The investors did not contend that the auditors participated in the fraud, only that they failed to conduct an appropriate investigation that might have exposed the scheme.

The federal district court summarily dismissed the suit holding that the auditors had complied with generally accepted auditing standards. Later, a federal appeals court held that the auditors had a common-law and a statutory duty of inquiry into the adequacy of First Securities's internal control system and that the investors were beneficiaries of that duty and the related duty to disclose material irregularities discovered during the inquiry. It ordered a trial to determine whether the auditors had, in fact, properly met these duties.

Upon further appeal, the U.S. Supreme Court dismissed the case and expressed its opinion that no action could be brought against the auditors under the 1934 Securities Act in the absence of intent on the part of the auditors to deceive, manipulate, or mislead. Relying extensively on the specific wording of the antifraud provisions of the act, the Court held that without proof that the auditors' state of mind involved knowing and willful misrepresentation there could be no cause for action under section 10(b) of the Securities Act of 1934.

THE CONTINENTAL VENDING MACHINE CORP. CASE

The fact that criminal charges as well as civil liability are a realistic threat was made clear to the accounting profession by the Continental Vending Machine Corp. case (*United States* v. *Simon,* 425 F. 2d 796 [1969]). Two partners and an audit manager of a national public accounting firm were found guilty of conspiracy, adopting a scheme to violate the federal criminal statutes prohibiting the filing of false statements with a governmental agency, and the use of the mails to perpetrate a fraud. The U.S. government did not attempt to prove that the accountants' motives included financial gain, but rather that they certified a statement which they knew to be false in an attempt to preserve their firm's reputation and to conceal their improper actions of prior years. The guilty verdict was reached by a jury after the first trial had resulted in a hung jury. The U.S. Court of Appeals upheld the conviction, and the U.S. Supreme Court refused to review the case. The public accounting firm settled for nearly $2 million in a $41 million civil suit filed by the trustee in bankruptcy for Continental.

The public accounting firm had served as Continental's auditors since 1956 and during this time was aware of the president's borrowings through an affiliated company, Valley Commercial Corp. The auditor's unqualified opinion on Continental's financial statements for the year ended September 30, 1962, contained a footnote that stated:

> 2. The amount receivable from Valley Commercial Corp. (an affiliated company of which Mr. Harold Roth is an officer, director and stockholder) bears interest at 12 per cent a year. Such amount, less the balance of the

notes payable to that company, is secured by the assignment to the Company of Valley's equity in certain marketable securities. As of February 16, 1963, the amount of such equity at current market quotations exceeded the net amount receivable.

The president of Continental managed the day-to-day operations of the Valley subsidiary from an office on the premises of Continental. From 1958 to 1962 he borrowed large sums of money to finance personal stock transactions through a system whereby Continental lent the money to Valley, who in turn lent it to him. Continental also borrowed money from Valley by issuing notes to Valley, who later discounted these notes at banks. As of the balance sheet date, Continental's borrowings from Valley amounted to about $1 million. This $1 million in payables to Valley was offset against the $3.5 million receivable from Valley to produce the net receivable referred to in the footnote. This offsetting of receivables and payables was improper because the bank, as ultimate holder of the discounted notes, differed from the debtor on the receivables. Although the footnote referred to the value of the securities on the report date, it failed to reveal that the receivable from Valley had subsequently increased to $3.9 million.

Not only did the U.S. government hold this offsetting to be improper, but it also held that the description of the marketable securities pledged as collateral was inadequate because of failure to reveal that securities of Continental composed a substantial portion of the collateral. The government contended that, if the auditors had included the pertinent facts which they knew, the footnote should have been stated as follows:

2. The amount receivable from Valley Commercial Corp. (an affiliated company of which Mr. Harold Roth is an officer, director, and stockholder), which bears interest at 12% a year, was uncollectible at September 30, 1962, since Valley had loaned approximately the same amount to Mr. Roth who was unable to pay. Since that date Mr. Roth and others have pledged as security for the repayment of his obligation to Valley and its obligation to Continental (now $3,900,000, against which Continental's liability to Valley cannot be offset) securities which as of February 15, 1963, had a market value of $2,978,000. Approximately 80% of such securities are stock and convertible debentures of the Company.

The government also contended that the market value of the pledged securities should have been reduced another $1 million because of liens of financial institutions about which the auditors should have been aware.

The auditors admitted to their error in netting the receivable and payable but contended that it was not material and that the error was unintentional. They claimed that the examination was properly performed and that the report was prepared in accordance with generally accepted accounting principles. The American Institute of Certified Public Accountants filed a brief as *amicus curiae* contending that the court was attempting to apply laymen's standards rather than looking at the balance sheet as accountants. Numerous expert witnesses testified that the footnote was prepared in accordance with generally accepted accounting principles.

In giving instructions to the jury at the second trial, the judge emphasized that the critical test was whether the financial statements as a whole fairly presented the financial condition of the company and results of its operations. Such fair presentation, he stated, must dominate over adherence to generally accepted accounting principles. Perhaps one important point for accountants to learn from this case is that the courts and the SEC will hold them to high standards of performance in communicating information to users of financial statements. Accountants should view financial statements as communication documents; and if the communication is only with other accountants or a few sophisticated investors, they have not fulfilled their purpose. Perhaps laymen's standards need to be considered in determining fair presentation by the preparers and attestors of financial statements, for certainly these are the standards employed by users of the statements. Communication can occur only if both the preparer and the users of financial statements employ the same standards.

THE NATIONAL STUDENT MARKETING CASE

Another case in which criminal liability under the federal securities laws was imposed on auditors is the National Student Marketing case (*United States* v. *Natelli* 527 F.2d 311 [1975]). In this case the partner in charge of the engagement and the audit supervisor were fined and received prison sentences for willfully and knowingly making and causing to be made false and misleading statements with respect to material facts in a proxy statement of National Student Marketing Corporation. The proxy statement was issued in connection with a special stockholders' meeting to authorize additional capital stock and to consider merger of six companies into National Student Marketing Corporation (NSMC). The proxy statement contained the audited financial statements for the year ended August 31, 1968, and the unaudited earnings statement for the nine months ended May 31, 1969.

The primary business of NSMC was that of providing for large corporate clients a diversified range of advertising and marketing services designed to reach the youth market. NSMC and the clients agreed on a fixed fee for NSMC to promote consumer products and services on college campuses primarily through posters and other literature distributed by campus representatives. In financial statements for the period ended May 31, 1968, included in a previously issued proxy statement, NSMC recognized income on these fixed-fee contracts at the time clients committed themselves to participate in the programs. The auditors determined that the percentage-of-completion method should be used to recognize income from these commitments for the annual period ended August 31, 1968. Many of the commitments that formed the basis of reporting the annual income were not in writing and were not recorded on the books during the fiscal year.

Had these oral commitments not been reflected on the financial statements, a net loss would have been reflected for the year. The auditors agreed to the recording of these "unbilled receivables" and accepted them without written confirmation. However, some commitments were verified with representatives of the corporations that had indicated intent to engage NSMC's services. By allowing "unbilled receivables" of $1.7 million to be recorded, a profit of $388,000 was reflected for the year.

Within five months of the issue of the 1968 fiscal year statements, over $1 million of the $1.7 million sales were written off as uncollectible. NSMC wrote off $350,000 of this loss against 1969 income and asked the auditors to suggest an entry to write off the balance against 1968 income. By reversing a tax item, an extraordinary tax credit was created of approximately the same amount as the 1968 sales write-off. The extraordinary tax item was netted with the unrelated bad debt adjustment thereby reflecting no reduction in the 1968 income. This netting procedure buried the retroactive adjustment which would have shown a material decrease in the 1968 income. In the proxy statement, the 1968 earnings statement was restated to reflect pooled earnings of companies acquired since the fiscal year end. The footnote reconciling the originally reported 1968 income with the adjusted pooled income did not disclose that $1 million of previously reported sales had been written off. The government in its case against the auditors asserted that making a mistake in the initial recording of unbilled receivables was not a crime, but attempting to cover up the mistake was.

During what appears to have been a frantic rush to get the proxy statements ready for printing, the partner in charge determined on August 15, 1969, that a "sale" of more than $1.2 million to the Pontiac Division of General Motors could not be included in earnings for the nine months ended May 31, 1969, because the letter from Pontiac did not form a binding commitment. This letter had been presented by NSMC two months after the end of the reporting period, but it was dated about a month before the end of the period. After learning of the rejection of the Pontiac sales, officials of NSMC were able to present on short notice a letter dated the preceding day from Eastern Airlines. This letter purported to confirm a commitment that Eastern had entered into a few days before the end of May. This commitment was for $820,000, and about $520,000 was booked as having already been earned under the percentage-of-completion method of accounting being used. The proxy statement reporting $700,000 net income for the nine-month period was printed with the Pontiac sale omitted and the Eastern commitment included. Although some discussions were held between the auditors and NSMC officials regarding write-offs, the proxy statement was filed on September 30, 1969, with the SEC. Undisclosed was the write-off of $1 million of NSMC's 1968 sales and over $2 million of the $3.3 million unbilled receivables recorded in 1968 and 1969.

In October, 1969, the auditors pointed out in a comfort letter issued in connection with NSMC's acquisition of a subsidiary that adjustments of NSMC's records would completely eliminate earnings of the first nine months as reported in the proxy statement. At the suggestion of the auditor in charge of the NSMC engagement, the auditing firm notified other businesses being acquired by NSMC of these adjustments although these businesses had not requested such a comfort letter. This action was too late apparently to overcome the action previously taken, for the courts decided against the auditors.

In its case against the auditors, the government contented that although professional standards do not require auditors to verify figures on unaudited financial statements with which they are associated, the standards do not permit auditors to disregard their knowledge of highly suspicious figures. Because the auditors did not investigate fully facts that on the surface appeared to be suspicious and did not insist on full disclosure of information known to them that would be of benefit to financial statement users, they were held to have violated their professional standards. The government, therefore, was successful in obtaining convictions of the auditors who were responsible for such conduct.

Accounting series releases

Accounting Series Releases, mentioned earlier in this chapter, are SEC notices of new and amended regulations, and of opinions of the chief accountant relating to accounting principles, independence of auditors, and the adequacy of the financial statements and the auditor's examination. The releases are also used to give notice of disciplinary sanctions imposed by the SEC, such as suspension of practice by accountants or firms before the SEC. The sanctions may be issued in settlement of cases arising under the civil liability sections of the securities acts, while cases involving the same parties may be progressing through the courts under the criminal liability sections of the acts.

Rule II(e) of the Security and Exchange Commission's Rules of Practice provides that the SEC may disqualify and deny either permanently or temporarily, the privilege of practicing before it to anyone whom the SEC finds to be lacking in character or integrity or who is guilty of improper professional conduct. Filing with the SEC any statements prepared by accountants or opinions expressed by accountants constitutes practice before the SEC. Even a short period of suspension may be not only embarrassing to the accountants, but also potentially damaging to their firm's practice. During the period of suspension, the firm's opinion may not be included in any registration statements or reports, no registration statements containing the firm's opinion may become effective, and accountants of the firm may not discuss any problems with the SEC.

The following provisions are representative of major requirements of settlements reached between an auditing firm and the SEC:

1. Agreement that the firm would submit to an investigation of its audit practices by another firm or outside committee approved by the SEC and would implement the committee's recommendations.
2. Agreement by the firm to undergo a quality control review.
3. Agreement by the firm to conduct training sessions for employees on accounting matters wherein weaknesses were discovered.
4. Agreement not to accept clients during a specified number of months (six, for example) if the clients' financial statements would be filed in documents with the SEC during a given period of time (such as one year).

Many cases in which CPA firms agree to settlements with the SEC could alternatively be settled in court. The process, however, takes months or years of trials and appeals, and during this time the firm incurs legal costs as well as possible unfavorable publicity. Even a favorable court decision, which certainly cannot be assured, costs the auditing firm heavily in time and financial resources. Consequently, auditors often choose to settle legal cases out of court in order to avoid the protracted court process.

Engagement letters

Particularly as they relate to unaudited engagements, engagement letters have increased in importance and have become more extensively used since the *1136 Tenants' Corporation* case. It is quite important that accountants and their clients have a clear understanding of the scope of the services to be rendered by the accountant and the uses for which the financial statements and the accountant's report will be employed. The existence of a written agreement specifying the terms of engagement will not necessarily eliminate litigation because there can be differences in interpretation of the written word. But there certainly should be fewer disputes than with the use of an oral agreement, where terms may not be recalled even if they are initially agreed upon.

Normally, an auditor and a client's representative will meet to discuss a forthcoming audit in terms of such matters as the period covered, the reliance of the auditor on the internal control system, the necessity of examining records and supporting evidence, the assistance expected by client personnel, the type of opinion to be expressed, the desired date of the report, tax returns and other specialized reports expected, fees to be charged, and, most likely, numerous other matters. The engagement letter follows up this verbal understanding and provides a written record of what is expected of the auditor. Auditors are responsible to whoever engages them; so, for a corporate client, the letter usually is addressed to the audit committee, the chairman of the board, the chief executive officer, or whoever represents the engaging authority. The letter must be tailored to meet the specific understanding with each client.

The scope of the services to be performed must be established in the engagement letter. If an opinion is to be expressed on the financial statements, the letter should state that the examination will be in accordance with *generally accepted auditing standards.* An explanation of this term should clarify that an essential feature is an examination of the client's internal accounting control system as it is designed and as it functions and that, based upon the evaluation of the internal accounting control system, tests will be made of other records and supporting evidence. Emphasis should be placed upon the fact that an audit consists of tests and not a detailed examination of all transactions, assets, and liabilities. Some accountants also present a brief listing of the auditing procedures contemplated. If a client has imposed any limitations on the scope of the examination, these should be described in the letter, along with a clear statement of the effect the restrictions will have on the opinion expressed. Clarification should be made in the letter of whether the auditor or client will be responsible for the preparation of income tax returns and any other specialized reports. Client personnel are frequently used to prepare certain schedules and analyses for the auditor, and the letter should describe this work and probably state the date on which the client has agreed such information will be available.

The letter should explicitly state that on an opinion audit the auditor is expressing a professional opinion about the fairness of the financial statements taken as a whole and is not guaranteeing the correctness of any specific figure appearing on the statements. The client's responsibility for the financial statements should be emphasized. Also, the letter should set forth a definite statement that the purpose of the examination is not to detect defalcations, and so the examination should not be relied upon for such purpose. Of course, the auditor is always alert for any irregularities and will bring them to the client's attention. Judging from statements of the court in the *1136 Tenants' Corporation* case, an engagement letter for write-up work should also specifically point out that the write-up work may not detect defalcations and that no one should expect such to be discovered from the work. The letter may state that the auditor will bring to the client's attention situations in the accounting system that should be altered to strengthen it.

Most accountants include in the engagement letter a paragraph in which fees are discussed. The per diem rates may be given for the various classes of auditors, and a statement may be included that the total fee is composed of travel expenses, other out-of-pocket costs, and the per diem charge, which depends upon the condition of the accounting system and records. A fee estimate or maximum fee may be stated for the engagement, emphasizing that any unexpected problems encountered during the examination will cause additional services and consequently additional fees. The method of billing—whether progress, monthly, or upon completion—may also be discussed.

At times independent accountants may be engaged by their clients merely to compile financial statements from the accounting records or to perform a review of the statements. In rendering either service, compilation or review, the accountants are not performing an audit and the financial statements are considered to be unaudited. The engagement letter should state specifically the nature of the engagement and should point out clearly that the accountants will not express an opinion as to the fairness of the financial statements in accordance with generally accepted accounting principles. When the accountants are engaged to perform a compilation service in connection with financial statements, the engagement letter should indicate that the service is limited to presenting the information provided by the client in financial statement format without any assurance as to whether material modifications should be made for the statements to be in conformity with generally accepted accounting principles. When a review service is to be provided, the accountants perform inquiry and analytical procedures. They give limited assurance that no material modifications are necessary for the financial statements to be in conformity with generally accepted accounting principles. The nature of the review should be described in the engagement letter, and there should be clarification of the limited assurance to be expressed by the accountants.

The clarification of terms for a new engagement is of utmost importance. The engagement letter is an essential element of the auditor's efforts to bring about a clear understanding between the auditor and the client. In repeat engagements, the auditor may choose to send a detailed engagement letter to the client each year. The auditor, however, may decide to send a renewal letter which indicates that the terms of the original engagement letter remain in effect or describes modifications to be made in the repeat engagements. To assure a meeting of minds on the terms of the engagement, officials of the client organization are asked to indicate agreement with the arrangements by signing and returning a copy of the engagement letter.

An example of an engagement letter appropriate for an audit in accordance with generally accepted auditing standards appears in Figure 4-2. An illustrative engagement letter for a compilation service is shown in Figure 4-3, and Figure 4-4 illustrates an engagement letter to be used in a review service.

Figure 4-2 Illustrative Engagement Letter: Audit in Accordance with Generally Accepted Auditing Standards

Ryman, Jackson & Co.
Certified Public Accountants
Denver, Colorado 80205

May 18, 1981

Audit Committee
Ace Corporation
Denver, Colorado 80209

Gentlemen:

This letter is to confirm our understanding of the arrangements to conduct an examination of the financial statements of Ace Corporation for the year ended December 31, 1981 for the purpose of expressing our professional opinion as to the fairness of the statements according to generally accepted accounting principles.

Our opinion will be based upon our examination of your books and records supporting the financial statements, our inspection of certain assets, our review of your accounting system, correspondence with various people and companies with whom you conduct business, and observation of your employees and officials. We will not review your activities in complete detail but will make tests. The extent of our tests will depend to a large extent upon our evaluation of your internal control system. Our examination will be in accordance with generally accepted auditing standards.

The primary responsibility for maintaining adequate accounting records and an effective system of internal control and for preparation of proper financial statements rests with officials of the company. The purpose of our examination is to enable us to express our opinion on the fair presentation of the statements and not for the detection of defalcations. Of course, we shall be alert for any indications of such irregularities and shall call them to your attention.

We shall perform interim work in your office during October, 1981, and shall return to perform the year-end work on approximately January 18, 1982. Also we shall have representatives present to observe your taking of physical inventory at the end of December, 1981. As agreed in our discussions, your personnel will have prepared the federal and state income tax returns, and will provide us with a detailed trial balance, an aging of accounts receivable, a listing of all additions to property, plant, and equipment, and a schedule of all payables at the time our representatives arrive in January, 1982. Also it was agreed that your personnel will assist us in locating and submitting to us vouchers, invoices, leases, contracts, minutes, and other corporate documents.

Our fee for this examination will be based upon our standard hourly rates for the various professional personnel engaged on the job plus travel and other direct costs. As we discussed earlier, we estimate that our fee will be between $18,000 and $23,000. Should we find conditions that indicate more audit time is necessary and therefore a higher fee, we shall advise you promptly. Invoices will be submitted periodically as the work progresses and are due upon presentation.

Although the timing of the issuance of our report is largely dependent upon our findings during the examination and an exact date cannot be set because of the many contingencies, we shall strive to have the report to you by April 1, 1982.

We are pleased to have been selected as auditors for Ace Corporation, and we look forward to a continuing pleasant relationship.

Please sign and return the enclosed copy of this letter to indicate your acceptance of the arrangements discussed.

Sincerely yours,

Ryman, Jackson & Co.

The terms of this letter
constitute our agreement.

____
Chairman, Audit Committee
Board of Directors
Ace Corporation

____
Date

Figure 4-3 Illustrative Engagement Letter: Compilation of Financial Statements (*AICPA adapted*)

Oliver and Thorn
Certified Public Accountants
1847 Jefferson Avenue
Memphis, Tennessee 38103

October 20, 1980

Mr. Francis B. Wooten, President
Briarmoor Company
185 Church Street
Memphis, Tennessee 38143

Dear Mr. Wooten:

This letter is to confirm our understanding of the terms of our engagement and the nature and extent of the services we will provide.

We will perform the following services:

1. We will compile, from information you provide, the annual and interim balance sheets and related statements of income, retained earnings, and changes in financial position of Briarmoor Company for the year 1981. We will not audit or review such financial statements. Our report on the annual financial statements of Briarmoor Company is presently expected to read as follows:

   We have performed a compilation service in connection with the accompanying balance sheet of Briarmoor Company as of December 31, 1981, and the related statements of income, retained earnings, and changes in financial position for the year then ended. All information included in these financial statements is the representation of the management of Briarmoor Company.

   Users of these financial statements should be aware that a compilation service is limited to the presentation in the form of financial statements of information supplied by management and that we have not achieved any assurance as to whether there are material modifications that should be made to the statements in order for them to be in conformity with generally accepted accounting principles.

   Our report on your interim financial statements, which statements will omit substantially all disclosures, will include an additional paragraph that will read as follows:

   Users of these financial statements should also be aware that management has elected to omit substantially all of the disclosures required by generally accepted accounting principles. If the omitted disclosures were included in the financial statements, they might influence the user's conclusions about the Company's financial position, results of operations, and changes in financial position.

If, for any reason, we are unable to complete the compilation of your financial statements, we will not issue a report on such statements as a result of this engagement.

2. We will also prepare the federal and state income tax returns of Briarmoor Company for the year 1981, and we will advise you on such income tax matters as you may bring to us for advice.

Our engagement should not be relied upon to disclose errors, irregularities, or illegal acts, including fraud or defalcations, that may exist. However, we will inform you of any matters that come to our attention which cause us to believe that such a condition may exist.

Our fees for these services will be computed at our standard rates and will be billed at the completion of our work. Bills for services are due when rendered.

We shall be pleased to discuss this letter with you at any time.

If the foregoing is in accordance with your understanding, please sign the copy of this letter in the space provided and return it to us.

Sincerely yours,

____
Oliver and Thorn
Certified Public Accountants

Acknowledged:
Briarmoor Company

____
President

____
Date

Figure 4-4 Illustrative Engagement Letter: Review of Financial Statements (*AICPA adapted*)

Doorn and Rosselli
Certified Public Accountants
481 Broad Street
Albuquerque, New Mexico 87103

May 18, 1980

Board of Directors
Sands Corporation
Western Plaza
Santa Fe, New Mexico 87505

Gentlemen:

This letter is to confirm our understanding of the terms of our engagement and the nature and extent of the services we will provide.

We will perform the following services:

1. We will perform a review of the balance sheet of Sands Corporation as of December 31, 1981, and the related statements of income, retained earnings, and changes in financial position for the year then ended, in accordance with standards promulgated by the American Institute of Certified Public Accountants. We will not audit such financial statements and, accordingly, we will not express an opinion on them. Our report on the financial statements is presently expected to read as follows:

   We have performed a review of the accompanying balance sheet of Sands Corporation as of December 31, 1981, and the related statements of income, retained earnings, and changes in financial position for the year then ended, in accordance with standards promulgated by the American Institute of Certified Public Accountants. All information included in these financial statements is the representation of the management of Sands Corporation.

   A review consists of inquiries of company personnel and analytical procedures applied to financial data. It is substantially less in scope than an examination in accordance with generally accepted auditing standards, the objective of which is the expression of an opinion regarding the financial statements taken as a whole. Accordingly, we do not express such an opinion.

   Based on our review, we are not aware of any material modifications that should be made to the accompanying financial statements in order for them to be in conformity with generally accepted accounting principles.

If, for any reason, we are unable to complete our review of your financial statements, we will not issue a report on such statements as a result of this engagement.

2. We will discuss with officers and directors of the company such suggestions and recommendations concerning the accounting methods and financial affairs of the company as may come to our attention in the course of our work.

3. We will prepare the federal and state income tax returns of Sands Corporation for the year 1981, and we will advise you on such tax matters as you may bring to us for advice.

Our engagement should not be relied upon to disclose errors, irregularities, or illegal acts, including fraud or defalcations, that may exist. However, we will inform you of any matters that come to our attention which cause us to believe that such a condition may exist.

Our fees for these services will be computed at our standard rates and will be billed monthly as work progresses. Bills for services are due when rendered.

Our fees for these services . . . .

We shall be pleased to discuss this letter with you at any time.

If the foregoing is in accordance with your understanding, please sign the copy of this letter in the space provided and return it to us.

Sincerely yours,

Doorn and Rosselli

Acknowledged:
Sands Corporation

____
Chairman, Board of Directors

____
Date

Avoidance of legal liability

Clearly the aim of all professional accountants is to avoid, if reasonably possible, legal liability; consequently, they should conduct themselves and perform their duties in a manner above reproach. Never should they approach their work with the attitude of doing the minimum allowable under the Code of Professional Ethics, SEC regulations, generally accepted auditing standards, or the law. Accountants should adopt the attitude that the public and their clients deserve the fairest presentation possible. The accounting profession must regulate itself to make sure that financial statements and reports serve both clients and the public, the consumers of its product. There is evidence that courts, espousing the attitude of protecting consumers, will force accountants to render the professional service desired by the consuming public unless the profession adopts such posture on its own. Legal liability probably can be minimized by adherence to the procedures discussed in the following paragraphs.

PROFESSIONAL ATTITUDE

Auditors should ask themselves if the financial statements present to users the information needed for decision making. They should not think that the statements have to be merely in accordance with generally accepted accounting principles but rather that they must also be a fair and meaningful presentation. If the statements are not a fair presentation to users who have no other knowledge of a company's activities, the auditor should consider requiring additional disclosure by the client. Additionally, if an auditor does not have sufficient knowledge to form an opinion on the overall fairness of the statements, the auditor has not gathered enough evidence to justify the audit report and must not express an unqualified opinion under the circumstances.

PROFESSIONAL GUIDELINES

Clarification and strengthening of auditing procedures, rules of professional conduct, and elimination of some alternative accounting principles represent some areas in which the profession can make changes to help avoid past mistakes and to serve the public better in the future. Pronouncements of professional groups on auditing standards and procedures should be strengthened in advance of legal action rather than subsequent to legal cases, as has often been the situation in the past.

The first Statement on Auditing Procedure by the AICPA, now Section 331 of *Statements on Auditing Standards,* was expressed in October 1939 after the famous McKesson & Robbins case had made headlines in December 1938. Included in the $87 million of assets on the 1937 financial statements were $10 million of fictitious inventory and $9 million of nonexisting accounts receivable resulting from an elaborate scheme by the president and his three brothers, each operating under assumed names. The president had learned that the company's auditors did not observe physical inventory or confirm accounts receivable, although these were practiced by some auditors in certain situations. Omission of these procedures permitted the fraudulent scheme to go undetected by the auditors. The corrective action taken by the AICPA after this case was to require the observation of physical inventory and the confirmation of accounts receivable where reasonable and practicable.

Subsequent to many legal cases cited in this chapter, a change was made to help rectify the situation that produced the original suit. A pronouncement, now SAS No. 1 (AU 710.08–710.10), dealing with the procedures for handling subsequent events in filings under the Securities Act of 1933, was issued by the AICPA Committee on Auditing Procedure after the *BarChris* case had raised issues in this area. In the Continental Vending case defalcations were taking place through a subsidiary, which was not audited by the auditors of the parent corporation. Subsequently, the AICPA Code of Professional Ethics was expanded to permit auditors to insist upon auditing any subsidiary or branch that they believed necessary to warrant the expression of an opinion. While the *1136 Tenants' Corporation* case was in the courts, the Committee on Auditing Procedure issued a pronouncement, now SAS No. 1 (AU 516), pertaining to unaudited financial statements; this clarified the conditions to be considered unaudited and specifically set forth the form in which an accountant should express a disclaimer. Many other sections of the *Statements on Auditing Standards* can be directly associated with court cases and SEC rulings of years past.

QUALIFIED PERSONNEL

The hiring and training of competent professional people is an essential ingredient of avoiding legal liability. Regardless of how well trained auditors are, a careful review of their work is desirable to determine that they are performing their duties carefully and as trained. With changes in accounting being almost constant, continuing professional education is a requisite for accountants to function in a professional manner.

SELECTION OF CLIENTS

A careful investigation of prospective clients is recommended. The relationship that develops between an auditor and a client is close, and in the eyes of many observers the auditor is seen to be sanctioning the activities of the client company. The association of the auditor's name with the financial statements of the company subjects the auditor to legal actions in many situations when the client is sued. If a prospective client company or its officials have a questionable history, an auditor probably should refuse the engagement.

In many cases where auditors have been sued, the client company was bankrupt or at least in financial difficulties. Creditors and investors are naturally concerned over their potential losses, and auditors and their firms may appear to be among those associated with the clients who are solvent and, therefore, are likely sources of recovery. All audits should be conducted with care, but those of companies in weak financial condition should be conducted with the greatest care possible.

ENGAGEMENT LETTER

A thorough understanding between auditor and client regarding the nature of the examination, the responsibilities of the client for the financial statements, and the meaning of the auditor's report is essential for all engagements. As discussed earlier in this chapter, this understanding should be evidenced by an engagement letter signed by both parties.

LIABILITY INSURANCE

Adequate liability insurance should be carried by all practicing public accountants or their firms. Never should the insurance protection for malpractice be viewed as justification for failing to perform in the highest professional manner possible; rather, good business practice dictates having adequate insurance in case all other defenses fail.

PROFESSIONAL CONDUCT OF EXAMINATION

The ultimate criterion for avoidance of legal liability is performance of the audit examination in a professional manner. The evidence that the auditor gathers should be in a form which will be meaningful to reviewers several years in the future, should the work be questioned. An excellent audit examination is extremely difficult, if not impossible, to defend if it is not supported by well-prepared and well-documented working papers. Execution of generally accepted auditing standards—accomplished by proper planning of the audit, supervision of audit personnel, thorough examination and evaluation of evidence, preparation of working papers, and a carefully written report—is essential for avoidance of legal liability.

Responsibilities in tax practice

Public accountants frequently serve clients by preparing annual income tax returns, rendering tax advice, and representing them before tax authorities. In general, accountants are legally liable for breach of contract or negligence in the performance of duties. Because there is not the same third-party reliance on tax returns, liability is more limited than in audit engagements.

The AICPA has issued a series of *Statements on Responsibilities in Tax Practice* that attempts to develop standards of responsibilities in tax practice and to foster an increased understanding of accountants' responsibilities by others. Additionally, these statements should reduce the possibility of accountants' being charged with misconduct when someone misunderstands the extent of their responsibilities. Accountants are also guided in their tax practice by the AICPA Code of Professional Ethics, by Treasury Department Circular No. 230, and by the Treasury Department's regulations on the liability of income tax preparers.

The preparer's declaration, which must be signed by the taxpayer as well as by the accountant when the latter prepares or advises a client in preparing the return, states:

> Under the penalties of perjury, I declare that I have examined this return, including accompanying schedules and statements, and to the best of my knowledge and belief it is true, correct, and complete. Declaration of preparer (other than taxpayer) is based on all information of which he has any knowledge.

Signing such a statement is not equivalent to the accountant's expressing an opinion on financial statements after conducting an audit examination. The accountant merely says that the return is complete and correct based upon known information, which may be incomplete. The accountant has no duty to conduct an examination to determine the correctness of data; however, if any of the material furnished by the client appears to be incorrect or incomplete, the accountant has a responsibility to ask questions. The client should be encouraged to provide appropriate supporting data and to allow the accountant to make reference to books and records of the client's business. If the Internal Revenue Code requires documentation for a particular deduction, the accountant should inquire if the requisite documentation exists. Additionally, by examining supporting evidence, the accountant can gather a more complete understanding of the transactions and determine the appropriate tax treatment, which may not have been evident from the limited information furnished by the client. If there are doubts about the accuracy of the information, the accountant should refuse to be associated with the return. Before accepting an engagement to prepare tax returns for a new client, the accountant should consider making inquiries as to the prospective client's reputation and possibly corresponding with the accountant who previously rendered tax services.

In some audit engagements, the accountant will have made a determination of the client's taxable income, will have reviewed the computations, or even will have reviewed the return prepared by the client in order to ascertain the reasonableness of the tax liability reflected on the financial statements. Unless substantial changes are made in the return as a result of such a review, the accountant has no responsibility for the return and is not required to sign the preparer's declaration. However, if the accountant acquires knowledge in making the review that is substantially equivalent to what would have been acquired in preparing the return, the accountant may sign the preparer's declaration and may co-sign the declaration if it was previously signed by the original preparer. Upon review of the tax return, the accountant may recommend that substantial changes be made in the return. If the changes are made in such a situation, the accountant is responsible and must sign the declaration.

Frequently, accountants are engaged to prepare a client's tax return from information that they compile from the client's books without performing an audit and from information supplied by the client. Although they may disclaim an opinion of the financial statements because they have not conducted an examination in accordance with generally accepted auditing standards, they must sign the preparer's declaration to reflect their responsibility.

Should an accountant learn of an error in a client's previously filed tax returns or learn of a failure to file a return in a previous year, the accountant should inform the client of the error and of the appropriate corrective action. The accountant should, preferably in writing, advise the client to file an amended return, file a claim for refund, or file an original return, whichever is necessary to correct the error. If there is a possibility of fraud, the client should be urged to consult an attorney before taking any action. The client has the complete responsibility to decide on the action to take, if any. The accountant is not obligated to inform the taxing authorities, and in fact would be wrong to do so without the client's permission. If the client does not correct the error, the accountant should seriously question whether to continue a professional relationship with the client.

An accountant may be engaged to represent a client in an administrative proceeding with the Internal Revenue Service or state tax authority. Should the return contain an error that would have caused the accountant to refuse to sign the preparer's declaration, the accountant should seek the client's permission to disclose the error to the tax authorities. If the client does not grant such permission, the accountant may determine that the best action is to withdraw from the engagement. The client should be aware that the accountant's confidential relation is not recognized under federal law and that the accountant will have to reveal matters known to him if questions are raised in court about the specific error.

A distinction should be made between obvious errors and debatable issues. Accountants have not only the right but also the responsibility to advocate for their clients the most favorable position on any issue for which there is reasonable support. They have no duty to reveal weaknesses that may be inherent in such a position.

Responsibilities in management advisory services

Legal liability may arise for accountants in rendering management advisory services just as in the areas of auditing or tax practice. The AICPA Management Advisory Services Executive Committee has issued a series of *Statements on Management Advisory Services* to guide accountants in this area. Contained in these statements is a set of management advisory service practice standards, which are quoted below.

1. *Personal Characteristics.* In performing management advisory services, a practitioner must act with integrity and objectivity and be independent in mental attitude.

2. *Competence.* Engagements are to be performed by practitioners having competence in the analytical approach and process, and in the technical subject matter under consideration.
3. *Due Care.* Due professional care is to be exercised in the performance of a management advisory services engagement.
4. *Client Benefit.* Before accepting an engagement, a practitioner is to notify the client of any reservations he has regarding anticipated benefits.
5. *Understanding with Client.* Before undertaking an engagement, a practitioner is to inform his client of all significant matters related to the engagement.
6. *Planning, Supervision, and Control.* Engagements are to be adequately planned, supervised, and controlled.
7. *Sufficient Relevant Data.* Sufficient relevant data is to be obtained, documented, and evaluated in developing conclusions and recommendations.
8. *Communication of Results.* All significant matters relating to the results of the engagement are to be communicated to the client.[2]

These standards apply to formal engagements in which the accountant is engaged to provide a consulting service to improve the client's use of its capabilities and resources. The accountant may apply an analytical approach, seeking out the facts, identifying the objectives, defining the problem, determining and evaluating alternative solutions, and presenting the findings and recommendations to the client. If the client selects an alternative and wants to proceed, the accountant may be involved in the planning, scheduling, and implementation of the program selected. These standards do not apply to informal advice rendered to clients in answering questions that arise in conjunction with rendering other professional services. The Statements on Management Advisory Services contain expanded comments and interpretations of these standards.

Supplementary readings

Burton, John C., ed. *Corporate Financial Reporting: Ethical and Other Problems.* New York: American Institute of Certified Public Accountants, 1972.

Causey, Denzil Y., Jr. *Duties and Liabilities of the CPA, Revised Edition.* Austin: Bureau of Business Research, The University of Texas, 1976.

———. "Newly Emerging Standards of Auditor Responsibility." *Accounting Review* (January 1976), 19–30.

[2] From *Statements on Management Advisory Services,* copyright © 1975 by the American Institute of Certified Public Accountants, Inc.

"The Continental Vending Case." *Journal of Accountancy* (November 1968), 54-62.

"Continental Vending Decision Affirmed." *Journal of Accountancy* (February 1970), 61-69.

Giacoletti, Robert R. "The Auditor's Liability for Fraud." *Management Accounting* (July 1977), 29-32.

Hampson, J. Jay. "Accountants' Liability—The Significance of Hochfelder." *Journal of Accountancy* (December 1976), 69-74.

Isbell, David B. "The Continental Vending Case: Lessons for the Profession." *Journal of Accountancy* (August 1970), 33-40.

Isbell, David B., and D. R. Carmichael. "Disclaimers and Liability—The Rhode Island Trust Case." *Journal of Accountancy* (April 1973), 37-42.

Kurland, Seymour. "Accountant's Legal Liability: Ultramares to BarChris." *Business Lawyer* (November 1969), 155-175.

Levy, Saul. *Accountants Legal Liability*. New York: American Institute of Accountants, 1954.

"McKesson & Robbins, Inc.: Summary of Findings and Conclusions of the SEC." *Journal of Accountancy* (January 1941), 90-95.

Reiling, Henry B., and Russell A. Taussig. "Recent Liability Cases—Implications for Accountants." *Journal of Accountancy* (September 1970), 39-53.

Robinson, Halden G. "10 Rules for Conducting a 'Defensive' Audit." *Practical Accountant* (July-August 1977), 62-68.

Schlesinger, Michael. "Hochfelder Decision: How It Will Affect Future Malpractice Suits Against Accountants." *Practical Accountant* (September-October 1976), 77-81.

Schnepper, Jeff A. "The Accountant's Liability under Rule 10b-5 and Section 10(b) of the Securities Exchange Act of 1934: The Hole in Hochfelder." *Accounting Review* (July 1977), 653-657.

Skousen, K. Fred. *An Introduction to the SEC*. Cincinnati: South-Western Publishing Co., 1976.

Slavin, Nathan S. "Elimination of Scienter in Determining the Auditor's Statutory Liability." *Accounting Review* (April 1977), 360-368.

Solomon, Kenneth I., Charles Chazen, and Barry L. Augenbraun. "Who Judges the Auditor, and How?" *Journal of Accountancy* (August 1976), 67-74.

"1136 Tenants' Corporation—Decision of the Appellate Division of the Supreme Court of the State of New York." *Journal of Accountancy* (November 1971), 67-73.

Review questions

4-1. Why are the ethical responsibilities of public accountants better defined than the legal responsibilities?

4-2. What degree of skill is a professional person expected to display when proclaiming to the public to be an independent auditor?

4-3. Under what circumstances are auditors subject to liability for negligence?

4-4. When an audit examination on financial statements has as its end and aim a specified person or a limited group, what has historically been the liability of the auditor for negligence? What is currently considered to be the liability?

4-5. What is meant by *contributory negligence*? Under what circumstances may the auditor use contributory negligence as a valid defense?

4-6. Distinguish between fraud and gross negligence.

4-7. To whom is an auditor liable for fraud or gross negligence?

4-8. What is the meaning of the term *to socialize the risk of error*? How is an auditor affected by the courts' tendency to socialize the cost of damages caused by negligence?

4-9. In what manner does the *Hochfelder* case seem to limit the liability of auditors?

4-10. What conditions led to the passage of the Securities Act of 1933 and the Securities Exchange Act of 1934?

4-11. Describe some of the major duties and responsibilities of the chief accountant of the Securities and Exchange Commission.

4-12. What is *Regulation S-X*?

4-13. What are *Accounting Series Releases*?

4-14. Describe the primary documents that must be filed with the SEC under the Securities Act of 1933.

4-15. What are comfort letters?

4-16. Why does an auditor perform an S-1 review?

4-17. Under what conditions may an accountant be sued by a purchaser of newly issued securities when the accountant has certified to the financial statements included in the registration statements?

4-18. What is due diligence?

4-19. Compare the type of security transactions covered by the Securities Act of 1933 with those transactions covered by the Securities Exchange Act of 1934.

4-20. Compare the liability of independent accountants under provisions of the Securities Act of 1933 with their liability under the Securities Exchange Act of 1934.

4-21. What are the implications for the accounting profession of the courts' establishing accounting procedures?

4-22. What appear to be the major points the accounting profession should learn from the Continental Vending Machine Corp. case?

4-23. What should the accountant in the *1136 Tenants' Corporation* case have included in the engagement letter that might have prevented the legal suit?

4-24. What information should a successor auditor obtain from the predecessor auditor? What is the reason for obtaining such information?

4-25. Why are some auditors willing to settle legal cases outside of court?

4-26. Discuss the major points to be covered in an engagement letter written to a new audit client by an independent auditor.

4-27. What matters should be included in an engagement letter for a compilation service that are not necessary in a letter for an opinion audit?

4-28. What matters should be included in an engagement letter for a limited review service that are not necessary in a letter for an opinion audit?

4-29. Describe some of the major steps an auditor should take in an effort to avoid legal liability.

4-30. "When a CPA signs the preparer's declaration on a client's income tax return, the CPA is in effect expressing an unqualified opinion on the attached financial statements as if a complete audit examination had been performed." Comment on this statement.

4-31. What benefits may ensue to a taxpayer by providing an accountant with supporting data when the accountant is reviewing or preparing the taxpayer's income tax return?

4-32. "When an accountant learns of a client's failure to file a previous year's tax return or of an error in the return, the accountant has no responsibility to inform the taxing authorities." Comment on this statement.

4-33. Explain why an accountant is not expected to be mentally independent when dealing with a client's income tax return and liability.

4-34. Describe the major concepts presented in the standards for a management advisory services practice.

Decision problems

4-35. Dora Conrad has recently been engaged to audit the financial statements of Springtime Preserves, Inc., a publicly held company. She has discussed the nature of the engagement with representatives of Springtime, has consulted with the previous auditor, and is ready to write the engagement letter.

a. List the items that should be included in the engagement letter under these conditons.

b. Describe the benefits to be gained from an engagement letter.

AICPA adapted

4-36. The CPA firm of Fairchild and Sojourner was engaged to perform an audit of Meridan Inc., which had been organized within the year. The auditors were aware that the financial statements accompanying their report would be the basis of a substantial loan from the Natchez National Bank. The financial statements, which were released six weeks after year end, reflected tremendous sales growth during the last two months of the year. The auditors had confirmed the accounts receivable as of year end, selecting the accounts on a random sampling basis.

The Natchez National Bank refused to grant the desired loan, but the Kingston State Bank did negotiate the loan. When the second installment became past due, Kingston State Bank investigated and discovered many of the sales near year end had been fictitious and that the confirmations had been returned to the auditors by company employees who had set up the fictitious companies using their own home addresses.

Kingston State Bank sued Fairchild and Sojourner for negligence in conduct of their audit and claimed damages equal to the amount of the defaulted loan.

a. Can the firm of Fairchild and Sojourner be held liable for ordinary negligence under the circumstances described?

b. What defense would you suggest the auditing firm present in this case?

c. What action do you think the CPAs could have taken to prevent such a suit from arising?

4-37. Brad Hoy was a junior staff member of an accounting firm. He began the audit of the Cosmos Corporation which manufactured and sold expensive watches. In the middle of the audit he quit. The accounting firm hired another person to continue the audit of Cosmos. Due to the changeover and the time pressure to finish the audit, the firm violated certain generally accepted auditing standards when they did not follow adequate procedures with respect to the physical inventory. Had the proper procedures been used during the examination they would have discovered that watches worth more than $20,000 were missing. The employee who was stealing the watches was able to steal an additional $30,000 worth before the thefts were discovered six months after the completion of the audit.

Discuss the legal problems of the accounting firm as a result of the above facts.

AICPA adapted

4-38. Barton and Co. has been engaged to examine the financial statements for Mirror Manufacturing Corporation for the year ended September 30, 1982. Mirror Manufacturing needed additional cash to continue its operations. To raise funds, it agreed to sell its common stock investment in a subsidiary. The buyers insisted upon having the proceeds placed in escrow because of the possibility of a major contingent tax liability. Carter, president of Mirror, explained this to Barton, the partner in charge of the Mirror audit. He indicated that he wished to show the proceeds from the sale of the subsidiary as an unrestricted current account receivable. He stated that in his opinion the government's claim was groundless and that he needed an "uncluttered" balance sheet and a "clean" auditor's opinion to obtain additional working capital. Barton acquiesced in this request. The government's claim proved to be valid and, pursuant to the agreement with the buyers, the purchase price of the subsidiary was reduced by $450,000. This, coupled with other adverse developments, caused Mirror to become insolvent with assets to cover only some of its liabilities. Barton and Co. is being sued by several of Mirror's creditors who loaned money in reliance upon the financial statements upon which it rendered an unqualified opinion.

What is the liability, if any, of Barton and Co. to the creditors of Mirror Manufacturing? Explain.

AICPA adapted

4-39. The CPA firm of Freeman & Arus was engaged by the Fast Cargo Company, a retailer, to examine its financial statements for the year ended August 31, 1982. It followed generally accepted auditing standards and examined transactions on a test basis. A sample of 100 disbursements was used to test vouchers payable, cash disbursements, and receiving and purchasing procedures. An investigation of the sample disclosed several instances where purchases had been recorded and paid for without the required receiving report being included in the file of supporting documents. This was properly noted in the working papers by Martin, the junior who did the sampling. Arus, the partner in charge, called these facts to the attention of Harris, Fast Cargo's chief accountant, who told him not to worry about it, that he would make certain that these receiving reports were properly included in the voucher file. Arus accepted this and did nothing further to investigate or follow up on this situation.

Harris was engaged in a fraudulent scheme whereby he diverted the merchandise to a private warehouse where he leased space and sent the invoices to Fast Cargo for payment. The scheme was discovered later by a special investigation and a preliminary estimate indicates that the loss to Fast Cargo will be in excess of $35,000.

a. What is the liability, if any, of Freeman & Arus in this situation? Discuss.

b. What addititional steps, if any, should have been taken by Arus? Explain.

AICPA adapted

4-40. Williams, Steinmitz, and Hall, CPAs, have been the auditors for the Pension Fund of the United Brotherhood of Construction Workers for the past three years. In the second year of their examination they wrote a letter to the treasurer pointing out that on a limited number of investments that year they found no evidence of proper authorization. The following year, the firm qualified their opinion because the authorization was missing on a substantial number of investments. Walter Williams, senior partner of the firm, discussed the qualified opinion with the treasurer before copies of the report were deliverd to him.

During the audit examination of the third year, the auditors discovered that a number of the new investments were made in newly established ventures organized by friends of the treasurer. The auditors completed their examination and expressed an adverse opinion on the financial statements because they did not believe "cost" of the investments was the proper valuation of the securities of these newly formed companies. All copies of the report were again delivered to the treasurer.

Several months later, the Board of Trustees of the Pension Fund of the United Brotherhood of Construction Workers sued the CPA firm for failure to communicate their findings to the proper authorities. The firm contended that all their dealings had been with the treasurer and that he was the one to whom they were responsible. They claimed they were being sued for losses actually caused by the trustees' failure to exercise proper control over the treasurer.

Comment on the issues involved in this case. What action would you have taken that might have prevented the legal suit had you been the auditor?

4-41. A CPA firm has been named as a defendant in a class action by purchasers of the shares of stock of the Newly Corporation. The offering was a public offering of securities within the meaning of the Securities Act of 1933. The plaintiffs alleged that the firm was either negligent or fraudulent in connection with the preparation of the audited financial statements which accompanied the registration statement filed with the SEC. Specifically, they allege that the CPA firm either intentionally disregarded, or failed to exercise reasonable care to discover, material facts which occurred subsequent to January 31, 1981, the date of the auditor's report. The securities were sold to the public on March 16, 1981. The plaintiffs have subpoenaed copies of the CPA firm's working papers. The CPA firm is considering refusing to relinquish the papers, asserting that they contain privileged communication between the CPA firm and its client. The CPA firm will, of course, defend on the merits irrespective of the questions regarding the working papers.

Answer the following, setting forth reasons for any conclusions stated.

a. Can the CPA firm rightfully refuse to surrender its working papers?

b. Discuss the liability of the CPA firm in respect to events which occur in the period between the date of the auditor's report and the effective date of the public offering of the securities.

AICPA adapted

4-42. In conducting the examination of the financial statements of the Farber Corporation for the year ended September 30, 1982, Jeanne Harper, a CPA, discovered that Mr. Nance, the president, who was also one of the principal stockholders, had borrowed substantial amounts of money from the corporation. He indicated that he owned 51 percent of the corporation, that the money would be promptly repaid, and that the financial statements were being prepared for internal use only. He requested that these loans not be accounted for separately in the financial statements, but be included in the other current accounts receivable. Harper acquiesced in this request. Nance was correct as to his stock ownership and the fact that the financial statements were for internal use only. However, he subsequently became insolvent and was unable to repay the loans.

What is Harper's liability? Explain.

AICPA adapted

4-43. Higgins, CPA, received a telephone call from Calhoun, the sole owner and manager of a small corporation. Calhoun asked Higgins to prepare the financial statements for the corporation and told Higgins that the statements were needed in two weeks for external financing purposes. Calhoun was vague when Higgins inquired about the intended use of the statements. Higgins was convinced that Calhoun thought Higgins' work would constitute an audit. To avoid confusion Higgins decided not to explain to Calhoun that the engagement would only be to prepare the financial statements. Higgins, with the understanding that a substantial fee would be paid if the work were completed in two weeks, accepted the engagement and started the work at once.

During the course of the work, Higgins discovered an accrued expense account labeled "professional fees" and learned that the balance in the account represented an accrual for the cost of Higgins' services. Higgins suggested to Calhoun's bookkeeper that the account name be changed to "fees for limited audit engagement." Higgins also reviewed several invoices to determine whether accounts were being properly classified. Some of the invoices were missing. Higgins listed the missing invoice numbers in the working papers with a note indicating that there should be a follow-up on the next engagement. Higgins also discovered that the available records included the fixed asset values at estimated current replacement costs. Based on the records available, Higgins prepared a balance sheet, income statement and statement of stockholder's equity. In addition, Higgins drafted the footnotes but decided that any mention of the replacement costs would only mislead the readers. Higgins suggested to Calhoun that readers of the financial statements would be better informed if they received a separate letter from Calhoun explaining the meaning and effect of the estimated replacement costs of the fixed assets. Higgins mailed the financial statements and footnotes to Calhoun with the following note included on each page:

"The accompanying financial statements are submitted to you without complete audit verification."

Identify the inappropriate actions of Higgins and indicate what Higgins should have done to avoid each inappropriate action.

AICPA adapted

4-44. For several years, Beulah O'Henry has performed a compilation service for her client, Kent Employment Service. She has been requested to perform a limited review of the financial statements for the quarter ended September 30, 1981.

Describe what changes, if any, O'Henry should make in the engagement letter to be sent to her client.

4-45. A major written understanding between a CPA and a client, in connection with an examination of financial statements, is the engagement letter.

a. 1. What are the objectives of the engagement letter?
2. Who should prepare and sign the engagement letter?
3. When should the engagement letter be sent?
4. Why should the engagement letter be renewed periodically?

b. A CPA's responsibilities for providing accounting services sometimes involve an association with unaudited financial statements. Discuss the need in this circumstance for an engagement letter.

AICPA adapted

4-46. Federal income tax returns provide for the signature of the individual or firm preparing the tax return.

Discuss whether a CPA is required to sign the tax return in each of the following independent sitauations:

a. The tax return was prepared by the CPA without compensation.
b. The tax return was prepared by the CPA who had rendered an adverse opinion in the auditor's report on the taxpayer's financial statements.

c. The tax return was prepared by the taxpayer's chief accountant who later submitted the return to the CPA for recommendations. The CPA recommended substantial changes, which were adopted.

AICPA adapted

4-47. Shortly before the due date, Daniel Cox requested that you prepare the 1982 federal income tax return for Cox Corporation, a small closely held service corporation which he controlled. Cox placed a package on your desk and said, "Here is all the information you need. I'll pay you $300 if you prepare the return in time for filing by the deadline with no extension—and if the tax liability is less than $2,000 I'll increase your fee to $800." The package contained the corporation's bank statements and paid checks, prior years' tax returns prepared on the accrual basis, and other financial and tax information. The books of account were not included because they were not posted up to date.

You found that deposits shown on the bank statements substantially exceeded Cox's sales figure and the expenses listed seemed rather large in relation to sales. Cox explained that he made several loans to the corporation during the year and expenses just seemed to mount up.

a. What ethical issues should you consider before deciding whether or not you should prepare the federal income tax return for Cox Corporation?

b. If you prepare this return, must you sign it? Explain.

c. If you sign the return, what does your signature imply?

AICPA adapted

4-48. In connection with the annual examination of the financial statements of the Thames Corporation, a CPA is reviewing the Federal Income Taxes Payable account. With the approval of its board of directors, the Thames Corporation made a sizable payment for advertising during the year being audited. The corporation deducted the full amount in its federal income tax return. The controller acknowledges that this deduction probably will be disallowed because it relates to political matters. He has not provided for this disallowance in his federal income tax provision and refuses to do so because he fears that this will cause the revenue agent to believe that the deduction is not valid. What is the CPA's responsibility in this situation? Explain.

AICPA adapted

4-49. Whitlow and Wyatt, CPAs, has been the independent auditor of Interstate Land Development Corporation for several years. During these years, Interstate prepared and filed its own annual income tax returns.

During 1984, Interstate requested Whitlow and Wyatt to examine all the necessary financial statements of the corporation to be submitted to the Securities and Exchange Commission (SEC) in connection with a multistate public offering of one million shares of Interstate common stock. This public offering came under the provisions of the Securities Act of 1933. The examination was performed carefully and the financial statements were fairly presented for the respective periods. These financial statements were included in the registration statement filed with the SEC.

While the registration statement was being processed by the SEC but prior to the effective date, the Internal Revenue Service (IRS) subpoenaed Whitlow and Wyatt to turn over all its working papers relating to Interstate for the years 1981-1983. Whitlow and Wyatt initially refused to comply for two reasons. First, Whitlow and Wyatt did not prepare Interstate's tax returns. Second, Whitlow and Wyatt claimed that the working papers were confidential matters subject to the privileged-communications rule. Subsequently, however, Whitlow and Wyatt did relinquish the subpoenaed working papers.

Upon receiving the subpoena, Wyatt called Dunkirk, the chairman of Interstate's board of directors and asked him about the IRS investigation. Dunkirk responded, "I'm sure the IRS people are on a fishing expedition and that they will not find any material deficiencies."

A few days later Dunkirk received written confirmation from the IRS that it was contending that Interstate had underpaid its taxes during the period under review. The confirmation revealed that Interstate was being assessed $500,000 including penalties and interest for the three years.

This $500,000 assessment was material relative to the financial statements as of December 31, 1984. The amount for each year individually exlusive of penalty and interest was not material relative to each respective year.

a. Discuss the additional liability assumed by Whitlow and Wyatt in connection with this SEC registration engagement.

b. Discuss the implications to Whitlow and Wyatt and its responsibilities with respect to the IRS assessment.

c. Could Whitlow and Wyatt have validly refused to surrender the subpoenaed materials? Explain.

AICPA adapted

5

The Auditor's Report

The auditor's report is the expression of a professional opinion or lack of opinion on a client's financial statements. Whereas the financial statements themselves are management's representations, the auditor's report, often referred to as the auditor's opinion, is solely the auditor's responsibility. The report usually should be addressed to the company being audited, its board of directors, or its stockholders, or a combination of the three.

Auditors should write their reports with the utmost care and consideration. The report is the only aspect of an auditor's work that the public sees. A public accountant's competence is likely to be judged by this report, and legal responsibility may be determined by it.

In rendering an opinion in an audit report, auditors are said to be performing the *attest function*—they are attesting to the fairness of the financial statements. This attestation is supported by their recognized expertise in accounting and auditing as well as by their carrying out an audit in accordance with generally accepted auditing standards.

Generally accepted auditing standards give broad criteria for writing the report. The first three standards relating to reporting instruct auditors to include in the report a statement regarding whether generally accepted accounting principles have been used in the financial statements, whether these principles have been used consistently, and whether disclosure is adequate. Furthermore, the fourth reporting standard requires that auditors give a clear expression of the degree of responsibility they are assuming in regard to the financial statements. It states, in part, "In all cases where an auditor's name is associated with financial statements the report should contain a clear-cut indication of the character of the auditor's examination, if any, and the degree of responsibility he is taking."

The unqualified opinion

The type of opinion rendered when an auditor has no reservations regarding the financial statements is the unqualified or "clean" opinion. Figure 5-1 is an example of an auditor's unqualified report.

The standard wording of the unqualified report is recommended by the AICPA and is widely used by auditors. The first paragraph is referred to as the *scope paragraph* and gives information concerning the extent and

Figure 5-1 Unqualified Opinion on Comparative Statements by Continuing Auditor

To the Shareholders and Board of Directors
of Red Giant Corporation

We have examined the consolidated statement of financial position of Red Giant Corporation and subsidiaries as of December 31, 19X5 and 19X4 and the related consolidated statements of earnings and retained earnings and of changes in financial position for the years then ended. Our examinations were made in accordance with generally accepted auditing standards and, accordingly, included such tests of the accounting records and such other auditing procedures as we considered necessary in the circumstances.

In our opinion, the aforementioned financial statements present fairly the financial position of Red Giant Corporation and subsidiaries at December 31, 19X5 and 19X4 and the results of their operations and changes in their financial position for the years then ended, in conformity with generally accepted accounting principles applied on a consistent basis.

Harris and Stephens
Certified Public Accountants

Atlanta, Georgia
February 18, 19X6

character of the auditors' examination. In the second, or *opinion paragraph,* auditors specifically state their opinion of the financial statements.

An analysis of the wording of the auditor's report reveals that a considerable amount of information is contained in the two paragraphs. The first sentence identifies the financial statements being referred to and states that the auditor has examined them. By so stating, the auditor indicates that the statements were prepared by management. Even if the auditor offers extensive advice and assistance in preparation of the statements, management has the responsibility for their content. The auditor then asserts that the examination was performed in a manner consistent with generally accepted auditing standards and that all procedures considered necessary were carried out. The reference to generally accepted auditing standards conveys information to the interested reader concerning the auditor's personal qualifications and independence and the care taken in performing the auditing function. In addition, it gives information regarding the type and extent of the field work as well as assurance that disclosure is adequate and that the auditor's opinion meets accepted criteria.

In the opinion paragraph the auditor states that the financial statements present fairly the information that they purport to present. The auditor's judgment regarding fairness is based on the adherence of the statements to generally accepted accounting principles and the consistent application thereof. Certain other information is generally considered to be implied by the auditor's report; namely, that

1. The audit is based on tests of the accounting records, not complete verification.
2. Immaterial errors are not considered.
3. Internal control is sufficient to the extent that the auditor is able to rely on the accounting data.
4. The financial statements agree with the books and records of the company.

Opinions other than unqualified

In some cases auditors are unable to render an unqualified opinion on a client's financial statements. Circumstances both within and beyond a client's control may make it necessary for an auditor to render an opinion other than an unqualified one. Types of audit opinions other than unqualified are

1. qualified opinion
2. adverse opinion
3. disclaimer

A distinctive feature of most other-than-unqualified opinions is the inclusion of one or more explanatory paragraphs. SAS No. 2 (AU 509) requires that an explanatory paragraph or paragraphs be included in all other-than-unqualified opinions except in cases of opinions that are qualified because of a change in accounting principles. In addition, the auditor may include explanatory material in an unqualified opinion when it is desired to emphasize a matter regarding the financial statements.

THE QUALIFIED OPINION

An opinion which expresses that the statements taken as a whole are, with certain reservations, fairly presented is called a *qualified opinion.* These opinions should include the phrases *except for, with the exception of,* or *subject to* in the opinion paragraph. Figure 5-2 illustrates an opinion which is qualified because of a change in accounting principles. Note that a separate explanatory paragraph is not required.

In all cases, auditors must take care that their reservations concerning the financial statements are not so material as to overshadow or, in effect, contradict their opinions regarding the overall fairness. Further, in all instances where a qualified opinion is rendered, except in typical cases of inconsistency, a separate explanatory paragraph(s) must be included in the opinion describing all circumstances leading to the qualification and the effects on the financial statements.

The conditions that require a qualified opinion by the auditor include the following:

1. *Inconsistency.* This situation arises when the client has been inconsistent in the application of accounting principles and there is a material effect on the financial statements. The qualification required for inconsistency differs from that required by the other conditions listed. The other qualifications disclose the auditor's reservations with respect to the fairness of the presentation, while in the consistency qualification, the auditor is calling attention to a change in method of presentation.
2. *Accounting principles violation.* This results from the client's employing accounting principles that are not generally accepted or that differ from a principle promulgated by authoritative bodies designated by the AICPA. The Financial Accounting Standards Board represents such a designated body.
3. *Inadequate disclosure.* Information required for fair presentation must be included in the financial statements or the notes thereto. Otherwise the statements cannot be considered fair, and the auditor must qualify the opinion. *This condition is a special case of accounting principle violation and is discussed separately to emphasize proper reporting procedures.*

Figure 5-2 Auditor's Opinion Qualified for Inconsistency

To the Shareholders and Board of Directors
of White Dwarf Corporation

We have examined the consolidated statement of financial position of White Dwarf Corporation and subsidiaries as of December 31, 19X5 and 19X4 and the related consolidated statements of earnings and retained earnings and of changes in financial position for the years then ended. Our examinations were made in accordance with generally accepted auditing standards and, accordingly, included such tests of the accounting records and such other auditing procedures as we considered necessary in the circumstances.

In our opinion, the aforementioned financial statements present fairly the financial position of White Dwarf Corporation and subsidiaries at December 31, 19X5 and 19X4 and the results of their operations and changes in their financial position for the years then ended, in conformity with generally accepted accounting principles consistently applied during the period except for the change, with which we concur, in the method of computing earned income as described in Note 4 to the financial statements.

Harris and Stephens
Certified Public Accountants

Atlanta, Georgia
March 3, 19X6

4. *Scope limitation.* If, for some reason, an auditor is precluded from carrying out all the procedures or from gathering all evidence considered necessary, a qualified opinion may be appropriate.
5. *Material contingency or uncertainty.* In business, situations often arise for which the outcome cannot be reasonably predicted. Common examples are lawsuits, contract renegotiation proceedings, and contested tax assessments. In these cases, a *subject to* type qualified opinion is often appropriate.

Figure 5-3 presents an example of an opinion that is qualified because of uncertainties. Some auditors believe that if uncertainties are accounted

Figure 5-3 Auditor's Opinion Qualified in Current Year for Uncertainty

To the Shareholders and Board of Directors
of Pulsar Paper Co.

We have examined the consolidated statement of financial position of Pulsar Paper Co. and subsidiaries as of December 31, 19X5 and 19X4 and the related consolidated statements of earnings and retained earnings and of changes in financial position for the years then ended. Our examinations were made in accordance with generally accepted auditing standards and, accordingly, included such tests of the accounting records and such other auditing procedures as we considered necessary in the circumstances.

As discussed in Note 4, there are uncertainties about the ability of the Company to consummate permanent long-term financing on certain constructed assets. The effects, if any, of the outcome of this matter are not presently determinable.

In our opinion, subject to the effects on the 19X5 financial statements of the matter referred to in the preceding paragraph, the aforementioned financial statements present fairly the financial position of Pulsar Paper Co. and subsidiaries at December 31, 19X5 and 19X4 and the results of their operations and changes in their financial position for the years then ended, in conformity with generally accepted accounting principles applied on a consistent basis.

Harris and Stephens
Certified Public Accountants

Atlanta, Georgia
March 8, 19X6

for properly on the financial statements and are adequately disclosed in the footnotes that the financial statements are, therefore, in accordance with generally accepted accounting principles and an unqualified opinion should be rendered. Although this view has merit, it is not currently the prevailing position and Statements on Auditing Standards provide for an other-than-unqualified opinion in such circumstances.

THE ADVERSE OPINION

An adverse opinion states that the auditor believes the financial statements are not fairly presented in accordance with generally accepted accounting principles. In rendering an adverse opinion the auditor must clearly disclose all the reasons therefor and the effects on the financial statements.

Further, in an adverse opinion the auditor should not make any references to consistency, since consistency implies the application of generally accepted accounting principles. A middle paragraph or paragraphs of the opinion should be used to describe the circumstances. Figure 5-4 illustrates an adverse opinion rendered because of a departure from generally accepted accounting principles.

Figure 5-4 Adverse Opinion on Comparative Financial Statements

To the Shareholders and Board of Directors
of Allied Semiconductors, Incorporated

We have examined the consolidated statement of financial position of Allied Semiconductors, Incorporated and subsidiaries as of December 31, 19X5 and 19X4 and the related consolidated statements of earnings and retained earnings and of changes in financial position for the years then ended. Our examinations were made in accordance with generally accepted auditing standards and, accordingly, included such tests of the accounting records and such other auditing procedures as we considered necessary in the circumstances.

As discussed in Notes 1 and 6, the Company follows the practice of capitalizing research and development costs and amortizing such costs over their expected useful life. This accounting practice is at variance with Statement of Financial Accounting Standards No. 2 and is not, in our opinion, in accordance with generally accepted accounting principles. Because of this departure from generally accepted accounting principles, as of December 31, 19X5 and 19X4, inventories have been increased $101,728 and $97,263 respectively; cost of goods sold has been increased $232,768 and $198,702 respectively; operating expenses have been decreased $464,720 and $384,280 respectively; net income has been increased by $231,952 and $185,578 respectively; and retained earnings have been increased by $784,667 and $552,715.

In our opinion, because of the effects of the matters discussed in the preceding paragraph, the financial statements referred to above do not present fairly, in conformity with generally accepted accounting principles, the financial position of Allied Semiconductors, Incorporated as of December 31, 19X5 and 19X4, or the results of its operations and changes in its financial position for the years then ended.

Harris and Stephens
Certified Public Accountants

Atlanta, Georgia
March 28, 19X6

An adverse opinion is not commonly rendered in actual practice, since clients typically prefer to change the accounting method in question rather than to receive an adverse opinion. However, it is an important and necessary reporting option for auditors when appropriate circumstances arise that cannot be rectified. The conditions that lead to an adverse opinion include the following:

1. accounting principles violation
2. inadequate disclosure (a special case of accounting principles violation)

These two conditions are also listed as conditions warranting a qualified opinion. Whether these conditions lead to a qualified or an adverse opinion is determined by the materiality of the effect on the financial statements. In this case, the auditor must decide whether the statements taken as a whole are fairly presented except for certain items or are not fairly presented because of these items. In the former case a qualified opinion is rendered; in the latter, an adverse opinion. Figure 5-6, on page 145 analyzes various interrelationships among the other-than-unqualified opinions.

THE DISCLAIMER

An opinion that is, more precisely, a declaration of no opinion is the *disclaimer.* In this audit report, the auditor states, for any of several reasons, an inability to express an opinion on the statements taken as a whole. In rendering a disclaimer, the auditor must clearly state *all* the reasons for this inability to form an opinion with respect to the financial statements. Again, a middle paragraph or paragraphs in the audit report should be used to describe the circumstances involved. Figure 5-5 presents an auditor's disclaimer of opinion based on material uncertainties. SAS No. 2 (AU 509.25) states that an auditor "should be able to form an opinion . . ." on financial statements affected by uncertainties and, therefore, render a qualified opinion rather than a disclaimer. However, the issuance of a disclaimer in such circumstances is not precluded by the Statement on Accounting Standards. In current practice both qualifications and disclaimers are issued as a result of uncertainties.

The following circumstances may cause an auditor to disclaim opinion on financial statements:

1. *Lack of independence.* Generally accepted auditing standards require auditors to maintain their independence, both in fact and in appearance. If circumstances exist so that an auditor is not independent of the client, an opinion cannot be rendered on the client's financial statements, since the auditor cannot perform an examination in accordance with generally accepted auditing standards. In these cases a disclaimer is appropriate.

Figure 5-5 Disclaimer of Opinion on Comparative Financial Statements

To the Shareholders and Board of Directors
of Quasar Products Corporation

We have examined the consolidated statement of financial position of Quasar Products Corporation and subsidiaries as of December 31, 19X5 and 19X4 and the related consolidated statements of earnings and retained earnings and of changes in financial position for the years then ended. Our examinations were made in accordance with generally accepted auditing standards and, accordingly, included such tests of the accounting records and such other auditing procedures as we considered necessary in the circumstances.

As discussed in Note 8, if the Company is not successful in obtaining continuing concessions from major creditors, the Company will not be able to meet current obligations and, therefore, might have to seek protection under Federal Bankruptcy laws or be forced to dispose of assets at less than carrying values. The outcome of this matter cannot be determined at this time.

As discussed in Note 9, a number of lawsuits have been filed against the Company. In certain instances counsel is of the opinion that the Company has adequate defenses and that the claims will not be sustained. However, in other cases, pending actions are in preliminary stages and, accordingly, counsel cannot express any opinion as to the final outcome of these actions at this time. Judgments against the Company, if any, could have a material effect on the liquidity of the Company.

Because of the significance of the matters discussed in the preceding paragraphs, we are unable to express, and we do not express, an opinion on the aforementioned financial statements of Quasar Products Corporation at December 31, 19X5 and 19X4 and for the years then ended.

Harris and Stephens
Certified Public Accountants

Atlanta, Georgia
April 7, 19X6

2. *Scope limitation.*
3. *Material contingency or uncertainty.*

The last two of these circumstances were also noted as conditions for a qualified opinion and represent further examples of interrelationships among opinions. In each of these two cases, the auditor has been unable to obtain sufficient evidence or information necessary to express an unqualified opinion. If the missing evidence or information is not so material as to overshadow the opinion on fairness, the auditor expresses a qualified opinion; if it is sufficiently material to make an opinion on the remaining items meaningless, he or she may disclaim an opinion.

THE PIECEMEAL OPINION

An opinion formerly used by auditors in conjunction with adverse opinions and disclaimers was the piecemeal opinion. This addition to an adverse opinion or disclaimer stated that certain parts of the financial statements were fairly presented even though (1) the financial statements taken as a whole were not fairly presented (when rendered in conjunction with an adverse opinion) or (2) the auditor expressed no opinion on the financial statements taken as a whole (when rendered in conjunction with a disclaimer).

Many auditors took the position that piecemeal opinions tended to mislead or confuse readers of financial statements. However, the use of piecemeal opinions was allowed until the issuance of SAS No. 2 (AU 509.48), which states, "Because piecemeal opinions tend to overshadow or contradict a disclaimer of opinion or an adverse opinion, they are inappropriate and should not be issued in any situation."

Interrelationships among opinions

It has been seen that a particular circumstance may be considered a causative condition for more than one type of opinion. In Figure 5-6 the other-than-unqualified opinions are presented along with their causative conditions. The auditor's decision regarding type of opinion must be based on the materiality of the condition as well as its nature. Figure 5-6 shows that accounting principles violations and inadequate disclosure may lead to either a qualified or an adverse opinion depending on the materiality of the condition. Similarly, the materiality of a scope limitation or contingency will determine whether a qualified opinion or disclaimer is appropriate. Also, it may be seen that an inconsistency can logically lead only to a qualified opinion and lack of independence results only in a disclaimer of opinion.

Figure 5-6 Opinion Interrelationships

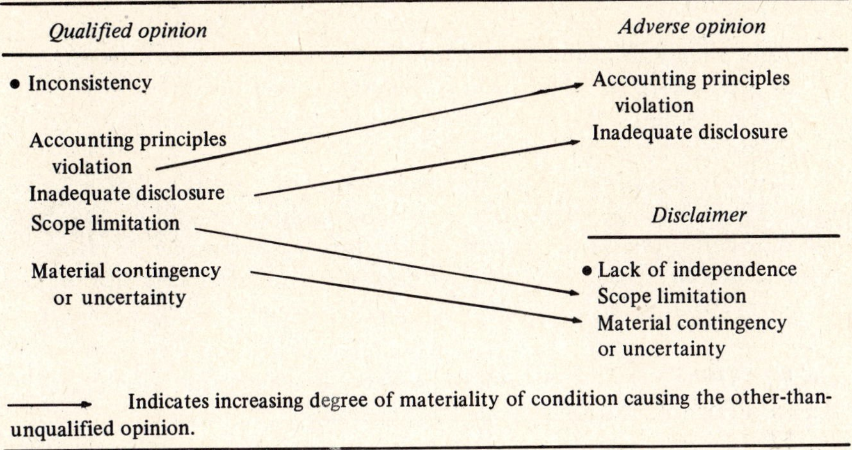

If the effect of an item or group of items is immaterial on the financial statements, no matter what type of error or violation is represented, an unqualified opinion is appropriate. In this regard, there is no exact point where the magnitude of an item dictates that it becomes material and that an other-than-unqualified opinion is necessary. This determination rests solely on the auditor's judgment.

In Figure 5-6 each condition is presumed to have been judged material. The degree of progression to extreme materiality is similarly not quantifiable and rests on the auditor's judgment.

Reporting on scope restrictions, inconsistency, and inadequate disclosure

In addition to indicating the type of opinion to be rendered, certain conditions require special reporting procedures. Scope restrictions must be analyzed to fully determine appropriate reporting. A scope restriction may be client-imposed or non-client-imposed. A client-imposed scope limitation leads the auditor to a qualified opinion or a disclaimer, as has been previously discussed. Of course, if the scope limitation is insignificant, an unqualified opinion may be rendered if otherwise justified. In the event of a non-client-imposed scope restriction, the auditor may decide to pursue other means, such as employing alternative auditing procedures or gathering other evidence. When auditors can satisfy themselves by these other means, they may render an unqualified opinion if it is otherwise justified.

If they do not or cannot satisfy themselves by other means and the scope restriction is significant, then they must render either a qualified opinion or a disclaimer. It should be noted that in cases of significant client-imposed scope limitations, auditors generally will not attempt to satisfy themselves by alternative procedures and, therefore, will disclaim an opinion. Figure 5-7 illustrates a disclaimer of opinion rendered as a result of a non-client-imposed scope restriction.

Another condition that requires special reporting procedures is inconsistency. In addition to rendering a qualified opinion in such a situation, auditors should disclose the nature of the inconsistency and its effect on the financial statements. This may be done in a middle paragraph of the

Figure 5-7 Disclaimer of Opinion because of Scope Limitation

To the Shareholders and Board of Directors
of Corbett Clothiers, Inc.

We have examined the statement of financial position of Corbett Clothiers, Inc. as of December 31, 19X5 and 19X4 and the related statements of earnings and retained earnings and of changes in financial position for the years then ended. Except as explained in the following paragraph, our examinations were made in accordance with generally accepted auditing standards and, accordingly, included such tests of the accounting records and such other auditing procedures as we considered necessary in the circumstances.

We did not observe the taking of the Company's physical inventories as of December 31, 19X5 and 19X4, which are stated at $124,397 and $102,728 respectively, since those dates were prior to the time that we were initially engaged to examine the financial statements. We were unable to satisfy ourselves as to the inventory quantities by means of other auditing procedures.

Because we did not observe the taking of the Company's physical inventories and were unable to apply adequate alternative procedures with regard to inventory quantities held by the Company on December 31, 19X5 and 19X4, as noted in the preceding paragraph, the scope of our work was not sufficient to enable us to express, and we do not express, an opinion on the abovementioned financial statements.

Harris and Stephens
Certified Public Accountants

Atlanta, Georgia
June 6, 19X6

opinion, or, as is more common, the opinion may refer to a note to the financial statements that describes the inconsistency. Also, it is appropriate for auditors to express in the opinion their approval of accounting principle changes when, upon examination of the circumstances, they consider the changes justifiable. A difference in meaning exists between a qualified opinion rendered due to inconsistency and one rendered due to other circumstances. The consistency qualification discloses an accounting change affecting the financial statements, whereas other qualifications express an auditor's reservations regarding the fairness of the financial statement presentation. Because of this difference in purpose, it may be useful to consider a consistency qualification as a less severe measure than a qualification for other purposes. Figure 5-2 illustrated an opinion qualified because of an inconsistency.

In the case of an audit of the first year of operation of a business, the auditor's opinion should not include any reference to consistency. However, in a first engagement to examine a previously existing client, the auditor must examine the prior year to the extent necessary to be assured that the accounting principles employed are consistent. Occasionally, there may be inconsistencies that have no material impact on the current financial statements but are likely to be significant in future financial reports. In these instances, a note to the financial statements in the year of change is required to describe the inconsistency, and no mention in the auditor's opinion is necessary.

Inadequate disclosure is another condition that requires special reporting. If the financial statements, including accompanying notes, fail to disclose information that is required by generally accepted accounting principles, the auditor should express a qualified or an adverse opinion because of the departure from those principles. In addition, the information should be provided in the audit report, if practicable, unless its omission from the audit report is authorized by a specific Statement on Auditing Standards. Examples of such appropriate omissions from the report are omissions of segment information and omission of the statement of changes in financial position. In these cases the omission is described in the audit report but the missing information need not be included in the auditor's opinion. Figure 5-8 presents an auditor's opinion qualified because of inadequate disclosure.

Long-form reports

The auditor's opinion or report discussed up to now is commonly referred to as the *short-form report.* It is the most widely used format for expressing an audit opinion. The complete short-form report often includes the auditor's opinion, the financial statements, and the notes thereto. It should

Figure 5-8 Auditor's Opinion Qualified for Inadequate Disclosure

To the Shareholders and Board of Directors
of Artistic Manufacturing Co.

We have examined the consolidated statement of financial position of Artistic Manufacturing Co. and subsidiaries as of December 31, 19X5 and 19X4 and the related consolidated statements of earnings and retained earnings and of changes in financial position for the years then ended. Our examinations were made in accordance with generally accepted auditing standards and, accordingly, included such tests of the accounting records and such other auditing procedures as we considered necessary in the circumstances.

On January 28, 19X6, the Company issued subordinated debentures in the amount of $2,750,000 for the purpose of expanding manufacturing facilities. The debt agreement prohibits the payment of cash dividends without the lender's consent after December 31, 19X5.

In our opinion, except for the omission of the information in the preceding paragraph, the aforementioned financial statements present fairly the financial position of Artistic Manufacturing Co. and subsidiaries at December 31, 19X5 and 19X4 and the results of their operations and changes in their financial position for the years then ended, in conformity with generally accepted accounting principles applied on a consistent basis.

Harris and Stephens
Certified Public Accountants

Atlanta, Georgia
February 26, 19X6

be noted here that the term *audit report* is used ambiguously to mean either the opinion alone or the opinion together with the statements and notes.

The *long-form report* is generally considered to include the auditor's opinion, the basic financial statements and notes, and additional financial information and schedules. The distinguishing feature of the long-form report is the inclusion of additional and often extensive financial information and analysis. This additional information may include such things as an aging of accounts receivable, detail analysis of certain accounts, schedule of insurance coverage, statistical analysis of operations, yield ratios of manufacturing operations, and other information desired by the client or specific users of the financial statements. A long-form report is usually prepared to render a service to the client or specific third parties. Often, a client may not have an accounting staff to produce various financial operating information needed. The auditor's long-form report may meet these needs of the client. Also, in many cases creditors or stockholders may request detailed financial information and the auditor, with the client's permission, may provide the necessary information in a long-form report.

In rendering a long-form report, auditors must clearly state what degree of responsibility they accept for the supplemental information. The degree of responsibility taken may range from none (in which case the auditors specifically disclaim opinion with respect to the supplemental information) to full audit responsibility (in which case the information is covered by the auditors' opinion of the financial statements).

Reliance on reports of other auditors

Frequently the principal auditor of the client will not perform the examination of all locations where the client does business. Foreign subsidiaries, divisions or branches at distant points, and other circumstances often lead to the appointment of other auditors for this work. In using the work of other auditors, the principal auditor has several decisions to make, including whether he or she is qualified to be the principal auditor. A principal auditor should be one who has done a material portion of the audit work and is in a position to express an opinion on the overall financial statements. The principal auditor also must decide the extent of responsibility to accept with respect to other auditors' work. If the principal auditor is willing to accept full responsibility for other auditors' work, then the fact that other auditors were involved is not mentioned in the principal auditor's opinion.

If, however, the principal auditor is willing to *rely* on the other auditors' work but is not willing to accept full responsibility, then special wording is required in the opinion. This wording, which should be in both the scope paragraph and the opinion paragraph, should make reference to the fact that parts of the audit were performed by other auditors, include a description of the significance of these segments of the company, and incorporate a statement that the opinion is based in part on such work of other auditors. In some cases, the principal auditor might not be willing to rely on the work of the other auditors. In these situations, the principal auditor should render a qualified opinion or a disclaimer as the circumstances dictate. At times the other auditors' report may be qualified for some item that is material on the financial statements covered by the report. When the financial statements are combined, this item may no longer be material. In this case, the principal auditor would not qualify the opinion but should explain why the qualification by the other auditors

Figure 5-9 Unqualified Opinion Making Reference to Examination of Other Auditors

To the Shareholders and Board of Directors
of Metric Conversion Corporation

We have examined the consolidated statement of financial position of Metric Conversion Corporation and subsidiaries as of December 31, 19X5 and 19X4 and the related consolidated statements of earnings and retained earnings and of changes in financial position for the years then ended. Our examinations were made in accordance with generally accepted auditing standards and, accordingly, included such tests of the accounting records and such other auditing procedures as we considered necessary in the circumstances. We did not examine the financial statements of Hectare Realty, Inc., a consolidated subsidiary, which statements reflect total assets constituting 19 percent and 21 percent of the related consolidated totals at December 31, 19X5 and 19X4 respectively and total revenues of 20 percent and 23 percent of the related consolidated totals for the years 19X5 and 19X4 respectively. These statements were examined by other auditors whose report thereon has been furnished to us, and our opinion expressed herein, insofar as it relates to the amounts included for Hectare Realty, Inc., is based solely upon the report of the other auditors.

In our opinion, based upon our examination and the report of other auditors, the aforementioned financial statements present fairly the financial position of Metric Conversion Corporation and subsidiaries at December 31, 19X5 and 19X4 and the results of their operations and changes in their financial position for the years then ended, in conformity with generally accepted accounting principles applied on a consistent basis.

Harris and Stephens
Certified Public Accountants

Atlanta, Georgia
February 25, 19X6

Figure 5-10 Time Line of Auditor's Responsibility for Reporting on Subsequent Events

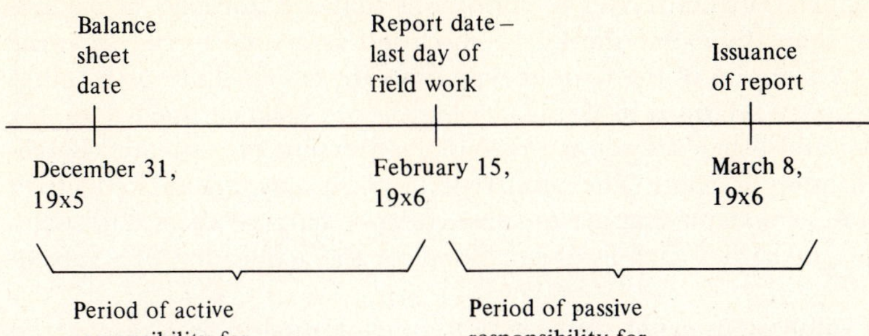

no longer applied, particularly if the other auditors' statements and opinion are presented. Figure 5-9 presents an unqualified opinion which makes reference to the work of other auditors. Note that the special wording does not constitute a qualification of the opinion.

Reporting on subsequent events and dating the report

The auditor's opinion should be dated as of the date the *field work* has been completed, that is, when audit procedures at the client's office have been finished. This date marks a change in the auditor's responsibility for *subsequent events* (events that happen after the balance sheet date but relate to the financial statements under audit). Prior to the opinion date, the auditor is responsible for *discovering* and *reporting on* any subsequent events (*active* responsibility). Between the opinion date and the date the opinion is delivered to the client, the auditor is responsible for reporting only on subsequent events that come to his or her attention (*passive* responsibility). In addition, the auditor's responsibility for discovering and reporting on subsequent events is extended when performing audits that relate to security issues under the Securities Act of 1933. Under this statute, the auditor has "active" responsibility for discovering and reporting on subsequent events that occur before the effective date of the registration statement. Figure 5-10 illustrates the time frame of the auditor's responsibility for discovering and reporting on subsequent events for engagements that do not involve the Securities Act of 1933.

The method for reporting on subsequent events discovered prior to the delivery of the opinion to the client is determined by the nature of the event. SAS No. 1 (AU 560) provides that if the event relates to a condition that existed at balance sheet date, then the financial statements should be adjusted to reflect the item. If, however, the subsequent event which affects the financial statements relates to conditions that did not exist at balance sheet date, then the event should be disclosed as a note to the financial statements. Examples of the former type of event may include such things as adverse court decisions in claims arising before balance sheet date, tax settlements, and other situations involving settlement of estimated liabilities or realization of assets. The latter type of event may include items such as settlement of a claim that arises subsequent to balance sheet date, sales of securities, casualties such as fire or flood, or the acquisition of a subsidiary.

When a subsequent event of the type requiring disclosure is discovered after the completion of field work but before the report is rendered, the auditor must modify the date of the report. The preferable method of modification is to use *dual-dating* whereby the report is dated as of the last day of field work with a reference to the date of the disclosed subsequent event. For example, "February 15, 19X6, except for Note 13 which is dated March 3, 19X6." An alternative method is to date the entire report as of the later date. This method, however, has the effect of lengthening the period of the auditor's "active" responsibility for subsequent events.

Audit procedures designed to aid in the discovery of subsequent events are discussed in Chapter 15.

Subsequent discovery of facts existing at report date

After the opinion is delivered to the client, the auditor has still another responsibility for reporting subsequent discovery of facts that existed at the date of the opinion and would have affected the opinion had the auditor been aware of them. In general, this responsibility requires the auditor to notify the client that such facts should be disclosed to all known users of the financial statements. If the client refuses to make the facts known to the appropriate parties, then the auditor should, unless the auditor's attorney recommends a different course of action, notify the appropriate parties, including any regulatory authorities having jurisdiction over the client, that the auditor's report should no longer be relied upon.

Figure 5-11 presents the time frame of the auditor's responsibility for such events. Note that the auditor's involvement may extend far beyond the date of issuance of the report. This responsibility ends only after sufficient time has elapsed that the auditor believes that no one is still relying on the financial statements in question.

Figure 5-11 Time Line of Subsequent Discovery of Facts Existing at the Date of Auditor's Report

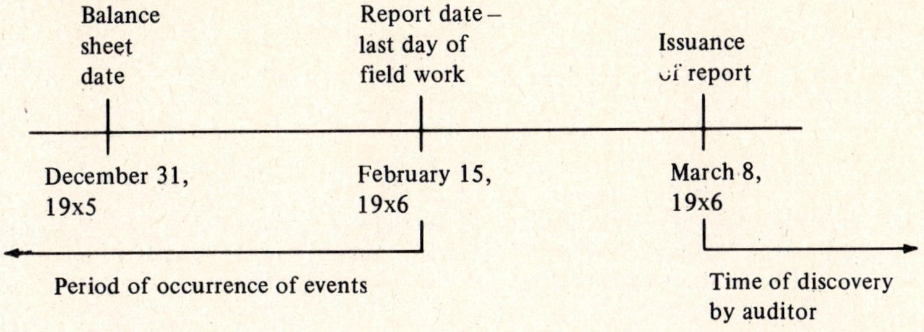

Unaudited financial statements

Auditors associated with unaudited financial statements are required to make disclosures regarding their responsibility with respect to the statements. The following paragraph from SAS No. 1 (AU 516.03) discusses the accountant's association with unaudited financial statements:

> A certified public accountant is associated with unaudited financial statements when he has consented to the use of his name in a report, document or written communication setting forth or containing the statements. Further, when a certified public accountant submits to his client or others, with or without a covering letter, unaudited financial statements which he has prepared or assisted in preparing, he is deemed to be associated with such statements. This association is deemed to exist even though the certified public accountant does not append his name to the financial statements or uses "plain paper" rather than his own stationery. However, association does not arise if the accountant, as an accommodation to his client, merely types on "plain paper" or reproduces unaudited financial statements so long as he has not prepared or otherwise assisted in preparing the statements and so long as he submits them only to his client.

When the accountant is associated with unaudited financial statements, the following disclosures are required:

1. Each page of the financial statements should be clearly marked that they are unaudited.
2. A disclaimer of opinion should accompany the financial statements.

Figure 5-12 illustrates a disclaimer on unaudited financial statements. Furthermore, if the accountant concludes, based on known facts, that the unaudited financial statements do not conform to generally accepted accounting principles, the accountant should insist that the statements be

Figure 5-12 Disclaimer on Unaudited Financial Statements

To the Stockholders and Board of Directors
of Masefield Publishing Company

The accompanying statement of financial position of Masefield Publishing Company as of December 31, 19X5 and 19X4 and the related statements of earnings and retained earnings and changes in financial position for the years then ended were not audited by us and accordingly we do not express an opinion on them.

Harris and Stephens
Certified Public Accountants

Atlanta, Georgia
January 28, 19X6

revised, should set forth reservations in the disclaimer, or, if necessary, should refuse to be associated with the statements.

These procedures for unaudited financial statements currently apply primarily to the unaudited financial statements of publicly held entities. Within this context exceptions exist including reports on reviews of interim financial information and letters to underwriters. Both these topics as well as the reports and procedures appropriate for compilation and review services on financial statements of non-publicly held entities are discussed in Chapter 6.

Lack of independence

Occasionally, auditors will perform auditing procedures for clients when independence is lacking. Since generally accepted auditing standards require auditor independence, auditors cannot render opinions in such cases nor can they state that they have performed an audit "in accordance with generally accepted auditing standards."

When the auditor is associated with financial statements and lacks independence, a disclaimer of opinion is required. Appropriate wording for

Figure 5-13 Disclaimer of Opinion When Auditor Who Is Not Independent Is Associated With Financial Statement

To the Stockholders and Board of Directors
of Meteor Mining Corporation

We are not independent with respect to Meteor Mining Corporation, and the accompanying statement of financial position as of December 31, 19X5 and 19X4 and the related statements of earnings and retained earnings and of changes in financial position for the years then ended were not audited by us; accordingly, we do not express an opinion on them.

Harris and Stephens
Certified Public Accountants

Atlanta, Georgia
February 7, 19X6

such a disclaimer is specified in SAS No. 1 (AU 517.03) and is illustrated in Figure 5-13. When rendering this disclaimer auditors should not explain the reasons that they lack independence nor should they make reference to any auditing procedures that may have been performed.

Currently, the only exception to this procedure is found in cases where the auditor performs compilation services on financial statements of non-publicly held entities. This topic is discussed in Chapter 6.

Reports on comparative financial statements

When financial statements of a prior period or periods are presented along with the statements of the current period being audited, SAS No. 15 (AU 505.02) requires that continuing auditors update their reports on the financial statements of the prior periods. A continuing auditor is one who has examined the financial statements of the current period and one or more consecutive periods immediately prior to the current period. "Update" means to re-express an opinion on or to express a different opinion on the statements of the prior periods. The opinions illustrated in this

Figure 5-14 Auditor's Updated Opinion Different from Previous Year

To the Stockholders and Board of Directors
of Burkett-Stickney Corporation

We have examined the consolidated statement of financial position of Burkett-Stickney Corporation and subsidiaries as of December 31, 19X5 and 19X4 and the related consolidated statements of earnings and retained earnings and of changes in financial position for the years then ended. Our examinations were made in accordance with generally accepted auditing standards and, accordingly, included such tests of the accounting records and such other auditing procedures as we considered necessary in the circumstances.

In our report dated March 6, 19X5, our opinion on the 19X4 financial statements was qualified as being subject to the effects on the 19X4 financial statements of such adjustments, if any, as might have been required had the outcome of certain litigation been known. As explained in Note 5, the litigation was settled on August 15, 19X5, with no material loss to the Company. Accordingly, our present opinion on the 19X4 financial statements, as presented herein, is different from that expressed in our previous report.

In our opinion, the aforementioned financial statements present fairly the financial position of Burkett-Stickney Corporation and subsidiaries at December 31, 19X5 and 19X4 and the results of their operations and changes in their financial position for the years then ended, in conformity with generally accepted accounting principles applied on a consistent basis.

Harris and Stephens
Certified Public Accountants

Atlanta, Georgia
March 12, 19X6

chapter are examples of updating. In Figure 5-1, the auditor expressed an unqualified opinion on the statements of 19X5 and re-expressed an unqualified opinion on the 19X4 statements. Similarly, in Figure 5-3 the auditor expressed a qualified opinion on the 19X5 statements and re-expressed an unqualified opinion on the 19X4 statements.

In some cases the auditor's updated opinion on prior-year financial statements will differ from the opinion originally expressed on those statements because of changed circumstances. Examples of changes in circumstances that will usually cause a change in an updated opinion include (1) subsequent resolution of an uncertainty, (2) discovery of an uncertainty in a later period, and (3) restatement of prior-period financial statements. In cases where the updated opinion differs from the previously expressed opinion, the auditor should disclose all substantive reasons for the change in a separate explanatory paragraph of the report. Further, SAS No. 15 (AU 505.07) provides that the explanatory paragraph should disclose (a) the date of the previous opinion, (b) the type of opinion previously expressed, (c) the circumstances causing the changed opinion, and (d) that the auditor's updated opinion is different from that previously expressed. Figure 5-14 illustrates an auditor's opinion with an updated opinion different from that previously expressed.

If the prior-year financial statements either were not audited or were audited by a predecessor auditor, modification of the report is required. Where the prior-year statements are unaudited, the auditor should disclaim an opinion on the unaudited statements in a separate paragraph in the report. Additionally, the statements should be clearly marked "unaudited."

When the prior-year statements were audited by a predecessor auditor, the predecessor auditor may reissue the previous report. If the predecessor auditor's report is not presented with the financial statements, the successor auditor should indicate the following in the scope paragraph of the current report: (1) that a predecessor auditor examined the prior year statements, (2) the date of the predecessor's report, (3) the type of opinion given by the predecessor, and (4) the reasons for a predecessor's other-than-unqualified opinion.

Negative assurance

Any attempt to temper an other-than-unqualified opinion with phrases meant to assure the reader must be avoided. An example of this negative assurance would be a statement, after a disclaimer, for example, such as the following: "However, nothing came to our attention that causes us to believe that the statements are not presented fairly." Such a statement is likely to mislead readers and should never be used in conjunction with an audit opinion on financial statements. Proper uses of negative assurance are discussed in Chapter 6.

Departures from statements of the Financial Accounting Standards Board

When the financial statements under audit employ accounting principles or practices that are at variance with statements of the Financial Accounting Standards Board, the auditor must disclose this departure in the opinion. Further, the auditor may not render an unqualified opinion unless it can be demonstrated that the financial statements would have been misleading otherwise. The auditor's disclosure should be in the form of a separate paragraph of the opinion and should describe the departure, the effects on the financial statements, and the reasons why compliance with the respective opinion would be misleading.

Audits of unincorporated businesses and personal financial statements

Audits of unincorporated business enterprises present special problems for an auditor because they do not represent complete legal entities. This causes the separation of business assets and liabilities from those of the owners of the business to be difficult at best. In these situations the auditor may find it advisable to include in the opinion an explanation that the financial statements under audit include only items which have been represented as relating to the business and that the statements could be materially affected by the owner's personal assets and liabilities.

Personal financial statements do not present the problem of legal entity identification for the auditor. A person's assets and liabilities represent a legal entity that can be segregated. Market values of assets represent information that users of personal financial statements often desire. Auditors should include market value information in personal financial statements as supplementary data if reliable appraisals are available.

Financial reporting checklist

Appendix C presents the Financial Reporting Checklist published by the Washington Society of CPAs. Such a checklist is useful to auditors in reviewing audit reports in that it helps them gain assurance that nothing has been overlooked. For students the checklist provides insight into the many individual considerations that need attention before an audit is completed.

Supplementary readings

Anderson, H. M., and J. W. Giese. "The Auditor's Belief and His Opinion—The Need for Consistency." *CPA Journal* (January 1973), 49-54.

Bernstein, L. A. "The Concept of Materiality." *Accounting Review* (January 1967), 86-95.

Carmichael, D. R. "Auditor's Reports—A Search for Criteria." *Journal of Accountancy* (September 1972), 67-74.

———. *The Auditor's Reporting Obligation, Auditing Research Monograph No. 1.* New York: American Institute of Certified Public Accountants, 1972.

Dominiak, Geraldine F., and Joseph G. Louderback, III. "Present Fairly and Generally Accepted Accounting Principles." *CPA Journal* (January 1972), 45-49.

Firth, Michael. "Qualified Audit Reports: Their Impact on Investment Decisions." *Accounting Review* (July 1978), 642-650.

Goodman, Hortense, and Leonard Lorensen. *Illustrations of Departures from the Auditor's Standard Report.* New York: American Institute of Certified Public Accountants, 1975.

Hill, Henry P. "Reporting on Uncertainties by Independent Auditors." *Journal of Accountancy* (January 1973), 55-60.

Hubbard, Thomas D., and Joyce C. Lambert. "Current and Proposed Unaudited Statement Standards." *CPA Journal* (August 1978), 35-41.

Isbell, David B., and D. R. Carmichael. "Disclaimers and Liability—The Rhode Island Trust Case." *Journal of Accountancy* (April 1973), 37-42.

Newton, Lauren K. "The Risk Factor in Materiality Decisions." *Accounting Review* (January 1977), 97-108.

Rosenfield, Paul, and Leonard Lorensen. "Auditors' Responsibilities and the Audit Report." *Journal of Accountancy* (September 1974), 73-83.

Review questions

5-1. What general criteria do auditors have for writing their reports?

5-2. What type of opinion is rendered when an auditor has no reservations regarding the financial statements?

5-3. What is the first paragraph of the standard short-form report called, and what general information does it contain?

5-4. What is the second paragraph of the standard short-form report called, and what information does it contain?

5-5. Who has the responsibility for the preparation of the financial statements, and how does the auditor make known who has this responsibility?

5-6. What is the purpose of referring to generally accepted auditing standards in the scope paragraph of the auditor's report?

5-7. Besides the explicit expression of an opinion on the financial statements, certain other information is implied in the auditor's report. Give four examples of this implied information.

5-8. Name three types of audit opinions other than a "clean" opinion.

5-9. Under what general conditions would an auditor issue a qualified opinion?

5-10. What are the specific conditions or violations that might lead to a qualified opinion?

5-11. In what way does a consistency exception differ from other exceptions or qualifications in a qualified opinion?

5-12. Under what circumstances would a qualified opinion be issued in which the phrase *subject to* would be used? List several examples.

5-13. Violation of a generally accepted accounting principle can lead to either a qualified opinion or an adverse opinion. What determines whether a qualified opinion or an adverse opinion will be issued when an accounting principle violation occurs?

5-14. What circumstances might cause an auditor to disclaim opinion on a client's financial statements?

5-15. In the format below indicate whether an unqualified opinion (*U*), a qualified opinion (*Q*), an adverse opinion (*A*), or a disclaimer (*D*) should be issued based on the degree of materiality shown. The first item has been completed as an example.

	Immaterial	Material	Grossly material
Inconsistency	U	Q	Q
Accounting principle violation			
Inadequate disclosure			
Scope limitation			
Contingency			

5-16. What violation or condition can lead only to a qualified opinion and no other type?

5-17. What special reporting procedures are required when a material inconsistency occurs?

5-18. What reference is made to consistency in the auditor's report when it is the auditor's first engagement to examine the financial statements of a previously existing client?

5-19. What is included in a long-form audit report, and how is it different from a short-form report?

5-20. What degree of responsibility does an auditor assume for supplemental information in a long-form report?

5-21. Where more than one auditor is performing an examination of financial statements, what decisions must the principal auditor make?

5-22. What should a principal auditor do if unwilling to rely on the work of another auditor who had examined a subsidiary's financial statements?

5-23. What is the auditor's responsibility for events occurring subsequent to the balance sheet date of financial statements the auditor is examining, assuming these events relate to the financial statements under audit?

5-24. How should a subsequent event that affects the financial statements but relates to a condition that did not exist at balance sheet date be reported? Give several examples of a subsequent event of this nature.

5-25. How should a subsequent event that related to a condition that existed at the balance sheet date be reflected in the financial statements? Give several examples of a subsequent event of this nature.

5-26. When an accountant is associated with unaudited financial statements, what disclosures are required?

5-27. When may an auditor render an unqualified opinion on financial statements that were prepared using an accounting practice that departs from a position of the Financial Accounting Standards Board?

5-28. What special problems are encountered in an audit of an unincorporated business?

5-29. What should the auditor do when facts that existed at the date of the report are discovered after rendering the report and such facts would have affected the auditor's opinion?

5-30. What is a "continuing" auditor?

5-31. What is meant by "updating" a prior audit report?

5-32. When should continuing auditors update their opinions on prior-period financial statements?

Decision problems

5-33. You have examined Hagren Appliance Corporation's financial statements for several years and have always rendered an unqualified opinion. To reduce its current auditing cost Hagren limited the scope of your examination of its financial statements for the year just ended to exclude accounts receivable and commissions payable. Hagren's officers stated that the type of auditor's opinion you would render was not important because your report would be used for internal management purposes only and would not be distributed externally. The materiality of the accounts not examined required you to disclaim an opinion on the fairness of the financial statements as a whole.

a. Why does a CPA prefer that the scope of the auditing engagement not be limited? Discuss.

b. How would a client's assurance to a CPA that the auditor's report will be used only for internal purposes affect the scope of the CPA's examination and the kind of opinion rendered? Discuss.

AICPA adapted

5-34. Pace Corporation, an audit client of yours, is a manufacturer of consumer products and has several wholly owned subsidiaries in foreign countries that are audited by other independent auditors in those countries. The financial statements of all subsidiaries were properly consolidated in the financial statements of the parent company and the foreign auditor's reports were furnished to your CPA firm.

You are now preparing your auditor's opinion on the consolidated balance sheet and statement of income and retained earnings for the year ended June 30, 1985. These statements were prepared on a comparative basis with those of last year.

a. How would you evaluate and accept the independence and professional reputations of the foreign auditors?

b. Under what circumstances may a principal auditor assume responsibility for the work of another auditor to the same extent as if the principal auditor had performed the work alone?

c. Assume that both last year and this year you were willing to utilize the reports of the other independent auditors in expressing your opinion on the consolidated financial statements but were unwilling to take full responsibility for performance of the work underlying their opinions. Assuming your examination of the parent company's financial statements would allow you to render an unqualified opinion, prepare (1) the necessary disclosure to be contained in the scope paragraph, and (2) the complete opinion paragraph of your auditor's report.

d. What modification(s), if any, would be necessary in your auditor's opinion if the financial statements for the prior year were unaudited?

AICPA adapted

5-35. The following draft of an auditor's report has been submitted for review:

To: Eric Jones, Chief Accountant
Sunshine Manufacturing Co.

We have examined the balance sheet of the Sunshine Manufacturing Co. for the year ended August 31, 1986 and the related statements of income and retained earnings. Our examination included such tests of the accounting records and such other auditing procedures as we considered necessary in the circumstances except that, in accordance with your instructions, we did not count the buyers' cash working fund.

In our opinion, subject to the limitation on our examination discussed above, the accompanying balance sheet and statements of income and earned surplus present fairly the financial position of the Sunshine Manufacturing Co. at August 31, 1986 and the results of its operations for the year then ended.

Frank George & Co.
August 31, 1986

It has been determined that:

a. Except for the omission of the count of the buyers' cash working fund there were no scope restrictions placed on the auditor's examination.

b. The Sunshine Manufacturing Co. has been in continuous operation since 1942, but its financial statements have not previously been audited.

1. Assuming that Frank George & Co. was able to perform alternative auditing procedures to satisfactorily substantiate the buyers' cash working fund and purchases through the fund, identify and discuss the deficiencies in the auditor's report.
2. Assuming that Frank George & Co. was unable to satisfactorily substantiate the buyers' cash working fund and purchases through the fund by alternative auditing procedures, discuss the appropriateness of the opinion qualification proposed by Frank George & Co.'s report.
3. Discuss the potential consequences to the CPA of issuing a substandard report or failing to adhere in his or her examination to generally accepted auditing standards.

AICPA adapted

5-36. In prior years your client, Noches, Inc., a manufacturing company, has used an accelerated depreciation method for its depreciable assets for both federal income taxes and financial reporting. At the beginning of 1989 the corporation changed to the straight-line method for financial reporting. As a result, depreciation expense for the year was $200,000 less for financial reporting than for income tax reporting, an amount that you consider to be material. The corporation did not use interperiod income tax allocation in 1989. Taxable income for 1989 was $600,000. Assume that the income tax rate was 48 percent.

a. Financial statement presentation:

1. Describe the effects of the accounting change on Noches's 1989 balance sheet, income statement, and funds statement. Cite specific amounts in your answer.
2. Explain what disclosure of the accounting change should be made in Noches's 1989 financial statements.

b. Auditor's report:

1. Assuming that the financial statement disclosure is considered to be adequately informative, discuss the effects that the change in depreciation methods should have on the auditor's report.
2. Assuming that the financial statement disclosure of the change in depreciation methods is not considered to be adequately informative, discuss the effects on the auditor's report.

3. Discuss whether the auditor's report should indicate approval of the change in depreciation methods.
4. Discuss the effects on the auditor's report of the failure to use interperiod tax allocation.

AICPA adapted

5-37. The CPA must comply with the generally accepted auditing standards of reporting when preparing an opinion on the client's financial statements. One of the reporting standards relates to consistency.

a. Discuss the statement regarding consistency that the CPA is required to include in the opinion. What is the objective of requiring the CPA to make this statement about consistency?

b. Discuss what mention of consistency, if any, the CPA must make in the opinion relating to the CPA's first audit of the financial statements of the following companies:

1. A newly organized company ending its first accounting period.
2. A company established for a number of years.

c. Discuss whether the changes described in each of the cases below would require recognition in the CPA's opinion as to consistency. (Assume the amounts are material.)

1. The company disposed of one of its three subsidiaries that had been included in its consolidated statements for prior years.
2. After two years of computing depreciation under the declining-balance method for income tax purposes and under the straight-line method for reporting purposes, the declining-balance method was adopted for reporting purposes.
3. The estimated remaining useful life of plant property was reduced because of obsolescence.

AICPA adapted

5-38. Presented below are three independent, unrelated auditor's reports. The corporation being reported on, in each case, is profit oriented and publishes general-purpose financial statements for distribution to owners, creditors, potential investors, and the general public. Each of the following reports contains deficiencies.

For each auditor's report describe the reporting deficiencies, explain the reasons therefor, and briefly discuss how the report should be corrected. Each report should be considered separately. When discussing one report, ignore the other two. Do not discuss the addressee, signatures, and date. Also do not rewrite any of the auditor's reports.

Auditor's Report I

We have examined the consolidated balance sheet of Belasco Corporation and subsidiaries as of December 31, 1984, and the related consolidated statements of income and retained earnings and changes in financial position for the year then ended. Our examination was made in accordance with generally accepted auditing standards and accordingly included such tests of the accounting records and such other auditing procedures as we considered necessary in the circumstances. We did not examine the financial statements of Seidel Company, a major consolidated subsidiary. These statements were examined by other auditors whose report thereon has been furnished to us, and our opinion expressed herein, insofar as it relates to Seidel Company, is based solely upon the report of the other auditors.

In our opinion, except for the report of the other auditors, the accompanying consolidated balance sheet and consolidated statements of income and retained earnings and changes in financial position present fairly the financial position of Belasco Corporation and subsidiaries at December 31, 1984, and the results of its operations and the changes in its financial position for the year then ended, in conformity with generally accepted accounting principles applied on a basis consistent with that of the preceding year.

Auditor's Report II

The accompanying balance sheet of Jones Corporation as of December 31, 1984, and the related statements of income and retained earnings and changes in financial position for the year then ended were not audited by us; however, we confirmed cash in the bank and performed a general review of the statements.

During our engagement, nothing came to our attention to indicate that the aforementioned financial statements do not present fairly the financial position of Jones Corporation at December 31, 1984, and the results of the operations and the changes in its financial position for the year then ended, in conformity with generally accepted accounting principles applied on a basis consistent with that of the preceding year; however, we do not express an opinion on them.

Auditor's Report III

I made my examination in accordance with generally accepted auditing standards. However, I am not independent with respect to Mavis Corporation because my wife owns 5 percent of the outstanding common stock of the company. The accompanying balance sheet as of December 31, 1984, and the related statements of income and retained earnings and changes in financial position for the year then ended were not audited by me; accordingly, I do not express an opinion on them.

AICPA adapted

5-39. Charles Burke, CPA, has completed field work for his examination of the Willingham Corporation for the year ended December 31, 1984, and now is in the process of determining whether to modify his report. Presented below are two independent, unrelated situations that have arisen.

Situation I

In September 1984, a lawsuit was filed against Willingham to have the court order it to install pollution-control equipment in one of its older plants. Willingham's legal counsel has informed Burke that it is not possible to forecast the outcome of this litigation; however, Willingham's management has informed Burke that the cost of the pollution-control equipment is not economically feasible and that the plant will be closed if the case is lost. In addition, Burke has been told by management that the plant and its production equipment would have only minimal resale values and that the production that would be lost could not be recovered at other plants.

Situation II

During 1984, Willingham purchased a franchise amounting to 20 percent of its assets for the exclusive right to produce and sell a newly patented product in the northeastern United States. There has been no production in marketable quantities of the product anywhere to date. Neither the franchisor nor any franchisee has conducted any market research with respect to the product.

a. Discuss factors that Burke must consider in reaching his reporting decision.

b. Draft the report and the accompanying disclosure that you consider appropriate.

AICPA adapted

5-40. Various types of "accounting changes" can affect the second reporting standard of the generally accepted auditing standards. This standard reads "The report shall state whether such principles have been consistently observed in the current period in relation to the preceding period."

Assume that the following list describes changes which have a material effect on a client's financial statements for the current year.

1. A change from the completed-contract method to the percentage-of-completion method of accounting for long-term construction-type contracts.
2. A change in the estimated useful life of previously recorded fixed assets based on newly acquired information.
3. Correction of a mathematical error in inventory pricing made in a prior period.
4. A change from prime costing to full absorption costing for inventory valuation.
5. A change from presentation of statements of individual companies to presentation of consolidated statements.
6. A change from deferring and amortizing pre-production costs to recording such costs as an expense when incurred because future benefits of the costs have become doubtful. The new accounting method was adopted in recognition of the change in estimated future benefits.
7. A change to including the employer share of FICA taxes as "Retirement benefits" on the income statement from including it with "Other taxes."
8. A change from the FIFO method of inventory pricing to the LIFO method of inventory pricing.

Identify the type of change which is described in each item above, state whether any modification is required in the auditor's report *as it relates to the second standard of reporting,* and state whether the prior year's financial statements should be restated when presented in comparative form with the current year's statements. Organize your answer sheet as shown below.

For example a change from the LIFO method of inventory pricing to the FIFO method of inventory pricing would appear as shown.

Item no.	*Type of change*	*Should auditor's report be modified?*	*Should prior year's statements be restated?*
Example	An accounting change from one generally accepted accounting principle to another generally accepted accounting principle.	Yes	Yes

AICPA adapted

5-41. Upon completion of all field work on September 23, 1985, the following "short-form" report was rendered by Tom Radigan to the directors of The Maser Corporation.

To the Directors of
The Maser Corporation:

We have examined the balance sheet and the related statement of income and retained earnings of The Maser Corporation as of July 31, 1985. In accordance with your instructions, a complete audit was conducted.

In many respects, this was an unusual year for The Maser Corporation. The weakening of the economy in the early part of the year and the strike of plant employees in the summer of 1985 led to a decline in sales and net income. After making several tests of sales records, nothing came to our attention that would indicate that sales have not been properly recorded.

In our opinion, with the explanation given above, and with the exception of some minor errors that are considered immaterial, the aforementioned financial statements present fairly the financial position of The Maser Corporation at July 31, 1985, and the results of its operations for the year then ended, in conformity with pronouncements of the Accounting Principles Board and the Financial Accounting Standards Board applied consistently throughout the period.

Tom Radigan, CPA
September 23, 1985

List and explain deficiencies and omissions in the auditor's report. The type of opinion (unqualified, qualified, adverse, or disclaimer) is of no consequence and need not be discussed.

Organize your answer sheet by paragraph (scope, explanatory, and opinion) of the auditor's report.

AICPA adapted

5-42. J. Childs, CPA, has completed the examination of the financial statements of Straw Corporation as of and for the year ended December 31, 1985. J. Childs also examined and reported on the Straw financial statements for the prior year. J. Childs drafted the following report for 1985.

March 15, 1986

We have examined the balance sheet and statements of income and retained earnings of Straw Corporation as of December 31, 1985. Our examination was made in accordance with generally accepted accounting standards and accordingly included such tests of the accounting records as we considered necessary in the circumstances.

In our opinion, the above mentioned financial statements are accurately prepared and fairly presented in accordance with generally accepted accounting principles in effect at December 31, 1985.

J. Childs, CPA
(Signed)

Other Information:

1. Straw is presenting comparative financial statements.
2. Straw does not wish to present a statement of changes in financial position for either year.
3. During 1986 Straw changed its method of accounting for long-term construction contracts and properly reflected the effect of the change in the current year's financial statements and restated the prior year's statements. J. Childs is satisfied with Straw's justification for making the change. The change is discussed in footnote number 12.
4. J. Childs was unable to perform normal accounts receivable confirmation procedures but alternate procedures were used to satisfy Childs as to the validity of the receivables.
5. Straw Corporation is the defendant in a litigation, the outcome of which is highly uncertain. If the case is settled in favor of the plaintiff, Straw will be required to pay a substantial amount of cash which might require the sale of certain fixed assets. The litigation and the possible effects have been properly disclosed in footnote number 11.
6. Straw issued debentures on January 31, 1984, in the amount of $10 million. The funds obtained from the issuance were used to finance the expansion of plant facilities. The debenture agreement restricts the payment of future cash dividends to earnings after December 31, 1990. Straw declined to disclose this essential data in the footnotes to the financial statements.

Consider all facts given and rewrite the auditor's report in acceptable and complete format incorporating any necessary departures from the standard (short-form) report.

Do not discuss the draft of Childs's report but identify and explain any items included in "*Other Information*" that need not be part of the auditor's report.

AICPA adapted

6

Special Reporting Situations

Most of the reporting considerations discussed in Chapter 5 concern audit situations involving financial statements purporting to be prepared in accordance with generally accepted accounting principles. In many cases, however, auditors are asked to report on statements not intended to conform to generally accepted accounting principles; or the requested reports may relate to services other than audit examinations of complete financial statements. These and other special reporting situations are discussed in this chapter. The topics covered include the following:

1. Reports on financial statements prepared on a comprehensive basis of accounting other than generally accepted accounting principles. *SAS No. 14 (AU 621)*
2. Reports on specific elements, accounts, or items within a financial statement. *SAS No. 14 (AU 621)*
3. Reports on compliance with contractual agreements or regulatory requirements. *SAS No. 14 (AU 621)*
4. Reports on prescribed forms. *SAS No. 14 (AU 621)*
5. The informal report or constructive comment letter.
6. Reports on internal control. *SAS No. 1 (AU 640)*
7. Reports on compilation and review services. *Statement on Standards for Accounting and Review Services No. 1*
8. Reports on reviews of interim financial information. *SAS No. 24 (AU 721)*
9. Other information in documents containing audited financial statements. *SAS No. 8 (AU 550)*

10. Letters for underwriters. *SAS No. 1 (AU 630)*
11. Reports filed with the SEC.
12. Reporting changes suggested by the Cohen Commission.

Comprehensive bases of accounting other than generally accepted accounting principles

Departures from generally accepted accounting principles in audited financial statements usually require auditors to render qualified or adverse opinions. This reporting consequence is appropriate in cases of financial statements that users will assume to be prepared in accordance with generally accepted accounting principles. However, a qualified or adverse opinion seems unduly severe for reports on financial statements that are not intended to be so prepared. Because of this, a special reporting format is available for financial statements that are *prepared in accordance with a comprehensive basis of accounting other than generally accepted accounting principles.*

SAS No. 14 (AU 621.04) defines such a comprehensive basis as one to which at least one of the following descriptions applies:

a. A basis of accounting that the reporting entity uses to comply with the requirements or financial-reporting provisions of a government regulatory agency to whose jurisdiction the entity is subject.
b. A basis of accounting that the reporting entity uses or expects to use to file its income tax return for the period covered by the financial statements.
c. The cash receipts and disbursements basis of accounting and modifications of the cash basis having substantial support, such as recording depreciation on fixed assets or accruing income taxes.
d. A definite set of criteria having substantial support that is applied to all material items appearing in financial statements, such as the price-level basis of accounting described in Accounting Principles Board Statement No. 3.

When one of the foregoing descriptions applies to financial statements, the auditor may render a special report having the following characteristics:

1. A scope paragraph identifying the statements that were examined and stating whether the audit was performed in accordance with generally accepted auditing standards.
2. An explanatory paragraph that (a) explains, or preferably refers to a note that explains, the basis of presentation of the financial statements, (b) refers to a note that explains how the presentation of the financial

statements differs from generally accepted accounting principles, and (c) states that the financial statements are not intended to conform to generally accepted accounting principles.

3. An opinion paragraph that expresses the auditor's opinion or disclaimer as to whether the statements are fairly and consistently presented on the basis described.

It should be stressed that if the statements do not conform to at least one of the four general descriptions of a comprehensive basis of accounting other than generally accepted accounting principles, the special report described above cannot be used.

An example of a special report rendered on an audit of an entity that is preparing cash basis financial statements adapted from SAS No. 14 (AU 621) is presented in Figure 6-1. Notice that terms such as *Balance Sheet* and *Income Statement* are not used since these terms tend to imply generally accepted accounting principles.

Reports on specified elements, accounts, or items of a financial statement

Auditors may be engaged to render opinions on specific portions of financial statements. In performing such engagements, special consideration must be given to the concept of materiality, since in dealing with only an element of a financial statement, a much smaller error will be material than if the financial statements taken as a whole were being considered. This situation usually requires the auditor to gather more evidence with respect to the item being reported on than would be necessary if the item were being examined as part of a general audit.

The reporting requirements for such an engagement are specified in SAS No. 14 (AU 621.13) and include the following:

1. Identification of the specified elements, accounts, or items examined.
2. A statement as to whether the examination was made in accordance with generally accepted auditing standards and, if applicable, that it was made in conjunction with an examination of financial statements. (Also, if applicable, any modification of the auditor's standard report on those statements should be indicated.)
3. An explanation of the basis on which the specified elements, accounts, or items are presented and, when applicable, any agreements specifying such basis.
4. A description and indication of the source of any significant interpretations by the client of contracts or agreements relevant to the engagement.

Figure 6-1 Special Report on Cash Basis Financial Statements

To the Shareholders and Board of Directors of
Bonmot Corporation

We have examined the statement of assets and liabilities arising from cash transactions of Bonmot Corporation as of December 31, 1985, and the related statement of revenue collected and expenses paid for the year then ended. Our examination was made in accordance with generally accepted auditing standards and, accordingly, included such tests of the accounting records and such other auditing procedures as we considered necessary in the circumstances.

As described in Note 4, the Company's policy is to prepare its financial statements on the basis of cash receipts and disbursements; consequently, certain revenue and the related assets are recognized when received rather than when earned, and certain expenses are recognized when paid rather than when the obligation is incurred. Accordingly, the accompanying financial statements are not intended to present financial position and results of operations in conformity with generally accepted accounting principles.

In our opinion, the financial statements referred to above present fairly the assets and liabilities arising from cash transactions of Bonmot Corporation as of December 31, 1985, and the revenue collected and expenses paid during the year then ended, on the basis of accounting described in Note 4, which basis has been applied in a manner consistent with that of the preceding year.

Harris and Stephens
Certified Public Accountants

Atlanta, Georgia
February 3, 1986

5. An opinion as to whether the specified elements, accounts, or items are presented fairly on the basis indicated.
6. If applicable, an opinion as to whether the disclosed basis has been applied in a manner consistent with that of the preceding period.

Figure 6-2 illustrates an example adapted from SAS No. 14 (AU 621.14) of a special report on the examination of specific items on a financial statement.

Figure 6-2 Special Report on Specific Items on a Financial Statement

Board of Directors
Banjo Corporation

We have examined the schedule of royalties applicable to production of the Ink Division of Banjo Corporation for the year ended December 31, 1984, under the terms of a license agreement dated April 16, 1976, between ABC Company and Banjo Corporation. Our examination was made in accordance with generally accepted auditing standards and, accordingly, included such tests of the accounting records and such other auditing procedures as we considered necessary in the circumstances.

We have been informed that, under Banjo Corporation's interpretation of the agreement referred to above, royalties were based on the ink produced after giving effect to product returns. This treatment is consistent with that followed in prior years.

In our opinion, the schedule of royalties referred to above presents fairly the products produced by the Ink Division of Banjo Corporation during the year ended December 31, 1984, and the amount of royalties applicable thereto under the license agreement referred to above, on the basis indicated in the preceding paragraph.

Reports on compliance with contractual agreements or regulatory requirements

Another special report auditors are frequently engaged to render concerns client compliance with specified agreements or regulatory requirements. For example, a creditor may request assurance from an auditor that the client has conformed to various requirements of a debt agreement. A request like this is usually satisfied by the auditor in the form of negative assurance. This type of report may be rendered separately or as an additional paragraph or paragraphs of the auditor's report on the financial statements. Such a report, however, may not be rendered unless the auditor has audited the financial statements of the client, and the special report should refer to the audit of the related statements. Figure 6-3 presents an example of a special report rendered separately from the audit report on the financial statements.

Figure 6-3 Special Report on Compliance with Contractual Agreement

(Addressed to the intended recipient.)

We have examined the balance sheet of Pallone Corporation as of December 31, 1984, and the related statements of income, retained earnings, and changes in financial position for the year then ended, and have issued our report thereon dated March 2, 1985. Our examination was made in accordance with generally accepted auditing standards and, accordingly, included such tests of the accounting records and such other auditing procedures as we considered necessary in the circumstances.

In connection with our examination, nothing came to our attention that caused us to believe that Pallone Corporation was not in compliance with the requirements of Articles K through N, inclusive, of the Debt Agreement dated October 6, 1979 with Venice Life Insurance Company. However, it should be noted that our examination was not directed primarily toward obtaining knowledge of such noncompliance.

Reports on prescribed forms

In some cases regulatory bodies and other entities request financial information and auditor's reports on prescribed forms or schedules. Often such prescribed forms for auditor's reports are not in conformity with appropriate professional reporting standards. In such cases, the auditor should modify or completely revise the report form as necessary to comply with generally accepted auditing standards.

The informal report or constructive comment letter

Most of the audit reports discussed previously are formal expressions of an auditor's opinion on financial statements, rendered to clients and third parties. In addition to this opinion, auditors frequently render an informal report, or constructive comment letter. This report is flexible as to format and concerns matters that the auditor has noted in the course of the engagement and wishes to call to management's attention. Common subjects of this report are internal control and the accounting system. These reports are rendered as constructive services to the client and should suggest system and control improvements as well as indicate deficiencies. They provide excellent vehicles for pointing out matters that need the client's attention; they can also benefit the auditor by improving client relations. Many firms follow a policy of rendering a constructive comment letter on every audit, believing that this is a necessary part of their service to the client.

Although constructive comment letters are not required to be rendered, they may be used to satisfy an audit requirement regarding internal control weaknesses. SAS No. 20 (AU 323.01)

> establishes a requirement that the auditor communicate to senior management and the board of directors or its audit committee material weaknesses in internal accounting control that come to his attention during an examination of financial statements made in accordance with generally accepted auditing standards.

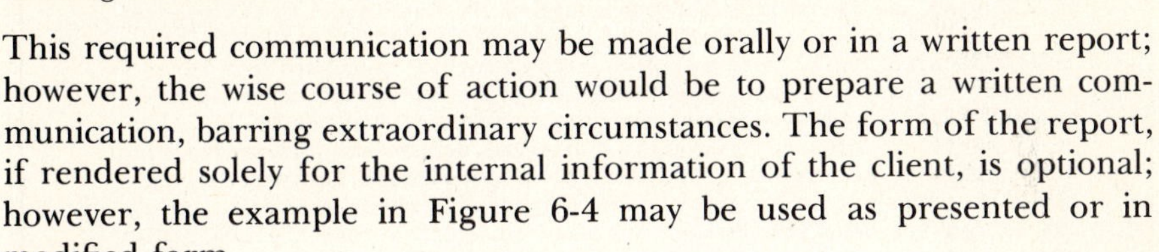
This required communication may be made orally or in a written report; however, the wise course of action would be to prepare a written communication, barring extraordinary circumstances. The form of the report, if rendered solely for the internal information of the client, is optional; however, the example in Figure 6-4 may be used as presented or in modified form.

Reports on internal control

Auditors are sometimes requested to render reports on their evaluation of the client's internal control. Such reports may be rendered to management, regulatory agencies, other independent auditors, or the general public. They may be based on the internal control evaluation performed as part of an audit examination or may result from an engagement to perform a *special study* in order to evaluate and report on internal control. Whether or not auditors are requested to furnish a report on internal control, they are required to communicate to the client any material weakness in internal control of which they are aware, in accordance with the preceding discussion.

An auditor should not render a report on internal control that is to be released to the general public if the report will be associated with unaudited financial statements. Such a report would be likely to mislead users into believing the financial statements were audited.

Form of the Report SAS No. 1 (AU 640.12) suggests a report form that is designed to minimize the risk that the report will be misunderstood by users. This is accomplished by describing in the report the objective and limitations of internal accounting control and the auditor's evaluation of it. Figure 6-4 represents an adaptation of the suggested report.

Figure 6-4 Report on Internal Control

(Addressed to the intended recipient.)

We have examined the financial statements of Meson Company for the year ended December 31, 1983, and have issued our report thereon dated February 23, 1984. As a part of our examination, we made a study and evaluation of the Company's system of internal accounting control to the extent we considered necessary to evaluate the system as required by generally accepted auditing standards. Under these standards, the purposes of such evaluation are to establish a basis for reliance on the system of internal accounting control in determining the nature, timing, and extent of other auditing procedures that are necessary for expressing an opinion on the financial statements and to assist the auditor in planning and performing the examination of the financial statements.

The objective of internal accounting control is to provide reasonable, but not absolute, assurance as to the safeguarding of assets against loss from unauthorized use or disposition, and the reliability of financial records for preparing financial statements and maintaining accountability for assets. The concept of reasonable assurance recognizes that the cost of a system of internal accounting control should not exceed the benefits derived and also recognizes that the evaluation of these factors necessarily requires estimates and judgments by management.

There are inherent limitations that should be recognized in considering the potential effectiveness of any system of internal accounting control. In the performance of most control procedures, errors can result from misunderstanding of instructions, mistakes of judgment, carelessness, or other personal factors. Control procedures whose effectiveness depends upon segregation of duties can be circumvented by collusion. Similarly, control procedures can be circumvented intentionally by management either with respect to the execution and recording of transactions or with respect to the estimates and judgments required in the preparation of financial statements. Further, projection of any evaluation of internal accounting control to future periods is subject to the risk that the procedures may become inadequate because of changes in conditions and that the degree of compliance with the procedures may deteriorate.

Our examination of the financial statements made in accordance with generally accepted auditing standards, including the study and evaluation of the Company's system of internal accounting control for the year ended December 31, 1983, that was made for the purposes set forth in the first paragraph of this report, would not necessarily disclose all weaknesses in the system because it was based on selective tests of accounting records and related data. However, such study and evaluation disclosed the following conditions that we believe to be material weaknesses. (A description of the material weaknesses that have come to the auditor's attention would follow.)

. . . .

The foregoing conditions were considered in determining the nature, timing, and extent of audit tests to be applied in our examination of the financial statements, and this report of such conditions does not modify our report dated February 23, 1984, on such financial statements.

Modifications of the Report Form There are a number of circumstances that may cause the auditor to modify the report form presented in Figure 6-4. For example, the auditor may want to include in the report recommendations for improvements in the system or corrective action with respect to the weaknesses. If the auditor found no weaknesses to be reported, the last sentence in the fourth paragraph should incorporate the word *no* in place of the phrase *the following.*

In cases where the report is rendered to other independent auditors or solely for the information of the client's management, the second and third paragraphs of the report, describing the objective and limitations of internal accounting control and the auditor's evaluation of it, may be omitted if considered unnecessary. In reports issued as a result of special studies of internal control, the first and fourth paragraphs of the report should be modified to reflect the purpose, scope, and limitations of the special study.

Compilation and review services for nonpublicly held entities

Many certified public accountants believe that the strict disclaimer procedures specified in Chapter 5 for situations in which auditors are associated with unaudited financial statements fail to serve adequately the needs of nonpublicly held entities and of those who prepare and use their financial statements. Often CPAs perform numerous verification procedures on financial statements; although they increase the reliability of the statements, they do not constitute an audit. Under the traditional requirements, the CPA must, in these cases, disclaim an opinion on such statements and refrain from referring to any verification procedures performed. In order to better meet the needs of users of unaudited financial statements of nonpublicly held entities, the AICPA has defined procedures and reporting standards for two levels of service that may be performed on unaudited financial statements. These services, *compilation of financial statements* and *review of financial statements,* lend assurance to financial statements, but they do not constitute an audit.

Compilation Services The AICPA's *Statement on Standards for Accounting and Review Services* No. 1, entitled "Compilation and Review of Financial Statements," defines compilation of financial statements as follows:

> To present in the form of financial statements information supplied by an entity without achieving any assurance as to whether there are material modifications that should be made to the statements in order for them to be in conformity with generally accepted accounting principles or, if applicable, with a comprehensive basis of accounting other than generally accepted accounting principles.

Standards that the CPA should adhere to in performing a compilation engagement, in addition to the general standards of the profession,[1] require the CPA to:

1. Obtain adequate knowledge of the accounting principles and practices of the industry in which the entity operates in order to be able to compile the financial statements appropriately.
2. Read the financial statements and consider whether they appear to be in proper form and free from obvious material errors.
3. If, during the compilation engagement, it becomes apparent that the information supplied by the client is incomplete, incorrect, or otherwise deficient, request that the client supply additional or revised information. If the client does not comply with the request, the CPA should withdraw from the engagement.
4. Include a reference to the CPA's report on each page of the compiled financial statements.

The report to be rendered on a compilation engagement should indicate (a) that a compilation service has been performed, (b) that all information in the statements is the representation of the client, and (c) the limitations of a compilation engagement. Figure 6-5 presents an appropriate report form adapted from the AICPA statement.

In some compilation engagements, the client may wish to omit some or all of the disclosures normally required. The CPA may compile the statements in this manner, provided the report clearly states that the disclosures are omitted and provided that the CPA is satisfied that the disclosures were not omitted in order to mislead users.

When entering into a compilation engagement, the CPA should obtain an appropriate engagement letter specifying the services to be performed and the report to be rendered. Engagement letters are discussed in Chapter 4.

A CPA may perform and report on a compilation engagement without being independent with respect to the client. In these situations, however, the CPA should indicate such lack of independence in the report.

Review Services The AICPA statement defines review of financial statements as follows:

> To achieve, through the performance of inquiry and analytical procedures, limited assurance that there are no material modifications that should be made to the statements in order for them to be in conformity with generally accepted accounting principles or, if applicable, with another comprehensive basis of accounting.

[1] From *Statements on Standards for Accounting and Review Services No. 1, "Compilation and Review of Financial Statements"* copyright © 1979 by the American Institute of Certified Public Accountants. The general standards of the profession, promulgated by the American Institute of Certified Public Accountants, apply to all major areas of accounting practice and are discussed in Chapter 3.

Figure 6-5 Report on Compilation Engagement

To the Shareholders and Board of Directors
of Ion, Incorporated

We have performed a compilation service in connection with the accompanying balance sheet of Ion, Incorporated as of December 31, 1983 and the related statements of income, retained earnings, and changes in financial position for the year then ended. All information included in these financial statements is the representation of the management of Ion, Incorporated.

Users of these financial statements should be aware that a compilation service is limited to the presentation in the form of financial statements of information supplied by management and that we have not achieved any assurance as to whether there are material modifications that should be made to the statements in order for them to be in conformity with generally accepted accounting principles.

Harris and Stephens
Certified Public Accountants

Atlanta, Georgia
January 23, 1984

Standards for the performance of a review service, in addition to the general standards of the profession, require the CPA to:

1. Obtain adequate knowledge of the accounting principles and practices of the industry in which the entity operates and an adequate understanding of the client's business in order to be able to perform the review procedures necessary to gain limited assurance that there are no material modifications that should be made to the financial statements.
2. Perform inquiry and analytical procedures consisting of the following:
   a. Inquiries concerning the accounting principles and practices of the client and the method of applying them.
   b. Inquiries concerning the client's procedures for processing accounting information.
   c. Analytical procedures designed to identify unusual items.
   d. Inquiries concerning proceedings of meetings of stockholders, board of directors, and so on.
   e. Reading the financial statements to consider reasonableness and conformity with appropriate accounting principles.

Figure 6-6 Report on Review Engagement

To the Shareholders and Board of Directors
of Bonnie Manufacturing Company

We have performed a review of the accompanying balance sheet of Bonnie Manufacturing Company as of December 31, 1982 and the related statements of income, retained earnings, and changes in financial position for the year then ended, in accordance with standards promulgated by the American Institute of Certified Public Accountants. All information included in these financial statements is the representation of the management of Bonnie Manufacturing Company.

A review consists of inquiries of Company personnel and analytical procedures applied to financial data. It is substantially less in scope than an examination in accordance with generally accepted auditing standards, the objective of which is the expression of an opinion regarding the financial statements taken as a whole. Accordingly we do not express such an opinion.

Based on our review, we are not aware of any material modifications that should be made to the accompanying financial statements in order for them to be in conformity with generally accepted accounting principles.

Harris and Stephens
Certified Public Accountants

Atlanta, Georgia
February 6, 1983

f. Inquiries of appropriate client officials and others regarding other relevant matters such as subsequent events, changes in accounting principles, and so on.

The CPA is not obligated to perform corroborative procedures to verify data. However, if the CPA believes that the data being reviewed are unsatisfactory, additional procedures will be necessary. The CPA should prepare appropriate working papers in connection with the review engagement and may wish to obtain a client representation letter, as well as an engagement letter.

The report accompanying a review engagement should state that a review service was performed in accordance with standards promulgated by the AICPA and that a review is substantially less in scope than an audit. The report should indicate too that all information in the statements is the representation of the client. The report then expresses, using negative assurance, that the CPA is not aware of any material modifications that should be made to the statements other than those, if any, indicated in the report. Each page of the financial statements should make reference to the report and the report should be dated as of the completion of the inquiry and analytical procedures. Figure 6-6 presents an example of a report on a review engagement adapted from the AICPA statement. A CPA may not issue a review report on the financial statements of an entity with respect to which he or she is not independent.

In reporting on either a compilation or a review service, CPAs must indicate any material departure from generally accepted accounting principles or other comprehensive basis of accounting that comes to their attention. If the departure is so material that the CPA believes that report disclosure is not adequate to inform users, then the accountant should withdraw from the engagement.

Reviews of interim financial information of publicly held entities

Auditors of publicly held entities frequently become associated with interim financial information of their clients. *Regulation S-X* of the Securities and Exchange Commission, which describes the appropriate form and content of financial statements filed with the commission, requires certain companies to disclose, in a note to the annual financial statements, selected interim financial data. This data may be designated "unaudited"; however, the auditor is deemed to be associated with the information since it is presented in conjunction with the audited financial statements. *Regulation S-X* further expresses the presumption that "appropriate professional standards and procedures with respect to the data in the note have been followed by the independent accountant who is associated with the unaudited footnote. . . ."

In addition, auditors may be engaged to review unaudited interim financial information of publicly held clients that is to be presented alone, such as in quarterly financial reports issued to stockholders, third parties, or the Securities and Exchange Commission.

SAS No. 24 prescribes appropriate procedures to be followed by the auditor in making reviews of unaudited interim data and provides examples of reports that may be issued.

Review Procedures The procedures prescribed in SAS No. 24 (AU 721.06) for reviews of interim financial information consist primarily of inquiries and analytical review procedures. These procedures are similar to those described in the previous discussion of review services for nonpublic companies; the primary differences are the requirement of a client representation letter and the incorporation of procedures specifically designed for interim financial statements. They are as follows:

a. Inquiry concerning (1) the accounting system, to obtain an understanding of the manner in which transactions are recorded, classified, and summarized in the preparation of interim financial information and (2) any significant changes in the system of internal accounting control, to ascertain their potential effect on the preparation of interim financial information.
b. Application of analytical review procedures to interim financial information to identify and provide a basis for inquiry about relationships and individual items that appear to be unusual. Analytical review procedures, for the purpose of this Statement, consist of (1) comparison of the financial information with comparable information for the immediately preceding interim period and for corresponding previous period(s), (2) comparison of the financial information with anticipated results, and (3) study of the relationships of elements of financial information that would be expected to conform to a predictable pattern based on the entity's experience. In applying these procedures, the accountant should consider the types of matters that in the preceding year or quarters have required accounting adjustments.
c. Reading the minutes of meetings of stockholders, board of directors, and committees of the board of directors to identify actions that may affect the interim financial information.
d. Reading the interim financial information to consider, on the basis of information coming to the accountant's attention, whether the information to be reported conforms with generally accepted accounting principles.
e. Obtaining reports from other accountants, if any, who have been engaged to make a review of the interim financial information of significant components of the reporting entity, its subsidiaries, or other investees.
f. Inquiry of officers and other executives having responsibility for financial and accounting matters concerning (1) whether the interim financial information has been prepared in conformity with generally accepted accounting principles consistently applied, (2) changes in the entity's business activities or accounting practices, (3) matters as to which questions have arisen in the course of applying the foregoing procedures, and (4) events subsequent to the date of the interim financial information that would have a material effect on the presentation of such information.
g. Obtaining written representations from management concerning its responsibility for the financial information, completeness of minutes, subsequent events, and other matters for which the accountant believes written representations are appropriate in the circumstances. . . .[2]

[2] Statements on this and the following page are from the *Statements on Auditing Standards* copyright © 1979 by the American Institute of Certified Public Accountants.

These procedures may be performed before the end of the interim period or at a later date and may be coordinated with the procedures performed as part of the annual audit. In addition, the auditor may determine the extent to which the procedures are applied based on knowledge of the client's internal accounting control, questions raised in the course of the review, and other considerations.

Form of Report Auditors are permitted to issue reports, based on performance of the specified review procedures, giving some assurance on interim financial information. The report may express negative assurance with respect to the interim information and should be dated as of the completion of the review. Each page of the interim financial information should be clearly marked "unaudited." The following requirements for the report are presented in SAS No. 24 (AU 721.17):

(a) a statement that the review of interim financial information was made in accordance with the standards for such reviews,
(b) an identification of the interim financial information reviewed,
(c) a description of the procedures for a review of interim financial information,
(d) a statement that a review of interim financial information is substantially less in scope than an examination in accordance with generally accepted auditing standards, the objective of which is an expression of opinion regarding the financial statements taken as a whole, and accordingly, no such opinion is expressed, and
(e) a statement about whether the accountant is aware of any material modifications that should be made to the accompanying financial information so that it conforms with generally accepted accounting principles.

Figure 6-7 presents an example of a report rendered on a quarterly financial statement. In cases where departures from generally accepted accounting principles are found, the report must be modified accordingly. When the auditor is associated with unaudited interim information presented in a footnote to audited financial statements, the standard audit report need not be modified unless the scope of the auditor's review of the interim information is restricted or if the interim information does not appear to conform to generally accepted accounting principles.

Other information in documents containing audited financial statements

Audited financial statements are commonly included in corporate annual reports and various other documents. These documents frequently include

Figure 6-7 Report on Review of Interim Financial Information

To the Shareholders and Board of Directors
of Rondo Corporation

We have made a review of the accompanying balance sheet of Rondo Corporation as of June 30, 1984 and 1983 and the related statements of income and retained earnings for the three-month and six-month periods then ended, in accordance with standards established by the American Institute of Certified Public Accountants.

A review of interim financial information consists principally of obtaining an understanding of the system for the preparation of interim financial information, applying analytical review procedures to financial data, and making inquiries of persons responsible for financial and accounting matters. It is substantially less in scope than an examination in accordance with generally accepted auditing standards, the objective of which is the expression of an opinion regarding the financial statements taken as a whole. Accordingly, we do not express such an opinion.

Based on our review, we are not aware of any material modifications that should be made to the accompanying financial statements for them to be in conformity with generally accepted accounting principles.

Harris and Stephens
Certified Public Accountants

Atlanta, Georgia
July 24, 1984

narrative and statistical data relating to the client and its operations, such as the president's letter to shareholders, financial highlights, and so on. Although the auditor's responsibilities do not extend beyond the financial information identified in the audit opinion, the auditor should read the other information in the document and consider if such information is inconsistent with information presented in the financial statements. If an inconsistency is found, the auditor should request that the inconsistent material be revised. If the client refuses to revise the information, the auditor must consider including an explanatory paragraph in the report, withholding the report, or withdrawing from the engagement. In cases of serious misstatement of fact in the other information and inability to resolve the matter with the client, the auditor should consider consulting legal counsel.

Letters for underwriters

As discussed in Chapter 4, underwriters of securities offerings usually request that auditors perform specified procedures and supply certain assurances with respect to audited and unaudited information contained in the registration statement. The auditor's response to such requests, commonly called a *comfort letter,* expresses negative assurance regarding certain matters of concern to the underwriter and provides other information. When supplying such a letter, the auditor normally attempts to provide the underwriter with the information and assurance requested while at the same time being careful not to extend audit responsibility beyond the intended limits. Since the procedures performed by the auditor to satisfy the underwriter's request do not constitute an audit, the degree of assurance that may be supplied is necessarily limited. In all cases, the auditor should prepare working papers to document the review procedures performed in order to substantiate that there existed a reasonable basis for the assurances supplied.

The contents of letters for underwriters will vary depending on the information requested and other matters. SAS No. 1 (AU 630) provides guidance to auditors rendering such letters and suggests the following matters as being typically covered:

a. A statement as to the independence of the accountants
b. An opinion as to whether the audited financial statements and schedules included in the registration statement comply as to form in all material respects with the applicable accounting requirements of the Act and the published rules and regulations thereunder
c. Negative assurances as to whether the unaudited financial statements and schedules included in the registration statement:
   (i) Comply as to form with the applicable accounting requirements of the Act and the published rules and regulations thereunder.
   (ii) Are fairly presented in conformity with generally accepted accounting principles on a basis substantially consistent with that of the audited financial statements and schedules included therein.
d. Negative assurances as to whether, during a specified period following the date of the latest financial statements in the registration statement and prospectus, there has been any change in capital stock or long-term debt or any decrease in other specified financial-statement items

In addition to the above items, the auditor is usually asked to provide assurance with respect to other information in the registration statement, such as statistics, tables, and other financial data.

Comfort letters are not required by federal securities laws and are not filed with the Securities and Exchange Commission. Due to the limited assurances contained in the letter, its contents would likely be misunderstood by the public, consequently, the letter itself should contain a statement limiting its use to the principal underwriter or other members of the underwriting group.

Reports filed with the SEC

Auditors frequently are involved with reports that the client must file with the Securities and Exchange Commission. The most commonly encountered of these reports are registration statements required to be filed in connection with the public offering of securities under the Securities Act of 1933 and the periodic reports required by the Securities Exchange Act of 1934. A brief description of several of these reports follows.

Registration Statements Registration statements (already mentioned in Chapter 4) must be filed in order to register securities that are offered for sale to the public. The most common registration statement form, Form S-1, is required for use by most commercial and industrial companies. Other statement forms, *Forms S-2* through *S-18,* are for use by companies in certain specialized industries and in other special circumstances. The registration statement is usually an extensive document containing narrative, statistical and financial data regarding the registrant. The audited financial statements required in Form S-1 include (1) the latest balance sheet of the company, (2) income statements for the latest three years, and (3) statements of changes in financial position for the latest three years. In addition, a five-year summary of operations, which is a form of condensed income statement, is required. This summary is not required to be audited but in most cases at least the latest three years will be covered by the auditor's opinion.

After filing a registration statement with the Securities and Exchange Commission, a waiting period follows during which the statement is reviewed by the SEC staff. Frequently, *letters of comment* are received by the prospective issuer from the SEC raising accounting questions and suggesting modifications with respect to the registration statement as originally filed. When any deficiencies in the registration statement are corrected and the SEC staff is satisfied that the document conforms to all requirements of the law, the registration statement is declared effective. As noted in Chapter 5, the *effective date* of the registration statement marks the end of the auditor's active responsibility for subsequent events. The effective date also marks the earliest date that the securities may be sold.

A prospectus is a brochure containing much of the same information included in the registration statement. Each buyer of the securities must be offered a prospectus describing the security in order to fulfill the requirements of the Securities Act of 1933. A final prospectus may not be distributed until the effective date of the registration statement; however, prior to that time a preliminary prospectus, termed a *red herring,* may be issued to provide information about the forthcoming securities.

Periodic Reports The Securities Exchange Act of 1934 imposes extensive periodic reporting requirements on registered companies. One distinction which may be drawn between the 1933 and 1934 acts is that under the 1933 act, a specific transaction, that is, a sale of securities, is registered. Under the 1934 act, a class of securities is registered, and the requirements of the act with respect to this class of securities continues indefinitely.

The following periodic reports are those most commonly encountered under the 1934 act:

Form 10-K. This is an annual report form required to be filed by most commercial and industrial registrants. Form 10-K requires, with certain exceptions, audited financial statements paralleling those required by Form S-1.

Form 10-Q. This is the quarterly report required to be filed by all registrants who file annual reports. A 10-Q must be filed for the first three quarters of each fiscal year. Form 10-Q is not required to be audited; however, auditors' reports issued on reviews of the registrant's interim financial statements may be submitted with the 10-Q.

Form 8-K. This report is required to be filed after the occurrence of a *material event.* Examples of events required to be reported on Form 8-K include:

1. change in control of the registrant,
2. acquisition or disposition of significant amounts of assets not in the normal course of business,
3. bankruptcy of the registrant,
4. change of the registrant's auditor.

Form 8-K does not require audited information; however, in cases of change of the registrant's auditor, a letter from the predecessor auditor stating agreement with statements made by the registrant in Form 8-K is required to be transmitted to the SEC along with the 8-K itself.

Proxy Statements. The final report to be discussed that is required under the 1934 act is the proxy statement. This statement is required to be given to shareholders at the time a proxy request is made. *Proxies,* which are authorizations given by shareholders directing someone to cast their votes at shareholders' meetings, are normally solicited prior to the meetings. Proxy statements usually do not contain financial statements since the corporate annual reports are normally distributed prior to the proxy request. In certain situations, however, audited financial statements are required. Material included in the proxy statement usually consists of narrative data with respect to election of directors, remuneration of directors and officers, relations with independent auditors, and other matters. Preliminary copies of proxy materials must be submitted to the SEC at least ten days prior to mailing to shareholders.

In addition to requiring the reports discussed above, the Securities and Exchange Commission exercises significant influence over the form and content of registrants' annual reports to shareholders. Although the annual report is not *filed* with the SEC, a copy must be sent to the commission. The SEC currently requires several specific disclosures in registrants' annual reports to shareholders, and because of these and other requirements, a growing similarity can be noted between shareholder reports and Form 10-K.

Proposed Revision of Forms An advisory committee to the SEC has proposed that a new reporting form, Form CD (for continuous disclosure), be adopted, which would replace all the current registration statement forms as well as all the periodic reporting forms. This new form is intended to reduce some duplication in the existing forms, but it would not change the basic requirements pertaining to the information to be disclosed. As of this writing the proposal is still under consideration.

Reporting changes suggested by the Cohen commission

The Commission on Auditors' Responsibilities, discussed in Chapter 1, has made numerous recommendations on a wide variety of topics related to auditing. The following are several recommendations of the commission that relate to the auditor's reporting function:

1. Elimination of the phrase "present fairly" from the report.
2. Elimination of the "subject to" qualified opinion in cases of financial statements affected by material uncertainties.
3. Expanded reporting on internal control.
4. Adoption of a more flexible reporting format containing more explicit phraseology.
5. Elimination of the reference to consistency.
6. Elimination of the reference to other auditors when they perform part of the examination.
7. Rendering a report in all cases where the auditor is associated with unaudited financial statements.
8. Inclusion of a report by management in addition to the auditor's report.

These and other recommendations of the commission deserve serious consideration as the auditing profession progresses and matures. The work of the Commission on Auditors' Responsibilities represents one of many responses of the accounting profession to the increased public awareness of the audit function.

Figures 6-8 and 6-9 present examples of the Report of Independent Auditors and the Report by Management that appear in the *Report, Conclusions and Recommendations* of the Commission on Auditors' Responsibilities.

Figure 6-8 Example of Report of Independent Auditors Suggested by the Commission on Auditors' Responsibilities (*Copyright © 1978 The Commission on Auditors' Responsibilities.*)

Report of Independent Auditors

Financial Statements

The accompanying consolidated balance sheet of XYZ Company as of December 31, 1976, and the related statements of consolidated income and changes in consolidated financial position for the year then ended, including the notes, are the representations of XYZ Company's management, as explained in the report by management.

In our opinion, those financial statements in all material respects present the financial position of XYZ Company at December 31, 1976, and the results of its operations and changes in financial position for the year then ended in conformity with generally accepted accounting principles appropriate in the circumstances.

We audited the financial statements and the accounting records supporting them in accordance with generally accepted auditing standards. Our audit included a study and evaluation of the company's accounting system and the related controls, tests of details of selected balances and transactions, and an analytical review of the information presented in the statements. We believe our auditing procedures were adequate in the circumstances to support our opinion.

Other Financial Information

We reviewed the information appearing in the annual report (or other document) in addition to the financial statements, and found nothing inconsistent in such other information with the statements or the knowledge obtained in the course of our audits. (Any other information reviewed, such as replacement cost data, would be identified.)

We reviewed the interim information released during the year. Our reviews were conducted each quarter (or times as explained) and consisted primarily of making appropriate inquiries to obtain knowledge of the internal accounting control system, the process followed in preparing such information and of financial and operating developments during the periods, and determining that the information appeared reasonable in the light of the knowledge we obtained from our inquiries during the current year, from any procedures completed to the interim date in connection with our audit for such year, and from our audits for preceding years. Any adjustments or additional disclosures we recommended have been reflected in the information.

Internal Accounting Controls

Based on our study and evaluation of the accounting system and related controls, we concur with the description of the system and controls in the report by management (or, Based on our study and evaluation of the accounting system and controls over it, we believe the system and controls have the following uncorrected material weaknesses not described in the report by management...) (or other disagreements with the description of the system and controls in the report by management) (or a description of uncorrected material weaknesses found if there is no report by management) Nevertheless, in the performance of most control procedures, errors can result from personal factors, and also, control procedures can be circumvented by collusion or overridden. Projection of any evaluation of internal accounting control to future periods is subject to the risk that changes in conditions may cause procedures to become inadequate and the degree of compliance with them to deteriorate.

Other Matters

We reviewed the company's policy statement on employee conduct, described in the report by management, and reviewed and tested the related controls and internal audit procedures. While no controls or procedures can prevent or detect all individual misconduct, we believe the controls and internal audit procedures have been appropriately designed and applied during the year.

We met with the audit committee (or the board of directors) of XYZ Company as often as we thought necessary to inform it of the scope of our audit and to discuss any significant accounting or auditing problems encountered and any other services provided to the company (or indication of failure to meet or insufficient meetings or failure to discuss pertinent problems).

Test Check & Co.
Certified Public Accountants

Figure 6-9 Example of Report by Management Suggested by the Commission on Auditors' Responsibilities *(Copyright © 1978 The Commission on Auditors' Responsibilities.)*

<u>Report by Management</u>

Financial Statements

We prepared the accompanying consolidated balance sheet of XYZ Company as of December 31, 1976, and the related statements of consolidated income and changes in consolidated financial position for the year then ended, including the notes (or, (the named statements) have been prepared on our behalf by our independent auditor from the company's records and other relevant sources.). The statements have been prepared in conformity with generally accepted accounting principles appropriate in the circumstances, and necessarily include some amounts that are based on our best estimates and judgments. The financial information in the remainder of this annual report (or other document) is consistent with that in the financial statements.

Internal Accounting Controls

The company maintains an accounting system and related controls to provide reasonable assurance that assets are safeguarded against loss from unauthorized use or disposition and that financial records are reliable for preparing financial statements and maintaining accountability for assets. There are inherent limitations that should be recognized in considering the potential effectiveness of any system of internal accounting control. The concept of reasonable assurance is based on the recognition that the cost of a system of internal control should not exceed the benefits derived and that the evaluation of those factors requires estimates and judgments by management. The company's system provides such reasonable assurance. We have corrected all material weaknesses of the accounting and control systems identified by our independent auditors, Test Check & Co., Certified Public Accountants (or, We are in the process of correcting all material weaknesses...) (or, We have corrected some of the material weaknesses but have not corrected others because....).

Other Matters

The functioning of the accounting system and related controls is under the general oversight of the board of directors (or the audit committee of the board of directors). The members of the audit committee are associated with the company only through being directors. The accounting system and related controls are reviewed by an extensive program of internal audits and by the company's independent auditors. The audit committee (or the board of directors) meets regularly with the internal auditors and the independent auditors and reviews and approves their fee arrangements, the scope and timing of their audits, and their findings.

We believe that the company's position in regard to litigation, claims and assessments is appropriately accounted for or disclosed in the financial statements. In this connection we have consulted with our legal counsel concerned with such matters and they concur with the presentation of the position.

The company has prepared and distributed to its employees a statement of its policies prohibiting certain activities deemed illegal, unethical, or against the best interests of the company. (The statement was included in the 197X annual report of the company; copies are available on request.) In consultation with our independent auditors we have developed and instituted additional internal controls and internal audit procedures designed to prevent or detect violations of those policies. We believe that the policies and procedures provide reasonable assurance that our operations are conducted in conformity with the law and with a high standard of business conduct.

(If applicable, During the past year our independent auditors provided the company with certain non-audit services. They advised us in the preparation of (or, if applicable, They prepared) the company's income tax return; they assisted in the design and installation of a new inventory control system; and they performed the actuarial computations in connection with the company's pension plan.)

(If applicable, The board of directors of the company in March, 1976 engaged Super, Sede & Co., Certified Public Accountants, as our independent auditors to replace Test Check & Co., following disagreements on (accounting principles, disclosures, or the scope of the examination). Test Check & Co. agrees with that description of disagreements.)

I. M. True
Chief Financial Officer

Supplementary readings

Commission on Auditors' Responsibilities. *Report, Conclusions and Recommendations.* New York: Commission on Auditors' Responsibilities, 1978.

Dillard, Jesse F., Richard J. Murdock, and John K. Shank. "CPAs' Attitudes Toward 'Subject To' Opinions." *CPA Journal* (August 1978), 43-47.

Foster, Taylor W., III, and Don Vickery. "The Incremental Information Content of the 10-K." *Accounting Review* (October 1978), 921-934.

Gregory, William R. "Unaudited, But OK?" *Journal of Accountancy* (February 1978), 61-65.

Reiss, Harry F., Jr. "Letters for Underwriters." *CPA Journal* (December 1971), 935-937.

Wade, Allison. "Launching a Stock Registration—A Joint Accountant-Attorney Effort to Lead the Client Through the Maze." *CPA Journal* (April 1972), 279-287; (May 1972), 399-402.

Review questions

6-1. What is a "comprehensive basis of accounting other than generally accepted accounting principles"?

6-2. How should the auditor report on financial statements prepared on a "comprehensive basis of accounting other than generally accepted accounting principles"?

6-3. How should the auditor report on financial statements that are not in accordance with generally accepted accounting principles and not in accordance with a "comprehensive basis of accounting other than generally accepted accounting principles"?

6-4. What are the requirements for audit reports on specified elements, accounts, or items of a financial statement?

6-5. How is the concept of materiality related to a report on a specified account on a financial statement?

6-6. May an auditor render a report on a client's compliance with a contractual agreement?

6-7. What is a report on a prescribed form?

6-8. What is the purpose of the informal report or constructive comment letter?

6-9. Are constructive comment letters required to be rendered?

6-10. What is required of an auditor when material weaknesses in internal accounting control are found?

6-11. To whom may the auditor be called upon to render reports on internal control?

6-12. Under what circumstances should an auditor not render a report on internal control that will be released to the general public?

6-13. What is a compilation service?

6-14. What is a review service?

6-15. What specific standards should a CPA adhere to when performing a compilation engagement?

6-16. May a CPA perform and report on a compilation engagement without being independent with respect to the client?

6-17. May a CPA perform and report on a review engagement without being independent with respect to the client?

6-18. What inquiry and analytical procedures should be performed in connection with a review engagement?
6-19. May an auditor render a report expressing assurance with respect to a review of unaudited interim financial information?
6-20. What are the requirements for a report on a review of unaudited interim financial information?
6-21. What responsibility does the auditor have regarding other information in documents containing audited financial statements?
6-22. What is a comfort letter and to whom is it rendered?
6-23. Why are comfort letters not released to the public?
6-24. What is a registration statement?
6-25. Of what importance is the effective date of a registration statement?
6-26. What is a prospectus?
6-27. What is the purpose of the proxy statement?
6-28. What federal securities act requires Form 10-K?
6-29. What is Form 8-K?
6-30. What are some reporting recommendations made by the Commission on Auditors' Responsibilities?

Decision problems

6-31. Ron Levy, CPA, has completed the audit of Rex Rentals, Inc., which rents various types of equipment to both industrial and individual customers. Except in recording the acquisition, disposal, and depreciation of its rental equipment, Rex prepares its financial statements on the cash receipts and disbursements basis. Levy has determined that material amounts of assets, liabilities, revenues, and expenses, which would have been recognized on the accrual basis, are not reflected on Rex's statements.

a. Assuming that Levy desires to render an unqualified opinion on Rex Rentals, Inc., draft the report that he should render for the current year.

b. Using assumed figures as necessary, prepare a footnote which, in your judgment, adequately explains Rex's accounting methods.

6-32. Your client, Reliable Electronics Corporation, has secured a long-term loan from The Industrial Life Insurance Company. After completing the audit and rendering an unqualified opinion on the Reliable Electronics financial statements, you are asked to render a separate report regarding Reliable's compliance with the provisions of the long-term loan agreement. This report will be submitted by your client to Industrial Life.

a. Draft a report to illustrate the appropriate format you should use for the separate report.

b. Under what circumstances should you not render such a report?

6-33. Jane Archer, CPA, in the course of her audit of Dunhill Wholesalers, Inc., discovers that the controller of the corporation has access to receipts from customers and has sole responsibility for bad debt write-offs, in addition to having the usual duties of a controller. Jane is able to gather adequate audit evidence and renders an unqualified opinion on the current year's financial statements.

a. Does this appear to be a material internal control weakness? Explain your reasoning for your answer.

b. Is Jane required to take any special action in the situation?

c. Assuming you concluded this was a material weakness, draft a report to Dunhill's management that you believe would be appropriate in the circumstances.

6-34. You have performed a compilation engagement involving the financial statements of a client corporation owned by your spouse. You have observed all the specific standards for compilation engagements promulgated by the AICPA.

a. Draft an appropriate report for this compilation engagement.

b. What changes would be necessary if this were a review engagement?

6-35. You have been engaged by your audit client, Monmouth Motors Corporation, to review the quarterly financial statements of the corporation prior to their being released to the public. You have performed similar reviews of interim financial statements for each of the past three years in addition to performing the annual audit. You have no reservations as to the fairness of the current quarter's statements nor have you had reservations regarding the statements of previous periods. Although you have not examined the interim financial statements in accordance with generally accepted auditing standards, you have adhered to the standard prescribed for interim reviews.

a. Draft a report on your review of the comparative financial statements for the quarters ending September 30, of the current and preceding years.

b. Comment on the degree of assurance this report conveys to the reader.

6-36. *a.* Evaluate the conventional audit report in light of the suggestions made by the Commission on Auditors' Responsibilities. In your discussion comment on the impact of each of the commission's suggestions given in the chapter as well as the overall effect of the suggestions on auditors' reports.

b. Do you believe that implementing the suggestions would have an effect on auditors' legal liability? On managements' responsibility regarding the financial statements? On the public's perception of the auditor's role?

6-37. The major result of a financial audit conducted by an independent accountant is the expression of an opinion by the auditor on the fairness of the financial statements. Although the auditor's report containing the opinion is the best known report issued by the independent auditor, other reports are often prepared during the course of a normal audit. One such report is the informal report or constructive comment letter.

a. What is the purpose of an informal report or constructive comment letter?

b. Identify the major types of information that are likely to be covered in such a letter.

CMA adapted

II

Techniques for Audit Decisions

Chapters 7 through 10 present several fundamental considerations that require an auditor's attention. These topics are somewhat broader than those commonly considered *procedures* and represent decision factors that underlie and direct much of auditors' detailed work.

In addition Chapter 11, the final chapter in Part II, describes certain auditing and reporting considerations that represent variations or extensions of conventional audit practice.

7

Internal Controls—Design and Review

More than any other single factor, internal control influences the nature of an audit conducted by either an internal auditor or an independent public accountant. The internal auditor's examination is principally concerned with a review of internal control to determine if management's directives are properly communicated and followed and if the reports flowing to management are accurate, timely, and complete with the necessary information to form the basis for managerial decisions. The review of internal control by an independent public accountant, as required by the second auditing standard regarding field work, is primarily designed to determine the reliability of the accounts and financial statements produced by the accounting system and to determine the extent of the other auditing procedures that must be followed in the conduct of the audit examination. Also, the review of internal control serves as the basis for: formal reports on the auditor's evaluation of the internal accounting control system; comments by the auditor on management's evaluation of the control system; and the auditor's constructive comment letter containing recommendations for improving the system.

Section One of this chapter discusses the design of an effective internal control system that the auditor must evaluate and rely upon. Section Two discusses the auditor's review of the system.

Section One—Design of the internal control system

Internal control defined

Internal control is the system within a company consisting of its plan of organization, the assignment of duties and responsibilities, the design of accounts and reports, and all measures and methods employed (1) to protect its assets, (2) to encourage the accuracy and reliability of accounting and other operating data and reports, (3) to promote and judge the operational efficiency of all aspects of the company's activities, and (4) to communicate managerial policies and to encourage and measure compliance therewith. A company's internal control system can be compared to a person's nervous system. It embraces the entire organization, serves as a two-way communication system, and is uniquely designed to meet the needs of the specific company. It includes much more than the accounting system, covering such things as employment and training practices, quality control, production planning, sales policies, and internal auditing.

Administrative and accounting controls

Internal controls are grouped in two categories, administrative and accounting. *Administrative controls* are procedures and methods that pertain primarily to the operations of an enterprise and to managerial directives, policies, and reports. Administrative controls relate only indirectly to financial statements. An administrative control is illustrated by the company requirement that all employees have an annual medical examination, or the company policy that no charge be made for delivery of merchandise within a one hundred-mile radius of the warehouse. The internal auditor may be concerned with the reasonableness of such policies, the relationship of the cost of carrying them out in comparison with the benefits, and the extent to which they are being implemented. An internal auditor may recommend that certain administrative controls be modified, replaced, or eliminated. In a typical audit situation, an independent public accountant would not make any investigation into administrative controls. However, nothing prevents an independent auditor from investigating administrative controls to the extent judged necessary.

Administrative control is described in SAS No. 1 (AU 320.27) as follows:

> Administrative control includes, but is not limited to, the plan of organization and the procedures and records that are concerned with the decision processes leading to management's authorization of transactions. Such authorization is a management function directly associated with the responsibility for achieving the objectives of the organization and is the starting point for establishing accounting control of transactions.

Internal accounting control consists of the methods, procedures, and plan of organization that pertain mainly to protection of the assets and to assurance that the accounts and financial reports are reliable. Independent auditors are concerned with such controls in order to determine the degree of reliance they can place on them to support the fairness of property, plant, and equipment shown on the balance sheet, to determine to what extent they should perform audit procedures regarding these assets and related accounts, and also to determine whether they should make any recommendations to the client concerning controls in this area.

Accounting control is described in SAS No. 1 (AU 320.28) as follows:

> Accounting control comprises the plan of organization and the procedures and records that are concerned with the safeguarding of assets and the reliability of financial records and consequently are designed to provide reasonable assurance that:
>
> *a.* Transactions are executed in accordance with management's general or specific authorization.
>
> *b.* Transactions are recorded as necessary (1) to permit preparation of financial statements in conformity with generally accepted accounting principles or any other criteria applicable to such statements and (2) to maintain accountability for assets.
>
> *c.* Access to assets is permitted only in accordance with management's authorization.
>
> *d.* The recorded accountability for assets is compared with the existing assets at reasonable intervals and appropriate action is taken with respect to any differences.

Responsibility for the internal accounting control system

To fulfill the financial reporting objective of providing information that is useful to investors and creditors in making rational economic decisions, management has the responsibility of designing and maintaining an internal accounting control system that produces reliable and timely financial information. Important aspects of this management function are monitoring the system for material weaknesses and taking corrective action. Weaknesses in the control system may be discovered at times by members of the management team or other company personnel, especially the internal auditor. Management also relies upon the independent auditor to notify it of weaknesses in the design or functioning of the system that are discovered during the auditor's examination. As pointed out in SAS No. 20 (AU 323.04), the independent auditor is required to report to senior management and to the board of directors or its audit committee any material weaknesses discovered during the audit.

There are limitations, however, to an auditor's responsibility for reporting weaknesses. Management and other users of audited financial statements should be aware that the auditor's review of internal accounting controls is primarily for the purposes of establishing reliance thereon and of determining the extent of other auditing procedures. There is no requirement that the auditor evaluate each control or identify all material weaknesses. In certain areas of the examination, the auditor may be able to determine the extent of the auditing procedures without relying on the specific internal controls in those areas. This condition arises when the time and effort needed for testing compliance with the controls would be greater than the time and effort required for performing extended auditing procedures using methods other than reliance on the controls. Since the audit is based on the concept of testing and consequently many items are not selected for examination, there is always the possibility that some material weaknesses may exist in the system and yet go undetected by the auditor. In the exercise of due professional care, however, an auditor must be alert throughout all phases of the audit for discovery of weaknesses in the accounting control system.

An auditor may decide to forgo reviewing internal accounting controls in certain areas that are not necessary for expression of an opinion on the financial statements taken as a whole. The client, however, may request a review in any area where such a review is important for purposes of management control, or in order to ensure that certain legal requirements are being met, such as provisions of the Foreign Corrupt Practices Act. For example, the auditor may have decided that the examination of a particular subsidiary is not necessary to express an opinion on the consolidated financial statements, but the client's audit committee may know of problems within the subsidiary's operations and want to expand the audit to include an examination of that subsidiary. The auditor should be willing to expand (but not to restrict) the scope of the examination to accommodate wishes of the client.

Although an independent auditor may advise management on the initial design of the internal accounting control system, may identify material weaknesses in the system, and may offer recommendations for revisions of the system, the responsibility for good internal control clearly rests with management. Regarding procedures of both administrative control and accounting control, management should be alert to the fact that changed conditions may make the original system no longer applicable. Thus, the system should be reviewed frequently to determine the appropriateness of each procedure. Also, constant review is necessary for assurance that personnel are performing duties as required by the internal control system.

In the initial design of an internal control system and in any subsequent revisions, both management and auditors should be conscious of the *cost-benefit concept,* which states that the costs of an internal control procedure should not exceed the expected benefits. Such a relationship is illustrated in Figure 7-1, which reflects the increasing costs of a greater degree of internal control and the resulting decline in costs resulting from theft, waste, and various inefficiencies. Admittedly, the benefits of a control that encourages adherence to management's directives or prevents the theft of some unknown amount of assets do not lend themselves to exact measurement. The total costs incurred in establishing and maintaining many internal controls are difficult, if not impossible, to determine. Subjective judgment must be used in reaching decisions about which internal control procedures are desirable and at what point the optimal expenditures have been incurred for internal controls. For instance, there is no justification of a control procedure that necessitates the employment of an additional employee at a salary of $12,000 annually when the only benefit is to prevent theft of shipping supplies that cost $9,000 annually. But usually control decisions do not have such obvious solutions.

Principles of internal accounting control

Each company's internal accounting control system is designed to meet the needs of its specific organizational, operational, and managerial goals;

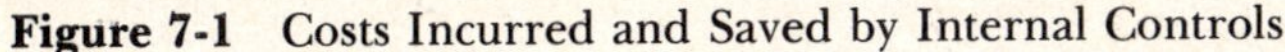

Figure 7-1 Costs Incurred and Saved by Internal Controls

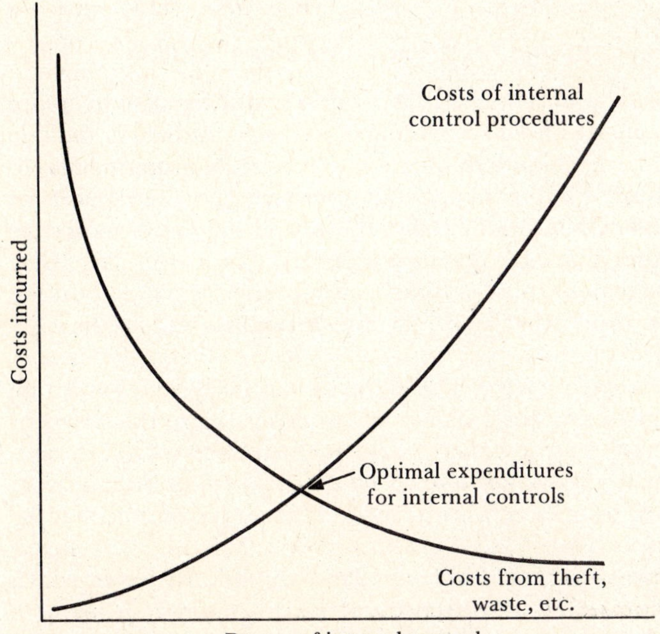

however, certain general principles are normally followed. The principles discussed in the following sections are: the control environment; authorization, accounting, and asset protection; the plan of organization; quality and training of personnel; system documentation; proofs of accuracy; and the internal auditing function. The more specific features and applications of internal control are discussed in later chapters as they relate to audit of accounts, transactions, and accounting cycles.

INTERNAL ACCOUNTING CONTROL ENVIRONMENT

When management maintains a business environment that emphasizes an appropriate level of control consciousness, a company is likely to have an effective internal control system. The internal control environment is reflected by management's policies that have control implications. Examples of such policies are: (1) a well-publicized statement on corporate conduct; (2) enforcement of corporate policies; (3) tight budgetary controls; (4) support of an effective internal auditing function; and (5) practices for hiring personnel with competence and integrity. Top management, the board of directors, and its audit committee are all influential in creating an appropriate internal control environment through effective organizational structure, sound management practices, adherence to appropriate standards of ethical conduct, and compliance with applicable laws and regulations. Management may achieve increased understanding and acceptance of these practices if they are expressed as written policies and procedures.

AUTHORIZATION, ACCOUNTABILITY, AND ASSET PROTECTION

An effective internal accounting control system contains features to assure the execution of transactions in accordance with management's desires. The accounting records should be maintained in such a manner as to establish accountability for the assets and to permit the preparation of proper financial statements. Additionally, the use of the assets should be restricted to purposes that management intended. To accomplish these desired goals, management must establish within the internal accounting control system various points at which its authorization is required.

General and Specific Authorization The ultimate authority in a corporate organization belongs to the stockholders and is delegated to the board of directors, officers, and other members of the management team. Management, in turn, delegates its authority to specific individuals or departments by authorizing them to take certain actions. This authorization may be general or specific.

General authorization establishes the standard conditions under which transactions are approved. Authorization relates to the identification of the general conditions to be met, whereas approval relates to a specific transaction meeting the conditions established in the general authorization. For example, management authorizes that credit be extended to customers who meet certain criteria. When a customer meeting these criteria applies for credit, the application is approved according to the general authorization.

Specific authorization embodies both the exact conditions and the particular individuals involved. The board of directors, in deciding to borrow $4.5 million from a particular financial institution, is granting specific authorization for such a transaction. In contrast, it is general authorization that extends to the purchasing department the right to obligate the company up to a maximum of $30,000 from a single vendor for regular operating supplies.

Execution of Transactions The term *transaction* refers both to (1) the exchange of assets and services between company and outside parties and (2) the transfer and use of assets and services internally within the company. The internal accounting control system should be designed so that each transaction executed is properly authorized, either generally or specifically. There usually should be some evidence to prove that the person approving the transaction is acting within authority. At times evidence that transactions are being executed as authorized may be available only by observing the transaction take place. If a purchase order is supposed to be placed only after obtaining three price quotations by telephone, observation is essential to determine that the proper authorization procedures are being followed.

Recording of Transactions The system of internal accounting controls should provide for the recording of transactions at the proper amount, in the proper account, and in the period in which the transaction occurred. The prompt recording of cash, marketable securities, and other items highly susceptible to errors and irregularities is extremely important. Once an initial record is made of a transaction, the risk of defalcation is reduced. Although the proper recording of transactions does not assure the preparation of fair financial statements, it is indispensable if such statements are to result. The use of prenumbered documents is a valuable aid in establishing that all transactions have been recorded. Of course, the use of prenumbered documents is of no value in itself; the value lies in accounting for all numbers and in explaining any missing documents.

Access to Assets A company owns assets for use in its business, and the success of the business is closely related to efficient use of the assets. The accounting control system should limit the use of the assets to purposes authorized by management. In safeguarding the assets, access to them should be limited to authorized personnel only. Access includes physical contact with the assets as well as indirect access through the authority to authorize their use and disposition. Limitation of physical access to assets may take such form as the supply of repair parts being kept in locked bins. Limitation of indirect access may be effected through the division of duties and well-defined requisition and authorization procedures.

Periodically a comparison should be made of the records and the physical assets actually on hand. Investigation of the causes of any differences may reveal weaknesses in the internal accounting control system either as it is designed or as it functions. Corrective action should be taken to rectify any weakness in the system, and of course the records should be adjusted to reflect the existing assets.

PLAN OF ORGANIZATION

A cardinal principle of internal accounting control is that there be a plan of organization to establish clearly the responsibility for the performance of all functions. When a person or department is given the responsibility for a particular function, the commensurate authority to act in that area must also be extended. Responsibility for activities should not be assigned to a person unless authority is also given.

A major concept of internal accounting control that should be implemented in a properly planned organization is the separation of incompatible functions; the lines of authority and responsibility should keep the functions of operations and custodianship separate from the function of recording. A person in a position to commit errors and irregularities should not be in a position to conceal them and the accounting controls should be designed to eliminate opportunities for such concealment. Thus, better controls exist if the person collecting cash from a customer is not the same person who records the entry in the accounts receivable records. Separation of the recording function from those of operations and custodianship prevents the person who has access to assets from appropriating some of those assets and then concealing the action through erroneous accounting entries.

In many cases, the nature of the activities makes the separation of the recording function from the operating and custodial functions a natural division. To illustrate, the workers on the production line typically have neither the training nor the desire to become involved with record keeping. In other cases, this division may not be so apparent. Handling cash receipts and disbursements, borrowing and repaying loans, extending credit, and collecting accounts receivable—which are functions of asset management—are not foreign to a person handling accounting functions. They all involve financial and other closely related matters. Whenever possible, the plan of organization would separate such incompatible functions. In any organization of sufficient size, a treasurer should be responsible for asset management, and a controller should be responsible for accounting matters.

Operations should be organized so that at least two persons or departments are involved in each transaction. In this way one person's work can be used to verify the accuracy of another person's work. In the absence of collusion between the two persons involved, errors and irregularities are likely to be discovered. Using several individuals to handle a single transaction takes advantage of each person's specialized training and should not result in duplication of work. For example, the filling of a sales order may involve someone in the sales department to take the order, a person in the credit department to verify the approval of credit, a person in the warehouse to select the physical goods, a billing clerk within the accounting department to produce records of the transaction, and a shipping clerk to verify the correctness of the items and to prepare them for delivery. Such specialization of labor not only adds to the efficiency of many operations but also enables internal accounting control to be implemented.

QUALITY AND TRAINING OF PERSONNEL

Even in the most automated operations, the success of the enterprise depends largely upon the quality of employees. Therefore, the success of any internal accounting control system is dependent for its design and implementation on qualified personnel. Careful screening of prospective employees should result in the selection of those who have the background and aptitude to perform their assigned duties. Regardless of their capabilities, however, in all likelihood individuals will not function properly in the job without adequate training. A thorough training program at all levels of operations in conjunction with frequent review and evaluation of each employee's performance contributes greatly to the success of an accounting control system.

Fidelity Bonds Fidelity bonds, a type of insurance, provide for indemnification of the company in case of defalcation by the employee covered by the bond. Each employee who has access to cash, negotiable assets, or other assets easily subject to misappropriation should be bonded. Even the most expertly designed system of internal accounting control can be circumvented by a person who is so determined; thus management should not assume that the company's system affords protection against defalcation to the extent that fidelity bonds are considered unnecessary. In addition to the indemnification in case of loss, fidelity bonds provide a psychological deterrent. The investigation conducted by an insurance company before an employee is bonded tends to discourage a person with intentions of committing defalcations from accepting a job that requires a bond. A further deterrent is the employee's knowledge that the insurance company will prosecute in an effort to recover any loss, whereas the employer might be persuaded to forgo prosecution.

Vacations and Job Rotation For most jobs it is desirable to have more than one employee trained to discharge the duties. By having the duties of a particular job performed by a substitute while the regular employee is on vacation, errors and irregularities in the usual performance of the job may become evident. When several employees are trained for one job, rotation of their assignments to the job discourages employees from devising any scheme for defalcation because they know someone else will be placed on the job after a short period of time and their scheme will likely be revealed. Since rotation of employees may not be the most efficient use of employee specialization, this cost of job rotation must be compared with the possible benefits derived from the strengthened accounting controls. In almost all situations the cost of having someone fill a job while the regular employee is on vacation is worth the benefit derived from the more effective accounting controls. Not only does the substitute have the opportunity to reveal any errors and irregularities in the manner in which the regular employee performs the job, but also there is likelihood that new ideas may be forthcoming to improve that area of responsibility.

SYSTEM DOCUMENTATION

In order that all persons involved may understand the overall internal accounting control system and, particularly, the responsibilities assigned to each individual, the lines of authority and responsibility and all policies and procedures should be clearly set forth in writing. The following paragraphs describe some of the fundamental documentation requirements.

Organization Chart The lines of authority and responsibility are presented in diagram form in an organization chart. The separation of the recording function from the operating and custodial functions should be quite apparent. Also, the organization chart should reflect the internal auditor as being in a staff position, preferably reporting to an audit committee of the board of directors or to a highly placed management official. The internal auditor should be in a position to investigate without restriction all necessary areas of business activities and should be independent of all units under examination. An organization chart, such as the one in Figure 7-2, gives a comprehensive view of the organizational structure of a company. However, details of company policy and responsibilities of each job are most likely provided by other documents.

Job Descriptions For each job within an organization there usually is a written description of the duties to be performed and of the authority and

Figure 7-2 Organization Chart

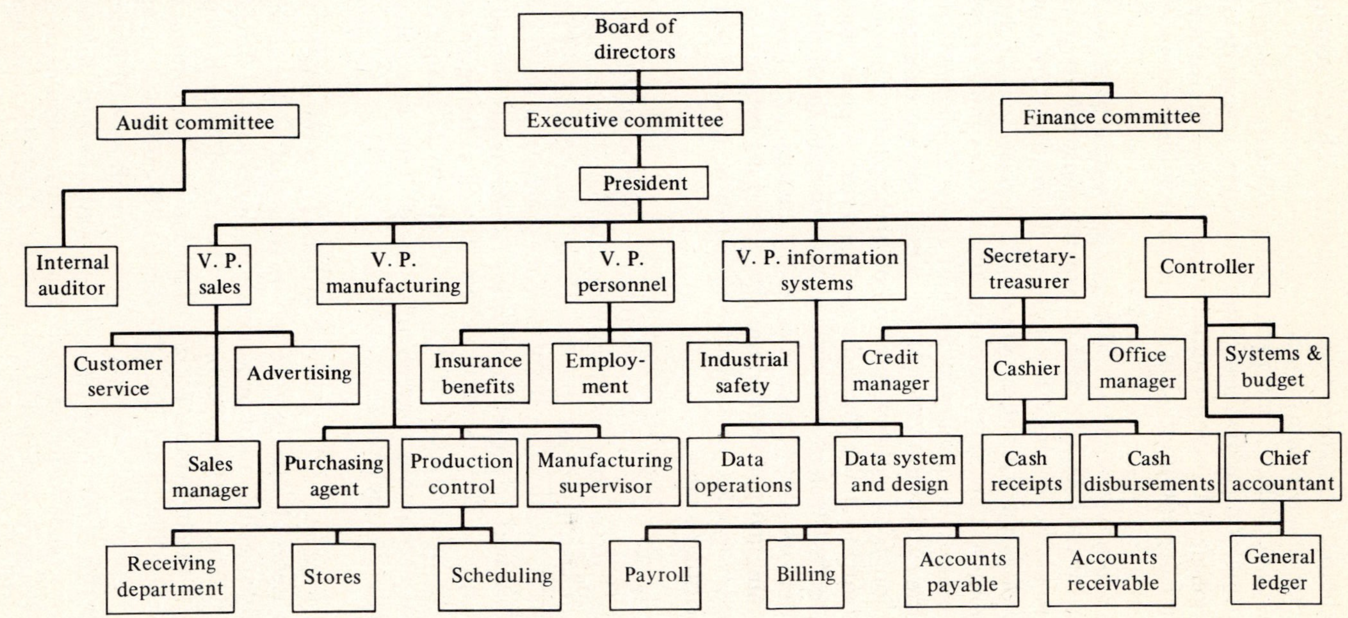

responsibility placed with the person filling that position. These job descriptions help an employee become familiar with the requirements of a new job. The superior to whom an employee reports should be constantly alert for any deviations from prescribed procedure through intent, misunderstanding, or carelessness, and corrective action should be taken where necessary. Changing conditions may cause the nature of a job to change, and the job description should be modified whenever necessary.

Policy and Procedures Manual Management's directives can be followed only when they are known, and one of the most effective ways to make them known is to set them forth clearly in writing. To assure uniform treatment of like items, there needs to be a statement of the method of accounting for various types of transactions. Policy must be established on such matters as the minimum amount to be capitalized in fixed asset accounts, the maximum amount for which the purchasing department may place an order without approval of higher authority, or the number of vacation days available for each year of service. A policy and procedures manual may be classified into sections according to the divisions or operations of the company. Employees in the factory may have available to them only the general section and those sections relating to production matters, whereas sales personnel would have the general section and the portion relating to sales.

System Flowchart A particularly effective method of reflecting relationships among the various functions of a company's operations is through the medium of a flowchart that shows the interrelations of the operating systems schematically. In an EDP system especially, it is necessary to have a system flowchart to reflect the various functions performed by humans and by machines. The system flowchart, as well as being an effective tool in the management of a business, is also useful to an auditor in evaluating the internal accounting controls of a client. This facet of the audit is discussed later in this chapter.

Other Documentation The chart of accounts is a document which helps assure that items of a like nature will be recorded in the same manner. It is effectively supplemented by a text of accounts to give further information about the type of transactions to be recorded in each account.

Because of the individual nature of an internal accounting control system, it is impossible to describe all necessary documentation applicable to a specific company. For instance, a company with an EDP system will have a computer-run manual describing the procedures to be followed in processing various types of information. Further discussion of documentation of an EDP system is included in Chapter 10, which discusses audits of EDP systems.

PROOFS OF ACCURACY

The internal accounting control system should use all available procedures to assure the proper functioning of the system and the fairness of the reports and statements produced. Examples of such proofs of accuracy are described below.

Control Accounts The use of control accounts is a simple procedure that can be quite effective as a proof of accuracy. If the accounts receivable control is posted from one source and the individual accounts are posted from another, the agreement of the control with the detailed accounts gives proof that the sources are in agreement. Irregularities may still exist, for there could be collusion between the two sources, and errors may result because the details are posted to the wrong customer's account.

Double-Entry Bookkeeping The mere use of the double-entry bookkeeping system is an internal accounting control procedure that gives a certain assurance of accuracy. The balancing of debits and credits assists in establishing clerical accuracy but does not guarantee it. The use of the double-entry system aids, for example, in establishing the accountability for assets. As assets are transferred through the production process from one form to another, or as they are transferred from one division to another, the use of debits and credits records the acceptance of accountability and the discharge of that accountability. As the usefulness of assets expires, the double-entry system reflects the transfer from asset status to expense. The double-entry bookkeeping system is essential in any effective accounting control system; consequently, any business, regardless of how small, should employ this fundamental procedure.

Batch Controls Establishing a control by batches is a procedure that is particularly applicable to EDP systems, but it can be employed effectively in many other situations. Any time a group of transactions is to be recorded or a group of data is to be manipulated in any way, a control figure should be established over that group. After the transactions have been posted or the data manipulated, the aggregate change on the resulting account or document should be the same as the control figure. If the effect produced is not in agreement with the batch control, the cause of the difference must be determined and any necessary corrections made. A batch control should be established over a relatively small number of items, for the location of differences is facilitated if there are not great numbers of transactions or data through which one must search to locate the source of the difference.

Imprest System The use of the imprest system is another type of control used to establish accuracy. The most common example is the petty cash account, whereby the custodian is responsible at all times for an established amount. This amount is represented either by money or by paid invoices. The fund is reimbursed and replenished to the established amount only by the presentation and cancellation of supporting invoices or receipts. A similar system can be used to establish control over the cash of a branch or division. Travel advances are also frequently operated on an imprest system.

INTERNAL AUDITING

Investigation and appraisal of the internal control system, both administrative controls and accounting controls, is a function of internal auditing. In many small- and medium-sized companies, this function may be performed by the owner or a member of top management. In larger organizations, the function is assigned to an internal auditor or to a staff of internal auditors. The internal auditing function is an essential element of an effective internal control system. An independent auditor views an internal control system as having a substantial weakness if no internal auditing function is performed.

The internal auditor's review is aimed at evaluation of the effectiveness of the design of the system as well as the effectiveness of its functioning. The auditor reviews reports going to management and questions whether those reports tell management what has happened or whether there is additional information that would be useful in formulating decisions. A more thorough discussion of the internal auditor's function is presented in Chapter 11 under the topics of internal financial auditing and internal operational auditing.

INTERNAL ACCOUNTING CONTROLS IN SMALL BUSINESSES

In many small businesses it is not practicable to implement all the internal accounting control concepts discussed earlier in this chapter. A small company very likely would have to engage additional employees merely to segregate duties and rotate jobs. In a small business the accounting system is usually quite simple and does not necessitate the employment of many people. Nevertheless, the system should be well organized, and there should be documentation so that all employees will know their duties and responsibilities. In a small business the control system is strengthened by the owner's involvement in the operation of the system. The owner should be involved in such duties as authorizing purchases, signing checks, distributing the payroll, opening the mail, reviewing the list of delinquent receivables, inspecting the inventory on hand, and observing employees as they go about their work. In fact, one may say that the owner at times functions as an internal auditor. The owner should require that financial statements be prepared at frequent intervals. These statements should be reviewed, perhaps in consultation with the company's independent accountant, and appropriate corrective action taken whenever necessary.

Section Two—Review of the internal control system

Modern auditing is based upon tests or samples rather than upon detailed examination of all transactions. For an auditor to rely upon tests, there must be evidence that the items included in the auditor's tests are representative of all similar items occurring during the accounting period and reflected on the financial statements. The internal accounting control system governs the manner in which transactions are treated during the accounting period. Consequently, if the internal accounting controls are functioning properly, transactions should be recorded in a manner that produces accurate accounts from which fairly presented financial statements may be prepared. The auditor makes tests of the adequacy of the internal controls, and if the tests indicate the system is reliable and functioning properly, the auditor depends upon the system to produce financial records upon which to rely. As stated by the second auditing standard, one of the essential purposes of reviewing internal controls is to determine the reliance thereon.

The second reason for reviewing the internal control system is to determine the extent of subsequent auditing procedures. Regardless of the strength of the accounting control system, the auditor must examine a certain amount of evidence to support directly the items appearing in the accounts and on the financial statements. There is always a risk that some errors will be reflected on the financial statements and not be detected. The objective in performing certain auditing procedures is to reduce this risk. The chance of errors being in the accounts and on the financial statements is greatest where the internal accounting controls are the weakest.

A third reason for reviewing internal controls is to form a basis for reports evaluating the control system and for recommendations to the client for improving the system. These recommendations, usually presented separately from the audit report, are discussed more thoroughly later in this chapter. At times, the implementation of the recommendations may improve the system to such an extent that the auditor can place greater reliance on it and thereby reduce the extent of the audit tests. One reason for reviewing the internal control system early in an examination, in particular with a new client, is so that the client may promptly make changes to strengthen the internal accounting control procedures. After the changes are implemented, the auditor can place greater reliance on the accounting controls for the remainder of the period under examination.

Organization of the auditor's review

The review of internal accounting controls should be made by the auditor in a systematic and rational manner. In selecting the approach to use for an individual company, the auditor should consider the size of the company, the location of its offices and operations, the nature of its business, its organization, and the information system used, as well as many other features. Although the specific steps of an internal accounting control review are unique for each company, several general concepts exist and are discussed in this section.

The size and nature of most businesses are such that the review of internal accounting controls and the conduct of other audit procedures need to be made separately on the different operating segments, or divisions. In some instances, the review of each segment will be assigned to different individuals on the audit team. Even a simple internal accounting control system for a relatively small business may need to be separated into several divisions to expedite the auditor's review.

In determining the specific segments of the operations, the auditor should give primary consideration to the relational nature of business functions and transactions, reviewing as a unit those functions that have a common data base, are under a common control, stem from similar events, or are closely related in some other manner. Some of the more common ways of segmenting a company's activities and transactions are by (1) cycles, (2) operating units, and (3) financial statement classifications.

CYCLES

When separating the internal control system into divisions by cycles, the auditor identifies within each cycle transactions or areas that are closely related. Since the accounting system is an interrelated composite of several cycles, obviously some accounts and transactions fall into more than one cycle. Cash, for example, is usually involved in nearly all cycles. Inventory may be considered in a sales cycle, in an expense and disbursement cycle, or possibly in a separate cycle dealing with inventory and cost of sales. Because of the interrelationships of cycles, questions arise as to where certain activities should be assigned. The answers depend upon the nature of the company under audit and to some extent the preference of the auditor performing the examination. An activity that can be included in more than one cycle should be assigned to a single cycle for review purposes. The assignment is usually made to the cycle where there is the greatest volume of activity, and all major aspects of that activity should be reviewed within that cycle.

A Special Advisory Committee of the AICPA[1] has given attention to a review of internal accounting controls using the following grouping of cycles:

1. the revenue cycle
2. the expenditures cycle
3. the production or conversion cycle
4. the financing cycle
5. the external financial reporting cycle

The committee developed criteria and examples of selected control procedures and techniques for each of these five cycles from the perspective of a hypothetical manufacturing entity. The committee pointed out that some businesses would have different characteristics and would have to develop different criteria and perhaps classify activities in different cycles. In order to illustrate the functions that may typically be classified within each of the cycles, the following excerpts from the AICPA's committee report are presented.

The revenue cycle The revenue cycle covers the functions involved in receiving and accepting requests for goods or services; delivering or otherwise providing goods or services; credit granting, cash receipts, and collection activities; billing; accounting for revenues, accounts receivable, commissions, warranties, bad debts, returned goods, and other adjustments.

The expenditures cycle The expenditures cycle is subdivided into purchasing, payroll, and disbursement functions.

Purchasing covers the functions involved in initiating requests for goods, other assets, and services ("goods"); obtaining information as to available vendors, prices, and other specifications; placing orders for goods; receiving and inspecting or otherwise accepting the goods delivered or provided; accounting for amounts payable to vendors, including freight-in, cash discounts, returned goods, and other adjustments. Payroll covers the functions involved in hiring employees and deciding their compensation, direct and indirect; reporting attendance and work performed; accounting for payroll costs, payroll deductions, employee benefits and other adjustments. Disbursement covers the functions involved in preparing, signing and issuing checks, or distributing cash.

[1] Adapted from *Report of the Special Advisory Committee on Internal Accounting Control* © 1979 by the American Institute of Certified Public Accountants, Inc.

The production or conversion cycle The production or conversion cycle covers the functions involved in production planning and control, inventory planning and control, property and deferred cost accounting, and cost accounting.

The financing cycle The financing cycle covers the functions involved with the issuance and redemption of capital stock and the recording of transactions therein; the payment of dividends; the investigation and selection of appropriate forms of financing, including lease transactions; debt management, including monitoring compliance with covenants; investment management and physical custody of securities.

The external financial reporting cycle The external financial reporting cycle covers the functions involved in preparing journal entries and posting transactions to the general ledger (to the extent such functions are not performed within other cycles); deciding the generally accepted accounting principles that the company should follow; gathering and consolidating the information required for the preparation of financial statements and other external historical financial reports, including related disclosures; preparing and reviewing the financial statements and other external reports.

OPERATING UNITS

The operating divisions of a business enterprise may form the segments that the auditor decides to use as the basis for the internal control review and other procedures of the audit examination. Some businesses are clearly divided into production, warehousing, selling, and administrative divisions. Although the activity of each division is distinct, there are information and accounting flows that are common, such as personnel and payroll. If the auditor selects the operating divisions around which to organize the audit, proper attention must be paid to the relational aspects of the divisions themselves as well as the information flows within and among the divisions.

FINANCIAL STATEMENT CLASSIFICATIONS

At times the financial statements, or even the trial balance, may form the basis around which an auditor organizes an examination. This approach is more likely in the examination of a small company with a simplified system of internal accounting control. Even in this arrangement of the audit steps, however, the auditor recognizes the interrelation of all accounts. One aspect of the cash receipts system, for example, is the collection of the accounts receivable, which in turn are a result of credit sales, in turn affecting inventory, which may have been increased by credit purchases reflected in the accounts payable. With transactions having effects on several related accounts, the auditor must decide through which account to concentrate each particular phase of the examination.

To summarize, the auditor may organize the review of an internal accounting control system on the basis of cycles, operating units, or financial statement classifications. Regardless of the organization decided upon—cycles, operating units, or financial statement classifications—the primary goal of the auditor's investigation is to acquire an understanding of the flow of information and data through the system. The interrelationship of various controls and functions should be viewed as they affect the accurate functioning of the entire accounting system and the fairness of the financial information produced. For example, an auditor may be engaged in the review of the controls over purchases of raw materials. Although the review may be organized on a financial statement classification basis, the auditor does not consider the purchases account alone but extends the review to cost of goods sold, gross profit, inventory of raw materials, work-in-process inventory, finished goods inventory, accounts payable, and perhaps other accounts also.

The review of internal accounting controls and the subsequent substantive testing and other auditing procedures frequently are organized on the same basis. However, it is possible to organize the review of internal controls on the cycle basis, for example, and to organize the other audit procedures on a financial statement classification basis, and such an arrangement is preferred by many auditors. In Part III of this text, which describes audit objectives and procedures, the relational aspects of balance sheet and operating accounts are emphasized. When selecting the organizational format of the internal control review and the organization of the other audit procedures, the auditor should choose the form that best suits the circumstances of the particular examination being performed.

Conduct of the auditor's review

By reviewing the system documentation, organization charts, job descriptions, procedure manuals, and system flowcharts—and by discussing the system with the controller, chief accountant, director of information systems, and other key personnel—the auditor should obtain a thorough knowledge of the design of the internal accounting control system. In fact, all the considerations discussed in the previous sections of this chapter as being desirable features of an internal accounting control system should be investigated by the independent auditor to determine if they exist and function properly. The auditor needs to document the review of the system to furnish evidence that auditing standards are being followed, and also to furnish a basis for modifying, if necessary, the substantive auditing procedures to be performed later. The auditor's documentation usually is a combination of flowcharts, narrative memoranda, and questionnaires, although at times, only one or two of these forms may be used.

FLOWCHARTS

Concentrating on the cycle, operating unit, or financial statement classification selected for review, the auditor reviews the client's manuals and other documentation and discusses the control system with client personnel to obtain an understanding of how the internal accounting control system operates. The auditor usually makes a flowchart of the system, which should include the flow of information, the division of duties, and records generated and maintained. When the client has flowcharts to document the company's own system, the auditor may use these along with other information as the basis for the flowcharts prepared for the auditor's working papers. Some narrative may supplement the flowcharts, especially when exceptions and nonroutine transactions are not clearly presented.

In order to prepare a flowchart of the internal accounting control system, an auditor must conduct a comprehensive survey and acquire a thorough understanding of the system. Such a schematic presentation enables the auditor to see quite readily the overall functioning of the system. Also, those reviewing the auditor's working papers can easily understand the system, and they can identify areas where either more or fewer auditing procedures need to be performed. Additionally, flowcharts often enable the auditor to make valuable recommendations to the client for improvements, since weaknesses in the system are easily identified.

Elements of systems flowcharting are presented in the final section of this chapter. Techniques of flowcharting are generally understood by auditors today, and such knowledge is viewed as essential for entering the auditing profession.

Significant time may be required in the initial preparation of flowcharts. However, in succeeding audits, the auditor may be able to modify previous years' flowcharts to reflect current changes, resulting in a considerable saving in audit time and cost.

Once the flowcharts are prepared, the auditor may find it desirable to have appropriate client personnel review them to assure their accuracy. Such a review should determine whether the auditor has properly interpreted and compiled information elicited from many different sources.

QUESTIONNAIRES

Auditors have traditionally used an internal control questionnaire as a primary method of obtaining information about the design of a client's internal accounting control system. The usual questionnaire is comprehensive and consists of numerous questions regarding all aspects of a business in general. A section of an internal control questionnaire on Marketable and Other Security Investments is shown in Figure 7-3. Generally, the auditor spends several hours with the controller or other key person asking questions and discussing the system. Answers to some of the more specific questions may be available only from operating personnel.

The questionnaire may be designed so that a *no* answer indicates a weakness in the internal accounting control system. Space is usually provided for elaboration when *yes* or *no* does not answer a question adequately. The questionnaire approach has the advantage of being quite thorough in the usual situation because standardized questionnaires are extremely extensive and comprehensive in their coverage.

On the other hand, the questionnaire approach has the disadvantage that it can omit some highly unusual area that is not included in the standardized form. Another disadvantage of the questionnaire in its standardized format is that many questions may not apply to a particular client, thereby requiring extensive modification in order to pursue those that are applicable. A common criticism of the questionnaire method is that the *yes* and *no* answer form lends itself to being treated in a superficial, routine manner. However, when used in conjunction with flowcharting and narrative memoranda, the internal control questionnaire contributes to the comprehensive nature of the review and helps the auditor to understand the overall functioning of the control system.

In order to be assured of a proper understanding of the documentation used by the client, the division of duties, the records maintained, and the detailed functioning of the system, the auditor may want to trace one test item in each functional area from its origin to its ultimate disposition. This tracing through the system of a representative transaction is sometimes called a *test of understanding*.

Upon completing the review of the accounting control system, the auditor is in a position to make a preliminary evaluation. As described in SAS No. 1 (AU 320.54), the auditor may be able to determine areas of weakness that are based exclusively upon the design of the system, and for those areas the auditor will normally decide not to conduct tests of compliance but to base the extent, timing, or nature of the substantive tests exclusively on the system design.

Internal Control Questionnaire for Small Businesses The independent auditor in reviewing the internal accounting controls of a small business will ordinarily follow the usual procedures of reviewing the system as planned, making tests to determine how well the system functions, and then evaluating the system. The auditor is aware of the important role of the owner and may choose to use a form of internal control questionnaire that is

Figure 7-3 Internal Accounting Control Questionnaire *(AICPA adapted)*

V. MARKETABLE AND OTHER SECURITY INVESTMENTS	Answer Yes	Answer No	Audit Implications
1. Are securities kept in a safe deposit vault in the name of the company?	___	___	___
2. If so:			
a. Does access thereto require the signatures or presence of two designated persons?	___	___	___
b. Is a record maintained by the client of visits to safe deposit vault?	___	___	___
3. If not:			
a. Are they kept in safekeeping by an independent person?	___	___	___
b. Are they kept in a safe place under control of an officer?	___	___	___
4. Is a record kept by the accounting or the financial department of each security, including certificate numbers?	___	___	___
5. Are all securities, except "bearer" bonds, in the name of the client?	___	___	___
6. Are securities periodically inspected and agreed with the record by internal auditors or other designated officers or employees?	___	___	___
7. Are purchases and sales of securities authorized by:			
a. The board of directors?	___	___	___
b. An officer?	___	___	___
c. The financial department?	___	___	___
8. Are securities, held for others or as collateral, recorded and safeguarded in similar manner to those owned by the client?	___	___	___
9. Are security investments which have been written off or fully reserved against followed up as to possible realization?	___	___	___
10. Are satisfactory records kept to insure the proper and prompt receipt of income on securities owned?	___	___	___

Conclusions on adequacy of internal accounting control: ______________________

____

____

____

____

Prepared by ______________________ Date ____________

Reviewed by ______________________ Date ____________

especially designed to determine the duties of the owner and other controls applicable in the small business. An abbreviated sample questionnaire of the type applicable to small businesses appears in Figure 7-4.

Verification of the system

The auditor's review of the system yields knowledge of the internal accounting controls primarily regarding their design. The auditor's review of job descriptions and procedures manuals as well as discussions with the controller furnish information concerning how the system is supposed to operate. How does the system actually function in its day-to-day operations? That is the question the auditor really wants answered.

TESTS OF COMPLIANCE

To be reasonably assured that the internal accounting control procedures are being applied as they are intended in the design of the system, the auditor makes some tests to determine compliance. These may be in the form of detailed tests of balances or tests of transactions. The tests of understanding may be a part of the tests of compliance. In making tests of compliance, the auditor selects several transactions in each functional area and traces them throughout the entire system, paying special attention to evidence about whether or not the control features are in operation. These tests of compliance are usually concentrated on the points of an internal accounting control system that the auditor considers critical. The testing of all aspects of control is not necessary for the auditor to obtain the desired level of assurance, and such extensive testing would be prohibitively expensive. Signatures on authorization forms, canceled supporting documents, verification notches on data processing cards, complete library records on use of EDP programs, and periodic reconciliation of perpetual inventory records with the physical count of the assets are only a few examples of evidence the auditor examines to determine whether operations are in compliance with the system as designed.

In some examinations, auditors may denote areas wherein they question a client's ability to comply with the system as designed. Consequently, in those areas they are likely to conduct more extensive compliance tests in order to determine the extent of the actual compliance.

In a manual system it is desirable to select tests of compliance from throughout the year because changes in personnel may have resulted in variance in the degree to which performance of duties conforms to prescribed procedures. Also, the same personnel may not be consistent in how they perform their duties at various times throughout the year. The same concept of testing throughout the year applies to a computerized

Figure 7-4 Internal Control Questionnaire for a Small Business*

	Yes	No
1. General		
a. Are accounting records kept up to date and balanced monthly?	___	___
b. Is a chart of accounts used?	___	___
c. Does the owner use a budget system for watching income and expenses?	___	___
d. Are cash projections made?	___	___
e. Are adequate monthly financial reports available to the owner?	___	___
f. Does the owner appear to take a direct and active interest in the financial affairs and reports which should be or are available?	___	___
g. Are the personal funds of the owner and his personal income and expenses completely segregated from the business?	___	___
h. Is the owner satisfied that all employees are honest?	___	___
i. Is the bookkeeper required to take annual vacations?	___	___
2. Cash Receipts		
a. Does the owner open the mail?	___	___
b. Does the owner list mail receipts before turning them over to the bookkeeper?	___	___
c. Is the listing of the receipts subsequently traced to the cash receipts journal?	___	___
d. Are over-the-counter receipts controlled by cash register tapes, counter receipts, etc.?	___	___
e. Are receipts deposited intact daily?	___	___
f. Are employees who handle funds bonded?	___	___
3. Cash Disbursements		
a. Are all disbursements made by check?	___	___
b. Are prenumbered checks used?	___	___
c. Is a controlled, mechanical check protector used?	___	___
d. Is the owner's signature required on checks?	___	___
e. Does the owner sign checks only after they are properly completed? (Checks should not be signed in blank.)	___	___
f. Does the owner approve and cancel the documentation in support of all disbursements?	___	___
g. Are all voided checks retained and accounted for?	___	___
h. Does the owner review the bank reconciliation?	___	___
i. Is an imprest petty cash fund used?	___	___
4. Accounts Receivable and Sales		
a. Are work order and/or sales invoices prenumbered and controlled?	___	___
b. Are customers' ledgers balanced regularly?	___	___
c. Are monthly statements sent to all customers?	___	___
d. Does the owner review statements before mailing them himself?	___	___
e. Are account write-offs and discounts approved only by the owner?	___	___
f. Is credit granted only by the owner?	___	___
5. Notes Receivable and Investments		
a. Does the owner have sole access to notes and investment certificates?	___	___
6. Inventories		
a. Is the person responsible for inventory someone other than the bookkeeper?	___	___
b. Are periodic physical inventories taken?	___	___
c. Is there physical control over inventory stock?	___	___
d. Are perpetual inventory records maintained?	___	___

* Herbert J. Seltzer, "Evaluation of Internal Control in Small Audits," *Journal of Accountancy* (November 1964), 58-59.

	Yes	No
7. Property Assets		
a. Are there detailed records available of property assets and allowances for depreciation?	___	___
b. Is the owner acquainted with property assets owned by the company?	___	___
c. Are retirements approved by the owner?	___	___
8. Accounts Payable and Purchases		
a. Are purchase orders used?	___	___
b. Does someone other than the bookkeeper always do the purchasing?	___	___
c. Are suppliers' monthly statements compared with recorded liabilities regularly?	___	___
d. Are suppliers' monthly statements checked by the owner periodically if disbursements are made from invoice only?	___	___

	Yes	No
9. Payroll		
a. Are the employees hired by the owner?	___	___
b. Would the owner be aware of the absence of any employee?	___	___
c. Does the owner approve, sign, and distribute payroll checks?	___	___

10. Brief Narrative of Auditor's Conclusion as to Adequacy of Internal Control

____
____
____
____
____
____
____
____
____
____
____
____
____

system because many EDP systems are heavily dependent on personnel and because program and system changes also may be implemented from time to time.

In performing tests of compliance auditors are particularly concerned that accounting procedures are executed independently. They must make sure that certain procedures are performed by persons having no incompatible functions. To illustrate, an auditor is not satisfied solely by verifying that the amount of cash deposited is in agreement with the total of the day's receipts. The auditor also verifies that the person depositing the cash has no responsibility in recording the receipts. Documentary evidence does not afford this type of verification. The auditor asks questions of various personnel and also observes the employees as they perform their duties. In some situations, in fact, the only way an auditor can determine compliance with internal accounting controls is by observing employees perform their duties. To the extent possible, the auditor should observe the employees without their knowledge, for only then can it be assumed that they are performing in their usual manner.

TIMING OF THE TESTS

Frequently, an auditor makes tests of compliance during the year under examination at the client's office during performance of interim work. Additional tests specifically designed to determine compliance may not be necessary during the remainder of the year. However, the auditor should inquire of management personnel regarding any changes in design or compliance, and in making substantive tests later in the examination, the auditor is alert for any indication that compliance with accounting controls has changed subsequent to the interim examination. The length of the time between performing the tests of compliance during the interim examination and the end of the accounting period influences the extent of the additional investigation. The auditor must have a reasonable degree of assurance that the accounting control procedures are in use during the entire accounting period. What constitutes a reasonable degree of assurance is a matter of judgment to be determined by the auditor on the basis of all evidence gathered.

Evaluation of the system

Having reviewed the design of the internal accounting control system and having verified by compliance testing the manner in which it is operating, the auditor is in a position to evaluate the system and to determine the degree of reliance upon the controls. This evaluation, in turn, determines the extent of substantive auditing procedures that follow.

STRENGTHS AND WEAKNESSES

In order to determine that the accounting controls are satisfactory in a particular area, an auditor must evaluate the review of the system and tests of compliance as revealing no condition considered to be a material weakness. As described in SAS No. 1 (AU 320.68), a material weakness exists whenever material errors or irregularities in the financial statements would not have been prevented or detected by employees' following the prescribed procedures with the degree of compliance indicated to be usual. As stated earlier, if the auditor determines from the review and preliminary evaluation of the system design that weaknesses in certain areas are so great that the controls cannot be relied on for limiting substantive tests, there is no need for conducting tests of compliance in those particular areas. Normally weaknesses in the accounting controls can be compensated for by increasing the extent of the substantive auditing procedures. Generally there is an inverse relationship between the strength of the control system and the degree of substantive tests; the greater the strength of the controls, the lesser the extent of substantive testing. Conversely, the greater the weaknesses of the controls, the more extensive the substantive testing. As illustrated in Figure 7-5, the stronger the internal control system, the lesser the required amount of substantive testing and other auditing procedures. The extent of reliance on the internal controls and the amount

Figure 7-5 Relationship of Substantive Testing and Strength of the Control System

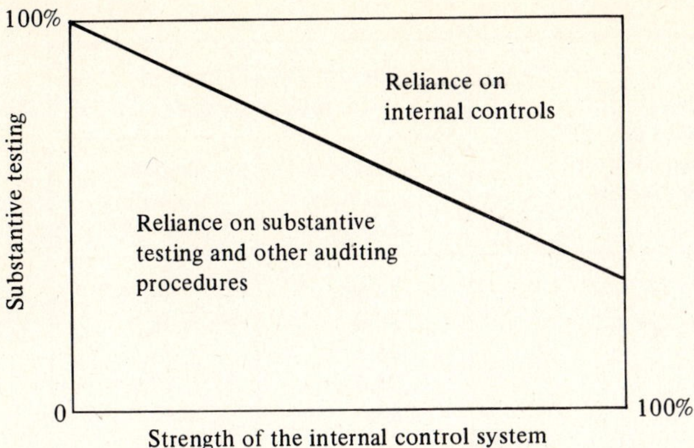

of substantive testing are matters of judgment, and the diagram in Figure 7-5 depicts only a general relationship and not specific percentages. No matter how strong the system of internal accounting controls, however, substantive testing and other auditing procedures can never be eliminated. The inherent limitations of an internal control system mean that there is always the possibility of errors and irregularities being present in the information generated by the system. Consequently, substantive auditing procedures must be performed, so that the auditor may be satisfied that the information is fair.

The auditor's judgment is the final authority as to the reliance to be placed on internal accounting controls and on substantive tests. However, SAS No. 1 (AU 320B.32-.35) states that the reliance assigned to internal accounting controls and other relevant factors in combination with the reliability level for substantive tests should produce the overall reliability level desired by the auditor. This concept is expressed by the following formula:

$$S = 1 - \frac{(1 - R)}{(1 - C)}$$

Where

S = Reliability level for substantive tests
R = Combined reliability level desired
C = Reliance assigned to internal accounting control and other relevant factors

Application of the formula with desired combined reliability levels set at 95 percent and 90 percent produced the data reflected in Figure 7-6.

Figure 7-6 Reliance Levels for Substantive Tests at 90% and 95% levels of combined reliability and different reliance levels assigned to internal accounting control.

Auditor's judgment as to reliance assigned to internal accounting controls and other relevant factors	Resulting reliability level for substantive tests	
	Combined reliability level 90%	Combined reliability level 95%
85%	33.3%	66.7%
80	50.0	75.0
70	66.7	83.3
60	75.0	87.5
50	80.0	90.0
40	83.3	91.7
30	85.7	92.9
20	87.5	93.8
10	88.9	94.4

It is noted that the reliability level for substantive tests rises rapidly as the reliance on internal control is reduced. A moderate reliance on internal controls makes necessary a high reliance on substantive tests.

In areas where the system is extremely weak in terms of design or compliance or both, auditors may request clients to reprocess certain records in a manner so that they can rely upon them. In extreme cases, they may determine that controls are so weak or completely missing that they will be unable to express an opinion on the financial statements. The usual procedure, as stated above, is for the auditor to adjust the extent of the substantive testing to compensate for any weaknesses in internal accounting controls.

Risks Auditors are concerned with two separate risks. The first is the risk that material errors or irregularities have occurred in the process of recording transactions and preparation of financial statements. Auditors rely upon internal accounting controls to reduce this risk. The second risk is that material errors have occurred, are reflected in the accounts and on the financial statements, and have not been detected. It is to reduce this risk that auditors perform substantive tests and examine other auditing evidence.

The strengths or weaknesses of internal accounting control as well as the nature of the item or the transaction itself affects the risk. For example, a highly liquid asset like cash, which is difficult to identify in terms of ownership and is easily abstracted, has a high degree of risk associated with it. On the other hand, an item like machinery has much less risk associated with it: ownership is easily established and it is difficult to remove and convert into cash.

SUBSTANTIVE TESTS

The nature and extent of substantive tests are influenced by the degree of risk associated with the accounts or transactions. Auditors design their substantive tests so that there is a high probability that they will detect any errors or irregularities affecting transactions and/or balances. By assessing the amount of risk associated with each accounting cycle, or each operating unit, or each group of related items on the financial statements, the auditor determines the extent and type of substantive auditing tests to perform.

These tests are of two general types as set forth in SAS No. 1 (AU 320.70). The first type is tests of details of transactions and balances, and the second type is an analytical review of significant ratios and trends along with investigation into unusual fluctuations, variances, and questionable items. The tests of details of transactions and balances are procedures in which sample transactions—representative of activities in a particular area—are selected and examined. These sample transactions may be examined to determine either the extent of compliance with internal controls or the reliability of recorded balances. In fact, in some cases the same procedure is performed as both a compliance test and a substantive test.

An analytical review consists of investigation of relationships. Financial data of the current period are compared with data projected for that period or with corresponding data of previous periods. The data projected for the current period may be contained in budgets, may be judgmental estimates or projected trends, or may be derived through regression analysis. If the actual result differs materially from the estimate, the auditor makes an investigation to determine the cause of the difference. As long as the activity and balances reflected on the financial statements approximate what is expected, there is little risk of error. Whenever there is a material variance from the expected, there is greater risk of error, and consequently, there is need for more extensive auditing procedures to be applied. These tests and other auditing procedures are discussed in later chapters.

Bridging Working Paper The auditor's working papers should show how the substantive auditing procedures are influenced by the review of internal control. One method of documenting this is illustrated in the bridging working paper shown in Figure 7-7. The auditor notes particular strengths and weaknesses of the internal controls and describes their audit implications. These weaknesses may be detected at any stage of review and

Figure 7-7 Bridging Working Paper

Royal Sales Company
Evaluation of Customer Orders, Shipping and Billing Controls - Revenue Cycle
Sales, Inventory, Cost of Sales, Accounts Receivable
12-31-83

I.C. Ref.	Audit Objective	Strengths of Internal Controls	Weaknesses of Controls	Implications for Audit	Procedures Modified
R-3	Proper approval of credit sales and recording of sales for goods shipped.	Customers orders are recorded on prenumbered six-part sales invoices.		Test that all prenumbered invoices are accounted for.	S-14
R-8			Copies #3 + 4 of invoice go to the warehouse for order to be filled prior to credit approval. Goods may be shipped in excess of credit limit.	Increase size of sample testing for Accounts Receivable balances in excess of credit limits.	S-32 increase %
R-11		Copy #4 returned from warehouse to billing clerk marked for exact items shipped and items backordered.		Test that customers are billed for items backordered.	S-19

documentation of existing controls. The illustrated bridging working paper indicates in the first column that the weaknesses and strengths were revealed by questions on the internal control questionnaire. The final column of that working paper indicates the specific audit procedure that was modified because of each strength and weakness.

INTERNAL AUDITOR'S WORK

One particular internal control feature that especially influences the substantive tests of an independent auditor is the work of the internal auditor. A company's internal control system is greatly strengthened by an effective internal auditor. When an internal auditor reviews and evaluates internal accounting controls by testing transactions and balances, additional assurance of accuracy is added to the company's accounting system beyond that contributed by the usual verification of accuracy performed by operating personnel. The work of the internal auditor can reduce the amount of substantive testing and other auditing procedures by the independent auditor. If, for example, the internal auditor has recently audited the revenue cycle and has confirmed a large percentage of accounts receivable, the independent auditor may be able to reduce substantially the number of accounts circularized for confirmation.

The independent auditor, before deciding upon the nature and extent of the substantive testing and other auditing procedures required, should consider the competence and objectivity of the internal audit staff members and evaluate their procedures. Inquiry about the training, education, and supervision of persons on the internal audit staff will enable the independent auditor to evaluate their competence. The objectivity of the internal auditors—their ability to act independently within the company—may be measured in several ways: (1) by noting the organizational level to which they report; (2) by reviewing recommendations contained in reports of the internal auditors; and (3) by reviewing documentary evidence of the internal auditor's work. As pointed out in SAS No. 9 (AU 322.08), the independent auditor should perform tests on the work of the internal auditors. In performing these tests, the independent auditor may examine some of the same evidence examined by the internal auditors, or may examine different, but similar, evidence. The independent auditor compares the results of the independent testing with the results of testing by the internal auditors. In order to rely upon the work of the internal auditors, conclusions reached by the independent auditor from the tests made should be similar to those reached by the internal auditors. If the independent auditor plans to rely to some extent upon the work of the internal auditors, informing them of this early in the period under audit not only is a matter of courtesy but also may result in work that will be more useful to the independent auditor. Clearly, however, the work of the internal auditors is only a supplement to the auditing procedures employed by the independent auditor and definitely not a substitute.

Letters and reports on internal accounting control

CONSTRUCTIVE COMMENT LETTERS

Having reviewed, verified, and evaluated the internal accounting control system of a company, the independent auditor is in an excellent position to present an evaluation of the accounting controls and to make recommendations regarding changes in the system. A constructive comment letter to management containing such recommendations is a valuable byproduct of an audit engagement. Some of the suggestions may be for improving the efficiency of the client's operations and may not be specifically related to the financial statements. This constructive comment letter should be directed to the appropriate personnel in the organization. Copies should be provided for the directors, audit committee, controller, or other individuals within management who will be concerned with decisions on implementation.

Auditors are protecting themselves as well as serving their clients in making recommendations for improving the accounting control system. An auditor will be able to reduce the substantive tests if the improvements are implemented, and perhaps reduce the legal liability. Should a defalcation occur in an area where the auditor has previously made a recommendation for improvement of the controls, the auditor would be able to claim contributory negligence by the client as part of self-defense in any negligence suit against the auditor if the improvement has not been implemented.

INTERNAL CONTROL REPORTS

Some external users of financial information have urged that reports on the auditor's evaluation of internal control be furnished to them. Serious questions exist regarding the benefit of such reports to external parties. They are likely to infer that a strong system of internal control, as reported upon in one period, will continue to be appropriate and be followed in the following period. Of course, conditions may change to make the prior system inappropriate, or it may be enforced to a much lesser degree. Conversely, external users of internal control reports may interpret a comment on a weakness as being more important than it actually is. A weakness in the system does not mean that any errors or irregularities exist in the accounts or statements, and untrained external users might place such an interpretation on comments regarding weaknesses in the system. Also there is danger of users' making false evaluations of management based upon the report on internal control. Management functions in many areas, and reports on its other functions usually are not furnished. It would be incorrect to infer that management performs in other areas in the same manner it performs in the area of internal accounting control.

There are conflicting views which hold that a report on internal control would help users evaluate unaudited financial statements produced through the same internal control system. Some also believe the report would be valuable in making decisions about management's performance. The present position of the AICPA, as expressed in SAS No. 1 (AU 640), is that the reports on the auditor's evaluation of internal accounting control may be issued to users to whom they can serve a useful purpose. These users are management, regulatory agencies, other independent auditors, and some or all of the general public as determined by management and/or a regulatory agency having proper jurisdiction. The auditor should never authorize the issuance of an internal control report in conjunction with unaudited financial statements, which are released to the general public.

In order to reduce the risk of misunderstanding, a specific form of the report on internal accounting control is recommended in SAS No. 1 (AU 640.12). This report was illustrated and discussed further in the preceding chapter.

Foreign Corrupt Practices Act of 1977

The United States Congress amended the Securities Act of 1934 to require certain registrants to maintain books, records, and accounts that, in reasonable detail, accurately and fairly reflect the transactions of the registrant and the disposal of its assets. Since these records derive their reliability to a considerable extent from the system of internal accounting controls, the Foreign Corrupt Practices Act of 1977 (FCPA) additionally requires that each registrant

> (2)(B) devise and maintain a system of internal accounting controls sufficient to provide reasonable assurances that—
>
> (i) transactions are executed in accordance with management's general and specific authorization;
>
> (ii) transactions are recorded as necessary (I) to permit preparation of financial statements in conformity with generally accepted accounting principles or any other criteria applicable to such statements, and (II) to maintain accountability for assets;
>
> (iii) access to assets is permitted only in accordance with management's general or specific authorization; and
>
> (iv) the recorded accountability for assets is compared with the existing assets at reasonable intervals and appropriate action is taken with respect to any differences.

These objectives of an internal accounting control system are taken directly from SAS No. 1 (AU 320.28).

The Securities and Exchange Commission has not prescribed detailed procedures and techniques to ensure compliance with FCPA but has held that management has such a responsibility. The SEC has identified five conceptual elements that it considers common to all evaluations. These are: (1) appraisal of the overall control environment; (2) translation of broad objectives into specific objectives; (3) consideration of detailed procedures and techniques to achieve specific objectives; (4) monitoring the control procedures to determine if they are functioning as intended; and (5) an evaluation of the system for reasonable assurance by considering the benefits and the costs that might result from additional or alternative controls.

A company's board of directors should determine whether the company's internal accounting control system meets the requirements of the FCPA. Such determination is to be made in the context of each company's circumstances with attention to matters such as the types of products or services rendered, types of customers, organization of the company, and the method of data processing used, if any. The board and its audit committee should encourage the establishment of an internal accounting control environment that will be conducive to the selection and implementation of effective accounting control procedures and techniques. Not only should the board and its audit committee oversee the establishment and maintenance of a strong control environment, but also they should oversee the procedures for evaluating the system of internal accounting controls.

Giving consideration to the circumstances of the particular company, management should design and implement a system of internal accounting controls with specific objectives that are consistent with the broad objectives stated in the FCPA. A process for monitoring the system should be established, through a transaction cycle review, a functional review, or some other approach, to determine if the procedures are accomplishing the desired objectives. Management needs to be assured that the system is appropriately designed and functions properly. Internal auditors fulfill an essential role in monitoring the compliance of a system, and additional emphasis on the importance of internal auditors is likely to result as the full impact of the FCPA is realized.

A proposed rule (No. 34-15772) of the SEC in April 1979 required that management include in annual reports to stockholders and in annual filings with the SEC a statement on internal controls. This statement must contain an expression of management's opinion as to whether the company's control system gives reasonable assurances of meeting each of the specific objectives of the FCPA. For reports issued between December 16, 1979 and December 15, 1980, management must state its opinion that the company's system as it existed at the balance sheet date provided such assurance and disclose any material control weaknesses communicated by the independent auditor that were uncorrected at year end. The independent auditor is required to report any material weaknesses at year end that management failed to report. For fiscal years ending after December 15, 1980, management's opinion on the internal accounting controls is to cover conditions that existed for the entire year, and the external auditor is required to examine and report upon management's representations. The auditor's opinion is in regard to two aspects of the representations by management: (1) whether the representations about the system of internal control are consistent with the results of management's evaluation of the system, and (2) whether the representations are reasonable with respect to transactions and assets that would be material in relation to the audited financial statements.

The purpose of an independent auditor's usual evaluation of an internal accounting control system is to establish a basis for reliance thereon in determining the nature, extent, and timing of audit tests to be applied in the examination of financial statements. As pointed out earlier in this chapter, at times auditors may not rely upon the controls to determine their tests in certain areas but rather determine the extent and nature of their substantive tests without a review of the controls in those specific areas. Consequently, the auditors may not be aware of weaknesses in those particular segments of the control system, since such weaknesses would have no effect on the usual auditing procedures. The proposed rule of the SEC requires that independent auditors increase the scope of their examination to evaluate segments of an internal accounting control system on which they do not rely for purposes of the usual audit.

The SEC's proposed requirement that the independent auditor express an opinion on the reasonableness of management's support for its statement on internal controls is a new responsibility for auditors. No auditing standards exist at the time of this writing for the auditor's review and evaluation of the underlying basis for management's conclusions as to the effectiveness of the design and functioning of the internal accounting control systems. A task force of the AICPA's Auditing Standards Board is studying the matter of reporting on internal accounting control, and an authoritative pronouncement establishing standards and procedures to be followed in such an examination and setting forth the form and content of a report thereon should be forthcoming.

Elements of systems flowcharting

Just as one idea may be expressed in a variety of ways, an accounting system may be represented in flowchart form through a variety of symbols in various arrangements. Although flowcharts usually reflect the preparer's individual method of expression, there are nevertheless a few standard symbols and conventions that are generally followed.

Five of the basic flowcharting symbols that are widely used are represented in Figure 7-8, and their use in a flowchart is illustrated in Figure 7-9.

The basic input/output symbol is used to indicate that a document or group of data has either entered into the system or has been produced by the system. A brief description of the data, the document, file, or process involved usually is written inside the appropriate symbol.

Since one of the basic purposes of flowcharting is to portray the flow of information throughout the accounting system, an input/output symbol representing such information must be joined with a flowline to show the direction in which the information flows. Flowlines connect each

Figure 7-8 Basic Flowcharting Symbols

Input/output Information available for processing (input), or recording of processed information (output).

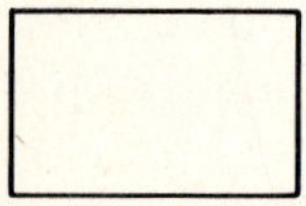

Process Any steps in the processing of information causing a change in value, form, or location of the information.

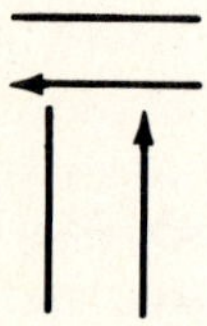

Flowlines Indicators of flow of information, normally left to right and top to bottom. Arrows indicating flow in direction opposite to normal are required and may be used to indicate flow at all times.

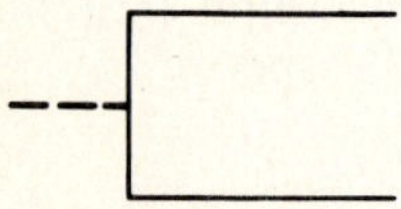

Comment or annotation Additional descriptive clarification associated with another symbol by a broken line.

Connector Exit from one sequence and entry into another sequence. Exit and entry points are referenced through labels appearing inside connector symbol.

Figure 7-9 Flowcharting of Cash Received by Mail

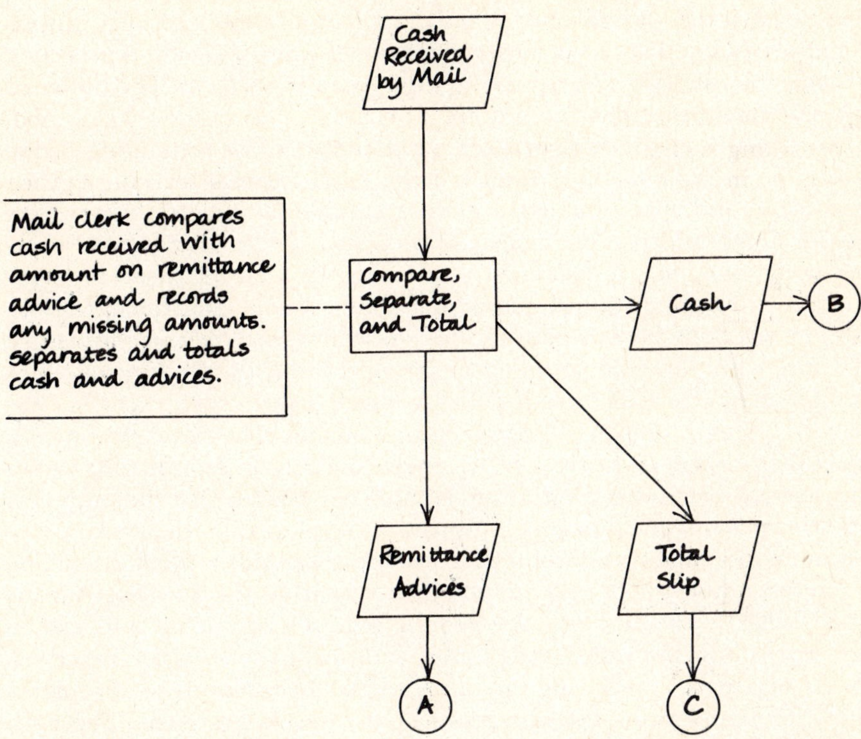

input/output symbol with one or more process symbols that explain the operations performed on the information, data, or document. If the process symbols and the brief description written within do not clearly depict the activity performed, additional information may be written on the flowchart and connected by the annotation symbol to the specific point being clarified.

One of the general rules of flowcharting is that the information flow normally is shown from top to bottom and from left to right. As long as the flow is in those directions, directional arrows are not necessarily used with the flowlines. Any time the flow of information is in a direction other than the usual, a directional arrow must be used.

Another rule of flowcharting is that an input/output symbol must always be connected directly to a process symbol. One document cannot produce another document, just as one group of data cannot produce another group of data, without some operation being performed, and this operation must be represented by a process symbol. On the other hand, one process symbol may be joined directly to one or more other process symbols, because the same data or document may flow through several processes before there is output of a new document or processed data.

A cardinal rule of flowcharting is that each input must lead to an output. All information, data, or documents introduced into a system is processed in some manner and always produces output in some form. The flowchart schematically delineates this process.

An effective method for preparing a flowchart of an accounting system is for the auditor to draw freehand the basic symbols to represent the documents and operations as the auditor acquires an understanding of the system. This information is usually procured in discussions with client personnel and may be obtained at the time of securing answers to the internal accounting control questionnaire or at some later time. The discussion normally is with one person concerning that person's duties, or activities within one department, or the operations of one function. The auditor may effectively use a separate sheet on which to represent the activities of each person, department, or function. The flowchart on each sheet then relates exclusively to the single function or department. Under this method of flowcharting, if the auditor determines that the output of one department or function is transferred to another department for further processing, the auditor may use the connector symbol containing a reference number or letter as the final symbol in the flowchart for the originating department. As the auditor acquires additional information and learns how the transferred information or documents are processed by the department receiving the information, the auditor uses a separate sheet for flowcharting the operations of the new department. The flowchart of the receiving department begins with the connector symbol referenced to the connector at the end of the previous operation. Figure 7-10 presents an illustration of this flowcharting method by reflecting further processing of the information originally illustrated in Figure 7-9.

Rather than using separate sheets for each function, the auditor may choose to use a multicolumn flowchart that reflects several departments in parallel vertical columns as shown in Figure 7-11. This form of flowchart is an excellent means of delineating the flow of information and documents throughout the entire system. The relationship of the different functions and the crosschecks and balances are clearly pictured. Drawing this type of flowchart while collecting the information and acquiring an understanding of the system may prove to be a formidable task for the auditor. The auditor may instead decide to gather the information by initially using separate flowcharts for each function or department and subsequently transferring the information to the multicolumn flowchart. However, since

Figure 7-10 Flowchart of Accounts Receivable Clerk's Processing of Remittance Advances

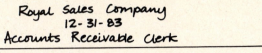

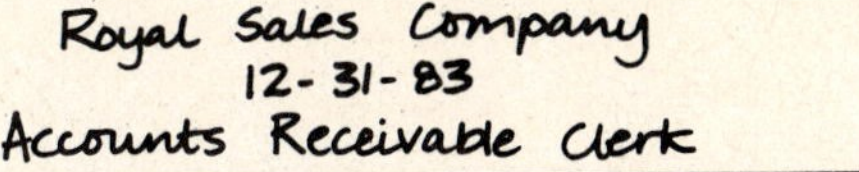

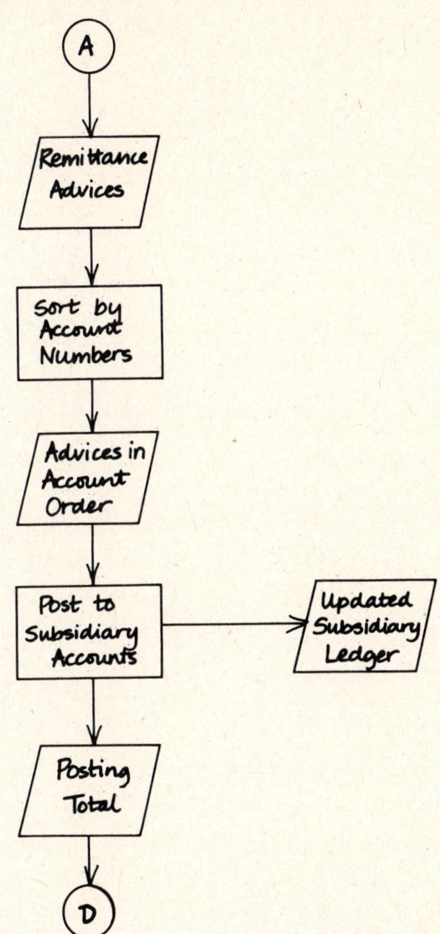

the original separate sheets contain all the pertinent information needed for an understanding and review of the system, these sheets may become a part of the auditor's working papers without any further processing.

When the multicolumn flowchart is used, the flowlines can be drawn from one department to another rather than using the connector symbol as described earlier. However, to prevent one flowline from crossing numerous other flowlines (thereby leading to possible confusion), the connector symbol may be used at the end of one function and repeated at

Figure 7-11 Multicolumn Flowchart

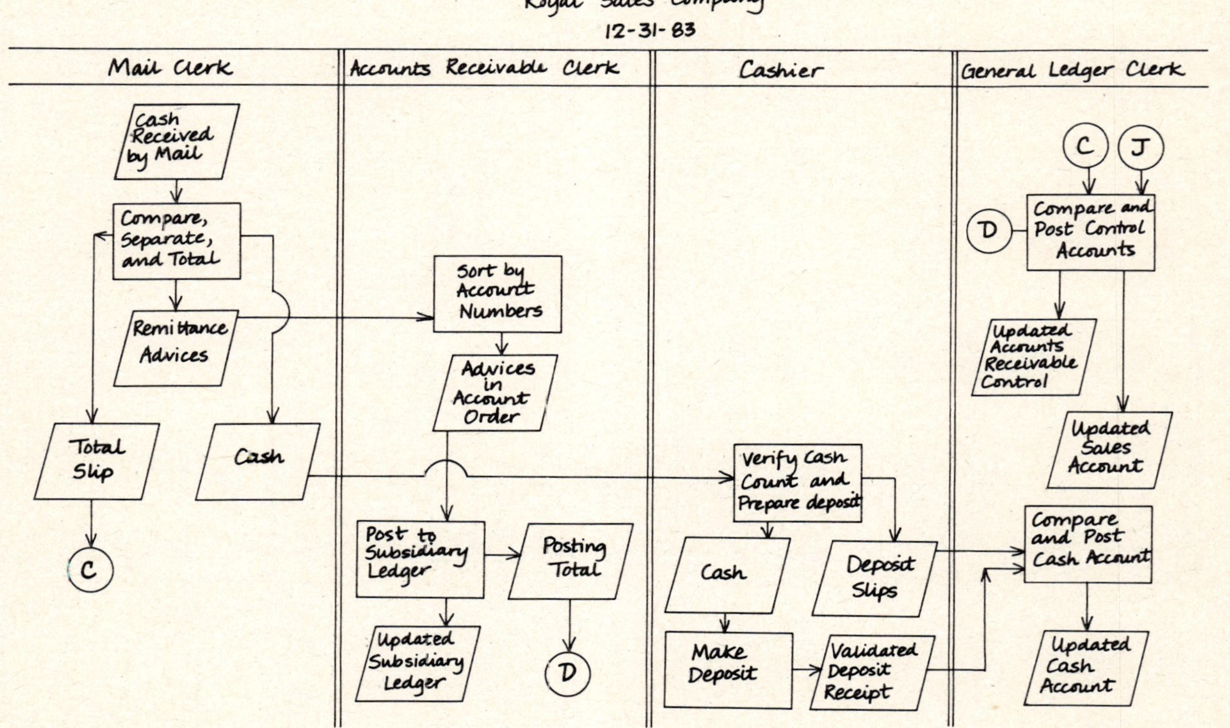

the beginning of another function. Both methods are illustrated in Figure 7-11.

An auditor may choose to use symbols that identify more specifically the form of the documents or the nature of the processing than is represented by the basic symbols. Some of these specialized symbols are shown in Figure 7-12. The use of the specialized symbols becomes more critical in the flowcharting of an Electronic Data Processing (EDP) system. The use of some of these specialized symbols in a multicolumn flowchart is illustrated in Figure 7-13.

Figure 7-12 Additional Flowcharting Symbols

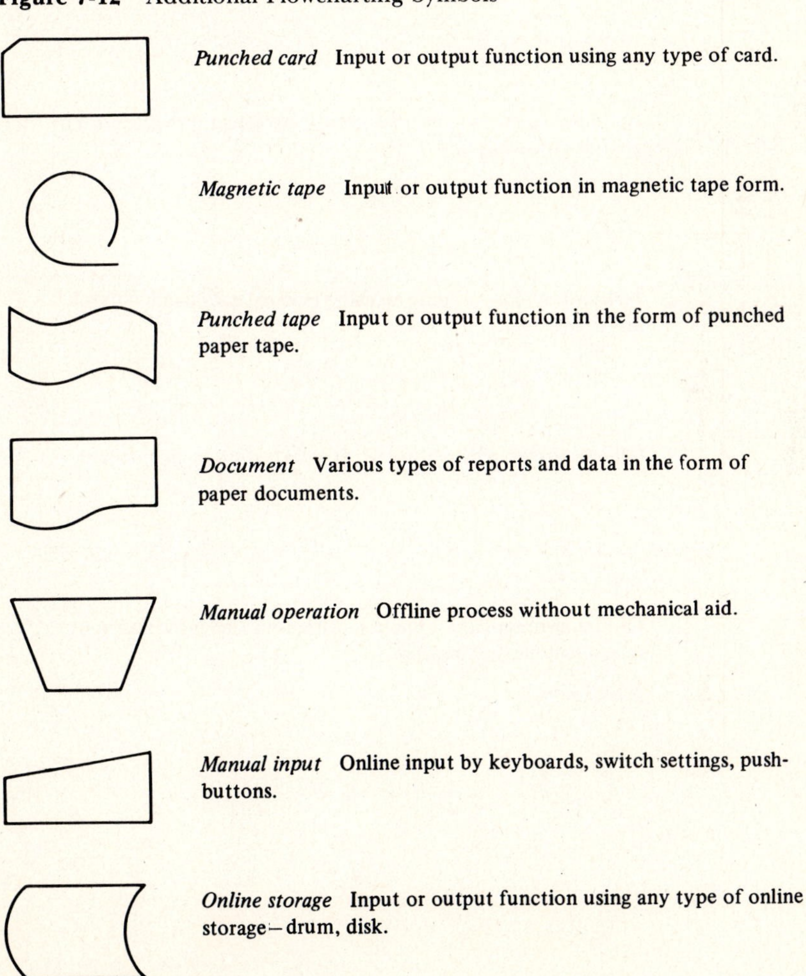

Punched card Input or output function using any type of card.
Magnetic tape Input or output function in magnetic tape form.
Punched tape Input or output function in the form of punched paper tape.
Document Various types of reports and data in the form of paper documents.
Manual operation Offline process without mechanical aid.
Manual input Online input by keyboards, switch settings, push-buttons.
Online storage Input or output function using any type of online storage—drum, disk.

Figure 7-12 (Continued)

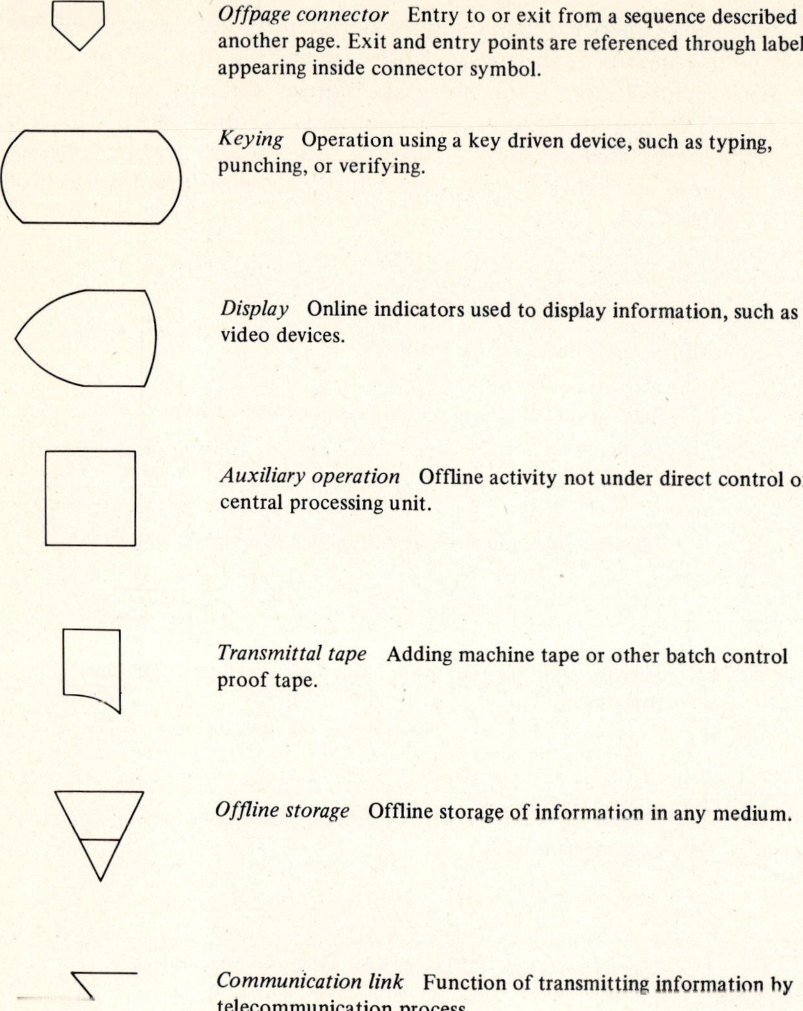

Offpage connector Entry to or exit from a sequence described on another page. Exit and entry points are referenced through labels appearing inside connector symbol.

Keying Operation using a key driven device, such as typing, punching, or verifying.

Display Online indicators used to display information, such as video devices.

Auxiliary operation Offline activity not under direct control of central processing unit.

Transmittal tape Adding machine tape or other batch control proof tape.

Offline storage Offline storage of information in any medium.

Communication link Function of transmitting information by telecommunication process.

Figure 7-13 Multicolumn Flowchart Using Specialized Symbols

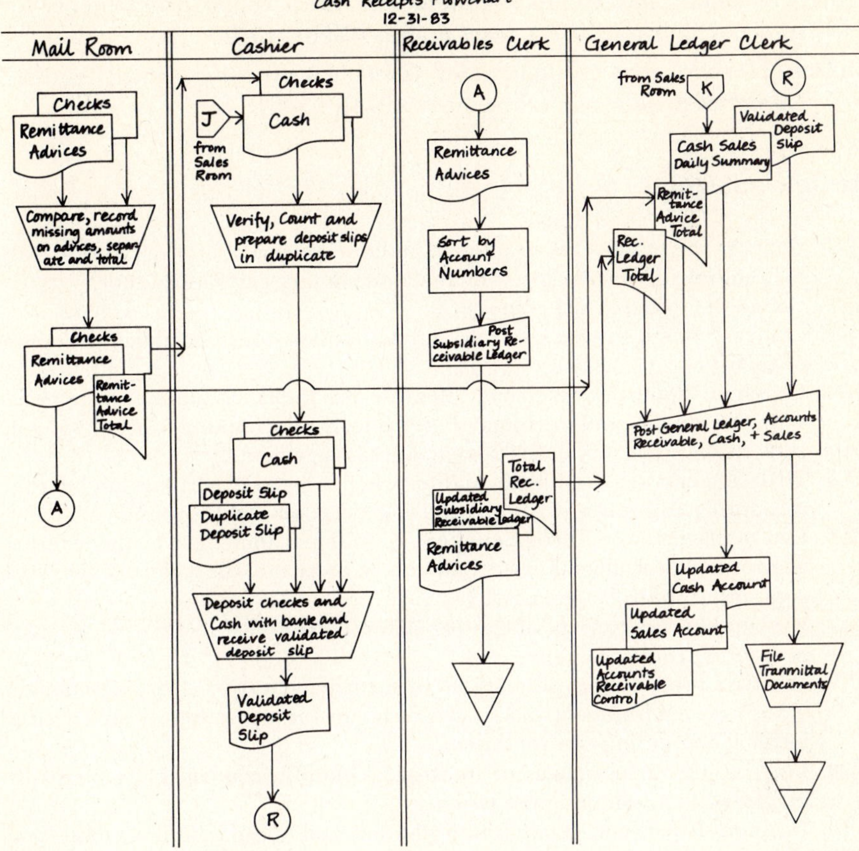

Supplementary readings

"Auditing Interpretations—Internal Accounting Control and the Foreign Corrupt Practices Act." *Journal of Accountancy* (October 1978), 130-131.

Barton, Larry M. "How to Prepare A Flowchart." *Practical Accountant,* (November-December 1977), 53-58.

Cushing, Barry E. "A Mathematical Approach to the Analysis and Design of Internal Control Systems." *Accounting Review* (January 1974), 24-41.

Grollman, William K., and Robert W. Colby. "Internal Control for Small Business." *Journal of Accountancy* (December 1978), 64-67.

Jancura, Elise G., and Fred L. Lilly. "SAS No. 3 and the Evaluation of Internal Control." *Journal of Accountancy* (March 1977), 69-74.

Morris, William, and Hershel Anderson. "Audit Scope Adjustments for Internal Control?" *CPA Journal* (July 1976), 15-20.

Stelzer, Herbert, Jr. "Evaluation of Internal Control in Small Audits." *Journal of Accountancy* (November 1974), 55-61.

Review questions

7-1. Contrast the reasons for an internal auditor's review of internal control with the reasons for such a review by the independent external auditor.

7-2. Define the term *internal control.*

7-3. Contrast administrative controls and accounting controls, giving examples of each.

7-4. Comment upon the statement, "Because the public accountant is involved with the design and revision of the internal accounting control system, responsibility for it is shared along with management."

7-5. What action is required by an auditor when a material weakness in internal accounting controls is discovered during the course of the audit?

7-6. Can management of a company rely upon the examination by the external auditor to detect all weaknesses that may be present in the company's internal accounting control system? Why?

7-7. Explain how the concept of cost-benefit enters into the design of an internal accounting control system.

7-8. What are some policies emphasized by management in its efforts to maintain a business environment that is conducive to the operation of an effective internal accounting control system?

7-9. List six general principles of internal accounting control that are usually employed in a well-designed system.

7-10. Distinguish between general authorization and specific authorization, and give examples of each.

7-11. Explain how proper recording of transactions is an essential feature of good internal accounting control.

7-12. Why should the operations and custodianship functions be separated from the recording function in a properly designed accounting system?

7-13. Explain how involving two persons or departments in one transaction strengthens accounting control and yet does not result in duplication of work.

7-14. Why should a company have any of its employees bonded when its accounting control system is considered extremely strong by both internal and external auditors?

7-15. Discuss the advantages and disadvantages, as related to an accounting system, of the practice of regularly rotating employees on a job and of requiring all employees to take vacations.

7-16. Describe the documentation an auditor would expect to find in order to understand the design of the client's accounting control system.

7-17. Describe some proofs of accuracy that are employed in an effective accounting control system.

7-18. Explain how a batch-control figure is used in an accounting system. Why should a batch control be established over only a relatively few items at one time?

7-19. Describe the approach an internal auditor takes in conducting an examination.

7-20. What is a test of understanding? Why does an auditor perform such a test?

7-21. Why are internal controls in a small business different from those of larger businesses?

7-22. The internal accounting controls for a small business involve the activities of one person to a considerable extent. Who is this person? Why are the activities of this person so important for the proper functioning of the internal accounting control system?

7-23. Name three ways in which an auditor may segment a company's activities in order to organize the auditor's review of the internal accounting control system.

7-24. Describe several arrangements of a company's business activities that would be appropriate for the auditor to use when employing the cycle approach.

7-25. How does the interrelation of accounts affect an auditor's review of internal accounting controls and subsequent auditing procedures?

7-26. Samuel Eidson has served as auditor of Harland Company for several years and has never found any errors or irregularities in the financial statements. In the current year he has again reviewed the system of internal accounting control and found it perfect both in design and function. After making tests of transactions to determine that the operations are in compliance with the system, Eidson tells his assistant, "We can now write our report on this examination without any substantive testing because this accounting control system is perfect any way you look at it." Comment.

7-27. Why should an internal accounting control system be reviewed by the auditor early in the examination?

7-28. Explain the purpose of tests of compliance and substantive tests.

7-29. Why does an auditor need to document the review of the client's internal accounting control system?

7-30. Discuss the manner in which an auditor might use each of the following methods of documenting the review of a company's internal accounting control system:

a. the narrative memorandum
b. flowcharts
c. the internal control questionnaire

7-31. Explain how the auditor's preliminary evaluation of an accounting control system may result in the elimination of tests of transactions for determining compliance with the system.

7-32. Why are tests of compliance selected from various periods throughout the year under examination?

7-33. Explain the correlation between the risk of error in an accounting control system and the extent of substantive tests by the auditor.

Figure 7-14 Selected Flowcharting Symbols

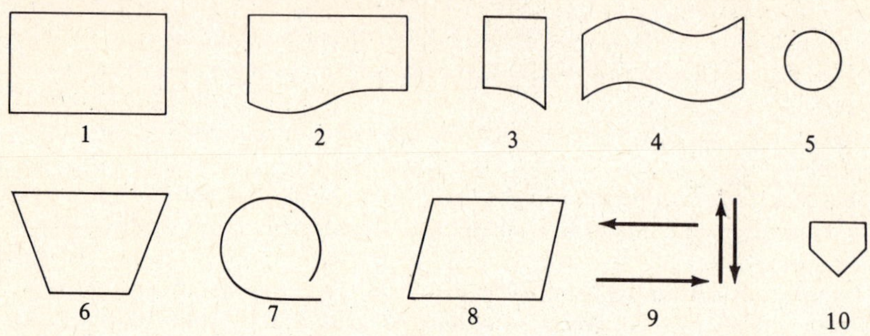

7-34. Under what circumstances is an auditor justified in making tests of compliance during an interim examination and not making further tests of compliance during that portion of the audit conducted at year end?

7-35. Explain how the nature of an asset affects the degree of risk and consequently the extent of the substantive auditing tests.

7-36. What are the two types of substantive tests and when is each used by the auditor?

7-37. Name each of the flowcharting symbols shown in Figure 7-14, and describe the use made of each.

Decision problems

7-38. In conducting an examination in accordance with generally accepted auditing standards, the CPA studies and evaluates the existing internal control of the client.

a. List and discuss the general elements or basic characteristics of a satisfactory system of internal control.

b. List the purposes for which the CPA reviews the client's system of internal control.

AICPA adapted

7-39. Management of the Northside Heating Company informed you that in its report to its stockholders it would be making a statement concerning the effectiveness of the company's internal control system. Management intends to use your review of the internal accounting controls as the basis for its report. Upon learning this information you requested a conference with the members of the audit committee of the company's board of directors.

Describe the major points you would bring up for discussion with the audit committee concerning reliance on your review of internal accounting controls as the basis of management's report to the company's stockholders.

7-40. As the independent auditor of Crescent Air Transport, Inc., you conducted a thorough review of the internal accounting control system during your interim examination for the nine months ended September 30, 1982. You completed this work on October 26, 1982. You found the system to be in excellent condition both in design and in operation.

Assume you have just arrived at the client's office on January 8, 1983, to perform the examination for expressing your opinion on the financial statements for the year ended December 31, 1982. Discuss the extent and nature of your review of internal accounting controls at this time.

7-41. An important procedure in the CPA's audit programs is the review of the client's system of internal control.

a. Distinguish between accounting controls and administrative controls in a properly coordinated system of internal control.

b. List the essential features of a sound system of accounting control.

c. Explain why the CPA is concerned about the separation of responsibilities for operating custodianship, financial custodianship, and controllership.

AICPA adapted

7-42. Internal auditing is a staff function found in virtually every large corporation. The internal audit function is also performed in many smaller companies as a part-time activity of individuals who may or may not be called internal auditors. The differences between the audits by independent public accountants and the work of internal auditors are more basic than is generally recognized.

a. Briefly discuss the auditing work performed by the independent public accountant and the internal auditor with regard to:
1. auditing objectives
2. general nature of auditing work

b. In conducting an audit, the independent public accountant must evaluate the work of the internal auditor. Discuss briefly the reason for this evaluation.

AICPA adapted

7-43. Jacquelyn Rau, one of the owners of Artistic Crafts Co., telephoned you, her auditor, and told you that she had just returned from a seminar on managing a small business. One of the topics discussed was internal control, and she wants your ideas on this topic. During the conversation she mentions two ideas she has that could help her internal controls: (1) employing temporary personnel so that duties can be properly separated, and (2) engaging you to do the write-up work rather than her partner continuing to perform that duty.

a. How would you reply to Rau regarding the two suggestions she has made?

b. Discuss some of the features of an effective internal accounting control system that can be implemented by many small businesses.

7-44. Carol Boyd, a local real estate broker, is a member of the board of directors of Suwannee Corporation. At a recent board meeting, called to discuss the financial plans for 1983, Boyd discovered two planned expenditures for auditing: in the controller's departmental budget there was an internal audit activity and in the treasurer's budget there was an estimate for the 1983 annual audit by a CPA firm.

Boyd could not understand the need for two different expenditures for auditing. Because the estimated fee for the CPA's annual audit was less than the cost of the internal audit activity, Boyd proposed eliminating the internal audit function.

a. Explain to Boyd the different purposes served by the two audit activities.
b. What benefits does the CPA firm performing an audit derive from existence of an internal audit function?

CMA adapted

7-45. Your client, Century Corporation, handled some government contracts during the year, and an auditor from a federal agency has just completed an examination, including a substantial review of year-end liabilities. The auditor has offered to allow you to review the working papers. Additionally, the internal auditor for Century Corporation had thoroughly audited the purchasing function about midyear and at that time had confirmed the balances with the vendors receiving a 72 percent response from all vendors. The internal auditor's working papers are also available to you.

Explain how the work of the auditor from the federal agency and the work of the company's internal auditor affect the auditing procedures you must follow as an independent external auditor.

7-46. A company's system of internal control (which consists of accounting and administrative controls) is strengthened by including in the system procedures that have specific functions or purposes. For example, the system of internal control may include a voucher system that provides for all invoices to be checked for accuracy, approved for propriety, and recorded before being paid. The system reduces the likelihood that an invoice will be mislaid or the discount lost, and it provides assurance that improper or unauthorized disbursements are not likely to be made.

Give the purposes or functions of the following procedures or techniques that may be included in a system of internal control, and explain how each purpose or function is helpful in strengthening accounting and administrative internal control.

a. fidelity bonding of employees
b. budgeting of capital expenditures
c. listing of mail remittances by the mail department when the mail is opened
d. maintaining a plant ledger for fixed assets

AICPA adapted

7-47. Neil Berkle was a highly regarded employee of Piedmont Manufacturing Company and had been in charge of raw material stores for seventeen years. The owner, Frank Paulk, regarded him as one of his most trusted employees. Mr. Paulk was shocked when the CPA's special investigation revealed that Berkle had stolen $400,000 in raw materials over the last ten years by entering incorrect receipts and withdrawals in the perpetual inventory records.

a. From the facts given, what most likely permitted this theft to go undetected?
b. What changes should be made in the accounting control system?

7-48. Jordan Finance Company opened four personal loan offices in neighboring cities on January 2, 1981. Small cash loans are made to borrowers who repay the principal with interest in monthly installments over a period not exceeding two years. Ralph Jordan, president of the company, uses one of the offices as a central office and vists the other offices periodically for supervision and internal auditing purposes.

Jordan is concerned about the honesty of his employees. He came to your office in December 1981 and stated, "I want to engage you to install a system to prohibit my employees from embezzling cash." He also stated, "Until I went into business for myself I worked for a nationwide loan company with 500 offices and I'm familiar with that company's system of accounting and internal control. I want to describe that system so you can install it for me because it will absolutely prevent fraud."

a. How would you advise Jordan on his request that you install the large company's system of accounting and internal control for his firm? Discuss.

b. How would you respond to the suggestion that the new system would prevent embezzlement? Discuss.

c. Assume that in addition to undertaking the systems engagement in 1982, you agreed to examine Jordan Finance Company's financial statements for the year ended December 31, 1981. No scope limitations were imposed.

1. How would you determine the scope necessary to satisfactorily complete your examination? Discuss.
2. Would you be responsible for the discovery of fraud in this examination? Discuss.

AICPA adapted

7-49. The accounting system illustrated by the flowchart in Figure 7-15 contains many weaknesses. Identify these weaknesses and discuss corrective action that you would recommend to strengthen the internal accounting control system.

7-50. Roz Galishoff, senior in charge of the audit on which you are currently working, asked you to prepare a bridging working paper to show how the strengths and weaknesses in the client's internal accounting controls should affect the auditing procedures.

a. Describe such a working paper.

b. Give an example of an internal accounting control that should reduce the auditing procedures necessary in the circumstances.

c. Give an example of an internal accounting control weakness that should increase the auditing procedures necessary in the circumstances.

7-51. As part of your annual audit of Call Camper Company, you have the responsibility for preparing a report on internal control to the management. Your work papers include a completed internal control questionnaire and documentation of other tests of the internal control system that you have reviewed. This review identified a number of material weaknesses; for some of these, corrective action by management is not practicable in the circumstances.

Discuss the form and content of the report on internal control to man-

Figure 7-15 Flowchart of Sales and Cash Receipts System (*AICPA adapted*)

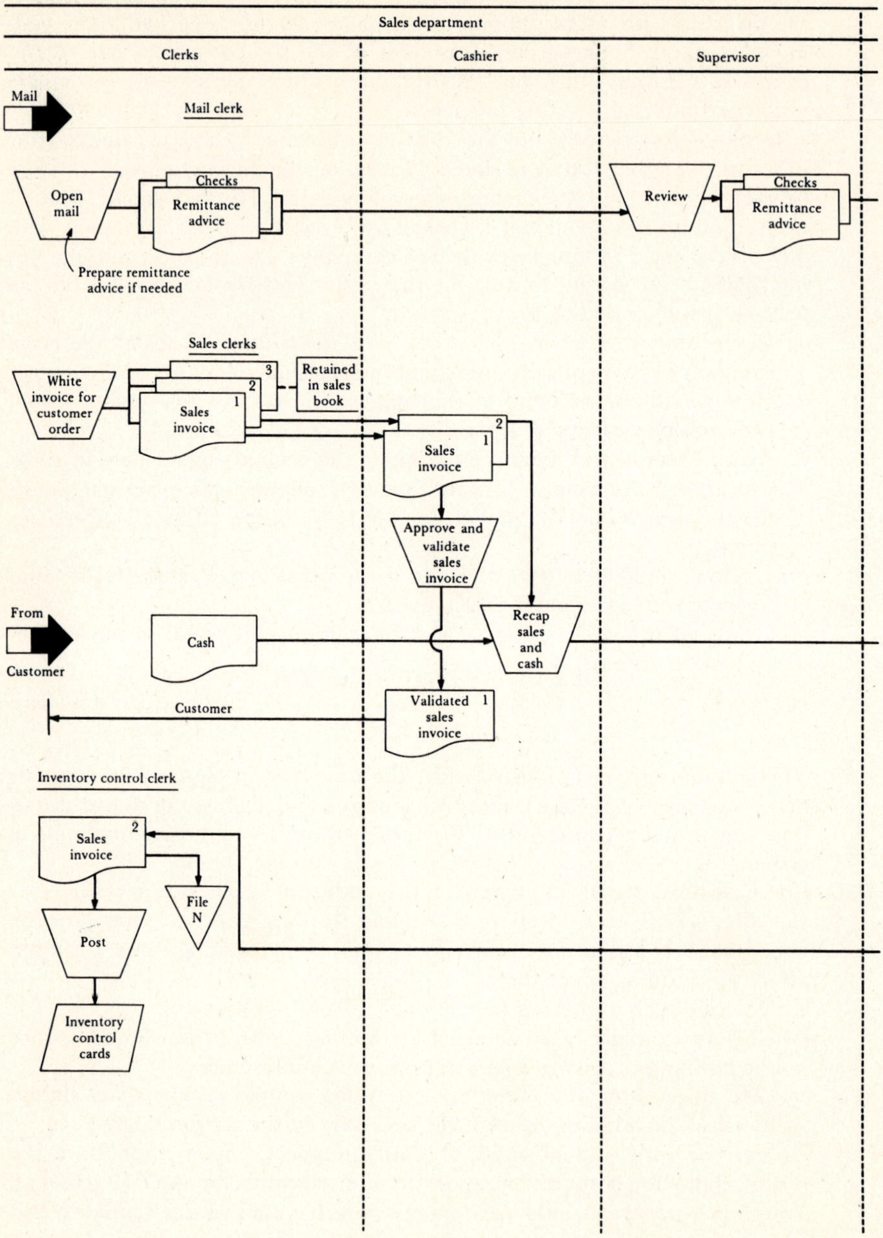

Sales department

Clerks | Cashier | Supervisor

Mail

Mail clerk

Open mail

Checks

Remittance advice

Prepare remittance advice if needed

Review

Checks

Remittance advice

Sales clerks

White invoice for customer order

3

2

1

Sales invoice

Retained in sales book

2

1

Sales invoice

Approve and validate sales invoice

From

Customer

Cash

Recap sales and cash

Customer

Validated sales invoice 1

Inventory control clerk

Sales invoice 2

File N

Post

Inventory control cards

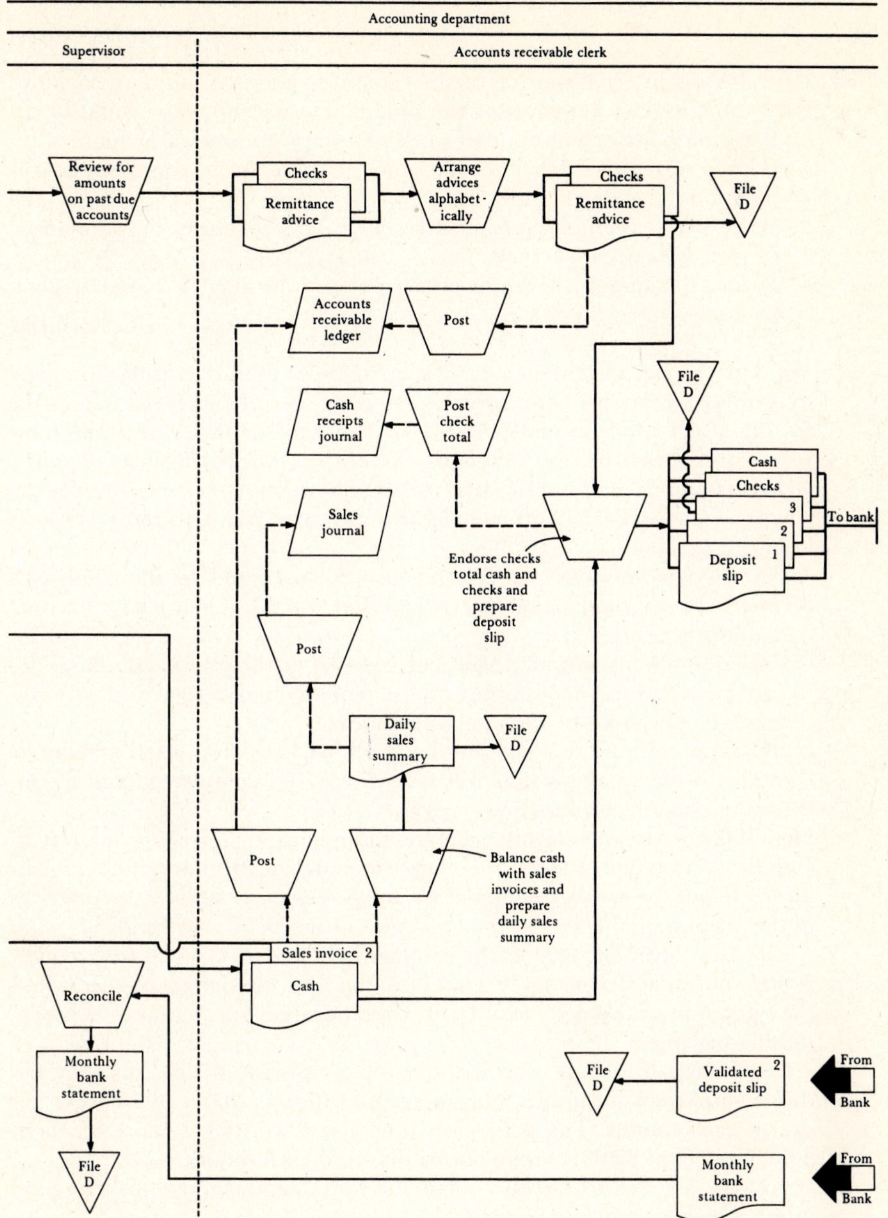
Accounting department
Supervisor
Accounts receivable clerk
Review for amounts on past due accounts
Checks
Remittance advice
Arrange advices alphabet-ically
Checks
Remittance advice
File D
Accounts receivable ledger
Post
Cash receipts journal
Post check total
File D
Cash
Checks
3
2
Deposit slip 1
To bank
Sales journal
Endorse checks total cash and checks and prepare deposit slip
Post
Daily sales summary
File D
Post
Balance cash with sales invoices and prepare daily sales summary
Sales invoice 2
Cash
Reconcile
Monthly bank statement
File D
File D
Validated deposit slip 2
From Bank
Monthly bank statement
From Bank

agement, based on your annual audit and the reasons or purposes for such a report. Do not write a report.

AICPA adapted

7-52. In evaluating internal control, the first step is to prepare an internal control questionnaire or a flowchart of the system. The second step should be to:

a. Determine the extent of audit work necessary to form an opinion.
b. Gather enough evidence to determine if the internal control system is functioning as described.
c. Write a letter to management describing the weaknesses in the internal control system.
d. Form a final judgment on the effectiveness of the internal control system.

AICPA adapted

7-53. You have recently been engaged by the Stephens Manufacturing Company to conduct an independent auditor's examination of its financial statements for the year ended December 31, 1981. During your first visit to the company's offices you discover that Marty Viverito, a college classmate of yours, is the company's chief internal auditor. He immediately welcomes you as the company's new CPA and offers to let you use any working papers or reports in his department.

a. How extensively can you rely on material prepared by the company's internal auditing department? What effect will this reliance have on your audit procedure?
b. Describe the investigation you may conduct of the internal auditing department before determining the extent of your reliance, if any, on material prepared by the internal auditors.
c. If you determine that the internal auditors have conducted a superior audit of the company's payroll system, can you completely omit all auditing procedures involving payrolls? Why?

7-54. Mrs. William Green recently acquired the financial controlling interest of Importers and Wholesalers, Inc., importers and distributors of cutlery. In her review of the duties of employees, Green became aware of loose practices in the signing of checks and the operation of the petty cash fund.

You have been engaged as the company's CPA, and Green's first request is that you suggest a system of sound practices for the signing of checks and the operation of the petty cash fund. Green prefers not to acquire a check-signing machine.

In addition to Green, who is the company president, the company has thirty employees including four corporate officers. About 500 checks are drawn each month. The petty cash fund has a working balance of about $400 and about $800 is expended by the fund each month.

Prepare a letter to Green containing your recommendations for good internal control procedures for:

a. Signing checks. (Green is unwilling to be drawn into routine check-signing duties. Assume that you decided to recommend two signatures on each check.)

b. Operation of the petty cash fund. (Where the effect of the control procedure is not evident, give the reason for the procedure.)

AICPA adapted

7-55. You have been engaged by the management of Rivera, Inc., to review its internal control over the purchase, receipt, storage, and issue of raw materials. You have prepared the following comments, which describe Rivera's procedures.

Raw materials, which consist mainly of high-cost electronic components, are kept in a locked storeroom. Storeroom personnel include a supervisor and four clerks. All are well trained, competent, and adequately bonded. Raw materials are removed from the storeroom only upon written or oral authorization of one of the production foremen.

There are no perpetual-inventory records; hence, the storeroom clerks do not keep records of goods received or issued. To compensate for the lack of perpetual records, a physical-inventory count is taken monthly by the storeroom clerks who are well supervised. Appropriate procedures are followed in making the inventory count.

After the physical count, the storeroom supervisor matches quantities counted against a predetermined reorder level. If the count for a given part is below the reorder level, the supervisor enters the part number on a materials-requisition list and sends this list to the accounts-payable clerk. The accounts-payable clerk prepares a purchase order for a predetermined reorder quantity for each part and mails the purchase order to the vendor from whom the part was last purchased.

When ordered materials arrive at Rivera, they are received by the storeroom clerks. The clerks count the merchandise and agree the counts to the shipper's bill of lading. All vendors' bills of lading are initialed, dated, and filed in the storeroom to serve as receiving reports.

Describe the weaknesses in internal control and recommend improvements of Rivera's procedures for the purchase, receipt, storage, and issue of raw materials.

AICPA adapted

7-56. The city of Lauraville recently opened a private parking lot in its downtown area for the benefit of city residents. A guard has been engaged to patrol the lot and to issue prenumbered parking stickers to residents who submit an application form and show evidence of residency. When the sticker is affixed to the car, the resident may park in the lot for twelve hours by placing four quarters in the parking meter. The guard inspects the stickers on all parked cars to determine that only residents are parking in the lot and also looks at the time gauges to see that the meter reflects the necessary fee has been paid. The completed application forms are maintained in the guard's office.

By using a master key, the guard takes the coins from the meters weekly and places them in a locked collection box. The guard delivers the box to the city storage department where a clerk opens it, manually counts the coins, puts the cash in a safe, and records the total on a weekly cash report. This report is sent to the city's accounting department. The day following the cash count, the city treasurer picks up the cash and manually recounts it, prepares the deposit slip, and makes the deposit at the bank. The deposit slip, authenticated by the bank teller, is sent to the accounting department where it is filed with the weekly cash report.

Describe weaknesses in the existing system and recommend for each weakness at least one improvement to strengthen the internal accounting control over the parking lot cash receipts for the city of Lauraville.

AICPA adapted

7-57. Herman Eisenberg, a new junior accountant with your firm, objects to your instructions when you ask him to prepare a flowchart of the client's purchasing system. He tells you that he spent many, many hours preparing flowcharts in a college course on accounting systems and that he is certain he can write up a narrative description of the client's purchasing system in much less time and with greater clarity than by use of flowcharts.

What advantages to flowcharting would you point out to Eisenberg? Would you change your instructions to Eisenberg in any manner?

7-58. George Koch, CPA, has been engaged to examine and report on the financial statements of Riverside Corporation. As part of the documentation of Riverside's internal accounting control system, Koch was given the flowchart for purchases which appears in Figure 7-16.

Identify the procedures relating to purchase requisitions and purchase orders that Koch would expect to find if Riverside Corporation's system of internal accounting control over purchases is effective. Do not comment on the effectiveness of the flow of documents as presented in the flowchart or on the separation of duties.

AICPA adapted

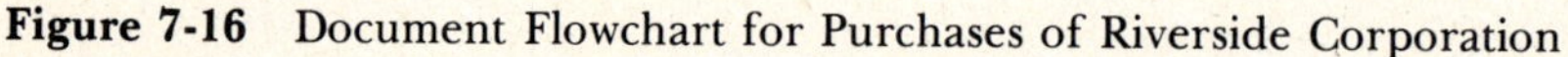

Figure 7-16 Document Flowchart for Purchases of Riverside Corporation

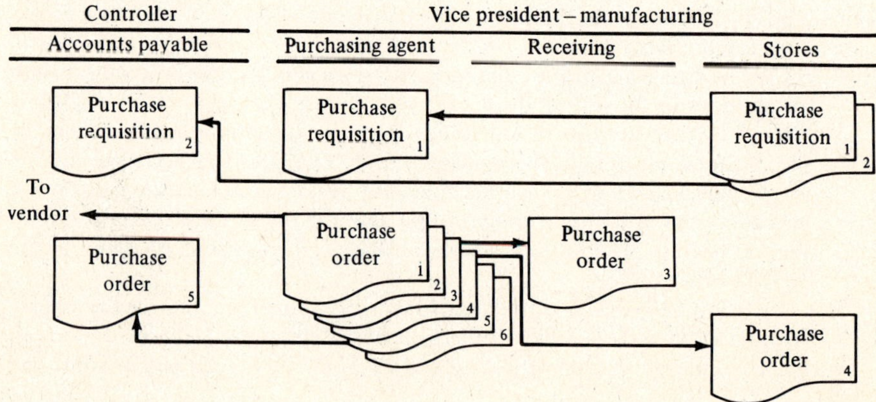

7-59. Kim Ecke, CPA, prepared the flowchart shown in Figure 7-17, on page 252, that portrays the raw-materials-purchasing function of one of Ecke's clients, a medium-sized manufacturing company, from the preparation of the initial documents through the vouching of invoices for payment in accounts payable. The flowchart was a portion of the work performed on the audit engagement to evaluate internal control.

Identify and explain the systems and control weaknesses evident from the flowchart shown in Figure 7-17. Include the internal control weaknesses resulting from activities performed or from those not performed. All documents are prenumbered.

AICPA adapted

7-60. The Gilmer Corporation became your client in 1982 when its former CPA died. You have completed your initial examination of Gilmer Corporation's financial statements for the year ended December 31, 1982 and have prepared a draft of your auditor's report containing your unqualified opinion, which was addressed to the board of directors according to instructions. In addition, you have drafted a special report in letter form outlining deficiencies in the system of internal control noted in the course of your examination and your recommendations for the correction of these deficiencies.

When you reviewed the drafts of these reports with Gilmer's president, he instructed you not to render the internal control letter. The president stated that he was aware the deficiencies existed and would give them his personal attention. Because he felt the board of directors should be concerned with major policy decisions and not with day-to-day management problems the president believed the board should not be burdened with such matters.

a. 1. What factors would you consider before deciding whether or not you should render the internal control letter?
   2. If you decide to render the internal control letter to Gilmer Corporation, should it be rendered to the board of directors or the president? Discuss.

b. Early in your examination you noted that the factory foreman approved time cards for hours worked and hourly rates and that he also distributed the factory payroll checks.
   1. Describe the alternative controls you would look for before concluding that an internal control weakness does in fact exist.
   2. If you find no alternative controls are in effect for the factory payroll, what steps in your factory payroll audit program would serve as a test for possible errors or irregularities? List only the procedures that would be of benefit in testing for this specific weakness.

AICPA adapted

7-61. The financial statements of the Tiber Company have never been audited by an independent CPA. Recently Tiber's management asked Anthony Burns, CPA, to conduct a special study of Tiber's internal control; this study will not include an examination of Tiber's financial statements. Following com-

Figure 7-17 Flowchart Prepared by Auditor

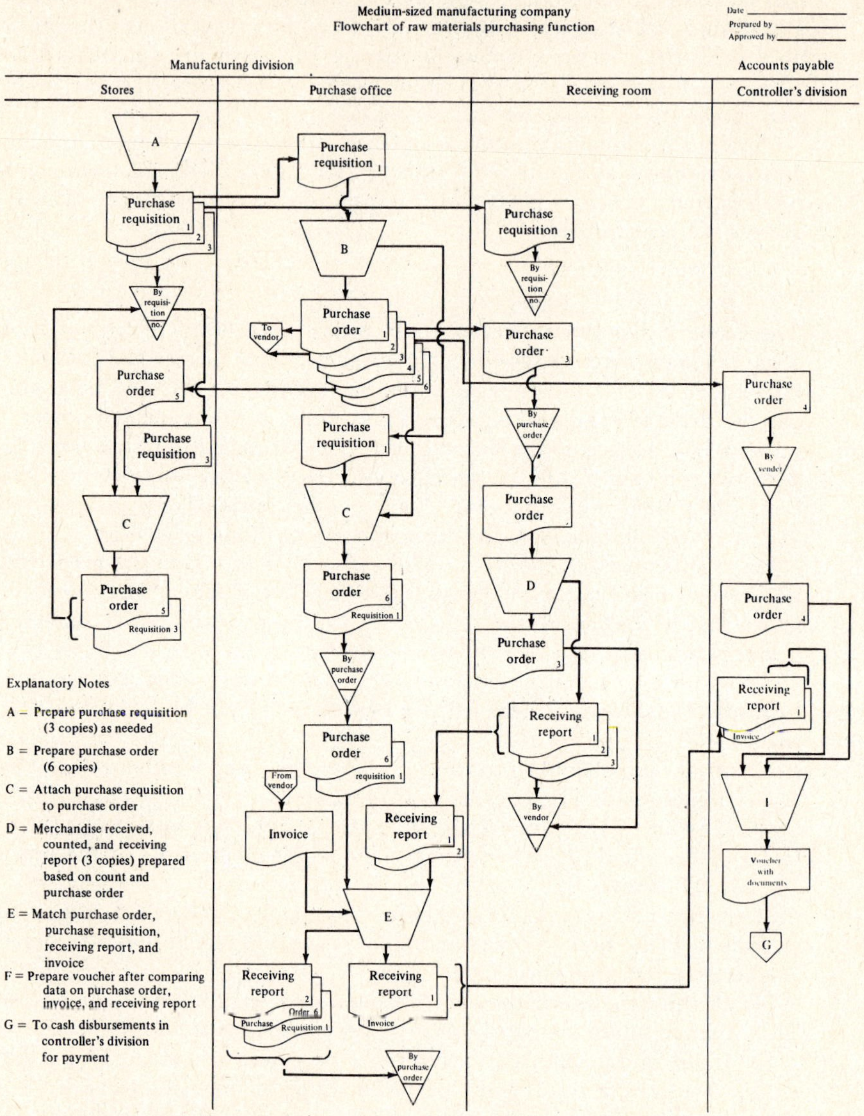
Medium-sized manufacturing company
Flowchart of raw materials purchasing function
Date
Prepared by
Approved by
Manufacturing division
Accounts payable
Stores
Purchase office
Receiving room
Controller's division
A
Purchase requisition 1 2 3
By requisition no.
Purchase order 5
Purchase requisition 3
C
Purchase order 5
Requisition 3
Purchase requisition 1
B
Purchase order 1 2 3 4 5 6
To vendor
Purchase requisition 1
C
Purchase order 6
Requisition 1
By purchase order
Purchase order 6
requisition 1
From vendor
Invoice
Receiving report 1 2
E
Receiving report 2
Order 6
Purchase
Requisition 1
Receiving report 1
Invoice
By purchase order
Purchase requisition 2
By requisition no.
Purchase order 3
By purchase order
Purchase order
D
Purchase order 3
Receiving report 1 2 3
By vendor
Purchase order 4
By vendor
Purchase order 4
Receiving report 1
Invoice
I
Voucher with documents
G
Explanatory Notes
A – Prepare purchase requisition (3 copies) as needed
B = Prepare purchase order (6 copies)
C = Attach purchase requisition to purchase order
D = Merchandise received, counted, and receiving report (3 copies) prepared based on count and purchase order
E = Match purchase order, purchase requisition, receiving report, and invoice
F = Prepare voucher after comparing data on purchase order, invoice, and receiving report
G = To cash disbursements in controller's division for payment

pletion of his special study, Burns plans to prepare a report that is consistent with the requirements of SAS section 640, "Reports on Internal Control."

a. Describe the inherent limitations that should be recognized in considering the potential effectiveness of any system of internal control.

b. Explain and contrast the review of internal control that Burns might make as part of an examination of financial statements with his special study of Tiber's internal control, covering each of the following:

1. objectives of review or study
2. scope of review or study
3. nature and content of reports

c. In connection with a loan application, Tiber plans to submit the CPA's report on his special study of internal control, together with its latest unaudited financial statements, to the Fourth National Bank.
Discuss the propriety of this use of the CPA's report on internal control.

AICPA adapted

7-62. You are reviewing audit work papers containing a narrative description of the Tenney Corporation's factory payroll system. A portion of that narrative is as follows:

Factory employees punch time clock cards each day when entering or leaving the shop. At the end of each week the timekeeping department collects the time cards and prepares duplicate batch-control slips by department showing total hours and number of employees. The time cards and original batch-control slips are sent to the payroll accounting section. The second copies of the batch-control slips are filed by date.

In the payroll accounting section payroll transaction cards are keypunched from the information on the time cards, and a batch total card for each batch is keypunched from the batch-control slip. The time cards and batch-control slips are then filed by batch for possible reference. The payroll transaction cards and batch total card are sent to data processing where they are sorted by employee number within batch. Each batch is edited by a computer program that checks the validity of employee number against a master employee tape file and the total hours and number of employees against the batch total card. A detail print-out by batch and employee number is produced, which indicates batches that do not balance and invalid employee numbers. This print-out is returned to payroll accounting to resolve all differences.

In searching for documentation you found a flowchart of the payroll system which included all appropriate symbols (American National Standards Institute, Inc.) but was only partially labeled. The portion of this flowchart described by the above narrative appears in Figure 7-18, on page 254.

a. Number your answer 1 through 17. Next to the corresponding number of your answer, supply the appropriate labeling (document name, process description, or file order) applicable to each numbered symbol on the flowchart.

b. Flowcharts are one aid auditors may use to determine and evaluate a client's internal control system. List advantages of using flowcharts in this context.

AICPA adapted

7-63. Over the last several years Springdale, Inc. has expanded and diversified its operations resulting in growth of sales and profit. Two years ago the Spring-

Figure 7-18 Tenney Corporation: Flowchart of Factory Payroll System

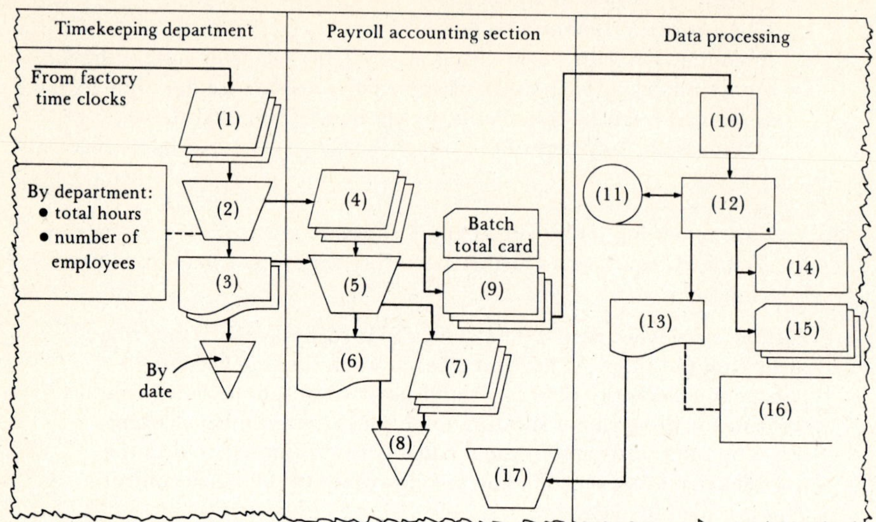

dale management established an internal audit function. The internal audit department is responsible for evaluating and recommending modifications in internal controls, reviewing operating practices to promote efficiency and economy, and conducting special inquiries at management's direction.

As in prior years, Springdale has engaged Anderson & May as its independent auditor. The partner from Anderson & May who is in charge of the Springdale audit has made an appointment with the manager of Springdale's internal audit department to discuss the development of the internal audit department, including new personnel and new activities, during its second year of operation.

The partner needs this information to plan the scope of the audit and to determine the amount of direct assistance, in the form of audit tests, to request from the internal audit department.

a. The scope of an audit can be modified if a good internal audit department exists in the client firm. What characteristics of Springdale's internal audit department and its work should Anderson & May evaluate when establishing the scope of its independent audit?

b. Explain, using one or two examples, the types of audit tests an external auditor could ask an internal audit department to perform in conjunction with the annual audit.

CMA adapted

8

Audit Evidence and Working Papers

The basis for an auditor's opinion on financial statements of a business enterprise is the examination that is performed in accordance with generally accepted auditing standards. The third standard of field work requires that sufficient competent evidential matter be obtained through inspection, observation, inquiries, and confirmation as a basis for the auditor's opinion. Consequently, the auditor's opinion is dependent upon obtaining sufficient evidence. Section One of this chapter considers the amount of evidence to be reviewed, the various types of evidence, and the methods of gathering the audit evidence. In Section Two, methods of accumulating the evidence in working papers are presented.

Section One—Audit evidence

Evidence consists of information and data that can be verified, are relevant to the matter under consideration, and can influence the auditor in arriving at an opinion. This information should display traits of genuineness and authenticity so that the auditor may rely upon it. The data concerning a business enterprise and its financial activities vary considerably in their nature and consequently in their degree of reliability. Auditors are presented with much data regarding a company's operations and financial statements, and they must select from the available information that which is reliable and has particular relevance to an expression of an opinion.

Amount of evidence

The final answer to the question of how much evidence an auditor should gather is that amount which is adequate in the auditor's judgment. Risk, materiality, and cost are factors that the auditor considers in applying judgment. Additionally, the reliability and quality of the evidence are major considerations.

RISK

The auditor needs greater assurance that items on the financial statements are fairly presented when the risk or chance of error or misstatement is greater. Risk is not associated with dollar amounts alone, for a misstatement can also be in the description of the item or in related comments and notations. Not only is there risk that an item included is in error, but there is also risk that necessary data will be omitted. The omission of data conveys information, just as erroneous inclusion does. If no marketable securities are shown on the balance sheet, for example, the user of the statements receives a message that the company does not own marketable investments as of the balance sheet date. The increased degree of assurance, which the auditor wants for items having a high degree of risk, may be obtained by acquiring a greater quantity of evidence or evidence that has a higher degree of reliability or a combination of both. As is indicated in the discussion later in this chapter, different types of evidence vary in their reliability.

One factor that affects the risk associated with an item is the effectiveness of the internal accounting controls related to the item. The stronger the accounting controls, the lower the degree of risk. Another factor influencing the risk is the environmental condition in which the company operates. If the economy is flourishing or if income tax rates are unusually high, there is risk that assets may be understated, liabilities overstated, and net income correspondingly reduced. On the other hand, if the company is in financial difficulty or if higher income tax rates are anticipated soon, there is risk that income will be overstated in the current period. If the company's trend of operations is opposite that of the industry, there is risk that misstatements will appear on the financial statements in order to make the company's operations fit closer to the industry's trend.

The nature of the items also influences the risk. A highly liquid item like cash, which is also hard to identify in terms of ownership, has a high degree of risk associated with it. Office equipment is an example of an asset with a low degree of risk as far as theft is concerned, yet there is some degree of risk associated with its improper use. Items like buildings and franchises have practically no risk of theft, but there is risk that incorrect amounts will be capitalized or that improper amounts will be allocated to annual expenses.

MATERIALITY

The concept of materiality is difficult to define and depends primarily upon the auditor's judgment for interpretation. A matter is considered to be material if its inclusion or exclusion will make a difference in the decision of the user of the information containing the matter. The vague term *matter* is used purposefully to indicate that to be material an item does not have to be expressed in dollars, not even in quantitative terms, and not necessarily in the body of the financial statements. Material matters may be such items as the disclosure of an accounting policy, the pro forma computation of a prior year's net income to reflect a subsequent accounting change, or the classification of an item on the balance sheet as a current asset as opposed to a noncurrent asset. If a matter is relevant to the decision of a user of financial statements, that matter—regardless of its form or location—is considered material.

Because materiality does not necessarily relate to quantitative matters, it frequently cannot be described in quantitative terms. Several attempts have been made to define materiality as some established percentage relationship, such as considering all items valued at more than 10 percent of net income to be material. Such attempts have generally been unsuccessful, for an item may have only a 10 percent effect on net income but at the same time have a 30 percent effect on current liabilities and a major effect on the current ratio. The percentage point at which matters make a difference to users is unknown; consequently, the decision regarding the point of materiality is left to the auditor's judgment.

The pervasiveness of an item's effect should be considered in judging its materiality. If the effect is contained entirely in the fixed-asset section of the balance sheet, the item is likely considered less material than another item of the same amount that affects the assets, owner's equity, statement of changes in financial position, and the income statement. To illustrate, assume fixed assets costing $300,000 were scrapped during the year and no entry was made to record the transaction. If the assets were fully depreciated, the failure to record the disposal has its effect contained entirely within the fixed-asset section of the balance sheet. Conversely, if the assets were not fully depreciated and the costs were being amortized at 12 percent a year, there would be, at the minimum, a misstatement of $36,000 on all major financial statements.

There are varying degrees of materiality. Matters shift from immaterial to material and from material to extremely material. A matter that is immaterial may be treated in any expedient manner without affecting the auditor's opinion, but once the matter is considered material, it is important enough to cause a qualification of the auditor's opinion. A matter with even greater materiality is considered to be extremely material and therefore sufficiently important to negate the auditor's opinion. An adverse opinion or a disclaimer of opinion must be rendered depending on whether the matter concerns an accounting principle or unavailability of information. Readers may wish to refer to Chapter 5 for further discussion of materiality as related to an auditor's opinion.

Since there are varying degrees of materiality, an auditor should seek more relevant evidence and/or a greater quantity of evidence for those matters that have a greater degree of materiality. Risk and materiality both vary in direct relationship with the quantity and quality of evidence; therefore, all should increase or decrease together.

COST OF EVIDENCE

An auditor must consider cost involved in obtaining evidence. The cost of acquiring evidence should be compared with the degree of assurance one will derive from the evidence. There is no exact measurement of either this cost or the degree of assurance; however, the auditor should be able to assess both with a fair degree of accuracy. In deciding if a particular type of evidence is worth the cost of acquiring it, the auditor should consider what alternative forms of evidence are available. As an illustration, the auditor does not have to incur the travel cost involved in personally examining inventory located in a distant city; another auditor may be engaged in the distant city to observe the inventory count as well as to examine some of the physical goods on hand. The degree of assurance should be only slightly lower; yet the cost savings should be considerable. The auditor should not omit an important element of evidence merely because it is costly to acquire, but rather should insist upon obtaining adequate evidence regardless of the cost. However, the auditor may settle for an alternative type of evidence because of cost considerations; and at times, if evidence is unavailable or is prohibitively costly to obtain, the auditor may have to disclaim or to qualify the opinion.

CONCLUSIVENESS

Audit evidence usually is not absolutely conclusive. It is considered to be persuasive rather than convincing. Regardless of the amount of evidence or its reliability, in all likelihood, the auditor will have some doubt regarding the fairness of the presentation of the matter involved. Examination of all evidence available, even presence at the client's office throughout the year, will not allow the auditor to have complete assurance about fair presentation or accuracy of items on the financial statements. The possibility of errors and misstatements always exists. Although the auditor cannot consider enough evidence to remove all doubt, evidence should be examined to the point of removing all substantial doubt.

Evidence classified by purpose

An auditor expresses an opinion on a company's financial statements taken as a whole, not on individual items on the statements. To arrive at this comprehensive opinion, the auditor reviews evidence that may be classified into three major groups according to the purpose of the review. The first is a broad group comprising general evidence relating to the overall welfare of the business enterprise. Evidence in this group enables the auditor to arrive at an opinion about the fairness of the financial statements in reflecting the general condition of the company in its environment. This evidence usually is reflected by events outside the accounting and financial system of the company. The second group comprises evidence that enables the auditor to determine whether the accounting system is functioning properly. The auditor seeks assurance that all authorized activities, and no others, are properly recorded, summarized, classified, and presented in correct form with the appropriate explanatory notations and comments. Evidence in this group is primarily contained in the financial records and financial statements of the company. As the most basic of all forms of evidence, the third group consists of facts relating to the authorization and occurrence of transactions, activities, and events. The first two groups involve processing the information and its presentation. The third group concerns fundamental facts showing that events occurred, assets exist, and transactions were authorized. These three groups of evidence are referred to in this chapter as (1) general evidence, (2) systems evidence, and (3) basic evidence.

GENERAL EVIDENCE

Information that relates to the environment in which the company or industry operates is considered general evidence. This represents facts that have already or likely will in the future affect the financial welfare of the business enterprise but have not entered into the financial records or statements. Illustrations of such matters are the forthcoming expiration of a patent that protects a major product, the nearing exhaustion or depletion of the supply of an essential raw material, and the approaching deadline to meet certain standards of environmental protection. These are examples of facts that can be verified and without question should be considered by the auditor; however, other evidence somewhat less verifiable may also need to be considered. The environmental conditions in which the company operates—reflected by such evidence as changing consumer demands, changing composition of the population, present and prospective legislation, changing economic conditions, and actions by competitors—are relevant to the overall condition of the enterprise, although the exact effect is impossible to predict. Some authorities advocate that the auditor give consideration to the effectiveness of management as evidence of the overall well-being of the company. These latter examples of general evidence are certainly not as verifiable as those first mentioned, and the necessary extent of the auditor's consideration is less well established.

General evidence is varied and differs for each business enterprise. To determine whether all such evidence has been considered, an auditor should ask whether the financial statements and related notes and comments furnish all facts necessary for informed decision making by users who depend entirely upon this source for their information. If the auditor believes that any general information available about the present or prospective financial and operating conditions of the company would be of benefit to users of the financial statements, the auditor should review the general evidence to determine whether the information should be disclosed.

SYSTEMS EVIDENCE

Auditors examine sufficient evidence to be assured that the financial statements fairly reflect a company's activities throughout the reporting period and the position of its economic resources and obligations at the end of the period. They examine facts which indicate that the activities, resources, and obligations were properly entered into the accounting system, were processed through the system, and are fairly presented on the financial statements. Evidence concerning the design of the internal accounting control system is of major interest to the auditor. To be familiar with the design and function of the accounting system, the auditor reviews evidence acquired from discussions with officials and with operating employees; evidence acquired by reviewing policy statements, procedure manuals, and job descriptions; and evidence acquired by observing the activities of the employees during the normal course of operations. Practically all types of evidence contribute to the auditor's understanding of the functioning of the accounting system.

BASIC EVIDENCE

The auditor requires assurance that all transactions occurring during the period are reflected in the financial records. The auditor wants assurance as well that all transactions recorded are legitimate activities of the business and are shown in the proper amounts. Whether the transaction involves revenue, expense, asset, or liability, the auditor reviews evidence to determine its validity. For assets, the best evidence is physical examination of the item itself or its physical representation in some documentary form. If the transaction involves an activity, the auditor usually wants to observe

Table 8-1 Classification of Evidence

	Purpose of evidence review		
Nature of evidence	General	Systems	Basic
Internal control		X	
Physical existence			X
Documents		X	X
Books of account		X	X
Oral statements	X	X	
Interrelated data	X	X	
Activities		X	X

the activity being performed. Basic evidence may be thought of as facts that are as close to their original form as possible.

Evidence classified as to its nature

In this section, evidence is presented by types, generally according to the nature or the characteristics of the facts represented. A particular item, when considered as evidence, may be classified in more than one category; for example, internal control is a classification that embraces several of the other types. Table 8-1 indicates how evidence may be classified both by the purpose of the review and by the nature of the evidence.

INTERNAL ACCOUNTING CONTROL

As described in Chapter 7, internal accounting control is the plan of organization and the procedures and records designed to give assurance that a company's transactions are executed in accordance with management's authorization and that the transactions are recorded in a manner to permit preparation of proper financial statements. Additionally, the records should be maintained in a manner to provide accountability for the assets, and the control system should provide for assets to be used only in accordance with management's authorization. The auditor's study and evaluation of a company's system of internal control serves two major purposes: (1) to indicate the reliability of the accounts and financial statements produced by the accounting system and (2) to determine the extent of the other auditing procedures necessary in the conduct of the audit. Internal accounting control, therefore, is a major form of evidence in itself as well as an indicator of how much additional evidence is necessary.

To evaluate an internal accounting control system, an auditor examines other forms of evidence to determine how well the system is designed and how well it is functioning. The auditor should review system documentation, organization charts, procedure manuals, and system flow charts to learn how the control system should work. Discussions with company officers, controller, chief accountant, and key employees form another type of evidence giving insight into the design of the internal accounting control system.

Before relying upon an internal accounting control system as evidence, an auditor normally makes tests to verify understanding of the system as well as tests of compliance to determine the extent to which the design of the system is implemented in the actual operations. The tests of understanding and of compliance make use of several other types of evidence since the auditor examines supporting documents for selected transactions, traces these transactions through the journals and ledgers, observes employees at work, and questions employees about actual duties performed.

It should be obvious that, in order to use internal accounting control as a form of evidence, many other types of evidence are also considered. These other types of evidence are reviewed to determine the design of the accounting control system and the degree of compliance therewith. The auditor evaluates the degree of reliance that can be placed on the control system and, consequently, decides on the amount of additional evidence that must be reviewed in the substantive tests. The evidence reviewed in the substantive testing is the same type of evidence reviewed in the tests of understanding and tests of compliance. For any area of weakness in the accounting control system, the auditor should require compensating evidence of another type. The quantity or quality of additional evidence should be in direct relationship to the degree of risk produced by the weakness in the control system. Stated in reverse form, the stronger the internal accounting controls, the less additional evidence the auditor needs to examine.

PHYSICAL EXISTENCE

Among the strongest types of evidence is physical existence. An auditor who sees a piece of machinery or a building or who counts cash on hand is certain of its existence. The auditor must be aware, however, that existence and ownership are two separate qualities; additional evidence must be reviewed to support ownership.

Since both quantity and quality affect financial representation, the auditor should consider these characteristics when they are evident in an item's physical existence. Usually the quantity of an item is clearly established by its physical existence; however, the quality may not be as obvious. For example, damage to inventory items may be easily detected, whereas obsolescence may be determined only upon examination of sales or production records or after a discussion with client personnel. Also, the physical existence of checks included in cash on hand proves nothing of quality or validity; these are determined when the checks are deposited and clear the banking system.

Assets such as cash in the bank, investments in securities, and franchises do not have physical existence but do have a form of physical representation. A bank statement represents cash in the bank or the company's claim for physical cash if desired; stock certificates represent the company's interest in other enterprises; and franchise contracts represent the legal rights bestowed upon the owner. The physical representation of items is generally accepted as the strongest evidence available for items that do not have physical existence or where the items are not available for examination. This physical representation takes the form of documents, and the reliability and limitations of the documentary form of evidence are discussed in the following section.

DOCUMENTS

Auditors rely upon documentary evidence more than any other type of evidence. Documents vary considerably in their degree of reliability, and one of the factors that affects their reliability is the ease with which they can be reproduced. For example, note receivable forms can be purchased at any office supply company and even at some variety stores. On the other hand, stock and bond certificates are printed on high-grade paper and bear a corporate seal, serial numbers, and official signatures, which increase the difficulty of reproduction. However, should a client's employee or officer set out to forge documents, it may be done with such skill that it would be difficult, if not impossible, for an auditor to detect it. The reliability of documents as evidence is also influenced by their source and the circulation they receive.

Documents Prepared Outside the Enterprise Documents prepared by outsiders have a high degree of reliability as evidence if they are sent directly to the auditor. The outside party should be independent and thoroughly competent on the matter at hand. The authority of the respondent influences the reliability of the testimony. If the documents containing the testimony are sent directly to the auditor, there is no chance for client personnel to modify the documents or to change the company records to agree with data on the documents. Documents of this type include accounts receivable confirmations returned by the client's customers, bank confirmations, letters from the client's attorney regarding ownership of property and any contingent liabilities, and letters from insurance companies concerning the insurance in force and the cash value of life policies on officers and key employees. Other examples are (1) confirmations from a bonded warehouseman regarding inventory stored, (2) communication from an investment broker of securities held for safekeeping, and (3) a statement from an actuary dealing with the adequacy of the pension provision. The last example illustrates the auditor's use of the work of a specialist to obtain competent evidential information. Before relying upon the work of a specialist, the auditor should make an investigation sufficient to be assured of the specialist's qualifications and reputation. As pointed out in SAS No. 11 (AU 336.08), the auditor should make some tests of the accounting information furnished the specialist to determine its appropriateness to the matter under review. The auditor should consider the reasonableness of the findings of the specialist before using them. If the specialist is related to the client, the auditor should make a more thorough review of the specialist's assumptions, methods, and findings than would be true if the specialist were not related.

Documentary evidence sent directly to the auditor at the client's request becomes part of the working papers and is retained as a valuable part of the support for the auditor's opinion. Documents prepared outside the company and in the client's possession have a slightly lower degree of reliability but nevertheless are an important type of evidence. The auditor, in all probability, examines more of this type of evidence than any other because it is the usual information maintained by a business enterprise to support all types of business activities, particularly expenditures. Invoices and statements received from outside creditors constitute a large volume of documentary evidence. Lease agreements, customers' orders, notes receivable, stock and bond investments, and bank statements are other examples of documents sent to the client by outsiders.

Internally Prepared Documents Documents prepared by personnel within the client company generally have less reliability as evidence than externally prepared documents. However, if the internally prepared document has circulated outside the company, it increases in reliability because of its acceptance by outsiders. Paid checks issued by the client are the primary example of this class of evidence. The payee's endorsing the check and the bank's honoring it contribute toward increased reliability. There is evidence that a transaction took place in the amount recorded on the check and that the related asset, expense, or liability reduction is a proper entry. There is always a possibility, however, that these documents were altered after they were returned to the client. The internal accounting controls should be designed so that such alterations are impossible to accomplish or are ineffective in covering up errors or misstatements. During the conduct of the audit, the auditor may request authority to pick up the bank statements from the bank, thereby giving evidence of greater reliability to the paid checks, since they have not been in the hands of client personnel after circulating outside the business. Although canceled checks constitute by far the majority of internally prepared documents circulating outside a company, other such documents are acknowledged purchase orders, a receipted bill of lading, a canceled note or bond payable, a lease agreement signed by the outside lessee, and a receipted bank deposit slip.

Internally prepared documents that circulate within the client's organization may have some degree of reliability as evidence. The extent of the reliability is closely related to the degree of internal accounting controls associated with the documents. For example, if the documents are serially numbered and accounted for and involve several persons in their preparation and approval, and if the preparer has no access to the assets or accounts to which the documents relate, in all likelihood they have a fairly high degree of reliability. A more specific example is a prenumbered shipping ticket prepared by a clerk who has access neither to accounts receivable records nor to the inventory of merchandise. The shipping ticket is approved by a supervisor before copies are sent to the warehouse and to the billing clerk. The auditor should be able to place reliance on such a shipping ticket.

Some documents may be prepared within the client's organization specifically for the auditor. When these documents are prepared by a person of authority, they may constitute reliable evidence. If the documents support evidence of another type, their reliability as evidence is increased. A statement of the president's own indebtedness to the company for a $5,000 advance is an example of such a document. Another example is a letter of representation in which officials of the company state that they are responsible for the accounting records, accounting system, and financial statements.

A letter of representation is a formal statement signed by one or more officers of the client company. In this document, the officials acknowledge their responsibility for the financial statements and state specifically that all financial records were available for the auditor's examination, the minutes of meetings of stockholders and the board of directors were complete, and that the financial statements are free of errors and unrecorded transactions. Other matters are described in SAS No. 19 (AU 333.05) that should be included in the written representation, such as information concerning material events that have occurred subsequent to the balance sheet date, information concerning transactions with related parties, intentions for refinancing certain liabilities, or the plans of management to discontinue a segment of the business. Statements regarding the quality of the inventory, the adequacy of the bad debt allowance, the marketability of investments, the proper disclosure of contingent liabilities, and many other details may be included in the letter of representation. During the examination the client may have made oral representations to the auditor concerning many of these matters. The written letter of representation confirms these oral statements, verifies the continuing appropriateness of such statements, and reduces the possibility of their being misunderstood.

Although a written letter of representation is essential documentary evidence, the auditor does not accept unquestioningly all statements made by management personnel. In many cases the auditor insists upon acquiring additional evidence to corroborate information contained in the letter of representation. However, certain representations, such as those describing management's plans for future action, are difficult or impossible to support with additional evidence. An illustration of a letter of representation appears in Chapter 15.

Documents prepared within the company and not circulating within the organization have the lowest degree of reliability of any internally created documents. These documents are not worthless as evidence, however, for they may corroborate other evidence or may have been prepared by someone in authority. A credit memorandum prepared by the credit manager becomes good evidence to support the write-off of an account receivable when it is supported by correspondence with the customer and perhaps with a collection agency. Minutes of the board of directors' meetings and meetings of important committees constitute reliable documentary evidence that does not circulate in the usual sense within the client's organization, and yet these documents are usually considered quite reliable.

A type of internally prepared documents relied upon by auditors is composed of general organizational records such as a written policy statement regarding company goals, objectives, and procedures. The company's budget, both long range and short range, could be included in this category. There should be extensive documentation of the company's electronic data processing system including systems flowcharts, program flowcharts, and procedure manuals. Documentation should describe the organization of the company, the design of the information system, the design of the accounting control system, the operating procedures, and duties prescribed for each job. Reliance on such documentation is essential if the auditor is to review and evaluate the internal control system, and extensive use of such evidence is made whenever the auditor performs an audit of management's performance.

Documents serve as both basic evidence and systems evidence. As basic evidence a document represents an actual event that took place involving a specific amount of funds, and as systems evidence a document indicates that the transaction was properly recorded and processed through the accounting system. A paid invoice for supply parts is an illustration. The invoice for the supplies supported by a purchase order and receiving report for the same quantity and description of items provides evidence that the actual acquisition of supplies took place. The fact that the three documents relate to the same event strongly suggests that the accounting control system is functioning properly. Further indications are such facts as the documents' being marked to indicate price verification, the account to be charged, check number, and date of payment. Other documents, such as the canceled check and supply requisitions, serve as corroborating evidence that the accounting system is functioning properly.

BOOKS OF ACCOUNT

A very basic form of evidence consists of a company's journals, ledgers, transaction tapes, master files, EDP programs, and other financial records collectively called *books of account.* When searching for evidence to substantiate an amount on the financial statements, an absolute requirement of the auditor is that the item be recorded in the books of account. This requirement is fundamental to the auditing process because the auditor should be able to trace an item from the financial statements backward through the ledger accounts to the journal or transaction tape and to the original source document. Perhaps the poorest single explanation an auditor can offer in justifying why a certain item appears on the financial statements is that it was recorded in the books of account. Yet this single explanation is an essential one to be combined with other forms of evidence.

An integral part of a company's books of account are controlling accounts and subsidiary ledgers. Their use throughout the year and agreement of balances at year end form evidence that the internal accounting control system is functioning properly. If the subsidiary records are maintained by a person other than the one maintaining the control account, this function of the accounting control system adds to the reliability of the evidence. On the other hand, if the control account is produced by a computer at the same time it processes the data appearing in the subsidiary accounts without other independently derived control totals, little significance can be placed on this type of evidence.

If the client company maintains its records in an electronic data processing system, the various programs used to process transactions constitute a major element of audit evidence. The auditor must acquire a thorough understanding of the processes and controls contained in the programs in order to assess the internal accounting control system and verify the proper handling of transactions. This subject is covered in Chapter 10.

ORAL STATEMENTS

The danger in relying on oral statements is the difficulty or sometimes impossibility of verification. Once a person has made an oral statement, there may be difficulty in later proving that that person made such a statement. There is also the possibility that the receiver of the oral message misunderstood the message or recorded the information incorrectly. In spite of the inherent dangers in using oral statements, as evidence they merit some degree of reliability.

The auditor in charge of an engagement properly spends considerable time in discussions with company officials regarding the objectives of the business enterprise, its progress during the year, major problems that have arisen, and prospects for the future. If there have been any major changes in the company's operations during the year under audit, or if any are anticipated during the forthcoming year, the auditor needs to discuss the present and prospective effects of such changes and the client's manner of disclosing them on the financial statements. Oral statements made during these discussions form a part of the general evidence that the auditor must have for conducting the examination and writing the report. As described earlier in this chapter, many matters discussed orally with client officials are presented as part of the written letter of representation.

Oral statements by the controller, or other official, in answering an internal control questionnaire constitute valid evidence. In obtaining facts to understand the internal accounting control system, the auditor considers oral statements made by employees at all levels regarding the nature of their duties and responsibilities.

In response to questions from the auditor, oral statements may be the only evidence available to explain an unusual entry, to explain why an item was classified as belonging in one account rather than another, or to explain the manner of making a computation such as an accrual of wages or taxes.

Oral statements on the more important matters should be reduced to writing by the auditor as soon as possible with a notation of who made the statement, the date, and under what circumstances. When possible, oral statements should be supported by other forms of corroborating evidence. The agreement of oral statements obtained from several employees adds reliability to this form of evidence. The fact that the auditor is told the same thing by several different sources makes the matter more believable than if it came from a single source.

INTERRELATED DATA

Auditors rely upon evidence provided by the interrelationship of data. Certain relationships normally exist, and any time there is a variance from the expected relationship, the auditors should seek evidence to explain the variance. The relationship may be expressed as a ratio, as a trend, simply as one account in comparison with another, or in many other ways. The rate of gross profit on sales and the comparison of interest expense with debt outstanding during the year are two examples of such interrelated data frequently considered by auditors. The relationships vary from company to company, and the auditors should determine which relationships are meaningful on each engagement and use only those related data as evidence. Some relationships are reflected in computations made by the client, whereas others may be made by the auditors.

ACTIVITIES

Activities by company employees, both operating and clerical, constitute a type of evidence. These activities usually produce recorded information in the books of account, documents, or reports. The auditor relies on the recorded information extensively but at times may want to see the actual operations being performed. For instance, evidence is acquired by observing the client's personnel take physical inventory that cannot be obtained from records. The auditor can observe the care with which the personnel count and their efforts for completeness and accuracy. Workers' clocking in, their activities on the production line, a distribution of paychecks, warehouse employees' filling orders, and cashiers' receipting customers are but a few of the possible activities that the auditor may wish to observe to acquire evidence. Evidence of this type is useful on any audit but has special significance for audits that take a systems approach or are designed to produce an opinion on operations or management.

SUBSTANCE OVER FORM

In some instances, the substance of business transactions may differ from their form. Generally the financial statements should reflect the substance of transactions regardless of their form. Because transactions with related parties may have a form different from their substance, the auditor should carefully review material transactions between the client and known related parties. Specific audit procedures are suggested in SAS No. 6 (AU 335) for the auditor to determine the existence of related parties. The procedures include such steps as inquiry of client personnel, review of SEC filings, determination of trustees and officers of pension and other trust funds, identification of principal stockholders, and review of material investment transactions. After identifying the related parties, the auditor should take special steps to identify transactions with these parties. Evidence revealing such transactions may be found in the minutes of meetings of board of directors, invoices from attorneys, loan agreements containing guarantee provisions, large and unusual transactions near year end, and special agreements with major customers or suppliers. The auditor should obtain an understanding of the business purpose of transactions with related parties, determine that there was appropriate approval, and consider the reasonableness of the disclosure on the financial statements including any representation by the client that the transactions with related parties were consummated on terms no less favorable than those that

Table 8-2 Relation of Audit Techniques and Audit Evidence

	Purpose of evidence review		
Audit techniques	General	Systems	Basic
Examination			X
Inspection		X	X
Confirmation		X	X
Recomputation		X	
Observation	X	X	X
Inquiry	X	X	
Comparison	X	X	

would have been obtained with unrelated parties. An extensive amount of evidence may be necessary to evaluate related party transactions and determine their substance.

Methods of gathering audit evidence

The various methods employed by an auditor to gather evidence are called *audit techniques.* Some of these methods have necessarily been mentioned in the discussion of audit evidence. The relationship of the various audit techniques to the three groups of evidence classified by purpose of review is shown in Table 8-2.

The discussion of audit techniques in this section relates to evidence gathering in general, although some specific examples are given. Auditing procedures, presented in Part III of this book, illustrate further how these techniques are applied in the process of gathering evidence as the auditor examines the assets, liabilities, owners' equity, and integrated operating activities.

The auditing process is one of critical analysis. Usually the auditor traces data from the financial statements, back through the accounting system, to the transactions that initially produced the data. In addition, the auditor frequently traces some transactions forward through the system, especially in compliance testing of internal accounting controls. The path followed by the auditor is known as the *audit trail.* In following the audit trail, the auditor analyzes many accounts that are reflected on the financial statements. In analyzing an account, the auditor identifies all the various data elements making up the balance. The auditor uses one or more of the audit techniques discussed in the following pages to obtain evidence regarding the items reflected in the account balance. At times the auditor may want to inspect evidence regarding each item, at other times may select only the material items, and at still other times may use a sampling procedure to select the items.

EXAMINATION

The audit technique whereby the auditor physically looks at an asset is called *examination.* By seeing the asset, the auditor identifies the item as being what it is purported to be and is assured that the item actually exists. Usually little regarding ownership is inferred from the evidence of existence. At the time of observing the physical existence, the auditor frequently determines the quantity on hand. In a large number of cases, the auditor is also able to reach a conclusion about the genuineness and quality of the item. Many items of inventory and equipment, for example, are common enough that the auditor's general knowledge is enough to determine their genuineness and quality. If the items are of an unusual nature, the auditor should call upon an independent advisor who has expert knowledge regarding the items for advice.

As discussed earlier in this chapter, many assets have a form of physical representation. The physical representation is examined in much the same way as an asset with physical existence is examined. Since the physical representation is usually in the form of a document, the audit technique is considered in this chapter as inspection of documentary evidence. In actual practice, the terms *inspection* and *examination* as applied to the review of physical and documentary evidence are used almost interchangeably.

INSPECTION

The auditor's technique of reviewing documentary evidence is called *inspection.* Since documentary evidence takes such a variety of forms, the actual steps performed by an auditor in the technique of inspection also vary.

Generally the auditor looks at a document to determine if it is genuine. The document should appear to be authentic; it should appear to be what the client represents it to be and should contain no indications of alteration. For example, an invoice that supposedly was received from a supplier should be on the supplier's statement form, should indicate shipment date, should bear an invoice number, and should show signs of having been sent through the mails.

Inspection includes determination that the item or transaction was authorized either specifically or generally. In many cases specific authorization is indicated by a signature on the document itself, such as a lease agreement. In other cases separate supporting documents contain the authorization. The supporting document may be attached to the primary document, such as a purchase order attached to an invoice for merchandise. At times reference may have to be made to the minutes of meetings of the board of directors to obtain evidence of both specific and general authorization. The auditor may have to determine general authorization by reference to policy statements from company officials. In the case of general authorization, the auditor should determine that the particular transaction or activity represented by the document under inspection meets the criteria established by the general authorization.

Also included in the inspection of documents is the determination that the transaction represented has been entered properly into the books of account. A common source of error in accounting records is the posting procedure. Often, journal totals are incorrectly transferred to ledger accounts or are entered in the wrong account. An important testing procedure is the verification of a representative number of postings to establish the accuracy of the records. Whenever a document authorizes a continuing process, the auditor should make tests to determine that the proper recording is made periodically.

The inspection technique is applied to all documents, records, and reports that come to the auditor's attention. In scrutinizing each document, the auditor is looking for the reasonableness of what is presented. By calling upon a total knowledge of accounting and business in general, the auditor can identify items or situations that appear to be unusual and to need further investigation. Entries that are large, that bear an unusual posting reference, or that possess any characteristic out of the ordinary should be investigated. In inspecting a list of inventory items, for example, the auditor may quickly spot an amount that is unreasonably large for that type of product. Investigation may reveal the item was priced at $10 each, rather than at $0.10 each, or perhaps the price was expressed in units of 1,000 but applied to a single unit count. Another example might occur during the auditor's inspection of the cash receipts journal and consist of the discovery of a loan of $50,000 recorded as a sale. The large, even amount would likely alert the auditor to make further investigation. The auditor should make a systematic review of the client's general journal entries as a part of the test of details. Frequently, transactions of audit interest require nonroutine journal entries, and an examination of the general journal may disclose such items.

Experience and constant alertness are characteristics of auditors that enable them to apply the inspection technique in a manner to detect the unusual. Some auditors use the term *scan* rather than inspection, as used in the sense of critical review of a document, record, or report.

In auditing, a variety of terms are used to describe the process of inspection. Rather than asking an assistant to *inspect* the supporting documents, the auditor might use the terms *vouch, agree, compare, sight,* or *examine.* A term that generally is avoided in auditing terminology is the verb *check.* To tell an assistant to "check the disbursements" can mean any number of things from putting a tick mark by each recorded disbursement, to inspecting the canceled checks, to inspecting the supporting invoices, to footing the column of monetary amounts. The use of any terms that have vague meanings should be avoided in auditing. In all cases auditors should be certain that those to whom they are communicating understand what their terms mean.

CONFIRMATION

The technique of confirmation consists of the auditor's obtaining directly from an outside authority a written statement to be used as evidence on some matter about which the authority has expertise. The confirming document should be received directly by the auditor so that there is no opportunity for the client to falsify the information. The request for the information must be made by an official of the client company, for the established relationship is between the client and the authority, not between the auditor and the authority. The information that the authority is asked to furnish may be considered confidential, and the client is the appropriate one to request that this be released to the auditor.

The confirmation technique is used widely in establishing the validity of accounts receivable. The specific process is described in Chapter 12. In addition, the auditor may ask the client to request that the company's attorney correspond directly with the auditor on such matters as title to property, contingent liabilities, and possible unasserted claims against the company. The matter of communication between the auditor and the client's attorney is discussed in Chapter 15. Banks, insurance companies, and creditors are others from whom confirmations frequently are requested. In all cases the client prepares the confirmation request as instructed by the auditor and returns it to the auditor. The auditor must be satisfied that the request asks for the proper information, that it is addressed to the proper authority, and that it includes instructions for the response to be sent directly to the auditor. Frequently a self-addressed envelope is included for the reply. After inspecting the confirmation request, the auditor mails it in an envelope marked with the auditor's return address to assure an awareness of all requests returned because of incorrect addresses. Standard forms for confirmation of cash balances, accounts receivable, accounts payable, and other frequently requested items are used widely. These forms reduce the amount of preparation time by the client, who usually has to add little more than the company's name, an authorized signature, the date, name, and address.

RECOMPUTATION

A part of all audits is the use of the technique of recomputation, whether it be in the form of footings, extensions, or some other. The recomputation process may be performed manually or by use of a computer program.

The auditor wants assurance that the computations in the client's accounting system, in the books of account, and on the financial statements are accurate. The auditor relies primarily on internal accounting controls for this assurance; however, some tests of the computations are always made.

Computer programs may be used to make many of the recomputations. A program to extend and foot the inventory is an example. The recomputation of depreciation expense and the recomputation of the allowance for doubtful accounts based upon an aged trial balance of the receivables are other illustrations of recomputations made by the computer. If these recomputations are made manually, they are usually on a test basis; but if made by a computer, a complete recomputation is usually expedient because of the great speed of electronic data processing equipment.

The recomputation does not have to be in the exact form of the original computation. The recomputation may be performed on total year-end figures, whereas the original computation may have been made on weekly or monthly data. For instance, payroll tax expense is computed by the client on weekly and monthly payrolls, but the auditor may base the recomputation upon annual payroll data.

Recomputation may initially seem unnecessary in situations where the client has an adding machine tape attached to the document to support the total. Even if the items on the tape compare exactly with the original data, the totals may be incorrect. It is possible that either positive or negative figures are included in the adding machine tape total but were printed on a part of the tape not included. Similarly, the client's computer program could contain instructions to print certain data but omit it from the totals or, vice versa, to add certain figures but not to print them.

The auditor should be alert to the possible error, intentional or not, of figures' being transferred or carried forward incorrectly. Although a group of figures may prove to be correct on recomputation, the total may not be the one used in subsequent processing. To illustrate, the auditor not only should recompute the total cash disbursements for the month but should also verify that the amount recorded as a credit in the cash account agrees with the total disbursements.

OBSERVATION

Throughout an audit auditors use the technique of observation. They should continually observe the activities around them and be alert to detect any deviations from prescribed procedures. Early in the audit they should request a tour of the facilities during which they observe the equipment and activities throughout the operations. Likely they may observe some matters that they will add to the audit program for further investigation. Observing two cashiers using the same cash drawer and observing new equipment only partially uncrated are examples of items needing further attention based upon the auditor's initial observation. One usual application of the observation technique is the auditor's observance of the client's personnel as they count physical inventory.

INQUIRY

The audit technique of asking questions is widely used. The questions may vary considerably in significance but should always be necessary. "Where are the voided checks located?" and "What is the company policy on capitalization of overhead on a construction project?" are questions of different significance, but the answers to each are essential information for the auditor. Inquiries also range from the very general to the specific. Questions about business conditions during the past year, for example, are very general but are an important aspect of planning an audit, since the responses may indicate areas in which special audit procedures should be applied. On the other hand, a question about the reasons for classifying an expenditure as travel expense rather than as advertising, for example, is quite specific.

Sometimes during normal conversation a casual inquiry about an employee's duties will indicate the extent to which internal control procedures are implemented. Specific questions about duties and responsibilities are asked during the formal review of internal control, but the auditor can learn much through more casual inquiries. For instance, inquiries during conversation at lunch with the vice-president of information systems may give the auditor new insight into the functioning of the data processing center.

COMPARISON

The auditor devotes the major portion of the audit to matters where the risk of error or misstatement is greatest. One method to determine areas of high risk is comparison. The auditor compares client data with what is expected to be normal, and variations from the norm are suspected to result from errors or mistakes. The variations must be investigated, using other audit techniques to determine the cause of variation.

Balances in accounts are subject to comparisons. The auditor may select all accounts or only certain accounts on the trial balance for the current year to compare with the corresponding accounts of the preceding year and then investigate major changes. Or the auditor may project the amounts on the trial balance of the preceding year to reflect normal growth and use these adjusted balances as a standard of comparison. Unusual fluctuations or variances often may be detected more readily by comparing the balances on a month-to-month basis rather than on an annual basis. The auditor either may compare balances for each month of the current year with the corresponding month of the preceding year or may compare balances of each month with other months of the same year. Whichever method of comparison is used, adjustment should be made for all normal variations so that they will not be investigated as unusual.

Some auditors use computer programs to make comparisons. An example is a program that projects expected monthly data based upon the trend established by historical data supplied over the past two or three years. The projected monthly data are compared by the computer with actual results, and variations that fall outside an acceptable range are identified for additional analysis and investigation.

Some comparisons are made with data that the auditor computes from the client's accounts and statements. The auditor may compute such ratios as gross profit percentage, inventory turnover, accounts receivable turnover, and bad debt ratio. These computations are compared with corresponding ones for previous years or with industry averages to determine variations that need further investigation.

Sometimes an auditor may make rough calculations about the expected balance in some account and then compare that estimate with the actual. For example, an auditor may calculate the expected amount of the sales staff's bonuses based upon sales. If the estimate differs significantly from the actual bonus expense recorded, the auditor should investigate to determine the cause of the variance. Other examples are a rough computation of the amount of insurance expense or property tax expense, based upon the beginning and ending prepayments and expenditures during the year, and then a comparison of this computed amount with the actual expense.

Another area in which the auditor can benefit from making comparisons is the client's budgeting system. Not only may the comparison of what was planned by management with actual performance lead the auditor to areas of the business that require expanded audit tests, but also a familiarity with the budget can expand the auditor's understanding of the client's accounting system and financial operations.

Comparison of actual account balances, ratios, and trends with those anticipated and investigation of any unusual or unexpected relationships is an auditing technique called *analytical review.* This technique identifies areas where there is a high risk of error or misstatement, and other techniques are then used for further investigation. The fact that an account balance or ratio is different from what the auditor anticipated does not mean that the variance resulted from any improper activities. Conversely, a variance may not necessarily arise when errors or irregularities are present. Analytical review is discussed further in Chapter 15.

Section Two—Working papers

Records of the different types of evidence accumulated by the auditor are known as *working papers.* Whatever the form of evidence and whatever the methods used in gathering it, some record should be made and maintained in the working papers. In SAS No. 1 (AU 338.03), working papers are defined as follows:

> Working papers are the records kept by the independent auditor of the procedures he followed, the tests he performed, the information he obtained, and the conclusions he reached pertinent to his examination. Working papers, accordingly, may include work programs, analyses, memoranda, letters of confirmation and representation, abstracts of company documents and schedules or commentaries prepared or obtained by the auditor.

The exact format of working papers varies with the size, complexity, and circumstances of each audit engagement. Additionally, each auditor or firm usually has a preference for the exact manner in which working papers should be prepared. A beginning auditor normally receives instructions in formal training sessions or from the supervisor on the job regarding the specific format. The presentation in this chapter deals mainly with general aspects of working papers, and each illustration should be viewed as an example and not necessarily as a model to be adopted.

Purposes of working papers

As an accumulation of all evidence gathered during the conduct of the audit, working papers serve several functions. The major purposes of working papers are to aid in organizing and coordinating the many phases of the audit examination, to provide information to be included in the audit report, and to serve as support for the auditor's opinion. Working papers also serve as evidence in case of legal suits, as a source of information for tax returns and other specialized reports, and as a guide for subsequent audit examinations. These major purposes are discussed in the following sections.

ORGANIZATION AND COORDINATION OF THE AUDIT EXAMINATION

Working papers are a means of organizing and coordinating the different phases of the audit as they are being performed. During the audit of a large company, assistants may be assigned to different phases of the examination. The working papers prepared by assistants are the vehicle by which the auditor in charge is able to supervise their work and review their findings, thus fulfilling the first standard of field work. When work is performed at different locations, such as at distant branches, the working papers serve to assure the auditor in charge that all phases of the examination have been completed. Frequently auditors cannot complete an entire phase of the audit at one time, and the working papers record the work completed to the point of interruption so that they know where to resume their work. As an example, an auditor may have analyzed the account Allowance for Doubtful Accounts but is unable to complete the working paper until the confirmation requests are returned. In order to assess the adequacy of the account balance, the auditor needs this additional evidence, which is available only later. Subsequently, when the confirmations are received, the auditor may complete the working paper to reflect an opinion on the adequacy of the Allowance and to make any recommendations for a change.

INFORMATION TO BE INCLUDED IN THE AUDIT REPORT

Working papers provide information to be included in the auditor's report. The usual short-form audit report consists of the financial statements, related notes, and the auditor's opinion. The evidence, in all its various forms, which is the basis for this report is in the working papers. Should a long-form or special report be required, the data for the additional schedules, comments, and recommendations are contained in the working papers. If the auditor prepares a separate report to management evaluating the internal control system and perhaps recommending improvements, the evidence that is used in preparing this report also is contained in the working papers.

SUPPORT FOR THE AUDITOR'S OPINION

The ultimate objective of an audit is the expression of the auditor's opinion on the financial statements. The working papers serve as support for this opinion. The auditor, in signing the standard auditor's report, states that the examination was conducted in accordance with generally accepted auditing standards. The working papers must contain evidence that the work was adequately planned and based upon a review of internal controls, that assistants were properly supervised, and that sufficient competent evidence was reviewed. Also, the auditor is attesting that the financial statements present fairly the position of the company and results of operations in accordance with generally accepted accounting principles. The working papers should contain evidence that all material presentations on the statements were reviewed to determine that they present fairly what actually transpired within the company. In a large public accounting firm, the partner responsible for the audit relies on supervisors, seniors, and assistants to perform most phases of the examination. The working papers should contain evidence of the work performed and conclusions reached by each of these staff persons and also evidence that the work at each level was properly reviewed by the immediate supervisor.

LEGAL EVIDENCE

Working papers constitute a form of evidence that may be used in legal action. Auditors may need to use working papers to substantiate their claim that they performed their audit in a professional manner, exercised due care, and were not negligent in the conduct of their examination. In reviewing the working papers prepared by assistants, the auditor at each level should question whether any of the information contained or the absence of any information could be used to attack the competence of the work at a later time when individuals might not be available to offer additional explanations. There should be in the working papers no contradictory statements, and any final conclusions that conflict with other evidence should be fully justified. For all questionable matters there must be adequate explanation for the conclusion reached. For example, a senior accountant may have questioned the obsolescence of some expensive metal parts that had not been used for over two years and were a material item within the inventory. Upon further investigation, the supervisor learned that these parts are used on equipment manufactured on special order for a limited number of customers. The client company is the exclusive manufacturer of this specialized equipment, which continues to be used by such customers. Orders from some customers are expected within the next year. The supervisor inspected a response to one of the customers written subsequent to the balance sheet date in which the client made a quotation on the estimated cost of this specialized equipment. The supervisor also saw where the costs of these metal parts were used in computing the quoted price. Evidence of the supervisor's additional findings and the conclusion that the inventory valuation did not need to be reduced because of obsolescence should be included in the working papers.

There is a possibility that an auditor assisting in the examination may not agree with the resolution of an accounting or auditing issue. Procedures should be established to allow those in disagreement to document their disagreement when they believe it necessary to dissociate themselves from the resolution. The working papers should contain evidence of this dissociation as well as evidence supporting the final resolution of the issue as recommended by SAS No. 22 (AU 311.12).

SPECIALIZED REPORTS

Another function of working papers is to provide the information needed for the preparation of reports to management on the adequacy of internal controls, or for the preparation of tax returns or reports to the SEC and other governmental agencies. At times clients need information from working papers for reports that they prepare themselves, or they may need data because their original records have been destroyed.

GUIDE FOR SUBSEQUENT AUDITS

An auditor usually carries working papers from the previous year's audit to the client's office to perform the current year's examination. The previous year's working papers give indications of matters of difficulty and the solution reached. The auditor is thus alerted to the possibility of a similar situation for the current year. Also, the auditor should be familiar with the description of the accounting system and controls from the previous audit in order to be aware of changes during the year and make necessary modifications in the audit program. There is great danger in following last year's working papers too closely. The auditor may profit by seeing the format of a particular analysis from last year but should use that same format only if it is suitable to the current year's situation. Duplicating the audit steps indicated in the preceding year's working papers may very well result in unnecessary and inappropriate steps as well as in the omission of some procedures essential for an adequate audit of the current year's activities and events.

Ownership of working papers

Working papers that auditors prepare are their property, and the information contained in them is generally regarded as confidential. Before releasing information in the working papers, the auditor usually obtains the client's consent. Upon receipt of a subpoena or a summons for information in the working papers, the auditor must release the information. Also, the auditor may have to reveal some information even against the client's wishes in order to comply with auditing standards, such as in cases involving the subsequent discovery of facts existing at the date of the auditor's report. When an auditor's practice is sold to another auditor, or when a client appoints a new auditor, the client must give permission before the working papers can be made available to the successor auditor.

The length of time that an auditor should retain working papers is difficult to establish. They should be kept as long as they are relevant to subsequent audits and to meet any legal requirements.

Types of working papers

Since working papers are the means of accumulating all evidence the auditor needs to express a professional opinion, the types of working papers necessarily must be quite varied. Some working papers follow a standard format, whereas others may be a simple memorandum of a discussion held in connection with the audit examination. The major types of working papers are (1) audit plans, (2) working trial balance and adjusting journal entries, (3) supporting schedules, (4) narrative summaries, (5) representations and confirmations, and (6) minutes and other records. The original draft of the auditor's report is also normally included in the working papers. Each working paper should be as complete as possible, leaving no questions concerning the matter to which it relates. Each of the major types of working papers is described in the following sections.

AUDIT PLANS

Working papers should contain evidence that the auditor has developed an overall strategy for the conduct and scope of the examination. Notations should be made as to the industry in which the client's business operates, conditions that may call for special audit procedures, any unusual accounting principles used, and the nature of any special reports to be rendered. The audit program, the planning document that sets forth the audit procedures expected to be necessary to accomplish the audit objectives, may be supported with an internal control questionnaire, flowcharts, an organization chart, and general evidence that helps shape the course of the examination. Memoranda prepared during the conduct of the examination on items to be investigated further, along with a complete explanation of the disposition of these matters, are included in the working papers.

WORKING TRIAL BALANCE

The trial balance is the connecting link between the client's books of account and the financial statements upon which the auditor is expressing an opinion. The working trial balance is the controlling schedule that shows the interrelationships of all the other schedules, other types of evidence, and the final report. The working trial balance for relatively small companies may be simply a listing of balances of each account in the general ledger arranged approximately in statement order. For most companies, a trial balance listing each account would extend over numerous work sheets and would be too lengthy; consequently, separate working sheets may be prepared for each major financial statement. This system of preparing and organizing working papers is illustrated in Figure 8-1 showing a working balance sheet; Figure 8-2, a working income statement; and Figure 8-3, a working statement of retained earnings. (Figures 8-1—8-13 begin on page 286.) Each item on these working sheets appears on the completed financial statements and usually represents the summary of several ledger accounts. This single amount on the working statement is supported by a grouping sheet, or lead schedule, that lists each general

Table 8-3 Working Papers Index—Selected Items

	Index references by type of working papers		
Working paper titles	Working financial statements	Grouping sheets	Supporting schedules
Working balance sheet	D-1		
Working income statement	D-2		
Working statement of retained earnings	D-3		
Cash		G	
Petty cash—office			G-1
Petty cash—warehouse			G-2
Security National Bank—operating			G-3
Citizens Trust Bank—payroll			G-6
Manufacturers State Bank—dividends			G-8
Prepaid expenses		L	
Prepaid business licenses			L-1
Prepaid postage			L-2
Unexpired insurance			L-3
Machinery and equipment		P	
Factory machinery and equipment			P-1
Office equipment and fixtures			P-2
Notes payable—banks		S	
Security National Bank			S-1
Manufacturers State Bank			S-3
Net sales		AA	
Sales—retail			AA-1
Sales—wholesale			AA-2
Sales cut-off tests			AA-5
Sales—tests of transactions			AA-7

ledger account that has been summarized into the single figure. For example, on the working balance sheet (Figure 8-1), the item cash is a summary of five ledger accounts (Figure 8-4), prepaid expenses is a summary of four ledger accounts (Figure 8-8), and machinery and equipment is a summary of two ledger accounts (Figure 8-10). The single amount on the working statements is similar to a control account balance, and the amounts on the grouping sheet are similar to the details contained in the subsidiary ledger.

Usually, for each set of working papers an index is prepared that clearly indicates the location within the working paper file of supporting schedules, groupings sheets, working financial statements, drafts of the auditor's report, all memoranda, and other data collected as evidence. Table 8-3 illustrates selected items from the index of the working papers presented in this chapter. The index references are classified by type of working paper for illustrative purposes only.

The following comments explain the function of the columns on the working financial statements (Figures 8-1, 8-2, and 8-3) and on the grouping sheets (Figures 8-4, 8-8, and 8-10). Column 1 is used as an index column. Each item appearing on these sheets is supported by another working paper, and the letter or number of that working paper should be shown in the reference column. For example, on the working balance sheet (Figure 8-1), for the item prepaid expenses, the letter L appears in the reference column. In order to determine what accounts are summarized as prepaid expenses, one would inspect the grouping sheet referenced L (Figure 8-8). On the grouping sheet, column 1 indicates the reference letter or number of the working papers that support each account listed. For example, unexpired insurance on the grouping sheet L (Figure 8-8) is referenced to working paper L-3 where the account is analyzed (Figure 8-9). The working papers should be so cross-referenced that a reviewer can readily locate all evidence that relates to each amount on the financial statements.

Column 2 on the working financial statements (Figures 8-1, 8-2, and 8-3) indicates the title to be shown on the finished financial statements. This same column on the grouping sheets (Figures 8-4, 8-8, and 8-10) indicates the general ledger account titles. Column 3 on the grouping sheets shows the general ledger account number, and all working papers that analyze an account should reflect the account number as well as the reference letter or number.

Last year's adjusted figures appear in column 4. With those figures appearing next to the current year's figures in column 5, the auditor can make a comparison and detect any major changes to be investigated further. The amounts in column 5 agree with the client's general ledger accounts after the client has posted all known adjustments and corrections. Adjustment column 6 contains the audit adjustments recommended to the client. For major companies with highly trained accountants on their staffs, routine audit adjustments are uncommon. On the other hand, for some smaller companies, the auditor may propose adjusting entries necessary to record such matters as depreciation expense, accrued salaries, and prepaid insurance. The client always should agree that the adjusting entries are necessary or desirable, because the responsibility for the books of account, including adjusting journal entries, is the client's, not the auditor's. Audit adjustments must be recorded by the client so that the adjusted figures, such as those in column 7 of the cash grouping sheet, appear in the ledger accounts. A separate working paper of adjusting journal entries accumulates all the entries and includes an explanation for each. Also, the adjustments are reflected on the supporting schedule for each account affected, for not only must the client's books agree with the adjusted figures in the working papers, but the supporting schedules also must tie in with the adjusted balances in the working papers.

Column 8 is used to record reclassifications that are necessary for proper statement presentation but are not to be recorded on the books. For instance, the working balance sheet (Figure 8-1) reflects the credit balance in accounts receivable of $3,841.06 reclassified to accounts payable and the deferred income tax charge of $6,345.29 reclassified as a deduction from deferred income tax credits.

Column 9 reflects the figures as they appear on the financial statements. In preparing working papers on the audit of large companies, many auditors use an additional column on the working financial statements to round the figures to the nearest thousand or ten thousand as they are to appear on published statements.

SUPPORTING SCHEDULES

An auditor may prepare various types of schedules to indicate the work performed in gathering evidence to support conclusions as to the accuracy of the accounts. Some schedules may be in the form of reconciliations, others may be complete analyses of all transactions in the accounts, others may compare month-to-month figures, and still others may be merely a listing of selected items from the accounts. Many schedules are prepared by the client and the supporting documents are assembled for inspection by the auditor. Supporting schedules may be in the form of computer print-outs resulting from a program designed by either the client or the auditor. The auditor must verify the accuracy of all working papers prepared by the client whether they are prepared manually or by computer. Several types of supporting schedules are illustrated on subsequent pages.

The supporting schedule of the petty cash fund kept in the warehouse is illustrated in Figure 8-5. This is an example of verification of the detail comprising a year-end balance. Figures 8-6 and 8-7 illustrate the bank reconciliation of the operating account as of the balance sheet date. This also is an example of verification of a year-end balance without analysis of transactions flowing through the account during the year. The auditor uses tick marks to reference the verification activity to the items verified. A variety of tick marks may be used, and their meaning should always be explained either on the face of the working paper or on a sheet defining standard tick marks used throughout the engagement. It should be noted that on Figure 8-6 the bank balance was initially reconciled to the year-end balance in the general ledger, although this was not the final figure to appear on the financial statements. After the general ledger figure is verified, any adjustments are then noted to reflect the adjusted balance for the current year.

Some accounts are analyzed for the entire period beginning with the adjusted balance from the preceding year's audit, and evidence is reviewed to substantiate each debit and credit entry recorded during the year. Supporting schedules of this type are illustrated by the analysis of unexpired insurance (Figure 8-9) and the analysis of factory machinery and equipment (Figure 8-11). The analysis of unexpired insurance illustrates a supporting schedule that records the simultaneous verification of two related accounts, insurance expense and the unexpired insurance asset account. This analysis also illustrates the point that only material items may be considered for adjustment. Although a mistake of $40 was discovered in the computation of insurance expense, no adjustment was made because of immateriality. The adjustment of factory machinery and equipment (Figure 8-11) further illustrates the point that the auditor's supporting schedule agrees initially with the general ledger balance at year-end and then reflects the adjustment necessary to present the adjusted balance.

The analysis of office equipment and fixtures (Figure 8-12) is an example of a supporting schedule where only selected items from an account are examined. In this case the auditor examined only those items that exceeded $250. In this situation the auditor may have had the client extract from the files the documents supporting these transactions for inspection. The auditor's conclusion is recorded on the supporting schedule itself.

Another working paper on which only selected items from an account are listed is illustrated in Figure 8-13, on pages 304–305. This working paper presents a portion of the tests of transactions for sales in which invoices, purchase orders, shipping tickets, and the related accounts receivable are inspected. As discussed in Chapter 15, a major aspect of the auditor's examination of sales is a test of transactions to establish that the accounting system is functioning as designed.

NARRATIVE SUMMARIES

One of the major forms of working papers in modern auditing is the narrative summary. All evidence gathered through inquiry, confirmation, inspection, and so forth, and all evidence reflected in questionnaires, flow charts, and supporting schedules is meaningless if the auditor does not reach a conclusion regarding the fairness of the presentations. The reviewers at various levels must indicate their conclusion regarding each phase of the audit performed for which they are responsible. The auditor's conclusion may be given by signing the audit program to indicate satisfactory completion of the specified procedure. The auditor may write a comment on the face of a supporting schedule or may write a separate narrative summary.

The staff assistant may merely sign the audit program if no exceptions were found in the audit steps performed or may make such a statement on the face of the related working papers. A narrative summary is more

(*Text continues on page* 303.)

Figure 8-1 Illustrative Working Balance Sheet

DeKalb Manufacturing Company — D-1

J.W.C. — Atlanta, Georgia

2-17-83 — Working Balance Sheet

December 31, 1982

Working Paper Reference	Description	Adjusted 12-31-81	Trial Balance Per Ledger 12-31-82
(1)	(2)	(4)	(5)
	Assets		
	Current Assets:		
G	Cash	3859103	2832048
H	Marketable Securities - Net	1602921	1583352
J	Receivables - Net	10452237	11815812
K	Inventories	17355858	17220461
L	Prepaid Expenses	2023016	2183229
	Total Current Assets	35293135	35634902
	Property, Plant and Equipment:		
M	Land	1055400	1055400
N	Buildings	8730325	9700626
P	Machinery and Equipment	15949347	17310645
	Total Property, Plant, and Equipment	25735072	28066671
Q	Less Accumulated Depreciation	13801418	13837035
	Net Property, Plant, and Equipment	11933654	14229636
R	Other Assets	426563	477893
	Total Assets	47653352	50342431
	Liabilities and Stockholders' Equity		
	Current Liabilities:		
S	Notes Payable - banks	4238400	4102100
T	Accounts Payable	6197369	5911256
U	Due to Affiliated Company	5455163	4766263
V	Other Accrued Liabilities	1584957	1699934
W	Income Taxes Payable	1757843	1787928
	Total Current Liabilities	19233732	18267481
X	Deferred Income Taxes	2391800	1838200
	Stockholder's Equity:		
Y	Common Stock	7904600	9454600
Y	Additional Paid in Capital	4864000	5365428
D-3	Retained Earnings	13259220	15416722
	Total Stockholders' Equity	26027820	30236750
	Total Liabilities and Stockholders' Equity	47653352	50342431

Adjustments dr. ⟨cr.⟩	Adjusted 12-31-82	Reclassifications dr. ⟨cr.⟩	Final 12-31-82
(6)	(7)	(8)	(9)
⟨6075⟩	2825973		2825973
	1583352		1583352
	11815812	384106	12199918
	17220461		17220461
⟨48700⟩	2134529	⟨634529⟩	1500000
	35580127		35329704
	1055400		1055400
	9700626		9700626
⟨58452⟩	17252193		17252193
	28008219		28008219
	13837035		13837035
	14171184		14171184
39127	517020		517020
⟨74100⟩	50268331	⟨250423⟩	50017908
	4102100		4102100
98421	5812835	⟨384106⟩	6196941
	4766263		4766263
⟨128400⟩	1828334		1828334
56565	1731363		1731363
	18240895		18625001
	1838200	634529	1203671
	9454600		9454600
	5365428		5365428
47514	15369208		15369208
	30189236		30189236
74100	50268331	250423	50017908

Figure 8-2 Illustrative Working Income Statement

DeKalb Manufacturing Company
Atlanta, Georgia
Working Income Statement
for the Year Ended December 31, 1982

D-2

Working Paper Reference	Description			Adjusted 12-31-81
(1)	(2)			(4)
AA	Net Sales			96559782
	Costs and Expenses			
CC	Cost of Sales			81044937
DD	Selling, Advertising, and Administrative			8393852
EE	Engineering and Development			3187214
HH	Interest Expense			608647
JJ	Provision for Income Taxes			1655916
	Total Costs and Expenses			94890566
	Net Income			1669216

Per Ledger 12-31-82	Adjustments dr. ⟨cr.⟩	Adjusted 12-31-82	Reclassifications dr. ⟨cr.⟩	Final 12-31-82
(5)	(6)	(7)	(8)	(9)
94737417		94737417		94737417
76373243	54775	76428018	437500	76865518
7775092	147725	7922817		7922817
2908426	⟨98421⟩	2810005	⟨437500⟩	2372505
564012		564012		564012
3519142	⟨56565⟩	3462577		3462577
91139915		91187429		91187429
3597502	47514	3549988		3549988

J.W.C.
2-17-83

Figure 8-3 Illustrative Working Statement of Retained Earnings

DeKalb Manufacturing Company — D-3
Atlanta, Georgia
Working Statement of Retained Earnings
for the Year Ended December 31, 1982

Working Paper Reference	Description			Adjusted 12-31-81
(1)	(2)			(4)
	Retained Earnings-beginning of year			12670004
D-2	Net Income			1669216
	Total			14339220
RR	Dividends			1080000
	Retained Earnings-end of year			13259220

Per Ledger 12-31-82	Adjustments dr.<cr.>	Adjusted 12-31-82	Reclassifications dr.<cr.>	Final 12-31-82		
(5)	(6)	(7)	(8)	(9)		
132592 20		132592 20		132592 20		
35975 02	475 14	35499 88		35499 88		
168567 22		168092 08		168092 08		
14400 00		14400 00		14400 00		
154167 22	475 14	153692 08		153692 08		

J.W.C.
2-17-83

Figure 8-4 Illustrative Grouping Sheet for Cash

DeKalb Manufacturing Company G
Atlanta, Georgia
Cash
December 31, 1982

Working Paper Reference	Account Title	Account Number	Adjusted 12-31-81
(1)	(2)	(3)	(4)
G-1	Petty Cash - office	101	50000
G-2	Petty Cash - warehouse	102	60000
G-3	Security National Bank - operating	105	3162103
G-6	Citizens Trust Bank - payroll	107	500000
G-8	Manufacturers State Bank - dividends	110	87000
	Total Cash (to D-1)		3859103

Per Ledger 12-31-82	Adjustments dr. ⟨cr.⟩	Adjusted 12-31-82	Reclassifications dr. ⟨cr.⟩	Final 12-31-82
(5)	(6)	(7)	(8)	(9)
50000	① ⟨16000⟩	34000		34000
75000		75000		75000
1871048	② 9925	1880973		1880973
700000		700000		700000
136000		136000		136000
2832048	⟨6075⟩	2825973		2825973

V.C.L.
1-20-83

Figure 8-5 Illustrative Supporting Schedule—Petty Cash Count

DeKalb Manufacturing Company — G-2
Atlanta, Georgia
#102 Petty Cash Count - Warehouse
December 31, 1982

	Quantity	Amount	Total
Currency:			
Twenties	12	240 00	
Tens	18	180 00	
Fives	6	30 00	
Ones	21	21 00	471 00
Coin:			
Ones	7	7 00	
Halves	1	50	
Quarters	13	3 25	
Dimes	26	2 60	
Nickels	42	2 10	
Pennies	17	17	15 62
Checks:			
Check payable to DeKalb Manufacturing Co. for $40.00 dated 1-1-83 drawn on Valley National Bank by A.R. Mulshaw, factory foreman. Attached note states "Authorized by S.B. McBrooks, manager."		✓✓	40 00
Total Cash			526 62
Paid Vouchers:			
Receipt from Hickory Pit Restaurant dated 1-1-83 for 20 lunches, marked "inventory counters."		128 73	
Invoice from World Freight Lines, marked "paid" and dated 1-2-83. Rush delivery of replacement valve M-4.		94 65	223 38
Total Imprest Balance			750 00
			to G

Above listed cash and cash items in the amount of $750.00 were returned to me intact after count by auditor at 10:15 a.m. on January 2, 1983.

Seth Kinnett cashier

✓✓ Exception to rule on cashing checks approved because of emergency during counting of inventory on holiday. — V.C.L. 1-2-83

Figure 8-6 Illustrative Supporting Schedule—Bank Reconciliation

DeKalb Manufacturing Company — G-3

Atlanta, Georgia

#105 — Bank Reconciliation - Operating Account

December 31, 1982

Security National Bank
Account #649-384-025

Balance per bank statement 12-31-82		√ ⊗ 2634632
Add: Deposit in transit (receipts of 12-30-82)	√√ √+ 359572	
Check drawn on account #469-384-025 encoded in error by bank and charged to this account	ϕ 71568	431140
Total		3065772
Less Outstanding checks - see list at G-4		1194724
Balance per general ledger 12-31-82		1871048
AJE #2 - Write off of old outstanding checks - see G-4		* 9925
Balance per adjusted general ledger 12-31-82		√√ 1880973
		to G

√ Traced to December 31, 1982 bank statement.
⊗ Confirmed by bank - see G-5.
√√ Traced to cut off bank statement of 1-13-83, received directly from bank.
ϕ Reviewed correspondence with bank.
√+ Traced to cash receipts book. Added receipts for 12-30-82 and total agrees with deposit.
* Discussed write off with treasurer on 1-13-83, agreed to adjustment.
√√ Agrees with adjusted general ledger.

V.C.L.
1-13-83

Figure 8-7 Illustrative Supporting Schedule—Outstanding Checks-Bank Reconciliation

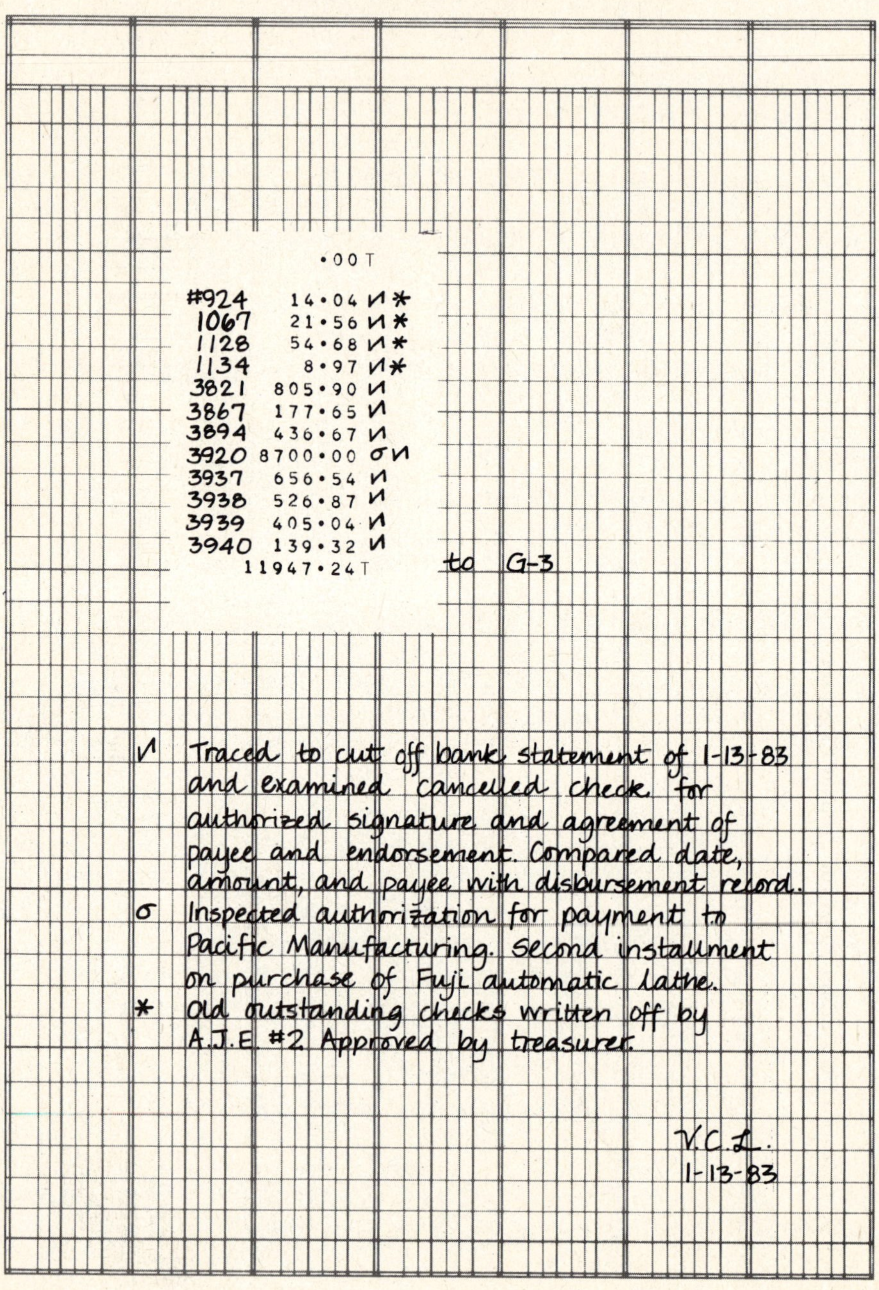
DeKalb Manufacturing Company
Atlanta, Georgia
Outstanding Checks - Operating Account
December 31, 1982

G-4

	•00T	
#924	14•04	✓*
1067	21•56	✓*
1128	54•68	✓*
1134	8•97	✓*
3821	805•90	✓
3867	177•65	✓
3894	436•67	✓
3920	8700•00	σ✓
3937	656•54	✓
3938	526•87	✓
3939	405•04	✓
3940	139•32	✓
	11947•24T	to G-3

✓ Traced to cut off bank statement of 1-13-83 and examined cancelled check for authorized signature and agreement of payee and endorsement. Compared date, amount, and payee with disbursement record.

σ Inspected authorization for payment to Pacific Manufacturing. Second installment on purchase of Fuji automatic lathe.

* Old outstanding checks written off by A.J.E. #2 Approved by treasurer.

V.C.L.
1-13-83

Figure 8-8 Illustrative Grouping Sheet for Prepaid Expenses

DeKalb Manufacturing Company
Atlanta, Georgia
Prepaid Expenses
December 31, 1982

L

Working Paper Reference	Account Title	Account Number	Adjusted 12-31-81	Per Ledger 12-31-82	Adjustments dr. <cr.>	Adjusted 12-31-82	Reclassifications dr. <cr.>	Final 12-31-82
(1)	(2)	(3)	(4)	(5)	(6)	(7)	(8)	(9)
L-1	Prepaid Rent	141	90000	90000		90000		90000
L-3	Unexpired Insurance	144	736762	1079500		1079500		1079500
L-6	Prepaid Taxes and Licenses	146	324150	379200	④ <48700>	330500		330500
L-7	Deferred Income Tax Expense	147	872104	634529		634529	<634529>	—
	Total Prepaid Expenses (to D-1)		2023016	2183229	48700	2134529	<634529>	1500000

C.P.S.
1-23-83

Figure 8-9 Illustrative Supporting Schedule—Analysis of Unexpired Insurance

DeKalb Manufacturing Company
Atlanta, Georgia
Unexpired Insurance
December 31, 1982

L-3

#144

Carrier		Policy Number	Coverage
Superior Insurance Co.	✓	R-147118	Fire and extended coverage on building and contents for $200,000
National Fire and Casualty	✓	83-M404D	Fire and extended coverage on inventory $175,000
(Renewal)	✓	83-M404G	✓ ✓ ✓ ✓ ✓
Mainline Insurance Co.	✓	WC2635	Workmen's Compensation $100,000
CMR Insurance Co.	✓	E 9386618	Fidelity bond coverage for $200,000 listed employees
Guardian Assurance Co.	✓	37-375-24	Use and occupancy - all plants and offices $130,000

✓ Inspected policy and noted type of coverage, amount, term, and premium. All policies were in the company's name.

m Inspected insurance company's invoice, credit in cash disbursement's journal, and cancelled check.

Ⓐ Agrees with last year's working papers.

ø Recomputed.

✓+ Error in computation - expense should be $40 more - no adjustment recommended.

✓✓ Agrees with general ledger accounts.

Reviewed correspondence with Century Insurance Agency in which the agent expressed an opinion on adequacy of coverage. Controller stated on 1-23-83 that there were no major changes in assets (including inventory) since date of agent's letter, 12-5-82.

Term		Premiums			
From	To	Unexpired 12-31-81	Paid	Expense	Unexpired 12-31-82
8-15-81	8-15-83	348039	—	√† ∅ 208133	√† 139906
6-1-79	6-1-82	45242	—	∅ 45242	
6-1-82	6-1-85	—	m 984654	∅ 192266	792388
1-1-82	12-31-82	—	m 323886	∅ 323886	—
1-1-82	12-31-82	—	m 45000	∅ 45000	—
9-30-81	9-30-83	343481	—	∅ 196275	147206
		Ⓐ 736762	1353540	W 1010802	W 1079500
				to CC-14	to L

C.P.S.
1-23-83

Figure 8-10 Illustrative Grouping Sheet for Machinery and Equipment

DeKalb Manufacturing Company
Atlanta, Georgia
Machinery and Equipment
December 31, 1982

P

Working Paper Reference	Account Title	Account Number	Adjusted 12-31-81	Per Ledger 12-31-82	Adjustments dr. <cr.>	Adjusted 12-31-82	Reclassifications dr. <cr.>	Final 12-31-82
(1)	(2)	(3)	(4)	(5)	(6)	(7)	(8)	(9)
P-1	Factory Machinery and Equipment	162	13659349	14696213	⑦ <58452>	14637761		14637761
P-2	Office Equipment and Fixtures	165	2289998	2614432		2614432		2614432
	Total Machinery and Equipment	(to D-1)	15949347	17310645	<58452>	17252193		17252193

BSB
2/3/83

Figure 8-11 Illustrative Supporting Schedule—Factory Machinery and Equipment

DeKalb Manufacturing Company — P-1
Atlanta, Georgia
#162 — Factory Machinery and Equipment
December 31, 1982

Date	Voucher Number	Payee	Description	Amount
		Balance per general ledger 12-31-81		√+ 136593 49
		Additions:		
4-8-82	3275	Circle Company	Fuji automatic lathe #3R84302	Ⓔ ϕ 28284 96
4-8-82	3279	Continental Freight Co.	Freight on lathe	ϕ 262 25
4-23-82	3654	Premier Equipment, Inc.	Installation of lathe	ϕ 481 00
7-18-82	6781	Republic Machine Works	Heliarc Welder #3675	ϕ 979 66
9-16-82	8396	Briardale Supply Co.	Ogawa radial drill #1457660	ϕ 1307 54
		Total Additions:		31315 41
		Deductions:		
5-6-82		P+A Used Machinery Co.	Sold old lathe for $2,650 - cost recorded 1-17-63	√† ∧∧ ⟨20946 77⟩
		Balance per general ledger 12-31-82		146962 13
		AJE #7- Remove installation and freight charges on old lathe that were not removed when sold		∧∧ ⊕ ⟨584 52⟩
		Balance per adjusted general ledger 12-31-82		√ 146377 61
				to P

√† Traced $2,650 to deposit in Security National Bank on 5-8-82.
√+ Agrees with ending balance in last year's working papers.
ϕ Inspected invoice. Amount agrees. Properly cancelled.
Ⓔ Examined the new lathe on 1-26-83.
⊕ Controller agreed on 1-27-83 to make entry.
∧∧ Traced to 1963 additions in property ledger. — B.S.B.
√ Agrees with adjusted general ledger. — 1-27-83

Figure 8-12 Illustrative Supporting Schedule—Office Equipment and Fixtures

DeKalb Manufacturing Company — P-2

Atlanta, Georgia

#165 — Office Equipment and Fixtures

December 31, 1982

Date	Voucher Number	Payee	Description		Amount
		Balance per general ledger 12-31-81		√+	2289998
		Additions:			
3-15-82	2485	Reliable Office Supply and Equipment Co.	Electronic typewriter #42336-104	√ϕ	184700
10-24-82	9641	Capitol Supply Co.	Duplicator # 37805	ϕ	46379
		Total of other items — all under $250 each			93355
		Balance per general ledger 12-31-82		√M	2614432
					to P

√+ Agrees with ending balance in last year's working papers.
ϕ Inspected invoices. Amount agrees. Properly cancelled.
√ Examined new typewriter on 2-3-83.
√M Agrees with general ledger.

All items capitalized appear to be appropriate and are adequately supported. All were properly authorized.

B.S.B.
2-3-83

frequently prepared by the senior accountant, summarizing the assigned activities and the conclusions reached on those phases of the examination. The supervisor usually expresses in a narrative summary the conclusions reached on all major divisions of the examination or on all major sections of the financial statements.

The partner in charge of the examination reviews the narrative summaries of all the audit staff, particularly those of the supervisors, and also reviews any supporting evidence in the working papers considered necessary. The partner in charge then prepares a narrative summary to the effect that the examination was conducted in accordance with generally accepted auditing standards and that an opinion should be expressed about the fairness of the financial statements in presenting the financial position and operating results of the client company in accordance with generally accepted accounting principles.

Some firms also use an overriding review team having no previous association with the audit to review the evidence and statements prior to the issuance of the report. This review team also would write a narrative summary of its conclusions and may make recommendations for modified auditing procedures in the subsequent year. In extreme cases, additional evidence or changed conclusions could be required for the current audit.

REPRESENTATIONS AND CONFIRMATIONS

The client's letters of representation and confirmations from customers, creditors, banks, attorneys, and so forth are all part of the working papers. The confirmation returns from customers may be in the form of punched cards to be processed by computer. Such forms are not filed with the other working papers. The method of maintaining files varies among public accounting firms. Regardless of the form, *working paper file* is the term generally used to describe the collection of evidence.

MINUTES AND OTHER RECORDS

Copies of minutes of meetings of the board of directors and of stockholders as well as copies of the charter and by-laws are a part of the working papers. Notes made on important contracts—such as leases, bond indentures, stock option plans, and deferred compensation plans—are also maintained in the working papers. Items of this type that do not change frequently and are applicable to more than one year are filed separately from the current working papers in what is known as a *permanent working paper file.* Other data that do not change frequently, like the organization chart and the analysis of the Land account, may also be included in the permanent working paper file.

Figure 8-13 Illustrative Supporting Schedule—Test of Transactions-Sales

DeKalb Manufacturing Company
Atlanta, Georgia
Test of Transactions - Sales - Detailed Invoice Test
December 31, 1982

AA-7

Date		Shipped To	Invoice Number	Amount
1-4-82	King Wholesalers, Inc.	Same	381	51 02
1-4	Garden View Builders	Same	382	147 26
1-4	Hunderup Designers	Portland Division	383	570 28
4-12	Rite-Way Products	Same	704	108 00
4-12	Advanced Systems Co.	Same	705	5 57
4-12	Krome-Brite Co.	Same	706	18 66
4-12	United Sales, Inc.	Same	VOID 707 708	149 07
4-12	Allied Installation Co.	Same	709	94 67
5-7	Central Service Corp.	Macon Distribution Cntr.	788	284 59
5-7	Royal Electric Assn.	Same	789	81 12
5-7	Econ-Style Products	Customer pick up	790	8 41
5-7	GAD-Albany, Inc.	Same	791	60 33
8-28	Silver Manufacturing	Same	1021	79 45
8-28	Certified Suppliers, Inc.	Same	1022	401 91
8-28	Fine Craft, Inc.	Customer pick up	1023	10 23
8-28	Stephens and Sons	Same	1024	53 11
11-3	Triangle Industries	Research Center	1295	81 73
11-3	General Appliance Co.	Same	1296	59 75
11-3	Hopkins Bros., Inc.	Same	1297	188 63
11-3	Greenbriar Contractors	Construction Site-N.C.	1298	424 84

Source - Invoice Numerical File

Randomly selected five days and inspected invoices for all sales on each day. Performed transaction tests indicated.

- √ Performed the procedure noted in the column heading
- √' Totalled all invoices bearing date selected.
- σ Traced daily total to monthly summary of sales.
- ① Quantity shipped was different from quantity ordered. Difference was automatically backordered.
- ② No purchase order prepared by customer-order placed orally.
- ③ Customer's purchase order used price from old price and old discounts. Invoice used current prices and terms.
- LDS Local Delivery Service used for shipment. LDS does not issue shipping tickets.

	From Order File				Traced To	
Total Sales for the Day	Quantities Agree	Terms Agree	Inspect Shipping Documents	Price Agrees to Price List	Sales Register	Accts. Receivable Ledger Card
	✓	✓	✓	✓	✓	✓
	✓	✓	✓	✓	✓	✓
v/σ 76856	✓	✓	✓	✓	✓	✓
	① no	✓	✓	✓	✓	✓
	✓	✓	LDS	✓	✓	✓
	②	②	✓	✓	✓	✓
	✓	✓	✓	✓	✓	✓
v/σ 37597	✓	✓	✓	✓	✓	✓
	✓	③ no	✓	③ no	✓	✓
	✓	✓	✓	✓	✓	✓
	②	②	N.A.	✓	✓	Cash
v/σ 43445	✓	✓	✓	✓	✓	✓
	✓	✓	✓	✓	✓	✓
	✓	✓	✓	✓	✓	✓
	②	②	N.A.	✓	✓	Cash
v/σ 54470	✓	✓	✓	✓	✓	✓
	✓	✓	LDS	✓	✓	✓
	✓	✓	LDS	✓	✓	✓
	✓	✓	✓	✓	✓	✓
v/σ 75495	✓	✓	✓	✓	✓	✓

Supplementary readings

Benis, Martin. "The Small Client and Representation Letters." *Journal of Accountancy* (September 1978), 78-84.

Fee, Francis X., Jr. "How to Handle the First Audit of a New Client." *Practical Accountant* (March-April 1977), 31-37.

Hollander, Morris. "The Audit Plan—A Tool for Improving Auditing Performance." *Practical Accountant* (September 1978), 37-40.

Hull, James C. "A Guide to Better Workpapers." *Journal of Accountancy* (February 1969), 44-52.

Kessinger, John N. "A General Theory of Evidence as the Conceptual Foundation in Auditing Theory: Some Comments and Extensions." *Accounting Review* (April 1977), 322-339.

Mautz, Robert K. "The Nature and Reliability of Audit Evidence." *Journal of Accountancy* (May 1958), 40-47.

Mautz, Robert K., and Hussein A. Sharaf. *The Philosophy of Auditing.* Sarasota, Fla.: American Accounting Association, 1961.

Ray, J. C. "Classification of Audit Evidence." *Journal of Accountancy* (March 1964), 42-47.

Toba, Yoshihide. "A General Theory of Evidence as the Conceptual Foundation in Auditing Theory." *Journal of Accountancy* (January 1975), 7-24.

Review questions

8-1. Define *audit evidence.*

8-2. What factors does an auditor consider in assessing the amount of risk associated with a matter under audit?

8-3. Define *materiality.*

8-4. If an item amounts to 3 percent of net income, is that item considered material? Describe the points that should be considered in determination of the materiality of an item.

8-5. What effect do risk and materiality have upon the quantity and the quality of the audit evidence considered by the auditor?

8-6. What consideration does the auditor give to costs in obtaining evidence?

8-7. Alicia Sanchez, a CPA, said she would never lose a suit for negligence in the conduct of an audit because she was always 100 percent sure of every figure on the financial statements on which she expressed an opinion. How much audit evidence must Sanchez review in order to reach this degree of confidence?

8-8. If classified by purpose of the review, evidence may be classified as general, systems, and basic. Describe the general characteristics of evidence in each classification.

8-9. Physical existence as a type of audit evidence may receive too much reliance by the auditor. Why is this true?

8-10. What causes documents to have different degrees of reliability? Which documents have the highest degree of reliability? Which the lowest degree of reliability? Why?

8-11. Under what circumstances do internally prepared documents have a fair degree of reliability?

8-12. What is a letter of representation? Why does the auditor obtain such evidence?

8-13. Explain the meaning of the following statement: Books of account constitute a poor but at the same time essential type of evidence.

8-14. Describe some conditions under which oral statements would be considered reliable evidence.

8-15. Define *audit techniques.*

8-16. What are auditors looking for when they physically examine items having physical existence?

8-17. In inspecting documents, what are the main matters the auditor considers?

8-18. In scanning documents and records, an auditor frequently is able to identify errors of various types. What enables an auditor to have this ability to spot errors, sometimes described as a "sixth sense"?

8-19. Auditors do not ask directly for an outside authority to confirm information to them. Why?

8-20. Describe the process of confirmation. Explain why each step is important.

8-21. The client company's records are maintained on a computerized system that has numerous built-in and programmed controls for accuracy. Why is it necessary for the auditor to make any recomputations?

8-22. Philip Jackson, a new staff member, told his supervisor that he would follow his college training and convey his independence to the client. "I don't want to be accused of being too friendly with client personnel; so I'll never ask a question of anyone until I've exhausted all other possibilities of obtaining the evidence I need." Comment on Jackson's statement.

8-23. The audit technique of comparisons is employed in selecting areas for additional auditing. Random sampling may also be used as a technique to select areas for additional auditing. Which technique is considered preferable? Explain.

8-24. What are the major purposes for which an auditor prepares working papers?

8-25. Auditors must be careful that evidence contained in their working papers cannot be used against them in case of legal action. What precautions should they exercise to reduce the possibility of this occurrence?

8-26. Describe the dangers involved in using the previous year's working papers as guides for preparation of the working papers for the current year.

8-27. Why is a single trial balance working paper not generally prepared for a large company? What substitutes for the working trial balance?

8-28. Distinguish between adjusting entries and reclassification entries.

8-29. What is the primary function of narrative summaries?

8-30. Describe the type working papers maintained in the permanent working paper file. Give specific examples.

Decision problems

8-31. In the examination of financial statements the auditor is concerned with the examination and accumulation of accounting evidence.

a. What are the objectives of the auditor's examination and accumulation of accounting evidence during the course of the audit?

b. The source of the accounting evidence is of primary importance in the evaluation of its quality. Accounting evidence may be classified according to source. For example, one class originates within the client's organization, passes through the hands of third parties, and returns to the client, where it may be examined by the auditor. List the classifications of accounting evidence according to source, briefly discussing the effect of the source on the reliability of the evidence.

c. In evaluating the quality of the accounting evidence the auditor also considers factors other than the sources of the evidence. Briefly discuss these other factors.

AICPA adapted

8-32. A factory foreman at Elkins Corporation discharged an hourly worker but did not notify the payroll department. On time cards and work tickets the foreman forged the worker's signature and, when giving out the payroll checks, he kept the check for that worker and cashed it himself. What audit evidence should enable this activity to be detected?

AICPA adapted

8-33. As auditor of The Phoenix Company, you are considering obtaining written representations from the client concerning the financial statements and matters pertinent to them.

a. What are the reasons for obtaining written representations from the client?

b. What reliance may the auditor place upon written representations from (1) the client, (2) independent experts, and (3) debtors?

AICPA adapted

8-34. In examination of financial statements the auditor evaluates the quality of the accounting evidence available. An audit procedure that may be employed in the examination of cash is to submit duplicate deposit slips to the depository bank to be authenticated.

a. Discuss the reliability of the authenticated duplicate deposit slips as accounting evidence.

b. What additional audit procedures are available to the auditor to verify the detail of deposits?

AICPA adapted

8-35. Discuss how each of the following factors affects the competence of evidential matter.
a. It has the qualities of being relevant, objective, and free from known bias.
b. There is enough of it to afford a reasonable basis for an opinion on financial statements.
c. It has been obtained by random selection.
d. It consists of written statements made by managers of the enterprise under audit.

AICPA adapted

8-36. Discuss the validity of each of the following criticisms of the reliability of audit evidence that the auditor physically observes.
a. The client may conceal items from the auditor.
b. The auditor may not be qualified to evaluate the items that he or she is observing.
c. Such evidence is too costly in relation to its reliability.
d. The observation must occur at a specific time, which is often difficult to arrange.

AICPA adapted

8-37. Describe the reliability of the following types of documentary evidence:
a. external documents held by the client
b. documentary evidence calculated by the auditor from company records
c. confirmations received directly from third parties
d. internal documents

AICPA adapted

8-38. The auditor of the Regency Corp. plans to gather audit evidence by comparing 1982 revenues and expenses with the prior year and then investigating all changes exceeding 12 percent.

Which of the following errors or questionable procedures has the best chance of being detected through the audit evidence described? Why?
a. The cashier began lapping accounts receivable in 1982.
b. Because of worsening economic conditions, the 1982 provision for uncollectible accounts was inadequate.
c. Regency Corp. changed its capitalization policy for small tools in 1982.
d. An increase in property tax rates has not been recognized in the Regency Corporation's 1982 accrual.

AICPA adapted

8-39. The third generally accepted auditing standard of field work requires that the auditor obtain sufficient competent evidential matter to afford a reasonable basis for an opinion regarding the financial statements under examination. In considering what constitutes sufficient competent evidential matter, a distinction should be made between underlying accounting data and all corroborating information available to the auditor.

a. Discuss the nature of evidential matter to be considered by the auditor in terms of the underlying accounting data, all corroborating information available to the auditor, and the methods by which the auditor tests or gathers competent evidential matter.

b. State the three general presumptions that can be made about the validity of evidential matter with respect to comparative assurance, persuasiveness, and reliability.

AICPA adapted

8-40. Auditors frequently refer to the terms *standards* and *procedures.* Standards deal with measures of the quality of the auditor's performance. Standards specifically refer to the ten generally accepted auditing standards. Procedures relate to those acts that are performed by the auditor while trying to gather evidence. Procedures specifically refer to the methods or techniques used by the auditor in the conduct of the examination.

List at least eight different types of procedures that an auditor would use during an examination of financial statements. For example, a type of procedure that an auditor would frequently use is the observation of activities and conditions. *Do not discuss specific accounts.*

AICPA adapted

8-41. The first generally accepted auditing standard of field work requires, in part, that "the work is to be adequately planned." An effective tool that aids the auditor in adequately planning the work is an audit program.

What is an audit program, and what purposes does it serve?

AICPA adapted

8-42. One technique of gathering audit evidence is the comparison of relationships. Explain how use of this technique might lead to detection of each of the following conditions:

a. inadequate Allowance for Doubtful Accounts Receivable

b. unrecorded retirements of Property, Plant, and Equipment

AICPA adapted

8-43. Evidential matter that supports financial statements consists of the underlying accounting data and all corroborating information available to the auditor. In the course of the audit of financial statements, the auditor performs detail tests of samples of transactions from various large-volume populations. The auditor may also audit various types of transactions by tracing a single transaction of each type through all stages of the accounting system.

What evidential matter would the auditor expect to gain from auditing various types of transactions by tracing a single transaction of each type through all stages of the accounting system?

AICPA adapted

8-44. In an examination of financial statements, an auditor must judge the validity of the audit evidence obtained.

Assume that you have evaluated internal control and found it satisfactory.

a. In the course of an examination, the auditor asks many questions of client officers and employees.
   1. Describe the factors that the auditor should consider in evaluating oral evidence provided by client officers and employees.
   2. Discuss the validity and limitations of oral evidence.

b. An auditor's examination may include computation of various balance-sheet and operating ratios for comparison to prior years and industry averages. Discuss the validity and limitations of ratio analysis.

c. In connection with an examination of the financial statements of a manufacturing company, the auditor observed the physical inventory of finished goods, which consisted of expensive, highly complex electronic equipment. Discuss the validity and limitations of the audit evidence provided by this procedure.

AICPA adapted

8-45. The CPA analyzes the Accrued Interest Payable account for the year, recomputes the amounts of payments and beginning and ending balances, and reconciles to the Interest Expense account.

Which of the following errors or questionable procedures is most likely to be detected by the audit evidence gathered through the auditing procedure described?

a. Interest revenue of $80 on a note receivable was credited against Miscellaneous Expense.

b. A provision of the client's loan agreement was violated. Dividends on common stock are prohibited if income available for interest and dividends is not three times interest requirements.

c. Interest paid on an open account was charged to the Raw Material Purchases account.

d. A note payable had not been recorded. Interest of $150 on the note was properly paid and charged to the Interest Expense account. Why?

AICPA adapted

8-46. The preparation of working papers is an integral part of an auditor's examination of financial statements. On a recurring engagement auditors review their audit programs and working papers from their prior examination while planning their current examination to determine the usefulness of the working papers for the current engagement.

a. 1. What are the purposes or functions of audit working papers?
   2. What records may be included in audit working papers?

b. What factors affect the auditor's judgment of the type and content of the working papers for a particular engagement?

c. To comply with generally accepted auditing standards, an auditor includes certain evidence in the working papers; for example, evidence that the engagement was planned and work of assistants was supervised and reviewed. What other evidence should an auditor include in audit working papers to comply with generally accepted auditing standards?

d. How can an auditor make the most effective use of the preceding year's audit programs in a recurring examination?

e. What advice should an auditor give a client about discontinuing the use of records needed in an examination, and how should one complete the examination when one finds that records reviewed in prior examinations have been discontinued by the client?

AICPA adapted

8-47. An important part of every examination of financial statements is the preparation of audit working papers.

a. Discuss the relationship of audit working papers to each of the standards of field work.

b. You are instructing an inexperienced assistant on a first auditing assignment. Your assistant is to examine an account. An analysis of the account has been prepared by the client for inclusion in the audit working papers. Prepare a list of the comments, commentaries, and notations that the staff person should make or have made on the account analysis to provide an adequate working paper as evidence of examination.

AICPA adapted

8-48. The Harris Company has a sales force of 120 men and women located throughout the United States. Rarely, if ever, do all the salespersons come to the home office in Boston at one time. However, they should all be present at a sales meeting to be held in Dallas. At that time the auditor could travel from Boston to Dallas and count the travel advance funds of $250 for which each salesperson is responsible.

a. In your opinion, is physical evidence of the travel funds of Harris Company necessary for your annual audit? Why?

b. What alternative forms of evidence would you suggest obtaining in lieu of the physical count?

8-49. An assistant auditor was instructed to compare the monthly sales of one division with the monthly sales of that same division for the preceding year. The assistant listed the sales on a working paper using the following columns:

	Amounts			*% of annual sales*		
Months	1982 Sales	1981 Sales	Increase (decrease)	1982 Sales	1981 Sales	Increase (decrease)
January						
February						
———						
December	———	———	———	———	———	———
Total	═══	═══	═══	═══	═══	═══

a. Is the form of this working paper adequate for the task assigned the assistant? Why?

b. Are the data on this working paper alone valuable evidence? Why?

c. What additional evidence or auditing procedures may be indicated by this working paper?

8-50. If you are a newly assigned auditor on an engagement that your firm has repeated for a number of years, how much use should you make of the working papers from the audit of the previous year?

8-51. The Ensley Corporation has an investment constituting 30 percent of the outstanding common stock of Wylam Company, which cost $276,000 four years ago. At the close of last year, the investment was reflected at $307,350 on the equity method.

The Ensley Corporation's fiscal year ends September 30, whereas the fiscal year of Wylam Company ends June 30. During the current year, Wylam's net income was reported at $124,000 in the annual report examined from the files of Ensley Corporation. Remittance advices and deposit slips indicate that during the current year Ensley received dividends from Wylam of $4,000 each quarter.

Based on the preceding information, prepare a working paper analyzing the account "Investment in Wylam Company" for the current year ending September 30.

8-52. The ledger account No. 130, Land, of Vinings Company reflected the following information for the year ended December 31, 1981.

		Dr.
	Balance, December 31, 1980	197,500
9/18	Deposit to J. B. Moore on lots 4 and 5 addition to Cummings Township	10,000
10/5	Balance on lot 4 to J. B. Moore	65,000
11/12	Excavation costs—cash to Norman Foundation Corp.	27,300
12/3	Title search—Jacobs & Langston Attorneys—200 shares of common—par $25—market $32	5,000
12/28	Rothchild Associates—architects fees on initial building plans	18,700
	Total	323,500

On January 6, 1982, Vinings Company received a check for $3,000 refund of deposit on lot 5, which was not purchased.

Assume that all supporting documents are available for inspection. Based upon the preceding data, prepare a working paper analyzing the Land account of Vinings Company as of December 31, 1981.

8-53. The auditor in charge of the audit of the Rockdale Company for the year ended December 31, 1981, found the working paper shown in Figure 8-14 (p. 314) in reviewing the work of assistants. Comment on the weaknesses of this working paper and suggest improvements to be made.

8-54. Theoretically, which of the following would *not* have an effect on the amount of audit evidence gathered by the auditor? Why?

a. the type of opinion to be issued
b. the auditor's evaluation of internal control
c. the types of audit evidence available to the auditor
d. whether or *not* the client reports to the Securities and Exchange Commission

AICPA adapted

Figure 8-14 Proof of Inventory Valuation

The Rockdale Company
Proof of Inventory Valuation

		D-7
Inventory, beginning		28742 ✓
Purchases - Material used		121640 ✓
Overhead - %		48656 ✓
Labor		193822 ✓
Total		392860 ✗
Sales for period	584735 ∅	
Est. G.P. - 40%	233894 ∅	
Est. C. of S. - 60%		350841 ∅
Estimated Inventory-end		42019 ∅
Inventory per count and pricing		40305
Difference investigated and satisfied-not adjusted		$ 1714
✓ Examined		PS
		1982

8-55. Nathan Pouse, CPA, has sold his public-accounting practice to Theodore Lyons, CPA. Which of the following actions must Pouse take?

a. Pouse must obtain permission from his clients before making available working papers and other documents to Lyons.

b. Pouse must obtain permission from his clients for only audit-related working papers and other documents before making them available to Lyons.

c. Pouse must return the working papers and other documents to his clients, and Lyons must solicit the clients for his use of the materials.

d. Pouse must obtain permission from his clients for only tax-related working papers and other documents before making them available to Lyons.

AICPA adapted

9

Statistical Sampling

A well-established principle is that the auditor's opinion must be based on evidence, and audit evidence is gathered by testing. Testing is normally employed in gathering audit evidence concerning such areas as internal control, results of operations, and financial position. A significant decision for auditors involves the determination of how much as well as what type of evidence to gather. An important aspect of this decision is answering the question, "How large a sample must be selected?"

Factors that the auditor must consider when determining sample sizes include the following:

1. internal control
2. materiality
3. relative risk

Internal control enters into an auditor's sample-size decision because the quantity of audit evidence required varies, within limits, inversely with the effectiveness of internal control. For example, relatively larger sample sizes are generally required for audits of companies with poor internal control than for those with good internal control.

Materiality must be considered when sample size is determined because other things being equal, the more material the area being tested, the more evidence usually required. Also, the relative audit risk associated with a particular area of the client's operations has an important bearing on the quantity of evidence required and, therefore, on the sample size. An example of this concept can be seen in comparing the relative risk involved in property, plant, and equipment with that of cash. While the absolute value of a company's property, plant, and equipment may far exceed the amount of cash on hand, it is quite possible that less audit evidence would be required to form an opinion concerning the property, plant, and equipment. This would result from the auditor's assessment that less audit risk is associated with the fixed assets because of factors such as the following:

1. less than universal desirability for the fixed assets, therefore less likelihood of theft
2. fewer fixed-asset transactions, therefore greater probability of noticing fraudulent entries
3. physical difficulties involved in theft of fixed assets because of size and permanence as compared to cash, therefore diminished opportunity for embezzlement

In determining appropriate sample sizes, auditors employ one of two approaches—judgment sampling or statistical sampling. In effectively applying either of these approaches, the auditor employs, implicitly or explicitly, the factors just discussed. For example, in properly using judgment sampling the auditor would subjectively incorporate internal control, materiality, and risk into the judgment regarding sample size. The auditor might do so without realizing it, attributing the judgment to a feel for the audit. However, it seems likely that an experienced auditor's feel for the job is shaped largely by these decision parameters. In employing statistical sampling these factors are incorporated in a more explicit manner, but in no way is the auditor's judgment supplanted. Statistical sampling may be considered a tool that aids auditors in forming judgments.

Judgment sampling procedures, while widely used, are frequently considered to have several theoretical drawbacks, which include the following:

1. Auditors do not have a quantitative estimate of the amount of risk taken.
2. Auditors do not have an objective, verifiable, systematic method for determining sample size or for showing that their samples were adequate.
3. Auditors have no objective method of evaluating the effect of errors they may find.
4. Auditors have no assurance that their samples are unbiased.
5. In some judgment sampling schemes, where blocks of records are examined for stated time periods (for example, two months' purchase invoices), auditors have little assurance that the periods examined represent the entire period under audit.

Many auditors believe that statistical sampling has great potential for overcoming these drawbacks.

Sampling objectives

Most often, the auditor's sampling objective is considered to be that of obtaining a sample that accurately represents the population. This is the primary sampling objective considered in this chapter and is known as *representative sampling.* In addition, auditors may have other sampling objectives that influence the sampling process. These additional objectives are usually integrated with the representation objective when actual audit samples are selected. Sampling procedures based on these other objectives are *corrective sampling, protective sampling,* and *preventive sampling.*

The objective of corrective sampling is to maximize the number of errors included in the sample in order that they can be found and corrected. Protective sampling is designed to maximize the dollar value of the items included in the sample. This provides the auditor with the assurance that a large proportion of the total population value has been examined. Preventive sampling is designed to select items from all areas of the accounting records so that the client will not consider any area to be free from audit examination. This procedure is intended to satisfy the objective of fraud prevention by creating uncertainty in the mind of the client as to which areas are to be examined.

In order to accomplish the desired sampling objectives, the auditor must define the population characteristics of interest and structure the population and the sampling procedure accordingly. For example, if corrective sampling is to be performed, the auditor must be able to determine which areas are most likely to contain errors and concentrate the sampling in those areas. Protective sampling usually requires stratification of the population according to item values and concentrating the sampling in the high-value strata. Preventive sampling requires selecting samples in such a way that no apparent pattern exists in order that the client may not be certain beforehand whether an area will or will not be examined.

Definitions of statistical terms

It is helpful, before launching into a discussion on more technical aspects of statistical sampling plans, to define certain terms that are germane to the subject. The following paragraphs explain selected statistical terms with emphasis on several that are peculiar to auditing applications.

Population—the entire group of individual elements from which a sample is to be selected and about which an inference is to be drawn. Typical populations of interest to auditors consist of elements such as documents, transactions, individual account balances, etc.

Random—the condition of being without bias or pattern. A random

Table 9-1 Random Number Table

Col. / Line	(1)	(2)	(3)	(4)	(5)	(6)	(7)
1	10480	15011	01536	02011	81647	91646	69179
2	22368	46573	25595	85393	30995	89198	27982
3	24130	48360	22527	97265	76393	64809	15179
4	42167	93093	06243	61680	07856	16376	39440
5	37570	39975	81837	16656	06121	91782	60468
6	77921	06907	11008	42751	27756	53498	18602
7	99562	72905	56420	69994	98872	31016	71194
8	96301	91977	05463	07972	18876	20922	94595
9	89579	14342	63661	10281	17453	18103	57740
10	85475	36857	53342	53988	53060	59533	38867
11	28918	69578	88231	33276	70997	79936	56865
12	63553	40961	48235	03427	49626	69445	18663
13	09429	93969	52636	92737	88974	33488	36320
14	10365	61129	87529	85689	48237	52267	67689
15	07119	97336	71048	08178	77233	13916	47564
16	51085	12765	51821	51259	77452	16308	60756
17	02368	21382	52404	60268	89368	19885	55322
18	01011	54092	33362	94904	31273	04146	18594
19	52162	53916	46369	58586	23216	14513	83149
20	07056	97628	33787	09998	42698	06691	76988
21	48663	91245	85828	14346	09172	30168	90229
22	54164	58492	22421	74103	47070	25306	76468
23	32639	32363	05597	24200	13363	38005	94342
24	29334	27001	87637	87308	58731	00256	45834
25	02488	33062	28834	07351	19731	92420	60952

Source: Table of 105,000 Random Decimal Digits. Statement 4914, Interstate Commerce Commission, Transport Economics and Statistics Bureau, May, 1949.

sample is one selected from a population wherein all elements of the population have an equal chance of being selected.

Random number table—a tabulation of digits occurring randomly. The user may select any sequence of digits from the table with assurance that no pattern or bias is present. Table 9-1 presents a portion of a random number table. The table may be entered at any point on a line or column and will provide digits in random sequence.

Random number generator (RNG)—computer hardware or software capable of producing random numbers.

Standard deviation—a measure of dispersion of a population. This measure is important in sampling theory and is directly related to the sample size. Another measure of dispersion, the *variance,* is the square of the standard deviation.[1]

Precision—the maximum amount of error, either in value or in occurrence rate, that the auditor is willing to accept in a sample estimate. It is determined by judgment and is related to what the auditor considers to be material in a particular circumstance. It is usually expressed as a range around the sample estimate or the expected error rate, for example, "the estimated value ±$13,500" or, "the expected error rate of 4 percent ±2 percent." Precision is inversely related to the sample size in that the "tighter" the precision requirements, the larger the sample, other things being equal.

Confidence (also called Reliability)—the degree of assurance desired by the auditor with respect to the statistical inferences drawn. This assurance is expressed as a percentage representing the probability that the inference is reliable. The level of confidence that the auditor specifies is determined by judgment and is based on such factors as previous experience with the client, the initial assessment of internal control, and the perceived level of relative audit risk. High confidence levels require relatively larger sample sizes and are required in instances involving weak internal control, high relative risk, and high incidence of errors.

Precision and confidence levels are interactive and must both be stated in order to specify sample requirements. For example, an auditor might state the requirements for a sample by expressing "a 90 percent confidence (reliability) level with a precision of ±$4,500." By this, the auditor states a requirement for a 90 percent probability that the value range formed by the sample estimate plus or minus $4,500 will include the true value of the population. In attribute sampling the requirements may be stated, for example, as "a 95 percent confidence (reliability) level with a precision of ±4 percent." Similarly, this states the requirement for a 95 percent probability that the range formed by the expected occurrence rate plus or minus 4 percent will include the true error rate in the population. If the expected error rate in the population is 5 percent, then the range formed by the stated precision around this occurrence rate is 1 percent to 9 percent. These boundaries of the precision range are known as the *lower precision limit (LPL)* and *upper precision limit (UPL),* respectively. In attribute

[1] Symbolically, the formula for calculating the standard deviation is

$$\sqrt{\Sigma(x - \bar{x})^2/n}$$

where the term $x - \bar{x}$ represents the deviation of each item in the population from the average value of all items and n represents the number of deviations. This calculation is laborious if performed manually but may be easily accomplished using EDP equipment.

A commonly used method of manually estimating the standard deviation of a population is to select randomly a preliminary sample of thirty to fifty items, calculate the standard deviation of these items, and use the resulting figure as the population standard deviation.

sampling only the upper precision limit is of importance since the auditor is normally interested in only the maximum rate of error.

Precision and confidence (reliability) are two of the variables that determine sample size. The complete set of parameters that determine the size of a sample is composed of:

1. precision
2. confidence (reliability)
3. standard deviation of the population
4. size of the population

Standard error of the mean—a value that is a derivative of the population standard deviation and is defined as the standard deviation of the means of all possible samples of a particular size drawn from a population. This distribution of the means of all possible samples of a particular size from a population is called the *sampling distribution,* and the standard error of the mean is often referred to as the *standard deviation of the sampling distribution.*

Standard normal deviate—This factor, often referred to as a *z value,* expresses the confidence level in terms of standard deviation units. For example, a 95 percent confidence level relates to a standard normal deviate of ±1.96. This means that 95 percent of the elements in a standard normal distribution are included in the area of 1.96 standard deviations above and below the mean.

The following tabulation presents several confidence levels and the associated *z* values:

Confidence level	*z Value*
99%	2.58
95%	1.96
90%	1.645
85%	1.44
80%	1.28
75%	1.15
70%	1.04

Confidence interval—a term widely used in sampling theory and frequently causing confusion because it is erroneously equated with the term *confidence.* Confidence intervals are formed by the product of a standard normal deviate and the standard error of the mean, and they represent to statisticians the same parameter as precision represents to auditors. Auditors refer, therefore, to the range of the confidence interval as *precision.* For example, if auditors require a precision of ± $2,000, they are, in equivalent statistical language, employing a confidence interval of $4,000.

Types of statistical sampling plans

The several types of statistical sampling plans used by auditors may be classified into two categories, *attribute* sampling plans and *variables* sampling plans. Attribute sampling is used to obtain a measure of the occurrence rate of a particular characteristic in a population. For example, the occurrence rate of a specified type of error in an accounting population may be investigated using an attribute sampling plan. Variables sampling plans are used to estimate a value range for a population characteristic. For example, the total value of an accounts receivable population may be estimated using variables sampling.

Whether the auditor selects attribute sampling or variables sampling will be determined by the audit objective of the particular test. If a *compliance test* is to be performed in conjunction with internal control evaluation, attribute sampling is appropriate. In this context, for example, an error might be defined as the failure to comply with a specific control feature, such as the countersigning of a document by a department head. Attribute sampling may then be used to estimate the occurrence rate of this error.

When *substantive tests* are being performed and book values are being examined for fairness, variables sampling is used. Such a plan, for example, will allow the auditor to estimate the total value of a population from a sample of items. This estimate is then compared to the value recorded on the client's records. If the disparity between the estimate and the recorded value is greater than the auditor is willing to accept, further investigation is warranted.

Types of Attribute Sampling Plans Two types of attribute sampling plans are frequently used by auditors. One plan, *estimation sampling for attributes,* is used to estimate the occurrence rate of a specified characteristic in the population or to determine whether the occurrence rate exceeds some pre-established limit. *Discovery sampling,* another form of attribute sampling, is typically used in cases of large populations where the occurrence rate is believed to be quite small. In using discovery sampling, the auditor's objective is not to estimate the occurrence rate in the population. Rather, the plan is designed to provide assurance to the auditor that if the occurrence rate in the population exceeds a specified level, the sample will include at least one occurrence. Thus, if no errors are found in the sample, the auditor has assurance that the population error rate does not exceed the level specified. Applications of both types of attribute sampling plans are discused later in this chapter.

Types of Variables Sampling Plans At least four different techniques for estimating variables are found in current practice. In one type plan, *mean-per-unit estimation,* the auditor is able to make a point estimate of the audited value of the total population or of the average item in the population.

Difference estimation, a second type, is particularly useful in cases of populations containing large numbers of errors. In this plan, an estimate is made based on the *differences* found between the audited values and the book values of items included in the sample. Similarly, *ratio estimation,* the third type, is used in populations with large numbers of errors. However, this technique bases the estimate on the *ratio* of the audited values of the sample items to their book values. Ratio and difference estimation techniques are particularly valuable in that for populations with certain characteristics (high variability and many homogeneous errors), much smaller sample sizes may be used as compared to mean-per-unit sampling.

A fourth plan, *dollar unit sampling,* also known as *cumulative monetary amount sampling,* combines certain aspects of attribute sampling with variables sampling. In this plan, each dollar in the population is viewed as a separate item or sampling unit. For example, an inventory with a book value of $3,400,828 may be viewed as a population with 3,400,828 items, each of which may be representative of a correctly stated or an incorrectly stated inventory item. In applying dollar unit sampling to this population, the auditor selects a random sample of individual dollars from the population of 3,400,828 and examines the specific inventory items which "contain" the individual dollars included in the sample.

The application of variables sampling is illustrated later in this chapter. This discussion emphasizes the mean-per-unit sampling technique which closely correlates with the material taught in most standard statistics courses.

Applications of attribute sampling

The first application of attribute sampling to be illustrated will be the use of estimation sampling for attributes in performing an internal control compliance test. Assume that in the client's cash disbursement system, authorizations for disbursements by check are initiated by several departments within the home office and are sent to the treasurer's department for execution. Each authorization for disbursement is signed by the initiating employee and countersigned by the respective department head. Each original authorization form is cancelled when the check is written and filed numerically in the treasurer's office.

The auditor considers that the department heads' countersigning the request is an important control feature in this system and desires to test compliance with this control. In this case an error is defined as the failure of a department head's signature to appear on a paid authorization form.

During the year under audit, approximately 12,000 authorizations for disbursements were processed. From past experience the auditor expects about a 3 percent error rate in this population. If the true error rate exceeded 5 percent, however, the auditor would conclude that this internal control feature was not effective. This conclusion would cause the auditor to revise the initial assessment of internal control over cash disbursements and consequently to expand the audit tests planned for that area.

Determining the Sample Size In determining sample sizes for either attribute or variables sampling, the four parameters for determining sample size—precision, confidence, population standard deviation, and population size—must be considered. In attribute sampling, tables are frequently used for determining sample sizes, whereas in variables sampling, calculation procedures are commonly employed.

In the present case, the precision has been set as a result of the auditor's determination that an error rate in excess of 5 percent would be unsatisfactory. This 5 percent upper precision limit, coupled with an expected error rate of 3 percent, indicates a precision of 2 percent. The tables incorporated in this chapter utilize precision in terms of (1) the expected occurrence rate and (2) the upper precision limit.

The confidence (reliability) level is determined by the auditor based on the relative audit risk involved in the situation. Audit areas with high perceived risk require relatively high confidence levels. In this case, assume that the auditor desires 95 percent assurance that the sample estimate is reliable. Most auditors would consider this to be a moderate to high confidence level.

In attribute sampling, the population standard deviation is a function of the occurrence rate in the population. Consequently, this parameter is determined when the estimated error rate is selected. Population size, the fourth parameter, is taken into account in that the tables in this chapter are based on infinite populations. This produces a slight conservative bias by yielding larger sample sizes, but the effect is not significant in typical audit situations.

The sample size may be determined based on the information provided thus far. Table 9-2b provides sample sizes for tests requiring a confidence (reliability) level of 95 percent. The sixth column in Table 9-2b is used with populations having an expected occurrence rate of 3 percent. Following that column downward provides upper precision limits that may be achieved with various sample sizes. The first upper precision limit in this column which is equal to or less than the 5 percent limit set by the auditor is 4.8 percent. This 4.8 percent upper precision limit indicates a sample size of 400 items, as shown in the first column in the table. The auditor now knows, by interpolation, that a sample of slightly less than 400 cash disbursement authorization forms must be randomly selected, examined, and evaluated in order to achieve the assurance desired from the test.

Table 9-2a Attribute Sampling Determination of Sample Size—Upper Precision Limits—90% Reliability

SAMPLE SIZE	OCCURRENCE RATE 0.0	.5	1.0	2.0	3.0	4.0	5.0	6.0	7.0	8.0	9.0	10.0	12.0	14.0	16.0	18.0	20.0	25.0	30.0	40.0	50.0
50	4.5			7.6		10.3		12.9		15.4		17.8	20.1	22.7	24.7	27.2	29.1		39.8	50.0	59.9
100	2.3		3.3	5.2	6.6	7.8	9.1	10.3	11.7	12.7	14.0	15.0	17.3	19.6	21.7	24.0	26.1	31.4	36.6	46.9	56.8
150	1.5			4.4		6.9		9.3		11.6		13.9	16.1	18.4	20.5	22.7	24.8		35.2	45.5	55.4
200	1.1	1.9	2.6	4.0	5.2	6.4	7.6	8.8	10.0	11.0	12.2	13.3	15.5	17.7	19.8	22.0	24.0	29.3	34.5	44.4	54.4
250	.9			3.7		6.1		8.4		10.7		12.9	15.1	17.2	19.3	21.5	23.6		33.7	43.7	53.7
300	.8		2.2	3.5	4.7	5.9	7.0	8.2	9.3	10.4	11.5	12.6	14.7	16.9	19.0	21.1	23.2	28.2	33.2	43.2	53.2
350	.7			3.3		5.7		8.0		10.2.		12.3	14.5	16.7	18.8	20.9	22.8		32.8	42.8	52.8
400	.6	1.3	2.0	3.2	4.4	5.6	6.7	7.8	8.9	10.0	11.1	12.2	14.3	16.5	18.5	20.5	22.5	27.5	32.5	42.5	52.5
450	.5			3.1		5.5		7.7		9.9		12.0	14.2	16.3	18.3	20.3	22.3		32.3	42.3	52.2
500	.5		1.8	3.1	4.2	5.4	6.5	7.6	8.7	9.8	10.9	11.9	14.1	16.1	18.1	20.1	22.1	27.1	32.1	42.1	52.0
550	.4			3.0		5.3		7.5		9.7		11.8	13.9	15.9	17.9	19.9	21.9		31.9	41.9	51.9
600	.4	1.1	1.7	2.9	4.1	5.2	6.3	7.4	8.5	9.6	10.7	11.7	13.7	15.7	17.7	19.7	21.7	26.7	31.7	41.7	51.7
650	.4			2.9		5.2		7.4		9.5		11.6	13.6	15.6	17.6	19.6	21.6		31.6	41.6	51.6
700	.3		1.7	2.9	4.0	5.1	6.2	7.3	8.4	9.5	10.5	11.5	13.5	15.5	17.5	19.5	21.5	26.5	31.5	41.5	51.5
750	.3			2.8		5.1		7.3		9.4		11.4	13.4	15.4	17.4	19.4	21.4		31.4	41.4	51.4
800	.3	1.0	1.6	2.8	3.9	5.0	6.1	7.2	8.3	9.3	10.3	11.3	13.3	15.3	17.3	19.3	21.3	26.3	31.3	41.3	51.3
850	.3			2.8		5.0		7.2		9.2		11.2	13.2	15.3	17.3	19.3	21.3		31.3	41.3	51.3
900	.3		1.6	2.7	3.9	5.0	6.0	7.1	8.2	9.2	10.2	11.2	13.2	15.2	17.2	19.2	21.2	26.2	31.2	41.2	51.2
950	.2			2.7		4.9		7.1		9.1		11.1	13.1	15.1	17.1	19.1	21.1		31.1	41.1	51.1
1000	.2	.9	1.5	2.7	3.8	4.9	6.0	7.1	8.1	9.1	10.1	11.1	13.1	15.1	17.1	19.1	21.1	26.1	31.1	41.1	51.1
1500	.2		1.4	2.5	3.6	4.7	5.7	6.7	7.7	8.7	9.7	10.7	12.7	14.7	16.7	18.7	20.7	25.7	30.7	40.7	50.7
2000	.1	.8	1.3	2.5	3.5	4.5	5.5	6.5	7.5	8.5	9.5	10.5	12.5	14.5	16.5	18.5	20.5	25.5	30.5	40.6	50.6
2500	.1		1.3	2.4	3.4	4.4	5.4	6.4	7.4	8.4	9.4	10.4	12.4	14.4	16.4	18.4	20.4	25.4	30.4	40.4	50.4
3000	.1	.7	1.3	2.4	3.4	4.4	5.4	6.4	7.4	8.4	9.4	10.4	12.4	14.4	16.4	18.4	20.4	25.4	30.4	40.4	50.4
4000	.1	.7	1.2	2.3	3.3	4.3	5.3	6.3	7.3	8.3	9.3	10.3	12.3	14.3	16.3	18.3	20.3	25.3	30.3	40.3	50.3
5000	.0	.7	1.2	2.3	3.2	4.2	5.2	6.2	7.2	8.2	9.2	10.2	12.2	14.2	16.2	18.2	20.2	25.2	30.2	40.2	50.2

Source: *An Auditor's Approach to Statistical Sampling,* Copyright © 1974, the American Institute of Certified Public Accountants, Inc.

Table 9-2b Attribute Sampling Determination of Sample Size—Upper Precision Limits—95% Reliability

SAMPLE SIZE	OCCURRENCE RATE 0.0	.5	1.0	2.0	3.0	4.0	5.0	6.0	7.0	8.0	9.0	10.0	12.0	14.0	16.0	18.0	20.0	25.0	30.0	40.0	50.0
50	5.8			9.1		12.1		14.8		17.4		19.9	22.3	25.1	27.0	29.6	31.6		42.4	52.6	62.4
100	3.0		4.7	6.2	7.6	8.9	10.2	11.5	13.0	14.0	15.4	16.4	18.7	21.2	23.3	25.6	27.7	33.1	38.4	48.7	56.6
150	2.0			5.1		7.7		10.2		12.6		15.0	17.3	19.6	21.7	24.0	26.1		36.7	47.0	56.8
200	1.5	2.4	3.1	4.5	5.8	7.1	8.3	9.5	10.8	11.9	13.1	14.2	16.4	18.7	20.9	23.1	25.2	30.5	35.7	45.7	55.6
250	1.2			4.2		6.7		9.1		11.4		13.7	15.9	18.1	20.3	22.4	24.6		34.8	44.8	54.7
300	1.0		2.6	3.9	5.2	6.4	7.6	8.8	10.0	11.1	12.2	13.3	15.5	17.7	19.8	22.0	24.1	29.1	34.1	44.1	54.1
350	.9			3.7		6.2		8.5		10.8		13.0	15.2	17.4	19.5	21.7	23.6		33.6	43.6	53.6
400	.7	1.6	2.3	3.6	4.8	6.0	7.2	8.3	9.5	10.6	11.7	12.8	15.0	17.2	19.2	21.2	23.2	28.2	33.2	43.2	53.2
450	.7			3.5		5.9		8.2		10.4		12.6	14.8	16.8	18.9	20.9	22.9		32.9	42.9	52.9
500	.6		2.1	3.4	4.6	5.8	6.9	8.0	9.2	10.3	11.4	12.5	14.6	16.7	18.6	20.7	22.6	27.6	32.6	42.6	52.6
550	.5			3.3		5.7		7.9		10.1		12.3	14.4	16.4	18.4	20.4	22.4		32.4	42.4	52.4
600	.5	1.3	2.0	3.2	4.4	5.6	6.7	7.8	9.0	10.0	11.2	12.2	14.2	16.2	18.2	20.2	22.2	27.2	32.2	42.2	52.2
650	.5			3.2		5.5		7.7		10.0		12.1	14.1	16.1	18.1	20.1	22.1		32.1	42.1	52.1
700	.4		1.9	3.1	4.3	5.4	6.6	7.7	8.8	9.9	10.8	11.9	13.9	15.9	17.9	19.9	21.9	26.9	31.9	41.9	51.9
750	.4			3.1		5.4		7.6		9.8		11.8	13.8	15.8	17.8	19.8	21.8		31.8	41.8	51.8
800	.4	1.1	1.8	3.0	4.2	5.3	6.4	7.5	8.7	9.7	10.7	11.7	13.7	15.7	17.7	19.7	21.7	26.7	31.7	41.7	51.7
850	.4			3.0		5.3		7.5		9.6		11.6	13.6	15.6	17.6	19.6	21.6		31.6	41.6	51.6
900	.3		1.7	3.0	4.1	5.2	6.3	7.5	8.5	9.5	10.5	11.5	13.5	15.5	17.5	19.5	21.5	26.5	31.5	41.5	51.5
950	.3			2.9		5.2		7.4		9.4		11.4	13.4	15.5	17.4	19.5	21.4		31.5	41.5	51.5
1000	.3	1.0	1.7	2.9	4.0	5.2	6.3	7.4	8.4	9.4	10.4	11.4	13.4	15.4	17.4	19.4	21.4	26.4	31.4	41.4	51.4
1500	.2		1.5	2.7	3.8	4.9	5.9	6.9	7.9	8.9	9.9	10.9	12.9	14.9	16.9	18.9	20.9	25.9	30.9	40.9	50.9
2000	.1	.8	1.4	2.6	3.7	4.7	5.7	6.7	7.7	8.7	9.7	10.7	12.7	14.7	16.7	18.7	20.7	25.7	30.7	40.7	50.7
2500	.1		1.4	2.6	3.6	4.6	5.6	6.6	7.6	8.6	9.6	10.6	12.6	14.6	16.6	18.6	20.6	25.6	30.6	40.6	50.6
3000	.1	.8	1.4	2.5	3.5	4.5	5.5	6.5	7.5	8.5	9.5	10.5	12.5	14.5	16.5	18.5	20.5	25.5	30.5	40.5	50.5
4000	.1	.7	1.3	2.4	3.4	4.4	5.4	6.4	7.4	8.4	9.4	10.4	12.4	14.4	16.4	18.4	20.4	25.4	30.4	40.4	50.4
5000	.1	.7	1.3	2.3	3.3	4.3	5.3	6.3	7.3	8.3	9.3	10.3	12.3	14.3	16.3	18.3	20.3	25.3	30.3	40.3	50.3

Source: *An Auditor's Approach to Statistical Sampling,* Copyright © 1974, the American Institute of Certified Public Accountants, Inc.

An alternative, graphical format of attribute sample size table is presented in Figures 9-1a, b, and c. For the present example, Figure 9-1b may be used. Each sloping curve on the graph is identified with an expected occurrence rate designated at the top. The vertical lines on the graph represent desired upper precision limits. At each point where a curve intersects a vertical line, a sample size may be read from the margin of the figure. Note that a sample size of approximately 375 is shown by this figure.

Figure 9-1a Attribute Sampling Graph—Reliability Level-90% (Figures 9-1a, 9-1b, and 9-1c are from *An Auditor's Approach to Statistical Sampling,* copyright © 1974 by the American Institute of Certified Public Accountants, Inc. These tables were adapted by the AICPA from materials furnished by The American Group of CPA Firms.)

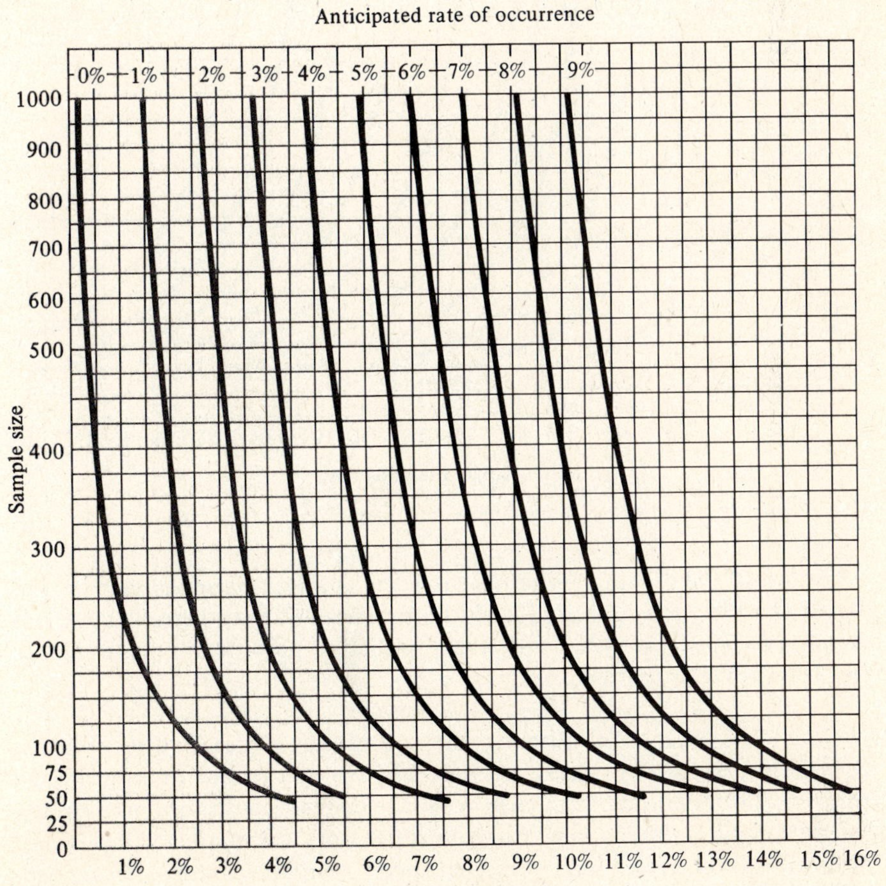

Figure 9-1b Attribute Sampling Graph—Reliability Level-95%

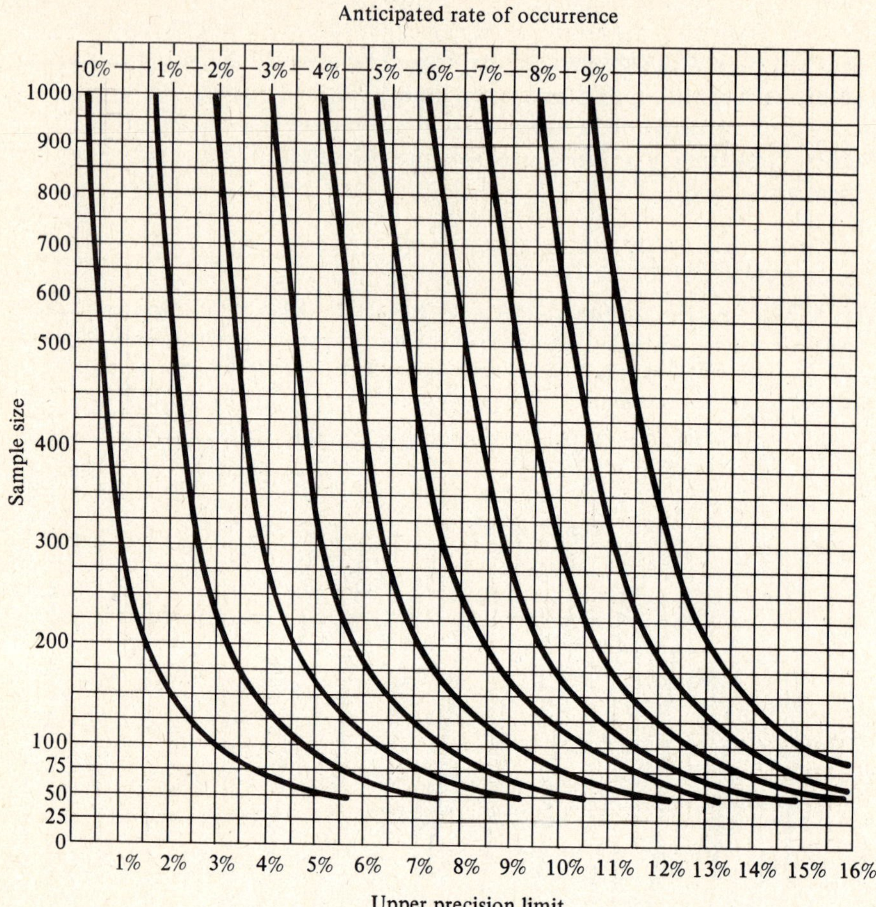

Assume that by using either format the auditor determines that the proper sample size is 375. It should be understood that the tables are not intended to be exact; rather they are designed to provide adequate sample sizes for audit applications.

Selecting the Sample In selecting the sample of 375 cash disbursement requisitions, the auditor must use a procedure that results in an unbiased selection. Two methods frequently used are unrestricted random sampling and systematic sampling with random start. Both techniques will produce unbiased sample selections when properly employed. Also, either approach may be employed manually or in conjunction with EDP equipment.

Figure 9-1c Attribute Sampling Graph—Reliability Level-99%

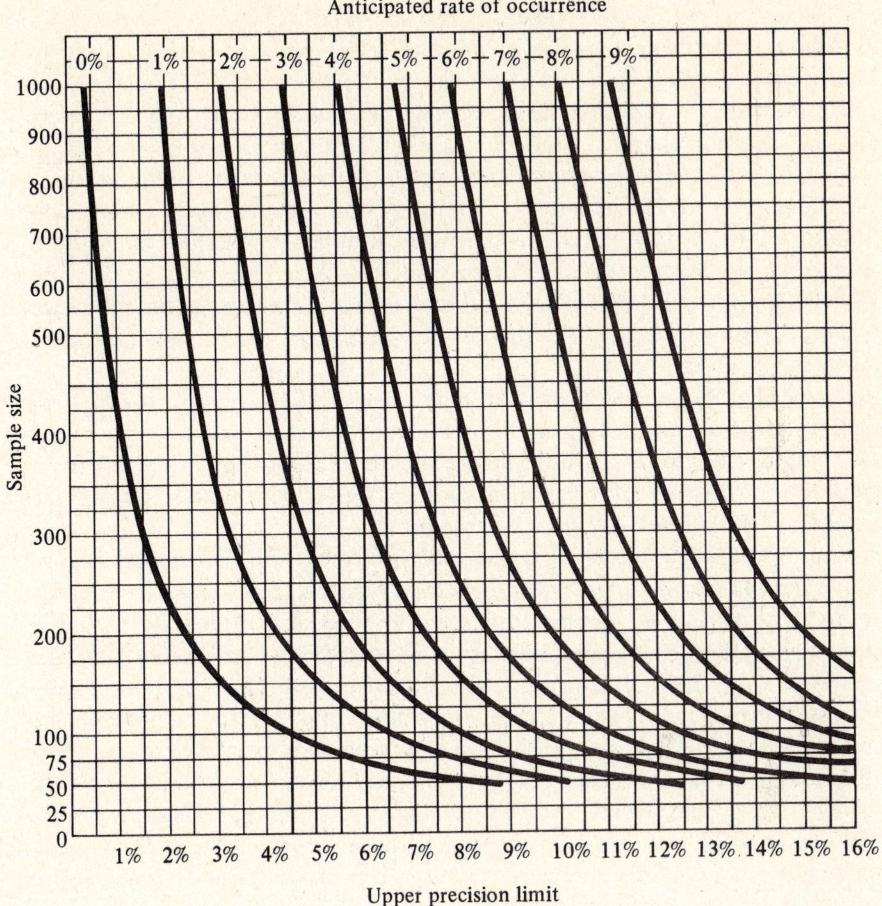

In employing unrestricted random sampling, the auditor may use a random number table or a random number generator computer routine to provide an unbiased selection guide. Since the disbursement requisition forms have identifying numbers, the random selection may be made on these numbers. In cases where no available identifying numbers are present, sequential numbering may be supplied. In addition, random selection may be made on the basis of sequential order, page position, or any other designating factor. In the current example, if the assumption is made that the forms are numbered sequentially from 1 to 12,000, a random number generator could be made to produce 375 random numbers between these values. Then the auditor would examine the forms designated by the random numbers. If no EDP equipment is available, the necessary random numbers may be manually selected from a random number table.

Systematic sample selection is often more convenient for auditors than random selection, especially in manual selection applications. Systematic selection procedure involves a selection rule that consists of two elements—a random start and a selection interval. The random start may be selected by the auditor from a random number table or by other means. The selection interval is determined by relating the number of items desired in the sample to the number of items in the population. In the current example, if the number of items in the population (12,000) is divided by the required sample size (375), the result is 32. This represents the required sampling interval. If an auditor selects a random number between 1 and 32 (inclusive), an appropriate random start will be obtained for use with this interval.

To implement the sampling rule just established, the auditor begins by selecting the account designated by the random start. Assuming a random start of 6, the auditor should select the sixth requisition form in the file and every thirty-second form thereafter. Upon completion, an unbiased sample of 375 items will have been selected.

Random sample selection is generally preferred on theoretical grounds, but often practical considerations favor systematic selections. It should be noted that additional precautions need to be taken when systematic selection is employed. Certain population characteristics can inject bias into a systematic sample. Clustering in the population is a common example of one of these characteristics. As an illustration of clustering, a payroll listing may be visualized that reports a weekly payroll for employees in several departments. Assume that there are twenty departments with thirty employees each. The payroll listing is arranged so that employees are grouped by department with the department supervisor listed first. If systematic selection is employed for this population, it is likely that a disproportionate number of supervisor items will be selected. Depending on the random start and the selection interval, the sample could contain all supervisor items, no supervisor items, or a disproportionately large or small number of supervisor items. Before employing systematic selection, the auditor should consider if any population characteristics, such as clustering or any order system, could inject bias into the sample. In cases with such characteristics, the auditor should employ random sampling or some other procedure to select an unbiased sample.

Application of either random or systematic selection is well within the capabilities of most EDP systems. This can relieve the auditor of much time-consuming and therefore costly routine work. Also, several generalized computer audit programs available include a sampling routine. This may further save time for both the auditor and the client's EDP personnel. Generalized computer audit programs are discussed further in Chapter 10.

Evaluating the Sample After the sample size has been determined and the sample selected, appropriate auditing procedures must be performed on the items in the sample. In the present example the only procedure necessary is to determine whether the disbursement requisition form has been countersigned by a department head. As this procedure is performed, the auditor should note in the working papers relevant information as to all errors found.

Once the number of errors in the sample has been determined, an inference as to the population error rate can be made. Assume that in the sample of 375 forms, the auditor found 9 that were not properly countersigned. To evaluate this result, reference is made to Table 9-3. By examining the section of Table 9-3 applicable to sample sizes of 375, the upper precision limit actually achieved may be determined. In this case it can be seen that with a 95 percent confidence (reliability) level, 9 occurrences indicates an upper precision limit (UPL) of 4.15 percent, well within the 5 percent specified by the auditor. Also, it can be seen that as many as 11 occurrences could have been found without exceeding the specified limit.

Since this compliance test has now indicated that the population error rate is within acceptable limits, the auditor may conclude that this specific internal control feature is being complied with. This reinforces the auditor's preliminary internal control evaluation and indicates that audit reliance may be placed on this control area.

USING DISCOVERY SAMPLING

To illustrate the use of discovery sampling, the facts of the previous example may be used with certain modifications. Since discovery sampling is usually used in cases where the expected occurrence rate is small and where the specific controls tested are critical, assume that the auditor requires 99 percent assurance that the population occurrence rate is less than 1 percent. Reference to Table 9-4c, on page 338, indicates that a sample size of 460 items provides 99 percent assurance that at least one occurrence will be included in the sample if the population occurrence rate equals or exceeds 1 percent.

One advantage of discovery sampling is the possibility of quickly determining if the occurrence rate in the population equals or exceeds the critical occurrence rate set by the auditor. This is because once a single error is found in the sample, the remaining items in the sample need not be examined since the objective of the test has been accomplished. If, however, the auditor wishes to estimate the rate of occurrence in the population, the remaining items in the sample may be examined and the results may be evaluated using the attribute tables as explained in the previous illustration.

(*Text continues on page* 339.)

Table 9-3 Attribute Sampling—Evaluation of Sample Results

	Number of Occur-rences	UPL* RELIABILITY LEVEL 90%	95%	99%
SAMPLE SIZE 25	0	8.80	11.29	16.82
	1	14.69	17.61	23.75
	2	19.91	23.10	29.59
	3	24.80	28.17	34.88
	4	29.47	32.96	39.79
SAMPLE SIZE 50	0	4.50	5.82	8.80
	1	7.56	9.14	12.55
	2	10.30	12.06	15.77
	3	12.88	14.78	18.72
	4	15.35	17.38	21.50
	5	17.76	19.88	24.15
	6	20.11	22.32	26.71
	8	24.69	27.02	31.61
SAMPLE SIZE 75	0	3.02	3.92	5.96
	1	5.09	6.17	8.53
	2	6.94	8.16	10.74
	3	8.69	10.01	12.78
	4	10.38	11.79	14.70
	5	12.02	13.51	16.55
	6	13.62	15.18	18.34
	7	15.20	16.82	20.08
	8	16.75	18.42	21.77
	12	22.78	24.63	28.25
SAMPLE SIZE 100	0	2.28	2.95	4.50
	1	3.83	4.66	6.45
	2	5.23	6.16	8.14
	3	6.56	7.57	9.70
	4	7.83	8.92	11.17
	5	9.08	10.23	12.58
	6	10.29	11.50	13.95
	7	11.49	12.75	15.29
	8	12.67	13.97	16.59
	9	13.83	15.18	17.87
	10	14.99	16.37	19.13
	11	16.13	17.55	20.37
	15	20.61	22.15	25.18
SAMPLE SIZE 125	0	1.83	2.37	3.62
	1	3.08	3.74	5.19
	2	4.20	4.95	6.55
	3	5.27	6.09	7.81
	4	6.29	7.17	9.00
	5	7.29	8.23	10.15
	6	8.27	9.25	11.26
	7	9.24	10.26	12.34
	8	10.19	11.25	13.40
	9	11.13	12.23	14.44
	10	12.06	13.19	15.47
	11	12.98	14.15	16.48
	12	13.89	15.09	17.47
	13	14.80	16.03	18.45
	19	20.14	21.50	24.16
SAMPLE SIZE 150	0	1.52	1.98	3.02
	1	2.57	3.12	4.34
	2	3.51	4.14	5.49
	3	4.40	5.09	6.54
	4	5.26	6.00	7.54
	5	6.10	6.88	8.50
	6	6.92	7.74	9.44
	7	7.72	8.59	10.35
	8	8.52	9.42	11.24
	9	9.31	10.24	12.12
	10	10.09	11.05	12.98
	11	10.86	11.85	13.83
	12	11.62	12.64	14.67
	13	12.39	13.43	15.50
	14	13.14	14.21	16.32
	15	13.89	14.98	17.13
	16	14.64	15.75	17.94
	23	19.79	21.02	23.42
SAMPLE SIZE 175	0	1.31	1.70	2.60
	1	2.20	2.68	3.73
	2	3.01	3.55	4.72
	3	3.78	4.37	5.63
	4	4.52	5.15	6.49
	5	5.24	5.91	7.32
	6	5.94	6.65	8.12
	7	6.63	7.38	8.91
	8	7.32	8.10	9.68
	9	8.00	8.80	10.43
	10	8.67	9.50	11.18
	11	9.33	10.19	11.91
	12	9.99	10.87	12.64
	13	10.65	11.55	13.36
	14	11.30	12.22	14.07
	15	11.95	12.89	14.77

*Upper Precision Limit

Source: *An Auditor's Approach to Statistical Sampling,* Copyright © 1974, the American Institute of Certified Public Accountants, Inc.

Table 9-3 (*cont.*)

	Number of Occur- rences	UPL RELIABILITY LEVEL 90%	95%	99%
	16	12.59	13.55	15.47
	17	13.23	14.21	16.16
	18	13.87	14.87	16.85
	27	19.51	20.64	22.84
SAMPLE SIZE 200	0	1.14	1.49	2.28
	1	1.93	2.35	3.27
	2	2.64	3.11	4.14
	3	3.31	3.83	4.93
	4	3.96	4.52	5.69
	5	4.59	5.18	6.42
	6	5.21	5.83	7.13
	7	5.82	6.47	7.82
	8	6.42	7.10	8.50
	9	7.01	7.72	9.16
	10	7.60	8.33	9.82
	11	8.18	8.94	10.46
	12	8.76	9.54	11.10
	13	9.34	10.14	11.73
	14	9.91	10.73	12.36
	15	10.48	11.31	12.98
	16	11.04	11.90	13.59
	17	11.61	12.48	14.20
	18	12.17	13.05	14.81
	19	12.73	13.63	15.41
	20	13.28	14.20	16.01
	21	13.84	14.77	16.60
	30	18.75	19.79	21.82
SAMPLE SIZE 225	0	1.02	1.32	2.03
	1	1.72	2.09	2.91
	2	2.35	2.77	3.68
	3	2.94	3.41	4.39
	4	3.52	4.02	5.07
	5	4.08	4.62	5.72
	6	4.63	5.19	6.35
	7	5.18	5.76	6.97
	8	5.71	6.32	7.57
	9	6.24	6.88	8.17
	10	6.76	7.42	8.75
	11	7.28	7.96	9.33
	12	7.80	8.50	9.90
	13	8.31	9.03	10.46
	14	8.82	9.56	11.02
	15	9.33	10.08	11.58
	16	9.83	10.60	12.12
	17	10.34	11.12	12.67

	Number of Occur- rences	UPL RELIABILITY LEVEL 90%	95%	99%
	18	10.84	11.63	13.21
	19	11.33	12.14	13.75
	20	11.83	12.65	14.28
	21	12.32	13.16	14.81
	22	12.82	13.67	15.34
	23	13.31	14.17	15.87
	34	18.63	19.60	21.50
SAMPLE SIZE 250	0	.92	1.19	1.83
	1	1.55	1.88	2.63
	2	2.11	2.50	3.32
	3	2.65	3.07	3.96
	4	3.17	3.62	4.57
	5	3.68	4.16	5.16
	6	4.17	4.68	5.73
	7	4.66	5.19	6.29
	8	5.15	5.70	6.83
	9	5.62	6.20	7.37
	10	6.10	6.69	7.89
	11	6.56	7.18	8.42
	12	7.03	7.66	8.93
	13	7.49	8.14	9.44
	14	7.95	8.62	9.95
	15	8.41	9.09	10.45
	16	8.86	9.56	10.94
	17	9.32	10.03	11.43
	18	9.77	10.49	11.92
	19	10.22	10.95	12.41
	20	10.66	11.41	12.89
	21	11.11	11.87	13.37
	22	11.55	12.33	13.85
	23	12.00	12.78	14.33
	24	12.44	13.23	14.80
	25	12.88	13.69	15.27
	26	13.32	14.14	15.74
	38	18.52	19.44	21.23
SAMPLE SIZE 275	0	.83	1.08	1.66
	1	1.41	1.71	2.39
	2	1.92	2.27	3.02
	3	2.41	2.80	3.61
	4	2.89	3.30	4.16
	5	3.35	3.78	4.70
	6	3.80	4.26	5.22
	7	4.24	4.73	5.72
	8	4.68	5.19	6.22
	9	5.12	5.64	6.71

Table 9-3 *(cont.)*

	Number of Occur-rences	UPL RELIABILITY LEVEL 90%	95%	99%
	10	5.55	6.09	7.19
	11	5.97	6.53	7.67
	12	6.40	6.97	8.14
	13	6.82	7.41	8.60
	14	7.24	7.84	9.06
	15	7.65	8.27	9.52
	16	8.07	8.70	9.97
	17	8.48	9.13	10.42
	18	8.89	9.55	10.87
	19	9.30	9.97	11.31
	20	9.71	10.39	11.75
	21	10.11	10.81	12.19
	22	10.52	11.23	12.62
	23	10.92	11.64	13.06
	24	11.32	12.05	13.49
	25	11.73	12.47	13.92
	26	12.13	12.88	14.35
	27	12.53	13.28	14.77
	28	12.92	13.69	15.20
	42	18.42	19.30	21.00
SAMPLE SIZE 300	0	.76	.99	1.52
	1	1.29	1.57	2.19
	2	1.76	2.08	2.77
	3	2.21	2.56	3.31
	4	2.65	3.02	3.82
	5	3.07	3.47	4.31
	6	3.48	3.91	4.79
	7	3.89	4.34	5.25
	8	4.30	4.76	5.71
	9	4.69	5.18	6.16
	10	5.09	5.59	6.60
	11	5.48	6.00	7.04
	12	5.87	6.40	7.47
	13	6.26	6.80	7.90
	14	6.64	7.20	8.32
	15	7.02	7.59	8.74
	16	7.40	7.99	9.16
	17	7.78	8.38	9.57
	18	8.16	8.77	9.98
	19	8.53	9.15	10.39
	20	8.91	9.54	10.79
	21	9.28	9.92	11.20
	22	9.65	10.31	11.60
	23	10.02	10.69	12.00
	24	10.39	11.07	12.39
	25	10.76	11.44	12.79
	26	11.13	11.82	13.18
	27	11.50	12.20	13.57

	Number of Occur-rences	UPL RELIABILITY LEVEL 90%	95%	99%
	28	11.86	12.57	13.96
	29	12.23	12.95	14.35
	30	12.59	13.32	14.74
	31	12.96	13.69	15.13
	45	17.98	18.81	20.42
SAMPLE SIZE 325	0	.71	.92	1.41
	1	1.19	1.45	2.02
	2	1.63	1.92	2.56
	3	2.04	2.37	3.06
	4	2.44	2.79	3.53
	5	2.83	3.21	3.98
	6	3.22	3.61	4.42
	7	3.60	4.01	4.85
	8	3.97	4.40	5.28
	9	4.34	4.78	5.69
	10	4.70	5.16	6.10
	11	5.06	5.54	6.51
	12	5.42	5.91	6.90
	13	5.78	6.28	7.30
	14	6.13	6.65	7.69
	15	6.49	7.02	8.08
	16	6.84	7.38	8.46
	17	7.19	7.74	8.85
	18	7.54	8.10	9.23
	19	7.88	8.46	9.60
	20	8.23	8.82	9.98
	21	8.58	9.17	10.35
	22	8.92	9.52	10.72
	23	9.26	9.88	11.09
	24	9.60	10.23	11.46
	25	9.94	10.58	11.83
	26	10.28	10.93	12.19
	27	10.62	11.27	12.55
	28	10.96	11.62	12.92
	29	11.30	11.97	13.28
	30	11.64	12.31	13.64
	31	11.97	12.66	13.99
	32	12.31	13.00	14.35
	33	12.64	13.34	14.71
	49	17.93	18.73	20.27
SAMPLE SIZE 350	0	.66	.85	1.31
	1	1.11	1.35	1.88
	2	1.51	1.79	2.38
	3	1.90	2.20	2.84
	4	2.27	2.60	3.28
	5	2.63	2.98	3.70

Table 9-3 (*cont.*)

Sample Size	Number of Occurrences	UPL Reliability Level 90%	95%	99%
	6	2.99	3.36	4.11
	7	3.34	3.72	4.51
	8	3.69	4.09	4.91
	9	4.03	4.44	5.29
	10	4.37	4.80	5.67
	11	4.70	5.15	6.05
	12	5.04	5.50	6.42
	13	5.37	5.84	6.79
	14	5 70	6.18	7.15
	15	6.03	6.52	7.51
	16	6.36	6.86	7.87
	17	6.68	7.20	8.23
	18	7.00	7.53	8.58
	19	7.33	7.86	8.93
	20	7.65	8.20	9.28
	21	7.97	8.53	9.63
	22	8.29	8.85	9.97
	23	8.61	9.18	10.32
	24	8.92	9.51	10.66
	25	9.24	9.83	11.00
	26	9.56	10.16	11.34
	27	9.87	10.48	11.68
	28	10.19	10.80	12.01
	29	10.50	11.13	12.35
	30	10.82	11.45	12.68
	31	11.13	11.77	13.02
	32	11.44	12.09	13.35
	33	11.75	12.40	13.68
	34	12.06	12.72	14.01
	35	12.37	13.04	14.34
	36	12.68	13.36	14.67
	53	17.89	18.66	20.14
SAMPLE SIZE 375	0	.61	.80	1.22
	1	1.03	1.26	1.76
	2	1.41	1.67	2.22
	3	1.77	2.05	2.65
	4	2.12	2.42	3.06
	5	2.46	2.78	3.46
	6	2.79	3.13	3.84
	7	3.12	3.48	4.22
	8	3.44	3.82	4.58
	9	3.76	4.15	4.94
	10	4.08	4.48	5.30
	11	4.39	4.81	5.65
	12	4.70	5.13	6.00
	13	5.01	5.45	6.34
	14	5.32	5.77	6.68
	15	5.63	6.09	7.02
	16	5.94	6.41	7.35
	17	6.24	6.72	7.69
	18	6.54	7.03	8.02
	19	6.84	7.35	8.35
	20	7.14	7.66	8.67
	21	7.44	7.96	9.00
	22	7.74	8.27	9.32
	23	8.04	8.58	9.64
	24	8.34	8.88	9.96
	25	8.63	9.19	10.28
	26	8.93	9.49	10.60
	27	9.22	9.79	10.91
	28	9.52	10.09	11.23
	29	9.81	10.39	11.54
	30	10.10	10.69	11.86
	31	10.39	10.99	12.17
	32	10.69	11.29	12.48
	33	10.98	11.59	12.79
	34	11.27	11.89	13.10
	35	11.56	12.18	13.41
	36	11.85	12.48	13.71
	37	12.14	12.77	14.02
	38	12.43	13.07	14.33
	57	17.85	18.59	20.01
SAMPLE SIZE 400	0	.57	.75	1.14
	1	.97	1.18	1.65
	2	1.32	1.57	2.08
	3	1.66	1.93	2.49
	4	1.99	2.27	2.87
	5	2.31	2.61	3.24
	6	2.62	2.94	3.60
	7	2.92	3.26	3.95
	8	3.23	3.58	4.30
	9	3.53	3.89	4.64
	10	3.83	4.20	4.97
	11	4.12	4.51	5.30
	12	4.41	4.82	5.63
	13	4.70	5.12	5.95
	14	4.99	5.42	6.27
	15	5.28	5.72	6.59
	16	5.57	6.01	6.90
	17	5.85	6.31	7.21
	18	6.14	6.60	7.52
	19	6.42	6.89	7.83
	20	6.70	7.18	8.14
	21	6.98	7.47	8.44
	22	7.26	7.76	8.75
	23	7.54	8.05	9.05

Table 9-3 *(cont.)*

Number of Occurrences	UPL RELIABILITY LEVEL 90%	95%	99%
24	7.82	8.33	9.35
25	8.10	8.62	9.65
26	8.38	8.90	9.95
27	8.65	9.19	10.25
28	8.93	9.47	10.54
29	9.20	9.75	10.84
30	9.48	10.03	11.13
31	9.75	10.32	11.42
32	10.03	10.60	11.71
33	10.30	10.88	12.01

Number of Occurrences	UPL RELIABILITY LEVEL 90%	95%	99%
34	10.57	11.15	12.30
35	10.84	11.43	12.59
36	11.12	11.71	12.87
37	11.39	11.99	13.16
38	11.66	12.27	13.45
39	11.93	12.54	13.74
40	12.20	12.82	14.02
41	12.47	13.09	14.31
60	17.54	18.25	19.62

Table 9-4a Discovery Sampling for Attributes for Populations Between 2,000 and 5,000

If the Population Occurrence Rate is:

The Probability of Discovering at Least One Occurrence in the Sample is:

Required Sample Size	.3%	.4%	.5%	.6%	.8%	1%	1.5%	2%
50	14%	18%	22%	26%	33%	40%	53%	64%
60	17	21	26	30	38	45	60	70
70	19	25	30	35	43	51	66	76
80	22	28	33	38	48	56	70	80
90	24	31	37	42	52	60	75	84
100	26	33	40	46	56	64	78	87
120	31	39	46	52	62	70	84	91
140	35	43	51	57	68	76	88	94
160	39	48	56	62	73	80	91	96
200	46	56	64	71	81	87	95	98
240	52	63	71	77	86	92	98	99
300	61	71	79	84	92	96	99	99+
340	65	76	83	88	94	97	99+	99+
400	71	81	88	92	96	98	99+	99+
460	77	86	91	95	98	99	99+	99+
500	79	88	93	96	99	99	99+	99+
600	85	92	96	98	99	99+	99+	99+
700	90	95	98	99	99+	99+	99+	99+
800	93	97	99	99	99+	99+	99+	99+
900	95	98	99	99+	99+	99+	99+	99+
1,000	97	99	99+	99+	99+	99+	99+	99+

Note: 99+ indicates a probability of 99.5% or greater.

Probabilities in these tables are rounded to the nearest 1%.

Source: *An Auditor's Approach to Statistical Sampling,* Copyright © 1974, the American Institute of Certified Public Accountants, Inc.

Table 9-4b Discovery Sampling for Attributes for Populations Between 5,000 and 10,000

Required Sample Size	If the Population Occurrence Rate is: .1%	.2%	.3%	.4%	.5%	.75%	1%	2%
	The Probability of Discovering at Least One Occurrence in the Sample is:							
50	5%	10%	14%	18%	22%	31%	40%	64%
60	6	11	17	21	26	36	45	70
70	7	13	19	25	30	41	51	76
80	8	15	21	28	33	45	55	80
90	9	17	24	30	36	49	60	84
100	10	18	26	33	40	53	64	87
120	11	21	30	38	45	60	70	91
140	13	25	35	43	51	65	76	94
160	15	28	38	48	55	70	80	96
200	18	33	45	56	64	78	87	98
240	22	39	52	62	70	84	91	99
300	26	46	60	70	78	90	95	99+
340	29	50	65	75	82	93	97	99+
400	34	56	71	81	87	95	98	99+
460	38	61	76	85	91	97	99	99+
500	40	64	79	87	92	98	99	99+
600	46	71	84	92	96	99	99+	99+
700	52	77	89	95	97	99+	99+	99+
800	57	81	92	96	98	99+	99+	99+
900	61	85	94	98	99	99+	99+	99+
1,000	65	88	96	99	99	99+	99+	99+
1,500	80	96	99	99+	99+	99+	99+	99+
2,000	89	99	99+	99+	99+	99+	99+	99+

Note: 99+ indicates a probability of 99.5% or greater.

Probabilities in these tables are rounded to the nearest 1%.

Source: *An Auditor's Approach to Statistical Sampling,* Copyright © 1974, the American Institute of Certified Public Accountants, Inc.

Table 9-4c Discovery Sampling for Attributes for Populations Over 10,000

Required Sample Size	If the Population Occurrence Rate is: .01%	.05%	.1%	.2%	.3%	.5%	1%	2%
	The Probability of Discovering at Least One Occurrence in the Sample is:							
50		2%	5%	9%	14%	22%	39%	64%
60	1%	3	6	11	16	26	45	70
70	1	3	7	13	19	30	51	76
80	1	4	8	15	21	33	55	80
90	1	4	9	16	24	36	60	84
100	1	5	10	18	26	39	63	87
120	1	6	11	21	30	45	70	91
140	1	7	13	24	34	50	76	94
160	2	8	15	27	38	55	80	96
200	2	10	18	33	45	63	87	98
240	2	11	21	38	51	70	91	99
300	3	14	26	45	59	78	95	99+
340	3	16	29	49	64	82	97	99+
400	4	18	33	55	70	87	98	99+
460	5	21	37	60	75	90	99	99+
500	5	22	39	63	78	92	99	99+
600	6	26	45	70	84	95	99+	99+
700	7	30	50	75	88	97	99+	99+
800	8	33	55	80	91	98	99+	99+
900	9	36	59	83	93	99	99+	99+
1,000	10	39	63	86	95	99	99+	99+
1,500	14	53	78	95	99	99+	99+	99+
2,000	18	63	86	98	99+	99+	99+	99+
2,500	22	71	92	99	99+	99+	99+	99+
3,000	26	78	95	99+	99+	99+	99+	99+

Note: 99+ indicates a probability of 99.5% or greater. Probabilities in these tables are rounded to the nearest 1%.

Source: *An Auditor's Approach to Statistical Sampling,* Copyright © 1974, the American Institute of Certified Public Accountants, Inc.

Applications of variables sampling

In employing the mean-per-unit technique, the auditor's usual objective is to estimate the "true" total value of the population from sample data and compare this estimate with the population value recorded in the client's records. In making the estimate the auditor must use audit judgment in specifying the level of assurance desired as to the reliability of the estimate. This level of reliability or confidence is expressed as a probability and is based on the level of risk that the auditor is willing to accept that the estimate may be wrong. For example, if the auditor is willing to accept no more than a 5 percent chance of the estimate being in error, then a 95 percent confidence (reliability) level is indicated. Since in many areas some reliability may be placed on internal control and other relevant factors, an overall reliability of 95 percent may be achieved using a somewhat lower confidence (reliability) level for substantive testing. This relationship between overall reliability requirements and that required for substantive tests is discussed in Chapter 7.

Another audit judgment that must enter into the construction of the statistical estimate is the maximum amount of difference the auditor will accept between the population value estimate and the book value. This difference, the precision, is related to what the auditor considers material. The relationship of materiality to the precision required by the auditor is discussed in a later section of this chapter.

In the application of mean-per-unit sampling to be illustrated, assume that the auditor wishes to perform substantive tests on an accounts receivable population. This population has a balance on the client's general ledger of $3,484,620 and consists of 2,659 individual accounts.

Determining the Sample Size In determining sample sizes for mean-per-unit sampling applications, standard statistical formulas may be used. The following formula incorporates the four parameters, mentioned earlier, which determine sample size: precision, confidence, population standard deviation, and population size.

$$n' = \left(\frac{zsN}{p}\right)^2 \tag{1}$$

Explanation of symbols:

p = precision desired
z = standard normal deviate or z value corresponding to the confidence (reliability) level desired
s = estimate of the standard deviation of the population
N = number of items in the population
n' = sample size with replacement

Formula (1) above relates to infinite populations, which, in the present context, implies *sampling with replacement.* Audit sampling is usually conducted *without replacement* in that when an item is selected it is not returned to the population. Formula (1) may be used in sampling without replacement but will provide samples that are larger than are necessary, especially in cases where the sample size is greater than approximately 5-10 percent of the population. In order to adjust the sample size calculation determined using formula (1) for the effects of sampling without replacement, the following formula should be used:

$$n = \frac{n'}{1 + (n'/N)} \qquad (2)$$

Explanation of symbols:

n' = sample size with replacement, from formula (1)
N = number of items in the population
n = sample size without replacement

In the present illustration, assume that the auditor requires a precision of ±$75,000 and a confidence level of 90 percent. Assume further that the standard deviation of the population is estimated, from a preliminary sample, to be $236.

At this point, all the necessary information for calculating the sample size has been given. It is summarized as follows:

p = $75,000, the precision selected by the auditor
z = 1.645, the z value representing a 90 percent confidence level
s = $236, the estimate of the population standard deviation
N = 2,659, the number of items in the population

When these values are incorporated in formula (1) the sample size is determined:

$$n' = \left(\frac{1.645 \times \$236 \times 2{,}659}{\$75{,}000}\right)^2$$

$$n' = 190$$

Using formula (2) to adjust for the effect of sampling without replacement yields the following sample size:

$$n = \frac{190}{1 + (190/2{,}659)}$$

$$n = 178$$

The auditor has now determined that the sample must consist of 178 items randomly selected from the population in order to meet the precision and confidence (reliability) specifications of the test.

Selecting the Sample Considerations relating to sample selection were discussed previously. Both unrestricted random selection and systematic selection are frequently employed by auditors. Assume that in this case the auditor wishes to employ systematic selection with a random start. As a first step, a sampling interval must be determined. This is done by dividing the number of items in the population by the number of items in the sample.

$$\text{sampling interval} = \frac{N}{n} = \frac{2{,}659}{178} \approx 15$$

After determining the sampling interval, a random starting point should be established in order that each item in the population has an equal chance of being selected. Assuming that the random starting point taken from a random number table is 6, the selection plan is to start with the sixth item in the population and select every fifteenth item thereafter.

Evaluating the Sample After the sample of 178 items has been selected, the auditor must perform the audit procedures considered necessary, using the items in the sample. In the case of accounts receivable these procedures usually will include (1) direct confirmation of the account balance with the customer, (2) examination of underlying evidence such as copies of sales invoices and shipping records, and (3) testing the recording of the transactions. If, during the examination, the auditor finds errors affecting the account balances of the sample items, the corrected balance of each such item should be determined.

After completing the examination of the sample items, an estimate of the population value may be made, based on the corrected values of the sample items. Assume that in the present example the total of the audited balances of the 178 accounts receivable included in the sample amounted to $231,222. To estimate the population value, this total is divided by the number of items in the sample to determine the average value per account. This average account value is then multiplied by the number of items in the population to provide the estimate. The procedure is shown as follows:

$$\text{average value per sampled account} = \frac{\$231{,}222}{178} = \$1{,}299$$

$$\text{population estimate} = \$1{,}299 \times 2{,}659 = \$3{,}454{,}041$$

As a next step, the auditor must determine if the accounts receivable book value lies within the precision limits achieved. The *desired precision,* as previously stated, was set at ±$75,000. Due to the possible difference between the estimated standard deviation used to determine the sample size and the actual standard deviation of the sample, however, the *achieved precision* of the estimate may differ from that desired. To determine the achieved precision of the estimate, the standard deviation of the audited values of the sample items must be calculated. Assume this is done and the result is $228. Next, by rearranging formula (1) and using the actual sample standard deviation, an achieved precision is determined:

$$p' = \frac{zsN}{\sqrt{n}} \tag{3}$$

$$p' = \frac{1.645 \times \$228 \times 2{,}659}{\sqrt{178}} = \$74{,}750$$

This result, since sampling without replacement is being used, must be corrected by use of the finite population multiplier formula as follows:

$$p'' = p' \sqrt{1 - (n/N)} \tag{4}$$

$$p'' = \$74{,}750 \times \sqrt{1 - (178/2{,}659)} = \$72{,}205$$

This achieved precision value (p'') is now used to construct the precision range.

The precision range is constructed by calculating the value of the sample estimate ($3,454,041) plus or minus the achieved precision ($72,205) or $3,381,836 to $3,526,246, as shown in Figure 9-2.

Since (1) the balance of the accounts receivable on the client's general ledger was $3,484,620, which is within the auditor's desired precision limits, and (2) the auditor's achieved precision is not greater than the desired precision, the auditor may conclude that the accounts receivable in this example are fairly stated.

In cases where the book value is not within the precision limits, the auditor must perform additional audit work. Usually the first step is to draw additional items from the population on a random or systematic basis. These items will be examined and corrected by employing procedures similar to those used for the initial sample. After the examination, the two samples may be pooled and a new estimate may be calculated. If the book value falls within the newly achieved precision limits, the auditor may accept the population. If it is still outside the acceptable range, the auditor may replicate the step just described and again pool the samples. At some point, if the book value remains outside the precision range, it may be necessary to perform a 100 percent verification of the population. Alternatively, the auditor may ask the client to recompute, or otherwise to correct, the items in the population so that it may be again subjected to testing.

In order to reduce the possibility that the achieved precision will exceed the desired precision, some auditors increase the calculated sample size by a small number of items. This is intended to compensate for any difference

Figure 9-2 Precision Range around Sample Estimate

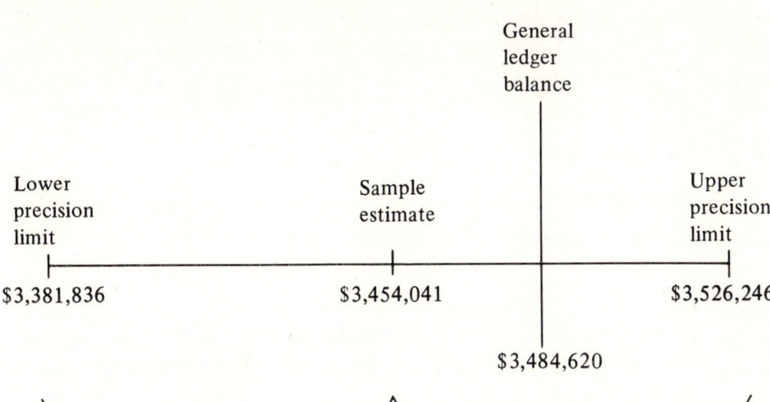

between the estimated standard deviation used in sample size determination and the standard deviation of the sample used to determine the achieved precision.

STRATIFICATION

Sampling for variables, as previously discussed, employed *unrestricted* random or systematic sampling. The *efficiency* of a sampling plan may be increased through the use of stratified sampling. The efficiency of a plan refers to achieving smaller sample sizes for given levels of confidence and precision or, equivalently, obtaining greater confidence and/or precision levels with a given sample size.

Stratified sampling is implemented by separating the population into value range classifications or strata. This has the effect of increasing the homogeneity of the separate groups and thereby decreasing their standard deviation. For example, the accounts receivable population used in the variable sampling illustration could have been divided into three (or any number of) strata, based on the dollar value of each item. A possible basis for division could have been

Stratum 1: $0 to $499.99
Stratum 2: $500.00 to $1,999.99
Stratum 3: $2,000.00 to ∞

After stratification, each stratum will be treated as a separate population for sample size calculation and selection. The characteristics of each population as well as the stratification points chosen by the auditor determine the efficiency achieved by employing stratified sampling. This technique is commonly used in audit applications, and the efficiency achieved from stratification in the form of reduced sample sizes usually far outweighs any extra time involved in its implementation. Computer programs have been developed that determine the optimum range for each stratum to provide maximum efficiency.

Relating precision to materiality: alpha and beta risk

In the discussion so far in this chapter, precision has been viewed as the maximum error in the estimate that the auditor is willing to accept. Additionally, it was noted that the value used as the precision is related to what the auditor considers material in the circumstances. In determining the appropriate precision level to be used in the sampling plan, the auditor must first, through the use of professional judgment, decide on the amount that is material in the circumstances. Conceptually, a material amount is one that will affect the decisions made by users of the financial statements. From the auditing viewpoint, a material item is one that, if left uncorrected, will affect the auditor's opinion by requiring a departure from the standard unqualified report. In making the materiality judgment, the auditor must consider a broad range of information including various current and prior financial statement values.

After the materiality decision is made, the precision is set by relating the precision amount to the amount considered material in order to control the risk inherent in the estimate. Two types of risk must be considered when precision is determined; these are designated *alpha risk* and *beta risk.* Alpha risk is the risk of the auditor's concluding that a material error exists in a population when in fact the population is materially correct. Alpha risk is initially controlled by the selection of the confidence (reliability) level. Beta risk is the risk of the auditor's concluding that the population is materially correct when in fact a material error exists. Beta risk, which is potentially the more important of the two risk types, is controlled by varying the ratio of precision to materiality.

Figure 9-3 illustrates the 5 percent alpha risk that results from the auditor's choice of a 95 percent confidence (reliability) level. In the diagram, a normal distribution of sample estimates drawn from a population with an assumed total value of $2,000,000 is shown, based on a sample of a given size. The distribution around the $2,000,000 value indicates the probability of sample estimates of various values being selected from this population. Assume further that the auditor determines that $100,000 represents a material amount (M) in this case and sets the precision level (P) at this amount so that $P = M$. This provides a precision range of $2,000,000 ± $100,000 or $1,900,000 to $2,100,000. Note that, for pur-

Figure 9-3 Diagram Showing 5% Alpha Risk

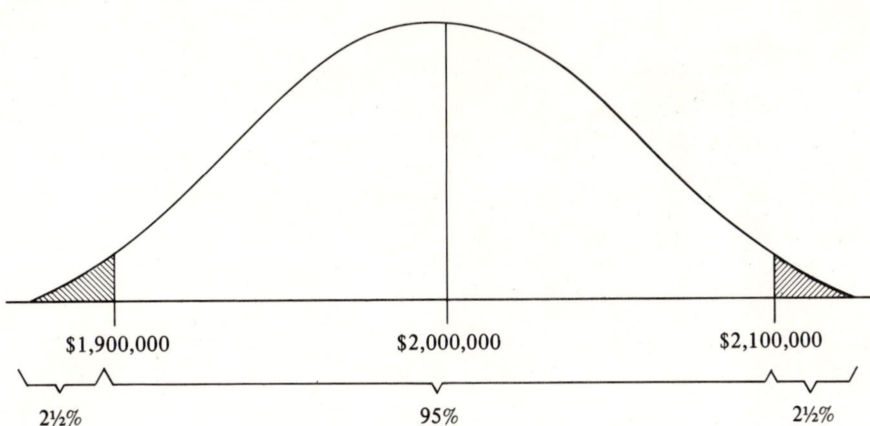

poses of illustration, the precision range is here viewed as a range around a book value, whereas earlier it was viewed as a range around an estimate.

If a sample drawn from the population shown in Figure 9-3 provides an estimate falling outside the precision range, the auditor may conclude, with 95 percent assurance, that a material error exists. However, there is a 5 percent probability that such a sample was in fact selected from this population and the $2,000,000 book value is correct. This 5 percent alpha risk is indicated by the shaded areas in the diagram and is composed of a 2½ percent risk in each "tail" of the distribution.

If the sample estimate in Figure 9-3 falls within the precision range, however, the auditor may not conclude, with 95 percent assurance, that the population is materially correct. The probability that a material error exists in this circumstance is the beta risk and is illustrated in Figure 9-4.

In Figure 9-4, it is assumed that while the book value of the population is stated at $2,000,000, the true value of this population is actually $1,899,000. This difference in the book value and the true value, $101,000, is material and should be disclosed by substantive tests. The part of the horizontal axis under the shaded area in Figure 9-4 represents the values of sample estimates, selected from the true population, that fall within the precision range around the erroneous book value. Any sample estimate falling under the shaded portion of the true distribution will be accepted by the auditor as coming from the distribution around the book value. This area represents the beta risk associated with this test. The closer that the true value of the population lies to either the upper or lower precision limit, the greater is the beta risk. The maximum beta risk approaches 50 percent when the true population value approaches a precision limit.

Figure 9-4 Beta Risk When Precision Equals Materiality

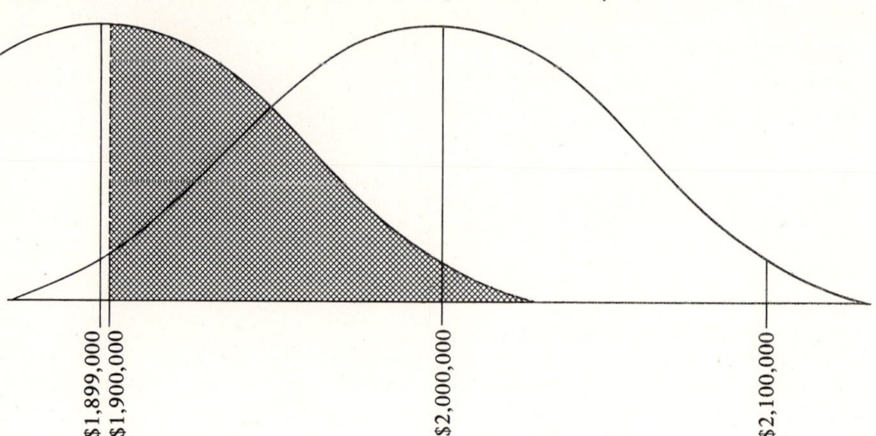

Figure 9-5 Beta Risk When Precision Equals One-Half Materiality

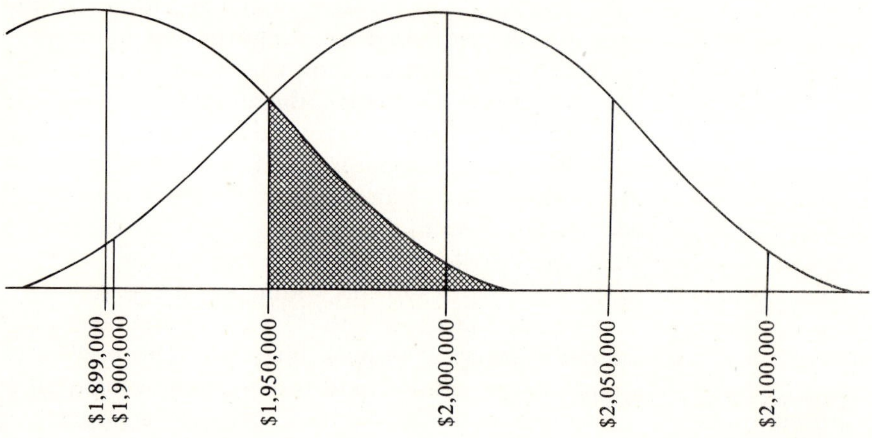

Figure 9-5 illustrates how beta risk is controlled by reducing the ratio of precision to materiality. In this diagram, the auditor has set precision at ±$50,000 or one-half the materiality value of $100,000. This provides a precision range of $1,950,000 to $2,050,000. The shaded area in Figure 9-5 again represents the beta risk associated with the test but is now seen to be much smaller. Note that while reducing the precision reduced beta risk, it concurrently increased the alpha risk inherent in the test. In order to decrease the alpha risk to the level specified by the auditor's confidence (reliability) requirement, the sample size must increase.

A formula[2] which may be used to determine the appropriate ratio of precision to materiality given the desired levels of alpha and beta risks that the auditor is willing to accept is

$$P = \frac{M}{1 + (Z_\beta / Z_{\alpha/2})} \qquad (5)$$

Explanation of symbols:

M = materiality level determined by the auditor
Z_β = the standard normal deviate or z value corresponding to $1 - (2 \times$ desired beta risk). For example, a desired beta risk of 5 percent requires a Z_β of 1.645: $1 - (2 \times 5\%) = 90\%$.
$Z_{\alpha/2}$ = the standard normal deviate or z value corresponding to the confidence (reliability) level selected
P = the appropriate precision amount

The approach to be used by the auditor to determine sample sizes and to evaluate sample results in applications of variables sampling may be summarized as follows:

1. Determine the amount of error which would be material in the circumstances.
2. Specify the overall confidence (reliability) level required considering both alpha and beta risks.
3. Calculate the appropriate precision level using formula (5).
4. Determine the sample size to be used using formulas (1) and (2).
5. Select the sample, perform audit procedures, and make the estimate.
6. Determine the achieved precision using formulas (3) and (4) and ascertain if the book value falls within both the achieved and the desired precision limits.

To illustrate the first three steps above, the accounts receivable example presented previously may be extended. In that example, the population consisted of 2,659 individual accounts and had a book value of $3,484,620. Assume that the auditor, using professional judgment, concludes that an error of $133,500 in the balance of this account would be material. Second, assume that the auditor is willing to accept a 10 percent alpha risk and a 10 percent beta risk for an overall confidence (reliability) level of 90

[2] Robert K. Elliott and John R. Rogers, "Relating Statistical Sampling to Audit Objectives," *Journal of Accountancy* (July 1972), 46–55.

percent. Based on these judgments the precision level may be calculated using formula (5) as follows:

$$M = \$133{,}500$$
$$Z_\beta = \text{the } z \text{ value of } 1 - (2 \times 10\%) = 80\% \text{ or } 1.28$$
$$Z_{\alpha/2} = \text{the } z \text{ value of } 90\% \text{ or } 1.645$$

$$P = \frac{\$133{,}500}{1 + (1.28/1.645)}$$

$$P = \$75{,}000$$

The auditor may now proceed with the test using a confidence (reliability) level of 90 percent and a precision of ±$75,000 as illustrated earlier in the chapter.

Ratio and difference estimation

Although ratio and difference estimation techniques are based on the same statistical concepts as mean-per-unit sampling, they may provide more efficient estimates in some audit applications. A principal disadvantage of mean-per-unit estimation is that large sample sizes often result when the population standard deviation is large. Stratification may be used in many cases to reduce the sample size but still the efficiency of the plan may not be increased to a practicable level. In many such situations, however, the *ratio* of the audited values of individual population items to their book values, or the *differences* between the audited values of individual items and their book values, may be estimated from a sample. Since the standard deviation of the populations of these ratios or differences may be smaller than the standard deviation of the population of individual items, the resulting sample sizes may be smaller than could be achieved using mean-per-unit techniques.

To illustrate the application of ratio estimation, assume the auditor is examining an accounts payable population consisting of 6,000 individual accounts with a book value of $3,600,000. The auditor wishes to employ ratio estimation to test the validity of the recorded payables and desires a precision of $80,000 and a confidence (reliability) level of 95 percent.

As an initial step, the auditor should randomly select a preliminary sample of at least 50 items. The items in this sample must be audited, employing appropriate procedures, and all differences between the audited values and the book values of the individual items recorded. From this distribution of differences, an estimate of the standard deviation of the population of ratios is made.

Assume that in the present example, 12 differences were discovered. From the number and amount of these differences, the auditor estimates the standard deviation of the population of ratios to be $102. The calculation procedure is somewhat laborious and will not be illustrated here.

At this point the auditor has the necessary data to calculate the appropriate sample size. Using the symbols and formulas discussed in conjunction with mean-per-unit sampling, the sample size calculation is as follows:

p = desired precision = $80,000
z = z value at 95% = 1.96
s = estimated standard deviation = $102
N = number of items in population = 6,000

$$n' = \left(\frac{zsN}{p}\right)^2 \quad (1)$$

$$n' = \left(\frac{1.96 \times 102 \times 6{,}000}{80{,}000}\right)^2$$

$$n' = 225$$

The above result is adjusted for the effect of sampling without replacement as follows:

$$n = \frac{n'}{1 + (n'/N)} \quad (2)$$

$$n = \frac{225}{1 + (225/6{,}000)}$$

$$n = 217$$

After calculating the sample size, the auditor randomly selects 167 additional items (which, when combined with the preliminary sample of 50 items yields a total sample of 217) and performs appropriate auditing procedures on these items. All differences between the audited and book values are recorded. Upon completion of the examination, the *ratio* of the total audited values to the total book values of the sample items is calculated. This ratio is used to estimate the audited value of the population. Assume that the ratio of the audited values to the book values computed from the sample was 1.019. Using this ratio, the estimated audited value of the population of accounts payable is $3,668,400 (1.019 × 3,600,000).

A final step is to determine the *achieved precision* of the estimate by recalculating the standard deviation of the ratio population based on the distribution of differences in the final sample and employing the procedures discussed previously.

Applications of difference estimation closely parallel ratio estimation procedures. The primary distinction is that in difference estimation the *average difference* in amount between the audited and book values in the sample is used to estimate the audited value of the population. The decision to use a ratio estimate or a difference estimate depends on the nature of the errors in the population. If the magnitude of errors tends to be unrelated to the size of the individual items, then difference estimation would be preferable. If, however, the errors tend to be proportional to the size of the related items, then ratio estimation is more appropriate.

Situations where ratio and difference estimation techniques are applicable include cases where (1) the book values of the individual items in the population are known, (2) the total of these book values equals the related ledger balance, and (3) errors are relatively frequent. Frequency of errors is an important consideration because, unless errors are relatively frequent, a large sample would be required to disclose a representative number of errors, thereby defeating a principal objective of employing ratio or difference estimation.

As in mean-per-unit estimation, stratification may be used to increase the efficiency of ratio or difference estimates.

Supplementary readings

Anderson, R. J., and A. D. Teitlebaum. "Dollar-Unit Sampling—A Solution to the Audit Sampling Dilemma." *CA Magazine* (April 1973), 30-39.

Arkin, Herbert. *Handbook of Sampling for Auditing and Accounting,* 2nd ed. New York: McGraw-Hill Book Company, 1974.

Bedingfield, James P. "The Current State of Statistical Sampling and Auditing." *Journal of Accountancy* (December 1975), 48-55.

Elliott, Robert K., and John R. Rogers. "Relating Statistical Sampling to Audit Objectives." *Journal of Accountancy* (July 1972), 46-55.

Finley, D. R. "Controlling Compliance Testing With Acceptance Sampling." *CPA Journal* (December 1978), 30-35.

Hansen, Don R., and Timothy L. Shaftel. "Sampling for Integrated Auditing Objectives." *Accounting Review* (January 1977), 109-123.

Ijiri, Yuji, and Robert S. Kaplan. "A Model for Integrating Sampling Objectives in Auditing." *Journal of Accounting Research* (Spring 1971), 73-87.

———. "The Four Objectives of Sampling in Auditing: Representative, Corrective, Protective, and Preventive." *Management Accounting* (December 1970), 42-44.

Neter, John, and James K. Loebbecke. *Behavior of Major Statistical Estimators in Sampling Accounting Populations, Auditing Research Monograph No. 2.* New York: American Institute of Certified Public Accountants, 1975.

Roberts, Donald M. *Statistical Auditing.* New York: American Institute of Certified Public Accountants, 1978.

———. "A Statistical Interpretation of SAP No. 54." *Journal of Accountancy* (March 1974), 47-53.

Smith, Kenneth A. "The Relationship of Internal Control Evaluation and Audit Sample Size." *Accounting Review* (April 1972), 260-269.

Review questions

9-1. In determining the appropriate sample size, what considerations must be taken into account by the auditor?

9-2. Why is less audit evidence required to form an opinion of fixed assets than of cash in most manufacturing companies?

9-3. What two approaches do auditors employ in determining an appropriate sample size?

9-4. What are the major disadvantages of judgment sampling?

9-5. What are two major categories of statistical sampling plans? What are the characteristics of each?

9-6. What type plan is most useful for compliance tests? For substantive tests?

9-7. What is mean-per-unit estimation?

9-8. Describe a discovery sampling plan and tell the circumstances in which it is usually employed.

9-9. What are ratio and difference estimation plans?

9-10. Briefly define the following statistical terms:
population
random
random number table
random number generator
standard deviation
precision
confidence
standard error of the mean
confidence interval
standard normal deviate

9-11. Using Tables 9-2a and b, determine the proper sample size for the following:

	Confidence (reliability)	*Expected occurrence rate*	*Upper precision limit*
Case A	90%	2%	4%
Case B	95%	5%	7.2%

9-12. Using Figures 9-1a, b, and c, determine the proper sample size for the following:

	Confidence (reliability)	*Expected occurrence rate*	*Upper precision limit*
Case C	90%	3%	5%
Case D	95%	4%	7%
Case E	99%	5%	9%

9-13. For the sample sizes determined in questions 9-11 and 9-12, determine the upper precision limit achieved in each case if the following number of occurrences were found when the samples were evaluated. Use Table 9-3.
Case A—4 occurrences
Case B—11 occurrences
Case C—7 occurrences
Case D—9 occurrences
Case E—7 occurrences

9-14. What two methods are frequently used by auditors in the selection of a sample?

9-15. Briefly describe an unrestricted random sampling procedure.

9-16. Briefly describe systematic sample selection.

9-17. What is the primary disadvantage or danger in using systematic selection?

9-18. Using Tables 9-4a, b, and c, determine the appropriate sample sizes for a discovery sampling plan given the following data:

Population size	*Population occurrence rate*	*Assurance desired*
3,500	1%	98%
7,800	.5%	96%
50,000	2%	99%

9-19. Calculate the required sample size for confirmation of accounts receivable assuming the following:
general ledger balance = $250,000
aggregate acceptable precision = ±$5,000
number of accounts = 2,000
desired confidence = 95%
estimated standard deviation = $25

9-20. Why is a finite population multiplier needed in calculating the sample size in mean-per-unit estimation?

9-21. Why might the achieved precision in a variables estimate differ from the desired precision?

9-22. What should the auditor do in cases wherein a sample estimator of a population parameter falls outside the precision limits?

9-23. How does the auditor benefit from stratification?

9-24. Define alpha and beta risks.

9-25. How is beta risk controlled by the auditor?

Decision problems

9-26. In evaluating internal control of your client, Cleary Corporation, you desire to perform a compliance test of certain controls that the client has indicated are in effect in the accounts payable area. The specific control in which you are interested relates to the matching of the purchase order, receiving report, and vendor invoice, prior to approving the invoice for payment. You are told that the three documents are compared, cancelled, and approved for payment by the accounts payable supervisor. After performing this operation, the supervisor indicates that the invoice is approved for payment, initials the invoice, staples the three documents together, and forwards them for processing. After processing, the documents are filed together in voucher number order. Each year, the voucher numbers begin at 0001. The last voucher number assigned during the current year is 8,178.

You define an error as being either (1) any approved invoice that does not agree in amount with the other two documents, (2) cases in which any of the three documents is missing, or (3) any paid invoice that does not bear the initials of the supervisor. In the past you have found an error rate in this population of approximately 2 percent and you expect this condition in the current year. If you found evidence that the error rate exceeded 4 percent, however, you would conclude that this control feature was ineffective. Because of the importance you place on this control, you decide to use a 95 percent confidence (reliability) level.

a. Determine the sample size appropriate in this case if the auditor uses estimation sampling for attributes.

b. Discuss the procedures you would use in selecting the sample.

c. What would you conclude if, in examining the items in the sample, five errors were found?

d. If eight errors were found in the sample, what would your conclusions be? What would be the effect on your audit?

9-27. Refer to the facts in decision problem 9-26 and assume that you have never in the past found the error rate in the population to be as great as 1 percent. Furthermore, you consider this control so important that if the error rate was found to be 1 percent or greater you would consider the control ineffective.

a. Determine the sample size appropriate in this case if the auditor uses discovery sampling and requires 95 percent assurance that the population error rate is less than 1 percent.

b. Discuss the advantages and disadvantages of discovery sampling with respect to estimation sampling for attributes.

c. If, in this case, the entire sample is evaluated and three errors are found, what statistical conclusions can be drawn with regard to the population?

9-28. Fran Ho, CPA, decides to use mean-per-unit estimation sampling for variables in performing substantive tests on the inventory of her client, Lombardy Coil Co. The client's inventory listing is obtained which presents each inventory item in stock designated by serial number. The listing includes 5,487 items and totals $4,883,430, the balance in Lombardy's general ledger inventory account.

As a first step, Fran selects a random sample of 40 items and calculates the standard deviation of this sample to be $167. Next, she decides that an error of $200,000 in the inventory would represent a material error. Finally, Fran decides that she requires 95 percent confidence (reliability) that the sample result is accurate, that is, she will accept no more than 5 percent alpha risk and 5 percent beta risk.

a. Based on the above information, determine Fran's desired precision limits.
b. Calculate the proper sample size for this test.
c. Discuss methods Fran might use to select this sample.
d. Assume that after the sample is selected and appropriate auditing procedures are applied to the sample items, the aggregate audited value of the items in the sample is $230,463 and the standard deviation of the sample items is $154. Determine the estimated value of the population and the achieved precision limits.
e. What conclusions may Fran draw as a result of this test?

9-29. The Cowslip Milk Company's principal activity is buying milk from dairy farmers, processing the milk, and delivering it to retail customers. You are engaged in auditing the retail accounts receivable of the company and determine the following:

a. The company has 50 retail routes; each route consists of 100 to 200 accounts, the number that can be serviced by a driver in a day.
b. The driver enters cash collections from the day's deliveries to each customer directly on a statement form in record books maintained for each route. Mail remittances are posted in the route record books by office personnel. At the end of the month the statements are priced, extended, and footed. Photocopies of the statements are prepared and left in the customers' milk boxes with the next milk delivery.
c. The statements are reviewed by the office manager, who prepares a list for each route of accounts with 90-day balances or older. The list is used for intensive collection action.
d. The audit program used in prior audits for the selection of retail accounts receivable for confirmation stated: "Select two accounts from each route, one to be chosen by opening the route book at random and the other as the third item on each list of 90-day or older accounts."

Your review of the accounts receivable leads you to conclude that statistical sampling techniques may be applied to their examination.

a. Since statistical sampling techniques do not relieve the CPA of responsibilities in the exercise of professional judgment, of what benefit are they to the CPA? Discuss.
b. Give the reasons why the audit procedure previously used for selection of accounts receivable for confirmation (as given in item *d* above) would not produce a valid statistical sample.
c. What are the audit objectives or purposes in selecting 90-day accounts for confirmation? Can the application of statistical sampling techniques help in attaining these objectives or purposes? Discuss.
d. Assume that the company has 10,000 accounts receivable and that your statistical sampling disclosed 6 errors in a sample of 200 accounts. Is it

reasonable to assume that 300 accounts in the entire population are in error? Explain.

AICPA adapted

9-30. You are now conducting your third annual audit of the financial statements of Teng Corporation for the year ended December 31, 1983. You decide to employ unrestricted random number statistical sampling techniques in testing the effectiveness of the company's internal control procedures relating to sales invoices, which are all serially numbered. In prior years, after selecting one representative two-week period during the year, you tested all invoices issued during that period and resolved all of the errors that were found to your satisfaction.

a. Explain the statistical procedures you would use to determine the size of the sample of sales invoices to be examined.

b. Once the sample size has been determined, how would you select the individual invoices to be included in the sample? Explain.

c. Would the use of statistical sampling procedures improve the examination of sales invoices as compared with the selection procedure used in prior years? Discuss.

d. Assume that the company issued 50,000 sales invoices during the year and the auditor specified a confidence level of 95 percent with a precision range of plus or minus 2 percent.

1. Does this mean that the auditor would be willing to accept the reliability of the sales invoice data if errors are found on no more than 4 sales invoices out of every 95 invoices examined? Discuss.
2. If the auditor specified a precision range of ±1 percent, would the confidence level be higher or lower than 95 percent assuming that the size of the sample remains constant? Why?

AICPA adapted

9-31. You desire to evaluate the reasonableness of the book value of the inventory of your client, Fang, Inc. You satisfied yourself earlier as to inventory quantities. During the examination of the pricing and extension of the inventory, the following data were gathered using appropriate unrestricted random sampling with replacement procedures.

- Total items in the inventory (N) 12,700
- Total items in the sample (n) 400
- Total audited value of items in the sample \$38,400

$\sum_{j=1}^{400} (x_j - \bar{x})^2$ 312,816

- Formula for estimated population standard deviation

$$S_{x_j} = \sqrt{\frac{\sum_{j=1}^{j=n} (x_j - \bar{x})^2}{n - 1}}$$

- Confidence level coefficient of the standard error of the mean at a 95 percent confidence (reliability) level ±1.96

a. Based on the sample results, what is the estimate of the total value of the inventory? Show computations in good form where appropriate.

b. What statistical conclusion can be reached regarding the estimated total inventory value calculated in item *a* above at the confidence level of 95 percent? Present computations in good form where appropriate.

c. Independent of your answers to items *a* and *b*, assume that the book value of Fang's inventory is $1,700,000, and based on the sample results the estimated total value of the inventory is $1,690,000. The auditor desires a confidence (reliability) level of 95 percent. Discuss the audit and statistical considerations the auditor must evaluate before deciding whether the sampling results support acceptance of the book value as a fair presentation of Fang's inventory.

AICPA adapted

9-32. During the course of an audit engagement, a CPA attempts to obtain satisfaction that there are no material misstatements in the accounts receivable of a client. Statistical sampling is a tool that the auditor often uses to obtain representative evidence to achieve the desired satisfaction. On a particular engagement an auditor determined that the precision would be $35,000. To obtain satisfaction the auditor had to be 95 percent confident that the population of accounts was not in error. The auditor decided to use unrestricted random sampling with replacement and took a preliminary random sample of 100 items (n) from a population of 1,000 items (N). The sample produced the following data:

Arithmetic mean of sample items ($\bar{x}$)	$4,000
Standard deviation of sample items (SD)	$ 200

The auditor also has available the following information:

Standard error of the mean (SE) $= SD \div \sqrt{n}$
Population precision (P) $= N \times R \times SE$

Partial list of reliability coefficients

If reliability coefficient (R) is	*Then reliability is*
1.70	91.086%
1.75	91.988
1.80	92.814
1.85	93.568
1.90	94.256
1.95	94.882
1.96	95.000
2.00	95.450
2.05	95.964
2.10	96.428
2.15	96.844

a. Define the statistical terms *reliability* and *precision* as applied to auditing.
b. If all necessary audit work is performed on the preliminary sample items and no errors are detected,
   1. What can the auditor say about the total amount of accounts receivable at the 95 percent reliability level?
   2. At what confidence level can the auditor say that the population is not in error by $35,000?
c. Assume that the preliminary sample was sufficient,
   1. Compute the auditor's estimate of the population total.
   2. Indicate how the auditor should relate this estimate to the client's recorded amount.

AICPA adapted

9-33. The use of statistical sampling techniques in an examination of financial statements does not eliminate judgmental decisions.
a. Identify and explain four areas where judgment may be exercised by a CPA in planning a statistical sampling test.
b. Assume that a CPA's sample shows an unacceptable error rate. Describe the various actions that the CPA may take based upon this finding.
c. A nonstratified sample of 80 accounts payable vouchers is to be selected from a population of 3,200. The vouchers are numbered consecutively from 1 to 3,200 and are listed, 40 to a page, in the voucher register. Describe four different techniques for selecting a random sample of vouchers for review.

AICPA adapted

9-34. In each of the following situations, indicate the type of statistical sampling application that would be most appropriate. Explain the reasons for each choice.
a. An auditor is interested in determining whether all credit sales are approved by the credit department prior to shipment. When this control feature is performed, the file copy of the invoice is initialed by the credit manager. The auditor wishes to gain assurance that less than 1 percent of such sales are shipped without approval.
b. An auditor is testing the client's perpetual inventory records with the objective of determining if the inventory value is fairly stated. The population has a very large standard deviation and numerous errors. The errors appear to be proportional to the size of the individual items.
c. In evaluating internal control over cash receipts, an auditor wishes to determine compliance with a client procedure requiring daily bank deposits. The auditor wishes to estimate the occurrence rate of delayed deposits during the year.
d. An auditor desires to estimate the value of the client's accounts receivable. In the past, this population has had a low standard deviation and the auditor has found few errors in the accounts receivable.
e. An accounts payable population is being examined and the auditor wishes to estimate the audited value of the payables. The population has a high

standard deviation and numerous errors. The magnitude of the errors does not appear to be related to the value of the associated payables.

9-35. In auditing an accounts receivable population, Hugh Kirby, CPA, decides to employ unstratified ratio estimation. The population has a book value of $6,025,500 and consists of 4,500 accounts. Kirby desires a confidence level of 90 percent and a precision of $100,000. A preliminary sample is selected and evaluated and the standard deviation of the population of ratios is estimated to be $175.

a. Calculate the sample size based on the above information.

b. Assume that the book value of the items in the final sample totaled $216,918 and the audited values of those items totalled $214,748. Estimate the total audited value of the population.

c. If the standard deviation of the population of ratios in the final sample was determined to be $160, calculate the achieved precision.

d. What conclusions may Kirby draw with respect to the client's accounts receivable based upon this test?

10

Auditing Computerized Systems

The application of electronic computers to the processing of data in business organizations has had a major impact upon the accounting profession. Virtually all the activities and services of both public and private accountants have been influenced by electronic data processing. Public accountants find that routine tax return preparation may be accomplished efficiently and economically through the use of a computer. For this, they may utilize a service bureau that specializes in this area or they may acquire their own computers to prepare the returns in their offices. Accountants whose practices include maintaining accounting records and preparing financial statements for clients often find that a computer can increase the efficiency with which this service can be performed.

In the management services aspect of public accountants' work, they often find that many of the services they are asked to render involve the computer. Examples include internal control studies for computerized systems, feasibility studies regarding proposed computer installations and applications, and system design and improvement engagements.

In no other area of the public accountant's practice, however, does the computer pose a greater challenge than in auditing. In auditing computerized systems, the auditor is faced with several distinct problems. One involves internal control. While the basic concepts of internal control are generally the same for computerized and manually prepared systems, the auditor must learn to evaluate a number of specific control mechanisms and applications related to computerized systems. Another problem the auditor sometimes must face in examining computerized systems is the reduction or elimination of *hard copy,* that is, printed records generated by the computer system, which may be interpreted visually. Traditionally, the auditor has depended upon readable records to provide the *audit trail,* whereby recorded transactions may be traced to source documents or other evidence. Other new difficulties sometimes encountered by auditors include obtaining necessary data from the system, devising methods to verify data generated by the system, determining that computer programs are properly processing data, and communicating effectively with EDP personnel.

Many problems and challenges of auditing computerized systems appear to be yet unsolved. As computer technology advances, audit techniques must change and develop also. Often, audit techniques appropriate for a given computer system configuration are ineffective in a more sophisticated system. This chapter discusses the audit of computerized systems in two parts; first, internal control evaluation and, second, auditing techniques and procedures.

Evaluating internal control in computerized systems

To evaluate adequately internal control in a computerized system, the auditor should possess knowledge of electronic data processing equipment and systems. This knowledge is necessary if the auditor is to conform to the first general auditing standard, which provides that an audit examination should be performed only by ". . . persons having adequate technical training and proficiency. . . ." SAS No. 3 (AU 321.04) provides the following guidance in this regard:

> If a client uses EDP in its accounting system, whether the application is simple or complex, the auditor needs to understand the entire system sufficiently to enable him to identify and evaluate its essential accounting control features. Situations involving more complex EDP applications ordinarily will require that the auditor apply specialized expertise in EDP in the performance of the necessary audit procedures.

In some auditing firms, teams of EDP audit specialists are utilized to evaluate internal control and direct some audit procedures for the examination of clients with computerized systems. Other firms endeavor to familiarize all members of the audit staff with EDP systems so that a single audit team is able to carry out the complete examination. Both approaches have merit and, if properly implemented, satisfy the requirements of generally accepted auditing standards.

Internal control procedures relating to computerized systems may be categorized into *general controls* and *application controls.* General controls apply broadly to EDP applications and include such considerations as:

1. organization of the EDP department
2. documentation procedures within the EDP department
3. access controls and other security measures

Application controls relate to specific data processing operations performed by the system. These are sometimes referred to as *data controls* or *procedural controls* and comprise the following elements:

1. input controls
2. processing controls
3. output controls

In evaluating the internal control over the EDP system, the auditor first should review the system to gain an understanding of the process and its control features. The second phase of the evaluation should consist of tests of compliance to provide the auditor with assurance that existing control features are functioning satisfactorily. The review of the system is usually performed using a special internal control questionnaire designed for EDP installations. An example of such a questionnaire is presented in Appendix D.

The following sections describe the features of the various elements of both general and application controls. An understanding of these elements is needed to evaluate properly the controls in an EDP system.

GENERAL CONTROLS

The general controls represent broad, policy-level controls adopted in the EDP department. They reflect control concepts which are valid in any data processing system.

Organization of the EDP Department Discussion of organizational considerations relating to computer installations may begin with an examination of where in the overall organization the EDP department should be placed. In reviewing the organizational structure of various companies, it may be found that the manager of the EDP department reports directly to the president, the comptroller, the vice-president for administration, or some other executive. Often the position is influenced by historical factors such as the nature of the first computer application employed in the company. The placement of the EDP department in the organization can be significant from the standpoint of internal control. This is because improper placement can interfere with the necessary separation of functions within the business. Basic functions that should be separated include (1) initiation and authorization of transactions, (2) recording of transactions, and (3) custody of assets. For example, in cases where the computer acts to authorize or initiate transactions in accordance with predetermined criteria, the necessary separation of functions may be violated. However, if adequate safeguards are taken, satisfactory control can be obtained with a number of different organizational patterns. A related consideration that the auditor should recognize is the centralization of functions caused by the EDP installation. This refers to the concentration in the EDP department of many functions that, prior to computerization, were performed in several different departments. Although this is a natural result of developing a separate EDP function, it is a situation that can lead to weaknesses in internal control.

Within the EDP department, several functions must be separated if there is to be adequate internal control. These functions, as illustrated in Figure 10-1 include:

1. systems analysis and programming
2. computer operations
3. program and file library
4. control unit

The separation of the systems analysis and programming function from computer operations is critical from an internal control standpoint. This division serves the purpose of separating those who possess the knowledge required to introduce unauthorized data into the system (analysts and programmers) from those who have access to the equipment necessary to implement such action (machine operators). Presumably, employees who design computer applications and write programs are familiar enough with each application to devise methods of introducing unauthorized program changes or unauthorized data into the computer operations. For this reason, routine computer operations should not be performed by employees from the systems and programming division. Machine operators should not be familiar with the details of the operating programs if this division is to be meaningful.

Figure 10-1 Division of Duties in an EDP Department

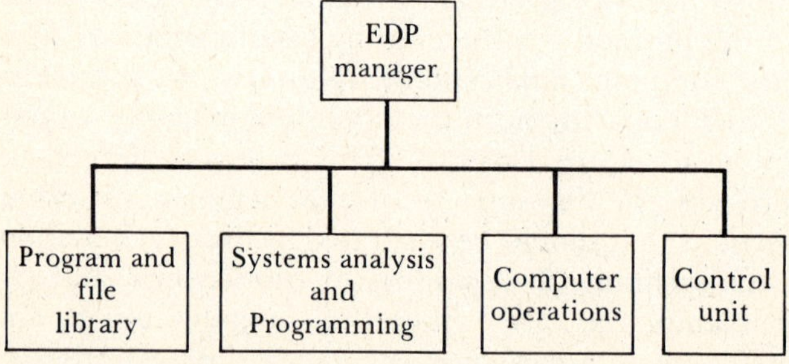

The program and file library should be separated from the other divisions of the department so that free access to programs and data files is not available. If control of these programs and records is not maintained, fraudulent changes can be introduced with little chance of detection. Adequate control procedures in this area should include checking-out materials as needed in accordance with the daily operating schedule or as otherwise authorized.

The control unit in the EDP department performs the audit function within the installation. This group should have sole access to the control data associated with the application controls. The control unit implements and monitors the application controls in order to assure accuracy of output. This group should be independent of the other departmental divisions and should perform no routine operating functions.

It can be seen that proper division of duties within the EDP departmental organization is necessary if adequate internal control is to be maintained. In very small installations, division of duties may be difficult because of personnel limitations. However, an awareness of the needed functional separation can often help in devising work routines that improve control in even the smallest system.

Documentation Procedures within the EDP Department Adequate control over the computer system requires that proper documentation procedures be in effect. These procedures should assure the creation and maintenance of records that describe the systems, programs, controls, and other operations of the department. These records provide the means whereby the essential elements of the EDP system can be interpreted and evaluated by management and auditors.

Such documentation procedures:

1. Provide management with a clear understanding of the EDP system and ensure that their policies are adhered to;
2. Serve as a basis for review of internal accounting controls by internal and external auditors; and
3. Provide a convenient reference for systems analysts and programmers responsible for maintaining and revising existing systems and programs.

Adequate documentation provides an intelligible description of the EDP system that can be used readily by outsiders to evaluate the computer operation. Therefore, inadequate documentation indicates a weakness in internal control over the EDP system. Without these explanatory materials, the detailed operations of a computer program, for example, may be known only to the programmer who created it. If this program is subsequently revised, possibly by a different programmer, no single person may understand the entire function of the program. With adequate documentation, however, records describing the details of the program as well as any program changes are on file and may be consulted as questions arise.

The following describes some of the documents that should be maintained with respect to two areas of the EDP department—systems and programs.

Systems Documentation The documentation for each system should include such materials as:

1. problem statement that provides an adequate definition of the purpose of the application and how it complements other operating systems
2. system flowchart
3. input and output requirements
4. methods of processing
5. equipment requirements
6. copies of authorizations for system changes
7. necessary controls

Program Documentation Each program documentation file should include:

1. problem statement that identifies the function of this program in the overall system
2. program flowchart
3. list of control features
4. record layouts specifying the characteristics of the data and fields on the computer file
5. operating instructions
6. program listing
7. details and approvals of program changes
8. description of input and output formats

Other areas of the EDP department that should have established documentation standards to provide a description of the respective operations include the library function, keypunch or other data conversion activity, the output section, machine operations, and the control unit.

Access Controls and other Security Measures Another important aspect of internal control over computerized systems is the consideration given to the security of computer hardware and software. Many companies have come to realize that the computer installation represents the virtual nerve center of the business. Because of this, a complete internal control system should include provision for physical protection of the EDP system and the data stored therein.

To promote physical security over computer hardware, policies should be developed regarding the admission of visitors to the computer center and the locking of doors, windows, and so forth. Adequate insurance coverage should be maintained to protect the company from losses due to theft or damage in the center. This coverage should include the cost of reconstructing lost data, rewriting programs, and using alternate equipment. In addition to these considerations, physical control over the equipment should include preventive maintenance procedures, regular servicing, and strict adherence to other recommended operating practices.

Adequate protection of computer software involves procedures for file reconstruction, off-premises data storage, and strict library control. A *file reconstruction plan* should incorporate procedures that provide for the maintenance of duplicate copies of programs and data files. Some plans call for the retention of predecessor data files so that all current data may be reconstructed if necessary. This is often referred to as a *grandfather-father-son* procedure. For file reconstruction procedures to be fully effective, the duplicates of all important master files and programs should be stored in a fireproof off-premises location. Many businesses utilize the services of firms specializing in protective custody of EDP software to provide adequate security for programs and data. Strict library procedures complement other software security measures by providing limited access to materials in order to guard against loss as well as against unauthorized use or alteration. Library procedures should limit the release of materials to authorized employees on a "need-to-know" basis. Programs and data files normally should be released to operators only in accordance with the current operating schedule and to others only upon specific authorization.

In some systems employing disk storage equipment, some programs and data files may not be physically removed from the computer. In these cases the library function must be modified to provide control over access to programs and data in this form.

Other types of general control, referred to as *hardware controls,* are features that are designed into the computer hardware by the manufacturer and include parity checks, duplicate circuitry, echo checks, file protection devices, overflow checks, and many others. These controls help assure that errors are not generated while data are in the computer.

APPLICATION CONTROLS

Specific application controls are measures taken in the design of the system or in the manufacture of the computer equipment to provide assurance that data are processed, recorded, and reported properly. These controls may be best discussed in the order in which they would affect data progressing through the system, that is, through input controls, processing controls, and output controls.

Input Controls The data input function of a computer system is often the area most susceptible to error. Although computer equipment has relatively error-free operation, the data input function requires the manipulation of data outside the equipment. Opportunities for error or data loss arise in the input area when data are recorded, converted into machine-sensible form, transmitted, and read into the computer.

Input controls should be developed that will provide assurance that input data are received, translated, and entered into the system without error. Some techniques used to accomplish this include:

1. accounting for all prenumbered input documents by the control unit
2. establishment of batch-control totals prior to keypunching and comparison of these totals with the totals of the keypunched data prior to processing
3. use of verifiers to control keypunch errors
4. maintenance of a controlled error-correction procedure
5. use of message counts or dual transmission procedures when data are transmitted between geographic locations
6. retention of source documents for reasonable periods so that data may be reconstructed if necessary

Processing Controls Controls over the processing of data should be written into the computer programs. Examples of programmed processing controls include:

1. Limit tests. This type of test could cause an error message to be produced if any computation in the program run is outside a predetermined limit.
2. Logic tests. This test could direct an error message to be generated if an illogical result were produced in a processing run—such as a negative paycheck.
3. Validity checks. These are tests that ascertain if certain data are valid—such as an employee number.
4. Header labels. These are magnetic identification codes written on data files that help assure proper identification of all data before processing.

Output Controls The basic concept of output control is that output totals should be compared with input control totals and any differences investigated and reconciled. This is an important function of the control unit in the EDP department. In many companies, user departments will perform a similar control function as an additional check. All error corrections should be performed and recorded in accordance with authorized procedures to prevent fraudulent entries at this point. Procedures for timely and proper delivery of output to users represent a further aspect of output control.

COMPLIANCE TESTS

The auditor's review of internal control over the EDP system should be designed to provide an understanding of how transactions flow through the system and the extent of controls over the process. SAS No. 3 (AU 321.24) describes this review as "an information-gathering process that depends on knowledgeable inquiries directed to client personnel, observation of job assignments and operating procedures, and reference to available documentation related to accounting control."

To supplement the review of internal control, an auditor should perform compliance tests for reasonable assurance that the internal control procedures described are being implemented. In performing these tests the auditor may observe error listings, examine documentation showing approvals, examine test transactions, and observe departmental organization. Other compliance tests may be performed by using the EDP equipment to process test data or to reprocess actual client data.

Upon completion of the internal control evaluation, the auditor must determine how much to rely on the internal accounting controls within the client's EDP department. If the controls provide a basis for reliance, the auditor may restrict the extent of the substantive transaction tests to be performed on EDP applications.

Auditing techniques and procedures in computerized systems

Which techniques and procedures are employed by the auditor in performing substantive tests of the accounting data depend to great extent on the design of the client's EDP system. The design and operation of the system defines the audit trail used in gathering evidence. This audit trail, or management trail, may be as well defined in a computerized system as it is in a properly designed manual accounting system. On the other hand, in an advanced EDP system with on-line capabilities and little hard copy, the audit trail could conceivably be nonexistent.

Numerous articles found in the literature of auditing suggest that in future EDP systems the conventional audit trail may be eliminated altogether, and they admonish auditors to develop procedures that are not dependent on such a trail. Since procedures designed to trace transactions back through the system to source documents using an audit trail represent basic operating technique for auditors, alternative procedures have not been easy to devise. Some alternative approaches have been developed, however, and will be discussed later in this chapter.

Whether or not the conventional audit trail will completely disappear from EDP applications in business is still unsettled. The possibility is supported by the fact that technical development of computers has advanced to a level where such systems are available. Further, certain operating efficiencies are achieved by these systems, such as speed of information delivery and reduction of paper usage.

On the other hand, there are valid reasons for businesses to maintain in their systems the capability to reconstruct or trace transactions. Some of these reasons are management uses of transaction detail, internal and external audit requirements, safeguards against system error or breakdown, and requirements of the Internal Revenue Service. In this regard, the position of the IRS is stated in Revenue Procedure 64-12 under the heading, "A.D.P. Record Guidelines":

> Supporting Documents and Audit Trails. The audit trail should be designed so that the details underlying the summary accounting data, such as invoices and vouchers, may be identified and made available to the Internal Revenue Service upon request.
>
> Recorded or Reconstructible Data. The records must provide the opportunity to trace any transaction back to the original source or forward to a final total. If printouts are not made of transactions at the time they are processed, then the system must have the ability to reconstruct these transactions.

The following discussion of auditing techniques and procedures with respect to EDP systems is divided into three sections addressing the topics of auditing *around, through,* and *with* computerized systems. These three topic areas comprise techniques auditors may consider when examining a client with an EDP installation. All these procedures concern auditors' substantive tests employed in gathering evidence regarding the validity of specific transactions and balances. However, many of the auditors' compliance tests, mentioned in the section on internal control evaluation, are performed in a similar manner.

AUDITING AROUND THE COMPUTER

In EDP systems where a detailed audit trail exists, auditors may be able to perform tests without utilizing the computer. In such cases the basic audit procedure involved is to obtain print-outs of the details of account balances and the transactions that comprise such balances. Specific transactions may then be selected manually and traced back through the accounting records to appropriate source documents. In auditing around the computer, the techniques used by auditors differ little from those used in auditing manual accounting systems.

In some applications, auditing around the computer provides adequate evidence upon which to form an opinion with respect to the data. Many auditors believe that in systems that provide enough hard copy to make tracing procedures feasible, around-the-computer techniques are both appropriate and desirable.

It would appear that much past criticism regarding auditing around the computer was advanced because this approach symbolized to many the auditor's fear and ignorance of computers. To the extent that these procedures are used by auditors because no alternatives are known, the criticism is justified. However, in situations where these direct procedures are feasible and informed audit judgment dictates their use, there is no reason for auditors to hesitate to use them.

AUDITING THROUGH THE COMPUTER

In EDP systems that provide little hard copy and do not have a discernible audit trail, techniques employed in auditing around the computer are likely to be inappropriate. Audit techniques that use the client's hardware and software to test data are usually required. This type of testing focuses on testing the computer programs used by the client to process data. Two methods frequently used to accomplish such tests are (1) use of test data and (2) reprocessing.

Use of Test Data In using test data to draw conclusions regarding the operation of a computer program, the auditor develops data similar to that normally processed by the program. Then, the test data are processed under controlled conditions using the client's program. When the resulting processed information is obtained, it is compared with predetermined results to ascertain whether the test data were processed properly.

In developing test data, auditors should include transactions that reflect those valid and invalid conditions that they wish to test. The test data approach gives auditors assurance regarding the operation of their client's program at one point in time. It tells an auditor little, however, about the operation of the program during the entire period under examination or about the data actually processed. "In order to satisfy auditing standards, use of the test data method must be coupled with an examination of source documents and other source evidence supporting the records that are being produced."[1]

Reprocessing This method of testing the operation of the client's EDP system requires that the auditor, under controlled conditions, reprocess samples of actual data from the period under examination. To perform the reprocessing operation the auditor either uses a program in the client's EDP department that previously has been tested or uses a duplicate program over which the auditor maintains control. After the reprocessing operation is completed, the result of the sample operation is compared with the original data as recorded in the client's records. This method

[1] Gordon B. Davis, *Auditing & EDP*, American Institute of Certified Public Accountants, New York, 1968, p. 160.

appears to have at least one advantage over the test data method in that the auditor may draw inferences regarding both the operation of the client's program and the validity of some of the data under audit.

As EDP systems become more advanced, through-the-computer techniques such as those described here, as well as others, will increase in importance. Procedures such as continuous monitoring of the client's EDP system may be required. More reliance may be placed on systems tests and internal control evaluation, and relatively less assurance may be obtained from the examination of source documents and tracing of transactions.

In any event, it seems likely that auditors will always require that a system provide some method of tracing a representative number of transactions and of examining some source documents. This indicates that a combination of around and through procedures will continue to be appropriate in auditing EDP systems in the future.

AUDITING WITH THE COMPUTER

The client's computer can provide the auditor extensive assistance in performing an examination. Computer programs can be devised so that numerous audit tasks can be efficiently performed using the client's, or outside, EDP equipment. *Generalized computer audit programs* are readily available that accomplish a wide range of audit tasks and are adaptable to a number of different EDP systems. In cases where appropriate software is not available in prepackaged form, auditors may wish to have programs written to their specifications.

Use of generalized computer audit programs provides the auditor increased access to the data stored in the client's EDP system. The programs also can be used to present the data in a more meaningful format than might otherwise be easily achieved. Such improved access and presentation of data can greatly facilitate audit decisions. Furthermore, the use of generalized audit software can lessen the auditor's dependence on the client's EDP personnel, increase the auditor's efficiency in performing necessary procedures, and enhance the auditor's understanding of the client's EDP system.

Uses of Computer Audit Programs Audit tasks that are commonly performed by generalized computer audit programs include:

1. statistical and judgmental selection of audit samples
2. mathematical verification of footings, extensions, and other calculations
3. multiple regression calculations or other procedures to select items for analytical review
4. data manipulation chores such as computation of subtotals, summarization, listing selectively, etc.
5. examining records for completeness and correctness
6. comparing data that appear on separate files

Other applications of computer audit programs include preparation of financial statements, preparation of accounts receivable aging analyses, printing and addressing confirmation requests, comparison of budgeted and actual amounts, computation of ratios and other statistics, listing slow-moving inventory items, matching credit limits to receivable balances, comparing physical inventory counts with master files, etc. It appears that the audit applications of computers are limited only by a system's capability and an auditor's ingenuity.

AUDITING DATA PROCESSED BY OUTSIDE SERVICE CENTERS

Many companies use data processing services of outside service centers. In such cases, the client has no direct control over and often little knowledge of the operation of the center. In using information processed by such a center, an auditor must obtain satisfaction regarding its reliability and the internal controls associated with its creation. To obtain such satisfaction the auditor must evaluate the system employed by the client to generate and control input data sent to the center as well as to utilize and control output received from the center. If the data processed by the center are material to the client's financial statements, the auditor should consider whether it is necessary to visit the center and evaluate the internal controls employed. Some service centers employ independent auditors to review their internal controls and issue reports thereon. These reports are sometimes relied upon by their customers' auditors to help them gain assurance regarding controls at the center.

GLOSSARY OF EDP TERMS

The following glossary presents brief definitions of many of the commonly used terms relating to EDP.

Glossary

Address—an identification that specifies the location of data in storage.

ADP—an acronym for *automatic data processing.* This term signifies the processing of data using electronic or electro-mechanical equipment.

Assembler—a computer program used to prepare a machine language program from one written in a symbolic language.

Batch processing—a procedure whereby groups of similar items are collected and processed together.

Check digit—a digit added to a number to enable a mathematical check to be performed. Also called a *residue check* and *self-checking digit.*

COBOL—a symbolic computer programming language. The name is formed by the acronym for *common business oriented language.*

Compiler—a computer program that transforms a program written in symbolic language into a machine language program. It performs the usual functions of an *assembler* but additionally utilizes the logical structure of the symbolic program.

Console—that part of the computer used for communication between the operator and the machine.

Console run book—a book of operator's instructions for a run.

Control clerk—a person having duties associated with the control function in an EDP installation.

Control total—a total of one type information from all items in a batch used for input and output control.

CPU—an acronym for *central processing unit.* This component interprets and executes the program instructions.

Debug—to eliminate errors from a program.

Deck—a group of computer cards.

Disk—a type of random access storage equipment consisting of circular magnetic plates.

Documentation—a record system that describes important aspects of the programs and other design factors of an installation.

Dual read—the duplicate reading of information by independent sensors and subsequent comparison for error detection.

Echo check—a data transmission control in which data received are transmitted back to their source and compared with the original input.

Edit—to modify the arrangement of data.

EDP—acronym for *electronic data processing.*

Error message—computer output informing the operator of errors or abnormal operation in a run.

External label—identification attached to the outside of files or programs.

Field—the location on a card or tape of a specific type of data.

File—a group of related records.

File protection ring—a mechanical device that prevents accidental destruction of information on a magnetic tape.

File reconstruction plan—procedures employed to enable the reconstruction of essential information in the event of accidental data loss.

Flowchart—a schematic diagram depicting the operation of a program or a system.

FORTRAN—acronym for *formula translating system,* a procedure-oriented programming language.

Generalized computer audit programs—any of several programs designed to perform various audit functions.

Hard copy—printed computer output.

Hardware—the electronic and mechanical components of the EDP system.

Hash total—a control total which is otherwise meaningless.

Header label—an internal, machine-readable identification that precedes the data on a file. This label is an important control device.

Library—the files and programs of the EDP installation usually stored collectively and controlled in terms of use.

Limit test—a programmed data control that causes attention to be directed to data that exceed certain predetermined limits.

Machine language—the basic numerical language used directly by the machine.

Master file—a file of relatively permanent records.

Memory—the internal information storage capability of the computer.

Memory dump—to output the contents of the computer memory.

Off-line—equipment that is not in direct communication with the CPU.

On-line—equipment kept in direct communication with the CPU.

Overflow—the condition of exceeding the capacity of the equipment involved.

Parity bit—an extra binary digit appended to a number to make the sum of the binary digits either odd or even.

Parity check—a test employing the parity bit that helps detect data loss during processing.

Patch—a minor modification of a program implemented in an expedient manner.

Peripheral equipment—the auxiliary equipment that with the CPU makes up the EDP installation.

Program—a set of instructions, written in a language that can be communicated to the computer, that directs the operations to be performed.

Programmer—an employee who writes computer programs.

Random access—a storage capability which allows data retrieval in such a manner that the access time is independent of the location of the data in the file.

Real-time—processing procedures and equipment that provide concurrent input and recording of data as well as immediate output.

Record layout—a diagram showing the data items comprised by a record.

Records—the related items in a file.

Routine—a set of instructions for a specific procedure.

Run—the performance of a set of instructions.

Sequential access—a data access procedure that involves movement along an ordered set of data.

Software—the programs and system design components of the EDP installation.

Sort—to arrange into a predetermined sequence.

Storage—computer memory.

Systems analyst—an employee who examines a function or activity and designs or modifies the procedures employed in its implementation.

Test deck—a set of simulated data used to check various computer operations.

Time sharing—the technique of using multiple input and output devices with a single CPU.

Update—to post current data to a master file.

Validity check—a test to determine if a data item is classified appropriately.

Verifier—peripheral equipment used to detect errors in input data.

Supplementary readings

Adams, Donald L., and John F. Mullarkey. "A Survey of Audit Software." *Journal of Accountancy* (September 1972), 39-66.

Allen, Brandt. "The Biggest Computer Frauds: Lessons for CPAs." *Journal of Accountancy* (May 1977), 52-62.

Cash, J. I., Jr., A. D. Bailey, Jr., and A. B. Whinston. "A Survey of Techniques for Auditing EDP-Based Accounting Information Systems." *Accounting Review* (October 1977), 813-832.

Computer Services Executive Committee. *Computer Assisted Audit Techniques* (Exposure Draft). New York: American Institute of Certified Public Accountants, 1978.

———. *The Auditor's Study and Evaluation of Internal Control in EDP Systems.* New York: American Institute of Certified Public Accountants, 1977.

Davis, Gordon B. *Auditing and EDP.* New York: American Institute of Certified Public Accountants, 1968.

Jancura, Elise G., and Fred L. Lilly. "SAS No. 3 and the Evaluation of Internal Control." *Journal of Accountancy* (March 1977), 69-74.

Porter, W. Thomas, and William E. Perry. *EDP: Controls and Auditing.* 2nd ed. Belmont, CA: Wadsworth Publishing Co., Inc., 1977.

Reneau, J. Hal. "Auditing in a Data Base Environment." *Journal of Accountancy* (December 1977), 59-65.

Rittenberg, Larry E., and Gordon B. Davis. "The Roles of Internal and External Auditors in Auditing EDP Systems." *Journal of Accountancy* (December 1977), 51-58.

Roussey, Robert S. "Third-Party Review of the Computer Service Center." *Journal of Accountancy* (August 1978), 78-82.

Review questions

10-1. Describe several areas in the work of both public and private accountants that have been directly affected by computers.

10-2. What is the *audit trail*?

10-3. How may computer systems change auditors' traditional concept of an audit trail?

10-4. How does the first general auditing standard relate to the examination of an audit client who has an EDP system?

10-5. Differentiate between *general controls* and *application controls* as these terms relate to internal control over EDP applications.

10-6. What are the internal control considerations regarding where in the corporate organization the EDP department is placed?

10-7. What basic functions within the EDP department should be separated, and why is such separation desirable?

10-8. What is the job of the control unit in the EDP department?

10-9. What purpose does documentation serve in an EDP installation?

10-10. What are some ways to promote physical security in a computer center?

10-11. What is a file reconstruction plan?

10-12. Define *auditing around, through,* and *with* the computer.

10-13. Why may auditing through the computer be necessary?
10-14. What techniques do auditors have for auditing through the computer? Explain each method named.
10-15. What is a *generalized computer audit program*?
10-16. What audit tasks can be performed by a computer?
10-17. How may auditors be satisfied regarding internal control applicable to client data processed by an outside service center?
10-18. In devising test data for auditing through the computer, what types of test transactions should be included?
10-19. In what cases might auditing around the computer be appropriate?
10-20. Why is it necessary to maintain strict library procedures in the computer center?

Decision problems

10-21. John Clinton, CPA, is examining the financial statements of the Rossville Sales Corporation, which recently installed an off-line electronic computer. The following comments have been extracted from Clinton's notes on computer operations and the processing and control of shipping notices and customer invoices:

> To minimize inconvenience Rossville converted without change its existing data processing system, which utilized tabulating equipment. The computer company supervised the conversion and has provided training to all computer department employees (except keypunch operators) in systems design, operations, and programming.
>
> Each computer run is assigned to a specific employee, who is responsible for making program changes, running the program, and answering questions. This procedure has the advantage of eliminating the need for records of computer operations because employees are responsible for their own computer runs.
>
> At least one computer department employee remains in the computer room during office hours, and only computer department employees have keys to the computer room.
>
> System documentation consists of those materials furnished by the computer company—a set of record formats and program listings. These and the tape library are kept in a corner of the computer department.
>
> The company considered the desirability of programmed controls but decided to retain the manual controls from its existing system.
>
> Company products are shipped directly from public warehouses, which forward shipping notices to general accounting. There a billing clerk enters the price of the item and accounts for the numerical sequence of shipping notices from each warehouse. The billing clerk also prepares daily adding machine tapes (control tapes) of the units shipped and the unit prices.

Shipping notices and control tapes are forwarded to the computer department for keypunching and processing. Extensions are made on the computer. Output consists of invoices (in six copies) and a daily sales register. The daily sales register shows the aggregate totals of units shipped and unit prices, which the computer operator compares to the control tapes.

All copies of the invoice are returned to the billing clerk. The clerk mails three copies to the customer, forwards one copy to the warehouse, maintains one copy in a numerical file, and retains one copy in an open invoice file that serves as a detail accounts receivable record.

Describe weaknesses in internal control over information and data flows and the procedures for processing shipping notices and customer invoices and recommend improvements in these controls and processing procedures. Organize your answer as follows:

Weakness	Recommended improvement

AICPA adapted

10-22. The audit of the financial statements of a client that uses the services of a computer for accounting functions compels the CPA to understand the operation of the client's electronic data processing (EDP) system.

a. The first requirement of an effective system of internal control is a satisfactory plan of organization. List the characteristics of a satisfactory plan of organization for an EDP department, including the relationship between the department and the rest of the organization.

b. An effective system of internal control also requires a sound system of recording, control of operations and transactions (source data and its flow) and of classification of data within the accounts. For an EDP system, these controls include input controls, processing controls, and output controls. List the characteristics of a satisfactory system of input controls. Confine your comments to a batch-controlled system employing punched cards and to the steps that occur prior to the processing of the input cards in the computer.

AICPA adapted

10-23. Harriet Stokes, CPA, has examined the financial statements of the Solt Manufacturing Company for several years and is making preliminary plans for the audit for the year ended June 30, 1983. During this examination Stokes plans to use a set of generalized computer audit programs. Solt's EDP manager has agreed to prepare special tapes of data from company records for the CPA's use with the generalized programs.

The following information is applicable to Stokes's examination of Solt's accounts payable and related procedures:

a. The formats of pertinent tapes are shown in Figure 10-2.

Figure 10-2 Tape Formats: Solt Manufacturing Company

Master File—Vendor Name

Vendor code	Recd type	Space	Blank	Vendor name	Blank	Card code 100

Master File—Vendor Address

Vendor code	Recd type	Space	Blank	Address—line 1	Address—line 2	Address—line 3	Blank	Card code 120

Transaction File—Expense Detail

Vendor code	Recd type	Voucher number	Blank	Batch	Voucher number	Voucher date	Vendor code	Invoice date	Due date	Invoice number	Purchase order number	Debit account	Prd type	Product code	Blank	Amount	Quantity	Card code 160

Transaction File—Payment Detail

Vendor code	Recd type	Voucher number	Blank	Batch	Voucher number	Voucher date	Vendor code	Invoice date	Due date	Invoice number	Purchase order number	Check number	Check date	Blank	Amount	Blank	Card code 170

b. The following monthly runs are prepared:
1. cash disbursements by check number
2. outstanding payables
3. purchase journals arranged (1) by account charged and (2) by vendor

c. Vouchers and supporting invoices, receiving reports, and purchase order copies are filed by vendor code. Purchase orders and checks are filed numerically.

d. Company records are maintained on magnetic tapes. All tapes are stored in a restricted area within the computer room. A grandfather-father-son policy is followed for retaining and safeguarding tape files.
1. Explain the grandfather-father-son policy. Describe how files could be reconstructed when this policy is used.
2. Discuss whether company policies for retaining and safeguarding the tape files provide adequate protection against losses of data.
3. Describe the controls that the CPA should maintain over:
   a. preparing the special tape
   b. processing the special tape with the generalized computer audit programs
4. Prepare a schedule for the EDP manager outlining the data that should be included on the special tape for the CPA's examination of accounts payable and related procedures. This schedule should show the:
   a. client tape from which the item should be extracted
   b. name of the item of data

AICPA adapted

10-24. CPAs may audit around or through computers in the examination of the financial statements of clients who utilize computers to process accounting data.

a. Describe the auditing approach referred to as auditing around the computer.

b. Under what conditions does the CPA decide to audit through the computer instead of around the computer?

c. In auditing through the computer, the CPA may use a *test deck.*
1. What is a test deck?
2. Why does the CPA use a test deck?

d. How can the CPA be satisfied that the computer program tapes presented are actually being used by the client to process its accounting data?

AICPA adapted

10-25. The Dalton Utility District is installing an electronic data processing system. The CPA who conducts the annual examination of the Utility District's financial statements has been asked to recommend controls for the new system. Discuss recommended controls over program documentation; EDP hardware; and tape files and software.

AICPA adapted

Figure 10-3 Time Cards, Job Tickets Diagram

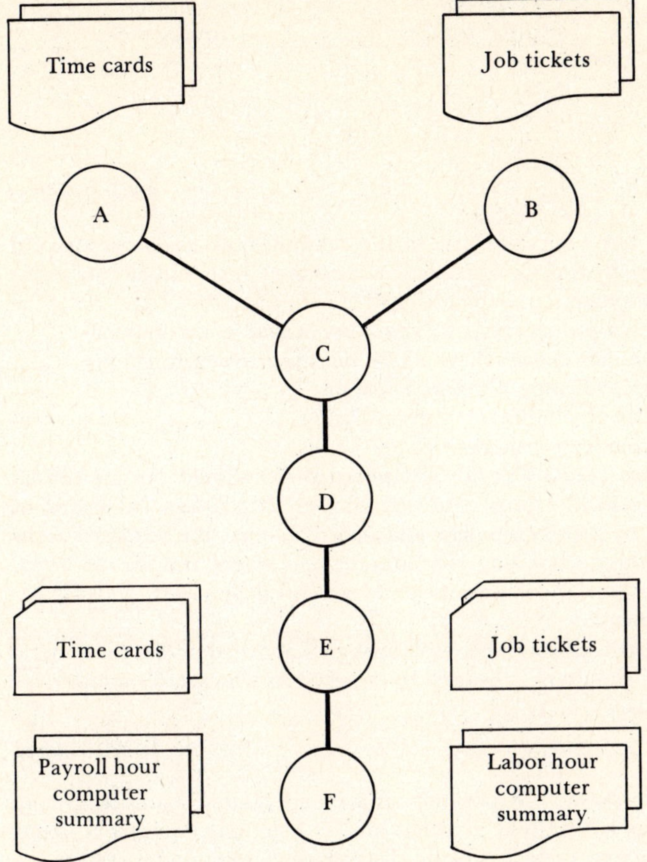

10-26. In connection with the examination of the financial statements of the Olympia Manufacturing Company, a CPA is reviewing procedures for accumulating direct labor hours. The CPA learns that all production is by job order and that all employees are paid hourly wages, with time-and-one-half for overtime hours.

Olympia's direct labor hour input process for payroll and job-cost determination is summarized in the flowchart illustrated in Figure 10-3.

Steps *A* and *C* are performed in timekeeping; step *B*, in the factory operating departments; step *D*, in payroll audit and control; step *E*, in data preparation (keypunch); and step *F*, in computer operations.

For each input processing step *A* through *F*:

a. List the possible errors or discrepancies that may occur.

b. Cite the corresponding control procedure that should be in effect for each error or discrepancy.

Organize your answer for each input-processing step as follows:

Step	Possible errors or discrepancies	Control procedures

AICPA adapted

10-27. The following five topics are part of the relevant body of knowledge for CPAs having field work or immediate supervisory responsibility in audits involving a computer:

1. Electronic data processing (EDP) equipment and its capabilities.
2. Organization and management of the data processing function.
3. Characteristics of computer based systems.
4. Fundamentals of computer programming.
5. Computer center operations.

CPAs who are responsible for computer audits should possess certain general knowledge with respect to each of these five topics. For example, on the subject of EDP equipment and its capabilities, the auditor should have a general understanding of computer equipment and should be familiar with the uses and capabilities of the central processor and the peripheral equipment.

For each of the topics numbered 2 through 5 above, describe the general knowledge that should be possessed by those CPAs who are responsible for computer audits.

AICPA adapted

10-28. A CPA's client, Quanta Corporation, is a medium-sized manufacturer of products for the leisure time activities market (camping equipment, scuba gear, bows and arrows, etc.). During the past year, a computer system was installed, and inventory records of finished goods and parts were converted to computer processing. The inventory master file is maintained on a disk. Each record of the file contains the following information:

Item or part number
Description
Size
Unit of measure code
Quantity on hand
Cost per unit
Total value of inventory on hand at cost
Date of last sale or usage
Quantity used or sold this year
Economic order quantity
Code number of major vendor
Code number of secondary vendor

In preparation for year-end inventory the client has two identical sets of preprinted inventory count cards. One set is for the client's inventory counts and the other is for the CPA's use to make audit test counts. The following information has been keypunched into the cards and interpreted on their face:

Item or part number
Description
Size
Unit of measure code

In taking the year-end inventory, the client's personnel will write the actual counted quantity on the face of each card. When all counts are complete, the counted quantity will be keypunched into the cards. The cards will be processed against the disk file, and quantity-on-hand figures will be adjusted to reflect the actual count. A computer listing will be prepared to show any missing inventory count cards and all quantity adjustments of more than $100 in value. These items will be investigated by client personnel, and all required adjustments will be made. When adjustments have been completed, the final year-end balances will be computed and posted to the general ledger.

The CPA has available a general purpose computer audit software package that will run on the client's computer and can process both card and disk files.

a. In general and without regard to the facts above, discuss the nature of general purpose computer audit software packages and list the various types and uses of such packages.

b. List and describe at least five ways a general purpose computer audit software package can be used to assist in all aspects of the audit of the inventory of Quanta Corporation. (For example, the package can be used to read the disk inventory master file and list items and parts with a high unit cost or total value. Such items can be included in the test counts to increase the dollar coverage of the audit verification.)

AICPA adapted

11

Operational, Management, and Comprehensive Auditing

Financial auditing performed by independent public accountants is the emphasis of the other chapters in this book. This chapter presents a discussion of other types of auditing.

Internal auditing, examinations performed by auditors within an enterprise, is discussed in two major divisions, internal financial auditing and internal operational auditing. Emphasis is placed on operational auditing as it relates to management's accomplishment of goals and objectives. Terminology is not uniform in the literature on this subject, and the terms *management auditing, functional auditing,* and *operations auditing* are used in the same sense as *operational auditing* in this chapter; they denote broadly based, wide-scope audits conducted by internal auditors.

Management auditing is the term in this chapter that designates the wide-scope audits conducted by public accountants. These audits result in an evaluation of management's performance.

Comprehensive auditing is the term employed to describe audits of governmental agencies and activities, whether performed by governmental auditors or independent public accountants. Three major aspects of comprehensive auditing are financial and compliance auditing, auditing for efficiency and economy, and performance auditing. Compliance auditing has applications within the private sector of business.

The chapter concludes with a brief discussion of the developing concept of *continuous auditing.* This type of auditing has been called by some writers *instant auditing,* because an auditor can express an opinion on financial statements prepared at a variety of dates without conducting an examination when the statements are issued.

Internal auditing

Almost every company of substantial size has a team of internal auditors, and many smaller companies have at least a single internal auditor. These persons are fulfilling the function of internal auditing, which developed to help keep management informed about its operations as the companies expanded to such an extent that the owner or manager could not personally oversee all operations. For some time after such expansion prevented personal supervision, owners and managers relied upon public auditors for assurance that the accounting records were properly maintained, that assets owned were on hand and properly safeguarded, and that appropriate internal controls were in effect. As companies continued to grow with increasing numbers of employees and widely scattered operations, the function of internal auditing developed to provide assurance to owners and managers that internal operations were functioning properly. At the same time, the services of external auditors came to be relied upon for assurance of fairness in financial statement presentations.

By using company personnel as internal auditors, a company may review its records and operations on somewhat more of a continual basis, rather than only when external auditors conduct a review. Additionally, internal auditors are able to become thoroughly familiar with the policies and practices of a company and to understand the peculiarities of its environment and personnel. Internal auditors can devote their attention to administrative and operational problems, which are beyond the usual realm of concern of external auditors. Furthermore, services of internal auditors are likely to be less costly than services of external auditors.

Indication of how recently internal auditing has developed as a major business function can be seen in the fact that the Institute of Internal Auditors, the national organization of internal auditors, was founded only in 1941. As might be expected with any young and developing profession, the nature and scope of internal auditing is continuously evolving. The internal auditing function within a company is designed to meet the needs of each particular organization and is shaped by the understanding that its management has of the role of the internal auditor. The size and stage of development of the company also influences the nature of the internal auditing function. Internal auditing must necessarily vary from any general description in order to meet the needs of an individual company.

Internal financial auditing

All early internal audits, and many even today, were concerned primarily with review and appraisal of financial or accounting activities of a company. In practically all audit situations, internal auditors are concerned with reviewing and appraising the soundness and adequacy of their company's internal accounting controls. For example, internal auditors may verify that the prenumbered cash receipts are prepared in triplicate by the cashier for all cash receipts, that all numbered receipts are properly accounted for, and that each day's cash collections are deposited intact at the close of a day's business.

Internal auditors historically have also been responsible for determining the extent to which company assets are properly accounted for and safeguarded from losses. Such activity may have specific significance for branches and divisions that are distant from home-office operations and in large companies where management is unlikely to have first-hand knowledge of assets either at the main location or at remote branch operations. Included in this function of internal auditing is the count of cash funds, the verification of inventories by taking or observing physical counts, determining the condition of inventory items, verifying that proper pricing policies are followed, and detailed examination of many other assets.

Another aspect of internal financial auditing is the auditor's establishing the reliability of accounting data maintained in the company's records and of the reports based upon these data. To accomplish this, the auditor examines supporting documents, tests for proper classification of transactions, and proves the agreement of subsidiary records with control accounts. In this aspect of the work, the internal auditor may make requests for confirmation of accounts receivable balances from customers. Such is an example of activities by the internal auditor that may reduce the amount of similar work performed by the external auditor.

Whereas in years past the financial aspects of an internal audit dominated in most companies, today in many companies financial auditing has become merely one aspect of a broadly based, wide-scope internal audit. In themselves the financial and accounting controls remain as important as ever for successful management and operation of a business; however, internal auditors now give them consideration along with other equally important controls.

As pointed out in previous chapters, the Foreign Corrupt Practices Act of 1977 (FCPA) requires management to devise and maintain a system of internal accounting controls sufficient to provide assurances that transactions are properly authorized and reflected in financial statements, and that existing assets are properly recorded and used only as authorized. Recommendations of the AICPA and the SEC indicate that corporate managements may be required to report publicly on the adequacy of their internal accounting control systems. Management personnel probably will place considerable reliance on the internal auditor's review, analysis, and recommendations regarding the control system as the basis for their reports. As the full impact of the FCPA and the required reports evolves, the importance of the internal auditing function is likely to increase.

Internal operational auditing

The opportunities for an internal auditor to expand the scope of an examination beyond the financial and accounting activities of a company were recognized in the early development of internal auditing. For example, the Institute of Internal Auditors said in its 1947 *Statement of Responsibilities* that internal auditing should deal primarily with accounting and financial matters but could deal also with matters of an operating nature. Determining the extent to which company policies and procedures were followed, evaluating these policies and procedures regarding adequacy of their design to accomplish goals of management, and appraising the quality of the performance of employees in carrying out these policies and procedures developed into a major aspect of the work of internal auditors.

Operational auditing is the term widely used to describe the extension of the internal auditing function into almost all aspects of a company's operations. Operational auditing is primarily oriented toward the future and improvements that can be made; whereas internal financial auditing is concerned essentially with the past, protection provided by existing controls, and the accuracy of data reflected in the financial records. Operational auditing is an extension of management that does what a good manager would do if present in all places at all times. The concern in internal operational auditing is over how well a department is performing in relation to the established objectives. The auditor considers how each function relates to the overall operation, not to discover minor violations of policy, but to help others understand the policy and accomplish the objectives of the activity. An internal auditor does not recommend a procedure because it is good in theory but because it will reduce costs or risks in an important and material operation of the business. Internal auditors should continuously question whether good management and business techniques are used in each department under review. But more important is the answer to the question, "Can these procedures be improved?"

The operational aspect of internal auditing is reflected in the scope-of-work section of the 1978 *Standards for the Professional Practice of Internal Auditing,* which follows. However, it should be noted that the financial and accounting aspects remain essential internal auditing activities.

Standards for the Professional Practice of Internal Auditing[1]

300 SCOPE OF WORK

The scope of the internal audit should encompass the examination and evaluation of the adequacy and effectiveness of the organization's system of internal control and the quality of performance in carrying out assigned responsibilities.

.01 The scope of internal auditing work, as specified in this standard, encompasses what audit work should be performed. It is recognized, however, that management and the board of directors provide general direction as to the scope of work and the activities to be audited.

.02 The purpose of the review for adequacy of the system of internal control is to ascertain whether the system established provides reasonable assurance that the organization's objectives and goals will be met efficiently and economically.

.03 The purpose of the review for effectiveness of the system of internal control is to ascertain whether the system is functioning as intended.

.04 The purpose of the review for quality of performance is to ascertain whether the organization's objectives and goals have been achieved.

.05 The primary objectives of internal control are to ensure:

.1 The reliability and integrity of information

.2 Compliance with policies, plans, procedures, laws, and regulations

.3 The safeguarding of assets

.4 The economical and efficient use of resources

.5 The accomplishment of established objectives and goals for operations or programs

310 RELIABILITY AND INTEGRITY OF INFORMATION

Internal auditors should review the reliability and integrity of financial and operating information and the means used to identify, measure, classify, and report such information.

.01 Information systems provide data for decision making, control, and compliance with external requirements. Therefore, internal auditors should examine information systems and, as appropriate, ascertain whether:

.1 Financial and operating records and reports contain accurate, reliable, timely, complete, and useful information.

.2 Controls over record keeping and reporting are adequate and effective.

[1] Used by permission of the Institute of Internal Auditors.

320 COMPLIANCE WITH POLICIES, PLANS, PROCEDURES, LAWS AND REGULATIONS

Internal auditors should review the systems established to ensure compliance with those policies, plans, procedures, laws, and regulations which could have a significant impact on operations and reports, and should determine whether the organization is in compliance.

.01 Management is responsible for establishing the systems designed to ensure compliance with such requirements as policies, plans, procedures, and applicable laws and regulations. Internal auditors are responsible for determining whether the systems are adequate and effective and whether the activities audited are complying with the appropriate requirements.

330 SAFEGUARDING OF ASSETS

Internal auditors should review the means of safeguarding assets and, as appropriate, verify the existence of such assets.

.01 Internal auditors should review the means used to safeguard assets from various types of losses such as those resulting from theft, fire, improper or illegal activities, and exposure to the elements.

.02 Internal auditors, when verifying the existence of assets, should use appropriate audit procedures.

340 ECONOMICAL AND EFFICIENT USE OF RESOURCES

Internal auditors should appraise the economy and efficiency with which resources are employed.

.01 Management is responsible for setting operating standards to measure an activity's economical and efficient use of resources. Internal auditors are responsible for determining whether:

- *.1* Operating standards have been established for measuring economy and efficiency.
- *.2* Established operating standards are understood and are being met.
- *.3* Deviations from operating standards are identified, analyzed, and communicated to those responsible for corrective action.
- *.4* Corrective action has been taken.

.02 Audits related to the economical and efficient use of resources should identify such conditions as:

- *.1* Underutilized facilities
- *.2* Nonproductive work
- *.3* Procedures which are not cost justified
- *.4* Overstaffing or understaffing

350 ACCOMPLISHMENT OF ESTABLISHED OBJECTIVES AND GOALS FOR OPERATIONS OR PROGRAMS

Internal auditors should review operations or programs to ascertain whether results are consistent with established objectives and goals and whether the operations or programs are being carried out as planned.

> *.01* Management is responsible for establishing operating or program objectives and goals, developing and implementing control procedures, and accomplishing desired operating or program results. Internal auditors should ascertain whether such objectives and goals conform with those of the organization and whether they are being met.
>
> *.02* Internal auditors can provide assistance to managers who are developing objectives, goals, and systems by determining whether the underlying assumptions are appropriate; whether accurate, current, and relevant information is being used; and whether suitable controls have been incorporated into the operations or programs.

DEFINITION OF INTERNAL OPERATIONAL AUDITING

Just as the entire function of internal auditing is continuously evolving and is shaped by the needs of management of each company, so too is operational auditing. Each company likely has its own description of the operational auditing function. The more common elements of such descriptions are reflected in the following definition:

> Operational auditing is a comprehensive examination and appraisal of business operations for the purpose of informing management whether or not the various operations are performed in a manner which complies with established policies directed toward management's objectives. Included in the audit is an appraisal of the efficient use of both human and physical resources as well as an appraisal of various operating procedures. The audit should also include recommendations of solutions to problems and of methods for increasing efficiency and profits.

MANAGEMENT'S OBJECTIVES

A major aspect of the work of an operational auditor is an appraisal of the operations toward accomplishing management's objectives. Obviously these objectives must be clearly defined, well documented, and properly disseminated.

The long-range goals of a company should be defined to provide for the overall direction of the company. Based upon these goals as long-term guides, management should develop short-term objectives. They should be in writing, be easily understood, and be distributed to all personnel concerned. Their terms should be sufficiently specific for an auditor to determine whether the objectives are being reached. A time period for accomplishing each objective should usually be established so that progress can be measured.

Whereas objectives are the results that management hopes to achieve, plans, policies, procedures, and strategies are the detailed steps necessary to accomplish the objectives. Plans, procedures, and strategies form the blueprint of how an organization intends to accomplish a specific objective. They constitute a commitment to a specific course of action. As such, they should be consistent with the environment in which the company operates and should recognize the financial, physical, and human resources of the company that are available for each specific undertaking. Obviously a budget is an essential part of each plan. Administrative and operational controls should be designed to assure management that the plans are implemented in accordance with prescribed procedures, which are designed with effectiveness and efficiency as guidelines.

For an internal auditor to perform an operational audit, the goals that management has for the company and the objectives that have been established must be thoroughly understood. As a representative of management, the internal auditor should have the same ideas as management, should think like management, and should be able to help communicate to others the goals and objectives of management. Although auditors usually do not question the goals and objectives established by management, they definitely have the responsibility to question plans and procedures regarding their appropriateness in the particular environment. With an orientation toward recommendations for future plans, internal auditors should not dwell on weaknesses of the present procedures but should concentrate on meaningful recommendations for future action. To the extent that they can make positive contributions toward helping managerial personnel at all levels better accomplish their jobs, the auditors are functioning as professional advisors to top management or as essential members of the management team itself.

ORGANIZATIONAL POSITION

Internal auditors should be positioned in the organizational structure of a company so that they may extend without restrictions their examinations over all aspects of the company's operations. The section of *Standards for the Professional Practice of Internal Auditing* on independence states that internal auditors should be responsible to an individual in the organization who has sufficient authority to assure the broad scope of their audits and to take action on their recommendations.

Some observers advocate that internal auditors report directly to the president, the audit committee of the board of directors, or the board of directors itself. These persons point out that the independence of internal auditors is enhanced by their reporting to the highest authority, thereby placing them in a position to review, appraise, and report on the operations on top management. One potential problem in reporting at this level is that persons in higher positions may not be close enough to the day-to-day operations of the company to evaluate the findings and recommendations of the internal auditors, and they may not be in a position to implement promptly necessary changes.

An alternative position is that internal auditors should be responsible to the financial vice president or controller. The person in this position is usually enough removed from the line operations to be objective in considerations of auditors' findings and recommendations, yet is at the same time well versed in the objectives, plans, procedures, and controls established by top management. It is important that internal auditors report to an authority who is in a position to take action on the recommendations in their report.

Independence, as discussed relative to external auditors, is essentially a state of mind for internal auditors also. As long as internal auditors are company employees, complete independence is probably impossible to attain. However, auditors should have sufficient independence within a company's organization so that their audit objectives will not be compromised. Management can do much to establish such an attitude of independence by allowing auditors ample freedom in selecting the particular operations for study and also by informing those responsible for the operations under audit that the investigation is fully sanctioned.

Regardless of what position internal auditors occupy on an organizational chart, their reputation, standing, and support from top management should be such that they can obtain information throughout the company whenever needed for a report. They should have access to executives who will give prompt and proper consideration to their opinions and recommendations. Because of the different structure of each company's organization, internal auditing may appear as a staff function in a wide variety of organizational positions.

Phases of operational auditing

The specific phases of an operational audit depend upon the nature of the company, the nature of the operational area being audited, and the size and expertise of the auditing team. Typical of the phases of an operational unit are the following steps which are discussed in greater detail subsequently:

1. selection of the operational area for audit
2. advance preparations
3. initial survey
4. audit program
5. investigation and analysis
6. evaluation and recommendations
7. final reporting

SELECTION OF THE OPERATIONAL AREA FOR AUDIT

The first phase of an operational audit is identification of the area or function to be covered by the examination. The area selected is usually based upon an activity, a system, or a function within the business; rarely, if ever, would the area be based upon an account classification. The purchasing function, the delivery system, the electronic data processing system, and the engineering activities are examples of areas designated for operational audits.

In some organizations internal auditors have the authority to select the operational area for audit without waiting for a request from management. The auditor takes the initiative in choosing the areas, for the auditor has the responsibility to audit all operations at all locations. Some companies may have a plan to audit all operations in a five-year period, for example. Naturally there must be a system of priorities, and high priority should be assigned to a request from top management to audit an area where problems exist or where profits are not satisfactory. The request may originate with the manager of the operational area itself.

The auditor considers many factors in selecting the audit area, and special priority should be given operations that involve large expenditures or investments. Also quite high in priority should be recently acquired companies or newly created divisions. In these situations, especially, the internal auditor has a responsibility to see that management's objectives and plans are known and that proper procedures are being followed. Distant operations that are infrequently visited by management personnel also merit similar attention. Another factor influencing the choice of an area for review is the length of time since the last audit. In addition, the auditor should attempt to maintain a balance between production and administrative operations that are audited. Frequently, when auditing a particular operation, questions or problems in other operations may be discovered, and these then become areas for future audits.

ADVANCE PREPARATIONS

After an operation has been selected for audit, the staff of the review team should be assigned as soon as possible. The auditors thereby have an opportunity to become knowledgeable about the area before actually starting the audit. Learning about the area includes studying job descriptions and procedures manuals, reading trade journals, and perhaps attending seminars related to the particular functional area. The talents, background, and experience of the auditors assigned to the review team influence the steps necessary for familiarization.

The designation of a staff person in the area under review to serve as liaison or resource person is usually of benefit in planning the audit as well as in its performance. This person can discuss technical matters with the auditors or direct them to the proper persons to obtain needed information.

Top management should notify the manager of the selected operational area of the forthcoming audit, who in turn should notify the personnel in that area. Shortly after notification, the auditor may meet with the personnel of the area to explain the nature of the operational audit, its objectives, the procedures that will be followed, and what will be the reporting process. Establishing the proper attitude of confidence and cooperation is extremely important for the conduct of a successful operational audit.

INITIAL SURVEY

The auditor should become familiar with management's general objectives for the operation under study and should become knowledgeable of the manner by which the personnel in the operational area attempt to accomplish these objectives, what procedures are followed, what controls are in effect, and what problems are encountered. The auditor should know the organizational structure within the area, the assignment of duties, the flow of work, and the nature and timing of reports.

Discussions with the assigned resource person and interviews with personnel in the operational area are the sources of much of the auditor's information. At this survey stage of the examination, the auditor may take some small samples of supporting evidence to substantiate what is reported. In taking these preliminary samples, one is following a procedure similar to making a test of understanding, which is discussed in Chapter 7.

Auditors document their findings by preparing working papers in a manner similar to that described for an external audit. Well-prepared working papers enable auditors to review with greater ease their findings and recommendations with personnel of the operational area. They are essential for keeping up with the work performed and for writing the final report.

AUDIT PROGRAM

Writing an audit program is a fundamental aspect of preparing for an operational audit. Only after becoming thoroughly familiar with the operation can an auditor determine all the steps of an audit program. Because the auditor's knowledge of the operation is increasing continuously throughout the conduct of the examination, the audit program is always subject to modification. Nevertheless, the auditor should draw up an initial audit program based upon a preliminary investigation. Consultation with the manager of the area under review on steps to be included in the audit program not only insures the inclusion of areas viewed as problems but also encourages an attitude of cooperation.

INVESTIGATION AND ANALYSIS

By following an audit program, the auditor seeks to discover the facts as to the operation of the area under study. The search usually is conducted on a sampling basis in which the auditor judgmentally rather than statistically selects items for examination. The number of items selected is increased if many errors or deviations from prescribed procedures are discovered. The auditor examines sufficient evidence to reach a conclusion about how closely the assignment of responsibilities and the conduct of the operations follow the procedures and controls established to reach management's objectives. The auditor ascertains whether operating records are accurate and whether reports are factual, complete, and issued in a timely and meaningful manner. Also the auditor determines whether internal controls are enforced and are coordinated properly with controls in other operational areas.

EVALUATION AND RECOMMENDATIONS

As auditors go through their investigation and analysis procedures, they simultaneously begin the evaluation of their findings. At the conclusion of the investigation and analysis phase of their examination, auditors take a comprehensive view of all facts; then they are in a position to evaluate the operational area in terms of the extent to which it follows proper procedures and the reasons for any deviations. They also can evaluate the adequacy of controls and the effectiveness of reporting systems.

Throughout the investigation and analysis phase and the evaluation phase of the audit, auditors in all likelihood discover numerous minor discrepancies. They should bring these matters to the attention of a supervisor at the lowest possible level who is in a position to authorize correction. Aside from notation in their working papers, no further action or reporting is usually required on minor items.

Also during the examination, auditors should discuss on an informal basis their findings and possible recommendations with the manager and appropriate supervisors of the operational area. Comments and reactions from these persons are important considerations in arriving at final recommendations.

FINAL REPORTING

Thinking as members of management, internal auditors are likely to recommend in their final report many specific steps for operational personnel to take in order to adhere more closely to prescribed procedures, to implement better controls, to prevent errors, and finally to improve profits. In all probability, there are some situations in which auditors' knowledge and experience do not permit them to make recommendations. In such situations, they should merely report their evaluation of the facts and let top management consult authorities who have the expertise to make meaningful recommendations.

Prior to putting their recommendations into final report form, internal auditors should meet with the manager and supervisors of the operational area under audit and discuss the recommendations. Perhaps they should have a preliminary draft of the report for review, and they should be willing to listen to opinions on all matters included in the report. At times the change of a single word to one considered by the manager more accurate or less harsh will mean the difference between a report that is accepted readily and one that is strongly resented. The auditors should also include in their report notation of any major changes in the operations implemented during the course of the examination. Where different, the recommendations of the operational area manager may be included. However, the more desirable situation is to obtain agreement from the area manager on the recommendations included in the report.

The audit report should be as concise as reasonably possible. It should omit matters that do not warrant an executive's attention and should clearly delineate fact from opinion. Emphasis should be placed on items that will improve the operation of the business and increase profits. Improvements of protective controls may best be justified as methods of reducing theft, waste, and other inefficiencies.

The format of the written report should include the purpose, scope, and limitations of the audit and the auditor's findings, opinions, evaluations, and recommendations. The report should be written in language that a business executive understands and should avoid technical terminology.

The final report should be sent to the financial executive or to whomever the auditor reports, as well as to the manager of the operational area audited. Copies of the report or pertinent excerpts also should be distributed to managers of all operational areas affected by the report.

No operational audit can ever completely exhaust all findings. Auditors usually must cease their fact-finding before they have discovered all possible evidence, and they cannot explore all possible solutions for a problem. The examination and the report, therefore, concentrate on major problems and recommendations. Each audit of an operational area probably identifies numerous related areas that are potential areas of future audits.

Management auditing

The term *management auditing* is used in this chapter to mean a comprehensive examination, analysis, and evaluation by an independent external auditor of the performance of management resulting in recommendations regarding the objectives, plans, procedures, and strategies of the business enterprise and in expression of an opinion on the effectiveness of management in performance of its responsibilities. Management auditing differs from operational auditing, discussed earlier in this chapter, in two major aspects. First, the examination is performed by external auditors and second, the report includes the expression of an opinion on the performance of the management function.

Since a management audit is performed by external auditors, there is opportunity for review and appraisal of management functions throughout the enterprise, including top management. A higher degree of independence and perhaps a greater degree of objectivity can be achieved when external auditors perform a management audit than when internal auditors perform an operational one.

The nature of the auditor's opinion on the evaluation of the management function is not established clearly. The type of opinion rendered is influenced to a large extent by who is the recipient of the report. If the report is to be kept by top management and used internally, it is likely to contain many recommendations designed to produce better performance, to help achieve objectives of the company, and to improve efficiencies and profits. An evaluation of how the company is organized, the process of assigning responsibilities, the communications system, and the capabilities of personnel for assigned tasks may all be included in a report designed for internal use. An overall opinion on the effectiveness of management may or may not be included.

Management audits may be performed for third parties outside a company. Some users of financial reports indicate a desire to have, in annual reports, independent attestation of much data that lie outside the usual financial statements. An independent auditor usually with little difficulty can expand the financial audit and thereby extend the opinion to cover data such as backlog of orders, turnover of employees, number of patents actively used and related revenues, composition of shareholders with percentage of equity owned, and various ratios and analyses.

Others who use financial statements indicate a desire to have an independent expression of opinion on the effectiveness of management. Only by greatly expanding the usual examination can an independent auditor express such an opinion, if at all. In undertaking such a management audit, an auditor expresses an opinion about the effectiveness or adequacy of the managerial decision-making *processes,* not about the *results* of the decisions. Management needs to document thoroughly their explicit goals and plans and the analysis of data used in reaching their decisions. The auditors should become familiar with accepted principles of management. Two essential criteria must exist before an auditor can express an opinion: (1) the data must be verifiable, and (2) there must be a standard for evaluation. If the decision-making processes of management can be documented adequately and if the principles of management are developed sufficiently, the auditor should be able to express an opinion on the effectiveness of the management function. Competence of the auditor is another requirement in conducting an audit and expressing an opinion. With the development of management auditing standards, an auditor should be able to acquire the requisite competence through training and experience.

Whether these independent management audits should be conducted by CPAs or by other professionals is an unsettled matter. Some CPAs fear that such close association with management in making detailed recommendations might cause observers to doubt their independence. Perhaps an even stronger fear relates to the possible legal liabilities associated with expressing opinions on the effectiveness of management. Other CPAs, however, consider the management audit a natural extension of the financial audit and see no reasons to hesitate in developing these expanded services.

Comprehensive auditing

The audits of governmental organizations, whether performed by governmental auditors or by independent accountants, and audits of external organizations performed for a governmental entity encompass a broader scope than the types of audits discussed previously. *Comprehensive auditing* is the term applied to this broad concept of auditing by the United States General Accounting Office (GAO), which is the independent internal auditing agency of the federal government established in 1921 within the legislative branch of the government and headed by the comptroller general.

The tremendous growth of the federal government during the depression years of the 1930s and the war years of the 1940s demanded that accounting be used not merely as a tool of bookkeeping but additionally as an instrument of management control. Audits were conducted to determine that the agencies spent and controlled their appropriations properly and that they complied with appropriate laws and regulations.

In the 1950s Congress began requesting information on the efficiency of performance by management of the various federal agencies. The GAO developed the capability to evaluate the deficiencies in management regardless of the type of activity involved. The purpose was to determine whether management was using personnel, property, funds, and other resources in an economical and efficient manner. These reviews and evaluations of management stressed the weaknesses in management processes, but they did not include an evaluation of a program in terms of its effectiveness in accomplishing the desired objectives.

In the latter part of the 1960s and the early 1970s, the GAO expanded its audit scope to embrace an evaluation of the effectiveness of a total program. Both the Congress and the agency heads needed such an evaluation by an independent nonadvocate of a program. With this evaluation available, they could make certain cost-benefit analyses. Although there may be difficulty in measuring some of the benefits, this information is necessary to determine whether desired results are obtained or whether other alternatives might better accomplish the desired aim of the legislation or program.

The Congress or individual representatives, in considering prospective legislation, may request the GAO to determine the needs for the proposed program, the possible costs of such a program, the possible degree of effectiveness, and consequently the cost-benefit relationship. Although such a determination of what might happen in the future differs considerably from audits of historical events, the GAO has expanded the scope of its operation to encompass these activities. In reporting on such audits, the auditor must delineate quite clearly in the report those aspects backed up by facts and those aspects based upon opinion.

Comprehensive auditing falls into three major divisions, somewhat according to its historical development. These divisions or elements are (1) financial and compliance, (2) economy and efficiency, and (3) program results or performance. The three elements are defined as follows:

1. *Financial and compliance*—determines (*a*) whether financial operations are properly conducted, (*b*) whether the financial reports of an audited entity are presented fairly, and (*c*) whether the entity has complied with applicable laws and regulations.
2. *Economy and efficiency*—determines whether the entity is managing or utilizing its resources (personnel, property, space, and so forth) in an economical and efficient manner and the causes of any inefficiencies or uneconomical practices, including inadequacies in management information systems, administrative procedures, or organizational structure.
3. *Program results*—determines whether the desired results or benefits are being achieved, whether the objectives established by the legislature or other authorizing body are being met, and whether the agency has considered alternatives which might yield desired results at a lower cost.[2]

These three elements of a comprehensive audit should generally be performed whenever a full audit of a governmental activity is undertaken. The most economical approach to the audit would be to perform the three elements simultaneously; however, such may not always be practical or possible. The official who authorizes a particular audit should give consideration to the potential needs of the users of the audit report and may in some instances determine that only one or two elements are appropriate at the time.

Many government programs involve funds and activities of federal,

[2] United States General Accounting Office, *Standards for Audit of Governmental Organizations, Programs, Activities & Functions,* Government Printing Office, Washington, D.C., 1972, p. 2.

state, and local governments and several agencies. To reduce the duplication of audit effort, cooperation of auditors from the various governments and agencies is encouraged. The audits usually do not comprehend all operations of an agency but rather are directed toward specific activities or program areas. The audit program developed for each program area should include a broad, comprehensive review regarding the laws, regulations, goals, and objectives of the program. Thus, a single review of these matters should satisfy auditors from all levels of government. Where possible the audit program should be designed to satisfy both the common and the specialized interests of each level of government. Auditors from the different levels of government and different governmental agencies may rely upon the work of one another if they are satisfied about the capabilities of the other and the proficiency with which the work is performed.

The comptroller general of the United States issued in 1972 *Standards for Audit of Governmental Organizations, Programs, Activities & Functions,* which set forth audit standards intended for application by auditors in all levels of government whether employed by the various governments or working as independent public accountants. These standards apply to all governmental organizations, programs, activities, and functions including internal auditing. They also apply to audits of contractors, grantees, and other external organizations performed by or for a governmental entity. Like the standards for financial auditing promulgated by the AICPA, these governmental auditing standards relate to the scope and quality of the examination and reports. The essence of the AICPA standards are included in the governmental auditing standards, but additional standards are prescribed to reflect the broader scope of governmental auditing. The standards for governmental auditing are divided into three divisions, general standards, examination and evaluation standards, and reporting standards. The standards are reproduced in Appendix E.

A brief description of each of the standards of governmental auditing appears on the following pages. Emphasis is placed on aspects that differ significantly from AICPA standards. For a more thorough discussion of the governmental auditing standards, readers are referred to *Standards for Audit of Governmental Organizations, Programs, Activities & Functions,* by the comptroller general of the United States.

GENERAL STANDARDS

The first general standard for governmental auditing states that the full scope of an examination should include a review and evaluation in the three areas of a comprehensive audit: (1) financial and compliance, (2) economy and efficiency, and (3) performance. The needs of the report's users also should be considered in determining the scope of each audit.

The financial and compliance element is designed to determine whether the audited agency is exercising appropriate controls over its assets, liabilities, receipts, and expenditures; maintaining the proper records of such items; and rendering accurate and useful reports in much the same manner as a traditional financial audit. The primary difference from financial auditing is the determination of the entity's compliance with the requirements of the applicable laws and regulations. One initial phase of a comprehensive audit is the auditor's familiarization with the enabling legislation. If necessary, legal opinion should be obtained to determine the appropriate interpretation. The auditor should determine not only that expenditures comply with legal requirements but also that all activities are within the intent of the law.

The second element in the scope of the governmental audit is a review of the efficiency and economy in the use of resources. For example, the auditor should seek to determine whether prescribed procedures are more costly than necessary, whether the activities of the employees contribute toward the stated goals, whether equipment is used efficiently, and whether materials and supplies are protected adequately and are used for appropriate activities in proper quantities. The auditor is not expected to be able to determine whether an entity has reached the maximum practical level of efficiency and economy in the use of resources; however, one should be able to note serious deviations from such a level.

The third element included in the full scope of a comprehensive governmental audit is a review to determine whether the desired results of the program are achieved effectively. This aspect is frequently called *performance auditing.* The auditor looks into the benefits ensuing from the program or activity and seeks to determine whether these benefits indicate that the program is meeting its established objectives. The agency under audit probably has established some criteria for evaluating the program's results, and the auditor should determine the reasonableness of the criteria used, the accuracy of the data collected, and also the appropriateness of the methods used by the agency itself to evaluate the program's effectiveness. Finally, the auditor should determine the reliability of the evaluation of the program's results as developed by the agency. In some cases the auditor may have to accumulate the data in order to evaluate the benefits of a program.

The benefits resulting from many programs cannot be measured in monetary terms and frequently not even in quantitative terms. Nevertheless, some methods of measuring benefits do exist. The expertise necessary to measure the benefits of many federal, state, and local government programs may be beyond the ability and knowledge of the usual auditor with only financial training. Consequently, persons with nonaccounting backgrounds are employed for such audits, and the team of auditors on a particular assignment may include individuals with training in the specialized area being audited. The second general standard of governmental auditing specifies that the auditors assigned to a particular audit should collectively possess adequate professional proficiency for the tasks required.

Independence of mental attitude is required by the third general standard of governmental auditing. Similar to the AICPA standard on independence, the interpretation of this standard is that auditors should be certain that their attitudes and beliefs allow them to be completely objective, and also that there is nothing in their situation which would lead others to doubt their independence. Auditors should consider whether there exist any personal, organizational, or external circumstances that would cause an impairment of independence.

Due professional care is required of auditors in conducting their examinations and in preparing their reports according to the fourth general standard of governmental auditing. An auditor's professional performance should be of a quality appropriate for the complexities of the particular assignment. Exercise of good judgment in selection of the audit tests and procedures and in writing the reports is evidence of due professional care. Obtaining an understanding of the audit scope and objectives with the officials who authorize the audit and with management of the agency under audit is also included in exercise of due professional care. Follow-up work to determine whether corrective action has been taken on recommendations is an additional aspect of due professional care.

EXAMINATION AND EVALUATION STANDARDS

The first standard of examination and evaluation requires that the work be adequately planned. As indicated earlier, audits of the same program may be required by several levels of government or by more than one agency. Planning should embrace, whenever possible, the requirements of all levels of government so that one audit may serve the needs of each interested level of government or agency.

A comprehensive audit usually begins with a preliminary survey to obtain information regarding applicable laws and regulations, general policies, and operating methods. Following this survey, a preliminary review is made to determine whether the agency's systems and procedures are effectively designed; whether they function as designed; whether the system provides satisfactory controls over costs, receipts, and resources; whether the practices followed comply with statutory requirements; and whether the controls result in efficient and economic operations. The preliminary review serves to indicate the appropriate subject matter to be examined in the detailed audit. Tests to determine the significance of items identified should be set out in the audit program. The audit program specifies the scope of the audit, the objectives of the audit, the type and quantity of evidence to be collected, the procedures to be followed, and the nature of the audit report to be prepared.

The second examination and evaluation standard for governmental auditing requires that assistants are to be supervised properly. The work assigned to assistants is expected to be commensurate with their training, experience, and ability.

A review of compliance with legal and regulatory requirements, as the third examination and evaluation standard, is particularly significant in governmental auditing. The auditor should consider applicable legal opinions, court cases, regulatory requirements, and related legislative history in addition to the specific enabling laws and implementing regulations. The auditor should first learn from officials of the audited entity the statutory and regulatory requirements that it is required to follow and then make a review to determine adherence to these requirements.

A review and evaluation of internal controls of the entity being audited is the fourth examination and evaluation standard. The purpose of internal control evaluation is to determine the extent that the system can be relied upon to produce accurate information, to assure compliance with statutory provisions, and to provide for efficient and effective operations. The auditor concentrates the review on those controls that are relevant to the objectives of the audit rather than on all internal controls effective in the entity.

The final examination and evaluation standard specifies that sufficient, competent, and relevant evidence should be obtained by the auditor to afford a reasonable basis for opinions, judgments, conclusions, and recommendations. The evidence may be in a variety of forms, such as physical, documentary, testimonial, and analytical. Testimonial evidence obtained by interviewing persons involved in conducting an entity's program, as well as those receiving services from the entity in some situations, can be extremely important evidence. All types of evidence should meet the tests for sufficiency, competence, and relevance. The test of sufficiency is met when there is enough evidence that another examiner would reach the same conclusion as the auditor. Statistical techniques may be used to establish sufficiency. The validity and completeness of the evidence helps the auditor determine its competence, whereas a logical relationship between the evidence and the issue involved is necessary to establish relevance.

REPORTING STANDARDS

The first standard of reporting concerns the distribution of the auditor's written report to as many interested officials as practicable. Unless the subject matter is classified for security purposes or other valid reasons, the report should be distributed to those officials who authorized the audit, to those designated by law to receive such reports, to those responsible for taking action on the recommendations, to legislators, and to those agencies providing funds. Generally, the reports should be available for distribution or inspection by interested members of the public unless there are statutory or regulatory restrictions.

In order for the information in the auditor's reports to be available to agency and legislative officials on a timely basis, the second reporting standard requires the reports to be issued as promptly as possible, and when required, on or before the dates specified by law or regulation. Interim communication of significant matters is recommended so that officials may be alerted to important findings as soon as possible and, if necessary, so that corrective measures may be instigated.

The content of the auditor's report is the subject of the third reporting standard for governmental auditing. Although the standard stresses conciseness, the auditor is cautioned not to be so concise so as not to fully inform the report's users. Accuracy, completeness, fairness, and objectivity are also stressed. The auditor is cautioned to guard against the tendency to exaggerate or overemphasize deficient performance noted during the audit. There should be adequate support for all data, findings, and conclusions presented in the report, but generally the detailed supporting data are not included in the report.

As with reports on operational auditing, the tone of the report of a comprehensive audit should encourage favorable reaction to the findings and recommendations. Although criticism of past performance may be necessary, the emphasis should be on needed improvements. To present a balanced report, information on satisfactory aspects and noteworthy accomplishments should be included. The auditor usually will make recommendations to effect compliance with legal or regulatory provisions, to attain greater efficiencies or economies, and to accomplish the program goals. When unable to make appropriate recommendations, the auditor should state why not and explain what additional work would be necessary to arrive at recommendations. If the scope of the audit did not extend into areas needing study, the auditor should recommend future examinations of those areas.

Again, like reports on operational auditing, the comprehensive audit report should be reviewed in draft form by officials and involved persons of the entity under audit. The report should contain comments on plans or activities in the entity to correct weaknesses pointed out. Statements of officials' opposition to recommendations should be included along with the auditor's reasons for opposing the position taken by the officials. On the other hand, the auditor should omit an item or modify a position if the original statement is determined to be incorrect.

The fourth and final reporting standard refers to responsibility assumed by the auditor for financial data included in the audit report. In addition to statements concerning fair presentation, use of generally accepted or prescribed accounting principles, and consistency of application, the report should contain information for the users to form an opinion on the effectiveness of the stewardship exercised by the responsible public officials. The auditor should comment if the statements do not provide sufficient disclosures of matters that have a material effect on the financial reports.

Frequently the users of comprehensive audit reports are quite concerned whether or not funds designated for certain purposes were spent for those purposes. Although auditors normally comment only on noncompliance, they may make a positive comment regarding the compliance of fund expenditures with applicable regulations. In commenting upon noncompliance, auditors should furnish sufficient data for the users to judge the extent of noncompliance.

COMPLIANCE AUDITING IN THE PRIVATE SECTOR

Compliance auditing by independent public accountants may become an important aspect of an auditor's work. As governmental regulations increase and business enterprises become subject to more controls in such areas as equal employment opportunities, pollution controls, wage and pension requirements, and pricing policies, the auditor has a responsibility to see that the client complies with applicable laws and regulations. Just as the auditor conducting the comprehensive governmental audit has to become familiar with appropriate laws, the public accountant must be knowledgeable about laws applying to the client. In reviewing the client's internal accounting control system, the auditor should inquire about the procedures and safeguards adopted to ensure their compliance with governmental regulations. A specific search for violations would not normally be within the scope of the usual examination. However, in examining evidence for other aspects of the audit, should the auditor discover evidence of noncompliance with the regulations, further inquiry should be made to reveal the extent of the violation. In some instances the matter may be outside an auditor's expertise, and the advice of other professionals may be required. If the client appears to be subject to penalties for noncompliance, the auditor should be certain that the appropriate liability is reflected on the financial statements. In extreme cases where violation of a government regulation could result in the operations being closed, the auditor should consider whether or not the financial statements should be prepared on a going-concern basis.

Some governmental agencies have developed in the form of audit guides and questionnaires criteria for evaluation of the internal controls of agencies with which they are concerned. Should an auditor be engaged to conduct a study of the procedures employed and to render an opinion based upon these criteria, the report should identify the matters studied and refer to the publication that sets forth the established criteria. As indicated in SAS No. 1 (AU 641), the auditor may express an opinion as to the compliance of the procedures under study with the criteria established by the agency. If material weaknesses are discovered during the study, the auditor's report should describe these in reasonable detail, although they may not be covered by the agency's criteria. Recommendations for action to bring the activities into compliance with the established criteria are usually made by the auditor.

Continuous auditing

As business enterprises increase their use of computers and develop comprehensive financial and management reporting systems, the practice of continuous auditing becomes a realistic possibility for public accountants. This concept of auditing, still somewhat in the developmental stage, proposes an annual review of the internal accounting control system and the financial reporting system. If these systems are designed properly and are functioning as designed, financial statements produced at any time should be reliable. Selected items appearing on the financial statements are chosen for an in-depth examination once every three or four years, and when selected, the examination covers activity for more than the latest year, probably going back to the last detailed review of the item. Rather than selecting items from the financial statements for review, the auditor may take a systems approach and identify a function for examination with activity in the functional area being reviewed for a three- or four-year period. Some audit procedures would not be performed in the current year, but they would have been performed in the last year or two or else would be scheduled for the next year or two as the auditor rotates the procedures over several audit periods. Another approach is for certain audit procedures to be performed each year, but with greater depth every three or four years. The areas selected for in-depth review are rotated so that some areas are audited in detail each year. Obviously, continuous auditing places great emphasis on the internal accounting control and financial reporting systems. Should an auditor detect a weakness in the system, the auditing procedures in the area of the weakness must be extended for the specific period of the audit.

Continuous auditing should enable an auditor to express an opinion on financial statements prepared at various dates. A requirement for the audit of quarterly financial statements issued by publicly held corporations would doubtlessly cause an expansion of the use of continuous auditing.

Supplementary readings

American Institute of Certified Public Accountants. Committee on Relations with the General Accounting Office. *Auditing Standards Estab-*

lished by the GAO—Their Meaning and Significance for CPAs. New York: American Institute of Certified Public Accountants, 1973.

Beisser, Frederick G. "Operational Auditing." *Journal of Accountancy* (October 1978), 59-64.

Bishop, David. "Management and Operations Auditing." *CPA Journal* (November 1974), 69-72.

Bromage, Mary C. "Wording the Management Audit Report." *Journal of Accountancy* (February 1972), 50-57.

Burton, John C. "Management Auditing." *Journal of Accountancy* (May 1968), 41-46.

Carolus, Roger N., and Michael J. Barrett. "Development of the Standards for the Professional Practice of Internal Auditing." *Internal Auditor* (December 1977), 12-14.

Griffin, Richard J., Jr. "Audit of Operational Controls and Non-Financial Data." *Internal Auditor* (June 1976), 73-75.

Hanson, Walter E. "The Role of the Internal Auditor is Changing." *Internal Auditor* (October 1977), 19-24.

Morse, Ellsworth H., Jr. "Performance and Operational Auditing." *Journal of Accountancy* (June 1971), 41-46.

Norgaard, Corine T. "Extending the Boundaries of the Attest Function." *Accounting Review* (July 1972), 433-442.

———. "Professional Accountant's View of Operational Auditing." *Journal of Accountancy* (December 1969), 45-48.

Pomeranz, Felix. "Public Sector Auditing: New Opportunities for CPAs." *Journal of Accountancy* (March 1978), 48-54.

Sawyer, Lawrence B. *The Practice of Modern Internal Auditing.* Orlando, Fla.: The Institute of Internal Auditors, Inc., 1973.

Secoy, Thomas G. "A CPA's Opinion on Management Performance." *Journal of Accountancy* (July 1971), 53-59.

"Standards for the Professional Practice of Internal Auditing." *Internal Auditor* (October 1978), 9-30.

Williams, Harold M. "The Emerging Responsibility of the Internal Auditor." *Internal Auditor* (October 1978), 45-52.

Review questions

11-1. Describe the function of internal auditors in the early days of the profession. How has their function changed in recent years?

11-2. What are the primary differences between internal financial auditing and internal operational auditing in terms of objectives and the nature of the work?

11-3. What is meant by the terms *management's goals, objectives,* and *procedures*? Why do internal auditors need to be familiar with each?

11-4. Present ideas to support the view that the internal auditor should report directly to:
a. the board of directors of the company
b. the financial executive of the company
Where within the company's organizational structure do you believe internal auditors should be located? Why?

11-5. What are some major factors that internal auditors should consider in selecting an area for an operational audit?

11-6. What are the advantages of assigning the staff members to an audit team soon after identification of the area of audit?

11-7. Describe the steps of advance preparation by auditors prior to beginning the investigation and analysis stage of the operational audit.

11-8. In the conduct of an operational audit, auditors usually find some minor deviations from prescribed procedures. To whom should they report such findings? When? In what manner?

11-9. Why is it advisable for operational auditors to review their report in draft stage with the manager and supervisors of the area being audited?

11-10. Describe the content and form of a typical operational audit report.

11-11. Contrast the nature and purpose of an operational audit and a management audit.

11-12. What is covered in the auditor's opinion on a management audit if the report is to be used internally? If used externally?

11-13. Describe the three major divisions of comprehensive auditing.

11-14. How is the audit team on a comprehensive audit able to measure the benefits resulting from government programs?

11-15. What constitutes due professional care in the conduct of a comprehensive audit?

11-16. Describe the steps in planning a comprehensive audit.

11-17. How do auditors determine whether the entity under audit is complying with legal requirements?

11-18. To whom should the audit report of a governmental entity be distributed?

11-19. Describe the contents, in general, of a comprehensive audit report.

11-20. How does continuous auditing differ from auditing on an annual basis?

11-21. What are the advantages of continuous auditing?

Decision problems

11-22. Both the Institute of Internal Auditors and the American Institute of Certified Public Accountants stress the importance of auditors' being independent.
a. Distinguish the difference in meaning, if any, of independence as used by the two organizations.
b. Can an equal degree of independence be attained by both internal auditors and external auditors? Why?

c. In what ways can internal auditors attain the greatest degree of independence within the corporate entity?

11-23. As an experienced auditor on the internal audit staff of Albany Company, you have been advised of a new assignment as the auditor in charge of the operational audit of the leasing activities of the company. You are told which members of the internal auditing staff are available for assignment. You are to plan and supervise the conduct of the audit and the writing of the report.

Describe the preparation and planning necessary prior to beginning the actual investigation and analysis phase of your operational audit. Point out the sources you would consult and the information you would seek from each. Also indicate any action you would take on selection of staff assistants and their instructions.

11-24. As the internal auditor of Cross Manufacturing Company, you are performing an operational audit of scrap sales. You have learned that large quantities of scrap metal are delivered daily from the production department to a special area adjoining the shipping dock. The area is under the supervision of the shipping clerk. About twice a month the shipping clerk calls a friend who is a scrap dealer to come pick up the scrap metal. In the presence of the shipping clerk, the dealer weighs the scrap and gives the clerk a check and receipt marked paid for the price of the scrap. The clerk signs the receipt and sends both receipt and check to the accounts receivable clerk for processing. A sales invoice is prepared, marked paid, and sent to the scrap dealer.

a. What additional information do you need to be able to complete your audit?

b. Based upon the information presented, what are the major points you would include in your report?

11-25. In performing an operational audit on the production operation of the Athens Manufacturing Company, the internal auditor seeks to review the determination of unit costs and variances.

Describe the major procedures the auditor would use in performing this phase of the examination.

11-26. The Ellis Manufacturing Company has branches located in numerous cities in several mid-Atlantic states. Each branch is small and only one office clerk is employed at each location. Cash and credit sales are made at the branches upon orders sent in by sales representatives who work out of each branch.

a. As internal auditor, what are some of the primary questions you would want answered in the conduct of your operational audit of the branch operations?

b. Based upon the limited information furnished, what recommendations do you make for improving the controls over inventory and cash?

11-27. Your client, Tifton Company, is under a court injunction to reduce by December 1, 1982 its pollution of the atmosphere by 60 percent from the level of pollution at December 1, 1979. You are performing interim-audit work for the year ended December 31, 1982, and have examined persuasive evidence that the $35 million pollution-control device just installed has reduced pollution by only 35 percent. Assume substantial evidence of a convincing nature is *not* available for you to examine by the time you do your year-end work to indicate a significantly greater reduction of pollution.

Describe the effect the situation presented will have on your audit report.

11-28. Dale Olliff, president of your company, has been discussing the company's internal operations with the presidents of several other multidivision companies. Olliff discovered that most of them have an internal audit staff. The activities of the staffs at other companies include financial audits, operational audits, and sometimes management audits.

Describe the meaning of the following terms as they relate to the internal audit function:

a. financial auditing
b. operational auditing
c. management auditing

CMA adapted

11-29. One definition and discussion of internal control states: "Internal control comprises the plan of organization and all of the coordinate methods and measures adopted within a business to safeguard its assets, check the accuracy and reliability of its accounting data, promote operational efficiency, and encourage adherence to prescribed managerial policies. This definition possibly is broader than the meaning sometimes attributed to the term. It recognizes that a 'system' of internal control extends beyond those matters which relate directly to the functions of the accounting and financial departments."

a. Identify the elements of this definition that are particularly applicable to operational audits performed by internal auditors and relate them to the objectives of operational auditing.
b. An operational audit of any particular functional segment of a business may entail three distinct, yet related areas of investigation: policy, control, and evaluation of performance. Discuss in general terms the audit methodology that might be applicable to each phase.

CMA adapted

11-30. Gollum and Cole, a local CPA firm, received an invitation to bid for the audit of a local, federally assisted program. The audit is to be conducted in accordance with the audit standards published by the General Accounting Office (GAO), a federal auditing agency. Gollum and Cole has become familiar with the GAO standards and recognizes that the GAO standards are not inconsistent with generally accepted auditing standards (GAAS). The GAO standards, unlike GAAS, are concerned with more than the financial aspects of an entity's operations. The GAO standards broaden the definition of auditing by establishing that the full scope of an audit should encompass the following elements:

a. an examination of *financial* transactions, accounts, and reports, including an evaluation of *compliance* with applicable laws and regulations
b. a review of *efficiency* and *economy* in the use of resources, such as personnel and equipment

c. a review to determine whether desired results are effectively achieved (*program results*)

Gollum and Cole has been engaged to perform the audit of the program and the audit is to encompass all three elements.

1. Gollum and Cole should perform sufficient audit work to satisfy the *financial* and *compliance* element of the GAO standards. What should such audit work determine?
2. After making appropriate review and inquiries, what uneconomical practices or inefficiencies should Gollum and Cole be alert to, in satisfying the *efficiency* and *economy* element encompassed by the GAO standards?
3. After making appropriate review and inquiries, what should Gollum and Cole consider to satisfy the *program results* element encompassed by the GAO standards?

AICPA adapted

11-31. Delta Machine Company is considering developing an internal audit department. A few years ago the company began an expansion program which included the acquisition of new businesses some of which are located quite distant from the home office. Delta has used the acquired managements in most past acquisitions and expects to continue to do so. The corporate organization is decentralized with the parent company (Delta Machine) setting the general policy. Divisions and subsidiary managements are quite autonomous; their performance is measured against budgets and return on investment targets established at the beginning of each year. The units of Delta manufacture and market their products. The present company-wide volume is $150,000,000.

Delta Machine has been audited by the CPA firm in which you are a manager. You have supervised the audit of Delta for the past three years. You have been asked by Delta to prepare a report on the activities that could be undertaken by an internal audit department.

a. Prepare a report which describes:
1. the different objectives of the external vs. internal auditor.
2. the types of audits that an internal audit department might be expected to perform.
3. the relationship of the internal auditor to the external auditor.

b. The company has indicated that you will be asked to head the internal audit department if it is established. Describe the change(s) in your audit philosophy and changes in your relationship to the firm management, if any, you believe should occur if you were to take this job.

CMA adapted

III

Audit Objectives and Procedures

Auditing procedures and the objectives they are to fulfill represent the emphasis of the chapters in Part III. These chapters are designed to convey an understanding of the process of determining audit objectives with respect to the various parts of financial statements and designing appropriate audit procedures to accomplish them. Audit objectives and procedures for several major financial statement areas are presented and explained.

12

Auditing Cash Balances, Receivables, Revenues, and Related Areas

The planning and execution of an audit is an exercise in defining, pursuing, and achieving objectives. In carrying out this exercise, auditors must organize the seemingly nebulous task of auditing a company so that the objectives and procedures are defined sharply. Also, the work must be planned so that it may be performed in a number of individual tasks which will, when completed, fit together into a comprehensive examination of the financial statements.

This organization process subdivides the audit so that several members of the audit team may simultaneously perform different aspects of the work. In addition, this process helps assure the auditor in charge of the engagement that no areas are left unexamined and that no duplication of effort arises. The format upon which the audit is organized may be based on cycles of business operations, operational units, or the financial statements. In any of these formats, the auditor conducts a coordinated examination of all related areas of the business. The material presented in the four chapters comprising this part assumes the modified financial statement format; however, the concepts presented may be applied by the auditor to any format selected.

The following examples of audit work organization reflect the interrelationships among various areas of a given business:

1. The audit of inventory may be coordinated with the examination of purchases and cost of goods sold.

2. The verification of property, plant, and equipment usually should be combined with the analysis of depreciation, accumulated depreciation, repair and maintenance expenses, and the examination of rental income.
3. The audit of investments usually should include the verification of investment income and any gains or losses realized upon the sale or exchange of investments.
4. The examination of accounts receivable frequently is coordinated with the audit of revenues and cash receipts.
5. Liabilities, interest expense, and cash disbursements may be audited concurrently.
6. The audit of capital stock and retained earnings should be integrated with the audit of dividends.

With some reflection, it can be seen that careful organization of audit assignments not only increases the efficiency with which the work is performed but also enhances the evidence gathered and the conclusions drawn by the auditor. This is because evidence gathered by one procedure in a well-organized audit will tend to either corroborate or disaffirm other audit evidence. For example, liabilities may tend to validate interest expense, and interest charges may be used as evidence to support the recorded liabilities. This line of thought is part of what is often termed the systems approach to auditing and is based on sound reasoning. This type of audit planning and execution gives auditors a deeper understanding of their clients' operations than they otherwise might achieve.

Planning the audit

The overall purpose of an audit examination is to give auditors sufficient evidence upon which to base an opinion on the financial statements as a whole. However, auditors cannot approach the audit by looking at all evidence at once, nor can the evidence be examined in a disorganized fashion. They must plan the audit and determine what procedures to employ in examining each account or related area. In planning the audit and developing the audit programs, the auditor in charge needs to consider three important questions about every area of the examination:

1. What is needed to provide good internal control over this area of the business and what degree of internal control presently exists?
2. What are the audit objectives in examining this area of the business? In other words, what should the auditor establish with regard to the account or accounts in question?
3. What audit procedures are necessary to enable the auditor to accomplish these objectives?

After these questions are answered and the answers are evaluated, *audit programs* may be prepared which provide detailed direction about specific audit procedures to be performed. This sequence of audit planning is essential for any well-executed examination. Desired objectives for each area of the audit must be clearly recognized by the auditor. *These objectives will logically suggest the major auditing procedures that are appropriate.* Internal control requirements and the degree of the client's compliance with the internal accounting control system have a strong influence on procedures selected and the extent of testing included in the required audit program.

Asset audit objectives

Although the audit objectives may vary slightly from one type of asset to another, general objectives apply to nearly all assets. These objectives are discussed in the following paragraphs and are illustrated by examples of their application to specific assets. The concept of determining appropriate audit procedures by reference to desired objectives should be noted throughout the discussion. Some general procedures customarily associated with various assets are presented, but specific auditing procedures are discussed later.

Existence Verifying existence should be a prime objective in the audit of every asset. A procedure logically suggested by this objective, especially in the case of tangible assets, is direct examination of the asset by the auditor. Confirmation (written inquiry) often provides evidence to support the existence of an asset, as do oral inquiry and inspection of documents. In some cases, qualitative as well as quantitative evidence is needed to establish the existence of an asset. In these circumstances special procedures are often required to give the auditor necessary assurance. These procedures could include retention of an expert to verify the existence of assets such as diamonds, exotic chemicals, and others. The qualitative aspects of existence are closely related to the objective of valuation discussed in the following paragraph.

Valuation Establishing market value is a primary audit objective for many assets and an objective of lesser importance for others. Inventories, receivables, and investments are examples of assets that normally require audit procedures designed to gather evidence regarding value. Fixed assets, for example, usually do not require such procedures. Examples of audit procedures used to obtain evidence regarding value include (1) reference to market quotations in the case of investments; (2) inspection of current price lists, catalogues, or other cost data, in the case of inventory;

(3) aging and confirmation, in the case of receivables; and (4) independent appraisal.

Authorization An auditor must be assured that the assets of a client represent authorized acquisitions. The authority for the acquisition may be stated in general terms, such as company policy that inventory be purchased upon requisition by the production department and after comparison of prices by the purchasing department. The authorization for accounts receivable is also usually general in that the credit policy authorizes credit sales to customers who meet prescribed credit requirements. Specific authorization usually is required for the acquisition of major fixed assets and investments in other companies. In such cases the board of directors, or perhaps an investment committee of the board, votes to approve the acquisitions. The auditor should follow the procedure of inspecting company procedures manuals and other documents to determine the authorized general policy and of reading minutes of meetings of the board of directors or other groups to verify specific authorizations. The signature of a properly designated employee on the purchase order for office supplies or the supervisor's signature on the voucher for a cash advance to an employee are examples of evidence the auditor should inspect in order to gain assurance of proper authorization.

Ownership The ownership of assets must be established to the auditor's satisfaction. In many cases possession of the asset, supported by a bill of sale or invoice, is sufficient to evidence ownership. This is usually true for inventory, securities, machinery, and most personal property. Ownership of accounts receivable can be evidenced by sales invoices and subsequent cash receipts. Vehicle ownership may be further evidenced by title certificates, registration documents, and tax receipts. Ownership of real property may be established by inspection of deeds, tax receipts, closing statements, and other legal documents. In some cases the auditor may consider further inquiry regarding real property ownership. Appropriate procedures for this inquiry could include title verification by an attorney and communication of the result directly to the auditor.

Restrictions An audit objective closely related to establishing ownership of assets is the determination of whether restrictions on ownership exist. Any ownership restrictions on assets must be disclosed in the financial statements. Further, these restrictions often require modified financial statement presentation for the particular asset. For these reasons, it is essential that the auditor employ procedures designed to call attention to any existing restrictions.

Common procedures used to detect asset restrictions include review of bond covenants or any agreements with creditors, examination of official public records to determine whether any liens are recorded against the client's property, and obtaining written representations from the client regarding the existence of pledged assets. In the case of some assets such as securities, the pledged property is often held by the secured party; thus, an attempt at physical examination will lead to discovery of the absence of the assets and the existence of the lien.

Accuracy of Amount An audit objective common to all assets is the determination that amounts are accurately presented. This objective is closely related to establishing the quantitative existence of the asset, but it focuses more specifically on mathematical accuracy. Audit procedures employed to attain this objective include physical and external verification such as counting and confirmation, as well as inspection and verification of the client's accounting records and supporting documents. Not only should the accuracy of the amount initially recorded be determined, but also the reasonableness and accuracy of any amounts subsequently allocated to expense should be established. The original cost of prepaid expenses, depreciable fixed assets, and intangibles usually is allocated over several future periods. The period over which a cost is spread should be reasonable in the auditor's judgment, and audit procedures should include a determination of the accuracy of the amount allocated to expense.

Usefulness For many assets, an audit objective is to form a conclusion regarding the use potential of the property. It was mentioned earlier that for property, plant, and equipment market values are often not relevant. An indication that an asset is obsolete or is used in the manufacture of a product line likely to be discontinued would be important information to the auditor. Further, inventories that are obsolete or otherwise unsalable are other examples of assets with impaired usefulness. In cases such as these, the diminished usefulness of the assets should result in a write-down or disclosure in the financial statements. Audit procedures designed to establish the degree of usefulness include studies of product-line sales records, inventory turnover, and physical examination of the asset.

Financial Statement Presentation A final, but critical, audit objective is the determination that the various assets are presented properly in the financial statements. This objective focuses specifically on financial statement classification and may be achieved by analysis of the characteristics of each asset and by consciously applying classification rules that include appropriate descriptions, methods of valuation, parenthetical disclosure of alternative values, references to footnotes, and description of liens and restrictions. The auditor should be aware that a misclassification or an improper description in the financial statements may be as serious as a misstatement of amount. Accordingly, each audit should include procedures to assure that proper financial statement presentation is employed.

Specific auditing procedures

In the following sections of this chapter and in Chapter 13, typical audit examinations for several important assets and related areas are described. Procedures appropriate for the audit of cash balances and of accounts receivable and related areas are described in the remaining sections of this chapter, and audits of inventories, fixed assets, investments and related areas are described in Chapter 13. In each case, the description of the audit examination is intended not to be exhaustive but rather to illustrate important procedures to readers.

The audit of cash balances

As in the audit of all phases of the business, procedures for auditing cash should be derived logically from the auditor's objectives in auditing the area. Since cash is considered a high risk asset that is relatively difficult to control, auditing procedures for cash tend to be more extensive and more detailed than procedures in some other areas. As in all cases, the auditor's evaluation of the client's internal accounting control over cash should heavily influence the extent and intensity of the auditing procedures employed.

Specific audit objectives that relate to cash include verification of existence, ownership, and the accuracy of amounts; discovery of any restrictions; and determination of proper financial statement presentation. From these objectives appropriate auditing procedures may be derived to compose the audit program for cash. The cash amount presented on the balance sheet of a company normally consists of two components, cash on hand and cash on deposit. Since each component has different characteristics, their audit procedures are considered separately.

CASH ON HAND

Cash on hand usually consists of both imprest cash funds and undeposited receipts from customers. The primary audit procedures employed for both types of cash on hand are (1) counting by the auditor, (2) subsequent agreement of count totals to the accounting records, (3) examination of items such as customers' checks and petty cash vouchers for regularity and apparent validity, and (4) observing the deposit of the customers' receipts in the client's bank.

Counting In counting cash on hand the auditor must exercise control over all cash and other negotiable assets to prevent *substitution.* Substitution refers to the act of concealing a cash shortage by transporting funds from one place to another or by converting other negotiable assets into cash so that the same funds are included more than once in the total. The auditor must maintain control over cash by *simultaneous verification* or by other means to prevent substitution of funds. Simultaneous verification may be accomplished by assigning staff auditors to each location of the business where cash and other negotiable assets are kept so that all cash may be counted at the same time. Other means of exercising control include having all cash brought to a central point for counting and the use of gummed paper seals for sealing all cash depositories so that they may be counted sequentially with assurance that there has been no substitution. Negotiable assets, such as notes receivable and marketable securities, must be controlled at the same time cash is controlled. This may be accomplished by having these items under the auditor's surveillance during the count, but more likely it is accomplished by assuring that no one has access to the items. Marketable securities, for example, may be in safe deposit at the bank with instructions that no one be admitted to the safe deposit box unless the auditor is present.

The auditor should insist on being observed by an employee of the client continuously while the cash count is underway. Many auditors prefer that the client's employees perform the actual count while the auditor observes and records the necessary information. The reason for such precautions is that, should a shortage in cash be exposed, the auditor may be blamed for it, since the custodian may easily charge, "It was all there when I gave it to you." After the count, the custodian may be asked to sign a statement acknowledging that the cash was returned intact as listed on the auditor's count sheet.

Agreement of Totals and Examination of Items After cash on hand has been counted, the petty cash totals should be compared to the general ledger, and the total of undeposited receipts should be traced to the cash receipts records. While the counts are underway, the particulars of any check, draft, disbursement voucher, or other item that appears questionable should be noted in the working papers. Questionable items should be investigated until a satisfactory explanation is determined for each matter. The working papers should contain a notation of the evidence or an explanation that the auditor used to answer these questions. Examples of questionable items are checks with old dates, personal checks of cash custodians, undated or old petty cash disbursement vouchers, IOUs, checks of affiliated companies, transfer checks, and so forth. As of the balance sheet date, all petty cash funds should be cleared of vouchers by replenishment so that cash and expenses will be stated properly on the financial statements. Unresolved questionable items or unreimbursed petty cash funds at year end may necessitate an audit adjusting entry.

Observing Deposit To complete the audit of cash on hand, the auditor should determine that all checks included in the cash on hand are deposited in the client's bank. This procedure gives the auditor assurance regarding the validity of these items. Should the checks be fraudulent or worthless, they will be returned by the bank, and the auditor will have the opportunity to detect this return when reviewing a subsequent bank statement. If the checks are not deposited while the auditor controls cash on hand, there is no assurance that a worthless check was not previously placed in the cash on hand as a device to conceal a cash shortage.

The presence of company transfer checks and checks of related companies in the cash on hand deserves special mention. If at year end these checks are included in cash on hand (or in transit to the bank), then they must be deducted as outstanding in the reconciliation of the account upon which they are drawn. Otherwise, cash will be overstated by the amount of the checks. This is essentially a form of the defalcation pattern known as *kiting,* which will be discussed later in this chapter. In this situation, each check of a related or affiliated company or each transfer check that is included in cash on hand should be traced to the outstanding check list of its respective bank reconciliation.

The Element of Surprise The element of *surprise* should be considered in all cash audits. In employing this tool, an auditor faces conflicting goals. First, if the auditor believes that it is necessary to verify cash as of balance sheet date, the surprise element is lost. If a surprise cash count is desired, the auditor cannot, year after year, verify cash only as of the year end. Many auditors believe that when internal control is adequate, surprise may be given priority, and a year-end verification is not necessary. In cases where poor internal control exists, the auditor typically insists on a year-end verification. A solution that may be feasible is two verifications, one on a surprise basis and the other at year end. In some cases surprise is accomplished by making two counts of the same fund during the audit period. The custodian may have "window dressed" the fund for the first count, assuming that the auditor would make the count. After the first count, the fictitious items, unapproved IOUs, and other inappropriate items may be replaced in the fund. A second count by the auditor is unusual, and such a surprise count might reveal irregularities. These dual procedures afford the auditor increased assurance regarding cash handling in the business.

CASH ON DEPOSIT

In verifying cash on deposit, an auditor employs quite different procedures from those used in auditing cash on hand. Rather than dealing with cash in the physical sense, as with cash on hand, the auditor deals with documentation that supports the existence of cash.

Preliminary Procedures Procedures for verification of cash on deposit should begin at the time cash on hand is verified, that is, on the *verification date.* One procedure that should be executed at that time is the collection of cash *cutoff data.* Cutoff data that are needed for the verification of cash on deposit include a record of all cash receipts and all cash disbursements immediately preceding the verification date. The auditor should record in the working papers the totals of cash receipts for the last few days of the period and the date, number, and amount of the last few checks written before the verification date. These amounts will later be agreed to information that supports the bank reconciliation prepared as of the verification date. For example, in a usual situation the auditor would expect cash receipts cutoff data to correspond to the bank deposits made near the end of the period. The last cash receipt recorded should agree with the count of undeposited receipts made on the verification date and with the "deposits-in-transit" shown on the bank reconciliation. The cash disbursement cutoff data collected usually should correspond to items that appear on the outstanding check list supporting the reconciliation. There should be no outstanding checks listed with a number subsequent to the last check recorded as cutoff data. Conversely, any check included in the cutoff data should either be returned by the bank in the current month's statement or be included in the list of outstanding checks. Any lack of agreement between the cutoff data and the information supporting the bank reconciliation can mean cash is misstated as of the verification date.

Another procedure relating to cash on deposit that may be performed on the verification date is preparation and mailing of *bank confirmations* (Figure 12-1), which are requests for information about the client's bank balances and transactions. These requests should be sent to all banks with which the client currently does business as well as those the client has dealt with in the recent past. The information received from the banks on the confirmation forms is used in the verification of cash on deposit as well as of liabilities and contingencies. Regarding cash, the primary information gained from the bank confirmation is the amount on deposit, account designation, and assurance from the bank that the funds are subject to withdrawal on demand.

Figure 12-1 Standard Bank Confirmation Inquiry

STANDARD BANK CONFIRMATION INQUIRY
Approved 1966 by
AMERICAN INSTITUTE OF CERTIFIED PUBLIC ACCOUNTANTS
and
BANK ADMINISTRATION INSTITUTE (FORMERLY NABAC)

ORIGINAL
To be mailed to accountant

_______________ 19____

Dear Sirs:

Your completion of the following report will be sincerely appreciated. IF THE ANSWER TO ANY ITEM IS "NONE," PLEASE SO STATE. Kindly mail it in the enclosed stamped, addressed envelope *direct* to the accountant named below.

Report from

Yours truly,

____
(ACCOUNT NAME PER BANK RECORDS)

(Bank) _______________

By _______________
Authorized Signature

____

Bank customer should check here if confirmation of bank balances only (item 1) is desired. ☐

____

NOTE—If the space provided is inadequate, please enter totals hereon and attach a statement giving full details as called for by the columnar headings below.

Accountant

Dear Sirs:

1. At the close of business on_______________19____our records showed the following balance(s) to the **credit** of the above named customer. In the event that we could readily ascertain whether there were any balances to the credit of the customer not designated in this request, the appropriate information is given below.

AMOUNT	ACCOUNT NAME	ACCOUNT NUMBER	Subject to Withdrawal by Check?	Interest Bearing? Give Rate
$				

2. The customer was directly liable to us in respect of loans, acceptances, etc., at the close of business on that date in the total amount of $____________, as follows:

AMOUNT	DATE OF LOAN OR DISCOUNT	DUE DATE	INTEREST		DESCRIPTION OF LIABILITY, COLLATERAL, SECURITY INTERESTS, LIENS, ENDORSERS, ETC.
			Rate	Paid to	
$					

3. The customer was contingently liable as endorser of notes discounted and/or as guarantor at the close of business on that date in the total amount of $____________, as below:

AMOUNT	NAME OF MAKER	DATE OF NOTE	DUE DATE	REMARKS
$				

4. Other direct or contingent liabilities, open letters of credit, and relative collateral, were

____

5. Security agreements under the Uniform Commercial Code or any other agreements providing for restrictions, not noted above, were as follows (if officially recorded, indicate date and office in which filed).

____

Yours truly, (Bank) _______________

Date_______________19____

By _______________
Authorized Signature

Additional copies of this form are available from the American Institute of CPAs, 1211 Avenue of the Americas, New York, N. Y. 10036

Further documentation that must be requested from the bank to support the auditor's verification of cash balances is the *cutoff bank statement*. This is a bank statement covering the period *subsequent* to the verification date. The auditor may wait and use the next regular monthly bank statement for this purpose; however, the auditor frequently will want to begin the verification work of cash on deposit before the end of the next month and so, with the client's authorization, will request that the bank send an early statement. Use of the cutoff bank statement also relieves the auditor from handling as many canceled checks as would be handled with the regular month-end statement. Many auditors use a minimum time period of ten business days after the verification date as the time to ask the bank to "cut off" the statement period and send the statement and canceled checks. Auditors commonly ask that they receive the cutoff statement directly from the bank so that they have assurance that the statement has not been tampered with before it is subjected to audit examination.

Final Procedures The final audit procedures for cash on deposit (that is, those necessarily accomplished sometime after the verification date) center upon the bank reconciliation. The auditor should obtain from the client a bank reconciliation as of the verification date, or, if necessary, should prepare one. A particularly useful form of bank reconciliation for audit purposes is the proof-of-cash (Figure 12-2). This expanded form of reconciliation analyzes bank transactions for a period (such as the month) preceding the verification date as well as the bank balance as of the verification date. The analysis of transactions during the period reveals any activity in the bank account that was not recorded on the books, or vice versa. For example, a cash shortage concealed by an unrecorded compensating deposit near year end would be detected by a proof-of-cash. Regardless of the form of reconciliation, the auditor must verify all the reconciling items, that is, those that explain the difference between the general ledger balance and the balance shown on the bank statement. The auditor should recognize that each reconciling item is a potential vehicle for covering, at least temporarily, a cash defalcation. The most common reconciling items together with the usual audit verification procedures are:

1. *Deposits-in-transit.* Certain cash shortages may be temporarily hidden simply by overstating deposits-in-transit. On the verification date, the auditor should have counted and, if necessary, should have controlled all cash on hand until deposited in the bank. Therefore, all deposits-in-transit shown on the reconciliation should agree with amounts recorded in the auditor's cash-count working papers. Cash is not verified to the extent that any deposits-in-transit are not counted by the auditor. Should it be discovered that deposits-in-transit are listed on the reconciliation which were not seen by the auditor on the verification date,

Figure 12-2 Proof-of-Cash

Eagle Corporation
Proof of Cash
December 31, 19X5

	Bank Reconciliation 11-30	December, 19X5 Receipts	Disbursements	Bank Reconciliation 12-31
Balances per Bank	7630842* ʌ	8460377 ʌ	8169089 ʌ	7922130 C √ ʌ
Deposits in Transit:				
11-30	578024*	⟨578024⟩ ʌ		ʌ
12-31		167207 ʌ		167207
Outstanding Checks:				
11-30	⟨348011⟩*		⟨348011⟩	√
12-31			544005 √	⟨544005⟩
Adjusted Bank Balances	7860855*	8049560	8365083	7545332 T/B
Balances Per Books	7860855*	8049560	8280450	7629965 √
N.S.F. Check Returned			84633 √+	⟨84633⟩ √+
Adjusted Book Balances	7860855*	8049560	8365083	7545332 T/B

Prepared by G.M.W. 1-19-x6
Reviewed by R.J.S. 1-28-x6

* Per client's 11-30 reconciliation.
ʌ Per December bank statement.
C Agreed to bank confirmation.
√ Agreed to cut off bank statement.
√ Per client's 12-31 outstanding check list. See verification work ⟨G-21⟩.
√+ Examined debit memo returned with bank statement. See adjusting entry at ⟨G-1⟩.
√ Agreed to G/L.
ʌ Counted and controlled to bank. See authenticated deposit slip at ⟨G-23⟩.
T/B Agreed to working trial balance.

extended procedures, such as a surprise second cash count, should be employed.

2. *Outstanding checks.* Omissions from the outstanding check list offer another method of temporarily hiding a cash shortage. The cutoff bank statement is used by the auditor to verify the accuracy of the list of outstanding checks. The canceled checks returned with the cutoff statement should be compared with the list of outstanding checks. Any canceled check that is dated on or before the verification date and is cleared by the bank after that date must, by definition, have been outstanding. If such a check has been omitted from the outstanding check list, the reason for its omission must be determined.

   The existence of old checks that are carried as outstanding for long periods afford a special opportunity for hiding a cash defalcation. Should a dishonest employee know it is unlikely that a particular outstanding check will be presented for payment, the employee could easily omit this check from the outstanding check list and thereby hide a cash shortage of like amount. Many auditors recommend that old outstanding checks be returned to cash on a regular basis to block this avenue for defalcation.

3. *Other reconciling items.* The verification of other reconciling items should be accomplished by examining appropriate documents that support the items. Many items, such as returned checks, bank collections, and service charges, will require adjustment of the cash account to achieve proper financial statement presentation.

Other procedures that remain to be performed before the cash audit is completed include:

1. Coordinate all cutoff data that were recorded on the verification date to the cutoff bank statement (for cash receipts data) and to the outstanding check list (for cash disbursements data).
2. Determine that all information on the bank confirmation agrees with information on the client's records and the audit work papers.
3. Ascertain from the cutoff statement, or from direct communication with the bank if necessary, whether any items contained in the deposits-in-transit were returned for insufficient funds or were otherwise uncollected. Should it be discovered that items were returned, appropriate adjusting entries may be necessary.
4. Checks that appear on the outstanding check list but that are not returned with the cutoff statement may need to be investigated by gathering further evidence of validity. Such investigation is especially important when the checks are for an unusually large amount, are to an affiliated company, are to a payee unfamiliar to the auditor, or indicate some other reason to question their validity. The investigation may be conducted by examining supporting documents and entries

such as paid invoices, check copies, entry in cash disbursement records, and so on. Further evidence may be gathered after the fact by examining the related canceled check during the next audit.

5. An integral part of the cash audit involves testing cash transactions during the year. Cash receipts and disbursement records should be tested for accuracy, proof-of-cash analyses may be prepared for interim periods, and supporting documents should be examined. The concept of testing transactions and its relationship to internal control are discussed further in Chapters 7, 8, and 15.
6. The auditor must ascertain what manner of financial statement presentation is appropriate. In many cases it is proper for the client to include aggregate cash balances under the single caption *Cash* on the balance sheet. Complicating factors such as overdrafts, compensating balances, time deposits, certificates of deposit, foreign deposits, and withdrawal restrictions dictate special reporting procedures.

INTERIM VERIFICATION

In the preceding discussion of the cash audit, it was assumed that the verification date and the balance sheet date coincided. Previously the conflict between the year-end and the surprise verification was discussed, and recommendations were made regarding resolution of this conflict. Most auditors contend that in proper circumstances cash may be verified at any date during the period under audit. When such an interim verification date is used, the transactions occurring between the verification date and the balance sheet date are reviewed as part of the year-end audit procedures.

INTERNAL CONTROL OVER CASH

Internal control concepts and techniques of evaluating internal accounting control were presented in Chapter 7. Some specific procedures that indicate good internal accounting control over cash are discussed in the following paragraphs. Differences in the operations and the accounting systems of various businesses make internal accounting control evaluation one of the more difficult judgments required of auditors. However, similarities in good control procedures enable a general study of this area.

Separation of Functions A cardinal principle in internal accounting control, as discussed in Chapter 7, is that the asset custody function should be separated in the organization from the record-keeping function. In the classical form of corporate organization, this principle, as it applies to cash, may be implemented by assigning the cash-handling function to the treasurer and the function of maintaining the general accounting records regarding cash to the controller.

Separation of Duties Within the functional areas described above, duties of individual employees should be so arranged that no single employee performs a complete transaction from beginning to end. For example, if in the treasurer's office, one employee receives cash, writes receipts, prepares the bank deposit, and conveys the deposit to the bank, several opportunities are likely to exist for the person to perpetrate and temporarily cover a cash defalcation. Should these duties be separated among several employees, the probability of defalcation would be lessened. In the controller's office, if one employee is empowered to make complete entries in the accounting records, that person may be able to permanently conceal errors and irregularities. For instance, the employee may credit a friend's account receivable and make a corresponding debit to an account such as Miscellaneous Expense.

Daily Intact Deposits Daily deposits of cash receipts are another feature of a good accounting control system. A daily deposit forces an additional accounting for cash receipts and tends to reduce the amount of cash on hand at any one time. Furthermore, in the event cash transactions need to be reconstructed or when cash is audited, this direct relationship between deposits and daily receipts is valuable. Additional benefits of depositing cash receipts intact are that company disbursements may not be made from cash receipts and that customer checks may not be cashed from daily receipts. Intact deposits create an item-by-item relationship between the bank deposit and cash receipts.

Use of Petty Cash Funds Imprest funds focus responsibility and allow the company to keep extraneous transactions out of daily receipts.

Well-Defined Disbursement Procedures Disbursement checks should be supported by a formal check request, which has been initiated and approved by individuals who have been delegated such authority. A check request normally should be accompanied by supporting documents, such as an invoice, purchase order, receiving report, and authorization voucher. The invoice should be canceled in some form to prevent duplicate payments. Checks should be signed only after the supporting documents have been reviewed and found to be in order. If the authorized signature is affixed to the check by some mechanical means, control of the device must be maintained in order to verify that the number of impressions made by the machine agrees with the number of checks authorized to be signed. Signed checks should not be returned to individuals who initiated or authorized the request but should be sent directly to payees. Supplies of blank checks should be controlled to minimize the opportunity for unauthorized use.

Bank Reconciliations Reconciliation of each bank account should be accomplished monthly, or, in the case of extremely active accounts, more frequently, preferably by a person who has no other cash responsibility. Punctual reconciliation is an effective method of assuring prompt discovery of errors. Since the bank reconciliation may be used to hide a cash defalcation, a person with no other cash responsibilities should perform this duty; presumably this person would have no motive to distort the cash balance.

Other Control Matters As discussed in Chapter 7, adequate internal control over cash should include use of fidelity bonds. These bonds do not alleviate the need for an adequate system of control, but they complement control procedures by further safeguarding assets. Also, the existence of an effective internal audit staff is another indication of strong internal control. Internal auditors enhance the effectiveness of the internal control system by employing procedures that insure the system is properly designed and employed. Examples of the cash procedures performed by the internal audit staff are surprise cash counts, review of bank reconciliations, analysis of the accounting control system for cash, and tests of compliance with the system.

CASH DEFALCATIONS

There have probably been as many methods devised to perpetrate cash defalcations as there have been perpetrators. For this reason, defalcation patterns are difficult to classify. One characteristic that may be used to help describe types of defalcations is concealment. Concealed defalcations usually are considered to be those for which a compensating entry has been made in the accounting records so that the shortage is not apparent. An example of a concealed defalcation is an abstraction of cash receipts followed by an entry debiting an expense and crediting cash. Usually, concealment can be accomplished only where internal accounting control is poor and allows a person access to cash as well as authority to make journal entries. An unconcealed defalcation is one that is not accompanied by a compensating accounting entry. Therefore, shortages resulting from unconcealed defalcations may be hidden only temporarily or not hidden at all.

Two patterns of unconcealed defalcations are common. These are *lapping* and *kiting*. Lapping is usually accomplished with collections on accounts receivable. The procedure employed is one of abstracting cash collections and replacing the cash abstracted with subsequent collections. The perpetrator involved in lapping is usually in a position to disguise the source of some receipts each day. After the initial abstraction, the employee reports some of the receipts of a subsequent day as being from customers who actually made payment on a preceding day. The customer will normally not be aware of a single day's delay in the posting of the account. If the delay is for several days, the customer may realize the discrepancy. An

Table 12-1 A Simple Lapping Operation

Date	*Customer and amount paid*	*Customer and amount recorded*	*Amount deposited*	*Amount withheld*
12/29	A — $100	$ 0	$ 0	$100
12/30	B — 100	A — 100	100	100
12/31	C — 60			
	D — 40	B — 100	100	100
1/2	E — 100	C — 60		
		D — 40	100	100

illustration of lapping is presented in Table 12-1. In this example the defalcation is accomplished through the one-day delay in recording and depositing customers' receipts. It can be seen that while a substitution, or lap, must be made each day to cover the cash abstraction, the perpetrator has use of company funds throughout the operation. Large-scale lapping schemes may require elaborate records and have in some cases been discovered because they became too complex for the perpetrator to operate. Well-executed lapping schemes may be difficult for the auditor to detect. In some cases, all the "borrowed" cash will be temporarily returned immediately before the verification date to elude the auditor. In other cases, the weakness of internal accounting control makes detection of lapping difficult. Audit procedures most effective in detecting lapping include:

1. Surprise cash counts.
2. Comparison of receipts and deposits. Any delay in depositing receipts may indicate a lapping scheme.
3. Confirmation of accounts receivable. This procedure, discussed in the next section, may help detect any delay in posting collections on accounts receivable, another indication of lapping.

Kiting is a cash defalcation pattern that involves cash disbursements. Essentially, it is a system of covering cash shortages with unrecorded transfer checks. A simple example might be as follows: In order to cover a cash shortage in bank account A, an employee, on December 31, deposited in account A a check for the amount of the shortage, drawn on bank account B. This transfer check would not be recorded as a December disbursement on account B but would be entered in January. When the bank accounts were reconciled as of December 31, the shortage would be hidden temporarily because of the time required for the transfer check to clear. This delay is often referred to as *float.* Kiting schemes may be very elaborate and involve numerous bank accounts in different geographical areas.

Detection of kiting is much easier than detection of lapping. If proper cash audit procedures are employed, any kiting at the verification date should be discovered. Effective audit procedures in the detection of kiting include:

1. Collection of cash cutoff data and subsequent agreement of these data to the list of outstanding checks.
2. Examination of undeposited receipts as of the verification date to ascertain whether any company checks are included therein.
3. Proper use of the cutoff bank statement.
4. Preparation of a schedule of all bank transfers for a reasonable period before and after the verification date. An example of this schedule is presented in Figure 12-3.

AUDIT PROGRAM FOR CASH BALANCES

The following is a representative audit program outlining the procedures performed in the verification of cash balances. Audit programs are retained in the working papers and normally include space for the auditor performing each step to indicate its completion by signing and dating the procedure. In this way, the audit program provides a permanent record of the audit work performed. In addition, audit programs are useful in (1) planning and organizing the audit, (2) providing guidance to the auditor in performing the field work, and (3) helping to determine the status of the audit as to work completed and work yet to be done. SAS No. 22 (AU 311.05) requires that the auditor prepare necessary programs in written form.

The form of audit programs may vary as may the extent of detail included. In many cases the written audit programs are modified during the course of the audit to recognize conditions differing from those anticipated.

I. Review internal controls over cash balances and transactions.

II. Plan the timing of the verification of cash balances considering client procedures, use of the element of surprise, and so on.

III. Cash on hand:

- **A.** Imprest or petty cash funds:
  - **1.** Ascertain the location of all funds. Plan the count of all funds so as to accomplish *simultaneous verification* in order to prevent substitution.
  - **2.** Count and record the contents of each fund. The auditor should count the fund in the presence of the custodian and obtain a signed statement that it was returned intact.
  - **3.** Examine each receipt, check, voucher, and so on, included in the fund to determine that it appears proper and is currently dated. Details of any questionable items should be included in the working papers.

Figure 12-3 Schedule of Bank Transfers

Clark-Mac Dowell Corporation
Schedule of Bank Transfers
December 31, 19X8

Transfer		Check		Disbursement Date		Receipt Date	
From	To	No.	Amount	Per Books	Per Bank	Per Books	Per Bank
Charlotte	Atlanta	1364	7500	12-23-X8 √	12-31-X8 √‾	12-30-X8 √ʼ	12-30-X8 √+
General	Payroll	678	13484	12-31-X8 √	12-31-X8 √‾	12-31-X8 √ʼ	12-31-X8 √+
Orlando	Atlanta	2224	4000	12-23-X8 √A	1-5-X9 √‾	1-2-X9 √ʼ √x	1-3-X9 √+
Atlanta	Birmingham	9064	6500	1-3-X9 √	1-7-X9 √‾	1-5-X9 √ʼ	1-5-X9 √+
Memphis	Atlanta	1117	5750	1-5-X9 √	1-12-X9 √‾	1-9-X9 √ʼ	1-10-X9 √+

√ per cash disbursement record
√ʼ per cash receipts book
√A agreed to Orlando outstanding check list
√x agreed to Atlanta General account deposits-in-transit
√‾ agreed to cancelled check
√+ agreed to deposit slip and bank statement

Prepared by: R. C. 1-29-X9
Reviewed by: R. J. S. 2-2-X9

4. Compare the total in each fund to the general ledger balance. Any shortage or overage should be acknowledged by the fund custodian.
5. If any items representing unreimbursed expenses are included in a fund on the verification date, consider proposing an appropriate audit adjusting entry.
6. Maintain control of all checks, drafts, or other items included in cash on hand at the verification date and verify their deposit.

B. Undeposited receipts:

1. Determine the location of all undeposited receipts. Coordinate the counting procedure to accomplish *simultaneous verification* in order to prevent substitution.
2. Count all undeposited receipts requesting that the custodian observe all counts.
3. Examine all checks, drafts, and other noncash items included in undeposited receipts to determine that they appear proper and are currently dated. Any items that appear questionable and any checks drawn on client bank accounts, subsidiaries, or affiliates should be noted in the working papers.
4. Agree total undeposited receipts to the cash receipts records. Investigate any difference found.
5. Control undeposited receipts, together with any checks, drafts, or other noncash items found in the cash funds, to the client's bank for deposit. Obtain a validated copy of the deposit slip to be included in the working papers.
6. Obtain cash cutoff data by recording in the working papers details of cash receipts and disbursements for a reasonable period prior to the verification date.

IV. Cash on deposit:

A. Send bank confirmations to banks and include responses in working papers. Confirmations should be sent to all banks with which the client currently maintains a banking relationship as well as any banks that the client has dealt with in the recent past.

B. Arrange for the client to request cutoff bank statements for all checking accounts. The statements should cover a reasonable period subsequent to the verification date (not less than ten business days) and should be received by the auditor directly from the bank.

C. Obtain a reconciliation of each account as of the verification date. Verify items on each reconciliation as follows:

1. Balance per bank. Agree balance per bank shown on reconciliation with bank confirmation and cutoff bank statement.
2. Deposits-in-transit. Agree deposits-in-transit per each reconciliation with the cash-count working papers and validated de-

posit slip prepared on the verification date as well as with the cutoff bank statement. Any amount shown as a deposit-in-transit that was not under the auditor's control on the verification date represents a potential cash irregularity and must be investigated.

3. Outstanding checks. Examine all checks returned with the cutoff bank statement to ascertain if any that were actually outstanding were not included on the list of outstanding checks. Proper examination of cancelled checks includes comparison of the date each check was recorded with the date of its deposit as well as comparison of check number, payee, and amount as shown on the check with corresponding data on the outstanding check list and the cash disbursement records. All checks listed on the outstanding check list that were not returned with the cutoff bank statement should be investigated by examining their entry in the cash disbursement records and the documents supporting the disbursement.
4. Other reconciling items. Other items on the reconciliation should be examined for validity. Audit adjusting entries should be considered if appropriate.
5. Balance per books. Agree book balance per the reconciliation with the respective general ledger cash account. Investigate any differences and propose adjusting entries where necessary.

D. Trace cash cutoff data obtained on verification date into the cash records to determine that no receipts or disbursements of the following period have been back-dated and entered in the current period.

E. Determine that all checks included in cash on hand on the verification date that were drawn on client bank accounts, subsidiaries, or affiliates are included on the outstanding check list of their respective accounts. If such transfer checks are numerous, prepare a schedule of bank transfers covering a reasonable period before and after the verification date.

F. In order to gain further assurance with respect to the client's internal control over cash and the propriety of the recorded cash transactions, prepare a *proof of cash* for the last month of the year as well as the month ending on the verification date if other than the last month. Additional months may be included if considered appropriate. The proof of cash may be combined with the reconciliation of the cash account as of the verification date if convenient.

V. Financial statement presentation. Consider appropriate presentation for cash balances and determine that client's statements conform to accepted reporting and disclosure standards.

The audit of receivables, revenues, and cash receipts

The intangible nature of receivables dictates audit procedures that differ in several respects from those described for cash. Receivables represent promises to pay, and, as such, have subjective aspects not present with cash. The auditor, in evaluating receivables, must form qualitative as well as quantitative judgments and must, for the most part, utilize indirect rather than direct evidence.

Objectives sought in the audit of receivables include verification of ownership, existence, and the accuracy of amount; assessment of the probability of collection; discovery of any liens relating to the receivables; and the determination of proper financial statement presentation. Since transactions giving rise to receivables are typically sales, the objectives of the audit of sales revenue may be accomplished in conjunction with the audit of receivables. Transactions reducing receivables usually involve cash receipts; therefore, the audits of cash receipts and accounts receivable may be performed jointly. In this way the related areas of the cash-generating cycle of the business are audited simultaneously. This approach provides greater assurance that no area escapes audit examination and affords increased audit efficiency.

Presented in the remainder of this chapter are discussions of the audits of accounts receivable, other receivables, sales and other revenues, and cash receipts, as well as the audit program for these areas.

Accounts receivable

Auditing procedures employed in the examination of accounts receivable may be classified for discussion as follows:

1. collection and examination of external evidence
2. examination of evidence internal to the firm
3. analytical procedures regarding the receivables balance and the Allowance for Doubtful Accounts

EXTERNAL EVIDENCE—CONFIRMATION

One of the most important auditing procedures regarding accounts receivable is direct confirmation of the account with the debtor. SAS No. 1 (AU 331.01) lists confirmation of receivables as representing a "generally accepted auditing procedure" and puts an auditor on notice as having the burden of justifying any opinion on financial statements where this procedure was not employed. The form of confirmation request used by auditors may be either positive or negative. Positive confirmation requests (Figure 12-4) ask that the debtor respond whether the information on the

Figure 12-4 Positive Form of Confirmation Request

No._______

Dear Sirs:

According to our records, the balance receivable from you as of   was $ If this agrees with your records, please sign this confirmation form in the space provided below; if it does not agree with your records, do not sign below but explain and sign on the reverse side. In either case, please return this form directly to our auditors, Spaulding, Robinson & Co., 706 Peachtree Street, N.E., Atlanta, Georgia 30301, for their use in connection with an examination of our accounts. A stamped and addressed envelope is enclosed for your reply.

____
SIGN HERE if the above is correct. (If incorrect, do not sign here but explain and sign on reverse side.)

____

BY____________________________

THIS IS NOT A REQUEST FOR PAYMENT

request is correct or incorrect. If it is incorrect, the debtor is asked to note what is in error. Negative confirmation requests (Figure 12-5) ask that the debtor respond only if the information is incorrect. The quality of evidence gained from positive confirmations is considered to be superior to that from negative confirmations because the auditor has no way of determining whether the lack of response to a negative confirmation request means debtor agreement, lack of delivery, or debtor neglect. Many auditors find it useful to use both types of requests simultaneously. In so doing, the auditor selects a sample of accounts (probably those with large balances) for positive confirmation and a larger group (possibly all the remaining accounts) for negative confirmation. This procedure achieves both high-quality evidence regarding the accounts positively confirmed and broad coverage of the accounts receivable balance through the negative confirmations.

The auditor selects the accounts for confirmation, and the request forms

Figure 12-5 Negative Form of Confirmation Request

```
        Please examine this statement carefully and if any
error is found please notify our auditors:

              Spaulding, Robinson & Co.
              706 Peachtree Street, N.E.
              Atlanta, Georgia  30301

A stamped, self-addressed envelope is enclosed for your
convenience.

            THIS IS NOT A REQUEST FOR PAYMENT
```

are prepared under audit supervision. The accounts to be confirmed are selected by using automated or manual methods that employ judgment or statistical sampling. Usually, some of the accounts written off as bad debts during the period should be included in the sample in order to support the validity of the recorded write-offs. The request forms should be prepared either by the auditor or under audit supervision.

The auditor controls the mailing of the requests to be assured that none of them are suppressed or altered. Also, the auditor's return address should appear on the envelope so that any nondeliverable requests will be returned directly to the auditor for attention. When a reasonable time has elapsed after mailing positive confirmation requests, second and perhaps even third requests are mailed. The auditor must examine other evidence to determine the validity of nonconfirming accounts. The best evidence of a valid account is its payment. However, the auditor must inspect remittance advices and deposit receipts in an effort to be assured that the payment was made by the customer. Sales contracts, shipping documents, and other internal evidence discussed in the next section are also valuable in establishing the validity of accounts receivable.

When customers disagree with the information on the confirmation request and call this to the auditor's attention, careful follow-up procedures should be implemented. In some cases, the customer's comments result from a misunderstanding of the request and must be disregarded by the auditor. Often, further correspondence with the customer is needed to clarify differences. In other cases, examination of the client's records will reveal errors regarding the account. Each confirmation exception should be carried to the point of satisfactory explanation, and the accounts should be adjusted if necessary. In cases where lapping of cash is being carried out, the only evidence of its presence may be customer disagreement with the account balance as shown on the confirmation.

INTERNAL EVIDENCE

In addition to the external evidence of existence and accuracy of the accounts receivable gained by confirmation, the auditor must collect and examine evidence that is internal to the firm. Procedures employed for this part of the audit are tests of the accounting records and examination of supporting documents. Accounting records that are used to record sales on account, cash receipts, bad-debt write-offs, credit memos, and other transactions affecting receivables should be tested for accuracy. Underlying documents such as copies of invoices, credit memos, cash receipts, bad-debt write-off authorizations, etc., should be examined on a test basis and compared to the accounting records. Such auditing procedures are termed *tests of transactions* and are described in the audit program for receivables.

ANALYTICAL PROCEDURES

Aside from the evidence gained from confirmation and transaction testing, the auditor may obtain assurance regarding collectibility of receivables by employing certain analytical procedures. One such procedure is the preparation of an *aging analysis* of the receivable balance. Such an analysis, which may be prepared by the client and verified by the auditor, indicates the composite age of the accounts receivable balance. Each account is classified by age into the proper column of the analysis. When completed, the column totals indicate the relative age of the accounts. This type of analysis aids the auditor in assessing the collectibility of the accounts, since older or past-due accounts, or a trend toward such accounts, usually indicate decreased collectibility. This information relates directly to the auditor's evaluation of the *adequacy of the Allowance for Doubtful Accounts.* Figure 12-6 presents an example of an aging analysis.

The adequacy of the Allowance account is critical if accounts receivable are to be presented fairly on the financial statements. Evaluating the Allowance requires sound audit judgment and additional information that can be used by the auditor to aid in the assessment of the adequacy of the Allowance includes (1) historical percentages of the receivables balance represented by the Allowance, (2) trends in bad-debt occurrence, (3) changes in credit granting policies, (4) receivable turnover calculations, (5) current economic conditions, and (6) the opinions of responsible client officials with respect to the collectibility of accounts.

INTERNAL CONTROL OVER RECEIVABLES

Several specific procedures that indicate good internal accounting control over accounts receivable follow. Controls over receivables naturally overlap

Figure 12-6 Accounts Receivable Aging Analysis

Villanow Industries
Accounts Receivable Aging Analysis
12-31-83

Account Name	Total	Current	1-30 Days Past Due	31-60 Days Past Due	61-90 Days Past Due	Over 90 Days Past Due
J. Albert	128467	128467				
R. Arner	323278		323278			
D. Attaway	94284			94284		
Autry Indus.	634040	634040				
B. Avery	191720	91720	100000			
Awnings, Inc.	1694077	1694077				
R. Bartlett	54080	54080				
Berry Shoes	177891		177891			
Wray Corp.	617077	617077				
WSBA Radio	54784	54784				
W.T. Corp.	907700			500000	316723	90977
Wunda Co.	193440	193440				
J. Yelverton	20288	20288				
R. Young	5477				5477	
V. Young	120000		120000			
Zell Milling Co.	1066834	1066834				
Total	12840377	9834445	1673101	792251	399336	141244
Percent	100.00%	76.59%	13.03%	6.17%	3.11%	1.10%
12-31-82 %	100.00%	74.60%	12.10%	7.08%	4.03%	2.19%
12-31-81 %	100.00%	73.78%	10.62%	8.04%	4.62%	2.94%

controls over other areas such as cash, sales, and sales returns. This reintroduces the concept of overlapping cycles of the business and the difficulty of isolating a single segment of a cycle without discovering interaction with other cycles.

Separation of Duties Persons maintaining accounts receivable details should not also be assigned duties relating to cash receipts, bad-debt write-off, issuance of credit memos, inventories, or billing. Such duty combinations can allow concealment of cash or inventory defalcations as well as unauthorized credits to selected accounts receivable.

Authorizations There should be formal procedures for the approval of bad-debt write-offs, sales returns, issuance of credit memos, or any transaction (other than routine cash receipts) that reduces accounts receivable. Any method of crediting accounts receivable without proper authorization can be used to perpetrate or conceal a defalcation. The auditor should be particularly concerned with noncash credits to accounts receivable. Should an account be paid and the cash abstracted, such activity can be hidden by entering a credit to the account for a sales return or a bad-debt write-off. Also, accounts set up to reflect sales to fictitious customers may be removed from the books by such noncash credits. The authorization for a sales return can be corroborated by inspection of the receiving report for the returned item, and a bad-debt write-off can be further substantiated by examination of correspondence files.

Billing Procedures In many cases unconcealed defalcations would be discovered were a customer to receive an erroneous account statement. Lapping, for example, will delay credit to a customer's account and thereby cause the account balance to be overstated. To prevent discovery, a dishonest employee may desire to suppress or intercept billing for particular accounts. To prevent this, internal control over billing should be designed so that billing duties are performed by someone who does not handle cash receipts or have access to inventories.

Further, invoicing or other initial billing should be coordinated with shipments of inventory. This assures that billing for shipments cannot be suppressed for certain accounts, permitting "free" merchandise to be shipped to selected customers.

FINANCIAL STATEMENT PRESENTATION OF RECEIVABLES

Trade Accounts Receivable are classified as current assets and presented on the balance sheet net of the Allowance for Doubtful Accounts. Receivables other than trade accounts may be current assets but usually should be classified under a separate caption such as *Other Receivables.* Credit balances in accounts receivable should, if material, be reclassified as current liabilities. Long-term receivables are presented in an appropriate noncurrent category under a descriptive caption. Advances to officers and employees of the client should be appropriately captioned. Intercompany accounts are usually noncurrent and should be appropriately described in the balance sheet.

Consignments of inventory relate to financial statement presentation of accounts receivable in that these amounts should be shown as inventory and not receivables. If a client engages in inventory consignment, the auditor should employ appropriate auditing procedures to gain assurance that proper accounting for the consignments has been made. Any liens with respect to receivables must be disclosed in the financial statements or the notes to the statements. Such disclosure should describe the nature of the lien and any other important aspects of the pledge.

Other receivables

Auditing procedures for other receivables are similar to those described for trade accounts receivable in that confirmation, examination of internal evidence, and analytical procedures are employed. If the other receivables are supported by documents such as promissory notes, these should be inspected as should any collateral held by the client to secure the receivables. The calculation and recording of interest income should be verified for all interest-bearing receivables. Collectibility of other receivables must be assessed by the auditor using an aging analysis or other procedures. If loans to officers or employees are made by the client, the auditor should obtain satisfaction that each such loan is properly authorized.

Financial statement presentation considerations for other receivables include the classification into current and noncurrent assets and proper description and disclosure. The existence of collateral-securing receivables or liens-pledging receivables should be disclosed as should the details of any receivables arising from transactions not in the normal course of business.

The audit of sales and other revenues

The objectives of auditing sales and other revenues include (1) determining that revenues recognized during the period under audit represent amounts earned by the client in accordance with generally accepted accounting principles, (2) determining that recorded revenues are neither overstated nor understated, and (3) ascertaining that revenues are properly presented on the financial statements and that disclosure is adequate.

Auditing procedures for sales and other revenues. The auditing techniques employed in the examination of sales and other revenue include both *tests of transactions* and *analytical review.* In performing tests of transactions the auditor must examine the accounting records and documentation supporting the recorded amounts. In order to test for both understatements and overstatements of revenues, the auditor should trace amounts recorded in the general ledger *backward* through the journals to source documents as well as *forward* by sampling source documents and tracing their entry through the records. In addition, the auditor should verify the mathematical accuracy of the accounting records as well as test for missing source documents by verifying the sequence of prenumbered forms. The revenue cutoff, that is, assigning revenue transactions occurring near year end to the proper period, may be verified by examining sales invoices and related shipping documents or other evidences of completed sales. This cutoff verification may often be more efficiently performed, however, in conjunction with the audit of inventories.

Analytical review is a technique in which the auditor examines interrelationships among accounting data in order to discover trends and fluctuations that require audit investigation. This *aggregative approach* often enables the auditor to perceive changes and tendencies in the accounting data that are not apparent from an examination of detail transactions alone. Analytical review is discussed further in Chapter 15.

INTERNAL CONTROL OVER SALES AND OTHER REVENUES

Internal control procedures in the areas of sales and other revenues should be designed to (1) insure the accuracy of recorded revenues, (2) preclude the possibility of any revenues being unrecorded, and (3) insure that all revenue transactions are properly authorized. Procedures that may be employed by the client to accomplish these internal control objectives include:

1. The use of prenumbered sales invoices and credit memoranda, and a procedure for maintaining numerical control.
2. An accounting system designed to coordinate and properly reflect the sales, shipping, billing, and collection functions.
3. An established procedure requiring proper authorization for sales, sales returns, and so on.
4. Control of miscellaneous revenue sources such as scrap materials and rentals to insure that these revenues are properly recorded.

FINANCIAL STATEMENT PRESENTATION OF REVENUES

Revenues are normally presented in the income statement at gross amount with related reductions shown as separate items. The nature of various revenues should be explained either in the footnotes or in the income statement itself. Special circumstances, such as large government contracts or a few major customers providing a large portion of the client's revenues, should be disclosed. Revenues of a special or nonrecurring nature should usually be presented separately in order to avoid distorting normal business trends.

The audit of cash receipts

Cash receipts are an integral part of the revenue generating cycle of the business and represent an area with a high risk of defalcation. The auditor must be concerned with the accuracy of the recorded receipts as well as the possibility that some receipts could be abstracted prior to entry in the records. These concerns give rise to the objectives of the cash receipts audit:

1. To determine that recorded cash receipts have been accurately accounted for.
2. To establish that all receipts of cash have been recorded.

Auditing procedures to accomplish the first objective of the cash receipts audit involve testing the accounting records for accuracy and for agreement with bank records. Individual cash receipts should be traced forward and backward from the record of original entry through the cash receipts journal into the general ledger accounts. Bank deposits, as recorded in the accounting records, should be agreed to entries on bank statements. Cash receipts records should be tested for mathematical accuracy by footing and cross-footing and should be scanned to detect unusual items.

To accomplish the second objective stated above, that is, gaining assurance that there are no unrecorded receipts, the auditor must rely heavily on internal control and analytical review. This is, of course, because detail tests of recorded transactions will not likely reveal unrecorded amounts or other omissions from the records.

INTERNAL CONTROL OVER CASH RECEIPTS

As discussed in Chapter 7, virtually all the general principles of internal control—separation of functions and duties, fidelity bonds, clear lines of authority and responsibility, limited access to assets, and so on—apply to cash receipts. In evaluating internal control over the cash receipts function, the auditor should determine that in all phases of the cash receipts system a separation is maintained between asset custody and record keeping. This may be accomplished initially by procedures requiring immediate, permanent recording of both mail and counter receipts. Subsequent to recording, the record of cash received should not be maintained by persons having direct access to cash. Daily intact bank deposits, adequate supervision, and regular bank reconciliation are other important elements of the cash receipts internal control system.

AUDIT PROGRAM FOR RECEIVABLES, REVENUES, AND CASH RECEIPTS

The following audit program summarizes auditing procedures for the examination of receivables, revenues, and cash receipts. As with all model audit programs used by auditors, individual differences in various industries and companies may require modification in the procedures. This program is designed for a small- to medium-sized company engaged in manufacturing or merchandising. Companies in service or extractive industries, or those not extending credit, for example, would require somewhat different procedures.

In addition, the program is designed to accommodate either statistical or judgment sampling as well as manual or most computerized accounting systems.

I. Review internal controls over receivables, revenues, and cash receipts.

II. Accounts receivable:

1. Obtain a detailed listing of accounts receivable as of the verification date. Foot the listing and agree total to the general ledger control account balance.

2. Select a sample of individual accounts receivable to be subjected to audit testing.

3. Send confirmations requests for accounts included in sample. Confirmation requests should be prepared by auditor or under direct auditor supervision and should be mailed by auditor.

4. After a reasonable period (ten business days or more), send second confirmation requests to nonrespondents.

5. Examine all confirmation replies and investigate all exceptions, differences, and comments noted by customers. Include record of investigations in working papers and propose any audit adjustments considered appropriate.

6. Examine subsequent collections and underlying sales and shipping documents of all accounts for which no confirmation reply is received.

7. Prepare a summary of confirmations requested, replies received, exceptions, and so on, and state the conclusion reached with respect to the adequacy of the confirmation procedure.

8. Test selected transactions underlying the individual accounts included in the sample:

a. Trace debit entries in accounts to entries in the sales journal.

b. Examine sales invoices and shipping reports supporting the sales transaction.
c. Trace credit entries to cash receipts journal and to initial cash receipts record.
d. Investigate any entries to individual accounts from records other than cash receipts and sales.
e. Foot accounts and prove ending balance.
f. Examine collections on account subsequent to verification date.

9. Test selected transactions recorded in accounts receivable control account:
a. Trace debit and credit entries to totals in cash receipts journal, sales journal, and sales returns record.
b. Investigate any entries to the accounts receivable control from records other than those examined in step 9a.
c. Foot the account and prove the ending balance.

III. Notes receivable and interest income:
In addition to procedures paralleling program steps 1-9 above,
1. Inspect the note document for items in the sample to determine that it appears proper and agrees with data recorded in the accounting records.
2. Verify the calculation and recording of interest income for items included in the sample.
3. Test interest revenue for overall reasonableness.

IV. Allowance for doubtful accounts and notes; bad debt expense:
1. Obtain an aging analysis of accounts and notes receivable as of the balance sheet date.
2. Review aging analysis, comparing totals with prior years to determine trends, and so on.
3. Consider adequacy of allowance account based on current age of receivables, discernible trends, discussion with client, and so on. Propose adjusting entry if appropriate.
4. Discuss client's procedures for bad debt write-offs with responsible officials. Obtain list of accounts and notes written off during year and inspect documentation supporting individual write-offs. Trace entries to receivable and allowance accounts.
5. Examine any other debit entries to the allowance account and all credit entries as well as all entries to bad debt expense. Foot accounts and prove the ending balance.
6. Send confirmation requests to representative number of accounts and notes written off during the period.

V. Sales and other revenues:
1. Test for an overstatement of sales by selecting a sample of re-

corded sales from the sales journal and examine the underlying sales invoices and shipping reports. If a perpetual inventory system is used, determine that the cost of the sale was recorded.

2. Test for unrecorded sales by selecting a sample sales invoice and tracing to entry in the sales journal.
3. Test numerical sequence of sales invoice copies on file.
4. Foot and cross-foot the sales journal and trace monthly totals to the cash, receivables, and sales accounts.
5. Examine credit memoranda for sales returns and allowances both during the year under audit and during a reasonable period following year end. If material credits are allowed after year end for sales recorded during the year under audit, consider whether an audit adjustment should be proposed.
6. Test available records or other data supporting miscellaneous revenues, such as sale of scrap, rent receipts, royalty receipts, and so on.
7. Examine the general ledger sales account and investigate any posting from a source other than the sales record. Note any unusual entries in the working papers.
8. Investigate whether any shipments recorded as sales were in reality consignment shipments. Assurance may be obtained through inquiry and by application of knowledge of client's mode of operation.
9. Analytically review sales and other revenues to determine if significant fluctuations exist necessitating audit investigation. (Analytical review techniques are discussed in Chapter 15.)

VI. Cash receipts:

1. Test the accuracy of the cash receipts journal by proving footings and cross-footings and tracing postings to the cash, accounts receivable, sales, or other accounts.
2. Trace totals in cash receipts journal to bank statements on test basis.
3. Trace individual cash receipts from remittance advices forward to entry in the cash receipts journal and from cash receipts journal backward to remittance advices.
4. Scan the cash receipts for large or unusual entries and investigate any such entries found.

VII. Financial statement presentation. Consider appropriate presentation for receivables and revenues, including such items as credit balances in receivables, nontrade receivables, miscellaneous income, sales returns, expense offsets, and so on. Determine that the client's statements conform to accepted reporting and disclosure standards.

Supplementary readings

Heath, Lloyd C., and Paul Rosenfield. "Solvency: The Forgotten Half of Financial Reporting." *Journal of Accountancy* (January 1979), 48-54.

Warren, Carl S. "Confirmation Reliability—The Evidence." *Journal of Accountancy* (February 1975), 85-89.

Review questions

12-1. What is the purpose, when organizing the audit, of subdividing the work?

12-2. What are some related areas of the audit that may be examined simultaneously?

12-3. In planning the audit, what are three questions an auditor needs to ask about every area of the audit?

12-4. What are some techniques employed by the auditor to determine existence?

12-5. What are some techniques employed by the auditor in establishing valuation?

12-6. Why are auditing procedures for cash often more extensive and more detailed than procedures in some other areas?

12-7. What are the usual audit procedures employed in the audit of cash on hand?

12-8. What is the primary information regarding cash gained from the bank confirmation?

12-9. What are the most common reconciling items on a bank reconciliation?

12-10. What are some internal control aspects and techniques employed in the area of cash?

12-11. Which audit procedures are most effective in detecting lapping? In detecting kiting?

12-12. Which three major areas of auditing procedures are employed in the examination of accounts receivable?

12-13. Explain the difference between positive and negative confirmations.

12-14. What information may be used by the auditor to help assess the adequacy of the Allowance for Doubtful Accounts?

12-15. Explain the concepts of *simultaneous verification* and *substitution.*

12-16. Why should petty cash funds be replenished as of the verification date?

12-17. Explain why all checks included in cash on hand at the verification date should be deposited immediately.

12-18. Any company transfer checks or checks of affiliated companies found in cash on hand as of the verification date require special attention. Explain.

12-19. Discuss the relative importance of the element of surprise and the year-end verification in auditing cash.

12-20. What are the purposes of the cutoff bank statement?

12-21. Of what do cash cutoff data consist and what are they used for?

12-22. Outline proper financial statement presentation for cash.

12-23. Of what audit use is an accounts receivable aging analysis?

12-24. Why is the billing function important to internal control over receivables?

12-25. Why should bank confirmations be sent to banks with which the client does not currently transact business?

12-26. Why must the auditor never have unsupervised control of cash funds when counting cash?

12-27. In the audit of assets, name a "generally accepted auditing procedure" as specified by the *Statements on Auditing Standards.*

12-28. Why should the auditor send confirmation requests to some accounts receivable that have been written off during the period under audit?

12-29. What are the auditor's objectives with respect to the audit of sales and other revenues?

12-30. List the audit procedures commonly employed in the audit of sales.

12-31. Why is it important for auditors to verify the numerical sequence of sales invoices?

12-32. Why should auditors examine credit memos for the period subsequent to the balance sheet date?

Decision problems

12-33. On December 31, the auditor counted all cash on hand at Link Co. The cashier had not completed the recording of cash receipts or made up the bank deposit for the day. The cash on hand comprised both checks and currency and totalled $24,572.06. The cashier is custodian of a $4,000 petty cash fund.

After the count, the auditor released control of the cash to the cashier. The auditor later found a deposit on the January bank statement dated January 2 in the amount of $20,572.06.

a. Did the auditor perform a satisfactory cash count?

b. What opportunities for defalcation are available to the cashier?

c. What other auditing procedures should have been carried out at the time of the cash count?

12-34. The auditor of Naturemate Corporation recorded cutoff information at the time of the year-end cash count showing check number 7,469 as being the last disbursement of the year on the general account. With the cutoff bank statement, however, the auditor receives check number 7,470, dated January 2 of the following year made payable to the corporation's payroll account. Upon inspection, the bank cancellation shows that this check was deposited in the payroll account on December 30.

a. What sort of irregularity would you suspect?

b. What usual audit procedures are designed to disclose such an irregularity?

12-35. Given the following information, prepare a proof of cash for August 1983 and indicate the proper cash balance for financial statement purposes.

Per Bank Statement:

Balance 7/31	$76,489
August Deposits	84,363
August Withdrawals	56,762

Outstanding Checks:

July 31	3,694
August 31	8,328

Deposit in Transit:

August 31	3,800

Per Books:

Balance 7/31	72,795
August Receipts	86,563
Balance 8/31	98,361

During August, four checks totalling $382 had been returned by the bank due to insufficient funds and are still on hand. No entry had been made for these checks as of August 31. On August 7, the bank deducted a service charge for $17. This was not discovered by the company until September. On August 12, the bank collected a note for $1,600 and credited the proceeds to the company's account. The company made an entry to record this collection on September 4.

12-36. The treasurer of one of your small clients decides to convert $2,500 of remittances from customers to his own use and to conceal the shortage in the following manner. (Assume that June 30 is the close of the client's fiscal year and that you visit the client's office and make a cash count on July 1 before the offices are open for business.)

1. Cash receipts of June 30 are recorded in the usual manner and the cashier prepares a deposit slip for the day's receipts.
2. The deposit slip and customers' checks are given to the treasurer, whose duties include mailing the deposit to a bank that is ten miles away.
3. Customers' checks aggregating $2,500 are diverted to the treasurer's own use so that the deposit that should be mailed at the close of business on June 30 cannot be mailed then. The treasurer merely places the remainder of the checks in his desk and waits until the next day.
4. $2,500 worth of receipts of July 1 are placed with the deposit slip of June 30, at which time the aggregate deposit is in the proper amount even though individual checks will not compare with entries on the deposit slip.
5. The deposit for June 30 is finally mailed to the bank at the close of business on July 1 and the bank credits your client's account as of July 2 or 3. (As in most such cases, the bank does not compare individual checks with the deposit slip, but merely ascertains that the total deposit agrees with the total shown on the deposit slip.)
6. When you attempt to count cash early on July 1, the June 30 receipts

are said to be in-transit, by mail, and are to be shown as in-transit on the June 30 bank reconciliation.

7. The shortage in the July 1 receipts is covered by using July 2 receipts in the same manner as described above, and the lapping process is continued indefinitely.

a. Would your routine auditing procedures detect this shortage? Which ones?

b. List auditing procedures that could be used that would increase the auditor's likelihood of detecting this fraud.

c. What internal control improvements would you suggest to prevent this type irregularity?

12-37. During the audit of Organic Industries, for the year ended December 31, 1984, the auditor's count of the petty cash fund disclosed the following items:

Bills and coin	$274.08
Stamps	16.00
Personal checks of the petty cash custodian dated December 29, 1984	23.96
Customer's check dated January 21, 1985	154.00
Personal check of an accounting department employee returned by bank for insufficient funds	35.00
Petty cash fund reimbursement check drawn on Organic Industries	94.68
Petty cash vouchers as follows:	
Freight charges	24.00
Travel advance to employee	125.00

Determine the proper amount of the petty cash fund to be included in the cash balance on the financial statements and present any adjusting entries that the auditor should propose. Assume that all amounts are material and that the balance shown in the general ledger petty cash account is $750.

12-38. In the course of the year-end audit as of December 31, 1983, the auditor discovers the following items affecting the client's accounts receivable:

1. During January 1984 the client issued credit memos for sales recorded in December 1983 in the amount of $3,754.12. The cost of these sales had been $2,200. The merchandise was returned in January.
2. A sale in the amount of $2,842.54 was made on December 30, and the merchandise was shipped on that date. Through a bookkeeping delay, the sale was not recorded until January 4, 1984. The physical inventory taken on December 31 did not include the shipment.
3. A consignment shipment made on December 15 was inadvertently recorded as a sale. The sales price of the shipment was $4,200, and the cost was $2,520. The goods were not included in the year-end physical inventory, and none had been sold by the dealer as of December 31, 1983.
4. Cash collections on accounts received in the mail on January 2, 1984, were recorded as of December 31, 1983. The envelopes were postmarked December 31, and the total of these receipts amounted to $748.

5. On January 12, the client received notice that a customer who owed $1,012.76 had been adjudicated bankrupt on December 28, and none of the debt would be collected.

a. For each situation describe the effects on the financial statements and indicate the appropriate adjusting entry that the auditor might propose. Treat all amounts as material and assume the client uses the periodic inventory method.

b. For each adjusting entry proposed in part *a*, determine whether the client should make a reversing entry in the subsequent period.

12-39. During the year-end examination of Finite Factors, Inc., the auditor's analysis of the Accounts Receivable—Trade account discloses the following items:

Debit balances—from sales of merchandise	$74,886
Credit balances—from sales returns and advance payments	5,604
Advances to sales representatives	1,782
Note receivable from customer	896
Subscriptions receivable from sale of common stock	2,000
Repossessed merchandise—carried at the remaining balance on the receivable	382
	$74,342

It was also established that, of the debit balances in the account, $5,400 were past due and considered uncollectible.

The Allowance for Doubtful Accounts shows a credit balance of $3,672. It is considered necessary for the Allowance account to be stated at 8 percent of the year-end balance in Accounts Receivable—Trade.

Present appropriate adjusting entries that the auditor might propose and show how the various receivables should appear on the balance sheet.

12-40. You are the auditor of Fox Manufacturing Company. A trial balance taken from the books of Fox one month prior to year end follows:

	Dr. (Cr.)
Cash in bank	$ 87,000
Trade accounts receivable	345,000
Notes receivable	125,000
Inventories	317,000
Land	66,000
Buildings, net	350,000
Furniture, fixtures, and equipment, net	325,000
Trade accounts payable	(235,000)
Mortgages payable	(400,000)
Capital stock	(300,000)
Retained earnings	(510,000)
Sales	(3,130,000)
Cost of sales	2,300,000
General and administrative expenses	622,000
Legal and professional fees	3,000
Interest expense	35,000

There are no inventories consigned either in or out. All notes receivable are due from outsiders and held by Fox.

Which accounts should be confirmed with outside sources? Briefly describe from whom they should be confirmed and the information that should be confirmed. Organize your answer in the following format.

Account name	From whom confirmed	Information to be confirmed

AICPA adapted

12-41. You have been engaged to examine the financial statements of Glenrich Corporation for the year ended December 31, 1986, and have begun your auditing procedures. Discuss the following questions relating to your examination:

a. Several accounts receivable confirmations have been returned with the notation that "verifications of vendors' statements are no longer possible because of our data-processing system." What alternative auditing procedures could be used to verify these accounts receivable?

b. You are considering obtaining written representations from the client concerning the financial statements and matters pertinent to them.

1. What matters would you want covered in the client representation letter?
2. What will be the benefits to the auditor of the client representation letter?
3. What degree of reliance may the auditor place on the client representation letter?

AICPA adapted

12-42. You have examined the financial statements of the Mill Glen Company for several years. The system of internal control for accounts receivable is very satisfactory. The Mill Glen Company is on a calendar year basis. An interim audit, which included confirmation of the accounts receivable, was performed at August 31 and indicated that the accounting for receivables was very reliable.

The company's sales are principally to manufacturing concerns. There are about 1,500 active trade accounts receivable of which about 35 percent in number represent 65 percent of the total dollar amount. The accounts receivable are maintained alphabetically in five subledgers, which are controlled by one general ledger account.

Sales are machine-posted in the subledgers by an operation that produces simultaneously the customer's ledger card, monthly statement, and the sales journal. All cash receipts are in the form of customers' checks and are machine-posted simultaneously on the customer's ledger card, monthly statement, and the cash receipts journal. Information for posting cash receipts is obtained from the remittance advice portions of the customers' checks. The bookkeeping machine operator compares the remittance advices with the list of checks that was prepared by another person when the mail was received.

Summary totals are produced monthly by the bookkeeping machine operations for posting to the appropriate general ledger accounts such as cash, sales, accounts receivable, and so on. Aged trial balances by subledgers are prepared monthly.

Sales returns and allowances and bad debt write-offs are summarized periodically and recorded by standard journal entries. Supporting documents for these journal entries are available. The usual documents arising from billing, shipping, and receiving are also available

Prepare in detail the audit program for the Mill Glen Company for the year-end examination of the trade accounts receivable. Do not give the program for the interim audit.

AICPA adapted

12-43. Drakeford, CPA, is examining the financial statements of a manufacturing company with a significant amount of trade accounts receivable. Drakeford is satisfied that the accounts are properly summarized and classified and that allocations, reclassifications, and valuations are made in accordance with generally accepted accounting principles. Drakeford is planning to use accounts-receivable confirmation requests to satisfy the third standard of field work as to trade accounts receivable.

a. Identify and describe the two forms of accounts-receivable confirmation requests and indicate what factors Drakeford will consider in determining when to use each.

b. Assume Drakeford has received a satisfactory response to the confirmation requests. Describe how Drakeford could evaluate collectibility of the trade accounts receivable.

AICPA adapted

12-44. Clone Corporation, a retail toy chain, honors two bank credit cards and makes daily deposits of credit card sales in two credit card bank accounts (Bank A and Bank B). Each day Clone batches its credit card sales slips, bank deposit slips, and authorized sales return documents, and keypunches cards for processing by its electronic data processing department. Each week detailed computer print-outs of the general ledger credit card cash accounts are prepared. Credit card banks have been instructed to make an automatic weekly transfer of cash to Clone's general bank account. The credit card banks charge back deposits that include sales to holders of stolen or expired cards.

The auditor conducting the examination of the 1986 Clone financial statements has obtained the following copies of the detailed general ledger cash account print-outs, a summary of the bank statements, and the manually prepared bank reconciliations, all for the week ended December 31, 1986.

CLONE Corporation
DETAILED GENERAL LEDGER CREDIT CARD
CASH ACCOUNT PRINT-OUTS
For the Week Ended December 31, 1986

	Bank A	*Bank B*
	Dr. or (Cr.)	*Dr. or (Cr.)*
Beginning Balance		
December 24, 1986	$12,100	$ 4,200
Deposits		
December 27, 1986	2,500	5,000
December 28, 1986	3,000	7,000
December 29, 1986	0	5,400
December 30, 1986	1,900	4,000
December 31, 1986	2,200	6,000
Cash Transfer		
December 27, 1986	(10,700)	0
Chargebacks		
Expired cards	(300)	(1,600)
Invalid deposits (physically deposited in wrong account)	(1,400)	(1,000)
Redeposit of invalid deposits	1,000	1,400
Sales returns for week ending December 31, 1986	(600)	(1,200)
Ending Balance		
December 31, 1986	$ 9,700	$29,200

SUMMARY OF THE BANK STATEMENTS
For the Week Ended December 31, 1986

	Bank A	*Bank B*
	(Charges)	*or Credits*
Beginning Balance		
December 24, 1986	$10,000	$ 0
Deposits dated		
December 24, 1986	2,100	4,200
December 27, 1986	2,500	5,000
December 28, 1986	3,000	7,000
December 29, 1986	2,000	5,500
December 30, 1986	1,900	4,000
Cash transfers to general bank account		
December 27, 1986	(10,700)	0
December 31, 1986	0	(22,600)
Chargebacks		
Stolen cards	(100)	0
Expired cards	(300)	(1,600)
Invalid deposits	(1,400)	(1,000)
Bank service charges	0	(500)
Bank charge (unexplained)	(400)	0
Ending Balance		
December 31, 1986	$ 8,600	$ 0

BANK RECONCILIATIONS
For the Week Ended December 31, 1986

Code No.		*Bank A*	*Bank B*
		Add or (Deduct)	
1.	Balance per bank statement December 31, 1986	$8,600	$ 0
2.	Deposits in transit December 31, 1986	2,200	6,000
3.	Redeposit of invalid deposits (physically deposited in wrong account)	1,000	1,400
4.	Difference in deposits of December 29, 1986	(2,000)	(100)
5.	Unexplained bank charge	400	0
6.	Bank cash transfer not yet recorded	0	22,600
7.	Bank service charges	0	500
8.	Chargebacks not recorded Stolen cards	100	0
9.	Sales returns recorded but not reported to the bank	(600)	(1,200)
10.	Balance per general ledger December 31, 1986	$9,700	$29,200

Based on a review of the December 31, 1986, bank reconciliations and the related information available in the print-outs and the summary of bank statements, describe what action(s) the auditor should take to obtain audit satisfaction *for each item* on the bank reconciliations.

Assume that all amounts are material and all computations are accurate.

Organize your answer sheet as follows using the appropriate code number *for each item* on the bank reconciliations:

Code No.	Action(s) to be taken by the auditor to obtain audit satisfaction
1.	

AICPA adapted

13

Auditing Inventories, Plant and Equipment, Investments, and Related Areas

In Chapter 12, audit objectives and procedures for cash balances, receivables, and related areas were described. Other categories commonly encountered by auditors which typically represent material amounts on clients' financial statements include inventories; property, plant, and equipment; investments; other assets; and related areas. This chapter describes audit objectives and procedures for these items. The categories of assets and related areas selected for analysis in this and the previous chapter were chosen because they are considered to require distinctive audit procedures, they are commonly encountered, and they usually represent material amounts. However, an understanding of the objectives and procedures appropriate for these areas should convey to readers the overall approach to the audit of any asset and its related areas.

The audit of inventories and cost of sales

Inventories represent a major asset category for many companies, and in these companies a considerable amount of audit time is usually devoted to the verification of inventories. Since inventories are tangible assets, auditors must be concerned with assessment of physical quantities and qualities as well as with calculations regarding value.

OBJECTIVES

Auditors' objectives regarding the examination of inventories and cost of sales include:

1. Ascertaining that adequate internal control exists regarding inventories
2. Verifying that the inventory is owned by the client
3. Ascertaining the physical quantities of inventory on hand
4. Being satisfied that the client has used proper inventory pricing
5. Determining whether any liens are applicable to the inventory
6. Assessing the salability of the inventory on hand by giving attention to indications of damaged goods, obsolete items, etc.
7. Ascertaining the propriety of cost of sales
8. Determining proper financial statement presentation

INVENTORY OBSERVATION

Another audit procedure that is specified by SAS No. 1 (AU 331.01) as one of the "generally accepted auditing procedures" is the observation of inventories. Inventory observation assists auditors in achieving several of the objectives, including those relating to ownership, quantities, existence, and salability.

A well-executed inventory observation should give the auditor assurance regarding the physical attributes, both quantitative and qualitative, of the inventories. The following paragraphs describe the client's count procedures as well as the primary activities of the auditor in a typical inventory observation. The discussion of the observation is presented as a series of procedures listed in an appropriate, but not inviolable, chronological order.

Client Procedures Prior to beginning the actual count of inventory, the client should give specific instructions to all employees regarding their duties during the count. Arrangements should be made for production to cease during the count, if feasible, and for any incoming and outgoing goods to be listed and physically separated. The items to be counted should be arranged for ease of count, with all like items placed together if possible. The auditor should review the client's written inventory plans in advance of the count date if possible and design the audit procedures accordingly. To discover on the count date that plans are inadequate may cause the necessary corrective action to come too late to insure an accurate count of inventory. In a well-controlled inventory count, the client will distribute prenumbered inventory count tickets for employees to use in recording counts and descriptions. These count tickets may be designed in various formats, with a two- or three-part ticket being common (Figure 13-1). The numbers of the tickets issued should be controlled, as should the collection of each of the ticket parts. An effective way to take inventory is to organize

Figure 13-1 Three-Part Inventory Count Ticket

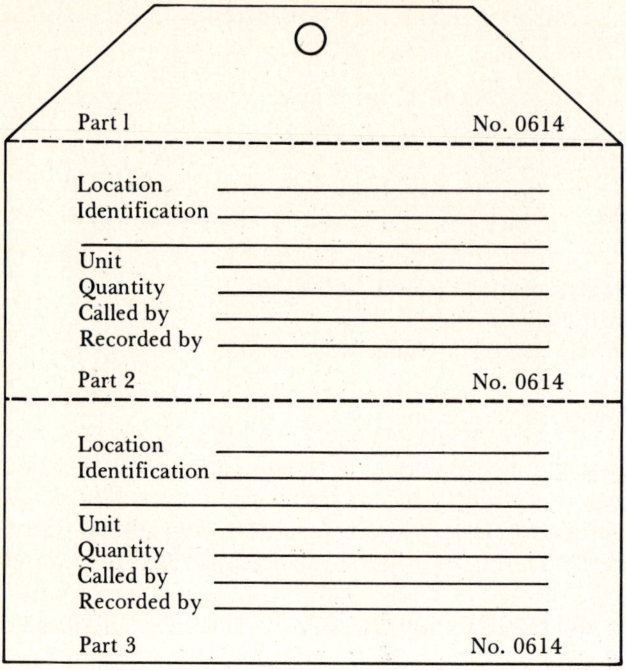

Part 1 No. 0614

Location ______________
Identification ______________
____
Unit ______________
Quantity ______________
Called by ______________
Recorded by ______________

Part 2 No. 0614

Location ______________
Identification ______________
____
Unit ______________
Quantity ______________
Called by ______________
Recorded by ______________

Part 3 No. 0614

count teams and to use "blind" second counts. Each count team generally is composed of two persons, one from within the department controlling the items (and therefore familiar with their location and description) and the second from outside the department (to encourage accuracy of the count). The count procedures then provide that the first count team go out into the inventory area, count the items, and fill out and collect part 3 of the inventory ticket. A second team will then independently count the inventory and fill out and collect part 2 of the ticket. Parts 2 and 3 of the tickets are then compared, and discrepancies are reconciled. In large inventories, inventory tickets may take the form of computer cards, and comparisons of first and second counts as well as inventory summaries and totals may be implemented through the use of EDP equipment.

The auditor's function in an inventory count and observation is not to count ("take") inventory but to verify counts on a test basis and, in general, to determine that an accurate physical inventory is taken. If the auditor finds errors in the inventory counts, the count team should be informed so that necessary corrections can be made. The auditor's recorded test counts should include some of these corrections for later verification that changes were made properly.

Ticket Accountability Early in the observation the auditor should establish strict accountability regarding the prenumbered inventory tickets. The auditor should record the numbers of the tickets that have been issued and used; those issued and unused; and those unissued. This accountability helps the auditor to guard against an overstatement of inventory perpetrated by filling in unused inventory tickets after the physical inventory. In addition to recording ticket numbers, the auditor should survey the inventory area to be satisfied not only that all items of inventory have been tagged but also that the issued tickets have been distributed and that none have been held back for later fraudulent use.

Cutoff Data During inventory observation, the auditor should record information regarding receipts and shipments immediately preceding the inventory date. This is to assure that proper coordination is achieved with respect to the recording of purchases, sales, and inventory on hand. This cutoff data will later be agreed to the last sales and last purchases recorded in the period.

Movement Closely related to gathering cutoff data is the procedure of gaining assurance regarding the movement of goods during the physical inventory count. Uncontrolled movement of goods into, out of, or within the inventory area during the count can lead to erroneous physical counts. During the entire period of observation, the auditor should be alert for inventory movements and be sure that any such movement is accounted for properly.

Test Counts During the observation the auditor should make numerous test counts to verify the accuracy of the client employees' work. Several test counts should be recorded in the audit work papers for later comparison with the inventory summaries. In making test counts the auditor should use judgment regarding the necessity of opening containers, unstacking cartons, etc., to be assured that actual quantities are what they appear to be. As a rule, the auditor will concentrate testing in those categories of the inventory where dollar value is the highest. The auditor may use a computer program to identify the higher-valued items or items meeting some other characteristic specified. A computer program could be designed to identify slow-moving items, those whose current balances are greatly increased over the balances of the preceding period, or perhaps those whose balances exceed the usual order quantity by some designated percentage. In such areas, the auditor is better able to use time efficiently with respect to the amount of assurance that may be obtained.

Evaluation of Physical Inventory During inventory observation, many auditors feel it desirable to record narrative comments in the working papers regarding the client's inventory-taking procedures, the condition of the inventory, and the auditor's own impressions of the physical counts. Such comments are valuable evidence for use in forming an opinion regarding inventories and in making constructive suggestions to the client.

In many inventory observation situations, the auditor needs ingenuity in order to be satisfied regarding the physical quantities observed. Examples of inventories that may pose such problems are (1) large piles of materials such as coal, (2) liquids in tanks (especially horizontal, cylindrical tanks), (3) large quantities of small parts, (4) work-in-process, and (5) logs in a river.

In other cases, the qualitative nature of the inventory may be difficult to assess. For example, materials said to be specific chemicals or jewels said to be of a given quality may represent circumstances that auditors cannot resolve. While auditors are not generally expected to be experts in appraisal, cases may arise in which they are uncomfortable in relying upon their own knowledge. In such cases, they should retain an expert to give further assurance regarding the inventory.

PROCEDURES FOLLOWING OBSERVATION

At some point following the inventory observation, the client will complete the listing, pricing, and extension of inventories on an *inventory listing* or *summary*. To complete verification work on inventories, the auditor should secure a copy of the listing for examination. The procedures that the auditor should perform in relation to this final listing and to other inventory records should be designed to substantiate the quantities, unit costs, mathematical operations, and total inventory value shown on the listing. These procedures include agreeing listed quantities to physical counts; reviewing price lists, purchase invoices, and cost records; examining cutoffs; and reviewing computations such as LIFO or retail method valuations.

The auditor should also employ procedures designed to achieve other audit objectives. For example, in order to be satisfied regarding the existence of liens, the auditor should review loan agreements, make inquiries, and, if necessary, review official public records to ascertain whether any secured transactions are recorded with respect to the client. While purchase invoices and possession tend to indicate ownership, the auditor should be alert for any indication that inventories are held on consignment. If, after examination, the auditor has reservations regarding the salability of inventory items, the auditor should discuss this with the client, compute inventory turnover statistics, and examine order backlog.

To gain assurance regarding the accuracy of the accounting data with respect to inventories and cost of sales, the auditor should test transactions and analytically review data relating to the receipt and shipment of inventory. Procedures should include the selection of source documents supporting receipts and shipments, tracing the entry of such documents into the accounting records, and ascertaining that these transactions are coordinated with authorized purchases and sales.

A *client representation,* including matters concerning inventories, should be obtained from responsible officials of the client. This representation serves the purpose of emphasizing the client's primary responsibility for the fairness and accuracy of the financial statements and is part of the evidence gathered by the auditor to support the opinion concerning inventories.

Information concerning inventories usually included in the client representation consists of (1) a summary of the various classes, valuation bases, and dollar amounts of the inventories on hand; (2) a statement regarding the extent to which inventory quantities were determined by physical count; (3) assurance that any liens against the inventories are properly disclosed; (4) assurance that all amounts included in inventory have been properly entered in the records as liabilities; (5) a statement that inventory has been presented on a basis that is consistent with the preceding year's; (6) assurance that there are no unsalable goods included in the inventory; (7) a statement that purchases and sales cutoffs were properly executed at year end; and (8) other assurances considered appropriate. Client representations are discussed further in Chapter 15.

INTERNAL CONTROL OVER INVENTORIES

Internal control over inventories properly includes accounting controls and physical controls. Good accounting control over inventories is indicated by a system in which the duties of employees are separated so that persons who control inventories are not also in charge of billing sales or entering purchases. The accounting system should be so designed that the flow of accounting data parallels the physical flow of inventory. Inventory should not be shipped until sales are approved and shipment authorized. Purchase invoices should not be entered or approved for payment until receiving reports are found to agree with the invoiced items. Frequent physical inventories are indications of good control, as is the existence of well-defined procedures regarding nonroutine transactions such as scrap sales or circumstances such as inventory shortages.

Physical control relates to protection of inventories from theft or deterioration. Evidence of such controls includes burglar alarms, night watchmen or guards, fences, locks, and other security measures. Situations such as warehoused inventory in disarray, inventory exposed to the elements, and storage buildings in disrepair indicate poor physical control from the standpoint of deterioration.

FINANCIAL STATEMENT PRESENTATION OF INVENTORIES

Inventories are presented as current assets on the balance sheet with disclosure of the basis for valuation. Acceptable valuation bases include cost or the lower of cost or market. If the auditor finds that market (adjusted current replacement cost) is less than the historical cost of the inventory, the auditor will usually insist that the inventory be written down to market. Obsolete or slow-moving inventory items may be carried at a nominal value. Aggregates of both cost and market value of the inventory are frequently disclosed as well as any other pertinent information regarding value or potential salability. Also the description of inventory should include an indication of the cost-flow method used, such as *first-in, first-out* or *weighted average.*

AUDIT PROGRAM FOR INVENTORIES AND COST OF SALES

The following is a representative audit program for inventories and cost of sales outlining appropriate auditing procedures for these areas.

I. Review internal control over inventories and cost of sales.

II. Inventories:

- **A.** Inventory observation:
  - **1.** Make arrangements to observe inventories at times that correlate with the client's own inventory taking and production schedule.
  - **2.** Ascertain the client's physical inventory procedures. Describe the procedures in the working papers and include the conclusions as to their adequacy. Comment on the extent to which the procedures are followed by employees during the physical inventory.
  - **3.** Determine inventory ticket accountability, recording details of ticket numbers issued, used, and unused in the working papers.
  - **4.** Obtain inventory cutoff data and record in working papers:
    - **a.** Receipts—list details of the last receiving report issued prior to the physical inventory and a reasonable number of those immediately preceding. Inspect unused, subsequently numbered receiving report forms.
    - **b.** Shipments—list details of the last shipping report issued prior to the physical inventory and a reasonable number of those immediately preceding. Inspect unused, subsequently numbered shipping report forms.
  - **5.** Ascertain if there is to be any inventory movement during the physical count. If movement is anticipated, make necessary arrangements with client to assure accurate count of goods received, shipped, or produced during the physical inventory.

List details of major inventory movement in the working papers.

6. Test the physical inventory counts made by the client's employees. Relatively heavier test counting should be performed on high value areas of the inventory. All errors found should be called to the attention of supervisory personnel and reconciled. Sufficient tests should be made to assure that an accurate inventory count is made. The details of a representative number of test counts should be recorded in the working papers for tracing into the final inventory listing.
7. Inquire if the client has inventory consigned-in or consigned-out. If inventory is held on consignment, obtain assurance that it has been excluded from the physical inventory count. Record details in the working papers. If inventory is out on consignment, arrange to observe or confirm physical quantities and record details in the working papers.
8. By means of overall observation of the physical inventories and by inquiry, determine if:
   a. Damaged, obsolete, or slow-moving inventory is on hand.
   b. Physical control over inventories is adequate. Include details and conclusions in the working papers.

B. Audit procedures following observation:

1. Obtain the final inventory listing prepared by the client summarizing quantities and prices of inventory on hand at the observation date.
2. Agree the test counts recorded in the working papers during the inventory observation to the physical quantities shown on the listing. Reconcile ticket accountability obtained during observation with the final listing.
3. Examine recent inventory purchase invoices to verify pricing and support ownership.
4. Verify extensions and footings on the inventory summary on a test basis.
5. Refer to current price lists, catalogues, or invoices to establish replacement cost of inventory. State conclusions regarding lower of cost or market valuation of the client's inventory.
6. Determine that any items noted during inventory observation as being damaged, obsolete, or slow moving have been properly valued.
7. Review calculations for cost-flow assumptions or special valuation methods used by the client (LIFO, FIFO, average, retail method, etc.).
8. If client is engaged in manufacturing, review the cost system to establish the validity of reported costs.

9. Trace cutoff data obtained at inventory observation to ascertain that shipments and receipts near the physical inventory date have been properly recorded:

a. Shipments—determine that shipments included in the cutoff data have been excluded from the physical inventory. Determine that such shipments have been recorded as sales and included in cost of sales in the proper period by examining the related sales invoices and tracing their entry into the sales record and cost of sales record. Determine that subsequent shipments and invoices are recorded in the subsequent period.

b. Receipts—determine that receipts included in the cutoff data have been included in the physical inventory. Determine that such receipts have been recorded in the purchases or inventory account in the proper period by examining the related purchase invoices and tracing their entry into the records. Determine that subsequent receipts and purchase invoices are recorded in the subsequent period.

10. Agree the inventory total per the inventory listing to the general ledger inventory account. Review any adjustment made for overage or shortage.

11. If client maintains a perpetual inventory, test recording of inventory received by selecting a sample of receiving reports and tracing items to entry in the general ledger inventory account.

12. Scan general ledger inventory account, investigate unusual entries, foot account, and prove ending balance.

III. Cost of sales—perpetual inventory records:

A. Select a sample of source documents giving rise to cost of sales entries. For each item selected, review the cost used, extensions, and footings. Trace the entry of the item into the cost of sales record.

B. Test the numerical sequence of source documents of cost of sales entries.

C. Foot and cross-foot the monthly totals of the cost of sales record and trace monthly totals to the cost of sales and inventory accounts.

D. Examine the general ledger cost of sales account and examine any posting from a source other than the cost of sales record.

E. Foot the inventory and cost of sales accounts and prove the ending balances.

F. Analytically review cost of sales to determine if significant fluctuations exist necessitating audit investigation. (Analytical review techniques are discussed in Chapter 15.)

IV. Cost of sales—periodic inventories:
- **A.** Scan general ledger purchases account and investigate any unusual entries.
- **B.** Foot account and prove ending balance.
- **C.** Test footings and cross-footings in purchases journal and trace postings to general ledger accounts. Scan entries in journal and investigate unusual items.
- **D.** Select a sample of individual entries in purchases journal. Review underlying purchase order, receiving report, and vendor invoice. Trace to entry in vendor account payable.
- **E.** Test numerical sequence of purchase orders and receiving reports on file.
- **F.** Select a sample of receiving reports and trace to entry in purchases record.
- **G.** Review calculation of cost of sales for the period under audit.

V. Financial statement presentation. Consider appropriate presentation for inventories and cost of sales, including such matters as manufacturing cost variances, inventory shortages and overages, work-in-process, obsolete or damaged inventory, and inventory replacement costs. Determine that the client's statements conform to accepted reporting and disclosure standards.

The audit of property, plant, and equipment and depreciation

Property, plant, and equipment often represents the largest dollar amounts of any caption on a company's balance sheet. In this class of assets there are usually fewer transactions than in current assets, but each individual transaction is typically larger than that found in current assets. This characteristic, coupled with the physical nature of property, plant, and equipment, is usually considered to reduce the relative audit risk associated with this asset class as compared with many other assets. The auditor should be mindful, however, that this reduced risk is only a probability statement and that opportunity for massive fraud does exist with respect to property, plant, and equipment.

OBJECTIVES

The auditor must pursue several objectives in the examination of property, plant, and equipment and depreciation. These objectives include:

1. Being satisfied that internal control over property, plant, and equipment is adequate and that financial statement presentation is proper
2. Establishing the physical existence of recorded assets
3. Verifying that the client owns the assets

4. Discovery and disclosure of any liens against property, plant, and equipment
5. Ascertaining whether any assets are not currently in use
6. Establishing the propriety of the client's policies for capitalization of expenditures, depreciation, and purchase authorization regarding property, plant, and equipment
7. Verifying the accuracy of the accounting records regarding additions, disposals, and retirements
8. Determining the propriety of amounts charged to depreciation expense

The following sections discuss the primary auditing procedures employed to achieve the auditor's objectives, described above.

PROCEDURES FOR INITIAL AUDITS

In the auditor's first engagement with a client, several procedures are required that may be unnecessary in subsequent engagements. For property, plant, and equipment, these initial procedures center upon establishing ownership of the various assets and verifying the cost of the assets. In the case of real property, it is often necessary for the auditor to examine deeds relating to the property, title abstracts and certificates, and other evidence of ownership. In special cases the auditor may examine official public records to establish proper recording of deeds and mortgages, although it is more common to ask the client to request that a confirmation of the proper recording be sent the auditor by the client's legal counsel. For personal property, original bills of sale are usually adequate to establish ownership as well as to provide evidence supporting the initial cost of the asset. If assets have been constructed, construction contracts, payments to contractors, invoices for materials, and cost allocations may be examined to establish the propriety of the recorded cost of the asset.

Once these initial procedures have been performed with respect to a client, only the current transactions in the property accounts need be verified in subsequent audits. Observation of assets in subsequent audits should comprehend tests of all property, plant, and equipment, however, and not be confined to current-year additions.

VERIFICATION OF CURRENT-YEAR ADDITIONS AND DISPOSALS

After the initial audit of a client, a substantial portion of the audit of property, plant, and equipment consists of the verification of current-year additions and disposals. Evidence regarding additions and disposals may be obtained by reviewing the proper authorization, such as minutes of the board of directors or the designated property committee, and by examining invoices, bills of sale, and other documents supporting the transactions. Gains and losses on asset disposals should be examined concurrently with the examination of other aspects of the transactions. In this manner, ending balances for property, plant, and equipment are established by applying audited current-year changes to the prior-year audited balances.

OBSERVATION OF PROPERTY, PLANT, AND EQUIPMENT

In addition to verification procedures performed on current-year property transactions, the auditor should physically observe items in the property, plant, and equipment accounts on a test basis. Such observation procedures are necessary to satisfy the audit objective of existence as well as to support the accuracy of the accounting records. Without this procedure, loss or theft of property may remain undiscovered for long periods. In addition, complete absence of physical observation procedures may encourage fraud in this area due to employee knowledge that there is a low probability of detection.

DEPRECIATION

Concurrent with the audit of property, plant, and equipment, it is efficient to perform the verification of current-year depreciation charges and accumulated depreciation balances. This usually may be accomplished by reviewing the client's depreciation schedules or calculations. The auditor, in addition to obtaining satisfaction regarding the mathematical accuracy of the computed depreciation, should also consider the reasonableness of the useful lives, depreciation methods, and salvage values used by the client.

FEDERAL INCOME TAX CONSIDERATIONS

Federal income tax considerations regarding property, plant, and equipment also should be considered at the time the other fixed-asset procedures are performed. Such matters as depreciation recapture, investment credit allowance and recapture, tax status of gains on disposals, allowability of useful lives, and depreciation methods should be examined; relevant data should be noted to facilitate either preparation of the tax return or review of the client's prepared return.

MAINTENANCE AND REPAIRS EXPENSE

Many auditors have found it beneficial to examine the maintenance and repair expense account concurrently with the property, plant, and equipment audit. This procedure is advisable because of the likelihood that capital expenditures may be charged erroneously to this expense. If such errors are discovered and appropriate adjustments are made prior to completing the audit of property, plant, and equipment, time-consuming changes in the working papers regarding asset balances, depreciation calculations, investment tax credits, and so forth may be minimized.

ADEQUACY OF INSURANCE COVERAGE

It is customary for the auditor to review the client's insurance coverage on tangible assets in order to be satisfied that adequate coverage exists. This review represents a constructive service to the client, who may have overlooked a needed coverage or may be paying for excessive coverage. Whether or not this procedure is necessary for the rendering of an opinion on financial statements is subject to question. Many auditors believe that financial statements users have a right to assume that the usual insurable risks are adequately covered and that circumstances to the contrary will be disclosed. That financial statement users do, in fact, implicitly make such an assumption appears reasonable, and this supports the desirability of the auditor's review of insurance coverage with disclosure of any inadequacies found.

INTERNAL CONTROL OVER PROPERTY, PLANT, AND EQUIPMENT

The internal control system relating to property, plant, and equipment should include physical as well as accounting controls. Accounting controls should include such features as:

1. Accountability for individual units or groups of assets
2. Authorization procedures to protect against unauthorized expenditures
3. Procedures to insure proper classification of expenditures
4. Procedures to control asset disposals and the proceeds of disposals

Physical controls over property, plant, and equipment should require a periodic physical inventory of the assets and comparison of the inventory counts with the accounting records. Also, procedures and policies should be designed to protect property, plant, and equipment from deterioration, theft, and damage.

FINANCIAL STATEMENT PRESENTATION OF PROPERTY, PLANT, AND EQUIPMENT AND DEPRECIATION

Property, plant, and equipment should be presented on the balance sheet as a noncurrent asset and should be captioned appropriately. Accumulated depreciation is shown as a deduction from the cost of related assets, with net book values being extended into the amount columns. All assets included in the property, plant, and equipment category should be in current use in the operations of the business or a part of essential standby equipment to be used in case of breakdowns or overloads of the regular equipment. All liens on assets must be disclosed prominently in the financial statements. Any assets considered to be in permanent disuse should be presented under another balance sheet caption, such as other assets. Depreciation should not be taken on such assets. The total depreciation expense for the period should be presented along with the balances of major classes of depreciable assets and major categories of accumulated depreciation. In addition, a general description of the depreciation methods used should be disclosed.

AUDIT PROGRAM FOR PROPERTY, PLANT, AND EQUIPMENT AND DEPRECIATION

The following audit program presents audit procedures appropriate for the examination of property, plant, and equipment and depreciation.

I. Review internal controls over property, plant, and equipment and depreciation.

II. Property, plant, and equipment:

1. Obtain a schedule of property, plant, and equipment detailing the beginning-of-period balances, current additions, current retirements, and ending balances.
2. Verify beginning-of-period balances by reference to prior year working papers for recurring audits. For initial audits, verify beginning balances by reviewing source documents and other evidence of cost and ownership from prior periods. Record details of initial audit procedures in working papers.
3. Test current-year additions by reference to source documents verifying recorded cost and trace entries into the accounting records.
4. Test current-year disposals verifying book value at disposition, gain or loss on disposal, and proper removal from the asset and accumulated depreciation accounts.
5. Review entries to the repairs and maintenance account to ascertain if property-related expenditures have been recorded in accordance with the client's capitalization policy.
6. Test the property records by systematically observing selected property items. Major items of equipment, current-year additions, and property that is easily transportable should be included in the selection. Tests should be made both by making selections from the property records then locating the physical items and by selecting physical items and tracing them into the records.
7. Foot the general ledger property accounts and prove the ending balance.
8. Review details and amounts of revenues from rentals, subleases, etc.
9. Make inquiries with respect to the existence of fully depreciated assets and assets not currently in use.

III. Depreciation and accumulated depreciation:

1. Obtain a schedule of accumulated depreciation detailing the beginning-of-period balances, current depreciation expense, current retirements, and ending balances.

2. Verify beginning-of-period balances by reference to prior-year working papers for recurring audits. For initial audits, verify beginning balances by recomputing prior year's depreciation.
3. Test current-year depreciation expense by recomputation and agree totals to general ledger depreciation expense accounts. Consider propriety of depreciation methods, useful lives, and salvage values used.

IV. Financial statement presentation. Consider appropriate presentation for property, plant, and equipment, accumulated depreciation, depreciation expense, and rental revenues. Include such matters as property not currently used, fully depreciated assets, liens against property, etc. Determine that client's statements conform to accepted reporting and disclosure standards.

V. Review of insurance coverage. Review the client's insurance coverage and note conclusions as to its adequacy in the working papers.

The audit of investments and investment income

For many companies, investments represent a substantial portion of total assets; for others, investments are only temporary assets or merely reflect incidental aspects of company operations. For the auditor, investments represent assets with high inherent audit risk because of their desirability and potential negotiability.

OBJECTIVES

The objectives sought by the auditor in the examination of investments and investment income include:

1. Establishing that an adequate system of internal control exists with respect to investments and income from investments
2. Ascertaining that the investments recorded in the client's records exist and are owned by the client
3. Establishing that the investments are properly valued and presented on the financial statements
4. Discovering and disclosing any liens applicable to investments
5. Determining that gains, losses, and investment income are properly recorded

Many auditing procedures used to satisfy the above-stated objectives are similar, in concept, to those used in the verification of several of the other areas already described. Some features of the investment audit, however, are peculiar to this type of asset, especially in the areas of valuation and the verification of investment income. SAS No. 1 (AU 332) provides auditors with specific guidance in gathering evidence regarding long-term investments.

EXAMINATION AND CONFIRMATION

Procedures designed to satisfy the auditor's objective regarding existence and ownership of investments usually include examination or confirmation. When securities are involved, it is considered good practice for the auditor to examine them and agree the count to the client's records. If this procedure is impracticable, confirmation with an outside custodian may be an acceptable alternative. Before relying on a confirmation of this nature, the auditor should carefully consider the risk of accepting such evidence and should evaluate the reputation and financial standing of the confirming party.

In performing a securities count, the auditor must design the procedures so that substitution of securities will be detected. First, the verification of securities must be performed simultaneously with that of other liquid assets. *Simultaneously* here means in a way that prevents someone from temporarily using the securities to aid in covering a shortage in some other account. For example, without simultaneous verification, the auditor might not discover a situation in which someone "borrowed" a negotiable security, pledged it for a loan, and used the loan proceeds to replenish a shortage in a cash account. After the auditor's verification of cash, but before verification of investments, the security could be redeemed and replaced without the auditor's knowledge. Simultaneous verification of investments and other liquid assets should enable the auditor to discover such activity. Simultaneity may be achieved by verifying all liquid assets at the same point in time or by judicious use of control devices to insure that no one has free access to liquid assets during the verification period.

During the securities count, the auditor should record serial numbers of securities. Comparison of serial numbers of securities on hand at year end with the recorded serial numbers of those on hand a year earlier will detect any changes made in the certificates and perhaps reveal unauthorized use of the securities during the year and their replacement at year end. These numbers may also be compared with broker's advices supporting the securities purchase in order to gain evidence that the certificates counted are in fact those owned by the client. In the case of registered securities, this may be unnecessary, since the certificates are issued in the name of the owner.

Confirmation with the issuer of investments when they are in the form of stocks and bonds is usually not made because of the high quality of other available evidence. However, when the investment is in a form such as a note or an advance to a related company, for example, confirmation is necessary. In cases of investments secured by collateral, the audit program should include an inspection and evaluation of the collateral.

VALUATION PROCEDURES

Investments commonly are presented on the financial statements at cost or the lower of cost or market. In cases where the investor exercises an element of control over the investee, the equity method is appropriate; and in cases of some regulated companies, investments are disclosed at market values. In practically every audit involving investments, the auditor must refer to some measure of the current market value of the investment to be satisfied that a proper asset value is reported.

Techniques for assessing the value of investments vary depending upon the investment in question. In the case of listed securities, reference to newspapers or other published data usually will provide adequate indication of current values. Often a situation arises in which a security is publicly held but infrequently traded. In many such cases, the most recent trade in the security is relevant. If the security is a bond, current prices of bonds with similar ratings and characteristics may be an adequate measure of current value.

When the investments being examined represent securities of a closely held corporation, examination of the financial statements of the investee corporation may offer the best indication of the investment's value. When investments are secured, as in the case of a mortgage or the pledge of other collateral, an appraisal of the existence, transferability, and value of the secured property may serve as audit evidence supporting the value of the investment.

The client's use of the equity method of accounting for investments in either subsidiaries or investees calls for the inclusion of a portion of another company's income or loss in the client's income statement and a corresponding change in the investment account. The auditor must be satisfied about the accuracy of this amount. Often the auditor may rely upon audited financial statements submitted by the other company, but in some cases he or she may insist on being allowed to make a personal examination of the financial statements and underlying evidence.

VERIFICATION OF ACQUISITIONS, DISPOSALS, GAINS, AND LOSSES

During the period under audit, the client may have engaged in investment transactions that must be verified by the auditor. Specific authorization for such transactions is usually granted by an investment committee or, in the case of major investments, by the board of directors; minutes of the meetings of these groups furnish evidence regarding the proper authorization. In the case of securities, brokers' advices may be used to support the transactions. These documents will indicate the dates and amounts of the various transactions as well as descriptions and identifying numbers of the securities involved. Should the auditor want further authentication, confirmation of transactions may be requested directly from the client's broker.

Other types of investment transactions normally will be documented by title conveyances, which usually will serve as audit evidence to support the recording of the transaction. Gains and losses on investment transactions may be verified by reference to the same documents used to determine cost and selling price of the investment sold. If the evidence available to the auditor regarding investment transactions is not deemed sufficient, the auditor should not hesitate to seek evidence external to the firm. Appropriate procedures in such cases include (1) confirmation requests to other parties to the transaction, (2) consultation with attorneys who represented the client in the transaction, and (3) reference to public records if the transaction has been so entered.

VERIFICATION OF INVESTMENT INCOME

In verifying income from investments, the auditor must examine evidence that the amounts recorded are neither overstated nor understated. Since investment income, in many cases, is received at irregular times and in irregular amounts, it is often difficult to control. Such unscheduled receipts may go undeposited and unrecorded for a number of days after receipt, offering an attractive opportunity for any dishonest employee who may have access to them. In cases of publicly held stock investments, the auditor may compare the recorded dividend income with published dividend records. Income from investments in bonds may be verified by calculation based on the face amount and the nominal interest rate. Accruals of interest and amortization of premium and discount also may be verified by calculation.

Rental income may be verified by reference to rental agreements. To verify dividend income on stock of closely held corporations and other investment income that is not evidenced by published data, the auditor may send confirmation requests to the payor.

INTERNAL CONTROL OVER INVESTMENTS AND INVESTMENT INCOME

Internal control systems relating to investments should provide both physical and accounting control over the assets. Physical control should be exercised to assure safe custody of the investments to prevent loss, theft, or unauthorized use. This control is often achieved, in the case of securities, by placing them with an outside custodian, such as a bank. If the company itself desires to maintain custody of the securities, they should be kept in an appropriate repository such as the company vault or a safety deposit box. Access to securities should be subject to dual control, whereby no person acting alone may gain possession of the securities.

Accounting controls over investments and investment income should provide accountability for individual investments. The investment accounting records should be kept by a person or persons who do not have access to the investments themselves. Further, persons with access to cash should not have control over the investments or the investment accounting records. Systematic procedures should be devised with respect to safeguarding investment income. It is often possible to prepare a schedule of expected investment income for a period and at a later time compare recorded income with expected income. There should be procedures for safeguarding the proceeds of sales of investments as well as systematic accounting for sales, purchases, gains, and losses.

FINANCIAL STATEMENT PRESENTATION OF INVESTMENTS AND INVESTMENT INCOME

Investments are normally presented on the financial statements at cost or the lower of cost or market, and it is usual to disclose both cost and market value of the investment portfolio. If the investment results in a significant degree of control in the investee, the equity method is appropriate for financial statement presentation. If investments are pledged or are otherwise subject to liens, this should be disclosed in the financial statements. If any collateral is held to secure the investment, this normally should be disclosed also.

Whether investments represent current or long-term assets depends upon the nature of the investment and the intent of management. To be classed as a current asset, an investment should be readily marketable, and it should be the intent of management to convert the investment to cash in the current period. Investments that are part of a fund and, consequently, are designated for a specific use should be so identified.

Valuation allowances should be used to reduce the portfolio of any marketable equity securities to market. The resulting loss (or recovery of loss) is reflected as an unrealized item on the income statement for current investments and in a special section of the owner's equity section for noncurrent and unclassified investments. Realized gains or losses may be recorded when marketable equity securities are reclassified from current to noncurrent, when there is a permanent impairment of the value of an investment, and upon disposal of an investment.

AUDIT PROGRAM FOR INVESTMENTS AND INVESTMENT INCOME

Representative auditing procedures for verification of investments and investment income are presented in the following audit program.

I. Review internal controls over investments and investment income.

II. Investments in securities:

1. Obtain a detailed schedule of securities held by the client, showing dates of acquisition, serial numbers, description, cost, carrying value, market value at balance sheet date, etc.
2. Verify dates, cost, descriptions, serial numbers, etc., recorded for current-year securities acquisitions by examining broker's advices

or other supporting documents and tracing to entries in the investments and cash disbursements records.

3. If data regarding securities acquisitions in prior years have not been verified in prior audits, examine documentation supporting the transactions and trace to entry in records.
4. Arrange to inspect securities. Determine that other liquid assets are under audit control in order to prevent substitution. Inspect securities agreeing serial numbers, descriptions, and amounts to schedule of investments. Determine that all securities in registered form are in the name of the client. If securities are held by an outside custodian, consider if confirmation rather than inspection is appropriate.
5. Test carrying values and market values at balance sheet date shown on the schedule of investments. Market values should be verified by reference to published sources when available.
6. Verify realized gains and losses recorded on dispositions of securities during the period by examining supporting documents, recalculating gain or loss, and tracing entries into the records.
7. Verify unrealized losses (and recoveries) resulting from presenting marketable equity securities at lower of cost or market.
8. Test extensions and footings of investment schedule and agree totals to general ledger.
9. Scan general ledger investment account for unusual entries, foot account and prove ending balance.

III. Other investments: verify cost, carrying value, and market value of client investments in real estate or other personal property. Inspect investments and include details of all verification procedures in working papers.

IV. Investment income:

1. Verify amounts of dividend income on stock investments by reference to published dividend records.
2. Verify amounts of bond interest recorded by recalculating interest received and interest accruals.
3. Verify investment income from stock investments carried on the equity method by reference to audited financial statements of the investee corporation.
4. Verify income from other investments such as rentals, royalties, etc., by examining underlying agreements, supporting documents, and entries in the accounting records.
5. Scan investment income accounts for unusual entries, foot accounts, and prove ending balances.
6. Analytically review investment income accounts. Consider reasonableness of amounts as well as unusual fluctuations. (Analytical review techniques are discussed in Chapter 15.)

V. Financial statement presentation. Consider appropriate presentation of investments and investment income, including such items as current or noncurrent classification and cost or market valuation. Determine that client's statements conform to accepted reporting and disclosure standards.

The audit of other assets and related areas

Auditing techniques appropriate for the examination of major assets and areas of the business related to those assets have been discussed in this and preceding chapters. Other assets such as prepaid expenses, leasehold improvements, patents, franchises, deposits, etc., also require audit verification. Audit procedures for such assets are similar to those described for the major asset areas and include techniques such as examination of source documents, confirmation, recalculation of cost expirations, tests of transactions, and analytical review. The following generalized audit program presents audit procedures appropriate for many of the types of miscellaneous assets encountered by auditors.

AUDIT PROGRAM FOR OTHER ASSETS AND RELATED AREAS

1. Review internal controls over other assets and related areas to include prepaid expenses, intangibles, and related expenses.
2. Obtain schedules of other assets showing beginning-of-period balances, additions, reductions, and ending balances.
3. Agree beginning-of-period balances to prior-year working papers. In initial audits, examine documentation supporting opening balances.
4. Test current-period additions by inspecting supporting documents and entry into accounting records.
5. Test current-period expirations by recomputation or other appropriate means. Consider propriety and consistency of amortization methods and useful lives for intangibles. Trace entries to asset accounts and related expense accounts on test basis.
6. Determine that carrying values of other assets are consistent with future benefits to be derived.
7. Obtain confirmations for any material prepayments or deposits.
8. Scan other asset accounts and related expense accounts in the general ledger. Investigate any unusual entries. On a test basis foot accounts and prove ending balances.
9. Consider appropriate presentation of other assets and related areas including the propriety of current or noncurrent classification. Determine that client's statements conform to accepted reporting and disclosure standards.

Review questions

13-1. What are an auditor's objectives regarding examination of inventories?

13-2. What audit objectives are achieved by inventory observations?

13-3. What is an auditor's function in an inventory count and observation?

13-4. What is the purpose of cutoff data and why should they be obtained at the time of inventory observation?

13-5. Why should an auditor concentrate test counts to the part of the inventory where dollar value is highest?

13-6. What audit procedures should be performed on the final inventory listing and other inventory records?

13-7. How are inventories properly presented on financial statements?

13-8. What two characteristics of property, plant, and equipment are considered to reduce the relative audit risk associated with this asset class?

13-9. What are the auditor's objectives in an examination of property, plant, and equipment?

13-10. What additional procedures are required on an initial audit in regard to property, plant, and equipment?

13-11. Discuss possible reasons why observation of property, plant, and equipment is not required, whereas observation of inventory is a generally accepted auditing procedure.

13-12. How is the audit of depreciation usually accomplished?

13-13. What other accounts are usually examined concurrently with property, plant, and equipment?

13-14. What are four features included in accounting controls over property, plant, and equipment?

13-15. What are an auditor's objectives in an examination of investments?

13-16. How are investments properly presented in financial statements?

13-17. How may acquisitions, disposals, gains, and losses of investments be verified by an auditor?

13-18. State how you might satisfy yourself regarding quantities in observing the following inventories:

a. Large pile of granular chemical
b. Logs in a river
c. Liquid in tanks
d. Small machine parts
e. Work-in-process

13-19. Why does an auditor review a client's insurance coverage?

13-20. How can an auditor *simultaneously* verify cash, investments, and all other liquid assets?

13-21. What are some procedures that may be used to verify investment income?

13-22. Why should auditors review a client's cost accounting system?

Decision problems

13-23. During the course of an audit of inventories, the auditor discovers the following items. His client uses a perpetual inventory system, and all differences between the physical inventory and the inventory account on the general ledger are adjusted at year end to the Inventory Over and Short account.

a. Merchandise held on consignment was included in the November 30 physical inventory count. Cost of such merchandise was $1,276.

b. An invoice for merchandise dated November 20 in the amount of $516 had not been recorded as of year end. The merchandise had been received and was included in the physical inventory.

c. Merchandise held on consignment at year end by a customer in the amount of $718 was inadvertently left off the physical inventory.

d. A purchase invoice dated November 28 in the amount of $1,263 for goods shipped FOB shipping point on that date was recorded at year end. The goods, however, had not been received and were excluded from the physical inventory.

e. Inventory in the amount of $1,874 had been listed on the physical inventory summary as $874.

f. A purchase invoice dated November 24 in the amount of $1,922 for goods shipped FOB destination on that date was recorded at year end. The goods had not been received and were not included in the year-end physical inventory.

1. Assuming all amounts are material, what adjusting entry would the auditor propose in each case for the year ended November 30, 1984?
2. For each adjusting entry proposed in part 1, determine whether the client should make a reversing entry in the subsequent period.

13-24. Consider the following situation:

In auditing a small, closely held corporation, Jennifer Leigh, CPA, experienced difficulty in determining the propriety of the valuation of a used motor launch the client had invested in. Leigh physically observed the ship accompanied by the comptroller of the corporation, who assured her that the investment was worth the $64,000 it had cost. When Leigh remarked that the ship appeared to be in poor physical condition, the comptroller assured her that company work crews would soon restore the craft and it would be sold at a sizeable profit.

Overhearing the conversation, the president of the client corporation walked up and remarked, "Confidentially, if you know anyone who will give $35,000 for this old tub, I'll take it." Leigh noted the various comments in the working papers along with her conclusion that an adjusting entry should be proposed writing-down the investment to $35,000.

Leigh's comments were reviewed by the partner-in-charge, who agreed with her conclusion and proposed the adjustment to the management of the corporation. The client reluctantly agreed and the adjustment was recorded.

Several months following the issuance of the audit report, Leigh read in the financial pages of the local newspaper that the president of the client corporation had purchased all the stock in the corporation from the former owners. The article went on to say that the purchase price was based on the book value of the corporation as determined by the latest audited financial statements.

a. Why are most asset auditing procedures designed to detect overstatements?
b. How could Leigh have better handled the situation described?
c. What are some motivations that management might have for understating assets and/or income?

13-25. What forms of audit evidence can the auditor obtain to assess the value of the following types of investments?
a. Common stock listed on the New York Stock Exchange
b. Corporate bonds not listed on any exchange
c. Mortgage loans on real estate
d. Common stock of an unlisted company
e. Municipal bonds
f. Warrants for the stock of a company whose stock is actively traded over-the-counter
g. U.S. Treasury bonds

13-26. You have been engaged to audit the December 31, 1984, financial statements of the Sunshine Equipment Corporation, which was formed in 1946 and sells or leases construction equipment such as bulldozers, road scrapers, dirt movers, etc., to contractors. The corporation at year end has fifty pieces of equipment leased to thirty contractors who are using the equipment at various locations throughout your state.

The Sunshine Equipment Corporation is identified as the owner of the leased equipment by a small metal tag that is attached to each machine. The tag is fastened by screws so that it can be removed if the machine is sold. During the audit you find that the contractors often buy the equipment that they have been leasing, but the identification tag is not always removed from the machine.

The corporation's principal asset is the equipment leased to the contractors. Although there is no plant ledger, each machine is accounted for by a file card that gives its description, cost, contractor-lessee, and rental payment records. The corporation's system of internal control is weak.

You were engaged upon the recommendation of the president of the local bank. The Sunshine Equipment Corporation, which had never had an audit, had applied to the bank for a sizable loan; the bank president had requested an audited balance sheet.

You barely know John Smith, the principal stockholder and president of Sunshine; he has a reputation for expensive personal tastes and for shrewd business dealings, some of which have bordered on being unethical. Nevertheless, Smith enjoys a strong personal allegiance from his contractor-lessees, whose favor he has carried by personal gifts and loans. The lessees look upon Smith as a personal friend for whom they would do almost anything. Often they overlook the fact that they are dealing with the corporation and make their checks payable to Smith, who endorses them over to the corporation.

a. List the audit procedures that you would employ in the examination of the asset account representing the equipment leased to the contractors.
b. Although your audit procedures, including those you described in answering part *a,* did not uncover any discrepancies, you have been unable

to dismiss your feeling that Smith and some of the contractor-lessees may have collaborated to deceive you. Under this condition discuss what action, if any, you would take and the effect, if any, of your feeling upon your auditor's opinion. (Assume that you would not withdraw from the engagement.)

AICPA adapted

13-27. As a result of highly profitable operations over a number of years, Mango Manufacturing Corporation accumulated a substantial investment portfolio. In the examination of the financial statements for the year ended December 31, 1984, the following information came to the attention of the corporation's CPA:

a. The manufacturing operations of the corporation resulted in an operating loss for the year.

b. In 1984 the corporation placed the securities making up the investment portfolio with a financial institution that will serve as custodian of the securities. Formerly the securities were kept in the corporation's safe deposit box in the local bank.

c. On December 22, 1984 the corporation sold and then repurchased on the same day a number of securities that had appreciated greatly in value. Management stated that the purpose of the sale and repurchases was to establish a higher cost and book value for the securities and to avoid the reporting of a loss for the year.

1. List the objectives of the CPA's examination of the Investment account.
2. Under what conditions would the CPA accept a confirmation of the securities on hand from the custodian in lieu of personally inspecting and counting the securities?
3. What disclosure, if any, of the sale and repurchase of the securities would the CPA recommend for the financial statements? If the client accepts the CPA's recommendations for disclosure, what effect, if any, would the sale and repurchase have upon the CPA's opinion on the financial statements? Discuss.

AICPA adapted

13-28. On January 10, 1985 you were engaged to make an examination of the financial statements of Cross Equipment Corporation for the year ended December 31, 1984. Cross has sold trucks and truck parts and accessories for many years, but has never had an audit. Cross maintains good perpetual records for all inventories and takes a complete physical inventory each December 31.

The Parts Inventory account includes the $2,500 cost of obsolete parts. Cross's executives acknowledge these parts have been worthless for several years but they have continued to carry the cost as an asset. The amount of $2,500 is material in relation to 1984 net income and year-end inventories, but not material in relation to total assets or capital at December 31, 1984.

a. List the procedures you would add to your inventory audit program for new trucks because you did not observe the physical inventory taken by the corporation as of December 31, 1984.

b. Should the $2,500 of obsolete parts be carried in inventory as an asset? Discuss.

c. Assume that your alternative auditing procedures satisfy you regarding the corporation's December 31, 1984 inventory but that you were unable to apply these alternative procedures to the December 31, 1983 inventory. Discuss (ignoring the obsolete parts) the effect this would have on your auditor's report in (1) the scope (or middle) paragraph and (2) the opinion paragraph.

AICPA adapted

13-29. In connection with her examination of the financial statements of Agricon Chemicals, Inc., Marjorie Kelly, CPA, is considering the necessity of inspecting marketable securities on the balance-sheet date, May 31, 1985, or at some other date. The marketable securities held by Agricon include negotiable bearer bonds, which are kept in a safe in the treasurer's office, and miscellaneous stocks and bonds kept in a safe deposit box at the Merchants Bank. Both the negotiable bearer bonds and the miscellaneous stocks and bonds are material to proper presentation of Agricon's financial position.

a. What factors should Kelly consider in determining the necessity for inspecting these securities on May 31, 1985 as opposed to other dates?

b. Assume that Kelly plans to send a member of her staff to Agricon's offices and the Merchants Bank on May 31, 1985, to make the security inspection. What instructions should she give to this staff member as to the conduct of the inspection and the evidence to be included in the audit working papers? Do not discuss the valuation of securities, the income from securities, or the examination of information contained in the books and records of the company.

c. Assume that Kelly finds it impracticable to send a member of her staff to Agricon's offices and the Merchants Bank on May 31, 1985. What alternative procedures may she employ to assure herself that the company had physical possession of its marketable securities on May 31, 1985, if the securities are inspected (1) May 28, 1985? (2) June 5, 1985?

AICPA adapted

13-30. In connection with a recurring examination of the financial statements of the Karen Manufacturing Company for the year ended December 31, 1983, you have been assigned the audit of the Manufacturing Equipment, Manufacturing Equipment-Accumulated Depreciation, and Repairs to Manufacturing Equipment accounts. Your review of Karen's policies has disclosed the following pertinent information:

a. The Manufacturing Equipment account includes the net invoice price plus related freight and installation costs for all of the equipment in Karen's manufacturing plant.

b. The Manufacturing Equipment-Accumulated Depreciation account is supported by a subsidiary ledger, which shows the cost and accumulated depreciation for each piece of equipment.

c. An annual budget for capital expenditures of $1,000 or more is prepared by the budget committee and approved by the board of directors.

Capital expenditures over $1,000, which are not included in this budget, must be approved by the board of directors, and variations of 20 percent or more must be explained to the board. Approval by the supervisor of production is required for capital expenditures under $1,000.

d. Company employees handle installation, removal, repair, and rebuilding of the machinery. Work orders are prepared for these activities and are subject to the same budgetary control as other expenditures. Work orders are not required for external expenditures.

1. Cite the major objectives of your audit of the Manufacturing Equipment, Manufacturing Equipment-Accumulated Depreciation, and Repairs to Manufacturing Equipment accounts. Do not include in this listing the auditing procedures designed to accomplish these objectives.
2. Prepare the portion of your audit program applicable to the review of 1983 additions to the Manufacturing Equipment account.

AICPA adapted

13-31. In connection with his examination of the financial statements of Papaya Products Co., an assembler of home appliances, for the year ended May 31, 1983, Terry Birt, CPA, is reviewing with Papaya's controller the plans for a physical inventory at the company warehouse on May 31, 1983. In answering the two parts of this question, do not discuss procedures for the physical inventory of work-in-process, inventory pricing, or other audit steps not directly related to the physical inventory taking.

a. Finished appliances, unassembled parts, and supplies are stored in the warehouse, which is attached to Papaya's assembly plant. The plant will operate during the count. On May 30 the warehouse will deliver to the plant the estimated quantities of unassembled parts and supplies required for May 31 production, but there may be emergency requisitions on May 31. During the count the warehouse will continue to receive parts and supplies and to ship finished appliances. However, appliances completed on May 31 will be held in the plant until after the physical inventory has been taken.

What procedures should the company establish to insure that the inventory count includes all items that should be included and that nothing is counted twice?

b. Warehouse employees will join with accounting department employees in counting the inventory. The inventory-takers will use a tag system.

What instructions should the company give to the inventory-takers?

AICPA adapted

13-32. You have assigned your assistant to the examination of the Cap Sales Company's fire insurance policies. All routine audit procedures with regard to the fire insurance register have been completed (i.e., vouching, footing, examination of cancelled checks, computation of insurance expense and prepayment, tracing of expense charges to appropriate expense accounts, etc.). Your assistant has never examined fire insurance policies before and asks for detailed instructions.

a. In addition to examining the policies for the amounts of insurance and premium and for effective and expiration dates, to what other details should your assistant give particular attention while examining the policies? Give the reasons for examining each detail. Confine your comments to fire insurance policies covering buildings, their contents, and inventories.

b. After reviewing your assistant's working papers, you concur in the conclusion that the insurance coverage against loss by fire is inadequate and that if loss occurs the company may have insufficient assets to liquidate its debts. After a discussion with you, management refuses to increase the amount of insurance coverage.

1. What mention will you make of this condition and contingency in your short-form report? Why?
2. What effect will this condition and contingency have upon your opinion? Give the reasons for your position.

AICPA adapted

13-33. You have just begun your examination of the financial statements of AMY Corporation for the year ended December 31, 1983. Analyses of the company's Unexpired Insurance and Insurance Expense accounts follow.

AMY Corporation
WORKSHEET FOR DISTRIBUTION OF INSURANCE
For Year Ended December 31, 1983

Date (1983)		*Unexpired Insurance*	*Folio*	*Amount* *Debit*	*Amount* *Credit*
January	1	Balance forward		$ 5,550	
	10	Premium on president's policy	CD	1,240	
	14	Deposit on workmen's compensation policy for 1983	CD	2,750	
	31	Monthly amortization	JE		$410
April	1	Down payment on fire policy (April 1, 1983, to April 1, 1988)	CD	1,000	
		Totals		$10,540	$410
		Insurance Expense			
January	10	Trip insurance on officers (Inspection tour of dealers in December 1982)	CD	$ 170	
	31	Monthly amortization	JE	410	

Date (1983)		Insurance Expense	Folio	Amount Debit	Amount Credit
February	21	Balance on workmen's compensation policy (Per payroll audit for policy year ending December 31, 1982)	CD	250	
April	10	Automobile collision policy (Policy year April 1, 1983, to April 1, 1984) ..	CD	2,500	
June	10	Increase in fire policy (May 1, 1983, to April 1, 1988)	CD	590	
August	10	Fleet public liability and property damage policy (September 1, 1983, to September 1, 1984)	CD	3,780	
	17	Check from insurance company for reduction in auto collision rate for entire policy year	CR		$120
October	1	Fire policy payment	CD	1,300	
	19	Cost of repair to automobile damaged in a collision	CD	400	
		Totals		$ 9,400	$120

Your examination also disclosed the following information:

a. Only one policy of those prepaid at January 1, 1983, remained in force on December 31, and it will expire on March 31, 1984. The policy was a 24-month policy and the total premium was $600.

b. Cash value of the life insurance policy of the president increased from $1,110 to $1,660 during 1983. The corporation is the beneficiary on the policy.

c. The corporation signed a note payable to an insurance company for the balance due on the fire insurance policy, which was effective as of April 1. The note called for nine additional $1,000 semiannual payments plus interest at 6 percent per annum on the unpaid balance (also paid semi-annually).

d. An accrual dated December 31, 1982, for $170 for insurance payable was included among accrued liabilities.

e. Included in miscellaneous income was a credit dated April 10 for $100 for a 4 percent dividend on the renewal of the automobile collision insurance policy. The insurance company is a mutual company. Also included in miscellaneous income was a credit dated November 2 for

$350 for a check from the same insurance company for a claim filed October 19.

f. An invoice dated November 15 for $1,560 for employee fidelity bonds from November 15, 1983, to November 15, 1984, was not paid or recorded.

g. An invoice dated January 13, 1984, for $2,800 for the 1984 workmen's compensation policy was not recorded. The net amount of the invoice was $2,660 after a credit of $140 from the payroll audit for the year ended December 31, 1983.

Prepare a worksheet to properly distribute all amounts related to insurance for 1983. The books have not been closed for the year. The worksheet should provide columns to show the distribution to unexpired insurance, to insurance expense, and to other accounts. The names of other accounts affected should be indicated. Formal journal entries are not required.

AICPA adapted

13-34. Mike Post, CPA, is the auditor for a manufacturing company with a balance sheet that includes the caption, property, plant, and equipment. Post has been asked by the company's management if audit adjustments or reclassifications are required for the following material items that have been included or excluded from property, plant, and equipment.

a. A tract of land was acquired during the year. The land is the future site of the client's new headquarters which will be constructed in the following year. Commissions were paid to the real estate agent used to acquire the land, and expenditures were made to relocate the previous owner's equipment. These commissions and expenditures were expensed and are excluded from property, plant, and equipment.

b. Clearing costs were incurred to make the land ready for construction. These costs were included in property, plant, and equipment.

c. During the land-clearing process, timber and gravel were recovered and sold. The proceeds from the sale were recorded as other income and are excluded from property, plant, and equipment.

d. A group of machines was purchased under a royalty agreement that provides royalty payments based on units of production from the machines. The cost of the machines, freight costs, unloading charges, and royalty payments were capitalized and are included in property, plant, and equipment.

1. Describe the general characteristics of assets, such as land, buildings, improvements, machinery, equipment, fixtures, etc., that should normally be classified as property, plant, and equipment, and identify audit objectives (i.e., how an auditor can obtain audit satisfaction) in connection with the examination of property, plant, and equipment. *Do not discuss specific audit procedures.*
2. Indicate whether each of the above items lettered *a* to *d* requires one or more audit adjustments or reclassifications, and explain why such adjustments or reclassifications are required or not required.

Organize your answer as follows:

Item number	Is audit adjustment or reclassification required? Yes or no	Reasons why audit adjustment or reclassification is required or not required

AICPA adapted

13-35. In connection with the annual examination of McCarley Corp., a manufacturer of janitorial supplies, you have been assigned to audit the fixed assets. The company maintains a detailed property ledger for all fixed assets. You prepared an audit program for the balances of property, plant, and equipment but have yet to prepare one for accumulated depreciation and depreciation expense.

Prepare a separate comprehensive audit program for the accumulated depreciation and depreciation expense accounts.

AICPA adapted

13-36. An auditor is conducting an examination of the financial statements of a wholesale cosmetics distributor with an inventory consisting of thousands of individual items. The distributor keeps its inventory in its own distribution center and in two public warehouses. An inventory computer file is maintained on a computer disk and at the end of each business day the file is updated. Each record of the inventory file contains the following data:

Item number
Location of item
Description of item
Quantity on hand
Cost per item
Date of last purchase
Date of last sale
Quantity sold during year

The auditor is planning to observe the distributor's physical count of inventories as of a given date. The auditor will have available a computer tape of the data on the inventory file on the date of the physical count and a general purpose computer software package.

The auditor is planning to perform basic inventory auditing procedures. Identify the basic inventory auditing procedures and describe how the use of the general purpose software package and the tape of the inventory file data might be helpful to the auditor in performing such auditing procedures.

Organize your answer as follows:

Basic inventory auditing procedure	How general purpose computer software package and tape of the inventory file data might be helpful
1. Observe the physical count, making and recording test counts where applicable.	*Determining which items are to be test counted by selecting a random sample of a representative number of items from the inventory file as of the date of the physical count.*

AICPA adapted

14

Auditing Liabilities, Owners' Equity, and Related Areas

The audit examination of liabilities, owners' equity, and related areas requires, in many ways, a different philosophy on the part of auditors than does the examination of assets. In the asset audit, auditors attempt to verify the existence and value of some tangible or intangible property. Usually, they are able to rely upon personal examination or direct confirmation to provide adequate evidence of an asset's existence. Such concrete evidence is not readily available to auditors in their verification of liabilities and owners' equity because, since liabilities and owners' equities are intangible in nature, physical observation is irrelevant. Another reason, especially applicable to liabilities, involves auditors' expectations regarding the manner in which financial statements might be deliberately misstated in an effort to improve the picture of the financial position or to cover up a defalcation. Stated concisely, these expectations are that assets are likely to be overstated and that liabilities are likely to be understated. These expectations set the basic direction for audit procedures in the two general areas. Asset audit procedures are primarily designed to detect overstatements; liability procedures focus on what may be a more difficult task, that of detecting omissions or understatements.

With the foregoing expectations in mind, auditors may be able to obtain satisfactory evidence that assets are not overstated through physical examination and confirmation procedures. However, no amount of verification work performed on the *recorded* liabilities will assure an auditor that all *existing* liabilities of a client have been recorded. For these reasons certain extended procedures and subjective considerations may be employed by the auditor to gain adequate assurance that liabilities and equities are properly stated. As a corollary, it should be noted that the conventional audit procedures described in the preceding chapters regarding assets are not primarily designed to disclose an understatement of assets. This is consistent with the expectations regarding fraud that have previously been stated but represents a condition that should be recognized and considered by the auditor.

Related areas to be considered concurrently with the audit of liabilities and owners' equity are cash disbursements, interest expense and accruals, and dividends. By examining these areas concurrently, the efficiency and effectiveness of the audit is enhanced. Audit efficiency is increased because areas of the accounting system that are verified by an examination of the same transactions and source documents are audited simultaneously, thereby eliminating multiple examinations of the same data. Coordination of audit procedures also increases the effectiveness of the audit because examination of the complete transactions at one time reduces the possibility that specific areas or transactions will escape audit scrutiny.

The audit of liabilities and related areas

In the liabilities audit, auditors should recognize that in many ways the level of objective evidence that can be gathered may be lower than in other areas of examination. This circumstance makes it more apparent why auditors should not serve clients they consider untrustworthy. Some auditors believe that certain areas of the financial statements can be misrepresented deliberately by an able but unscrupulous client, probably without being discovered. The liabilities section represents one such high-risk area. Because of this risk, an auditor is wise to investigate carefully the background and reputation of a prospective client and decline to accept any client whose character is questionable.

OBJECTIVES AND PROCEDURES

The objectives of the auditor in verifying liabilities and related areas include:

1. Establishing that satisfactory internal control over liabilities exists
2. Ascertaining the reasonableness and propriety of the recorded liabilities
3. Being satisfied that *all* liabilities have been recorded, i.e., that *no* unrecorded liabilities exist
4. Determining that liabilities are presented properly on the financial statements

5. Ascertaining that transactions that create and discharge liabilities are properly recorded

Auditing procedures for accounts payable, cash disbursements, long-term debt, other liabilities, and related areas are presented in the remainder of this section. Also presented are discussions of the auditor's search for unrecorded liabilities, internal control considerations, and financial statement presentation. Audit programs summarizing the audit procedures to be performed follow the discussions.

Accounts payable audit procedures

In pursuing the objective for liabilities regarding the reasonableness and propriety of the recorded items, the auditor obtains a listing of the individual accounts payable that compose the account balance. This list should be tested for mathematical accuracy and agreed, in total, to the client's accounting records. On a test basis, the auditor examines invoices or other documents supporting the individual accounts payable on the list. Any accounts found to be overdue or otherwise irregular should be investigated and pursued to a satisfactory conclusion. For example, the auditor may find, upon investigation, that a particular account is past due because it is disputed. Finding this situation, the auditor must investigate further in order to assess the probable outcome of the dispute. Upon gathering all necessary evidence regarding the matter, the auditor will reach a conclusion about whether the payable is properly stated or whether an adjustment should be proposed.

CONFIRMATION OF ACCOUNTS PAYABLE

To gain further assurance regarding the validity of the recorded accounts payable, the auditor should consider sending confirmation requests to the creditors whose accounts appear on the list of accounts payable. Furthermore, if the auditor becomes aware of vendors with whom the client customarily deals but whose accounts are not shown to have payable balances, it would be wise to obtain confirmation of these accounts to verify the zero balances. This procedure provides additional assurance that unrecorded liabilities do not exist.

The confirmation of accounts payable has not gained the status of being a required auditing procedure as has accounts receivable confirmation. Some auditors believe that since the major audit risk associated with payables relates to unrecorded items, confirmation of recorded payables is of reduced value. However, some unrecorded liability schemes may involve the reduction of a liability rather than its deletion from the year-end listing. In these cases, confirmations may prove effective in uncovering the scheme. Furthermore, confirmations can also disclose much about the client's internal control over liabilities, since errors and other information may be noted by vendors on confirmation replies. Because of its value as audit evidence, the confirmation of accounts payable is suggested as an effective procedure that should be performed routinely.

TEST OF TRANSACTIONS

The audit of accounts payable also should include a test of the transactions associated with the client's system for creation and discharge of payables. The tests of this system are integrated with the auditor's tests of the cash disbursements system. The testing procedures are most commonly executed by selecting invoices, tracing these documents into the client's accounting records, and ascertaining that the invoices have been properly recorded. The auditor should determine that invoices are supported by purchase orders and receiving reports if the client has such procedures in effect. The auditor's tests of the discharge of payables should involve tracing the accounting entries for the cash disbursements through the client's records to ascertain that proper procedures are employed. If the client utilizes a voucher system, the auditor's testing procedures should be modified as necessary and expanded to include an examination of all relevant entries in the voucher register.

Cash disbursements audit procedures

The verification of the cash disbursement records may be coordinated with the testing of the accounts payable transactions in order to verify the complete liability-discharge system. In verifying the cash disbursement records, a sample of individual items is selected, including items from the payables test as well as additional disbursement items, and traced to supporting records and documents. Such records and documents include the check register, vendors' invoices, contracts and agreements, cancelled checks, and so on. The debit side of each transaction should be reviewed and traced to entry in the appropriate account. The cash disbursement journal should be tested for mathematical accuracy by footing and crossfooting and should be scanned by the auditor in a search for unusual entries.

Search for unrecorded liabilities

An important procedure specifically designed to give the auditor further assurance regarding liabilities is the search for unrecorded liabilities. This procedure affords the auditor a systematic approach to the examination of data that could disclose the existence of unrecorded liabilities. It should be performed as near as possible to the last day of field work in order to encompass as long a subsequent period as possible and to correspond to the date of the opinion.

In implementing the search for unrecorded liabilities, the first step is the examination, perhaps on a test basis, of cash disbursements for a period after the close of the year under audit. Often the auditor chooses to examine all material disbursements during the period chosen; alternatively, the auditor may employ statistical sampling or other selection techniques. Upon selecting the items, each disbursement is examined to determine whether or not it is in payment of an item that represented a liability at year end. This normally is readily determinable by examining the documents supporting the disbursement. If the disbursement is in payment of a year-end liability, then the auditor should determine whether the item was included on the year-end accounts payable listing. If the item is not included on the accounts payable listing, then it represents an unrecorded liability. A diagram of this procedure is presented in Figure 14-1.

After examining the cash disbursements of the subsequent period, the auditor should request a list of all payables as of the end of the subsequent period. This list is examined to determine if any of the items included represent liabilities of the year under audit. If there are items that do not appear as liabilities as of the year end, they also represent unrecorded liabilities. Upon completion of the above steps, the auditor determines the total unrecorded liabilities discovered and, if material, considers the necessity of an adjusting entry to record such liabilities.

The auditor should be alert for other indications of unrecorded liabilities. In reviewing evidence supporting additions to property, plant, and equipment, the auditor should ascertain that any related liabilities are properly reflected. The presence of a *mortgage payee* provision on insurance policies covering fixed assets indicates the existence of a mortgage and related payable, which should be shown on the financial statements. Another example is in the area of investments where the auditor should be sure that the liability is reflected for any securities purchased on margin. Agreeing interest expense with notes and bonds payable during the period may enable the auditor to detect the existence of unrecorded interest payable on debt or possibly the existence of unrecorded debt upon which interest is being paid. The auditor should review the client's computations of accrued wages, commissions, and bonuses to be assured that the liabilities are correct. Accrued payroll taxes, both the client's portion and amounts withheld from employees, is an area the auditor investigates to determine the accuracy of the liability. Review of the accounting controls and recomputation of amounts on a test basis are the most practical methods of gaining assurance as to the accuracy of payroll tax accruals. Further

Figure 14-1 Diagram of Search for Unrecorded Liabilities

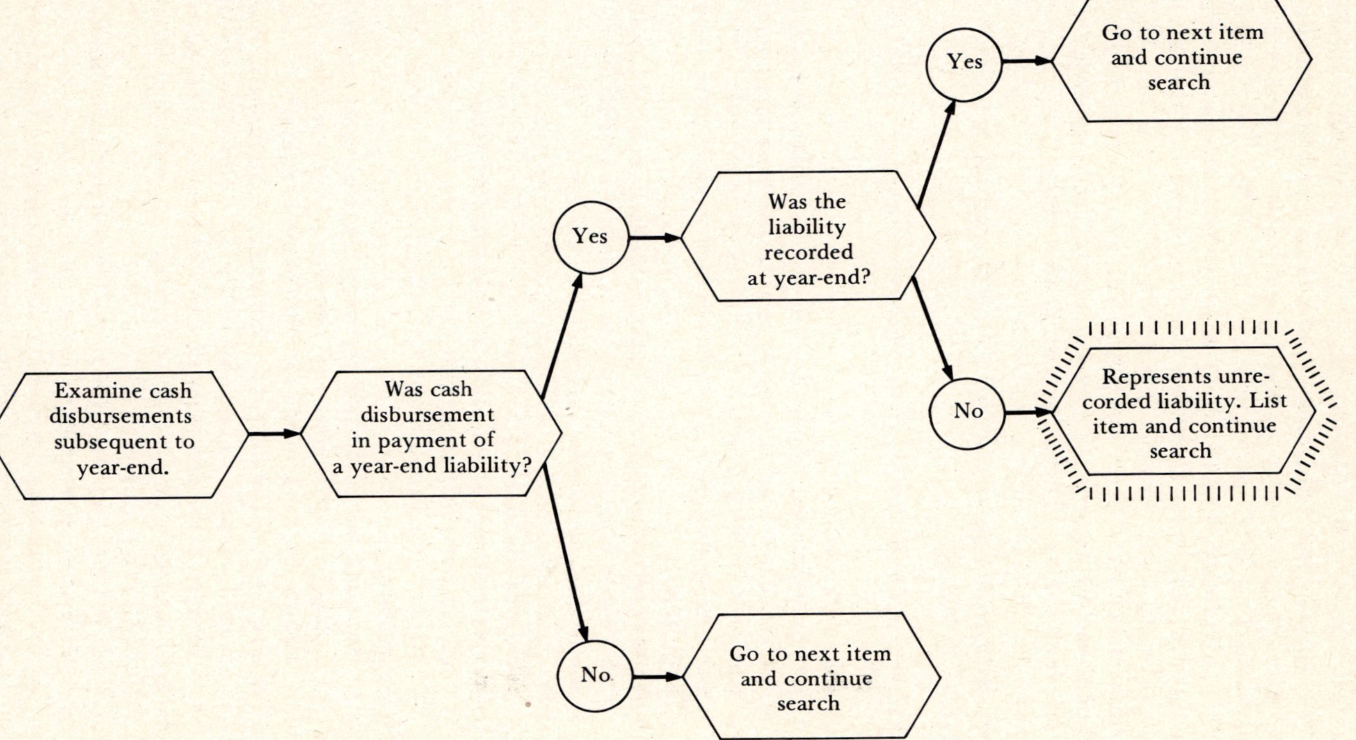

assurance regarding unrecorded liabilities is obtained from the bank confirmation replies received by the auditor. This form, illustrated in Figure 12-1, includes questions regarding both direct and contingent liabilities about which the client's banks may have knowledge. For this reason, auditors usually follow the practice of sending the confirmation request not only to banks with which the client currently deals but also to any other banks the client is known to have dealt with in the recent past. If this were not done, the client might secure a loan with a bank other than one shown on the accounting records as being a depository, fail to record the liability, and risk little chance of detection during an audit.

AUDIT PROGRAM FOR ACCOUNTS PAYABLE AND CASH DISBURSEMENTS

I. Review internal control over accounts payable and cash disbursements.

II. Accounts payable:

1. Obtain a detailed listing of trade accounts payable as of the verification date. Foot the listing and agree total to general ledger control account balance.

2. Select a sample of individual accounts payable to be subjected to audit testing.

3. Send confirmations for accounts included in sample. Confirmation requests should be prepared by auditor or under direct auditor supervision and should be mailed by auditor.

a. After a reasonable period send second confirmation requests to nonrespondents.

b. Examine all confirmation replies and investigate all exceptions noted by vendors. Include record of investigations in working papers and propose any audit adjustments considered appropriate.

c. Examine purchase and receiving records, vendors' statements, subsequent payments and relevant correspondence for all accounts not responding to confirmation requests.

d. Prepare a summary of confirmations requested, replies received, exceptions, etc., and state the conclusion reached with respect to the adequacy of the confirmation procedure.

4. Test selected transactions underlying the individual payables included in the sample:

a. Examine purchase orders, receiving reports, vendors' invoices and statements supporting the payable.

b. Trace credit entries in accounts to corresponding entry in purchases, inventory, expense, or other record.

c. Trace debit entries to cash disbursements record.

   - **d.** Investigate any entries to individual accounts from records other than cash disbursements and customary purchase, asset, expense, etc., accounts.
   - **e.** Foot accounts and prove ending balances.
5. Test selected transactions recorded in accounts payable control account:
   - **a.** Trace debit and credit entries to totals in cash disbursements, inventory, or other records.
   - **b.** Scan account and investigate any unusual entries.
   - **c.** Foot the account and prove ending balance.

III. Cash disbursements:

1. Test the accuracy of the cash disbursements journal by proving footings and cross-footings and tracing postings to cash and other general ledger accounts.
2. Trace individual cash disbursements to supporting documents, check register, and canceled checks.
3. Scan cash disbursement record and investigate unusual entries.

IV. Search for unrecorded liabilities:

1. Select a sample of cash disbursements for a reasonable period following the balance sheet date.
2. Determine by reference to source documents if any items in the sample represent unrecorded liabilities at year end.
3. Examine on a test basis unpaid invoices on hand at end of period selected in step 1. Determine if any represent unrecorded liabilities.
4. Consider proposing audit adjusting entry for any unrecorded liabilities discovered.

V. Financial statement presentation. Consider appropriate presentation for accounts payable and determine that the client's presentation conforms to accepted reporting and disclosure standards.

Audit procedures for long-term debt, other liabilities, and related areas

Notes, bonds, and other liabilities commonly represent substantial amounts on the client's financial statements and have fewer transactions per account than are found in the case of accounts payable. The audit of these accounts usually includes three primary procedures: (1) confirmation of the account balances, (2) analysis of changes in the accounts during the period under audit, and (3) computation of interest expense and related accruals.

The confirmations should be requested from the creditors involved, the trustee, as is often appropriate in the case of a bond issue, or other responsible party. The information requested in the confirmation letter commonly includes data regarding the original amount of the debt, the current balance, the interest rate, any arrearages as to the payment of interest or principal, the maturity schedule, the sinking fund requirement, security interests, and any supplementary agreements that may exist such as compensating balances.

Changes during the period under audit in the liability accounts and in related accounts should be analyzed and examined for propriety and internal consistency. Changes commonly found in the primary liability accounts reflect decreases in the debt due to repayment, issuances of new debt, and refunding. Related accounts that should be analyzed at the time of the audit of liabilities include bond discount or premium, interest expense, and sinking funds. Verification of discount or premium and interest expense usually is accomplished by independently calculating the appropriate amounts and comparing these calculations with amounts recorded. The audit of the sinking fund usually involves verification of contributions to the fund, review of investment transactions during the year, and confirmation of fund assets, income, and expenses with the trustee.

AUDIT PROGRAM FOR LONG-TERM DEBT, OTHER LIABILITIES, AND RELATED AREAS

I. Review internal controls over long-term debt, other liabilities, and related areas.

II. Long-term debt:

1. Review provisions of bond indentures, notes, mortgages, or other debt agreements. Determine if client is in compliance with all restrictive provisions.
2. Confirm amount, interest rate, maturity, and other particulars with outside trustee or with lender.
3. Review responses on bank confirmations and agree data with client's records.
4. Verify increases and decreases in long-term debt during the period by examining source documents and tracing entries into records.
5. Verify interest expense, amortization of premium and discount, and interest accruals by recomputation, and trace entries into records.
6. Analytically review interest expense recorded for the period and correlate with outstanding debt.

III. Other liabilities:

1. Obtain schedules of other liabilities showing beginning balances, ending balances, and summaries of increases and decreases during the year.

2. Test changes in accounts during year by recomputing accruals, examining underlying documents, and tracing entries to cash, expense, and other accounts.
3. Investigate and explain any unusual entries during the period or significant change in the liability balance from the beginning to the end of the period.

IV. Financial statement presentation. Consider appropriate presentation for long-term debt, other liabilities, interest expense, and related items, including the propriety of current or noncurrent classifications. Determine that client's statements conform to accepted reporting and disclosure standards.

INTERNAL CONTROL OVER LIABILITIES, CASH DISBURSEMENTS, AND RELATED AREAS

The system of internal control over liabilities must give assurance that liabilities are reported accurately, that all liabilities of the company are entered in the accounting records, that all liabilities recorded represent valid obligations of the firm, and that liabilities are discharged in accordance with company policy. Control over cash disbursements must provide assurance that amounts disbursed are properly authorized and are for valid business obligations. Access to cash, blank checks, and check-signing equipment should be limited to authorized personnel. Checks should be prepared and signed only when accompanied by properly approved check requisitions. All documentation supporting disbursements should be marked paid or otherwise cancelled in order to avoid duplicate payments. Duties should be arranged so that employees who prepare checks do not also reconcile bank accounts. Bank reconciliation procedures should be thorough and performed by an employee who has neither access to cash nor other duties in the cash receipts or disbursements system. Examples of procedures designed to insure the foregoing conditions include:

1. A comparison of the purchase order, invoice, and receiving report before entering any payable into the accounting records. This procedure helps to insure that a liability is a valid obligation of the company, that its incurrence was properly authorized, and that the goods or services giving rise to the obligation were received.
2. Use of a voucher system or some equivalent procedure designed to call attention to the appropriate payment date of individual liabilities. Such a system helps insure that liabilities are not paid late, thereby causing lost discounts and possibly a damaged credit rating, or early, thereby causing less than optimum cash utilization.
3. All invoices should be marked, perforated, or canceled in some manner at the time of payment to prevent their being paid more than once.

4. Employment of a system for controlling purchase returns and claims against vendors.
5. Regular balancing of the detail listing of accounts payable with the general ledger control account.
6. A strict system of authorization for cash disbursements to protect against improper transactions.
7. Separation of duties in the cash disbursement function to provide that employees preparing or signing checks do not reconcile bank accounts or perform other incompatible duties.
8. Dual signatures on checks or dual control of check-signing equipment.

FINANCIAL STATEMENT PRESENTATION OF LIABILITIES

Two primary aspects of the financial statement presentation of liabilities are proper classification and adequate disclosure. Proper classification of liabilities requires that accounts be assigned to either current or long-term categories. Within these categories there may be an ordering based on maturity date, subordination, or other criteria. The current portion of long-term liabilities normally must be calculated and reported as a current liability.

Adequate disclosure for liabilities should include information regarding maturity dates, interest rates, liens on assets to secure the liabilities, compensating cash balance requirements, lease payment schedules, dividend restrictions, and sinking fund requirements. Information regarding contingent liabilities and subsequent events also should be included in the financial statements or in the footnotes. Explanatory notes often are appropriate in the cases of liabilities such as deferred taxes, product warranties, lease commitments, and other items.

The audit of owners' equity and dividends

In auditing the owners' equity accounts, the auditor must be concerned not only that the accounts are presented in accordance with acceptable accounting principles but also that the corporation is conforming both to the provisions of its charter and to applicable state corporation laws. Such matters as legal capital of the corporation, the number and type of shares authorized, the legality of dividend payments, and limitations on purchase of treasury stock have legal as well as accounting implications, and in some cases may require the services of an attorney for proper resolution. The auditor should also ascertain that provisions for corporate meetings, appropriate records, and so on, are being adhered to.

AUDIT OBJECTIVES

The objectives of the audit of owners' equity include:

1. Ascertaining that adequate internal control over owners' equity exists
2. Verifying the number of shares of stock outstanding
3. Determining whether the outstanding shares have been fully paid for and recorded at the proper value
4. Ascertaining that dividend payments have been properly authorized and have been properly disbursed both as to total amount and as to amounts paid individual shareholders
5. Determining that the retained earnings account includes only earned increments
6. Ascertaining that all appropriations of retained earnings are reasonably justified and have been created or released with proper authorization
7. Investigating the propriety of the accounting for items such as treasury stock, stock option or purchase plans, securities offerings, warrants, convertibility options, right offerings, and so on
8. Determining that all elements of paid-in capital are properly identified
9. Determining that financial statement presentation is proper

Audit procedures for capital stock, dividends, paid-in capital, and retained earnings

Auditing procedures for the various areas of owners' equity are described separately, but this should not overshadow the interrelationships among the various equity accounts. The following sections illustrate usual auditing procedures for owners' equity accounts.

CAPITAL STOCK

A primary concern in the examination of this area relates to the number of shares of stock recorded as outstanding and the valuation of those recorded shares. Large, publicly held corporations usually utilize the services of a registrar and a transfer agent who are independent of the company. The registrar, usually a bank, has the responsibility for controlling the total number of the corporation's shares that are outstanding. For example, each time shares of the company are sold by one stockholder to a new stockholder, the registrar will determine that the old stock certificate is canceled before issuing new certificates for the same number of shares. The transfer agent, also usually a bank, has the responsibility for maintaining the individual stockholder records. For example, when shares of stock are sold by one shareholder to another, the transfer agent reduces the number of shares on record for the selling shareholder and records the identifying information and number of shares of the new shareholder. Usually for a stock certificate to be valid, it must be signed by both the registrar and the transfer agent. When the client corporation utilizes an outside registrar and transfer agent, the auditor will normally confirm the number of shares outstanding with one or both of these parties.

Smaller and closely held corporations often maintain their own stock records. In such cases the auditor must obtain these records and perform tests sufficient to be convinced of their validity. Commonly these records consist of a stock certificate book and a stockholders' ledger. The stock certificate book contains information regarding each individual stock certificate issued, perhaps on a stub similar to a check stub, as well as all unissued certificates. The stockholders' ledger contains information regarding individual shareowners. These records operate together to record all transations in the corporations' stock. The tests performed by the auditor include (1) totalling the number of shares recorded in both records and agreeing the totals to the general ledger, (2) testing agreement of detail information between the two records, (3) examining canceled certificates to verify that cancellation actually was accomplished, and (4) examining unissued certificates to gain assurance that none has been issued without authorization.

DIVIDENDS

Further assurance regarding the capital stock accounts may be obtained in the audit examination of dividends. All dividend declarations should be traced to the minutes of the board of directors. The total dividend payments may be proved arithmetically by multiplying the per-share amounts by the number of shares recorded as outstanding. The auditor may obtain a listing of individual dividend payments to shareholders as well as canceled dividend checks. These individual payments may be compared with information in the stockholders' ledger on a test basis to ascertain that dividends paid the shareholders are appropriate for the number of shares reportedly held by each.

The authorization for stock dividends will also be found in the minutes of the board of directors meeting. The amount capitalized may be at market value or at par depending on the intent of the board of directors and the size of the dividend. The auditor should determine that the amount capitalized is proper according to generally accepted accounting principles and should, in addition, determine that the amount allocated to capital stock and the appropriate paid-in capital account is proper.

Often the client will employ a computerized system for dividend payments. Such applications give the auditor the opportunity to utilize computer audit programs to assist in the verification work. Such a program may perform such tasks as statistically sampling individual dividend payments to be examined and verifying the mathematical computation of each individual dividend check or, in the case of stock dividends, each dividend share and fractional share.

PAID-IN CAPITAL

The primary audit technique for verifying the paid-in capital accounts is examination of the transaction that gave rise to the recorded amounts. Entries recording such transactions should be traced through the accounting records and compared with any other supporting evidence available. When paid-in capital is associated with issuances of new stock, audit verification of both items should be correlated.

RETAINED EARNINGS AUDIT PROCEDURES

Audit procedures for retained earnings may, in the simplest cases, involve little more than mathematically proving the account balance. Since quite often the changes in retained earnings during a year consist only of net income and dividends, little additional verification work is necessary.

In other cases, retained earnings may have been affected by prior-year items. These items must be examined by the auditor to establish the propriety of the accounting treatment. Additionally, the auditor should review the accuracy of the computations and the method of reflecting the adjustment on both the current and prior year's financial statements. Earnings-per-share data may require adjustment also. The auditor should be certain that all historical comparisons the client presents to users of financial statements reflect properly such adjustments.

Special audit procedures must be employed regarding retained earnings in initial audits. In the first examination of a corporation, the auditor must obtain assurance that the amount represented as retained earnings at the beginning of the year was all *earned* in previous periods, as opposed to being paid in, donated, or otherwise created through a *non-earnings* transaction. If the company has been examined by another auditor previously, the audited financial statements from the previous periods will offer valuable evidence regarding the retained earnings balance. If there have been no previous examinations, the auditor must utilize the client's unaudited financial statements and accounting records to reconstruct the retained earnings account from the inception of the corporation.

INTERNAL CONTROL OVER OWNERS' EQUITY

A primary function of a well-designed internal control system for owners' equity accounts is to give assurance that all owners' equity transactions are authorized properly. Unissued stock certificates, the stock certificate book, and the stockholders' ledger should be controlled in order to prevent the possibility of fraudulent stock issuance or transfer. The retention of an outside registrar and transfer agent usually affords a satisfactory degree of control over the capital stock accounts. If these functions are handled within the company, a system of authorizations and separation of duties should be devised to afford control. As an example, the functions of dividend payment, stock issuance, and stockholders' ledger maintenance should be performed by different employees, where possible. This division affords a series of controls in that an error in one of the functions will likely be noticed in the course of performing one of the other functions.

FINANCIAL STATEMENT PRESENTATION OF THE OWNERS' EQUITY ACCOUNTS

The auditor must be satisfied that the owners' equity section of the balance sheet is presented properly and is accompanied by adequate disclosure. Certain basic rules of disclosure, which should be followed, include:

1. A separation must be maintained between earned and paid-in amounts.
2. Capital stock must be presented at values appropriate to its nature, such as par value, stated value, and so on.
3. The source of various elements of paid-in capital should usually be disclosed.
4. Appropriations of retained earnings should be identified and should be based on reasonable assumptions.
5. Restrictions applicable to dividend payments or retained earnings levels should be adequately disclosed.
6. Changes in any element of owners' equity during the year should be fully explained on the face of the financial statements or in the footnotes.

The auditor also should be satisfied about the propriety of amounts and disclosures regarding such items as treasury stock, authorized shares, shares issued, shares outstanding, convertibility features, preferred dividend arrearages, stock option plans, dividend restrictions, and other matters.

AUDIT PROGRAM FOR OWNERS' EQUITY AND DIVIDENDS

I. Review internal controls over owners' equity and dividend transactions.

II. Capital stock and paid-in capital:

1. Review the corporate charter and other documents to verify details of all classes of stock, such as authorized shares, par values, call or redemption values, preferences, etc.

2. Obtain analysis of all capital stock accounts detailing any changes during the period.
3. Verify all capital stock issuances or retirements during the year by examining supporting documents and tracing entries into the records. Examine any changes in paid-in capital accounts.
4. Compare beginning-of-period balances with prior-year working papers. On initial audits, all stock transactions of prior periods should be examined.
5. If the client utilizes an independent registrar and transfer agent, confirm the outstanding shares with the outside parties.
6. If the client acts as its own registrar and transfer agent, examine the stock records as follows:
   a. Foot the total shares outstanding as reflected by both the stockholders' ledger and the stock certificate book and agree the totals to the general ledger account.
   b. Trace the details of individual certificates issued as shown in the stock certificate book to the individual stockholders' accounts in the stockholders' ledger on a test basis.
   c. Trace, on a test basis, individual entries in stockholders' accounts in the stockholders' ledger to the record of the related certificate shown in the stock certificate book.
   d. Examine all certificates canceled during the period.
   e. Consider confirming stock ownership with selected shareholders.
7. Examine all treasury stock owned by the client and verify all treasury stock transactions by examining supporting documents and tracing to records.
8. Review details of any existing stock option plans, stock warrants, or stock rights. Review all related transactions and determine that client is in compliance with all related provisions.
9. Test computation of earnings per share.

III. Dividends and retained earnings:
1. Select a sample of individual dividend payments made throughout the year.
2. For items selected, verify per-share amount with board of directors' minutes.
3. Agree the number of shares reflected by the payment to the number of shares shown in individual shareholders' accounts in stockholders' ledger or other record.
4. Examine canceled dividend checks for items in sample and agree to record.
5. Examine all other changes in retained earnings account, agree beginning-of-period balance with prior-year working papers and

prove ending balance mathematically. On initial audits, obtain a summary reconstruction of retained earnings since the client's inception and review all changes.

IV. Financial statement presentation. Consider appropriate presentation for owners' equity and dividends including adequate disclosure in notes to financial statements. Determine that client's statements conform to accepted reporting and disclosure standards.

Review questions

14-1. Why is the examination of liabilities considered a high-risk area of the audit?

14-2. What are the objectives of auditors in verifying liabilities and related areas?

14-3. What are the proper procedures for the examination of accounts payable?

14-4. Explain the audit benefits and limitations of confirmation procedures for accounts payable.

14-5. What steps are required in a search for unrecorded liabilities?

14-6. Name two primary procedures involved in the audit of notes, bonds, and other liabilities.

14-7. What related accounts are usually examined concurrently with liabilities?

14-8. What are the advantages of integrating the audit of accounts payable with that of cash disbursements?

14-9. What are some desirable internal control features of a cash disbursements system?

14-10. Name several procedures that indicate adequate internal accounting control over liabilities.

14-11. Name the general requirements for proper financial statement presentation of liabilities.

14-12. What are the objectives of the audit of owners' equity?

14-13. List procedures that should be employed in the audit of dividends.

14-14. In an initial audit, how are retained earnings verified?

14-15. What are the basic considerations for financial statement presentation of owners' equity?

14-16. How does use of a voucher system affect the internal control over payables and disbursements?

14-17. Why is the investigation of the background and reputation of a client important to the auditor?

14-18. What specific transaction tests should be accomplished in the audit of accounts payable?

14-19. Distinguish between a *reserve* and a *fund*.

14-20. In performing the search for unrecorded liabilities, why does the auditor request a list of payables as of the end of the subsequent period?

14-21. Why should the auditor send bank confirmations to banks at which the client has no current account?

14-22. Outline the characteristics of a good internal accounting control system over the owners' equity accounts.

Decision problems

14-23. Near the end of your client's fiscal year, the controller of the company obtained from the accounts payable clerk several invoices for shipments of inventory received prior to year end. The invoices had not been recorded in the accounting records at the time the controller secured them. The controller then held the invoices, which aggregated $12,000, without recording or paying them until your field work was completed at the end of the month subsequent to the balance sheet date.

a. What effect did this action have on the financial statements?

b. What difference would there be in the accounting records as a result of this act if the client kept periodic or perpetual inventory data?

c. What audit procedures would enable you to detect this irregularity?

d. What improvements in internal control would you suggest to lessen the possibility of this type of irregularity?

14-24. During your examination of the financial statements of the Sittig Manufacturing Company for the year ended December 31, 1985, you find that at January 1, 1985, the company had installed the following punched-card processing system for recording raw material purchases:

a. Vendors' invoices are sent directly to the accounts payable department by the mail department.

b. All supporting documents to the invoices are accumulated in the accounts payable department and are attached to the invoices. After being checked and cash discounts computed, the invoices are accumulated in batches and adding machine tapes prepared of the net invoice amounts to provide predetermined totals. Then the batches of invoices and tapes are sent to the tabulating department.

c. In the tabulating department keypunch operators prepare for each invoice an accounts payable punched card and one or more punched cards for the related debit distribution to several departmental inventories.

d. The invoice register is prepared by tab runs of the distribution cards and accounts payable cards. In this run, totals of distribution cards are compared by the tabulating machine with the amounts punched for the related accounts payable cards. Tab run subtotals by invoice batches are taken for checking to the predetermined totals.

e. The general ledger control account is posted monthly from the totals shown in the invoice register and all other journals.

f. The distribution and accounts payable cards are separated by sorting. The distribution cards are filed for further processing. The accounts payable cards are sorted by due dates and tab runs are prepared to determine cash requirements.

g. On the due dates the accounts payable cards are processed to prepare combined check and remittance statements.

h. At the end of the month the accounts payable cards in the unpaid file are tabulated for comparison with the general ledger control account.

What audit procedures would you employ to satisfy yourself as to the reasonableness of the accounts payable balance at December 31, 1985?

AICPA adapted

14-25. You were in the final stages of your examination of the financial statements of Clouse Corporation for the year ended December 31, 1987, when you were consulted by the corporation's president, who believes there is no point to your examining the 1988 voucher register and testing data in support of 1988 entries. The president stated that (*a*) bills pertaining to 1987 that were received too late to be included in the December voucher register were recorded as of the year end by the corporation by journal entry, (*b*) the internal auditor made tests after the year end, and (*c*) the president would furnish you with a letter certifying that there were no unrecorded liabilities.

a. Should a CPA's test for unrecorded liabilities be affected by the fact that the client made a journal entry to record 1987 bills that were received late? Explain.

b. Should a CPA's test for unrecorded liabilities be affected by the fact that a letter is obtained in which a responsible management official certifies that to the best of the official's knowledge all liabilities have been recorded? Explain.

c. Should a CPA's test for unrecorded liabilities be eliminated or reduced because of the internal audit tests? Explain.

d. Assume that the corporation, which handled some government contracts, had no internal auditor, but that an auditor for a federal agency spent three weeks auditing the records and was just completing work at this time. How would the CPA's unrecorded liability test be affected by the work of the auditor for a federal agency?

e. What sources in addition to the 1988 voucher register should the CPA consider to locate possible unrecorded liabilities?

AICPA adapted

14-26. You were engaged on May 1, 1985 by a committee of stockholders to perform a special audit as of December 31, 1984 of the stockholders' equity of the Chalmers Corporation, whose stock is actively traded on a stock exchange. The group of stockholders who engaged you believe that the information contained in the stockholders' equity section of the published annual report for the year ended December 31, 1984, is not correct. If your examination confirms their suspicions, they intend to use the report in a proxy fight.

Management agrees to permit your audit but refuses to permit any direct confirmation with stockholders. To secure cooperation in the audit, the committee of stockholders has agreed to this limitation and you have been instructed to limit your audit in this respect. You have been instructed also to exclude the audit of revenue and expense accounts for the year.

a. Prepare a general audit program for the usual examination of the stockholders' equity section of a corporation's balance sheet, assuming no limitation on the scope of your examination. Exclude the audit of revenue and expense accounts.

b. Describe any special auditing procedures you would undertake in view of the limitations and other special circumstances of your examination of the Chalmers Corporation's stockholders' equity accounts.

c. Discuss the content of your auditor's report for the special engagement including comments on the opinion that you would render. Do not prepare your auditor's report.

AICPA adapted

14-27. The Glass Company manufactures household appliances that are sold through independent franchised retail dealers. The electric motors in the appliances are guarantied for five years from the date of sale of the appliances to the consumer. Under the guaranty, defective motors are replaced by the dealers without charge.

Inventories of replacement motors are kept in the dealers' stores and are carried at cost in the Glass Company's records. After replacing a defective motor, the dealer notifies the factory and returns the defective motor to the factory for reconditioning. After the defective motor is received by the factory, the dealer's account is credited with an agreed fee for the replacement service.

When the appliance is brought to the dealer after the guaranty period has elapsed, the dealer charges the owner for installing the new motor. The dealer notifies the factory of the installation and returns the replaced motor for reconditioning. The motor installed is then charged to the dealer's account at a price in excess of its inventory value. In this instance, to encourage the return of replaced motors, the dealer's account is credited with a nominal value for the returned motor.

Dealers submit quarterly inventory reports of the motors on hand. The reports are later verified by factory salesmen. Dealers are billed for inventory shortages determined by comparison of the dealers' inventory reports and the factory's perpetual records of the dealers' inventories. The dealers order additional motors as they need them. One motor is used for all appliances in a given year, but the motors are changed in basic design each model year.

The Glass Company has established an account, Estimated Liability for Product Guaranties, in connection with the guaranties. An amount representing the estimated guaranty cost prorated per sales unit is credited to the Estimated Liability account for each appliance sold and the debit is charged to a Provision account. The Estimated Liability account is debited for the service fees credited to the dealers' accounts and for the inventory cost of the motors installed under the guaranties.

The engineering department keeps statistical records of the number of units of each model sold in each year and the replacements that were made.

The effect of improvements in design and construction is under continuous study by the engineering department, and the estimated guaranty cost per unit is adjusted annually on the basis of experience and improvements in design. Experience shows that, for a given motor model, the number of guaranties made good varies widely from year to year during the guaranty period, but the total number of guaranties to be made good can be reliably predicted.

Prepare an audit program to satisfy yourself as to the propriety of the transactions recorded in the Estimated Liability for Product Guaranties account for the year ended December 31, 1987.

AICPA adapted

14-28. You are a CPA engaged in an examination of the financial statements of McCollough Corporation for the year ended December 31, 1985. The financial statements and records of McCollough Corporation have not been audited by a CPA in prior years.

The stockholders' equity section of McCollough Corporation's balance sheet at December 31, 1985, follows:

Stockholders' equity:	
Capital stock—10,000 shares of $10 par value authorized; 5,000 shares issued and outstanding	$ 50,000
Capital contributed in excess of par value of capital stock	32,580
Retained earnings	47,320
Total stockholders' equity	$129,900

McCollough Corporation was founded in 1965. The corporation has ten stockholders and serves as its own registrar and transfer agent. There are no capital stock subscription contracts in effect.

a. Prepare the detailed audit program for the examination of the three accounts comprised by the stockholders' equity section of McCollough Corporation's balance sheet. Do not include in the audit program the verification of the results of the current year's operations.

b. After every other figure on the balance sheet has been audited by the CPA, it might appear that the retained earnings figure is a balancing figure and requires no further verification. Why are the retained earnings verified by the CPA as are the other figures on the balance sheet? Discuss.

AICPA adapted

14-29. You were engaged to examine the financial statements of Alba Corporation for the year ended June 30, 1986.

On May 1, 1986, the corporation borrowed $500,000 from Second National Bank to finance plant expansion. The long-term note agreement provided for the annual payment of principal and interest over five years. The existing plant was pledged as a security for the loan.

Due to unexpected difficulties in acquiring the building site, the plant expansion had not begun at June 30, 1986. To make use of the borrowed funds, management decided to invest in stocks and bonds, and on May 16, 1986, the $500,000 was invested in securities.

a. What are the audit objectives in the examination of long-term debt?

b. Prepare an audit program for the examination of the long-term note agreement between Alba and Second National Bank.

AICPA adapted

14-30. In connection with the examination of Morningside, Inc., for the year ended December 31, 1985, Lawson Jolly, CPA, is aware that certain events and transactions that took place after December 31, 1985, but before the report dated February 28, 1986, is issued, may affect the company's financial statements.

The following material events or transactions have come to Jolly's attention.

a. On January 3, 1986 Morningside received a shipment of raw materials from Canada. The materials had been ordered in October 1985 and shipped FOB shipping point in November 1985.

b. On January 15, 1986, the company settled and paid a personal injury claim of a former employee as the result of an accident that occurred in March 1985. The company had not previously recorded a liability for the claim.

c. On January 25, 1986, the company agreed to purchase for cash the outstanding stock of Elizabeth Electrical Co. The acquisition is likely to double the sales volume of Morningside, Inc.

d. On February 1, 1986, a plant owned by Morningside, Inc., was damaged by a flood resulting in an uninsured loss of inventory.

e. On February 5, 1986, Morningside, Inc., issued and sold to the general public $2 million in convertible bonds.

For each of the above events or transactions, indicate the audit procedures that should have brought the item to the attention of the auditor, and the form of disclosure in the financial statements, including the reasons for such disclosures.

Arrange your answer in the following format.

Item No.	Audit procedures	Required disclosure and reasons

AICPA adapted

14-31. Ron Wagner, CPA, is the auditor of the Eastern Electric Corporation. Wagner is considering the audit work to be performed in the accounts payable area for the current year's engagement.

The prior year's working papers show that confirmation requests were mailed to one hundred of Eastern's one thousand suppliers. The selected suppliers were based on Wagner's sample that was designed to select accounts with large dollar balances. A substantial number of hours were spent by Eastern and Wagner resolving relatively minor differences between the confirmation replies and Eastern's accounting records. Alternate audit procedures were used for those suppliers who did not respond to the confirmation requests.

a. Identify the accounts payable audit objectives that Wagner must consider in determining the audit procedures to be followed.

b. Identify situations when Wagner should use accounts payable confirmations and discuss whether Wagner is required to use them.

c. Discuss why the use of large dollar balances as the basis for selecting accounts payable for confirmation might not be the most efficient approach and indicate what more efficient procedures could be followed when selecting accounts payable for confirmation.

AICPA adapted

15

Auditing Payrolls and other Revenues and Expenses; Completing the Audit

Audits of business enterprises may be organized in varying formats depending on the personal preference of the auditor. Audit objectives may be accomplished through any of several organizational patterns. Many audits are organized in a fashion that closely follows a financial statement format; that is, the various aspects of the examination are planned and executed in a manner paralleling the accounts on the financial statements.

Other organizational plans adhere less strictly to financial statement elements and focus on the functional systems within the enterprise. Proponents of this approach believe that it provides for a more efficient and effective audit. Efficiency is increased by auditing related areas of the enterprise concurrently: the auditor verifies several items at once, thus avoiding examining the same record or transaction several times while performing separate verifications of all the areas affected by that transaction. For example, a procedure usually incorporated in the verification of accounts payable transactions during the year is to examine the paid invoices and other supporting documentation and trace the entry to the cash disbursements record. This same procedure is employed in the verification of cash disbursements. By examining these two areas concurrently, the procedure is performed once to help support both accounts payable and cash disbursement transactions.

Audit effectiveness also may be increased by organizing the audit plan in the format of related functional areas. This improvement results because the detection of errors or irregularities is more likely when an entire

Table 15-1 Areas Concurrently Verified

Financial statement captions	*Related areas*
Accounts Receivable	Sales, other revenues, cash receipts, bad debt expense, allowance for doubtful accounts
Inventories	Cost of sales, purchases
Property, Plant, and Equipment	Depreciation, accumulated depreciation, gains and losses on disposals
Investments	Investment income, gains and losses on disposals
Accounts Payable	Cash disbursements
Long-Term Debt	Interest expense
Capital Stock and Retained Earnings	Dividends
Prepaid Insurance	Insurance expense
Payroll Tax Accruals	Payroll tax expense
Current and Deferred Income Tax Accruals	Income tax expense
Various Prepaid, Accrued, and Deferred Asset and Liability Items	Miscellaneous income and expense items

transaction is examined simultaneously than when the various aspects of the transaction are examined piecemeal.

Table 15-1 reviews areas that often are audited concurrently. It includes major financial statement captions and those related areas that the auditor may integrate in their examination. The auditor may find that in examining different companies and different accounting systems, other audit organization formats would be appropriate.

Auditing procedures appropriate for many of the major areas of the business have been discussed in Chapters 12, 13, and 14. The primary areas not yet covered are other income items, payrolls, and other selling, general, and administrative expenses. A discussion of the audit of these items is presented in this chapter as well as additional topics relating to procedures employed by the auditor in completing the audit engagement.

Objectives of the audit of payrolls and other revenues and expenses

The overall objectives of the audit of payrolls and other revenues and expenses differ from many of the major objectives sought in the examination of balance sheet accounts such as existence, ownership, valuation, and so on. The objectives of this aspect of the audit tend to focus on establishing the proper determination of income and proper disclosure and presentation of the items appearing on the income statement. The following items represent the major audit objectives with respect to payrolls and other revenues and expenses:

1. Establishing that satisfactory internal control exists over revenues and expenses
2. Determining the accuracy and propriety of recorded amounts of revenues and expenses
3. Establishing that end-of-period cutoffs, matching of revenues and associated expenses, and timing of transactions have been properly executed
4. Determining that revenues and expenses are appropriately classified
5. Ascertaining that proper financial statement presentation has been accomplished

Audit procedures—general approaches

SAS No. 1 (AU 320.70) refers to two types of substantive tests: (1) analytical review procedures and (2) tests of details of transactions and balances. In discussing the application of these procedures to audits of payrolls and other revenues and expenses, the procedures are classified into three general categories: (1) analytical review, (2) tests of transactions, and (3) detailed account analysis.

ANALYTICAL REVIEW

Analytical review procedures, as defined by SAS No. 23 (AU 318.02), are substantive tests of financial information made by a study and comparison of relationships among data and consist of various techniques. The auditor utilizes analytical review to discover significant fluctuations or unusual relationships in the data that should be investigated. Analytical review techniques include such procedures as ratio analysis, trend analysis, search for fluctuations in accounting data series, regression analysis, graphical analysis, absolute comparison of year-to-year and month-to-month account balances, and other statistical methods. Analytical review techniques may be used to identify accounts that require further testing as well as to isolate variations in the operating data that require explanation.

An example of a commonly used analytical review technique is the month-to-month and year-to-year comparison of account activity. In applying this technique to expenses, for example, the auditor should prepare, or have the client prepare, a worksheet listing each expense account vertically on the margin and recording the monthly charge to each account horizontally across the page. After the data are arranged in this fashion, the auditor may visually examine the monthly charges to each account and note any significant increases, decreases, or trends. Each significant fluctuation or trend should then be investigated and explained. To complete this procedure, the year-end balance of each expense account should be compared with the balances in prior years and any fluctuations or trends noted should be explained similarly. If the client has EDP equipment available to the auditor, a computer program may be developed that will select fluctuations and trends in accounting data based on predetermined criteria. The auditor may then investigate the items selected and reported.

Another application of analytical review techniques is the use of graphical analysis. In many businesses it is known that certain operating accounts should experience predictable variation throughout a year. Line graphs are often prepared either by the auditor or at the auditor's direction that visually convey such variations. Department stores, for example, usually experience very predictable seasonal variation in sales and related accounts. If sales, cost of sales, and variable expenses are plotted on a line graph on a monthly basis, the expected seasonal trend of these items may be examined and any deviation can then be investigated.

Calculation of ratios and comparison with prior periods, with budgeted data or with industry standards may disclose unusual variations that should be investigated by the auditor. Examples of significant ratios that are useful for this purpose are the gross profit ratio, accounts receivable turnover, inventory turnover (preferably on a product-line basis), ratio of sales returns and allowances to gross sales, and an overall ratio analysis of income statement classifications.

Regression analysis is a statistical technique that may be used in analytical review to detect trends and variations in data series that may escape a visual analysis. The availability of EDP equipment and appropriate statistical programs serve to make sophisticated statistical analysis capability easily accessible to the auditor.

Many auditors feel that extensive analytical review is necessary on every audit in order to gather proper evidence to support the opinion. This is because some types of errors and irregularities are difficult to detect through the use of any other auditing techniques. Examples of the types of errors, irregularities, and other items of interest that may be best detected by the use of analytical review include:

1. omissions or decreases in accounts
2. posting errors
3. accounting changes
4. changes in products, markets, and pricing
5. policy changes affecting the financial statements
6. other items that may have been disguised in the details of the accounting records

In addition to their application to the audit of revenue and expense accounts, analytical review techniques are beneficial in the examination of balance sheet accounts. Often significant trends and fluctuations that exist in balance sheet items need investigation by the auditor and may only be detected through systematic analytical review techniques.

TESTS OF TRANSACTIONS

Other auditing procedures widely used in the verification of revenue and expense accounts are tests of transactions. These techniques involve detailed verification of the recording of selected transactions or groups of transactions in the accounting records. This verification may involve the examination of source documents, tracing postings, verifying totals, proving calculations, verifying cutoffs, and other procedures. These procedures provide the auditor with additional assurance regarding the extent to which the internal accounting control system is functioning effectively, as well as with evidence supporting the validity of the transactions in particular accounts. The extent of the tests of transactions performed in each audit is determined by the auditor's evaluation of internal control. This initial determination of the extent of tests may be modified if the testing indicates that the initial assessment of the degree of internal control is inaccurate.

For example, if the initial internal control evaluation indicated that control over nonroutine maintenance expense was strong because all such work orders were approved by the plant manager, only limited tests of transactions might be planned for this area of the audit. However, if these limited tests, when performed, disclosed that in numerous cases the plant manager's approval was not secured for the work order, then the testing in this area should be expanded and the conclusion regarding internal control modified.

DETAILED ACCOUNT ANALYSIS

Some revenue and expense accounts, in addition to being subjected to analytical review and tests of transactions, should be analyzed in more detail to determine the nature and propriety of the individual charges and credits comprising their balance. The procedure employed in analyzing accounts begins with a review of entries recorded in the account during the period and selecting either all or a representative number for verification. Following selection, each item is verified using such procedures as (1) comparison with source documents like invoices or remittance advices, (2) establishing that proper approval existed for the item, (3) determining that the accounting treatment of the item is appropriate, and (4) determining that the item is a proper revenue or expense for the company.

The auditor may select certain accounts for detailed analysis on a random sampling basis. In addition, the nature of some accounts makes it desirable for the auditor to ascertain information regarding the composition of their balances. Accounts that usually are selected for detailed analysis, and some of the audit considerations supporting their selection, include:

Repairs and Maintenance The auditor recognizes the possibility that charges to the Repairs and Maintenance account may represent capital expenditures. For this reason, the auditor usually carefully examines all material entries recorded in Repairs and Maintenance. Many auditors find that this procedure should be performed early in the examination so that any required adjustments are made prior to verifying depreciation, preparing tax returns, and so on, in order to prevent the necessity of reworking those aspects of the audit.

Taxes The auditor usually is interested in the details of taxes paid in order to consider the various assessments that have or have not been paid. In addition, schedules of taxes paid may be required for tax return preparation and for financial statement disclosures.

Legal Fees Every invoice for legal services should be inspected so that the auditor may consider whether or not any previously undetected legal action exists. The services described on an attorney's statement may provide the auditor's first indication of items that must be disclosed or entered on the financial statements.

Auditing and Accounting Services The auditor is interested in any auditing or accounting services provided the client by another professional. Aside from a personal interest, such services could indicate the existence of problems or activities within the realm of audit interest that had not been called to the auditor's attention.

Contributions In typical corporations, contributions require the approval of the board of directors. Further, political or various other types of contributions may be prohibited by law. In order to verify that proper approval has been obtained and that contributions are not in conflict with legal requirements, the auditor usually examines the details of the Contributions account.

Cost Variances Any significant variances in the elements of manufacturing costs should be investigated by the auditor. This procedure may be accomplished at the time of the auditor's review of the cost system and should adequately explain the cause of any significant amounts.

Miscellaneous Expense This type expense account may be frequently used to record unusual items. Such items are often of interest to the auditor since they may indicate transactions or events that require disclosure or other action.

Officers' Compensation Because of the sensitive nature of this account and because of the importance of proper approval for amounts contained therein, auditors frequently consider it necessary to analyze officers' salary payments and fringe benefits on an individual basis and verify that board of directors' authorization has been obtained.

Other Accounts In addition to the accounts indicated above as usually requiring detailed analysis, the auditor may, in specific cases, analyze additional accounts. Advertising expense, research and development, supplies, consulting fees, and others are common candidates for detailed analysis in specific cases.

The audit of payrolls

The accounting aspects of payrolls are more complex than most of the other expenses incurred by the business. In addition to the usual approval and disbursement procedures necessary for most expense items, payrolls require additional procedures involving timekeeping, wage rates, tax withholdings, and other details. The auditor, in turn, has additional objectives in the examination of payrolls. For example, the auditor seeks to establish that the recipients of payroll checks actually exist, are employees of the firm, and have performed services for the period indicated. Other factors such as pension agreements, labor contracts, and vacation pay also are objectives of audit verification when encountered by the auditor.

In order to ascertain that employees that the records show are being paid actually exist and are employed by the company, the auditor should observe the distribution of a sample of paychecks whenever possible. The details of any unclaimed paychecks should be recorded and further audit investigation should be performed with respect to these items. For further assurance, the auditor may compare endorsements on paychecks with employee signatures found in personnel records.

The following audit program presents typical procedures included in the audit of payrolls.

AUDIT PROGRAM FOR PAYROLLS

1. Review internal controls over payrolls.
2. Select a sample of individual wage payments from the client's payroll records.

3. Verify gross pay for each item selected by reference to time cards, salary authorizations, union contracts, or other wage records.
4. Determine that deductions from gross pay have been calculated correctly and are properly authorized.
5. Obtain canceled checks associated with each item selected and agree to payroll record. Compare endorsement with employee's W-4 Form or other signed document.
6. Test client's payroll records by verifying footings and extensions on selected payroll listings and tracing postings to the general ledger.
7. Observe the distribution of a selected number of paychecks to the employees. Record in the working papers the details of any unclaimed paychecks and perform follow-up procedures to insure that these items are not indications of irregularities.
8. Determine that all officers' salaries paid are in agreement with amounts approved by the board of directors.
9. Verify computations related to vacation pay, pensions, and profit-sharing plans.
10. Analytically review payroll data and investigate any unusual relationships or significant fluctuations.
11. Consider financial statement presentation related to payrolls and determine that the client's practices are appropriate.
12. If applicable, review standard labor rates for applying labor cost to manufacturing. Investigate treatment of any year-end labor cost variances.

The audit of other revenues and expenses

Auditing other revenues and expenses requires application of the three general approaches discussed previously: analytical review, tests of transactions, and detailed account analysis. The following audit program presents procedures usually performed in this area of the examination.

AUDIT PROGRAM FOR OTHER REVENUES AND EXPENSES

I. Review internal controls over other revenues and expenses.

II. Analytical review:

1. Obtain schedules of revenues and expenses for the period and comparable data for prior years. If available, obtain budgeted, as well as actual, data.
2. Review revenue and expense data and note any unusual fluctuations, trends, or budget variances.
3. Calculate relevant ratios, percentages, and other relationships and note any unusual fluctuations or trends.
4. Investigate all unusual fluctuations, trends, and budget variances

noted. Through analysis, client inquiry, and examination of accounting records and other documentation, obtain explanation of all unusual items and include in working papers.

III. Tests of transactions:

1. Select a sample of individual revenue and expense accounts for testing.

2. On a test basis, trace debit and credit entries into the accounting records, and examine source documents to determine authenticity of items and propriety of classification and recording.

3. Foot accounts and prove ending balance.

IV. Detailed account analysis:

1. Obtain schedule of revenue and expense account for which detailed analysis is desired.

2. Examine source documents supporting all entries in accounts selected. Consider carefully the propriety and implication of each item.

V. Financial statement presentation. Consider appropriate presentation for all revenues and expenses. Determine that client's statements conform to accepted reporting and disclosure standards.

Internal control over payrolls and other revenues and expenses

Internal control considerations regarding payrolls and other revenues and expenses closely parallel the internal control over cash receipts and disbursements, accounts receivable, and accounts payable. Special requirements regarding revenues include controls over sales approvals and issuance of credit memorandums, adequate procedures to control miscellaneous income items, and procedures to assure proper classification of various types of revenue.

Major considerations of internal control over expenses include procedures to assure that all expenses are properly authorized and approved for payment as well as that the respective goods or services were actually received. Further, the auditor must ascertain that a system exists to insure that expenses are properly classified as to nature and purpose. Also, regarding payrolls, the system should provide assurance that amounts representing employee compensation are properly related to services performed.

Financial statement presentation for payrolls and other revenues and expenses

Proper financial statement presentation and disclosure rank along with accuracy of reported amounts in audit importance. The auditor must ascertain that the various elements of revenue and expense are properly captioned, explained, and positioned on the income statement. Revenues, in appropriate cases, should be identified by source, and nonoperating revenues should be properly identified.

In the expense section of the income statement, operating and nonoperating expenses commonly are distinguished, making possible the presentation of an operating income subtotal where appropriate.

Presentation of unusual, nonrecurring items should be considered carefully to determine whether such gains and losses represent extraordinary items or should be presented as separate statement items as determined in accordance with the criteria presented in authoritative opinions. Statement presentation, as well as accounting principles, must be consistent from year to year. Any accounting changes or statement presentation changes in the current year require specific treatment and disclosure and often require mention in the auditor's opinion. Earnings-per-share calculations presented on the income statement must be examined by the auditor to substantiate the accuracy of the calculations as well as the propriety of the statement presentation format.

Completing the audit

To complete the audit process and fulfill the requirement that sufficient competent evidential matter be gathered in order to support the opinion, the auditor needs assurance with respect to many matters that may not be reflected in the accounting records of the period. One concern of the auditor is whether any events have occurred subsequent to the balance sheet date that affect the financial statements under audit. Another item needed by the auditor to complete the examination is written assurance by the client that all information given to the auditor during the course of the engagement has been truthful and accurate to the best of the client's knowledge. A third matter about which the auditor requires assurance concerns the existence and status of claims, potential claims, litigation, and other contingencies faced by the client.

This section covers the auditor's procedures for obtaining assurance regarding the above matters.

SUBSEQUENT EVENTS

As was discussed in Chapter 5, the auditor has a significant responsibility for reporting on the effects of some events that occur subsequent to the balance sheet date. In order to become aware of such events and properly discharge audit responsibility in this area, the auditor must devise appropriate procedures designed to disclose any happenings in the subsequent period that will require attention. Such procedures are in addition to the search for unrecorded liabilities discussed in Chapter 14, which is primarily related to substantiation of events and transactions occurring prior to or on the balance sheet date.

The following audit program presents appropriate procedures for the investigation of subsequent events. Further discussion of the items called for in steps 5 and 6 of the program is found in succeeding sections.

AUDIT PROGRAM FOR SUBSEQUENT EVENTS

1. The procedures in this audit program should be performed as of the last day of field work and should cover the period from balance sheet date to the date of the opinion. Record in the working papers the date each procedure is executed and details of the work performed.
2. Review the interim financial statements for periods subsequent to the balance sheet date. Investigate any significant fluctuations to determine if they were caused by subsequent events requiring adjustment of or disclosure in the financial statements. For periods for which no interim statements are available, scan appropriate accounting records and investigate any unusual transactions.
3. Review the minutes of all meetings of directors, stockholders, and appropriate corporate committees. Investigate any matters that may indicate the existence of subsequent events. If such meetings have been held for which minutes are not available, make inquiries as to the nature of the proceedings.
4. Make inquiries of responsible officials as to any events or conditions occurring subsequent to balance sheet date that might require adjustment of or disclosure in the financial statements being reported on. Include in the discussion matters such as unusual transactions or adjustments subsequent to balance sheet date; litigation, commitments, uncertainties, or other contingent liabilities; significant changes in the capital or debt structure of the company; and other matters.
5. Obtain from appropriate officials a client representation concerning pertinent matters occurring both during and subsequent to the period under audit. The representation should be dated as of the date of the opinion and should be signed by the chief executive officer and the chief financial officer.
6. Obtain a letter from the client's legal counsel describing and evaluating any litigation, pending litigation, claims, or contingencies of which he or she has knowledge.

CLIENT REPRESENTATIONS

SAS No. 19 (AU 333.01) requires that the auditor obtain written representations from management covering various aspects of the audit. In this letter, the client's management acknowledges its responsibility for the fairness of financial statements and confirms many of the oral representations given to the auditor during the course of the engagement.

The client representation letter is not a substitute for conventional auditing procedures but serves to corroborate much of the evidence already gathered by the auditor. In addition, the representation letter often provides assurance for the auditor in areas where evidence that can be obtained by other auditing procedures is limited. Further, a written representation from the client lends support to the auditor's contention that there was sufficient reason to believe in the fairness of the financial statements. Finally, the client representation letter serves the purpose of explicitly reminding the client that management has primary responsibility for the fairness of the financial statements.

Since the auditor is concerned with events occurring both during the period under audit and during the subsequent period, the client representation letter should be dated as of the last day of field work to correspond with the date of the auditor's report. The letter should be addressed to the auditor and signed by responsible client officials, usually the chief executive officer and the chief financial officer. If management officials should refuse to furnish the auditor with a written representation concerning essential matters, such a refusal would constitute a scope limitation sufficient to cause a qualified opinion or disclaimer. In addition, such a refusal should cause the auditor to consider whether information provided by the client during the course of the audit was reliable.

Figure 15-1 presents an example of a comprehensive client representation letter. In each audit, the specific representations obtained from the client should depend on the circumstances of the particular client and the engagement. In order for the client to be aware of all items that should be included in the letter of representation, the auditor normally prepares a draft and presents it to the client to be used as a model.

INVESTIGATION OF LITIGATION, CLAIMS, AND ASSESSMENTS

In order to obtain assurance with regard to proper reporting of litigation, claims, and assessments against the client, the auditor should perform procedures designed to provide adequate evidence with respect to the circumstances surrounding the litigation, claim, or assessment; the probability of an unfavorable outcome; and an estimate of the potential loss. Audit procedures appropriate for this purpose follow.

1. Obtain from management a description and evaluation of all litigation, claims, and assessments existing at balance sheet date and during the subsequent period. The list should identify those matters referred to legal counsel. Written assurance should be obtained from the client, usually in the client representation letter, that all such matters are

Figure 15-1 Client Representation Letter

Financial Software Corporation
1607 Arthur Street
Albany, New York 12201

February 18, 1984

Friedman and Montag
Certified Public Accountants
716 Fifth Avenue
Albany, New York 12201

Gentlemen:

In connection with your examination of the balance sheet of Financial Software Corporation as of December 31, 1983 and the related statements of income, retained earnings and changes in financial position for the year then ended, we represent the following to you to the best of our knowledge and belief.

In making these representations, except in matters relating to items a, b, c, and h, any amounts aggregating less than $1,000 have not been considered.

a. We acknowledge our responsibility for the fair presentation of the financial statements referred to above in conformity with generally accepted accounting principles.

b. We have made available to you all financial records and related data of the Company.

c. All minutes of meetings of stockholders, directors and committees of directors have been made available to you in complete form.

d. There are no errors in the financial statements and there are no unrecorded transactions.

e. Any related party transactions, including any associated receivables or payables, have been properly recorded or disclosed in the financial statements.

f. All aspects of contractual agreements, noncompliance with which would affect the financial statements, have been complied with.

g. No events have occurred subsequent to the balance sheet date which would require disclosure in or adjustment to the financial statements.

h. There have been no irregularities involving management or employees.

i. There have been no communications from regulatory agencies concerning noncompliance with, or deficiencies in financial reporting practices.

j. The Company has no plans or intentions which may have an effect on either the carrying value or classification of assets or liabilities.

Friedman and Montag
February 18, 1984
Page 2

k. All arrangements involving compensating balances, other restrictions on cash balances, lines-of-credit, and similar matters have been properly recorded or disclosed.

l. Any excess, obsolete or damaged inventories have been reduced to net realizable value.

m. There are no losses to be sustained in connection with sales commitments.

n. The Company holds satisfactory title to all owned assets and all liens or encumbrances on assets and all pledges of assets have been disclosed.

o. There are no agreements to repurchase assets previously sold.

p. There are no losses to be sustained in connection with any purchase commitments.

q. There have been no violations or possible violations of laws or regulations whose effects should be considered for disclosure in the financial statements or as a basis for recording a loss contingency.

r. There are no other liabilities or gain or loss contingencies which should be accrued or disclosed as required by Statement of Financial Accounting Standards No. 5.

s. There are no unasserted claims or assessments which our attorney has advised are probable of assertion and therefore require disclosure in accordance with Statement of Financial Accounting Standards No. 5.

t. There are no capital stock repurchase agreements and all capital stock reserved for options, warrants, conversions or other purposes is properly disclosed.

Sincerely yours,

Graham Williams, Jr.

Graham Williams, Jr., President
Chief Executive Officer

Aaron Blount

Aaron J. Blount, V.P. and
Comptroller
Chief Financial Officer

Figure 15-2 Inquiry Letter to Legal Counsel

Financia' Software Corporation
1607 Arthur Street
Albany, New York 12201

January 16, 1984

Hale and Hale
Attorneys-At-Law
1702 Morningside Drive
Gloucester City, NJ 08030

Gentlemen:

In connection with an examination of our financial statements at December 31, 1983, and for the year then ended, management of the Company has prepared, and furnished to our auditors, Friedman and Montag, Certified Public Accountants, 716 Fifth Avenue, Albany, New York 12201, a description and evaluation of certain contingencies, including those set forth below involving matters with respect to which you have been engaged and to which you have devoted substantive attention on behalf of the Company in the form of legal consultation or representation. These contingencies are regarded by management of the Company as material for this purpose. Your response should include matters that existed at December 31, 1983 and during the period from that date to the date of your response.

Pending or Threatened Litigation:

Damage suit brought by Jones Manufacturing Co. for alleged product failure and filed in United States District Court. Case to be heard in May, 1984. Management intends to contest the case vigorously. In the opinion of management the likelihood of an unfavorable outcome is remote and that in the event of an unfavorable outcome the maximum damages would not exceed $50,000.

Please furnish to our auditors such explanation, if any, that you consider necessary to supplement the foregoing information, including an explanation of those matters as to which your views may differ from those stated and an identification of the omission of any pending or threatened litigation, claims, and assessments or a statement that the list of such matters is complete.

Unasserted Claims and Assessments:

In connection with products and services provided during the current year to a customer, Mary's Vineyard, Inc., significant dissatisfaction has been expressed. Litigation has not been threatened but management considers it probable that a claim will be asserted and that if asserted there is a reasonable possibility of an unfavorable outcome. Management intends to contest the claim vigorously if asserted and believes that an unfavorable outcome is not probable. In the event of an unfavorable outcome of such claim if asserted, management believes that the total loss would not exceed $100,000. Please furnish to our auditors such explanation, if any, that you consider necessary to supplement the foregoing information, including an explanation of those matters as to which your views may differ from those stated.

Hale and Hale
January 16, 1984
Page 2

We understand that whenever, in the course of performing legal services for us with respect to a matter recognized to involve an unasserted possible claim or assessment that may call for financial statement disclosure, if you have formed a professional conclusion that we should disclose or consider disclosure concerning such possible claim or assessment, as a matter of professional responsibility to us, you will so advise us and will consult with us concerning the question of such disclosure and the applicable requirements of Statement of Financial Accounting Standards No. 5. Please specifically confirm to our auditors that our understanding is correct.

In addition, please specifically identify the nature of and reasons for any limitation on your response.

Sincerely yours,

Roger J. Elkins

Roger J. Elkins,
Vice President and General Counsel

properly disclosed in accordance with the provisions of Statement of Financial Accounting Standards No. 5.

2. Obtain assurance from the client that all unasserted claims have been disclosed that legal counsel has advised require disclosure in accordance with Statement of Financial Accounting Standards No. 5. The auditor should, with the client's permission, inform the attorney that such assurance has been obtained.
3. Examine all documentation relating to any litigation, claims, or assessments, and discuss with management their procedures for identifying, evaluating, and accounting for such contingencies.
4. Request that the client send a letter of inquiry to those attorneys who have been consulted with respect to litigation, claims, or assessments. This letter provides a means of corroborating evidence the auditor has gathered regarding such matters. In the letter, the attorney is asked to confirm, directly to the auditor, the information provided by the client.

Figure 15-2 provides an example of an inquiry letter sent to the client's legal counsel. The attorney's response to the letter should provide the auditor with the additional assurance needed to form a conclusion with respect to the presentation of litigation, claims, assessments, or other contingencies. If the auditor is unable to secure a satisfactory response from the attorney because of the attorney's refusal or inability to respond, this usually will constitute a scope limitation sufficient to require a qualification or disclaimer of opinion.

Supplementary readings

Benis, Martin. "The Small Client and Representation Letters." *Journal of Accountancy* (September 1978), 78-84.

Benson, Benjamin. "Lawyers' Responses to Audit Inquiries—A Continuing Controversy." *Journal of Accountancy* (July 1977), 72-78.

Kinney, William R., Jr. "ARIMA and Regression in Analytical Review: an Empirical Test." *Accounting Review* (January 1978;, 48-60.

Review questions

15-1. Why are some revenue and expense accounts verified in conjunction with the examination of balance sheet accounts?

15-2. Which revenue and expense accounts usually are examined concurrently with related balance sheet accounts?

15-3. What are the primary audit objectives in auditors' examinations of revenues and expenses?

15-4. Name the three general groups of audit procedures employed in the verification of revenues and expenses.

15-5. What is analytical review?

15-6. What items of audit interest are best disclosed by analytical review?

15-7. What specific audit procedures are included in tests of transactions?

15-8. What determines the extent of the transaction tests performed by an auditor?

15-9. What is the purpose of tests of transactions?

15-10. Why is the auditor concerned with events that occur after the date of the financial statements being audited?

15-11. What are the purposes of the client representation letter?

15-12. How should the auditor respond if the client refuses to sign the client representation letter?

15-13. What is the purpose of the inquiry letter to the client's legal counsel?

15-14. What would the auditor's course of action be if the client's attorney is unable or unwilling to provide a satisfactory response to the inquiry letter?

15-15. Why are certain expense accounts frequently selected for detailed analysis?

15-16. How do auditors perform a detailed analysis of an expense account?

15-17. What are some expense accounts usually analyzed in detail and why is their analysis desirable?

15-18. What is payroll padding?

15-19. How do auditors gain assurance that a client's payroll is not padded?

15-20. Why should auditors carefully analyze the compensation of corporate officers?

15-21. What are the major internal control considerations with respect to revenues and expenses?

15-22. What are the significant factors involved in determining proper financial statement presentation of revenues and expenses?

Decision problems

15-23. Your client is a large construction company with contracts in progress at several job sites. At each site, the construction foreman is in charge of hiring and dismissal of employees in addition to overall supervision of the work. Each Thursday, the foreman makes up the payroll from job time cards and submits it to the home office for processing. On Friday the payroll is recorded in the accounting records and the paychecks are prepared. The checks are returned to the foreman for distribution at the end of work Friday. When an employee is hired or terminated, the foreman has the necessary paperwork prepared and submits it to the home office along with the payroll.

The controller of the company informs you that she is concerned that some foremen may "pad" the payrolls. She further asks that you examine this area with care and that you make suggestions that could improve the client's system.

a. What opportunities are available on the job foremen to defraud the company?

b. Prepare an audit program for the examination of construction payrolls for this client. Note any procedures that are specifically designed to detect payroll "padding."

c. What system improvements would you suggest with regard to construction payrolls?

15-24. On January 11, 1988, at the beginning of your annual audit of the Meteor Manufacturing Company's financial statements for the year ended December 31, 1987, the company president confides in you that an employee is living on a scale in excess of that which her salary would support.

The employee has been a buyer in the purchasing department for six years and has charge of purchasing all general materials and supplies. She is authorized to sign purchase orders for amounts up to $200. Purchase orders in excess of $200 require the countersignature of the general purchasing agent.

The president understands that the usual examination of financial statements is not designed, and cannot be relied upon, to disclose fraud or conflicts of interest, although their discovery may result. The president authorizes you, however, to expand your regular audit procedures and to apply additional audit procedures to determine whether there is any evidence that the buyer has been misappropriating company funds or has been engaged in activities that were conflicts of interest.

a. List the audit procedures that you would apply to the company records and documents in an attempt to

1. Discover evidence within the purchasing department of defalcations being committed by the buyer. Give the purpose of each procedure.
2. Provide leads as to possible collusion between the buyer and suppliers. Give the purpose of each audit procedure.

b. Assume that your investigation disclosed that some suppliers have been charging the Meteor Manufacturing Company in excess of their usual prices and apparently have been making kickbacks to the buyer. The excess charges are material in amount.

What effect, if any, would the defalcation have upon (1) the financial statements that were prepared before the defalcation was uncovered and (2) your auditor's report? Discuss.

AICPA adapted

15-25. Your client, ABC Manufacturing Company, acquired XYZ Equipment Corporation three years ago in a cash purchase transaction. In reviewing the files of XYZ, the management of ABC has found evidence that XYZ, in the past, engaged in activities that violated certain antitrust statutes. The last illegal act occurred about five years ago and the statute of limitations for such acts is seven years. If the activities of XYZ's former management are discovered, and the injured parties assert claims prior to the running out of the statute of limitations, ABC will likely be required to pay substantial damages.

In preparing the audit report for the current year, you are concerned with adequate disclosure in light of your knowledge of the above situation. You realize that if the situation is disclosed in the footnotes, the timely discovery of the claims and their assertion is practically assured. On the other hand, if the situation is not disclosed and the claims are asserted nevertheless, you and the client will be in a very difficult position with respect to the lack of disclosure.

How should you resolve the above situation in reporting on the fairness of the financial statements?

15-26. Your client is the Dunwoody Shopping Center, Inc., a shopping center with thirty store tenants. All leases with the store tenants provide for a fixed rent plus a percentage of sales, net of sales taxes, in excess of a fixed dollar amount computed on an annual basis. Each lease also provides that the landlord may engage a CPA to audit all records of the tenant for assurance that sales are being properly reported to the landlord.

You have been requested by your client to audit the records of the Rangoon Restaurant to determine that the sales totaling $390,000 for the year ended December 31, 1983, have been properly reported to the landlord. The restaurant and the shopping center entered into a five-year lease on January 1, 1983. The Rangoon Restaurant offers only table service. No liquor is served. During mealtimes there are four or five waitresses in attendance who prepare handwritten prenumbered restaurant checks for the customers. Payment is made at a cash register, manned by the proprietor, as the customer leaves. All sales are for cash. The proprietor also is the bookkeeper. Complete files are kept of restaurant checks and cash register tapes. A daily sales book and general ledger are also maintained.

a. List the auditing procedures that you would employ to verify the total annual sales of the Rangoon Restaurant. Disregard vending machine sales and counter sales of chewing gum, candy, etc.

b. Prepare the auditor's report that you would submit to the Dunwoody Shopping Center, Inc. Assume that your examination of the records of the Rangoon Restaurant disclosed that sales were properly reported to the shopping center.

AICPA adapted

15-27. You are completing the audit of Archer Industries for the year ended December 31, 19X1. The last day of field work is to be February 14, 19X2. You believe that you have been able to gather sufficient, competent evidence to support your opinion on the financial statements; also, you believe that Archer's management has been open and candid with you in all matters.

a. Is a client representation letter needed in these circumstances?

b. What purpose does a client representation letter serve?

c. Draft an appropriate client representation letter for this situation. Supply names and dates as needed.

15-28. In auditing the financial statements of a manufacturing company that were prepared from data processed by electronic data processing equipment, the CPA has found that the traditional audit trail has been obscured. As a result, the CPA may place increased emphasis upon overall checks of the data under audit. These overall checks, which are also applied in auditing visibly posted accounting records, include the computation of ratios, which are compared to prior-year ratios or to industry-wide norms. Examples of such overall checks or ratios are the computation of the rate of inventory turnover and computation of the number of days' sales in receivables.

a. Discuss the advantages to the CPA of the use of ratios as overall checks in an audit.

b. In addition to the computations given above, list the ratios that a CPA may compute during an audit as overall checks on balance sheet accounts and related nominal accounts. For each ratio listed name the two (or more) accounts used in its computation.

c. When a CPA discovers that there has been a significant change in the ratio when compared to the prior year's ratio, the possible reasons for the change are considered. Give the possible reasons for the following significant changes in ratios:

1. The rate of inventory turnover (ratio of cost of sales and average inventory) has decreased from the prior year's rate.
2. The number of days' sales in receivables (ratio of average daily accounts receivable and sales) has increased over the prior year.

AICPA adapted

15-29. Your client, Arbor Associates, Inc., is involved in several situations at year end that you believe may require adjustment to or disclosure in the financial statements. In this connection you have obtained the following written information from management:

Litigation, claims, and assessments existing at December 31, 19X2 and during the period from that date to February 22, 19X3:

a. Claim by X Factors, Inc. against the company with respect to alleged product defects in the amount of $28,000. Matter not referred to legal counsel since management considers that the claim has no merit.

b. Suit filed by Martini Ready-Mix, Inc. against the company for alleged product liability in the amount of $140,000. Management intends to contest this action vigorously; however, an unfavorable outcome of the case is reasonably possible. The suit is to be heard in United States District Court in July, 19X3. In the event of an unfavorable outcome, management believes the amount of loss would not exceed $100,000. The corporation's legal counsel has been engaged to prepare the defense.

Unasserted claims:

There exists one unasserted claim that, in management's opinion, is probable of assertion and if asserted would have at least a reasonable possibility of an unfavorable outcome. This claim is in connection with a product defect, now corrected, which was discovered through the company's product testing program. This matter has been referred to legal counsel who has advised the company that the claim should be disclosed in accordance with Statement of Financial Accounting Standards No. 5. Accordingly, appropriate disclosure has been made. If such claim is asserted, management intends to seek an out-of-court settlement with the claimants. Management believes that the potential loss from this claim, if asserted, would fall in the range of $50,000–$75,000.

1. What additional auditing procedures should be performed to provide adequate assurance with respect to litigation, claims, assessments, and unasserted claims?
2. Draft an appropriate inquiry letter to the client's legal counsel with respect to the above matters. Supply names and dates as needed.
3. What action would be required if the client's attorney was unwilling or unable to provide a satisfactory response to the inquiry letter?

15-30. The client's cost system is often the focal point in the CPA's examination of the financial statements of a manufacturing company.

a. For what purposes does the CPA review the cost system?

b. The Holly Bell Manufacturing Company employs standard costs in its cost accounting system. List the audit procedures that you would apply to satisfy yourself that Holly Bell's cost standards and related variance amounts are acceptable and have not distorted the financial statements.

AICPA adapted

15-31. In connection with the examination of the financial statements of Keister Wholesalers, Inc. for the year ended June 30, 1986, a CPA performs several cutoff tests.

a. 1. What is a cutoff test?

2. Why must cutoff tests be performed for both the beginning and the end of the audit period?

b. The CPA wishes to test Keister's sales cutoff at June 30, 1986. Describe the steps that should be included in the test.

AICPA adapted

15-32. You are engaged in your first audit of the Hinds Pest Control Company for the year ended December 31, 1984. The company began doing business in January 1984 and provides pest control services for industrial enterprises.

Additional information includes the following:

a. The office staff consists of a bookkeeper, a typist, and the president, Mr. Hinds. In addition, the company employs twenty servicemen on an hourly basis who are assigned to individual territories to make both monthly and emergency visits to customers' premises. The servicemen submit weekly time reports that include the customer's name and the time devoted to each customer. Time charges for emergency visits are shown separately from regular monthly visits on the report.

b. Customers are required to sign annual contracts, which are prenumbered and prepared in duplicate. The original is filed in numerical order by contract anniversary date and the copy is given to the customer. The contract entitles the customer to pest control services once each month. Emergency visits are billed separately.

c. Fees for monthly services are payable in advance—quarterly, semiannually, or annually—and are recorded on the books as *income from services* when the cash is received. All payments are by checks received by mail.

d. Prenumbered invoices for contract renewals are prepared in triplicate from information on the contract file. The original invoice is sent to the customer twenty days prior to the due date of payment, the duplicate copy is filed chronologically by due date, and the triplicate copy is filed alphabetically by customer. If payment is not received by fifteen days after the due date, a cancellation notice is sent to the customer and a copy of the notice is attached to the customer's contract. The bookkeeper notifies the serviceman of all contract cancellations and reinstatements and requires written acknowledgement of receipt of such notices. Hinds himself approves all cancellations and reinstatements of contracts.

e. Prenumbered invoices for emergency services are prepared weekly from information shown on servicemen's time reports. The customer is billed at 200 percent of the serviceman's hourly rate. These invoices, prepared in triplicate and distributed as shown above, are recorded on the books as *income from services* at the billing date. Payment is due thirty days after the invoice date.

f. All remittances are received by the typist, who prepares a daily list of collections and stamps a restrictive endorsement on the checks. A copy of the list is forwarded with the checks to the bookkeeper, who posts the date and amount received on the copies of the invoice in both the alphabetical and chronological files. After posting, the copy of the invoice is transferred from the chronological file to the daily cash receipts binder, which serves as a subsidiary record for the cash receipts book. The bookkeeper totals the amounts of all remittances received, posts this total to the cash receipts book and attaches the daily remittance tapes to the paid invoices in the daily cash receipts binder.

g. The bookkeeper prepares a daily bank deposit slip and compares the total with the total amount shown on the daily remittance tapes. All remittances are deposited in the bank the day they are received. Cash receipts from sources other than services need not be considered.

h. Financial statements are prepared on the accrual basis.

List the audit procedures you would employ in the examination of the Income from Services account for 1984.

AICPA adapted

15-33. During your audit of the accounts of the Eloise Manufacturing Corporation, your assistant tells you of errors found in the computation of the wages of factory workers and that you should verify the work.

Your assistant has extracted from the union contract the following description of the systems for computing wages in various departments of the company. The contract provides that the minimum wage for a worker is the worker's base rate, which is also paid for any *down time,* i.e., time when the worker's machine is under repair or the worker is without work. The standard work week is forty hours. The union contract also provides that workers be paid 150 percent of base rates for overtime production. The company is engaged in interstate commerce.

a. Straight piecework. The worker is paid at the rate of 20 cents per piece produced.

b. Percentage bonus plan. Standard quantities of production per hour are established by the engineering department. The worker's average hourly production, determined from total hours worked and production, is divided by the standard quantity of production to determine the worker's efficiency ratio. The efficiency ratio is then applied to the worker's base rate to determine the hourly earnings for the period.

c. Emerson Efficiency System. A minimum wage is paid for production up to 66⅔ percent of the standard output, or *efficiency.* When the worker's production exceeds 66⅔ percent of the standard output, payment is at a bonus rate. The bonus rate is determined from the following table:

Efficiency	*Bonus*
Up to 66⅔%	0%
66⅔%—79%	10%
80—99%	20%
100—125%	45%

Your assistant has prepared the following schedule of information pertaining to certain workers for a weekly payroll selected for examination:

Worker	*Wage incentive plan*	*Total hours*	*Down time hours*	*Units produced*	*Standard units*	*Base rate*	*Gross wages per books*
Long	Straight piecework	40	5	400		$1.80	$ 82.00
Loro	Straight piecework	46		455[1]		1.80	91.00
Huck	Straight piecework	44	4	420[2]		1.80	84.00
Nini	Percentage bonus plan	40		250	200	2.20	120.00
Boro	Percentage bonus plan	40		180	200	1.90	67.00
Wiss	Emerson	40		240	300	2.10	92.00
Alan	Emerson	40	2	590	600[3]	2.00	118.00

[1] Includes forty-five pieces produced during the six overtime hours.

[2] Includes fifty pieces produced during the four overtime hours. The overtime, which was brought about by the down time, was necessary to meet a production deadline.

[3] Standard units for forty hours production.

a. Prepare a schedule comparing each individual's gross wages per books and gross wages per your calculation. Computations of workers' wages should be in good form and labeled with the workers' names.

b. All the above errors, as well as others, were found in a weekly payroll selected for examination. The total number of errors was substantial. Discuss the courses of action you can take.

AICPA adapted

15-34. *a.* In a properly planned examination of financial statements, the auditor coordinates the review of specific balance-sheet and income-statement accounts. Why should the auditor coordinate examinations of balance-sheet accounts and income-statement accounts? Discuss and illustrate by examples.

b. A properly designed audit program enables the auditor to determine conditions or establish relationships in more than one way.
Cite various procedures that the auditor employs that might lead to detection of each of the following two conditions:
1. Inadequate allowance for doubtful accounts receivable
2. Unrecorded retirements of property, plant, and equipment

AICPA adapted

15-35. Haly, CPA, is examining the financial statements of the Jill Corporation as of and for the period ended September 30, 1987. Haly plans to complete the field work and sign the auditor's report on November 15, 1987. Haly's audit work is primarily designed to obtain evidence that will provide a reasonable degree of assurance that the Jill Corporation's September 30, 1987, financial statements present fairly the financial position, results of operations, and changes in financial position of that enterprise in accordance with generally accepted accounting principles consistently applied. Haly is concerned, however, about events and transactions of Jill Corporation that occur after September 30, 1987, since Haly does not have the same degree of assurance for such events as for those that occurred in the period ending September 30, 1987.

a. Define what is commonly referred to in auditing as a subsequent event and describe the two general types of subsequent events that require consideration by the management of Jill Corporation and evaluation by Haly.

b. Identify those auditing procedures that Haly should follow to obtain the necessary assurances concerning subsequent events.

AICPA adapted

15-36. J. Levy, CPA, is auditing the McCrary Manufacturing Company as of February 28, 1985. As with all engagements, one of Levy's initial procedures is to analytically review the client's financial data by determining significant ratios and trends so that he has a better understanding of the business and can determine where to concentrate his audit efforts.

The financial statements showing audited 1984 figures and preliminary 1985 figures are presented below in condensed form.

McCRARY Manufacturing Company
CONDENSED BALANCE SHEETS
February 28, 1985 and 1984

Assets	*1985*	*1984*
Cash	$ 12,000	$ 15,000
Accounts receivable, net	93,000	50,000
Inventory	72,000	67,000
Other current assets	5,000	6,000
Plant and equipment, net of depreciation	60,000	80,000
	$242,000	$218,000
Equities		
Accounts payable	$ 38,000	$ 41,000
Federal income tax payable	30,000	14,400
Long-term liabilities	20,000	40,000
Common stock	70,000	70,000
Retained earnings	84,000	52,600
	$242,000	$218,000

McCRARY Manufacturing Company
CONDENSED INCOME STATEMENTS
Years Ended February 28, 1985 and 1984

	1985	*1984*
Net sales	$1,684,000	$1,250,000
Cost of goods sold	927,000	710,000
Gross margin on sales	757,000	540,000
Selling and administrative expenses	682,000	504,000
Income before federal income taxes	75,000	36,000
Income tax expense	30,000	14,400
Net income	$ 45,000	$ 21,600

Additional information:
The company has only an insignificant amount of cash sales.
The end-of-year figures are comparable to the average for each respective year.

For each year compute the current ratio and a turnover ratio for accounts receivable. Based on these ratios, identify and discuss audit procedures that should be included in Levy's audit of (1) accounts receivable and (2) accounts payable.

AICPA adapted

15-37. The complete set of financial sttatements for the Huffman Corporation for the year ended August 31, 1985, is presented below:

The HUFFMAN Corporation
BALANCE SHEET
(In Thousands of Dollars)
August 31, 1985

Assets

Cash		$ 103
Marketable securities, at cost which approximates market value		54
Trade accounts receivable (net of $65,000 allowance for doubtful accounts)		917
Inventories, at cost		775
Property, plant, and equipment	$3,200	
Less: Accumulated depreciation	1,475	1,725
Prepayments and other assets		125
Total assets		$3,699

Liabilities and Stockholders' Equity

Accounts payable	$ 221
Accrued taxes	62
Bank loans and long-term debt	1,580
Total liabilities	1,863
Capital stock, $10 par value (authorized 50,000 shares, issued and outstanding 42,400 shares)	424
Paid-in capital in excess of par value	366
Retained earnings	1,046
Total stockholders' equity	1,836
Total liabilities and stockholders' equity	$3,699

The HUFFMAN Corporation
STATEMENT OF INCOME AND RETAINED EARNINGS
(In Thousands of Dollars)
For the Year Ended August 31, 1985

Product sales (net of $850,000 sales returns and allowances)		$10,700
Cost of goods sold		8,700
Gross profit on sales		2,000
Operating expenses:		
Selling expenses	$1,500	
General and administrative expenses	940	2,440
Operating loss		(440)
Interest expense		150
Net loss		(590)
Retained earnings, September 1, 1984		1,700
		1,110
Dividends:		
Cash—$1 per share	40	
Stock—6% of shares outstanding	24	64
Retained earnings, August 31, 1985		$1,046

List deficiencies and omissions in The Huffman Corporation's financial statements and discuss the probable effect of the deficiency or omission on the auditor's report. Assume that The Huffman Corporation is unwilling to change the financial statements or make additional disclosures therein.

Consider each deficiency or omission separately, and do *not* consider the cumulative effect on the deficiencies and omissions on the auditor's report. There are no arithmetical errors in the statements.

Organize your answer sheet in two columns as indicated below and write your answer in the order of appearance within the general headings of Balance Sheet, Statement of Income and Retained Earnings, and Other.

Financial statement deficiency or omission	Discussion of effect on auditor's report

AICPA adapted

APPENDIX A

AMERICAN INSTITUTE OF CERTIFIED PUBLIC ACCOUNTANTS

Code of Professional Ethics[1]

Concepts of Professional Ethics

A man should *be* upright; not be *kept* upright.
—MARCUS AURELIUS

A distinguishing mark of a professional is his acceptance of responsibility to the public. All true professions have therefore deemed it essential to promulgate codes of ethics and to establish means for ensuring their observance.

The reliance of the public, the government and the business community on sound financial reporting and advice on business affairs, and the importance of these matters to the economic and social aspects of life impose particular obligations on certified public accountants.

Ordinarily those who depend upon a certified public accountant find it difficult to assess the quality of his services; they have a right to expect, however, that he is a person of competence and integrity. A man or woman who enters the profession of accountancy is assumed to accept an obligation to uphold its principles, to work for the increase of knowledge in the art and for the improvement of methods, and to abide by the profession's ethical and technical standards.

The ethical Code of the American Institute emphasizes the profession's responsibility to the public, a responsibility that has grown as the number of investors has grown, as the relationship between corporate managers and stockholders has be-

[1] Copyright 1972, © 1975, 1978, and 1979 by the American Institute of Certified Public Accountants, Inc., 1211 Avenue of the Americas, New York, New York, 10036.

come more impersonal and as government increasingly relies on accounting information.

The Code also stresses the CPA's responsibility to clients and colleagues, since his behavior in these relationships cannot fail to affect the responsibilities of the profession as a whole to the public.

The Institute's Rules of Conduct set forth minimum levels of acceptable conduct and are mandatory and enforceable. However, it is in the best interests of the profession that CPAs strive for conduct beyond that indicated merely by prohibitions. Ethical conduct, in the true sense, is more than merely abiding by the letter of explicit prohibitions. Rather it requires unswerving commitment to honorable behavior, even at the sacrifice of personal advantage.

The conduct toward which CPAs should strive is embodied in five broad concepts stated as affirmative Ethical Principles:

Independence, integrity and objectivity. A certified public accountant should maintain his integrity and objectivity and, when engaged in the practice of public accounting, be independent of those he serves.

General and technical standards. A certified public accountant should observe the profession's technical standards and strive continually to improve his competence and the quality of his services.

Responsibilities to clients. A certified public accountant should be fair and candid with his clients and serve them to the best of his ability, with professional concern for their best interests, consistent with his responsibilities to the public.

Responsibilities to colleagues. A certified public accountant should conduct himself in a manner which will promote cooperation and good relations among members of the profession.

Other responsibilities and practices. A certified public accountant should conduct himself in a manner which will enhance the stature of the profession and its ability to serve the public.

The foregoing Ethical Principles are intended as broad guidelines as distinguished from enforceable Rules of Conduct. Even though they do not provide a basis for disciplinary action, they constitute the philosophical foundation upon which the Rules of Conduct are based.

The following discussion is intended to elaborate on each of the Ethical Principles and provide rationale for their support.

Independence, integrity and objectivity

A certified public accountant should maintain his integrity and objectivity and, when engaged in the practice of public accounting, be independent of those he serves.

The public expects a number of character traits in a certified public accountant but primarily integrity and objectivity and, in the practice of public accounting, independence.

Independence has always been a concept fundamental to the accounting profession, the cornerstone of its philosophical structure. For no matter how competent any CPA may be, his opinion on financial statements will be of little value to those who rely on him—whether they be clients or any of his unseen audience of credit grantors, investors, governmental agencies and the like—unless he maintains his independence.

Independence has traditionally been defined by the profession as the ability to act with integrity and objectivity.

Integrity is an element of character which is fundamental to reliance on the CPA. This quality may be difficult to judge, however, since a particular fault of omission or commission may be the result either of honest error or a lack of integrity.

Objectivity refers to a CPA's ability to maintain an impartial attitude on all matters which come under his review. Since this attitude involves an individual's mental processes, the evaluation of objectivity must be based largely on actions and relationships viewed in the context of ascertainable circumstances.

While recognizing that the qualities of integrity and objectivity are not precisely measurable, the profession nevertheless constantly holds them up to members as an imperative. This is done essentially by education and by the Rules of Conduct which the profession adopts and enforces.

CPAs cannot practice their calling and participate in the world's affairs without being exposed to situations that involve the possibility of pressures upon their integrity and objectivity. To define and proscribe all such situations would be impracticable. To ignore the problem for that reason, however, and to set no limits at all would be irresponsible.

It follows that the concept of independence should not be interpreted so loosely as to permit relationships likely to impair the CPA's integrity or the impartiality of his judgment, nor so strictly as to inhibit the rendering of useful services when the likelihood of such impairment is relatively remote.

While it may be difficult for a CPA always to appear completely independent even in normal relationships with clients, pressures upon his integrity or objectivity are offset by powerful countervailing forces and restraints. These include the possibility of legal liability, professional discipline ranging up to revocation of the right to practice as a CPA, loss of reputation and, by no means least, the inculcated resistance of a disciplined professional to any infringement upon his basic integrity and objectivity. Accordingly, in deciding which types of relationships should be specifically prohibited, both the magnitude of the threat posed by a relationship and the force of countervailing pressures have to be weighed.

In establishing rules relating to independence, the profession uses the criterion of whether reasonable men, having knowledge of all the facts and taking into consideration normal strength of character and normal behavior under the circumstances, would conclude that a specified relationship between a CPA and a client poses an unacceptable threat to the CPA's integrity or objectivity.

When a CPA expresses an opinion on financial statements, not only the fact but also the appearance of integrity and objectivity is of particular importance. For this reason, the profession has adopted rules to prohibit the expression of such an opinion when relationships exist which might pose such a threat to integrity and objectivity as to exceed the strength of countervailing forces and restraints. These relationships fall into two general categories: (1) certain financial relationships with clients and (2) relationships in which a CPA is virtually part of management or an employee under management's control.

Although the appearance of independence is not required in the case of management advisory services and tax practice, a CPA is encouraged to avoid the proscribed relationships with clients regardless of the type of services being rendered. In any event, the CPA, in all types of engagements, should refuse to subordinate his professional judgment to others and should express his conclusions honestly and objectively.

The financial relationships proscribed when an opinion is expressed on financial statements make no reference to fees paid to a CPA by a client. Remuneration to providers of services is necessary for the continued provision of those services. Indeed, a principal reason for the development and persistence in the professions of the client-practitioner relationship and of remuneration by fee (as contrasted with an employer-employee relationship and remuneration by salary) is that these arrangements are seen as a safeguard of independence.

The above reference to an employer-employee relationship is pertinent to a question sometimes raised as to whether a CPA's objectivity in expressing an opinion on financial statements will be impaired by his being involved with his client in the decision-making process.

CPAs continually provide advice to their clients, and they expect that this advice will usually be followed. Decisions based on such advice may have a significant effect on a client's financial condition or operating results. This is the case not only in tax engagements and management advisory services but in the audit function as well.

If a CPA disagrees with a client on a significant matter during the course of an audit, the client has three choices—he can modify the financial statements (which is usually the case), he can accept a qualified report or he can discharge the CPA. While the ultimate decision and the resulting financial statements clearly are those of the client, the CPA has obviously been a significant factor in the decision-making process. Indeed, no responsible user of financial statements would want it otherwise.

It must be noted that when a CPA expresses an opinion on financial statements, the judgments involved pertain to whether the results of operating decisions of the client are fairly presented in the statements and not on the underlying wisdom of such decisions. It is highly unlikely therefore that being a factor in the client's decision-making process would impair the CPA's objectivity in judging the fairness of presentation.

The more important question is whether a CPA would deliberately compromise his integrity by expressing an unqualified opinion on financial statements which were prepared in such a way as to cover up a poor business decision by the client and on which the CPA has rendered advice. The basic character traits of the CPA as well as the risks arising from such a compromise of integrity, including liability to third parties, disciplinary action and loss of right to practice, should preclude such action.

Providing advice or recommendations which may or may not involve skills logically related to a client's information and control system, and which may affect the client's decision making, does not in itself indicate lack of independence. However, the CPA must be alert to the possibility that undue identification with the management of the client or involvement with a client's affairs to such a degree as to place him virtually in the position of being an employee, may impair the appearance of independence.

To sum up, CPAs cannot avoid external pressures on their integrity and objectivity in the course of their professional work, but they are expected to resist these pressures. They must, in fact, retain their integrity and objectivity in all phases of their practice and, when expressing opinions on financial statements, avoid involvement in situations that would impair the credibility of their independence in the minds of reasonable men familiar with the facts.

General and technical standards

A certified public accountant should observe the profession's general and technical standards and strive continually to improve his competence and the quality of his services.

Since accounting information is of great importance to all segments of the public, all CPAs, whether in public practice, government service, private employment or academic pursuits, should perform their work at a high level of professionalism.

A CPA should maintain and seek always to improve his competence in all areas of accountancy in which he engages. Satisfaction of the requirements for the CPA certificate is evidence of basic competence at the time the certificate is granted, but it does not justify an assumption that this competence is maintained without continuing effort. Further, it does not necessarily justify undertaking complex engagements without additional study and experience.

A CPA should not render professional services without being aware of, and complying with, the applicable general or technical standards as interpreted by bodies designated by Council. Moreover, since published general and technical standards can never cover the whole field of accountancy, he must keep broadly informed.

Observance of the rule on general and technical standards calls for a determination by a CPA with respect to each engagement undertaken that there is a reasonable expectation it can be completed with the exercise of due professional care, with adequate planning and supervision and with the gathering of sufficient relevant data to afford a reasonable basis for conclusions and recommendations. If a CPA is unable to bring such professional competence to the engagement he should suggest, in fairness to his client and the public, the engagement of someone competent to perform the needed service, either independently or as an associate.

The standards referred to in the rules are elaborated and refined to meet changing conditions, and it is each CPA's responsibility to keep himself up to date in this respect.

Responsibilities to clients

A certified public accountant should be fair and candid with his clients and serve them to the best of his ability, with professional concern for their best interests, consistent with his responsibilities to the public.

As a professional person, the CPA should serve his clients with competence and with professional concern for their best interests. He must not permit his regard for a client's interest, however, to override his obligation to the public to maintain his independence, integrity and objectivity. The discharge of this dual responsibility to both clients and the public requires a high degree of ethical perception and conduct.

It is fundamental that the CPA hold in strict confidence all information concerning a client's affairs which he acquires in the course of his engagement. This does not mean, however, that he should acquiesce in a client's unwillingness to make disclosures in financial reports which are necessary to fair presentation.

Exploitation of relations with a client for personal advantage is improper. For example, acceptance of a commission from any vendor for recommending his product or service to a client is prohibited.

A CPA should be frank and straightforward with clients. While tact and diplomacy are desirable, a client should never be left in doubt about the CPA's position on any issue of significance. No truly professional man will subordinate his own judgment or conceal or modify his honest opinion merely to please. This admonition applies to all services including those related to management and tax problems.

When accepting an engagement, a CPA should bear in mind that he may find it necessary to resign if conflict arises on an important question of principle. In cases of irreconcilable difference, he will have to judge whether the importance of the matter requires such an action. In weighing this question, he can feel assured that the practitioner who is independent, fair and candid is the better respected for these qualities and will not lack opportunities for constructive service.

Responsibilities to colleagues

A certified public accountant should conduct himself in a manner which will promote cooperation and good relations among members of the profession.

The support of a profession by its members and their cooperation with one another are essential elements of professional character. The public confidence and respect which a CPA enjoys is largely the result of the cumulative accomplishments of all CPAs, past and present. It is, therefore, in the CPA's own interest, as well as that of the general public, to support the collective efforts of colleagues through professional societies and organizations and to deal with fellow practitioners in a manner which will not detract from their reputation and well-being.

Although the reluctance of a professional to give testimony that may be damaging to a colleague is understandable, the obligation of professional courtesy and fraternal consideration can never excuse lack of complete candor if the CPA is testifying as an expert witness in a judicial proceeding or properly constituted inquiry.

A CPA has the obligation to assist his fellows in complying with the Code of Professional Ethics and should also assist appropriate disciplinary authorities in enforcing the Code. To condone serious fault can be as bad as to commit it. It may be even worse, in fact, since some errors may result from ignorance rather than intent and, if let pass without action, will probably be repeated. In situations of this kind, the welfare of the public should be the guide to a member's action.

While the Code proscribes certain specific actions in the area of relationships with colleagues, it should be understood that these proscriptions do not define the limits of desirable intraprofessional conduct. Rather, such conduct encompasses the professional consideration and courtesies which each CPA would like to have fellow practitioners extend to him.

It is natural that a CPA will seek to develop his practice. However, in doing so he should not seek to displace another accountant in a client relationship by any means which will lessen the effectiveness of his technical performance or lessen his concern for the rights of third parties to reliable information. Further, he should not act in any way that reflects negatively on fellow practitioners.

A CPA may provide service to those who request it, even though they may be served by another practitioner in another area of service, or he may succeed another practitioner at a client's request. In such circumstances it is always desirable and required in some situations before accepting an engagement that the CPA who has been approached should advise the accountant already serving the client. Such action is indicated not only by considerations of professional courtesy but by good business judgment.

A client may sometimes request services requiring highly specialized knowledge. If the CPA lacks the expertise necessary to render such services, he should call upon a fellow practitioner for assistance or refer the entire engagement to another. Such assistance or referral brings to bear on the client's needs both the referring practitioner's knowledge of the client's affairs and the technical expertise of the specialist brought into the engagement. If both serve the client best in their own area of ability, all parties are well served as is the public.

Other responsibilities and practices

A certified public accountant should conduct himself in a manner which will enhance the stature of the profession and its ability to serve the public.

In light of the importance of their function, CPAs and their firms should have a keen consciousness of the public interest and the needs of society. Thus, they should support efforts to achieve equality of opportunity for all, regardless of race, religious background or sex, and should contribute to this goal by their own service relationships and employment practices.

The CPA is a beneficiary of the organization and character of his profession. Since he is seen as a representative of the profession by those who come in contact with him, he should behave honorably both in his personal and professional life and avoid any conduct that might erode public respect and confidence.

Solicitation to obtain clients through false, misleading and deceptive statements or acts is prohibited under the Rules of Conduct because it will lessen the professional effectiveness and the independence toward clients which is essential to the best interests of the public.

Advertising, which is false, misleading and deceptive, is also prohibited because such representations will mislead some of the public and thereby reduce or destroy the profession's usefulness to society. A CPA should seek to establish a reputation for competence and character, through actions rather than words. There are many ways this can be done such as by making himself known through public service, by civic and political activities, and by joining associations and clubs. It is desirable for him to share his knowledge with interested groups by accepting requests to make speeches and write articles. Whatever publicity occurs as a natural by-product of such activities is entirely proper.

In his work, the CPA should be motivated more by desire for excellence in performance than for material reward. This does not mean that he need be indifferent about compensation. Indeed, a professional man who cannot maintain a respectable standard of living is unlikely to inspire confidence or to enjoy sufficient peace of mind to do his best work.

In determining fees, a CPA may assess the degree of responsibility assumed by undertaking an engagement as well as the time, manpower and skills required to perform the service in conformity with the standards of the profession. He may also take into account the value of the service to the client, the customary charges of professional colleagues and other considerations. No single factor is necessarily controlling.

Clients have a right to know in advance what rates will be charged and approximately how much an engagement will cost. However, when professional judgments are involved, it is usually not possible to set a fair charge until an engagement has been completed. For this reason CPAs should state their fees for proposed engagements in the form of estimates which may be subject to change as the work progresses.

Other practices prohibited by the Rules of Conduct include using any firm designation or description which might be misleading, or practicing as a professional corporation or association which fails to comply with provisions established by Council to protect the public interest.

A member, while practicing public accounting, may not engage in a business or occupation which is incompatible therewith. While certain occupations are clearly incompatible with the practice of public accounting, the profession has never attempted to list them, for in most cases the individual circumstances indicate whether there is a problem. For example, there would be a problem of conflict of interest if a practicing CPA were to serve on a tax assessment board since he would be open to accusations of favoring his clients whether this was done or not. Moreover, they might, under some circumstances, create a conflict of interest in the CPA's independence relationship with his clients.

Paying a commission to outsiders is prohibited in order to eliminate the temptation to compensate anyone for referring a client. Receipt of a commission is proscribed since practitioners should look to the client, and not to others, for compensation for services rendered. The practice of paying a fee to a referring CPA irrespective of any service performed or responsibility assumed by him is proscribed because there is no justification for a CPA to share in a fee for accounting services where his sole contribution was to make a referral.

Over the years the vast majority of CPAs have endeavored to earn and maintain a reputation for competence, integrity and objectivity. The success of these efforts has been largely responsible for the wide public acceptance of accounting as an honorable profession. This acceptance is a valuable asset which should never be taken for granted. Every CPA should constantly strive to see that it continues to be deserved.

Rules of Conduct

(As amended through May 22, 1979)

Definitions

The following definitions of terminology are applicable wherever such terminology is used in the Rules and Interpretations.

Client. The person(s) or entity which retains a member or his firm, engaged in the practice of public accounting, for the performance of professional services.

Council. The Council of the American Institute of Certified Public Accountants.

Enterprise. Any person(s) or entity, whether organized for profit or not, for which a CPA provides services.

Firm. A proprietorship, partnership, or professional corporation or association engaged in the practice of public accounting, including individual partners or shareholders thereof.

Financial statements. Statements and footnotes related thereto that purport to show financial position which relates to a point in time or changes in financial position which relate to a period of time, and statements which use a cash or other incomplete basis of accounting. Balance sheets, statements of income, statements of retained earnings, statements of changes in financial position, and statements of changes in owners' equity are financial statements.

Incidental financial data included in management advisory services reports to support recommendations to a client, and tax returns and supporting schedules do not, for this purpose, constitute financial statements; and the statement, affidavit, or signature of preparers required on tax returns neither constitutes an opinion on financial statements nor requires a disclaimer of such opinion.

Institute. The American Institute of Certified Public Accountants.

Interpretations of Rules of Conduct. Pronouncements issued by the division of professional ethics to provide guidelines as to the scope and application of the Rules of Conduct.

Member. A member, associate member, or international associate of the American Institute of Certified Public Accountants.

Practice of public accounting. Holding out to be a CPA or public accountant and at the same time performing for a client one or more types of services rendered by public accountants. The term shall not be limited by a more restrictive definition which might be found in the accountancy law under which a member practices.

Professional services. One or more types of services performed in the practice of public accounting.

Applicability of rules

The Institute's Code of Professional Ethics derives its authority from the bylaws of the Institute which provide that the Trial Board may, after a hearing, admonish, suspend, or expel a member who is found guilty of infringing any of the bylaws or any provisions of the Rules of Conduct.[2]

The Rules of Conduct which follow apply to all services performed in the practice of public accounting including tax and management advisory services except (a) where the wording of the rule indicates otherwise and (b) that a member who is practicing outside the United States will not be subject to discipline for departing from any of the rules stated herein so long as his conduct is in accord with the rules of the organized accounting profession in the country in which he is practicing. However, where a member's name is associated with financial statements in such a manner as to imply that he is acting as an independent public accountant and under circumstances that would entitle the reader to assume that United States practices were followed, he must comply with the requirements of Rules 202 and 203.

A member may be held responsible for compliance with the Rules of Conduct by all persons associated with him in the practice of public accounting who are either under his supervision or are his partners or shareholders in the practice.

A member engaged in the practice of public accounting must observe all the Rules of Conduct. A member not engaged in the practice of public accounting must observe only Rules 102 and 501 since all other Rules of Conduct relate solely to the practice of public accounting.

A member shall not permit others to carry out on his behalf, either with or without compensation, acts which, if carried out by the member, would place him in violation of the Rules of Conduct.

Independence, integrity and objectivity

Rule 101—Independence. A member or a firm of which he is a partner or shareholder shall not express an opinion on financial statements of an enterprise unless he and his firm are independent with respect to such enterprise. Independence will be considered to be impaired if, for example:

A. During the period of his professional engagement, or at the time of expressing his opinion, he or his firm
   1. (a) Had or was committed to acquire any direct or material indirect financial interest in the enterprise; or
      (b) Was a trustee of any trust or executor or administrator of any estate if such trust or estate had or was committed to acquire any direct or material indirect financial interest in the enterprise; or
   2. Had any joint closely held business investment with the enterprise or any officer, director, or principal stockholder thereof which was material in relation to his or his firm's net worth; or
   3. Had any loan to or from the enterprise or any officer, director, or principal stockholder thereof. This latter proscription does not apply to the following loans from a financial institution when made under normal lending procedures, terms, and requirements:

[2] Bylaw Section 7.4.

(a) Loans obtained by a member or his firm which are not material in relation to the net worth of such borrower.
(b) Home mortgages.
(c) Other secured loans, except loans guaranteed by a member's firm which are otherwise unsecured.

B. During the period covered by the financial statements, during the period of the professional engagement, or at the time of expressing an opinion, he or his firm
1. Was connected with the enterprise as a promoter, underwriter, or voting trustee, a director or officer or in any capacity equivalent to that of a member of management or of an employee; or
2. Was a trustee for any pension or profit-sharing trust of the enterprise.

The above examples are not intended to be all-inclusive.

Rule 102—Integrity and Objectivity. A member shall not knowingly misrepresent facts, and when engaged in the practice of public accounting, including the rendering of tax and management advisory services, shall not subordinate his judgment to others. In tax practice, a member may resolve doubt in favor of his client as long as there is reasonable support for his position.

General and technical standards

Rule 201—General Standards. A member shall comply with the following general standards as interpreted by bodies designated by Council and must justify any departures therefrom.

A. *Professional competence.* A member shall undertake only those engagements which he or his firm can reasonably expect to complete with professional competence.
B. *Due professional care.* A member shall exercise due professional care in the performance of an engagement.
C. *Planning and supervision.* A member shall adequately plan and supervise an engagement.
D. *Sufficient relevant data.* A member shall obtain sufficient relevant data to afford a reasonable basis for conclusions or recommendations in relation to an engagement.
E. *Forecasts.* A member shall not permit his name to be used in conjunction with any forecast of future transactions in a manner which may lead to the belief that the member vouches for the achievability of the forecast.

Rule 202—Auditing Standards. A member shall not permit his name to be associated with financial statements in such a manner as to imply that he is acting as an independent public accountant unless he has complied with the applicable generally accepted auding standards promulgated by the Institute. Statements on auditing standards issued by the Institute's auditing standards executive committee are, for purposes of this rule, considered to be interpretations of the generally accepted auditing standards, and departures from such statements must be justified by those who do not follow them.

Rule 203—Accounting Principles. A member shall not express an opinion that financial statements are presented in conformity with generally accepted accounting principles if such statements contain any departure from an accounting principle promulgated by the body designated by Council[3] to establish such principles which has a material effect on the statements taken as a whole, unless the member can demonstrate that due to unusual circumstances the financial statements would otherwise have been misleading. In such cases his report must describe the departure, the approximate effects thereof, if practicable, and the reasons why compliance with the principle would result in a misleading statement.

Rule 204—Other Technical Standards. A member shall comply with other technical standards promulgated by bodies designated by Council[4] to establish such standards, and departures therefrom must be justified by those who do not follow them.

Responsibilities to clients

Rule 301—Confidential Client Information. A member shall not disclose any confidential information obtained in the course of a professional engagement except with the consent of the client.

This rule shall not be construed (a) to relieve a member of his obligation under Rules 202 and 203, (b) to affect in any way his compliance with a validly issued subpoena or summons enforceable by order of a court, (c) to prohibit review of a member's professional practices as a part of voluntary quality review under Institute authorization or (d) to preclude a member from responding to any inquiry made by the ethics division or Trial Board of the Institute, by a duly constituted investigative or disciplinary body of a state CPA society, or under state statutes.

Members of the ethics division and Trial Board of the Institute and professional practice reviewers under Institute authorization shall not disclose any confidential client information which comes to their attention from members in disciplinary proceedings or otherwise in carrying out their official responsibilities. However, this prohibition shall not restrict the exchange of information with an aforementioned duly constituted investigative or disciplinary body.

Rule 302—Contingent Fees. Professional services shall not be offered or rendered under an arrangement whereby no fee will be charged unless a specified finding or result is attained, or where the fee is otherwise contingent upon the findings or results of such services. However, a member's fees may vary depending, for example, on the complexity of the service rendered.

[3] See Resolution A appearing at the end of Rules of Conduct.
[4] See Resolutions B, C, and D appearing at end of Rules of Conduct.

Fees are not regarded as being contingent if fixed by courts or other public authorities or, in tax matters, if determined based on the results of judicial proceedings or the findings of governmental agencies.

Responsibilities to colleagues

(All Rules of Conduct under this section have been repealed by vote of the membership of the AICPA.)

Other responsibilities and practices

Rule 501—Acts Discreditable. A member shall not commit an act discreditable to the profession.

Rule 502—Advertising and Other Forms of Solicitation. A member shall not seek to obtain clients by advertising or other forms of solicitation in a manner that is false, misleading, or deceptive.

Rule 503—Commission. A member shall not pay a commission to obtain a client, nor shall he accept a commission for a referral to a client of products or services of others. This rule shall not prohibit payments for the purchase of an accounting practice or retirement payments to individuals formerly engaged in the practice of public accounting or payments to their heirs or estates.

Rule 504—Incompatible Occupations. A member who is engaged in the practice of public accounting shall not concurrently engage in any business or occupation which would create a conflict of interest in rendering professional services.

Rule 505—Form of Practice and Name. A member may practice public accounting, whether as an owner or employee, only in the form of a proprietorship, a partnership, or a professional corporation whose characteristics conform to resolutions of Council.[5]

A member shall not practice under a firm name which includes any fictitious name, indicates specialization, or is misleading as to the type of organization (proprietorship, partnership, or corporation). However, names of one or more past partners or shareholders may be included in the firm name of a successor partnership or corporation. Also, a partner surviving the death or withdrawal of all other partners may continue to practice under the partnership name for up to two years after becoming a sole practitioner.

A firm may not designate itself as "Members of the American Institute of Certified Public Accountants" unless all of its partners or shareholders are members of the Institute.

[5] See Resolution E appearing at end of Rules of Conduct.

Council Resolutions

Resolution A

The following resolution of Council was approved at the spring meeting of Council on May 7, 1973:

WHEREAS in 1959 the Council designated the Accounting Principles Board to establish accounting principles, and
WHEREAS the Council is advised that the Financial Accounting Standards Board has become operational, it is
RESOLVED, that as of the date hereof the Financial Accounting Standards Board, in respect of statements of financial accounting standards finally adopted by such board in accordance with its rules of procedure and the bylaws of the Financial Accounting Foundation, be, and hereby is, designated by this Council as the body to establish accounting principles pursuant to the rule 203 of the Rules of Conduct of the American Institute of Certified Public Accountants; provided, however, any Accounting Research Bulletins, or Opinions of the Accounting Principles Board presently issued or approved for exposure by the Accounting Principles Board prior to April 1, 1973, and finally adopted by such Board on or before June 30, 1973, shall constitute statements of accounting principles promulgated by a body designated by Council as contemplated in rule 203 of the Rules of Conduct unless and until such time as they are expressly superseded by action of the FASB.

Resolution B

The following resolution of Council was adopted October 21, 1978:

WHEREAS: The membership of the Institute has adopted Rule 204 of the Rules of Conduct which authorizes the Council to designate bodies to promulgate technical standards with which members must comply, and therefore it is
RESOLVED: That the Management Advisory Services Executive Committee is hereby designated to promulgate technical standards under Rule 204 with respect to the offering of management advisory services provided, however, that such standards do not deal with the broad question of what, if any, services should be proscribed, and provided further that any such statements are subject to review by affected senior technical committees of the Institute prior to issuance.

Resolution C

The following resolution of Council was adopted May 7, 1979:

WHEREAS: The membership of the Institute has adopted Rule 204 of the Rules of Conduct which authorizes the Council to designate bodies to promulgate technical standards with which members must comply, and therefore it is

RESOLVED: That the Accounting and Review Services Committee is hereby designated to promulgate technical standards under Rule 204 with respect to unaudited financial statements or other unaudited financial information of an entity that is not required to file financial statements with a regulatory agency in connection with the sale or trading of its securities in a public market provided, however, that any such statements are subject to review by affected senior technical committees of the Institute prior to issuance.

Resolution D

The following resolution of Council was adopted May 7, 1979:

WHEREAS: The membership of the Institute has adopted Rule 204 of the Rules of Conduct which authorizes the Council to designate bodies to promulgate technical standards with which members must comply, and therefore it is
RESOLVED: That the Auditing Standards Board shall establish under statements on auditing standards the responsibilities of members with respect to standards of disclosure of financial information outside financial statements in published financial reports containing financial statements. For this purpose, the council designates the FASB as the body, under Rule 204 of the Rules of Conduct, to establish standards for the disclosure of such information.

Resolution E

The following resolution of Council was approved at the spring meeting of Council on May 6, 1969, and amended at the fall meeting of the Council on October 12, 1974:

RESOLVED, that members may be officers, directors, stockholders, representatives, or agents of a corporation offering services of a type performed by public accountants only when the professional corporation or association has the following characteristics:

1. *Name.* The name under which the professional corporation or association renders professional services shall contain only the names of one or more of the present or former shareholders or of partners who were associated with a predecessor accounting firm. Impersonal or fictitious names, as well as names which indicate a specialty, are prohibited.
2. *Purpose.* The professional corporation or association shall not provide services that are incompatible with the practice of public accounting.
3. *Ownership.* All shareholders of the corporation or association shall be persons engaged in the practice of public accounting as defined by the Code of Professional Ethics. Shareholders shall at all times own their shares in their own right and shall be the beneficial owners of the equity capital ascribed to them.
4. *Transfer of Shares.* Provision shall be made requiring any shareholder who ceases to be eligible to be a shareholder to dispose of all of his shares within a reasonable period to a person qualified to be a shareholder or to the corporation or association.

5. *Directors and Officers.* The principal executive officer shall be a shareholder and a director, and to the extent possible, all other directors and officers shall be certified public accountants. Lay directors and officers shall not exercise any authority whatsoever over professional matters.
6. *Conduct.* The right to practice as a corporation or association shall not change the obligation of its shareholders, directors, officers, and other employees to comply with the standards of professional conduct established by the American Institute of Certified Public Accountants.
7. *Liability.* The stockholders of professional corporations or associations shall be jointly and severally liable for the acts of a corporation or association, or its employees—except where professional liability insurance is carried, or capitalization is maintained, in amounts deemed sufficient to offer adequate protection to the public. Liability shall not be limited by the formation of subsidiary or affiliated corporations or associations each with its own limited and unrelated liability.

In a report approved by Council at the fall 1969 meeting, the board of directors recommended that professional liability insurance or capitalization in the amount of $50,000 per shareholder/officer and professional employee to a maximum of $2,000,000 would offer adequate protection to the public. Members contemplating the formation of a corporation under this rule should ascertain that no further modifications in the characteristics have been made.

Interpretations of Rules of Conduct

Interpretations of the Rules of Conduct are issued by the division of professional ethics to provide guidelines as to the scope and application of such rules. Members who depart from such guidelines shall have the burden of justifying such departure in any disciplinary hearing.

Interpretations under Rule 101—Independence

101-1—Honorary Directorships and Trusteeships. Members are often asked to lend the prestige of their names to not-for-profit organizations that limit their activities to those of a charitable, religious, civic or similar nature by being named as a director or a trustee. A member who permits his name to be used in this manner and who is associated with the financial statements of the organization would not be considered lacking in independence under Rule 101 so long as (1) his position is purely honorary, (2) it is identified as honorary in all letterheads and externally circulated materials in which he is named as a director or trustee, (3) he restricts his participation to the use of his name, and (4) he does not vote or otherwise participate in management functions.

It is presumed that organizations to which members lend only the prestige of their names will have sufficiently large boards of directors or trustees to clearly permit the member to limit his participation consistent with the foregoing restriction.

101-2—Retired Partners and Firm Independence. A retired partner having a relationship of a type specified in Rule 101 with a client of his former firm would not be considered as impairing the firm's independence with respect to the client provided that he is no longer active in the firm, that the fees received from such client do not have a material effect on his retirement benefits and that he is not held out as being associated with his former partnership.

101-3—Accounting Services. Members in public practice are sometimes asked to provide manual or automated bookkeeping or data processing services to clients who are of insufficient size to employ an adequate internal accounting staff. Computer systems design and programming assistance are also rendered by members either in conjunction with data processing services or as a separate engagement. Members who perform such services and who are engaged in the practice of public accounting are subject to the bylaws and Rules of Conduct.

On occasion members also rent "block time" on their computers to their clients but are not involved in the processing of transactions or maintaining the client's accounting records. In such cases the sale of block time constitutes a business rather than a professional relationship and must be considered together with all other relationships between the member and his client to determine if their aggregate impact is such as to impair the member's independence.

When a member performs manual or automated bookkeeping services, concern may arise whether the performance of such services would impair his audit independence—that the performance of such basic accounting services would cause his audit to be lacking in a review of mechanical accuracy or that the accounting judgments made by him in recording transactions may somehow be less reliable than if made by him in connection with the subsequent audit.

Members are skilled in, and well accustomed to, applying techniques to control mechanical accuracy, and the performance of the record-keeping function should have no effect on application of such techniques. With regard to accounting judgments, if third parties have confidence in a member's judgment in performing an audit, it is difficult to contend that they would have less confidence where the same judgment is applied in the process of preparing the underlying accounting records.

Nevertheless, a member performing accounting services for an audit client must meet the following requirements to retain the appearance that he is not virtually an employee and therefore lacking in independence in the eyes of a reasonable observer.

1. The CPA must not have any relationship or combination of relationships with the client or any conflict of interest which would impair his integrity and objectivity.
2. The client must accept the responsibility for the financial statements as his own. A small client may not have anyone in his employ to maintain accounting records and may rely on the CPA for this purpose. Nevertheless, the client

must be sufficiently knowledgeable of the enterprise's activities and financial condition and the applicable accounting principles so that he can reasonably accept such responsibility, including, specifically, fairness of valuation and presentation and adequacy of disclosure. When necessary, the CPA must discuss accounting matters with the client to be sure that the client has the required degree of understanding.

3. The CPA must not assume the role of employee or of management conducting the operations of an enterprise. For example, the CPA shall not consummate transactions, have custody of assets or exercise authority on behalf of the client. The client must prepare the source documents on all transactions in sufficient detail to identify clearly the nature and amount of such transactions and maintain an accounting control over data processed by the CPA such as control totals and document counts. The CPA should not make changes in such basic data without the concurrence of the client.
4. The CPA, in making an examination of financial statements prepared from books and records which he has maintained completely or in part, must conform to generally accepted auditing standards. The fact that he has processed or maintained certain records does not eliminate the need to make sufficient audit tests.

When a client's securities become subject to regulation by the Securities and Exchange Commission or other federal or state regulatory body, responsibility for maintenance of the accounting records, including accounting classification decisions, must be assumed by accounting personnel employed by the client. The assumption of this responsibility must commence with the first fiscal year after which the client's securities qualify for such regulation.

101-4—Effect of Family Relationships on Independence. Rule of Conduct 101 proscribes relationships which impair a member's independence through direct financial interests, material indirect financial interests, or other involvements. Relationships which arise through family bloodlines and marriage may give rise to circumstances that may impair a member's independence.

Financial and business relationships ascribed to the member. It is well accepted that the independence of a member may be impaired by the financial interests and business relationships of the member's spouse, dependent children, or any relative living in a common household with or supported by the member. The financial interests or business relationships of such family, dependents or relatives in a member's client are ascribed to the member; in such circumstances the independence of the member or his firm would be impaired under Rule 101.

Financial and business relationships that may be ascribed to the member—close kin. Family relationships may also involve other circumstances in which the appearance of independence is lacking. However, it is not reasonable to assume that all kinships, per se, will impair the appearance of independence since some kinships are too remote. The following guidelines to the effect of kinship on the appearance of independence have evolved over the years:

A presumption that the appearance of independence is impaired arises from a significant financial interest, investment, or business relationship by the following close kin in a member's client: nondependent children, brothers and sisters, grandparents, parents, parents-in-law, and the respective spouses of any of the foregoing.

If the close kin's financial interest in a member's client is material in relationship to the kin's net worth, a third party could conclude that the member's objectivity is impaired with respect to the client since the kinship is so close. In addition, financial interests held by close kin may result in an indirect financial interest being ascribed to the member.

The presumption that the appearance of independence is impaired would also prevail where a close kin has an important role or responsible executive position (e.g., director, chief executive or financial officer) with a client.

Geographical separation from the close kin and infrequent contact may mitigate such impairment except with respect to:

a. A partner working on the engagement or located in the office responsible for the engagement,
b. A partner in the same office or one who maintained close personal relationships with partners working on the engagement,
c. A partner who, as a result of his administrative or advisory positions, is involved in the engagement, or
d. A staff member participating in the engagement or located in an office participating in a significant portion of the engagement.

If a member does not or could not reasonably be expected to have knowledge of the financial interests, investments and business relationships of his close kin, such lack of knowledge would preclude an impairment of objectivity and appearance of independence.

Financial and business relationships that are not normally ascribed to the member—remote kin. A presumption that the appearance of independence is impaired would not normally arise from the financial interests and business relationships of remote kin: uncles, aunts, cousins, nephews, nieces, other in-laws, and other kin who are not close.

The financial interests and business relationships of these remote kin are not considered either direct or indirect interests ascribed to the member. However, the presumption of no impairment with remote kin would be negated if other factors indicating a closeness exist, such as living in the same household with the member, having financial ties, or jointly participating in other business enterprises.

Summary. Members must be aware that it is impossible to enumerate all circumstances wherein the appearance of a member's independence might be questioned by third parties because of family relationships. In situations involving the assessment of relationships with both close and remote kin, members must consider whether geographical proximity, strength of personal and other business relationships and other factors—when viewed together with financial interests in question—would lead a reasonable observer to conclude that the specified relationships pose an unacceptable threat to the member's objectivity and appearance of independence.

101-5—Meaning of the Term "Normal Lending Procedures, Terms and Requirements." Rule 101(A)(3) prohibits loans to a member from his client except for certain specified kinds of loans from a client financial institution when made under "normal lending procedures, terms and requirements." The member would meet the criteria prescribed by this rule if the procedures, terms and requirements relating to his loan are reasonably comparable to those relating to other loans of a similar character committed to other borrowers during the period in which the loan to the member is committed. Accordingly, in making such comparison and in evaluating whether his loan was made under "normal lending procedures, terms and requirements", the member should consider all the circumstances under which the loan was granted including

1. The amount of the loan in relation to the value of the collateral pledged as security and the credit standing of the member or his firm.
2. Repayment terms.
3. Interest rate, including "points".
4. Requirement to pay closing costs in accordance with the lender's usual practice.
5. General availability of such loans to the public.

Related prohibitions (which may be more restrictive) are prescribed by certain state and federal agencies having regulatory authority over such financial institutions.

101-6—The Effect of Actual or Threatened Litigation on Independence. Rule of Conduct 101 prohibits the expression of an opinion on financial statements of an enterprise unless a member and his firm are independent with respect to the enterprise. In some circumstances, independence may be considered to be impaired as a result of litigation or the expressed intention to commence litigation.

LITIGATION BETWEEN CLIENT AND AUDITOR

In order for the auditor to fulfill his obligation to render an informed, objective opinion on the client company's financial statements, the relationship between the management of the client and the auditor must be characterized by complete candor and full disclosure regarding all aspects of the client's business operations. In addition, there must be an absence of bias on the part of the auditor so that he can exercise dispassionate professional judgment on the financial reporting decisions made by the management. When the present management of a client company commences, or expresses an intention to commence, legal action against the auditor, the auditor and the client management may be placed in adversary positions in which the management's willingness to make complete disclosures and the auditor's objectivity may be affected by self-interest.

For the reasons outlined above, independence may be impaired whenever the auditor and his client company or its management are in threatened or actual positions of material adverse interests by reason of actual or intended litigation. Because of the complexity and diversity of the situations of adverse interests which may arise, however, it is difficult to prescribe precise points at which independence may be impaired. The following criteria are offered as guidelines:

1. The commencement of litigation by the present management alleging deficiencies in audit work for the client would be considered to impair independence.
2. The commencement of litigation by the auditor against the present manage-

ment alleging management fraud or deceit would be considered to impair independence.

3. An expressed intention by the present management to commence litigation against the auditor alleging deficiencies in audit work for the client is considered to impair independence if the auditor concludes that there is a strong possibility that such a claim will be filed.
4. Litigation not related to audit work for the client (whether threatened or actual) for an amount not material to the member's firm[6] or to the financial statements of the client company would not usually be considered to affect the relationship in such a way as to impair independence. Such claims may arise, for example, out of disputes as to billings for services, results of tax or management services advice or similar matters.

LITIGATION BY SECURITY HOLDERS

The auditor may also become involved in litigation ("primary litigation") in which he and the client company or its management are defendants. Such litigation may arise, for example, when one or more stockholders bring a stockholders' derivative action or a so-called "class action" against the client company or its management, its officers, directors, underwriters and auditors under the securities laws. Such primary litigation in itself would not alter fundamental relationships between the client company or its management and auditor and therefore should not be deemed to have an adverse impact on the auditor's independence. These situations should be examined carefully, however, since the potential for adverse interests may exist if cross-claims are filed against the auditor alleging that he is responsible for any deficiencies or if the auditor alleges fraud or deceit by the present management as a defense. In assessing the extent to which his independence may be impaired under these conditions, the auditor should consider the following additional guidelines:

1. The existence of cross-claims filed by the client, its management, or any of its directors to protect a right to legal redress in the event of a future adverse decision in the primary litigation (or, in lieu of cross-claims, agreements to extend the statute of limitations) would not normally affect the relationship between client management and auditor in such a way as to impair independence, unless there exists a significant risk that the cross-claim will result in a settlement or judgment in an amount material to the member's firm[6] or to the financial statements of the client.
2. The assertion of cross-claims against the auditor by underwriters would not usually impair independence if no such claims are asserted by the company or the present management.
3. If any of the persons who file cross-claims against the auditor are also officers or directors of other clients of the auditor, the auditor's independence with respect to such other clients would not usually be impaired.

[6] Because of the complexities of litigation and the circumstances under which it may arise, it is not possible to prescribe meaningful criteria for measuring materiality; accordingly, the member should consider the nature of the controversy underlying the litigation and all other relevant factors in reaching a judgment.

OTHER THIRD-PARTY LITIGATION

Another type of third-party litigation against the auditor may be commenced by a lending institution, other creditor, security holder or insurance company who alleges reliance on financial statements of the client examined by the auditor as a basis for extending credit or insurance coverage to the client. In some instances, an insurance company may commence litigation (under subrogation rights) against the auditor in the name of the client to recover losses reimbursed to the client. These types of litigation would not normally affect the auditor's independence with respect to a client who is either not the plaintiff or is only the nominal plaintiff, since the relationship between the auditor and client management would not be affected. They should be examined carefully, however, since the potential for adverse interests may exist if the auditor alleges, in his defense, fraud or deceit by the present management.

If the real party in interest in the litigation (e.g., the insurance company) is also a client of the auditor ("the plaintiff client"), the auditor's independence with respect to the plaintiff client may be impaired if the litigation involves a significant risk of a settlement or judgment in an amount which would be material to the member's firm or to the financial statements of the plaintiff client. If the auditor concludes that such litigation is not material to the plaintiff client or his firm and thus his independence is not impaired, he should nevertheless ensure that professional personnel assigned to the audit of either of the two clients have no involvement with the audit of the other.

EFFECTS OF IMPAIRMENT OF INDEPENDENCE

If the auditor believes that the circumstances would lead a reasonable person having knowledge of the facts to conclude that the actual or intended litigation poses an unacceptable threat to the auditor's independence he should either (a) disengage himself to avoid the appearance that his self-interest would affect his objectivity, or (b) disclaim an opinion because of lack of independence as prescribed by Section 517 of *Statement on Auditing Standards No. 1.* Such disengagement may take the form of resignation or cessation of any audit work then in progress pending resolution of the issues between the parties.

TERMINATION OF IMPAIRMENT

The conditions giving rise to a lack of independence are usually eliminated when a final resolution is reached and the matters at issue no longer affect the relationship between auditor and client. The auditor should carefully review the conditions of such resolution to determine that all impairments to his objectivity have been removed.

ACTIONS PERMITTED WHILE INDEPENDENCE IS IMPAIRED

If the auditor was independent when his report was initially rendered, he may re-sign such report or consent to its use at a later date while his independence is impaired provided that no post-audit work is performed by such auditor during the period of impairment. The term "post-audit work", in this context, does not include inquiries of subsequent auditors, reading of subsequent financial statements, or such procedures as may be necessary to assess the effect of subsequently discovered facts on the financial statements covered by his previously issued report.

101-7—Application of Rule 101 to Professional Personnel. The term "he and his firm" as used in the first sentence of Rule 101 means (1) all partners or shareholders in the firm and (2) all full and part-time professional employees participating in the engagement or located in an office participating in a significant portion of the engagement.

101-8—Effect on Independence of Financial Interests in Nonclients Having Investor or Investee Relationships with a Member's Client.

INTRODUCTION

Rule 101, Independence, provides in part that "A member or a firm of which he is a partner or shareholder shall not express an opinion on financial statements of an enterprise unless he and his firm are independent with respect to such enterprise. Independence will be considered to be impaired if for example, (A) . . . during the period of his professional engagement, or at the time of expressing his opinion, he or his firm . . . had or was committed to acquire any direct or material indirect financial interest in the enterprise . . . (B) during the period covered by the financial statements, during the period of the professional engagement, or at the time of expressing an opinion, he or his firm . . . was connected with the enterprise . . . in any capacity equivalent to that of a member of management . . ."

This interpretation deals with the effect on the appearance of independence of financial interests in nonclients that are related in various ways to a client. Some of the relationships discussed herein result in a financial interest in the client, while others would place the member in a capacity equivalent to that of a member of management.

Situations in which the nonclient investor is a partnership are not covered in this interpretation because the interests of the partnership are ascribed directly to the partners. A member holding a direct financial interest in a partnership that invests in his client has, as a result, a direct financial interest in the client, which impairs his independence.

TERMINOLOGY

The following specially identified terms are used in this Interpretation as indicated:

1. *Client.* The enterprise with whose financial statements the member is associated.
2. *Member.* In this Interpretation the term "member" means (a) a partner or shareholder in the firm or (b) a full or part-time professional employee participating in the engagement or located in an office participating in a significant portion of the engagement.
3. *Investor.* In this Interpretation the term "investor" means (a) a parent or (b) another investor (including a natural person but not a partnership) that holds

an interest in another company ("investee"), but only if the interest gives such other investor the ability to exercise significant influence over operating and financial policies of the investee. The criteria established in paragraph 17 of Accounting Principles Board Opinion Number 18 shall apply in determining the ability of an investor to exercise such influence.

4. *Investee.* In this Interpretation, the term "investee" means (a) a subsidiary or (b) an entity that is subject to significant influence from an investor. A limited partnership in which a client-investor holds a limited partnership interest would not be considered as "investee" subject to this interpretation unless the limited partner were in a position to exercise significant influence over operating and financial policies of the limited partnership.
5. *Material Investee.* An investee is presumed to be material if:
   a. the investor's aggregate carrying amount of investment in and advances to the investee exceeds 5% of the investor's consolidated total assets, or
   b. the investor's equity in the investee's income from continuing operations before income taxes exceeds 5% of the investor's consolidated income from continuing operations before income taxes.

   When the investor is a nonclient and its carrying amount of investments in and advances to the client investee is not readily available, the investor's proportionate share of the client investee's total assets may be used in the calculation described in (a) abovc.

   If the income of an investor or investee from continuing operations before income taxes of the most recent year is clearly not indicative of the past or expected future amounts of such income, the reference point for materiality determinations should be the average of the incomes from continuing operations before income taxes of the preceding 3 years.

   If a member has a financial interest in more than one nonclient investee of a client investor, the investments in and advances to such investees, and the equity in the income from continuing operations before income taxes of all such investees must be aggregated for purposes of determining whether such investees are material to the investor.

   The 5% guidelines for identifying a material investee are to be applied to financial information available at the beginning of the engagement. A minor change in the percentage resulting from later financial information, which a member does not and could not be expected to anticipate at the beginning, may be ignored.
6. *Material Financial Interest.* A financial interest is presumed to be material to a member if it exceeds 5% of the member's net worth. If the member has financial interests in more than one investee of one investor, such interests must be aggregated for purposes of determining whether the member has a material financial interest as described in the preceding sentence.

INTERPRETATION

Where a nonclient investee is material to a client investor, any direct or material indirect financial interest of a member in the nonclient investee would be considered to impair the member's independence with respect to the client. Likewise, where a client investee is material to a nonclient investor, any direct or material indirect financial interest of a member in the nonclient investor would be considered to impair the member's independence with respect to the client.

The remainder of this Interpretation discusses whether, in the other situations listed below, a member's financial interest in nonclient investor or nonclient investee of an audit client will impair the member's independence.

These situations are discussed in the following sections:

1. Nonclient investee is not material to client investor.
2. Client investee is not material to nonclient investor.

Other relationships, such as those involving brother-sister common control or client-nonclient joint ventures, may affect the appearance of independence. The member should make a reasonable inquiry to determine whether such relationships exist, and where they do, careful consideration should be given to whether the financial interests in question would lead a reasonable observer to conclude that the specified relationships pose an unacceptable threat to the member's independence.

In general, in brother-sister common control situations, an immaterial financial interest of a member in the nonclient investee would not impair the independence of a member with respect to the client investee provided the member could not significantly influence the nonclient investor. In like manner in a joint venture situation, an immaterial financial interest of a member in the nonclient investor would not impair the independence of the member with respect to the client investor provided that the member could not significantly influence the nonclient investor.

If a member does not and could not reasonably be expected to have knowledge of the financial interests or relationships described in this interpretation, such lack of knowledge would preclude an impairment of independence.

(1) NONCLIENT INVESTEE IS NOT MATERIAL TO CLIENT INVESTOR

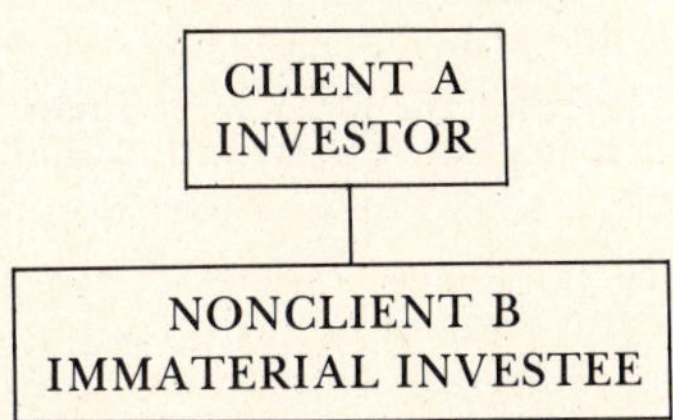

An immaterial financial interest of a member in Nonclient B (investee) would not be considered to impair the member's independence with respect to Client A (investor). A material financial interest of a member in Nonclient B would be considered to impair the member's independence with respect to Client A. The reason for this is that through its ability to influence Nonclient B, Client A could enhance or diminish the value of the member's financial interest in Nonclient B by an amount material to the member's net worth without a material effect on its own financial statements. As a result, the member would not appear to be independent when reporting on the financial statements of Client A.

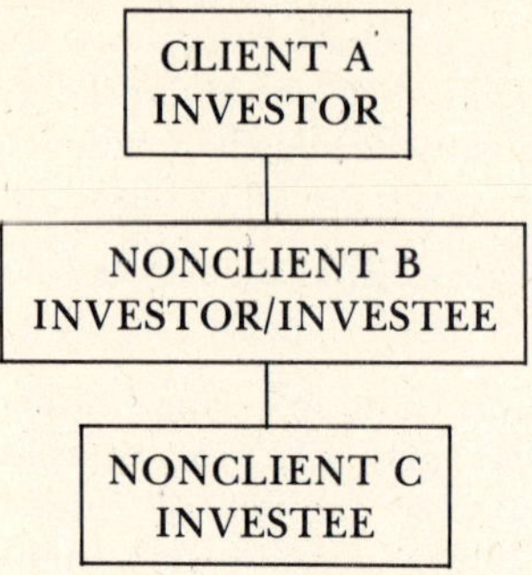

If Nonclient B (investee of Client A) had an investee, Nonclient C, the determination as to whether a financial interest in Nonclient C would be considered to impair the member's independence would be based on the same rules as above for Nonclient B, except that the materiality of Nonclient C is measured in relation to Client A, rather than to Nonclient B.

(2) CLIENT INVESTEE IS NOT MATERIAL TO NONCLIENT INVESTOR

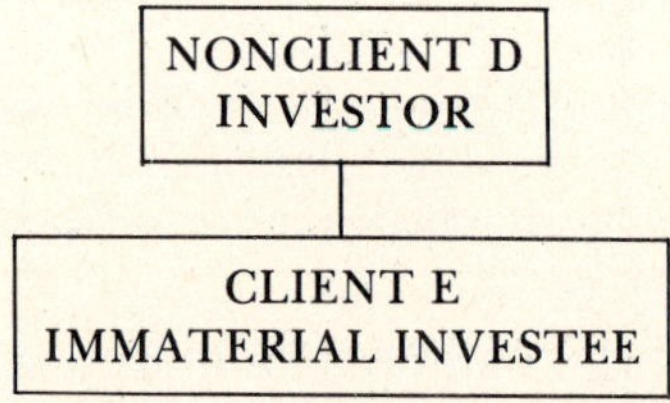

Except as indicated in the next paragraph, a financial interest of a member in Nonclient D (investor) would not be considered to impair the member's independence with respect to Client E (investee) even if the financial interest in Nonclient D were material to the member's net worth. The reason for this is that, since Client E is immaterial to Nonclient D, the member would not appear to be in a position to enhance his investment in Nonclient D.

If the member's financial interest in Nonclient D (investor) is sufficiently large to allow the member to significantly influence the actions of Nonclient D, the member's independence would be considered to be impaired. The reason for this is that a financial interest sufficient to allow the member to significantly influence the actions (operating and financial policies, intercompany transactions, etc.) of the investor could permit the member to exercise a degree of control over the client that would place the member in a capacity equivalent to that of a member of management. Such relationship would be considered to impair independence under Rule 101(b)(1).

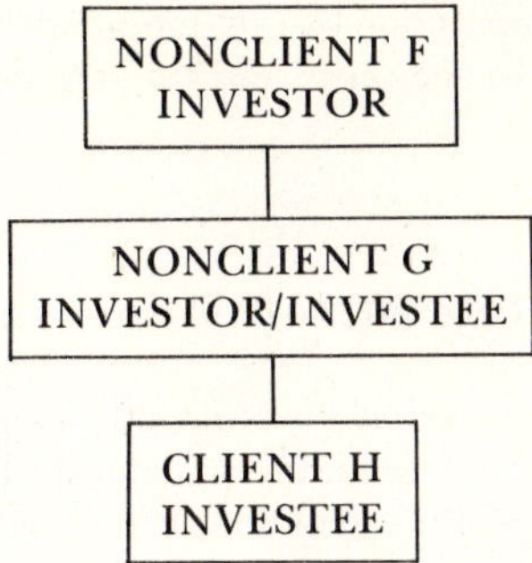

If Client H were an investee of Nonclient G, who was an investee of another investor, Nonclient F, the determination as to whether a financial interest in Nonclient F would be considered to impair the member's independence would be based on the same rules as above for Nonclient G, except that the materiality of Client H is measured in relation to Nonclient F, rather than to Nonclient G.

Interpretations under Rule 201—General standards

201-1—Competence. A member who accepts a professional engagement implies that he has the necessary competence to complete the engagement according to professional standards, applying his knowledge and skill with reasonable care and diligence, but he does not assume a responsibility for infallibility of knowledge or judgment.

Competence in the practice of public accounting involves both the technical qualifications of the member and his staff and his ability to supervise and evaluate the quality of the work performed. Competence relates both to knowledge of the profession's standards, techniques and the technical subject matter involved, and to the capability to exercise sound judgment in applying such knowledge to each engagement.

The member may have the knowledge required to complete an engagement professionally before undertaking it. In many cases, however, additional research or consultation with others may be necessary during the course of the engagement. This does not ordinarily represent a lack of competence, but rather is a normal part of the professional conduct of an engagement.

However, if a CPA is unable to gain sufficient competence through these means, he should suggest, in fairness to his client and the public, the engagement of someone competent to perform the needed service, either independently or as an associate.

201-2—Forecasts. Rule 201 does not prohibit a member from preparing, or assisting a client in the preparation of, forecasts of the results of future transactions. When a member's name is associated with such forecasts, there shall be the presumption that such data may be used by parties other than the client. Therefore, full disclosure must be made of the sources of the information used and the major assumptions made in the preparation of the statements and analyses, the character of the work performed by the member, and the degree of the responsibility he is taking.

Interpretation under Rule 202—Auditing standards

202-1—Unaudited Financial Statements. Rule 202 does not preclude a member from associating himself with the unaudited financial statements of his clients. The Rule states in part that "A member shall not permit his name to be associated with financial statements in such a manner as to imply that he is acting as an independent public accountant unless he has complied with the *applicable* generally accepted auditing standards promulgated by the Institute." (Emphasis supplied.)

In applying this provision to situations in which a member's name is associated with unaudited financial statements, it is necessary to recognize that the standards were specifically written to apply to audited financial statements. The fourth reporting standard, however, was made sufficiently broad to be applicable to unaudited financial statements as well.

The fourth reporting standard states in part: ". . . In *all* cases where an auditor's name is associated with financial statements, the report should contain a clear-cut indication of the character of the auditor's examination, *if any,* and the degree of responsibility he is taking." (Emphasis supplied.)

Those sections of Statements on Auditing Standards and related guides which deal with unaudited financial statements provide guidance to members associated with such statements.

Interpretations under Rule 203—Accounting principles

203-1—Departures from Established Accounting Principles. Rule 203 was adopted to require compliance with accounting principles promulgated by the body designated by Council to establish such principles. There is a strong presumption that adherence to officially established accounting principles would in nearly all instances result in financial statements that are not misleading.

However, in the establishment of accounting principles it is difficult to anticipate all of the circumstances to which such principles might be applied. This rule therefore recognizes that upon occasion there may be unusual circumstances where the literal application of pronouncements on accounting principles would have the effect of rendering financial statements misleading. In such cases, the proper accounting treatment is that which will render the financial statements not misleading.

The question of what constitutes unusual circumstances as referred to in Rule 203 is a matter of professional judgment involving the ability to support the position that adherence to a promulgated principle would be regarded generally by reasonable men as producing a misleading result.

Examples of events which may justify departures from a principle are new legislation or the evolution of a new form of business transaction. An unusual degree of materiality or the existence of conflicting industry practices are examples of circumstances which would not ordinarily be regarded as unusual in the context of Rule 203.

203-2—Status of FASB Interpretations. Council is authorized under Rule 203 to designate a body to establish accounting principles and has designated the Financial Accounting Standards Board as such body. Council also has resolved that FASB Statements of Financial Accounting Standards, together with those Accounting Research Bulletins and APB Opinions which are not superseded by action of the FASB, constitute accounting principles as contemplated in Rule 203.

In determining the existence of a departure from an accounting principle established by a Statement of Financial Accounting Standards, Accounting Research Bulletin or APB Opinion encompassed by Rule 203, the division of professional ethics will construe such Statement, Bulletin or Opinion in the light of any interpretations thereof issued by the FASB.

Interpretation under Rule 301—Confidential client information

301-1—Confidential Information and Technical Standards. The prohibition against disclosure of confidential information obtained in the course of a professional engagement does not apply to disclosure of such information when required to properly discharge the member's responsibility according to the profession's standards. The prohibition would not apply, for example, to disclosure, as required by Section 561 of *Statement on Auditing Standards No. 1,* of subsequent discovery of facts existing at the date of the auditor's report which would have affected the auditor's report had he been aware of such facts.

Interpretations under Rule 501—Acts discreditable

501-1—Client's Records and Accountant's Workpapers. Retention of client records after a demand is made for them is an act discreditable to the profession in violation of Rule 501. The fact that the statutes of the state in which a member practices may specifically grant him a lien on all client records in his possession does not change the ethical standard that it would be a violation of the Code to retain the records to enforce payment.

A member's working papers are his property and need not be surrendered to the client. However, in some instances a member's working papers will contain data which should properly be reflected in the client's books and records but which for convenience have not been duplicated therein, with the result that the client's records are incomplete. In such instances, the portion of the working papers containing such data constitutes part of the client's records, and copies should be made available to the client upon request.

If a member is engaged to perform certain work for a client and the engagement is terminated prior to the completion of such work, the member is required to return or furnish copies of only those records originally given to the member by the client.

Examples of working papers that are considered to be client's records would include:

a. Worksheets in lieu of books of original entry (e.g., listings and distributions of cash receipts or cash disbursements on columnar working paper).
b. Worksheets in lieu of general ledger or subsidiary ledgers, such as accounts receivable, job cost and equipment ledgers or similar depreciation records.
c. All adjusting and closing journal entries and supporting details. (If the supporting details are not fully set forth in the explanation of the journal entry, but are contained in analyses of accounts in the accountant's working papers, then copies of such analyses must be furnished to the client.)
d. Consolidating or combining journal entries and worksheets and supporting detail used in arriving at final figures incorporated in an end product such as financial statements or tax returns.

Any working papers developed by the member incident to the performance of his engagement which do not result in changes to the clients' records or are not in themselves part of the records ordinarily maintained by such clients, are considered to be solely "accountant's working papers" and are not the property of the client, e.g.:

The member may make extensive analyses of inventory or other accounts as part of his selective audit procedures. Even if such analyses have been prepared by client personnel at the request of the member, they nevertheless are considered to be part of the accountant's working papers.

Only to the extent such analyses result in changes to the client's records would the member be required to furnish the details from his working papers in support of the journal entries recording such changes unless the journal entries themselves contain all necessary details.

Once the member has returned the client's records to him or furnished him with copies of such records and/or necessary supporting data, he has discharged his obligation in this regard and need not comply with any subsequent requests to again furnish such records.

If the member has retained in his files copies of a client's records already in possession of the client, the member is not required to return such copies to the client.

501-2—Discrimination in Employment Practices. Discrimination based on race, color, religion, sex, age or national origin in hiring, promotion or salary practices is presumed to constitute an act discreditable to the profession in violation of Rule 501.

Interpretations under Rule 502—Advertising and other forms of solicitation

502-1—Informational Advertising. Advertising that is informative and objective is permitted. Such advertising should be in good taste and be professionally dignified. There are no other restrictions, such as on the type of advertising media, frequency of placement, size, artwork, or type style. Some examples of informative and objective content are—

1. Information about the member and the member's firm, such as—
   a. Names, addresses, telephone numbers, number of partners, shareholders or employees, office hours, foreign language competence, and date the firm was established.
   b. Services offered and fees for such services, including hourly rates and fixed fees.
   c. Educational and professional attainments, including date and place of certifications, schools attended, dates of graduation, degrees received, and memberships in professional associations.
2. Statements of policy or position made by a member or a member's firm related to the practice of public accounting or addressed to a subject of public interest.

502-2—False, Misleading, or Deceptive Acts. Advertising or other forms of solicitation that are false, misleading, or deceptive are not in the public interest and are prohibited. Such activities include those that—

1. Create false or unjustified expectations of favorable results.
2. Imply the ability to influence any court, tribunal, regulatory agency, or similar body or official.
3. Consist of self-laudatory statements that are not based on verifiable facts.
4. Make comparisons with other CPAs.
5. Contain testimonials or endorsements.
6. Contain any other representations that would be likely to cause a reasonable person to misunderstand or be deceived.

[*502-3*]—[Deleted]

502-4—Self-Designation as Expert or Specialist. Claiming to be an expert or specialist is prohibited because an AICPA program with methods for recognizing competence in specialized fields has not been developed and self-designation would be likely to cause misunderstanding or deception.

502-5—Engagements Obtained Through Efforts of Third Parties. Members are often asked to render professional services to clients or customers of third parties. Such third parties may have obtained such clients or customers as the result of their advertising and solicitation efforts.

Members are permitted to enter into such engagements. The member has the responsibility to ascertain that all promotional efforts are within the bounds of the Rules of Conduct. Such action is required because the members will receive the benefits of such efforts by third parties, and members must not do through others what they are prohibited from doing themselves by the Rules of Conduct.

Interpretation under Rule 503—Commissions

503-1—Fees in Payment for Services. Rule 503, which prohibits payment of a commission to obtain a client, was adopted to avoid a client's having to pay fees for which he did not receive commensurate services. However, payment of fees to a referring public accountant for professional services to the successor firm or to the client in connection with the engagement is not prohibited.

Interpretation under Rule 505—Form of practice and name

505-1—Investment in Commercial Accounting Corporation. A member in the practice of public accounting may have a financial interest in a commercial corporation which performs for the public services of a type performed by public accountants and whose characteristics do not conform to resolutions of Council, provided such interest is not material to the corporation's net worth, and the member's interest in and relation to the corporation is solely that of an investor.

APPENDIX B

Certified Internal Auditor Code of Ethics[1]

The Certified Internal Auditor has an obligation to his profession, management, stockholders, and the general public to maintain high standards of professional conduct in the performance of his profession. In recognition of these obligations the board of regents has adopted the following Code of Ethics.

Adherence to this code, which is based on the Code of Ethics of The Institute of Internal Auditors, Inc., is a prerequisite to maintaining the designation Certified Internal Auditor. A Certified Internal Auditor who is judged in violation of the provisions of the code by the ethics committee of the board of regents shall forfeit the CIA designation.

Preamble

The provisions of this Code of Ethics cover basic principles in the various disciplines of internal auditing practice. A Certified Internal Auditor shall realize that individual judgment is required in the application of these principles. He has a responsibility to conduct himself so that his good faith and integrity should not be open to question. While having due regard for the limit of his technical skills, he will promote the highest possible internal auditing standards to the end of advancing the interest of his company or organization.

[1] Reprinted with permission of The Institute of Internal Auditors, Inc., 249 Maitland Avenue, Altamonte Springs, Florida 32701. From *Standards for the Professional Practice of Internal Auditing.*

Articles

I. A Certified Internal Auditor shall have an obligation to exercise honesty, objectivity, and diligence in the performance of his duties and responsibilities.

II. A Certified Internal Auditor, in holding the trust of his employer, shall exhibit loyalty in all matters pertaining to the affairs of the employer or to whomever he may be rendering a service. However, a Certified Internal Auditor shall not knowingly be a party to any illegal or improper activity.

III. A Certified Internal Auditor shall refrain from entering into any activity which may be in conflict with the interest of his employer or which would prejudice his ability to carry out objectively his duties and responsibilities.

IV. A Certified Internal Auditor shall not accept a fee or a gift from an employee, a client, a customer, or a business associate of his employer without the knowledge and consent of his senior management.

V. A Certified Internal Auditor shall be prudent in the use of information acquired in the course of his duties. He shall not use confidential information for any personal gain or in a manner which would be detrimental to the welfare of his employer.

VI. A Certified Internal Auditor, in expressing an opinion, shall use all reasonable care to obtain sufficient factual evidence to warrant such expression. In his reporting, a Certified Internal Auditor shall reveal such material facts known to him which, if not revealed, could either distort the report of the results of operations under review or conceal unlawful practice.

VII. A Certified Internal Auditor shall continually strive for improvement in the proficiency and effectiveness of his service.

APPENDIX C

Financial Reporting Checklist[1]

This checklist is intended primarily as a guide to disclosures required in reports and financial statements of commercial and industrial entities organized for profit. It is not intended to present minimum reporting requirements for all circumstances, and in many cases merely directs the user to appropriate authority for specific situations. Further, the checklist does not cover the requirements of the various regulatory bodies or unusual or unique problems associated with certain types of industries or organizations. Use of the checklist cannot be a substitute for judgment or an overall review of financial statements for fairness of presentation. The references in the checklist are to both the original pronouncements and to the Commerce Clearing House looseleaf reference volumes (the "Ac" and "Au" references, are to AICPA Professional Standards, Vol. I, III & IV, *CCH). A practitioner using the original pronouncements should exercise care to be sure that superseded material is not relied upon.*

I. Accountants' report

	YES	NO	N/A
1. Are all financial statements, supplemental schedules and supplemental commentary dealt with in the report? (SAS 1: Par. 610.01-.06; SAS 2: Par. 4-6) & (Au: 610.01; 509.04-.06)	☐	☐	☐
2. Are names, dates and addresses correctly indicated, including the same dates on co-existing long and shortform reports? (SAS 1: Par. 530.01-.08; 610.04; SAS 2: Par. 8) & (Au: 530.01-.08; 610.04; 509.08)	☐	☐	☐

[1] Reproduced by permission of the Washington Society of Certified Public Accountants. Edition of 12/31/78. This checklist may be ordered from: Washington Society of CPAs, 347 Logan Building, Seattle, WA 98101.

	YES	NO	N/A
3. Is the subject of the examination indicated to be the financial statements or other appropriate material rather than the accounts or records of the client? (SAS 2: Par. 4–5) & (Au: 509.04–.05)	☐	☐	☐
4. Does the report mention generally accepted auditing standards and tests or, if not, is such omission appropriate? (SAS 1: Par. 516.04; SAS 2: Par. 7; 10–13; 40) & (Au: 516.04; 509.07, .10–.13, .40)	☐	☐	☐
5. If the standard scope paragraph is not appropriate, is the scope of the examination adequately disclosed? (SAS 1: Par. 542.05–.06; SAS 2: Par. 10–13; .40) & (Au: 542.05–.06; 509.10–.13, .40)	☐	☐	☐
6. Are conclusions expressed as an opinion rather than as statement of fact? (SAS 1: Par. 610.06; SAS 2: Par. 4–8, .28–.48) & (Au: 610.06; 509.04–.08; .28–.48)	☐	☐	☐
7. Is the basis on which the statements or other material have been prepared indicated to be in conformity with generally accepted accounting principles? (SAS 1: Par. 410.01–.02; 544.02–.04; SAS 2: Par. 36; SAS 5) & (Au: 410.01–.02; 411; 544.02–.04; 509.36), or another comprehensive basis of accounting? (SAS 14) & (Au: 621)	☐	☐	☐
8. Is consistency mentioned or, if not, is the omission appropriate? (SAS 1: 420.01–.21) & (Au: 420.01–.21)	☐	☐	☐
9. If accounting principles are not consistently applied has the appropriate qualification been made? (SAS 1: Par. 546.01–.17; SAS 2: Par. 20) & (Au: 546.01–.17; 509.20)	☐	☐	☐
10. Have accounting changes explained in APB 20 having a material effect on the financial statements been disclosed as to consistency in the report? (SAS 1: Par. 420.01–.21) & (Au: 420.01–.21)	☐	☐	☐
11. Have qualifications, because of scope restrictions, referred to the specific items in the financial statements with respect to which the qualification relates rather than to the scope limitation itself? (SAS 2: Par. 29–31; 35; 40) & (Au: 509.29–.31, .35, .40)	☐	☐	☐
12. If the opinion contains a qualification regarding conformity with generally accepted accounting principles is the effect of the qualification on the financial statements clearly stated in a separate explanatory paragraph in the auditor's report? (SAS 1: Par. 544.02–.04; 545.01–.05; SAS 2: Par. 15–17; 29–40; SAS 14; SAS 21: Par. 8–18) & (Au: 544.02–.04; 545.01–.05; 509.15–.17; .29–.40; 621; 435.08–.18)	☐	☐	☐
13. Are qualifications clearly stated so the reader will understand the position of the accountant? (SAS 1: Par. 544.02–.04; 545.01–.05; SAS 2: Par. 9–40; SAS 14; SAS 21: Par. 8–18) & (Au: 544.02–.04; 545.01–.05; 509.09–.40; 621; 435.08–.18)	☐	☐	☐
14. Do the supplementary data in the long-form report exclude items that would support a contention of inadequate disclosure in the short-form report? (SAS 1: Par. 610.01–.06) & (Au: 610.01–.06)	☐	☐	☐
15. Does an appropriate disclaimer of opinion (or adverse opinion, if required) accompany unaudited financial statements? (SAS 1: Par.			

YES NO N/A

516.01-.13; SAS 15: Par. 13-15) & (Au: 516.01-.10; .13-.14; 505.13-.15) ☐ ☐ ☐

16. Does the report comply with Statement on Standards for Accounting and Review Services No. 1 for periods ending on or after July 1, 1979? (SSARA 1) (Note: The Washington State Society is developing separate Review Services and Compilation Services Checklists.) ☐ ☐ ☐
17. Does an appropriate disclaimer of opinion (conforming to the requirements of SAS No. 10) accompany interim financial information subject to limited review? (SAS 10: Par. 19-22; SAS 13: Par. 4-9) & (Au: 519.04-.09; 720.19-.20) ☐ ☐ ☐
18. Has lack of independence, if any, been disclosed in the disclaimer of opinion? (SAS 1: Par. 517.01-.06) & (Au: 517.01-.06) ☐ ☐ ☐
19. Have limitations in auditing procedures relating to beginning balances on new engagements been disclosed in the opinion? (SAS 1: Par. 542.05; SAS 2: Par. 10-13; 40) & (Au: 542.05; 509.10-.13, .40) ☐ ☐ ☐
20. Does the scope indicate reliance on work of other auditors, if any? (SAS 1: Par. 543.01-.17; SAS 15: Par. 8-12) & (Au: 543.01-.17; 505.08-.12) ☐ ☐ ☐
21. Have limitations in the examination of long-term investments been disclosed? (SAS 1: Par. 542.06) & (Au: 542.06) ☐ ☐ ☐
22. When financial statements of the prior year are presented together with those of the current year, does the auditor's report cover the prior year? (SAS 15) & (Au: 505) ☐ ☐ ☐
23. Has a piecemeal opinion been avoided in all circumstances? (SAS 2: Par. 48) & (Au: 509.48) ☐ ☐ ☐
24. When the auditor's examination indicates the presence of errors or possible irregularities, and the auditor remains uncertain whether these errors or irregularities may materially affect the financial statements, he should issue a qualified opinion or a disclaimer. (SAS 16) & (Au: 327) ☐ ☐ ☐
25. If illegal acts are detected, do the financial statements disclose the effects of such illegal acts? (SAS 17) & (Au: 328) ☐ ☐ ☐

II. Financial statement presentation

YES NO N/A

A. GENERAL

1. Is a description of all significant accounting policies of the reporting entity included with the financial statements? (APB 22) & (Ac: 2045) ☐ ☐ ☐
2. Do the financial statements and/or accountants' report clearly indicate the nature of the organization reported upon? If the entity is a trust, association, partnership, proprietorship, or non-profit

	YES	NO	N/A
corporation, this should be described in a footnote or on the face of the statements.	☐	☐	☐
3. Have disclosure requirements been met for related party transactions? (SAS 6: Par. 16–18) & (Au: 355.16–.18)	☐	☐	☐
4. Do footnotes for proprietorship or partnership statements indicate that the statements only include items relating to the business of the proprietorship or partnership?	☐	☐	☐
5. Is the exact legal name of the reporting entity used?	☐	☐	☐
6. Are unaudited statements including notes thereto clearly marked on each page as "UNAUDITED"? (SAS 1: Par. 516.04) & (Au: 516.04)	☐	☐	☐
7. Is unaudited replacement cost information that is included with or in notes to audited financial statements clearly marked as "UNAUDITED"? (SAS 18: Par. .9) & (Au: 730.09)	☐	☐	☐
8. Has the use of *Guide for Engagements of CPAs to Prepare Unaudited Financial Statements,* AICPA, been considered when appropriate?	☐	☐	☐
9. Has the accounting for nonmonetary transactions entered into after September 30, 1973 been based on the fair values of the assets (or services) involved, where such fair values are reasonably determinable (except for reorganizations, liquidations, or exchanges which are not essentially the culmination of an earning process) and do the financial statements disclose the nature of such transactions, the basis of accounting for the assets transferred and gains or losses recognized? (APB 29) & (Ac: 1041)	☐	☐	☐
10. For "Development Stage Enterprises" have the special reporting requirements been considered? (FASB 7; FASB Interpretation 7) & (Ac: 2062; 2062-1)	☐	☐	☐
11. For interim financial statements have the special reporting requirements been considered? (APB 28; FASB Interpretation 18) & (Ac: 2071; 2071-1)	☐	☐	☐
12. Have the accounting and reporting requirements for foreign operations been complied with? (ARB 43, Ch 12; FASB 8; FASB 20; FASB Interpretation 15; FASB Interpretation 17) & (Ac: 1081; 1083; 1084; 1083-1; 1083-2)	☐	☐	☐
13. For oil and gas producers, have the special accounting principles and reporting requirements been complied with? (FASB 19) & (Ac: 6021)	☐	☐	☐

14. Have accounting and auditing standards set forth in AICPA accounting guides, auditing guides, or statements of position been followed? Those currently available include:

   a. Industry Audit Guides—Internal Control in EDP Systems, Banks, Brokers and Dealers in Securities, Colleges and Universities, Construction Contractors, Employee Health & Welfare Benefit Funds, Finance Companies, Fire & Casualty Insurance Companies, Government Contractors, Investment Companies, Personal Financial Statements, Savings & Loan Association, Service-Center Produced Records, State & Local Government

YES NO N/A

Units, Stock Life Insurance Companies and Voluntary Health and Welfare Organizations, Unaudited Financial Statements, Hospitals, Medicare. ☐ ☐ ☐

b. Industry Accounting Guides—Franchise Fee Revenue, Retail Land Sales, Profit Recognition on Sales of Real Estate, Motion Picture Films. ☐ ☐ ☐

c. Statements of Position—Auditors' Reports on Fire & Casualty Insurance Companies, Brokers and Dealers in Securities, Hospital Malpractice Loss Contingencies, Confirmation of Insurance Policies in Force, Sales of Receivables with Recourse, Colleges and Universities, Face-amount Certificate Companies, Mortgage Banking, Revenue Recognition when Right of Return Exists, REITs, Accrual or Revenues & Expenditures by State and Local Governmental Units, Financial Forecasts, Broadcasting, Questions concerning Profit Recognition on Sales of Real Estate, Record and Music Industry, Origination Costs and Commitment Fees in the Mortgage Banking Industry, ESOTs, Investment Companies, Interfund Transfers of State and Local Governmental Units, Certain Marketable Equity Securities of Hospitals, Costs to Sell and Rent and Initial Rental Operations of Real Estate Projects, Methods in Accounting for Sales of Real Estate, Advance Refundings of Tax Exempt Debt, Property and Liability Insurance Companies, Hospitals Operated by a Governmental Unit, Product Financial Arrangements, Investments in Real Estate Ventures, Certain Non-profit Organizations. ☐ ☐ ☐

15. Have events subsequent to the balance sheet date been considered as to their effect on the financial statements or accountants' report? (SAS 1: Par 530.03-.05; 560.01-.12) & (Au: 530.03-.05; 560.01-.12) ☐ ☐ ☐
16. Has "other information" provided by an entity in annual reports and other documents been read for consistency? (SAS 8: Par 4-6) & (Au: 550.04-.06) ☐ ☐ ☐
17. Are all leasing transactions properly accounted for from the viewpoint of a lessor and/or lessee? (FASB 13; FASB 17; FASB 22; FASB 23; FASB Interpretations 19, 21, 23, 24 & 26) & (Ac: 4053; 4054; 4055; 4056; 4053-1-4053-6) ☐ ☐ ☐
18. If the provisions of FASB 13 (Ac: 4053) are not applied initially on a retroactive basis to those leases existing or committed at Dec. 31, 1976, are the alternative disclosures of the effects of those leases presented? (FASB 13: Par. 50) & (Ac: 4053.050) ☐ ☐ ☐
19. Has the need for reporting the financial results of segments of the enterprise been considered? (FASB 14; FASB 18; FASB 21; FASB 24) & (Ac: 2081-2084) ☐ ☐ ☐

B. COMPARATIVE FINANCIAL STATEMENTS

1. Have comparative statements been considered? (ARB 43: Ch 2, Par 1) & (Ac: 2041.1) ☐ ☐ ☐

	YES	NO	N/A
2. Have notes and other disclosures relating to the financial statements for the preceding period been repeated, or at least referred to, to the extent that they continue to be of significance in the current period? (ARB 43: Ch 2, Par 2) & (Ac: 2041.2)	☐	☐	☐
3. Are prior-period figures in fact comparable with those for the current period? (ARB 43: Ch 2, Par 3) & (Ac: 2041.3)	☐	☐	☐

C. CONSOLIDATED FINANCIAL STATEMENTS

	YES	NO	N/A
1. When entities are under common control, and particularly when intercompany transactions are present, combined statements, including disclosure of the basis of combination, may be necessary for fair presentation. Has this been considered? (ARB 51: Par 22) & (Ac: 2051.21)	☐	☐	☐
2. When one of the companies in a group directly or indirectly has a controlling financial interest in the other companies, there is a presumption that for a fair presentation consolidated financial statements are usually necessary. Have all controlled companies been consolidated? (ARB 51: Par 2) & (Ac: 2051.3)	☐	☐	☐
3. Do the financial statements disclose the principles of consolidation or combination? (ARB 51: Par 5, 22) & (Ac: 2051.06)	☐	☐	☐
4. Have material inter-company balances and transactions been eliminated? (ARB 51: Par 6) & (Ac: 2051.07)	☐	☐	☐
5. When there is a difference in fiscal periods between a consolidated subsidiary and that of the parent (normally not more than three months allowed) has the effect of intervening events which materially affect the financial statements been disclosed? (ARB 51: Par. 4), (FASB Interpretation 13) & (Ac: 2051.05, 5132, 5132-4)	☐	☐	☐
6. Do consolidated statements in which the parent company is a manufacturing entity exclude subsidiaries which are banks, finance or insurance companies where more meaningful information is presented by separate statements? (ARB 51: Par 2-3) & (Ac: 2051.3-.4)	☐	☐	☐
7. Have subsidiaries whose principal business activity is leasing property or facilities to their parents or other affiliates been consolidated? (FASB 13: Par. 31) & (Ac: 4053.031)	☐	☐	☐
8. Where the parent includes realized gains and losses on marketable securities in the determination of net income and the subsidiary does not, has the accounting practice of the subsidiary been conformed to that of the parent? (FASB 12: Par 18) & (Ac: 5132.18)	☐	☐	☐

D. ACCOUNTING CHANGES

	YES	NO	N/A
1. In applying the concept of materiality to disclosure of changes have you considered materiality for items (1) individually and in the aggregate, (2) in relation to net income for the current period and the trend of earnings, (3) which are reasonably certain to have a material effect in later periods? (APB 20: Par. 38; SAS 1: Par. 420.18) & (Ac: 1051-38; Au: 420.18)	☐	☐	☐

YES NO N/A

2. For those changes in principle requiring restatement of financial statements of prior periods (those changes specifically required by FASB statements, change from LIFO, long-term construction contract reporting, to or from "full cost" method in extractive industries, and change in entity) has the nature of and justification for change, and effect on net income and earnings per share been disclosed for all periods presented? (APB 20: Par. 27, 28, 34 and 35; FASB 16: Par. 12; FASB Interpretation 1; SAS 1: Par. 420.19) & (Ac: 1051.27, .28, .34 & .35; 2014.12; 1051-1; Au: 420.19) ☐ ☐ ☐
3. For changes in accounting estimates and other changes in principle (not requiring retroactive adjustment), have you disclosed nature of and justification of change, effect on net income and earnings per share of the period of change, and required pro-forma data on face of income statement? (APB 20: Par. 19, 31-33; SAS 1: Par 420.19) & (Ac: 1051.19, .31-.33; Au: 420.19) ☐ ☐ ☐
4. Has the correction of an error in previously issued financial statements been reported as a prior period adjustment and the nature of the error and effect on income and earnings per share disclosed in the period in which the error was discovered and corrected? (APB 20: Par 36) & (Ac: 1051.36) ☐ ☐ ☐
5. Has consideration been given to a special exemption from change reporting rules on initial issue of financials for (1) obtaining equity capital (2) effecting a business combination or (3) registering securities? (APB 20: Par 29; SAS 1: Par 420.19) & (Ac: 1051.29; Au: 420.19) ☐ ☐ ☐
6. Have accounting changes been reported appropriately on interim financial statements? (FASB 3) & (Ac: 2072) ☐ ☐ ☐

E. BUSINESS COMBINATIONS

1. For any business combination, a whole series of difficult accounting issues and reporting requirements come into force. Examples are the use of purchase or pooling treatment, effects on reported earnings, treatment of goodwill disclosure and restatement of financials. Have you considered these issues carefully? (APB 16; APB 17; FASB 10; FASB Interpretations 9 & 11) & (Ac: 1091; 5141; 1092; 1091-1; 4053-2) ☐ ☐ ☐

III. Balance sheet

YES NO N/A

A. GENERAL

1. Have allowances for depreciation and depletion and asset valuation allowances for losses, such as those on receivables and investments, been deducted from the related asset with appropriate disclosure? (APB 12: Par 2-3) & (Ac: 2044) ☐ ☐ ☐

	YES	NO	N/A
2. Is the carrying amount of assets pledged or otherwise encumbered for indebtedness disclosed? (SAS 1: Par 430.02) & (Au: 430.02)	☐	☐	☐
3. Are components of working capital (current assets and current liabilities) disclosed if appropriate for the industry? (Stmt No. 4 of APB: Par 198) & (Ac: 1027.25)	☐	☐	☐

Assets

B. CASH

1. Do the financial statements show funds subject to withdrawal restrictions (consider noncurrent classification) and bank overdrafts in banks not having other free balances in an amount sufficient to offset (classify as current liabilities)?	☐	☐	☐

C. MARKETABLE SECURITIES

1. Are the current and non current portions of marketable securities carried at the lower of cost or market? (FASB 12; FASB Interpretation 10; FASB Interpretation 11; FASB Interpretation 16) & (Ac: 5132; 5132-1; 5132-2; 5132-5)	☐	☐	☐
2. Do the financial statements or notes disclose the carrying basis and the aggregate market value of marketable securities, and the gross unrealized gains and losses? (ARB 43: Ch 3A, Par 9), (FASB 12: Par 12) & (Ac: 5132.12)	☐	☐	☐
3. Are all securities which are listed on an exchange and/or have a ready market included in marketable securities (unless they should be excluded from current classification because of purpose held, etc.)?	☐	☐	☐
4. Has any balance in an existing valuation allowance account established prior to the issuance of FASB Statement No. 12, which reduced the carrying amount of individual marketable equity securities to market value, been eliminated and credited to income and has the valuation allowance then been determined in accordance with provisions of FASB Statement No. 12? (FASB Interpretation No. 12) & (Ac: 5132-3)	☐	☐	☐

D. RECEIVABLES

1. Are material non-trade receivables classified by source including amounts due from parent, subsidiaries, affiliated companies, employees, stockholders, etc.? (ARB 43: Ch 1A, Par 5) & (Ac: 5111)	☐	☐	☐
2. Are amounts due from affiliates or subsidiaries classified as current only if it is the company's practice to liquidate them periodically and if the current position of the affiliate or subsidiary warrants this treatment? (ARB 43: Ch 3A, Par 4) & (Ac: 2031.4)	☐	☐	☐
3. Has hypothecation or the contingent liability on receivables sold or discounted been disclosed? (SAS 1: Par 430.02) & (Au: 430.02)	☐	☐	☐

	YES	NO	N/A
4. Are unearned discounts, finance charges and interest included in the face amount of receivables deducted from the related receivables? (APB 6: Par 14) & (Ac: 2031)	☐	☐	☐
5. Are unbilled receivables, including unbilled costs and fees under CPFF contracts, shown separately from billed accounts receivable? (ARB 43: Ch 11A, Par 4) & (Ac: 4041.4)	☐	☐	☐
6. Are allowances for uncollectible accounts deducted from the receivables or group of receivables to which they relate and the amounts thereof disclosed? (APB 12: Par 3) & (Ac: 2044)	☐	☐	☐
7. If a note has been received for property, goods or service, has consideration been given as to whether it is appropriate to record a premium or discount on the receivable? If applicable, have the following been disclosed:	☐	☐	☐
a. Discount reported as a deduction from the face amount? (APB 21: Par 16) & (Ac: 4111.15)	☐	☐	☐
b. Face amount and stated interest and imputed interest rates? (APB 21: Par 16) & (Ac: 4111.15)	☐	☐	☐
8. Has a debt restructuring as defined in FASB 15 occurred and, if so, have appropriate disclosures been made? (FASB 15: Par 40–41) & (Ac: 5363.040–.041)	☐	☐	☐

E. INVENTORIES

1. Do the financial statements or notes disclose the basis for carrying inventories, and the method of determining cost? (ARB 43: Ch 3A, Par 9; APB 22: Par 13) & (Ac: 2031.9; 2051.13)	☐	☐	☐
2. Has overhead been allocated to the cost of inventory? (ARB 43: Ch 4, Par 5) & (Ac: 5121.5)	☐	☐	☐
3. Are the major classes of inventory disclosed (i.e., finished goods, work-in-process, raw materials and supplies)? (ARB 43: Ch 3A, Par 9) & (Ac: 2031.9)	☐	☐	☐
4. Are accrued net losses on firm purchase commitments for inventory, if material, recognized in the accounts and have the amounts thereof as well as substantial or unusual losses resulting from valuing inventories at the lower of cost or market been properly disclosed? (ARB 43: Ch 4, Par 14, 17) & (Ac: 5121.14, .17)	☐	☐	☐

F. PREPAID EXPENSES

1. Have long-term prepayments been classified as noncurrent assets? (ARB 43: Ch 3A, Par 6) & (Ac: 2031.6)	☐	☐	☐

G. PROPERTY, PLANT AND EQUIPMENT

1. Do the financial statements or the notes disclose the following information:			
a. Balances of major classes of depreciable assets at the balance sheet date? (APB 12: Par 5) & (Ac: 2043)	☐	☐	☐
b. Allowances for depreciation, by class or in total, at the balance sheet date? (APB 12: Par 5) & (Ac: 2043)	☐	☐	☐

	YES	NO	N/A
c. A general description of the method or methods used in computing depreciation for major classes of depreciable assets? (APB 12: Par 5; APB 22: Par 13) & (Ac: 2043; 2045.13)	☐	☐	☐
d. Basis of valuation? (SAS 1: Par 430.02) & (Au: 430.02)	☐	☐	☐
2. Are there capitalized leases (lessee) and, if so, are the major asset classifications and accumulated amortization separately identified? (FASB 13: Par 13, 16) & (Ac: 4053.013, .016)	☐	☐	☐
3. Do the financial statements or notes disclose the following information for lessor's property and equipment held for lease:			
a. Operating leases—cost of leased property by major classes and accumulated depreciation? (FASB 13: Par 23) & (Ac: 4053.023)	☐	☐	☐
b. Sales-type or direct financing leases—components of net investment? (FASB 13: Par 23) & (Ac: 4053.023)	☐	☐	☐
c. Leveraged leases—components of net investment? (FASB 13: Par 47) & (Ac: 4053.047)	☐	☐	☐
4. Are the details of any important sale-and-leaseback transactions during the period disclosed? (FASB 13: Par 32-34) & (Ac: 4053.032-.034)	☐	☐	☐
5. Is the carrying amount of property not a part of operating plant (i.e., plant that is idle or held for investment or sale) segregated?	☐	☐	☐
6. Where "boot" has been received on a nonmonetary transaction has gain or loss been properly reported? (APB 29: Par 22) & (Ac: 1041.22)	☐	☐	☐

H. INVESTMENTS IN COMMON STOCK

1. Has the equity method of accounting been applied to account for investments in common stock of:			
a. Unconsolidated subsidiaries? (APB 18: Par 14-17) & (Ac: 5131.14-.17)	☐	☐	☐
b. Corporate joint ventures? (APB 18: Par 14-17) & (Ac: 5131.14-.17)	☐	☐	☐
c. Other issuers, 50% or less owned, over whose operating and financial policies the investor is able to exercise "significant influence"? (APB 18: Par 14-17) & (Ac: 5131.14-.17)	☐	☐	☐

If answer to a, b or c is "yes", refer to APB 18, Paragraph 20 and APB 23 and 24 for disclosure requirements. (Ac: 5131.20; 4095; 4096) If answer is "no", see III C—Marketable Securities.

I. OTHER ASSETS AND DEFERRED CHARGES

1. Are significant deferred charges and intangible assets segregated by type? (Stmt No. 4 of APB: Par 198) & (Ac: 1027.25)	☐	☐	☐
2. Is the carrying basis of intangible assets and other investments disclosed?	☐	☐	☐
3. Are the method and period of amortization of intangible assets disclosed? (APB 17: Par 30) & (Ac: 5141-30)	☐	☐	☐
4. Are issue costs of debt reported as deferred charges? (APB 21: Par 16) & (Ac: 4111.15)	☐	☐	☐

Liabilities and stockholders' equity

	YES	NO	N/A
J. COMMITMENTS AND CONTINGENT LIABILITIES			
1. Are all material commitments and guarantees disclosed? (ARB 50: Par. 6 and FASB 5: Par 12) & (Ac: 5514.6 and 4311.12)	☐	☐	☐
2. Have all material loss contingencies been disclosed? (FASB 5: Par 9-13 and FASB Interpretation 14: Par 3) & (Ac: 4311.9-.13 and 4311-1.03)	☐	☐	☐
3. Do the financial statements or notes disclose the required information about lease commitments:			
a. For lessees of property under capital or operating leases? (FASB 13: Par 16) & (Ac: 4053.016)	☐	☐	☐
b. For lessors of property under sales-type, direct financing, or operating leases? (FASB 13: Par 23) & (Ac: 4053.023)	☐	☐	☐
K. CURRENT LIABILITIES			
1. Are current liabilities segregated by type (e.g., accounts payable, current portion of notes payable, accrued liabilities, etc.) (Stmt No. 4 of APB: Par 198) & (Ac: 1027.25)	☐	☐	☐
L. INCOME TAXES			
1. Has proper segregation been made between current and non-current deferred taxes with appropriate disclosure? (APB 11: Par 60) & (Ac: 4091.59)	☐	☐	☐
M. NOTES PAYABLE AND OTHER LONG-TERM DEBT			
1. Are the terms and interest rates of all long-term debts disclosed?	☐	☐	☐
2. Is the existence of property pledged to secure the debt, restrictions on retained earnings, sinking fund requirements, etc. disclosed? (SAS 1: Par 430.02) & (Au: 430.02)	☐	☐	☐
3. Is the current portion of long-term debt properly classified as a current liability? (Stmt No. 4 of APB: Par. 198) & (Ac: 1027.25)	☐	☐	☐
4. Has convertible debt been accounted for solely as debt? (APB 14: Par 12) & (Ac: 5516.10)	☐	☐	☐
5. Has that portion of the proceeds of debt issued with detachable stock purchase warrants which is allocable to the warrants been accounted for as paid-in capital? (APB 14: Par 16) & (Ac: 5516.14)	☐	☐	☐
6. Are obligations arising from capitalized leases properly segregated on the balance sheet? (FASB 13: Par 13) & (Ac: 4053.013)	☐	☐	☐
7. If a note has been issued for property, goods, or service, has consideration been given to whether it is appropriate to record and disclose a premium or discount on the obligation? (APB 21: Par 16) & (Ac: 4111.15)	☐	☐	☐
8. Are short-term obligations classified as long-term debt due to refinancing plans defined in FASB 6 properly disclosed? (FASB 6: Par 15; FASB Interpretation 8) & (Ac: 2033.15; 2033-1)	☐	☐	☐

	YES	NO	N/A
9. Has a debt restructuring as defined by FASB 15 occurred and, if so, have appropriate disclosures been made? (FASB 15: Par 25-26) & (Ac: 5363.025-.026)	□	□	□

N. SHAREHOLDERS' EQUITY

1. For capital stock, have the following been disclosed?			
a. Title of issue, par or stated value per share, and number of shares authorized, issued, and outstanding. (Stmt No. 4 of APB: Par 198) & (Ac: 1027.25)	□	□	□
b. Call price, basis of conversion, cumulative features, and dividend arrearages on preferred stock. (APB 15: Par 19 and APB 9: Par 35) & (Ac: 2011.19)	□	□	□
c. Carrying basis and number of shares of treasury stock with cost normally shown as reduction of equity. (APB 6: Par 12-13) & (Ac: 5542.13-.14)	□	□	□
d. Shares reserved for options, warrants, and conversions. (ARB 43: Ch. 13B, Par 15) & (Ac: 4061.15)	□	□	□
e. Option prices, number of shares, date of grant, expiration dates or periods exercisable for stock options. Also, as to options exercised during the period, the number of shares involved and prices thereof. (ARB 43: Ch 13B, Par 15) & (Ac: 4061.15)	□	□	□
f. Details of stock subscriptions.	□	□	□
2. Do capital surplus transactions exclude items which should be charged to current or future years income? (ARB 43: Ch 1A, Par 2) & (Ac: 5511)	□	□	□
3. If the company has contingency reserves, were the reserves created by a segregation or appropriation of retained earnings with no costs or losses being charged to them? (FASB 5: Par 15) & (Ac: 4311.15)	□	□	□
4. Have stock dividends (less than 20 to 25% on previously outstanding shares) been accounted for by transfer from retained earnings to permanent capital accounts, based on the fair value of shares issued? (ARB 43: Ch 7B, Par 10) & (Ac: 5561.10)	□	□	□
5. Are all changes in the separate accounts comprising stockholders' equity and in the number of shares of equity securities disclosed? (APB 12: Par 10) & (Ac: 2042.2)	□	□	□
6. Are restrictions as to dividend payments disclosed? (SAS 1: Par 430.01) & (Au: 430.01)	□	□	□

IV. Statement of income

	YES	NO	N/A
1. Are material intra-company transactions eliminated? (ARB 51: Par 6) & (Ac: 2051.7)	□	□	□
2. Do financial statements disclose the method of recognizing income under long-term construction type contracts? (ARB 45) & (Ac: 4031)	□	□	□

	YES	NO	N/A
3. Do the financial statements disclose the method of reporting revenues under cost reimbursement type contracts? (ARB 43: Ch 11A) & (Ac: 4041)	☐	☐	☐
4. Is the accounting method used in accounting for leasing activities in statements of lessors disclosed? (FASB 13: Par 23)	☐	☐	☐
5. Has the Company recognized revenues when sales were effected (in contrast to installment method)? (APB 10: Par 12) & (Ac: 4020)	☐	☐	☐
6. Concerning affiliated companies of which 20% to 50% of the stock is owned:			
a. Had equity in earnings of such companies been included in the determination of net income? (APB 18) & (Ac: 5131)	☐	☐	☐
b. Has the investor's share of the investee's extraordinary items and prior period adjustments been classified as such in the investor's financial statements? (APB 18) & (Ac: 5131)	☐	☐	☐
7. If there is a pension or profit-sharing plan:			
a. Is the accounting method used for the plan appropriate? (APB 8: Par 9–45) & (Ac: 4063.9–.45)	☐	☐	☐
b. Are proper disclosures made? (APB 8: Par 46; FASB Interpretation 3: Par 4) & (Ac: 4063.46; 4063-1)	☐	☐	☐
8. If there is a plan for issuance of stock as compensation:			
a. Is compensation expense properly accrued and are income tax benefits or expense recorded in the proper period? (APB 25: Par 10–13; 16–17; FASB Interpretation 28) & (Ac: 4062.10–.17 & 4062-1)	☐	☐	☐
b. Has adequate disclosure been made? (ARB 43: Ch 13B) & (Ac: 4061)	☐	☐	☐
9. Is depreciation expense for the period separately classified, or disclosed parenthetically or in a footnote? (APB 12: Par 5) & (Ac: 2043.2)	☐	☐	☐
10. Is interest expense segregated, if significant?	☐	☐	☐
11. Are any gains or losses on early debt extinguishment identified separately in the statement of income? (APB 26: Par 20; FASB 4: Par 8–9) & (Ac: 2013, 5362.20)	☐	☐	☐
12. Have research and development costs been charged to expense and the amount disclosed in the financial statements? (FASB 2, FASB Interpretations 4, 5 & 6) & (Ac: 4211)	☐	☐	☐
13. Have appropriate net realizable gains or losses relating to marketable equity securities been included in determination of net income and have they been adequately disclosed? (FASB 12: Par 12) & (Ac: 5132.12)	☐	☐	☐
14. Are material gains or losses resulting from foreign currency transactions adequately disclosed? (FASB 8: Par 32 & 34) & (Ac: 1083)	☐	☐	☐
15. Discontinued operations:			
a. Have results of discontinued operations and any gain or loss from disposal of a segment of a business been reported separately from results of continuing operations and all required disclosures made? (APB 30: Par 8) & (Ac: 2012.8)	☐	☐	☐
b. Has the amount of income tax applicable thereto (separately			

	YES	NO	N/A
allocated to results of discontinued operations and any gain or loss on disposal) been disclosed on the face of the income statement or related notes? (APB 30: Par 8 & 9) & (Ac: 2012.8)	☐	☐	☐
c. Has a provision been made for expected losses from proposed disposal of a segment of a business, if appropriate? (APB 30: Par 15) & (Ac: 2012.15)	☐	☐	☐
16. Extraordinary items:			
a. Has consideration been given as to whether or not there are any extraordinary items? (APB 30: Par 19–24) & (Ac: 2012.19–.24)	☐	☐	☐
b. Do items reported as extraordinary items meet the criteria that they are of an unusual nature and would not reasonably be expected to recur in the foreseeable future? (APB 30: Par 19–24) & (Ac: 2012.19–.24)	☐	☐	☐
c. Are material events or transactions that are either unusual in nature or occur infrequently, but not both (therefore do not meet both criteria for classification as an extraordinary item), reported as a separate component of income from continuing operations? (APB 30: Par 26) & (Ac: 2012.26)	☐	☐	☐
d. If there are extraordinary items:			
(1) Have they been segregated from the results of ordinary operations and shown separately in the statement of income with disclosure of the nature and principal items thereof? (APB 30: Par 11) & (Ac: 2012.11)	☐	☐	☐
(2) Has the amount of income tax applicable thereto been disclosed, either on the face of the income statement or in a note thereto? (APB 30: Par 11) & (Ac: 2012.11)	☐	☐	☐
17. Income taxes: (APB 11, FASB 9) & (Ac: 4091-4091A, 4097) [Note: FASB 9 (Ac: 4097) has been superseded effective for financial statements for years beginning after Dec. 15, 1978 by FASB 19 (Ac: 6021).]	☐	☐	☐
a. Do the statements disclose that taxes are not provided for partnerships, Subchapter S Corporations or proprietorships?	☐	☐	☐
b. Is income tax based on pretax book income?	☐	☐	☐
c. Are tax effects of any realizable loss carrybacks recognized in the loss period?	☐	☐	☐
d. Are tax benefits of any book operating loss carry-forward (not recognized in loss period) reported as an extraordinary item in the period realized? (APB 11: Par 61) & (Ac: 4091.60)	☐	☐	☐
e. Is there disclosure of the income tax components, i.e., taxes estimated to be currently payable, tax effects of timing differences and tax effects of operating losses? (APB 11: Par 60) & (Ac: 4091.59)	☐	☐	☐
f. Are taxes allocated to (a) income from continuing operations, (b) effects of discontinued operations (c) cumulative effect of a change in accounting principle, (d) extraordinary items, and (e) prior period adjustments? (APB 11: Par 60, APB 20: Par			

YES NO N/A

20; APB 30; Par 8 and 11) & (Ac: 4091.59; 1051.20; 2012.8-.11) ☐ ☐ ☐

g. Are unused amounts of both book and tax operating loss carryforwards, together with expiration dates, disclosed? (APB 11: Par 63(a)) & (Ac: 4091.62(a)) ☐ ☐ ☐

h. Are reasons for significant variations in customary relationships between income tax expense and pretax accounting income explained? (APB 11: Par 63(c)) & (Ac: 4091.62(c)) ☐ ☐ ☐

i. Has information been disclosed in notes to financial statements concerning undistributed earnings of a subsidiary or corporate joint venture for which income taxes have not been accrued? (APB 23; Par. 14 and 18; FASB Interpretation 22) & (Ac: 4095.14-.18; 4091-1) ☐ ☐ ☐

j. Have timing differences related to recognized, but unrealized, changes in the carrying value of marketable securities been considered? (FASB 12: Par 22) & (Ac: 5132.22) ☐ ☐ ☐

18. Investment Credits:

a. Has the accounting method used for the investment credit and amounts involved been disclosed? (APB 4: Par 11) & (Ac: 4094.18) ☐ ☐ ☐

b. Has the amount of any unused investment credit been disclosed? (APB 2: Par 16; FASB Interpretation 25) & (Ac: 4094.21; 4094-1) ☐ ☐ ☐

19. If there are any prior period adjustments (as defined in FASB 16, Par 11-12 (Ac: 2014.11-12); APB 16, Par 52 (Ac: 1091.52); APB 20, Par 34 (Ac: 1051.34); APB 20, Par 27, 29 (Ac: 1051.27, 1051.29)): ☐ ☐ ☐

a. Have the resulting effects (both gross and net of applicable income tax) on the net income and net income per share of prior periods been disclosed in the annual report for the year in which the adjustments are made? (APB 9: Par 18,26) & (Ac: 2010.17, 2010.25) ☐ ☐ ☐

b. If financial statements for a single period only are presented, have the effects of the restatement on the balance of retained earnings at the beginning of the period and on net income and net income per share of the immediately preceding period been disclosed? (APB 9: Par 26) & (Ac: 2010.25) ☐ ☐ ☐

c. If financial statements for more than one period are presented, have the effects for each of the periods included in the statements been disclosed? (APB 9: Par 26) & (Ac: 2010.25) ☐ ☐ ☐

d. Have historical summaries of financial data which are excluded from the accountants' report been restated to the extent necessary to properly reflect prior period adjustments? (APB 9: Par 27) & (Ac: 2010.26) ☐ ☐ ☐

20. Earnings per share: (Note: FASB 21 (Ac: 2083) suspends reporting of earnings per share by nonpublic enterprises)

a. Have earnings or net loss per share data been shown on face

	YES	NO	N/A
of income statement? If there is a complex capital structure, refer to APB 15 for disclosure requirements. (APB 15: Par 12,17) & (Ac: 2011.12,17)	☐	☐	☐
b. Have earnings per share data been shown for the cumulative effect of an accounting change, if any? (APB 20: Par 20) & (Ac: 1051.20)	☐	☐	☐
c. Has earnings per share data for income before extraordinary items been shown? (APB 30: Par 12) & (Ac: 2012)	☐	☐	☐
d. Is the basis for the computation of earnings per share disclosed? (APB 15: Par 20) & (Ac: 2011.20)	☐	☐	☐
21. Have dividends per share been disclosed and adjusted for stock splits and stock dividends?	☐	☐	☐
22. Have transactions in the company's own capital stock been excluded from the determination of income? (APB 9: Par 28) & (Ac: 2010.27)	☐	☐	☐

V. Statement of changes in financial position

	YES	NO	N/A
1. When financial statements purporting to present both financial position and results of operations are issued, is a statement of changes in financial position also included? (APB 19: Par 7) & (Ac: 2021.7)	☐	☐	☐
2. Does the statement disclose all important aspects of financing and investing activities, including net changes in each element of working capital (as customarily defined)? (APB 19: Par 9) & (Ac: 2021.9)	☐	☐	☐

VI. Subsequent pronouncements

	YES	NO	N/A
1. This Checklist covers pronouncements through SAS 23, SSARS 1, FASB 24 and FASB Interpretation No. 28. Do the financial statements conform to subsequent pronouncements?	☐	☐	☐

APPENDIX D

Questionnaire for Evaluation of Internal Control in Electronic Data Processing[1]

This appendix contains a model questionnaire for obtaining information on internal control in an electronic data processing installation.

The questionnaire is divided into two major parts:

1. questions relating to the operation of the electronic data processing installation
2. questions relating to an individual data processing application

This division reflects the fact that the organization, the policies, and the procedures of the installation provide an environment in which individual applications are run. This environment must be understood before the controls associated with individual applications can be evaluated.

The review of a computer processing application should be carried out in the context of the entire processing cycle, including both computer and noncomputer processing and controls. The firm's internal review questionnaire (or other method used to obtain information) should cover the noncomputer procedures and controls; the application questionnaire is structured to provide only the added questions related to computer processing.

The number of questions to be included in a review questionnaire depends somewhat on how broadly the auditor views his audit assignment—whether he looks at items affecting operational efficiency as well as items directly affecting the audit. The control significance of the response to a particular question often, however, depends on the characteristics of the system being evaluated and the total picture of internal control. Each question in the model is coded A, B, or C according to its general control significance. This code is only an indicator to aid the auditor; he must evaluate the significance in each particular case.

[1] This questionnaire is adapted from Appendix E of *Auditing & EDP* by Gordon B. Davis. Copyright © 1968 by the American Institute of Certified Public Accountants, Inc.

Code	*In general, question relates to:*
A	control element which may affect the auditor's evaluation of internal control
B	control element which tends to affect data processing safeguards but is, however, not likely to affect audit procedures
C	element affecting operational effectiveness or efficiency

All yes-or-no questions are worded so that "yes" is a favorable response and "no" indicates that further investigation or evaluation is required. The auditor may also wish to expand and clarify his answers by adding comments.

Part I: Questionnaire for operation of the electronic data processing installation

1. BACKGROUND

1-1. Where is the computer located? ______________________

1-2. Give a brief description of equipment ______________________

____

(a) Manufacturer and model number of computer (this can be obtained from a copy of the manufacturer's invoice) ______________

(b) Internal memory size ______________________

(c) File storage devices

Magnetic tape (no. units ______) ☐

Disk (no. drives ______) ☐

Other (describe) ☐

____

____

____

(d) Input/output devices

Card reader ☐

Card punch ☐

Printer ☐

Other (list) ☐

____

____

____

1-3. Applications

Cash ☐

Receivables ☐

Inventory ☐

Property, plant, and equipment ☐

Payables ☐

Sales ☐

Payroll ☐

Cost and expenses ☐

Other (list major ones on next page) ☐

____

____

____

2. ORGANIZATION

	YES	NO	
2-1. Prepare or obtain an organization chart of the EDP organization. Determine position titles, job descriptions, and names of persons in these positions.			
2-2. Is there a segregation of duties such that:			
(a) The functions and duties of system design and programming are separate from computer operation?	☐	☐	A
(b) Programmers do not operate the computer for regular processing runs?	☐	☐	A
(c) Computer operators are restricted from access to data and program information not necessary for performing their assigned task?	☐	☐	B
(d) The employees in data processing are separated from all duties relating to the initiation of transactions and initiation of requests for changes to the master files?	☐	☐	A
2-3. Are the operators assigned to individual application runs rotated periodically?	☐	☐	A
2-4. Are the computer operators required to take vacations?	☐	☐	B
2-5. Is supervision of operators sufficient to verify operator's adherence to prescribed operating procedures?	☐	☐	B

3. THE CONTROL FUNCTION

	YES	NO	
3-1. Is there a person or group charged with responsibility for the control function in the data processing department? Obtain description of duties. These duties will normally include:			
(a) Control over receipt of input data and recording of control information?	☐	☐	
(b) Reconciliation of control information (batch control with computer control totals, run-to-run controls, etc.)?	☐	☐	
(c) Control over distribution of output?	☐	☐	
(d) Control over errors to ensure that they are reported, corrected and reprocessed?	☐	☐	
(e) Review of console logs, error listings, and other evidence of error detection and control?	☐	☐	
3-2. Is the person or group responsible for control over processing by the data processing department independent from the person or group responsible for the operation of the equipment?	☐	☐	A
3-3. If there is an internal auditing group, does it perform EDP control activities related to:			
(a) Review or audit?	☐	☐	A

	YES	NO	
(b) Day-to-day control activities? If "yes" note the nature and extent of these activities.	☐	☐	**A**
3-4. Are master file changes or changes in program data factors authorized in writing by initiating departments?	☐	☐	**A**
3-5. Are departments that initiate changes in master file data or program data factors furnished with notices or a register showing changes actually made? (Examples of such changes are changes in pay rates, selling prices, credit limits, and commission tables.)	☐	☐	**A**

4. CONTROL OVER THE CONSOLE

4-1. Are provisions adequate to prevent unauthorized entry of program changes and/or data through the console? The following questions reflect the types of controls which may be used.

(a) Are adequate machine operation logs being maintained? For each run, these should include information covering the run identification, operator, start and stop time, error halts and delays, and details of reruns. Idle time, down time, program testing, etc., should also be logged.	☐	☐	**B**
(b) Is there an independent examination of computer logs to check the operator performance and machine efficiency?	☐	☐	**B**

If "yes,"

(1) How often ______________________

(2) By whom ______________________

(3) How carried out ______________________

____

____

____

(c) If the computer has a typewriter console, is there an independent examination of the console print-outs to detect operator problems and unauthorized intervention?	☐	☐	**B**

(1) How often ______________________

(2) By whom ______________________

(3) How performed ______________________

____

____

____

5. MANAGEMENT PRACTICES

5-1. Is there a written plan for future changes to be made to the system?	☐	☐	**C**
5-2. Is approval for each application supported by a study of cost and benefit?	☐	☐	**C**

	YES	NO	
5-3. Is a schedule of implementation prepared showing actual versus planned progress?	☐	☐	**C**
5-4. Is there a systems and procedures manual for the activities of the installation?	☐	☐	**C**

6. DOCUMENTATION

	YES	NO	
6-1. Is a run manual prepared for each computer run?	☐	☐	**C**
6-2. Are operator instructions prepared for each run?	☐	☐	**C**
6-3. Are documentation practices adequate?	☐	☐	**C**
Does the normal documentation for an application include the following?			
Problem statement	☐	☐	
System flowchart	☐	☐	
Record layouts	☐	☐	
Program flowcharts	☐	☐	
Program listing	☐	☐	
Test data	☐	☐	
Operator instructions	☐	☐	
Summary of controls	☐	☐	
Approval and change record	☐	☐	
6-4. Is there supervisory review of documentation to ensure that it is adequate?	☐	☐	**B**
6-5. Is documentation kept up to date?	☐	☐	**C**

7. PROGRAM REVISIONS

	YES	NO	
7-1. Is each program revision authorized by a request for change properly approved by management or supervisory personnel?	☐	☐	**B**
(a) Who authorizes? ____________________			
(b) How evidenced? ____________________			
7-2. Are program changes, together with their effective dates, documented in a manner which preserves an accurate chronological record of the system?	☐	☐	**C**
7-3. Are program revisions tested in the same manner as new programs?	☐	☐	**B**

8. HARDWARE CONTROLS

Unless there is evidence of hardware-based processing difficulties, the auditor can usually rely on the hardware. No review is ordinarily required for audit purposes.

9. CONTROL OVER INPUT AND OUTPUT DATA

Although the control over input and output data must be exercised for each application, general questions regarding these controls may be used to ascertain policy regarding the use of control procedures.

		YES	NO	
9-1.	Are initiating departments required to establish independent control data submitted for processing (through the use of batch totals, document counts, or otherwise)?	☐	☐	**A**
9-2.	Is a schedule maintained of the reports and documents to be produced by the EDP system?	☐	☐	**B**
9-3.	Are output reports and documents reviewed before distribution to ascertain the reasonableness of the output?	☐	☐	**A**
9-4.	Are there adequate procedures for control over the distribution of reports?	☐	☐	**B**

10. PROGRAMMED CONTROL OVER PROCESSING

Programmed controls must be evaluated in terms of each application.

11. CONTROLLING ERROR INVESTIGATIONS

		YES	NO	
11-1.	Are all error corrections reviewed and approved by persons who are independent of the data processing department?	☐	☐	**A**
11-2.	Are records maintained of errors occurring in the EDP system?	☐	☐	**C**
11-3.	Are these error records periodically reviewed by someone independent of data processing?	☐	☐	**C**

12. PHYSICAL SAFEGUARDS OVER FILES

		YES	NO	
12-1.	Are important computer programs, essential documentation, records, and files kept in fire-proof storage?	☐	☐	**C**
12-2.	Are copies of important programs, essential documentation, records, and files stored in off-premises locations?	☐	☐	**C**

13. PROCEDURAL CONTROLS FOR SAFEGUARDING FILES

		YES	NO	
13-1.	Are external labels used on all files?	☐	☐	**B**
13-2.	Are internal labels used on all magnetic tape files?	☐	☐	**B**
13-3.	Are file header labels checked by programs using the files?	☐	☐	**B**
13-4.	Are file protection rings used on all magnetic tape files to be preserved?	☐	☐	**B**
13-5.	Is the responsibility for issuing and storing magnetic tape or portable disk packs assigned to a tape librarian, either as a full-time or part-time duty?	☐	☐	**C**

14. CAPABILITY FOR FILE RECONSTRUCTION

		YES	NO	
14-1.	Are there provisions for the use of alternative facilities in the event of fire or other lengthy interruption?	☐	☐	**C**

YES NO

14-2. Is there adequate data processing insurance (other than fire coverage)? ☐ ☐ **B**

14-3. Are data processing personnel covered by fidelity insurance? ☐ ☐ **B**

Part II. Questionnaire for individual applications

The questions in this section are expected to supplement an internal review questionnaire or any other information-obtaining method. They should enable the auditor to obtain information on whether or not various control techniques have been used in the computer processing phase of a particular application.

The questionnaire is organized around the following control points:

1. Adequacy of control over input data
   (a) Verification of correctness of input data
   (b) Control over transmittal of data for processing
   (c) Validity tests and other tests of input data
2. Adequacy of control over processing
   (a) Control for completeness of processing
   (b) Checks for correctness of processing
   (c) Handling of rejects
   (d) Management trail or audit trail
3. Adequacy of control over programs and data files
   (a) Documentation
   (b) Control over changes to master files
   (c) Back-up procedures

The questions are numbered from 101 to distinguish them from questions in the general questionnaire. In cases where a control can be implemented by two or more methods, the related question is followed by a check-list of common control procedures. For each application (or run) related to the audit, the auditor should obtain information sufficient for answering all the relevant questions.

A data processing control review sheet may be used as a means of describing the input, processing, and output controls for a particular application (see Figure 1, page 596). It may be used in place of or in addition to questions 101 and 102.

101. CONTROL OVER INPUT AND OUTPUT FOR AN APPLICATION

YES NO

101-1. Are there adequate controls over the creation of data and its conversion to machine-readable form? ☐ ☐ **A**
   (a) Procedural controls ☐
   (b) Mechanical or visual verification ☐
   (c) Check digit ☐

101-2. Is there adequate control over transmittal and input of data to detect loss or nonprocessing? Note data field controlled. ☐ ☐ **A**

Figure 1

Data processing control review sheet

Application ____________________ Prepared by ____________________ Date ________

Reviewed by ____________________ Date ________

Run no. and run name	Description of control field or control item	Type of control	Controls established by				Controls verified by			
			Department sending data	Data processing department control section	Computer program	Preceding run (run-to-run)	Computer program		Data processing department control section	User or other outside department
							Control information output	Exception output only		

YES NO

FIELD

(a) Financial control totals ________
(b) Hash control totals ________
(c) Document counts ________
(d) Sequential numbering of input documents ________
(e) Other ________

101-3. Are the input control totals and run-to-run control totals for each application by someone other than the equipment operator? ☐ ☐ A
By whom? ________

101-4. If data transmission is used, are controls adequate to determine that transmission is correct and no messages are lost? ☐ ☐ B
(a) Message counts ☐
(b) Character counts ☐
(c) Dual transmission ☐
(d) Other ________

101-5. Is input data adequately tested for validity, correctness, and sequence? ☐ ☐ B
Note: Questions may have to be applied to each important data field of the input being reviewed by the auditor.

FIELDS TESTED

(a) Validity tests:
(1) Valid code ________
(2) Valid character ________
(3) Valid field ________
(4) Valid transaction ________
(5) Valid combinations ________
(6) Missing data ________
(b) Sequence ________
(c) Limit ________
(d) Reasonableness ________
(e) Other ________

101-6. Is control over distribution of output adequate? Describe. ☐ ☐ B

101-7. Describe the control function, if any, for evaluating quality of output.

102. PROGRAMMED CONTROL OVER PROCESSING

102-1. Are control totals used to check for completeness of processing? These may include trailer file labels, run-to-run totals, etc. ☐ ☐ B

102-2. Are programmed controls used to test processing of significant items? ☐ ☐ B

Item applied to

(a) Limit and reasonableness test ________
(b) Cross-footing test ________

		YES	NO	
102-3.	Does the program check for improper switch settings (if sense switches are used)?	☐	☐	**C**

103. CONTROL OVER HANDLING OF ERRORS

103-1.	Does the program provide an adequate console print-out of control information (switch settings, control violations, operator intervention, etc.)?	☐	☐	**B**
103-2.	When a program is interrupted, are there adequate provisions for re-start?	☐	☐	**C**
103-3.	Are there adequate controls over the process of identifying, correcting and reprocessing data rejected by the program?	☐	☐	**B**
103-4.	Inquire into handling of unmatched transactions (no master record corresponding to transaction record). Is it adequate?	☐	☐	**A**

(a) Reject and note on error log ☐
(b) Reject and write on suspense record ☐
(c) Other ________________

104. CONTROL OVER PROGRAM AND DATA FILES

104-1.	Is there adequate up-to-date documentation for the application?	☐	☐	**C**

	YES	NO
(a) Application summary	☐	☐
(b) Run manuals	☐	☐
(c) Operator instructions	☐	☐

104-2.	Is test data documented and kept up to date?	☐	☐	**C**
104-3.	Are controls over master file changes adequate?	☐	☐	**B**

	YES	NO
(a) Written request for change from outside data processing	☐	☐
(b) Register of all changes reviewed by initiating department	☐	☐
(c) Supervisory or other review of changes	☐	☐

104-4.	Are there adequate provisions for periodically checking master file contents?	☐	☐	**B**

	YES	NO
(a) Periodic print-out and review	☐	☐
(b) Periodic test against physical count	☐	☐
(c) Other ________________		

104-5.	Are the back-up and reconstruction provisions adequate?	☐	☐	**B**

105. MANAGEMENT OR AUDIT TRAIL

105-1. Do the records or references provide the means to adequately:

	YES	NO	
(a) Trace any transaction forward to a final total?	☐	☐	**A**
(b) Trace any transaction back to the original source document or input?	☐	☐	**A**
(c) Trace any final total back to the component transactions?	☐	☐	**A**
105-2. When ledgers (general or subsidiary) are maintained on computer media, does the system of processing provide:			
(a) An historical record of activity in the accounts?	☐	☐	**B**
(b) A periodic trial balance of the accounts?	☐	☐	**B**
105-3. Are source documents retained for an adequate period of time in a manner which allows identification with related output records and documents?	☐	☐	**C**

APPENDIX E

Standards of Governmental Auditing[1]

General standards

1. The full scope of an audit of a governmental program, function, activity, or organization should encompass:
   a. an examination of financial transactions, accounts, and reports, including an evaluation of compliance with applicable laws and regulations.
   b. a review of efficiency and economy in the use of resources.
   c. a review to determine whether desired results are effectively achieved.

   In determining the scope for a particular audit, responsible officials should give consideration to the needs of the potential users of the results of that audit.
2. The auditors assigned to perform the audit must collectively possess adequate professional proficiency for the tasks required.
3. In all matters relating to the audit work, the audit organization and the individual auditors shall maintain an independent attitude.
4. Due professional care is to be used in conducting the audit and in preparing related reports.

Examination and evaluation standards

1. Work is to be adequately planned.
2. Assistants are to be properly supervised.
3. A review is to be made of compliance with legal and regulatory requirements.
4. An evaluation is to be made of the system of internal control to assess the extent it can be relied upon to ensure accurate information, to ensure compliance with laws and regulations, and to provide for efficient and effective operations.

[1] United States General Accounting Office, *Standards for Audit of Governmental Organizations, Programs, Activities, & Functions,* Washington, D.C., Government Printing Office, 1972, pp. 6–9.

5. Sufficient, competent, and relevant evidence is to be obtained to afford a reasonable basis for the auditor's opinions, judgments, conclusions, and recommendations.

Reporting standards

1. Written audit reports are to be submitted to the appropriate officials of the organizations requiring or arranging for the audits. Copies of the reports should be sent to other officials who may be responsible for taking action on audit findings and recommendations and to others responsible or authorized to receive such reports. Copies should also be made available for public inspection.
2. Reports are to be issued on or before the dates specified by law, regulation, or other arrangement and, in any event, as promptly as possible so as to make the information available for timely use by management and by legislative officials.
3. Each report shall:
   a. Be as concise as possible but, at the same time, clear and complete enough to be understood by the users.
   b. Present factual matter accurately, completely, and fairly.
   c. Present findings and conclusions objectively and in language as clear and simple as the subject matter permits.
   d. Include only factual information, findings, and conclusions that are adequately supported by enough evidence in the auditor's working papers to demonstrate or prove, when called upon, the bases for the matters reported and their correctness and reasonableness. Detailed supporting information should be included in the report to the extent necessary to make a convincing presentation.
   e. Include, when possible, the auditor's recommendations for actions to effect improvements in problem areas noted in his audit and to otherwise make improvements in operations. Information on underlying causes of problems reported should be included to assist in implementing or devising corrective actions.
   f. Place primary emphasis on improvement rather than on criticism of the past; critical comments should be presented in balanced perspective, recognizing any unusual difficulties or circumstances faced by the operating officials concerned.
   g. Identify and explain issues and questions needing further study and consideration by the auditor or others.
   h. Include recognition of noteworthy accomplishments, particularly when management improvements in one program or activity may be applicable elsewhere.
   i. Include recognition of the views of responsible officials of the organization, program, function, or activity audited on the auditor's findings, conclusions, and recommendations. Except where the possibility of fraud or other compelling reason may require different treatment, the auditor's tentative findings and conclusions should be reviewed with such officials. When possible, without undue delay, their views should be obtained in writing and objectively considered and presented in preparing the final report.

j. Clearly explain the scope and objectives of the audit.
k. State whether any significant pertinent information has been omitted because it is deemed privileged or confidential. The nature of such information should be described, and the law or other basis under which it is withheld should be stated.

4. Each audit report containing financial reports shall:
   a. Contain an expression of the auditor's opinion on whether the information contained in the financial reports is presented fairly. If the auditor cannot express an opinion, the reasons therefor should be stated in the audit report.
   b. State whether the financial reports have been prepared in accordance with generally accepted or prescribed accounting principles applicable to the organization, program, function, or activity audited and on a consistent basis from one period to the next. Material changes in accounting policies and procedures and their effect on the financial reports are to be explained in the audit report.
   c. Contain appropriate supplementary explanatory information about the contents of the financial reports as may be necessary for full and informative disclosure about the financial operations of the organization, program, function, or activity audited. Violations of legal or other regulatory requirements, including instances of noncompliance, shall be explained in the audit report.

Index

BCDEFGHIJ-H-821